REPORTS

OF

PRIZE CASES

DETERMINED IN THE

HIGH COURT OF ADMIRALTY,

BEFORE THE

LORDS COMMISSIONERS OF APPEALS IN PRIZE CAUSES,

AND BEFORE THE

JUDICIAL COMMITTEE OF THE PRIVY COUNCIL,

FROM

1745 TO 1859.

EDITED BY

E. S. ROSCOE,

BARRISTER-AT-LAW,

ADMIRALTY REGISTRAR OF THE SUPREME COURT.

VOL. I.

LONDON:

STEVENS AND SONS, LIMITED,

119 & 120, CHANCERY LANE,

Law Publishers.

1905.

PREFACE.

THE desirability of a single edition of the Prize Cases which are contained in a number of separate Admiralty Reports was pointed out in the Report of the Inter-Departmental Committee of 1902 on Prize Law. An arrangement was therefore, in 1904, come to between His Majesty's Government and Messrs. Stevens & Sons, Limited, for the publication of a uniform edition of these Cases, with the preparation of which I have been entrusted. In regard to the general plan of the work I have had the advantage of the advice of the EARL OF DESART, K.C.B., Solicitor to the Treasury, and Mr. W. E. DAVIDSON, K.C., C.B., of the Foreign Office, two members of the Committee already mentioned, to whom is due the realization of its recommendation, and who have taken a personal interest in this publication. For the execution of it I am, however, solely responsible.

I desire here to thank Mr. JOHN GEORGE SMITH, late Registrar of the Admiralty Court, for his kind and valuable assistance—by perusing the proof sheets of these two volumes, and by many important suggestions in regard to the phraseology of the head-notes. To Mr. JOHN ASPINALL, Barrister-at-Law, I am also much indebted, for his important assistance in the troublesome work of preparing an Index to each of these volumes.

This edition, it may be stated, is not a selection of Leading Cases, but, as far as may be, an edition which contains all the reported cases which remain of value.

In order to accomplish this end within the contemplated space several means have been employed. The purely Admiralty Cases contained in the several Reports—those known technically as cases decided in the Instance Court—have, of course, been rejected, and also cases on the Navigation, Slave Trade and Revenue Acts. Questions of fact have usually not been reprinted, unless, as in some of the earlier Reports, they are illustrative of the evolution of British Prize Law, or as in the cases arising out of the war with Russia in 1854—5, they are the latest modern examples of the application of this law. Sometimes, also, it has been possible—especially in cases relating to joint capture—to reprint only the decision on a point of law, whilst where more than in one case the same legal principle has been repeated, it has usually been considered desirable not to print each case. It has also been possible to reject cases reiterating points of practice, and some on the interpretation of the special wording of licences, not involving questions of principle. In the six volumes of Sir Christopher Robinson's Reports the arguments of Counsel are stated at length. In those of Sir John Dodson they are entirely omitted, and as Lord Stowell's judgments are so clear and exhaustive the arguments add little to the value of the decision, and therefore they have generally been entirely excluded from this republication. A few decisions only have been reprinted from Acton's Appeal Cases, because the decisions of the Court below being usually affirmed without reasons stated, it is impossible to obtain any guidance from most of these Reports.

Headnotes in the form which is now usual in modern Law Reports have been inserted uniformly throughout the two volumes, but those published in Moore's Privy Council Reports have been retained, with an occasional verbal amendment. Occasional cross-references are also given. The reference in the margin to the original report will facilitate the discovery of cases in current text-books.

The full titles and dates of the Reports from which the present collection has been made are given in the Table of Reports. In addition to the general Table of Cases with headnotes, a short subsidiary Table has been prepared, showing such cases as have been printed in footnotes. In the original Reports some valuable decisions were, from some cause or other, placed in notes; these have when desirable, as in the leading case of *The Sally*, been placed in the text. Other cases which were reported in the body of the former works have been placed in notes appended to cases of a more leading character. Such cases have the reference to the original report placed in the margin, in order to distinguish them from decisions originally printed by the reporters in a note. A Chronological Table has also been compiled to make the course of British Prize Law more clear. The most remarkable feature of that body of jurisprudence is the extraordinary influence upon it of a single judge—Lord Stowell—whose decisions form the basis of British Prize Law. During the

Crimean War, the last occasion on which a British Prize Court was at work, those judgments gained in credit and permanence, since criticisms to which they were subjected served only to show their soundness and value. Lord Stowell was singularly fortunate. When, in 1798, he was appointed judge of the High Court of Admiralty, and then became judge of the Prize Court, the war with France had already continued for five years, and the Prize Court was overflowing with business. But there was little definite law to guide either Bench or Bar, there was no code of British Prize Law, and but few judicial decisions were to be found recorded, and these, for the most part, but imperfectly reported. The time and the man thus came together. Lord Stowell had a remarkable power of lucid exposition, he was a master of maritime and international law, and he had a keen sense of the dignity of his office and of the unique opportunity which lay before him. Unhampered by judicial dicta, or by statutes, he set out to lay down a series of propositions which, as has been said, now form the basis of English Prize Law. For the most part they are contained—as was to be expected—in the judgments which were given during the first ten years of his tenure of office, a period conterminous with the Reports of Sir Christopher Robinson. After that time his decisions are, generally speaking, illustrative rather than expository, for the chief part of the work of this great jurist and judge was finished.

E. S. ROSCOE.

June, 1905.

Chronological Table.

Date.		Events.
1756	May......	Commencement of the Seven Years' War.
1762	Jan. 2 ...	War declared by Great Britain against Spain.
1762	Nov. 2 ...	Preliminaries of Peace.
1763	Feb. 10	Treaty of Paris. End of Seven Years' War.
1775	June ...	American War of Independence. (Bunker's Hill, June 17.)
1778	March ...	Declaration of War against France on her Alliance with the American Colonies.
1778	July 29	Order of Reprisals against France.
1779	June 16	Declaration of War by Spain against Great Britain.
1779	June 18	Order of Reprisals against Spain.
1783	Sept. 3...	Treaties of Versailles. (Separate treaties between Great Britain, and France, Spain, and the United States.)
1793	Feb.......	Declaration of War by France against Great Britain.
1793	Feb. 14	Order of Reprisals against France.
1793	....	33 George III. c. 66 (Prize Act, 1793) (*a*).
1795	Sept. 15	Order of Reprisals against Holland.
1796	Nov. 9 ...	Order of Reprisals against Spain.
1798	Oct. 26...	Sir William Scott (Lord Stowell) appointed Judge of the High Court of Admiralty.
1801	Oct. 10...	Ratification of the Preliminaries of Peace exchanged between Great Britain and France.

(*a*) 6 Ann. c. 37 (1708) has been called the first general Prize Act, but 4 & 5 Will. & Mary, c. 25, gave one-third of a prize captured by a man-of-war to the crew, and four-fifths in case of a privateer; in 1649 an Ordinance of the Commonwealth gave a moiety of a prize to the captors. A Prize Act was passed at the beginning of each war. The Naval Prize Act (27 & 28 Vict. c. 25) was a permanent act. See further, the *Elsebe*, Vol. I., p. 450, note; and Collectanea Maritima, being a Collection of Public Instruments tending to illustrate the History and Practice of Prize Law (p. 188 *et seq.*, note), by Chr. Robinson, LL.D. London: J. White and J. Butterworth, Fleet Street. 1801.

Date.		Events.
1802	Mar. 27	Treaty of Amiens.
1803	Jan. 11...	Declaration of War by Great Britain against Spain.
1803	May 16	Declaration of War by Great Britain against France.
1803	....	43 George III. c. 160 (Prize Act, 1803).
1803	June 16	Declaration of War by Great Britain against Holland.
1806	May 14	Declaration of War by Great Britain against Prussia.
1805	....	45 George III. c. 72 (Prize Act, 1805), wholly incorporating Prize Act, 1803.
1806	Mar. 28	North Sea Ports closed by Prussia against British Ships.
1806	April 5...	Embargo on Prussian Ships in, or which may enter, British Ports.
1807	Oct. 26...	Declaration of War by Russia against Great Britain.
1807	Dec. 1 ...	Declaration of War by Great Britain against Russia.
1814	April 4...	Abdication of Napoleon.
1814	May 30...	First Treaty of Paris.
1815	March ...	War renewed against Napoleon.
1815	Nov. 20	Second Treaty of Paris.
1834	....	Privy Council created Appeal Court in Prize Cases (3 & 4 Will. IV. c. 41).
1854	Mar. 29	Declaration of War against Russia.
1854	Mar. 29	Order in Council granting Reprisals against Russia, and establishing the High Court of Admiralty and the several Courts of Admiralty within Her Majesty's Dominions as Prize Courts.
1854	....	Prize Act, 1854 (17 & 18 Vict. c. 18).
1856	Mar. 30	Treaty of Paris.
1856	April 16	Declaration of Paris. (1) Privateering is and remains abolished. (2) The Neutral Flag covers Enemy's Goods with the exception of Contraband of War. (3) Neutral Goods, with the exception of Contraband of War, are not liable to capture under Enemy's Flag. (4) Blockades, in order to be binding, must be effective.
1864	....	Naval Prize Act, 1864 (27 & 28 Vict. c. 25), creating the High Court of Admiralty and Vice-Admiralty Courts Prize Courts.

Date.		Events.
1891	....	Judicature Act, 1891 (54 & 55 Vict. c. 53), by s. 4, the High Court to be a Prize Court within meaning of Naval Prize Act, 1864, and all Prize Causes to be assigned to the Probate, Divorce and Admiralty Division.
1894	....	Prize Court Act (57 & 58 Vict. c. 39)—contains Regulations as to Prize Courts, and authorizes the making of Rules of Court.
1898	Oct. 20...	Order in Council approving new Rules of Court touching Practice in Prize Proceedings, with Forms and Tables of Fees.
1898	July 18...	Order in Council approving Rules of Court for Vice-Admiralty Courts.

JUDGES OF THE HIGH COURT OF ADMIRALTY (PRIZE COURT) FROM 1702.

Sir CHARLES HEDGES	June, 1702	—	1714 (*a*).
H. HENCHMAN, LL.D.	June, 1714	—	1714 (*b*).
H. NEWTON, LL.D.	Oct. 1714	—	1715 (*c*).
Sir HENRY PENRICE	Aug. 1715	—	1751 (*d*).
Sir THOMAS SALUSBURY	Dec. 1751	—	1773 (*e*).
Sir GEORGE HAY	Nov. 1773	—	1778 (*f*).
Sir JAMES MARRIOTT	Oct. 1778	—	1798 (*g*).
Sir WILLIAM SCOTT (Lord Stowell)	Oct. 26, 1798	—	1828 (*h*).
*Sir CHRISTOPHER ROBINSON	Feb. 1828	—	1833 (*i*).
*Sir JOHN NICHOLL	May, 1833	—	1838 (*j*).
Right Hon. STEPHEN LUSHINGTON, LL.D.	Oct. 1838	—	1867 (*k*).
*Sir ROBERT J. PHILLIMORE	Aug. 1867	—	High Court of Admiralty incorporated in Supreme Court of Judicature, 1873 (*l*).

(*a*) Admiralty Muniment Book, Vol. 5, p. 121.
(*b*) ,, ,, ,, ,, 6, p. 121.
(*c*) ,, ,, ,, ,, 6, p. 139.
(*d*) ,, ,, ,, ,, 7, p. 139.
(*e*) ,, ,, ,, ,, 9, p. 80.
(*f*) ,, ,, ,, ,, 10, p. 147.
(*g*) ,, ,, ,, ,, 10, p. 212.
(*h*) ,, ,, ,, ,, 12, p. 99.
(*i*) ,, ,, ,, ,, 15, p. 266.
(*j*) ,, ,, ,, ,, 18, p. 1.
(*k*) ,, ,, ,, ,, 19, p. 20.
(*l*) ,, ,, ,, ,, 22, p. 394.

* These Judges had no occasion to sit as Judges of the Prize Court.

TABLE OF REPORTS.

Volume I.

Volume II.

TABLE OF CASES.

Contraband — Cargo — Ship — Same Owner — False Destination and Papers—Forfeiture of Freight.

If a ship carrying a contraband cargo is owned by the cargo owner, or is sailing under a false destination, or with false papers, she is liable to condemnation.

Carriage of contraband is a cause of forfeiture of freight.

Blockade—Port of actual Shipment not Blockaded—Goods ordered for Blockaded Port.

When goods were ordered for shipment from a blockaded port, but were actually shipped from a non-blockaded port: Held, that there had been no breach of blockade (1).

Recapture — Salvage — Essentials of Capture — Prize Act — General Maritime Law.

In order to constitute a case of capture it is sufficient if a vessel become under the control of an enemy ship. The placing of a prize crew on board is not essential to constitute a capture.

For a vessel rescued, but not actually "retaken," salvage awarded under the general maritime law.

Joint Capture—Associated Service—Squadron not in Sight of Main Fleet—Sight—Detached Service.

Where a capture was made by several ships of a fleet which had been ordered to undertake a certain operation, and the main body of which, owing to a haze, was not in sight of the capture: Held, that as these ships were not detached on special service, but were acting in co-operation with the main body of the fleet, the latter were entitled to share in the capture (a).

Blockade—Non-European State.

The rules of the Law of Nations as to blockades are binding on merchants of non-European nations.

*Evidence—Further Proof—*Primâ facie *Neutral Cargo—Illegal Origin of Cargo—False Papers—Captors' Expenses.*

The Court will not, on an application for further proofs, usually admit evidence not connected with the original evidence.

Application for further proof to show an illegal course of trade, there being nothing in the original evidence pointing to such a suspicion, rejected, and the cargo restored.

The ship's papers being false, captors' expenses allowed.

CASES REPUBLISHED IN NOTES.

⁂ *See also Cases Republished in Notes, Vol. II.*

ALPHABETICAL TABLE OF CASES.

REPORTS

OF

PRIZE CASES.

THE MED GUDS HIELPE. [Pratt, 191(a)]

Contraband—Principles of Law—Pitch and Tar—Liability of Ship.

Pitch and tar are contraband of war. The different classes of contraband enumerated. A neutral ship condemned for carrying contraband.

PER CURIAM. [Sir Henry Penrice.] The question is, whether this Swedish ship is well seized by the *Eagle* privateer. This ship has not a passport in the form directed by the treaty with Sweden in 1661, and therefore the privateer had good reason to bring in this ship. Her whole cargo is pitch and tar, and there is no doubt but that it was designed for the use of the French. 1745 *Aug.* 9; affirmed *June* 29, 1750.

Pitch and tar are not enumerated in the 11th Article (*b*) of the Swedish Treaty, but I rather think those enumerated were mentioned rather for example than by way of exclusion, and that there are other contraband goods than what are mentioned in that article.

Three species of goods—

1st. For immediate use of war in the manner they are, and those are contraband.

2nd. Of a mixed nature, which may be of use for war and for other purposes, and these sometimes are, and sometimes are not, contraband.

3rd. Things for pleasure, and which are of no use in war, and those are not contraband.

Pitch and tar are of a mixed nature; may be used for civil purposes, and also for fitting ships of war. Sovereign Princes at

(*a*) The Law of Contraband of War, by F. T. Pratt, LL.D. London, 1856. [In this work are collected a number of short reports from the MS. notes of Sir George Lee (1700—1758), D.C.L., P.C., M.P. Besides being an Advocate of Doctors' Commons with a large business, Lee was from 1751 to 1758 Dean of Arches.]

(*b*) Dumont, Vol. VI., p. 386.

1745 Aug. 9. war may declare such and such things to be contraband, and, after notice to their allies, their subjects may certainly seize them.

THE MED GUDS HIELPE. The *Arms of Plymouth*, in 1692, is the strongest case that has been cited for condemning this ship.

In the old instructions the 11th and 12th Articles of the Swedish Treaty were inserted. Now they are not inserted, and I suppose the reason was, because by the present instructions pitch and tar in Swedish ships are expressly declared to be contraband.

A privateer who pursues his instructions, does right. The *Eagle* privateer has pursued the King's instructions, and therefore I declare and pronounce that this ship and her cargo of pitch and tar are good and lawful prize, and was rightly and duly seized and taken by the *Eagle* privateer, Captain Bazeley, Commander.

Nov. 12th, 1745.—The above judgment was appealed against, and came on for argument before the Lords of Appeal.

Dr. Paul, for appellants. Treaties by Cromwell enumerate contraband, and nothing else is so.

Pitch and tar have been ordered to be sold in England.—Attentat by selling.

N.B. *Treaties with Cromwell not confirmed.*

Mr. Solicitor-General, for respondents. Contraband is every thing that is of use in carrying on the war.

Dr. Paul's argument. Pitch and tar are not useful without tallow. 9th Article of Instructions directs treaties to be observed.

Mr. Attorney-General, same side for appellants. First, consider the ship only. No instance mentioned of condemning the ship for having contraband goods.

Secondly, consider the goods. With regard to the Law of Nations. Every good purpose is supported by detaining the goods that may be made use of in war.

Bynkershoek. Does not say pitch and tar. Treaty with Sweden, 1661. Nothing contraband but what is enumerated in the 11th Article.

Christiana Margaretta. Sir Lionel Jenkins, 2 vols. 751.

On the 29th of June, 1750, the Lords met and confirmed the sentence of the Judge of the Admiralty, pronouncing that the cargo is contraband by the laws of nations and within the treaty with Sweden, and condemned both ship and cargo. [See *post*, p. 38.] 1750 *June* 29. THE MED GUDS HIELPE.

Present at this sentence, Duke of Dorset, Lord President, Lord Chief Justice Willes, and Mr. Doddington. The Duke of Bedford and Earl of Harrington heard the cause, but were absent when the sentence was given, but sent their approbation and consent to it.

In the *Jonge Tobias*, December 14th, 1747, salt consigned to a port of naval equipment was pronounced contraband. [Pratt, p. 190.]

In the *Young Andreas*, March 22nd, 1747, a Prussian ship bound from Dublin to Rochfort with butter, tallow, and coals, was captured on 3rd November, the tallow and 20 tons of butter were condemned as contraband. [Pratt, p. 99.]

THE LA PACIFIQUE.

[Burrell, 158.]

Capture—Prize—Admiral—Right to Share of Prize.

An admiral was appointed to take command of a squadron. *Held*, that he was not entitled to share of prize taken by a ship of such squadron, the captain of which ship at the time of the capture had not yet received orders from him, such ship being on a cruise out of reach of communication with the squadron, and acting under orders from the Admiralty.

A FRENCH ship was taken, March, 1758, in lat. 48, off Cape Finisterre, by his Majesty's ship *Windsor*, Captain Lane Falkner. 6th May, the ship was condemned in the Admiralty Court, when an appearance was given for Sir Edw. Hawke, claiming one-eighth as admiral, under whose command the prize was taken. Captain F. denied his interest, which was propounded in an allegation pleading that, 5th March, 1758, Sir E. H. was appointed by the Lords of the Admiralty commander of a squadron of men-of-war to be employed in the Channel soundings, or wherever else his Majesty's service should require; and he was thereby required to take on him the command of said squadron, and all captains and officers belonging to said ships were charged to be obedient to 1761, 1764

1761, 1764

THE LA PACIFIQUE.

him as their commander-in-chief. That annexed to said commission was a list of what ships the squadron was to consist, amongst which is the *Windsor*, particularly described to be off Finisterre, then between Cape Ortugal and Ushant. That by reason of the premises, the *Windsor* was, on 13th March, 1758, under the command of said Sir E. H., who was at that time on board the *Ramillies*, proceeding to the westward. Captain F. in his answers admitted Sir E. H.'s command as pleaded, and gave an allegation pleading that, 14th Feb., 1758, he received an order of that date from the Commissioners of the Admiralty, directing him to take the *Coventry* to sea and cruise between lat. 48 and 50 till he should get 120 leagues to the westward, and directing him to stretch off Cape Finisterre and cruise between Cape Ortugal and Ushant, taking care to return to Plymouth Sound with both ships by the expiration of one month from his departure. That Captain F. sailed for Plymouth with the *Windsor* and *Coventry*, 24th Feb., 1758, and 13th March following took the *Pacifique* in lat. 48, with which he returned to Plymouth, 26th March, and then, and not before, received from Admiral Harrison, then commander-in-chief at Plymouth, an order from Sir E. H., dated Spithead, 1st (*a*) March, requiring him as captain of the *Windsor* to put himself under his command, and to complete his water and stores and provisions to four months, and to keep in constant readiness for the sea. (Sir E. H. sailed from Spithead on 11th of March.) Captain F. did not at that time act under any order of Sir E. H., but solely under the aforesaid order of 14th February, 1758, from the Lords of the Admiralty. The facts pleaded in this allegation were admitted by Sir E. Hawke in his answer.

13th May, 1761.—The Judge of the Admiralty pronounced for Sir E. Hawke's interest, and that under his Majesty's proclamation he was and is, as admiral under whose command the prize in question was taken, entitled to one-eighth of the prize, and decreed the same to him accordingly.

Captain F. appealed, and the Lords, 28th July, 1764, reversed the sentence of the Judge below, and pronounced against Sir E. Hawke's interest.

(*a*) Query this date. On p. 3, Sir E. H. is said to have been appointed on 5th March—four days after the date of this order.

THE DIE VIER GEBROEDERS.

[Burrell, 159.]

Blockade—Evidence—Enemy Cargo.

A blockade must be proved strictly, and when this was not done the parties were, by the Judges' Delegates, given time to plead, and the sentence of the Court below was for the time being reversed.

1759, 1760

2nd July, 1759.—A SHIP was seized by an English privateer at anchor under Dunge Ness laden wholly with brandy and salt. The master had entered into a charter party at Rochelle, 13th June, 1759, with one Queurt, an inhabitant of that city, to sail from thence to Sendees, near St. Martins, in France, there to take his full lading of brandy and salt and carry it to Dunkirk, the port of his unlading. The master gave in a claim for the ship as the property of Jacobs and others, merchants, of Amsterdam, and for the cargo as privileged, as being laden in a ship belonging to subjects of the States General.

13th November, 1759.—The Judge of the Admiralty decreed the ship to be restored to the claimants, but that Dunkirk being blocked up at the time of the capture, the cargo thereby, by its nature, became contraband, and therefore condemned it as lawful prize.

15th July, 1760.—On appeal, 15th July, 1760, the Lords declared that, it not appearing judicially in this cause what the state of Dunkirk was, or that his Majesty's fleet lay before it, 2nd July, 1759, though of public notoriety, and the cargo indisputably belonging to the enemy, and the claimant having no otherwise interest than in the privilege of the ship, and it being just that any further examination should be at the peril of costs, upon the claimants giving good security in 500*l.* within two months to pay such costs as may be awarded, reversed that part of the sentence which condemned the cargo, and ordered the parties to plead and prove within three months, and in default of the claimants giving such security within the time aforesaid the sentence to be affirmed.

[Burrell, 160.]

THE ST. JACOB.

Cargo—Contraband—Oil.

A cargo of oil was held by the Court of Appeal not to be contraband. Judgment of the Court of Admiralty reversed.

1759 A DANISH ship took in a cargo of oil and a quantity of lemons, with which she was taken on her voyage to Havre de Grace. The Judge of the Admiralty pronounced that the goods were of the nature of contraband, or as the goods of enemies, or otherwise liable to confiscation, and condemned the same, but pronounced that the ship belonged to Danish subjects, and that the lemons belonged to the master, and decreed the ship and money produced by the sale of the lemons to be restored to the master for the use of himself and the owners thereof.

28th June, 1759.—The Lords reversed the sentence; declared that under the circumstances of the case, the cargo or any part thereof ought not to be deemed contraband; pronounced it to belong as claimed, and decreed that the net produce of the sale be restored to the proctor for the owners.

[Burrell, 164.]

THE JESUS.

Contraband—Neutral Cargo—Saltpetre.

Saltpetre is contraband of war.

1756, 1759, 1761 A SPANISH ship was taken in her voyage from Corunna to St. Sebastian, with a loading of coffee, *saltpetre*, dye-wood, pepper, and India bail goods, which was all on board from a French East India ship then lying there, by a Spaniard for account of a person resident at St. Sebastian to whom they were consigned. The cargo was claimed as the property of a Spanish subject, and likewise as laden on board a ship belonging to the King of Spain. The master on his examination said that the voyage on which he was taken was to have ended in France, and that he believed the lading belonged to French subjects, and that Spanish coasting vessels were made use of to protect said goods from the English cruisers. Four other of the mariners swore to the same effect. 1756, 1759, 1761

THE JESUS.

27th Dec., 1756.—The Judge of the Admiralty pronounced just cause of seizure, and condemned the claimant in expenses; furthermore pronounced that the saltpetre seized is in the nature of contraband, and condemned it as lawful prize to the captor; but pronounced that the ship and rest of the goods belonged to the claimant, and directed the same to be restored, paying expenses. An appeal was interposed, to which the respondent adhered, forasmuch as the Judge had not condemned the ship and all the cargo as lawful prize.

15th July, 1759.—The Lords assigned the claimant to make proof that the ship and cargo were Spanish property, and that the ship when taken was bound from Corunna to St. Sebastian, and to no other port within two months. An allegation was accordingly given, and was examined 17th December, 1760. The Lords took time to deliberate till the first Court after the holidays.

5th Sept., 1761.—Respondent's proctor presented a petition desiring to withdraw his adhesion to the appeal, which he was permitted to do, and the Lords affirmed the decrees of the Judge below and decreed the cause to be remitted.

THE DE FORTUYN.

[Burrell, 175.]

Capture—Neutral Port—Enemy Ship.

An enemy ship captured in a neutral port was ordered to be restored to the owner.

A DUTCH ship bound for Cape François with a licence from the French king to trade there, being arrived off Hispaniola put into Monte Christi, a Spanish port in that island, and anchored there, and whilst at anchor was seized by three English privateers; notwithstanding the Spanish Governor came on board and remonstrated against the seizure, the privateers carried her to Jamaica, where ship and cargo were condemned. 1760

1760

THE DE FORTUYN.

12th June, 1760.—The Lords of Appeal declared that ship and cargo were liable to confiscation, but by reason that this ship was attacked and taken whilst she lay at anchor in one of the ports of the King of Spain, within reach of his cannon and under his protection, contrary to the remonstrances of his Governor, reversed the sentence and decreed ship and cargo or the full value to be restored to the claimant.

[Burrell, 178.]

THE YONG VROW ADRIANA.

Neutral Ship—Enemy Goods—Bills of Lading—Fictitious Transhipment.

A neutral ship was put up for general freight at Cadiz, and took on board as part of her cargo goods, originally destined for Marseilles, from two enemy ships lying near. The bills of lading stated that the goods were shipped on account and at the risk of neutrals, and were going to a neutral port. *Held*, that having regard to the facts, the goods were enemy goods destined for an enemy port, and so were liable to condemnation.

1758, 1761, 1764

A DUTCH ship was put up at general freight at Cadiz, and took on board a cargo of coffee, sugar, indigo, cochineal, wool, and other merchandise, great part of which was brought from two French ships then lying in the bay. There were 157 bills of lading on board, signed as well by the captain as the owners of the goods, and all declared the goods shipped for the account and at the risk of subjects of the King of Spain and other neutrals. There was likewise on board an affidavit of thirty persons, attested by a notary, that the goods on board the said ship, being the whole cargo, belong entirely to the declarants, and that no other person had any concern therein. The master and mariners swore that they knew no more of the property of the cargo than the bills of lading and manifest showed. 2nd May, 1758, the ship was taken by the *Nelly's Resolution*, privateer, within a mile of the port of Cadiz, and carried into Gibraltar. After the capture several further affidavits of their property in the cargo were made by the owners at Cadiz and transmitted to Gibraltar.

15th July, 1758.—The Judge of the Vice-Admiralty at Gibraltar restored the ship as the property of subjects of the States General; pronounced that some part of the cargo specified in the sentence, consisting chiefly of wine and money, were not liable to confiscation, and decreed them to be restored to the claimants; but condemned the rest of the cargo, consisting of West India produce. The captors acquiesced in the restitution of the ship, and paid the captain his freight.

26th July, 1758.—Nicholas Tardy, on behalf of himself and the several claimants, appealed from that part of the sentence condemning the rest of the goods. 31st August, 1759, Seeke Jeekes, the master of the ship, to prevent the expenses that must have arisen from prosecuting several appeals in consequence of the several claims given for the owners of different parts of the cargo in the Court below, empowered Pet. Erricarte of London, merchant, to claim the several goods condemned in the Court below in his name, which was accordingly done.

An appearance was given for the respondent under protestation, for that the present appeal was prosecuted in the name of Seeke Jeekes, the master, and that the claim given in before the Lords was also in his name, whereas in the Court of Gibraltar Jeekes did not claim any of the goods schedulate, but some were claimed by Nicholas Tardy and others, and that Jeekes never appealed from the sentence in the Court below condemning said goods, but on the contrary petitioned the Judge to be paid his freight by the captors, which was decreed; therefore he cannot now appeal therefrom; wherefore respondent prayed to be dismissed.

20th December, 1760.—The Lords declared that the captain is not now at liberty to appeal, under privilege of the ship, but that the owners may use him on the appeal as a claimant of their property.

27th June, 1761.—The Lords having heard informations in the cause, and respondents having made many objections to the credibility of a real sale at Cadiz of a cargo going to Marseilles, the place of its first destination, to be delivered to the original consignees, as appeared manifestly in many instances, and alleging that by the law of Spain and France the goods must have been cleared out and transboarded, and have paid the duty at Cadiz, and must have entered at Marseilles as continuing French property, and also urging that the oaths in support of the claims are evasive; and the appellants insisting that neither the law of Spain nor France was as alleged, and averring that no evasion was intended nor could fairly be insinuated from the oaths in support of the claim; their Lordships thought it reasonable that some opportunity should be given for further explanation by affidavits as to the laws and practice of Spain in relation to transboarding goods from French to neutral ships, and as to the laws and practice of France in relation to the importation of the produce of French settlements in America into France on board a neutral bottom from a port in Europe; and that the claimants should be at liberty to supply the oaths and depositions already made by declaring whether the property was to continue theirs after the arrival and delivery of the goods at Marseilles, and likewise to supply the defect in their oaths by declaring that the price was actually and *bonâ fide* paid to the original proprietors, and how and where.

In obedience to their Lordships' order, affidavits and proofs respecting the laws of France and Spain were given in on both sides, and on 30th June, 1764, the matter came on again, when the Lords declared, from the evidence on both sides, that the transboarding on this occasion was not done in any fair course of trade or commerce, which ever did, or ever can exist in time of peace, but was a fraudulent contrivance merely on account of the war to continue the original voyage and cover the *goods* of the *enemy* to their destined port, entitled to the same privileges and liable to the same duties and consequences as if they had arrived on board the same ship on which they were first laden, and therefore an actual sale for a consideration really paid ought not to be allowed to screen, but ought to be considered merely as a mode of unfair assistance to complete the original voyage in favour of the original proprietors, the original consignees, and the public revenue of the enemy arising from the duties.

THE GOOD CHRISTIAN.

[Burrell, 216 and 217.]

Neutral—Trade with Colony of Belligerent—Restoration of Ship.

A neutral ship and cargo were captured and condemned as lawful prize on the ground that the vessel was trading to a French West India Island as a French ship. On appeal the decree was reversed, and the ship and cargo were ordered to be restored (*a*).

A DANISH ship was taken in her voyage from St. Croix to St. 1760
Domingo; had on board a Dutch pass for trade amongst all the West India Islands; a bill of lading expressing the voyage to be to St. Domingo, and that the goods are on account and risk of a Danish subject; a clearance at St. Croix for Cape François. The master and mariners said they were bound to St. Domingo or Cape François, where the cargo was to be sold to any person that would buy it. The ship was carried to North Carolina, and proceeded against as prize. Claim was given for ship and cargo as the property of Danish subjects.

20th December, 1760.—The Judge condemned both as prizes, ordering claimant to pay costs pursuant to stipulation. The Lords declared that on all the evidences and circumstances of the case they are of opinion there is not sufficient ground to presume that the voyage in which the ship *Good Christian* was taken was allowed by the French king or his officers, or undertaken on any assurance, agreement, or authoritative intimation that the ship would be received at Cape François on the foot of a French ship or treated in such a manner as only French ships have a right to be treated in time of peace. They ordered both ship and cargo to be restored.

[(*a*) This case illustrates an attempt to extend the rule of the War of 1756, by which Dutch ships and cargoes trading to the French West India colonies were condemned on the ground that the French Government having given exceptional privileges to the Dutch by allowing them to trade with their colonies, the Dutch ships were, in fact, incorporated with the French mercantile marine. Sir W. Burrell notes in a few lines a number of cases of neutral ships either condemned or restored by the application of this rule.]

[Hay & Marriott, 152.]

THE JOHN.

Recapture—Privateer—Salvage.

An English ship was taken by the French, and remained in their possession for ninety-six hours; she did not enter any port, and was recaptured by a British privateer. The Court decreed one-eighth salvage.

1778 *Nov.* 23.

An English ship, retaken from the French by a privateer, and having been in possession of the enemy near ninety-six hours, although not carried into any port, a question was made whether, there being no Act of Parliament to regulate proceedings in cases of French captures and recaptures, the old rules should not be observed in favour of privateers retaking, to give a salvage according to the time in the possession of the enemy. That larger salvage has always been allowed to the privateers than to the King's ships in all former Acts till the American Act, which now equally confined both to one-eighth salvage. That it must have been a slip in the legislature, in the American Act; as the King's ships are doing their duty, fitted out at the public expense, but the privateers at the extraordinary expenses of particulars.

The Court said that whether it was a slip or not, in the drawers of the American Acts, yet it would be very awkward to have two different rules; one for American, another for French, recaptures. That as in this case the Court was not bound by the Acts in former wars, which expired with them, so it was not bound in this case of French reprisals by the American Act of letters of marque. That the divisions of point of time for more or less salvage was always a bad rule, borrowed from the oldest Dutch placarts, and seemed calculated for increasing litigations and disputes. The simplest rule was the best in everything, and that the decision in the French cases of recapture should square with the clause in the American Act; therefore pronounced for an eighth salvage, yet not so as to preclude the discretion of the Court to give a greater, and even a very great salvage, in other cases, where there should be very great merit in retaking.

There was no resistance in this case on the part of the enemy; but when the action should be attended with loss of lives and blood, and damage of recaptors, they might expect a proportionable salvage; observing that this country owed much at this time to the activity of private armaments; and while privateers observed strictly the law and the King's instructions, in doing no injury to British or neutral innocent subjects, they would meet with every suitable and just encouragement. 1778 *Nov.* 23. THE JOHN.

THE VRYHEID (No. 1).

[Hay & Marriott, 188.]

Contraband—Masts—Pre-emption—Payment of Freight—Treaty of December 11th, 1674.

A Dutch ship bound for Rochfort with a cargo of masts for the French Government was captured. The Court ordered the cargo to be sold for the use of his Majesty, all freight, expenses, and charges to be paid by his Majesty.

A DUTCH ship, taken on the 26th of August by his Majesty's cutter the *Kite*, Lieutenant Trollope commander, bound from Riga to Rochfort, the cargo 71 masts of above 90 feet in length fit for first-rate ships of war, 12 small ditto, 460 boat-masts, 100 spars, 2,900 deals, laden by Blanchenhagen of Riga, who ordered the master to touch at Elsineur in Denmark, and to apply to the French Consul for orders in regard to the destination. The master deposed to this fact, and that the French Consul directed him accordingly to carry the naval stores to Rochfort, and that a broker there would instruct him to whom they were to be delivered. The Dutch master claimed his ship as Dutch property, having a sea-brief from the States, and duly documented; and the cargo as privileged under the treaty of December 11th, 1674, with all costs and damages. The advocate for the captor consented to restitution of the ship with freight, but prayed condemnation of the stores as for the account of the French king. He strongly pressed that the privileges had never been yet allowed that the Dutch should carry the naval stores of the enemy's Government; that the privilege in such an extent as claimed was never in contemplation of the contracting parties, who were at the time of this treaty entering into an alliance offensive and defensive, and understood as engaging to have always the same friends and the same enemies; that the great federal union between England and Holland had since then 1778 *Dec.* 2.

1778 Dec. 2. THE VRYHEID.

been established if possible in a firmer manner. On the part of the Dutch claimant was urged the IVth Article of the treaty as explicit, that "masts, planks, boards, and beams of any kind of wood, and all other materials requisite for building or repairing ships shall be wholly reputed free goods, so that the same may be freely transported and carried by the subjects of the States to places under the obedience of the enemies of his said Majesty, except only to places besieged, blocked up or invested."

The Proctor and Advocate of the Admiralty moved, that the stores might be sold on a fair valuation to the Commissioners of the Navy for his Majesty's use. The freight, the expenses of proceeding, and all other charges due to the Dutch claimant to make a part of the price.

The Judge gave his opinion nearly in the following terms:—

This question, of the highest national importance, turns, in my opinion, upon a great extent of comprehensive argument. To give the utmost force to the treaty of 1674, relied on by the claimants as the fort of their pretensions, the IVth Article must be admitted to to be in the terms as stated. The Ist Article stipulates, "Freedom to exercise all manner of traffic."

Article II. "This freedom of commerce is not to be interrupted by reason of any war as to any kind of merchandize, but shall extend to all commodities which may be carried in time of peace; those only excepted which are described under the name of contraband." There follows the IIIrd Article, affirming what shall be contraband, specifically naming the sorts of arms and ordnance; and lastly, in general words, "all other instruments of war."

The IVth Article is negative of contraband; and masts, &c. are excepted from being contraband.

By the general law and usage of nations (treaties and extraordinary stipulations out of the question) there are two sorts of things confiscable: 1st, all those, generally, which belong to an enemy, found on board the ships of a friend; 2ndly, those which belong to a friend, but which will aid the enemy to maintain war. These latter are *contraband;* so that one of the ideas inseparably annexed to contraband, and to the exception of contraband, is, that the goods excepted belong to a friend; from which it is clear that the goods of the Dutch subject, specially or generally enumerated in

Article III., are contraband; and that masts, &c., &c., and all other materials requisite for building and repairing ships, excepted in Article IV., do mean such masts, &c., which do also belong to the friend, and are going in the ordinary merchandize and for mercantile purposes. This must be the natural sense of the stipulation. For to admit a right of being the privileged carriers of the enemy to the royal docks would work such an adoption of a hostile character, would defeat every idea of alliance and confederacy of the contracting parties, and transfer the federal union over to the other belligerent.

1778. *Dec. 2.*

THE VRYHEID.

The great argument is that all subsisting treaties of commerce and alliance, offensive and defensive, are to be taken as one contract, *uno contextu*, and the spirit of the federal union is to interpret the letter, so that no one treaty, or article of the treaty, is to be taken substantive, or standing alone and single from the rest.

The secret Article of Westminster, 1673-4, is as strong as possible. The words are: "Neither of the said parties shall give nor consent that any of their subjects or inhabitants shall give any aid, favour, or counsel, directly or indirectly, by land or by sea, or on the fresh waters, nor shall furnish nor consent that the subjects and inhabitants of their dominions and countries shall furnish any *ships*, soldiers, mariners, provisions, money, instruments of war, gunpowder, or any other things necessary for making war, to the enemies of the other party, of any rank or condition whatsoever." It is very clear that ships may be furnished by piecemeal, as completely as if they sailed out of the Texel with all their furniture.

If one Dutch ship carries masts, another anchors, another sails, another a ship's frame (and such there is now taken, of size for a seventy-gun ship), a whole fleet may go by detail from Holland for the King of France's service.

It could never be the intention of the contracting parties that Dutch ships, or English, *vice versâ*, should become the transports of an enemy's government for carrying free its stores of war either for sea or land.

Besides all this, the usage of nations is the best interpreter of all contracts; and it always has been the usage to pay the Dutch carrier for the enemy's stores, and for his freight; and the prece-

1778 Dec. 2. dents of the usage universally acquiesced in during the last wars are worth all the reasonings of Grotius and Puffendorf.

THE VRYHEID. By decreeing naval stores to be sold to the public, and the freight and all incidental charges, as between merchant and merchant, made a part of the price, the carrier has the benefit of the treaty. The great object is his cabotage or carrying trade; give him that, the spirit of the treaty is fulfilled. As to necessity, by the XXIVth Article of the Treaty of Bredah, "the persons of merchants, masters, and mariners of either party, their ships, goods, wares, and merchandizes may be arrested or detained in the port of the other, to serve in war, or for any other service upon an extraordinary necessity, and then just satisfaction shall be made."

Holland, in case of such necessity, may press English ships and seamen, and England may do the same *vice versâ*. The *casus fœderis* exists: the dominions of Great Britain in America and her commerce on the ocean are invaded by France. The necessity is and can only be judged of by the party who claims the assistance; because if it rested with the other confederates to judge of the necessity he would judge in his own cause, and elude the contract.

Whenever it comes to that, it may be urged with equal reason and plain sense: "I say, I am in necessity, and want your assistance." You say, "I am not in necessity, and you will not give the assistance." The reply is obvious: "I know best my own wants and necessities, which I feel, and not you; if therefore you will not allow my demand, I will not allow yours. All is reciprocal. As you do not admit my necessity, I am under a necessity to refuse your privilege."

As to England having enjoyed the privilege of the treaty, it was but once (above a century ago). But Holland, on the contrary, has used it so often as almost *to wear it out*.

In the present state of things, England, in a most extraordinary position, never possible in contemplation in the utmost range of the imagination of the contracting parties, engaged in a civil war with her own subjects of the whole continent of British America, and assailed, first privately and then publicly, by France, cannot admit of the privilege of carrying the naval stores of the enemy, in the extent claimed by the States, without opening her breast to all her enemies without defence.

She is obliged by every principle of self-preservation to snatch the sword from the hand of her assailants, let who will interfere, and not to afford arms to that restless and malignant nation who, in the weakness or destruction of Great Britain, will most assuredly involve the fate of Holland.

1778 *Dec.* 2.

THE VRYHEID.

The Judge decreed the ship to be restored to the Dutch claimants, together with the value of the cargo; the naval stores to be sold, according to former precedents, for the use of his Majesty; all freight, expenses and charges, both of the captor and claimant, to be paid by his Majesty. From this sentence the Proctor of the captor appealed; but the Court ordered the execution of the sentence not to be suspended, and the captor to give adequate security to answer the appeal.

THE RENARD.

[Hay & Marriott, 222.]

Recapture—Restoration—Salvage—Amount.

A British ship was captured by the enemy and was judicially condemned, then fitted out as a privateer, and subsequently re-taken by a British privateer. The Court ordered the ship to be restored to her original owners, and decreed a moiety of her value to the recaptors as salvage.

1778 *Dec.* 9.

THIS vessel was first taken by the French, carried by them into Havre de Grace, condemned judicially, and by them fitted out as a privateer; retaken by the *Lark* privateer. A claim was given by one Mr. Lad and others, as their property. The French witnesses deposed that she was an English prize; objection was taken by the counsel for the captors to the identification, there being a variation of tonnage between the French papers and the affidavit of the claimant. But the great question was, whether (this vessel having been completely in the enemy's port and possession, and condemned in France) the property of the original British owner was not entirely defeated; and if not, that the quantum of salvage to be allowed was to be considered? because there is no Prize Act, in the present case, of hostilities with France; and that the American Privateer Act gives only one-eighth even to privateers, which in former Prize Acts, in time of war, used always to give to privateers a salvage proportionable to the number of hours any ship, retaken from the enemy, shall have been in the enemy's possession;

1778 *Dec. 9.* THE RENARD. although men-of-war had never more than an eighth salvage. In support of the argument that no salvage was due, quotations were made from Grotius, who considers occupancy by the enemy for twenty-four hours as a divesting of the original property, and as good a transfer, by the law of nations, as bargain and sale by the civil law.

Bynkershoek, a modern Dutch writer, now much in esteem and fashion, opposes the sentiments of Grotius, and says that an occupancy of twenty-four hours is not sufficient; but there must be such a bringing into port as that all hope of recovery is lost with the ship.

This idea of Bynkershoek was said to agree with the common law of England, as laid down in Brooke's Abridgement, tit. Property, forfeiture 38: "If an enemy takes an Englishman's goods, the former owner," says he, "shall lose his property; and it becomes indefeasibly vested in the first taker, unless it shall be retaken the *same* day, and the first owner puts in his claim before sunset." From whence a conclusion is to be drawn that a possession of a certain time, even without a sentence, defeases the first owner.

JUDGMENT:

The Court [Sir J. Marriott] observed, that there is something ridiculous in the decisive manner each lawyer, as quoted, had given his opinion. Grotius might as well have laid down, for a rule, twelve hours, as twenty-four; or forty-eight as twelve. A pedantic man in his closet dictates the law of nations; everybody quotes, and nobody minds him. The usage is plainly as arbitrary as it is uncertain; and who shall decide when dictators disagree? Bynkershoek, as it is natural to every writer or speaker who comes after another, is delighted to contradict Grotius: his rule is, that the prize must not only be brought, *infra præsidia*, into the port and under the guns of the enemy, but so that all hope of recovery is lost. But this rule will not do, it is plain, because the fact is the ship is recovered.

As to Master Brooke's rule, there is neither sense nor justice in it. The property, he says, is lost between an Englishman and Englishman, unless it is retaken in twelve hours; and besides that,

1778 *Dec.* 9. THE RENARD. Sir J. Marriott.

it must be reclaimed before sunset. What! when the original owner at land knows nothing of his ship being taken by the enemy at sea? and how, and where, and from whom can he reclaim her? From the enemy? The rule is nonsensical, for it is impossible. I take the general law to be, and it is equity, that a British subject has always a right to his own again, when found in the hands of another British subject, and can maintain his suit for it, paying a salvage proportionable to the expense and danger, and other circumstances.

This doctrine is just, in the relation in which one British subject stands to another British subject, and does not at all controvert the principle that a lawful enemy in war may acquire property by occupancy, and may transfer it to a third party, who is not forbid from such purchase by any especial treaty.

In the present case, the state of hostilities is more favourable to the claimant than a declared war. What is declared, then? Reprisals upon the French King, his subjects, and the inhabitants of his territories. But British subjects, generally (the case of the Americans being out of the question), are not to make reprisals upon one another; there is no authority for that. Clearly, the American Act does not extend to the present question of salvage. There is no act relative to recaptures from the French. It rests then with the Court. By what rule can it direct its discretion? The old War Prize Acts have pointed out a rule which the Court may adopt, not as binding on the judgment of the Court, but as declaring the practice. A man-of-war, being paid by the public and fitted out at the national expense, had by the Act only an eighth of the recapture if a merchant ship; but a privateer retaking after a ship had been in the possession above ninety-six hours, was to have a moiety, and a man-of-war, as well as a privateer, retaking a British ship, the same being fitted out for war by the enemy, had a moiety. In this case, the recaptured vessel appears to have been fitted out as a privateer, and therefore I have no doubt to decree a moiety as salvage and restore the ship to the original owners; the variation of the tonnage is accounted for by the difference of the French and English computation, and admitted by the counsel.

[Hay & Marriott, 245.]

THE POSTILION.

Capture—Cargo—Domicile—Enemy Subject Resident in Neutral Territory—Restoration—Costs and Damages.

Great Britain being at war with France, the cargo of a Frenchman, domiciled in Hamburgh, was captured on a neutral ship. The cargo ordered to be restored with costs and damages since the owner must be considered a Hamburgher.

1779 Jan. 8.

A Lubeck ship was restored to the Lubeckers and the cargo to M. Lienau, the owner, who, though a Frenchman, was domiciled at Hamburgh; and it appearing by evidence, and by a certificate of the magistrates on board the ship, that the cargo was his sole property, though consigned to his brothers in France, the cargo was also restored, and the privateer condemned in costs and damages. The ground of the decision was that a native of Hamburgh, resident in France, would have his property condemned by the law of nations as an adopted Frenchman, *pro hâc vice;* and so the King's declaration of reprisals expresses it, that the ships and goods of persons inhabiting the territories of the French King shall be subject to reprisals; and therefore the same equity operates the other way, that a Frenchman resident at Hamburgh should be considered as a Hamburgher, and have the advantages of protection if he is the sole proprietor.

[Hay & Marriott, 247.]

THE MARIA MAGDALENA.

Cargo—British Owners—Declaration of Reprisals—Capture—Condemnation—False Affidavits.

A neutral ship sailed from the Thames after a declaration of reprisals, having on board a cargo consigned to France by British traders. *Held*, that war *de facto* existed between Great Britain and France, and that the cargo must be condemned.

1779 Jan. 11.

This was a Swedish ship, taken by his Majesty's cutter, the *Kite*, upon the 26th of August, bound from the port of London to Nantes. She was laden by several merchants of French houses of eminence in London, and the cargo put on board between the 7th of July and the 21st of August, cleared and sailed out of the river Thames on the 24th of August, as appeared upon the evidence of the Swedish master and mate. Separate claims were given, and one of the claimants very honestly in his affidavit confessed that if the goods got safe to Nantes they were to be French property, but if taken upon the high seas then they were to be British property. This shows the artful manner in which merchants cover their trade with the enemy, and the necessity of parties being required to prove a *continued* and *complete* property for their own account and risk at the time of their lading, at the time of their being taken, and at the time of their unlading at the place of their final destination. One of the claimants had made an affidavit that his goods were shipped the beginning of August, but being deceived, as his counsel said, by his broker, he now made another affidavit that they were shipped in July, on a day before his Majesty's declaration of reprisals, which was on the 29th of July. They all of them swore roundly that their respective cargoes were shipped for Ostend; and it appeared by the evidence of the master that the ship was never intended for, nor did it touch at, Ostend, and that he flung overboard all his English Custom House papers the moment he got out of the river. All the bills of lading were made out in the French language, and as of goods shipped at Ostend in foreign names of Arnoldus Hoys and others. The counsel for the claimants urged that the present state of hostilities was not such a state of war as to make British subjects liable to confiscation, or any other legal inconvenience, for holding correspondence with France; that nothing but a declaration of war could restrain the subject; but a declaration of reprisals went no farther than to confiscate the goods of enemies and of others residing within their territories, under their protection and government, and not those of British subjects. If there was meant to have been a prohibition of that kind, it ought to have been expressed, to have put British merchants upon their guard; that it was well known in the commercial world that by the laws of France British manufactures cannot be imported directly into France without an extraordinary duty, which duty is avoided by carrying them to Ostend, and from Ostend to French ports; that this trade, by connivance, is greatly for the advantage of England, and as such to be tolerated, being like to the profits acquired by insuring the goods of the enemy, and the balance in favour of this kingdom. That it appears by Rymer's Foedera in the time of Edward the Third, that commerce

1779 Jan. 11. THE MARIA MAGDALENA.

was allowed between English and French subjects, although the two kingdoms were in a state of war, and that no prohibition can legally take place till there is a declaration of war, which, like that in 1752, forbids the subject to hold any kind of correspondence; that the packets to this moment sail between Dover and Calais; that it is not even clear that the French Minister, or his representative, have quitted this country; and an Order of Council for reprisals is not equal to a declaration of war in many respects; otherwise, why does this Court decree that naval stores, laden on board neutral vessels, before the time limited by his Majesty's notification, and destined for his enemies, should be sold to his Majesty for the benefit of the proprietors? To this it was answered, that the fact was clear on the part of the captors that the ship had sailed a month after, in defiance of the King's declaration of reprisals, from the port of London to the port of an enemy. If such trade was thought useful, upon a representation to his Majesty's Government, passports and letters of safe conduct should be applied for, and licences obtained. The master deposing that the bills of lading were all colourable and false is a sufficient ground for condemnation. The present state of hostilities is a state of war, *de facto*, to all intents and purposes, and the parties claiming suffered the vessel to sail a month after the King's declaration, with their eyes open to all the consequences of such an act.

In the case of the *Stadt Bergen*, in 1758, in the *Rengender Jacob*, and the *Notre Dame de Grace*, where British subjects claimed goods on board neutral ships destined for the ports of the enemy, the goods were condemned, upon this principle, that no claims can be admitted to contradict the ship's papers, and that English merchants shall not consign falsely; that the truth of the matter seems to be, that the present claimants are shippers and insurers for the French, but not ultimately and truly the owners: if they are the owners, such a trade is illegal.

JUDGMENT:

The judge [Sir J. Marriott] delivered his opinion as follows: The fact is, that merchants in England have cleared out a vessel in the river Thames falsely, and have furnished her with false bills of lading; and the English clearances have been destroyed. They have sworn

1779 Jan. 11.

THE MARIA MAGDALENA.

Sir J. Marriott.

most equivocally in their affidavits that the goods were shipped for Ostend, whereas they were shipped in reality for Nantz, in France, the capital port for the rebel American trade. The several parcels of goods were put on board at different times, some before, and others entirely after his Majesty's declaration of general reprisals, on the 29th of July, against France. They could not but know also, being French houses, of the King of France declaring in terms, on the 10th of July, that he was engaged in actual hostilities with England. This point has already been decided by the Admiralty Courts of both kingdoms. Where is the difference, whether a war is proclaimed by a herald at the Royal Exchange, with his trumpets, and on the Pont Neuf at Paris, and by reading and affixing a printed paper on public buildings; or whether war is announced by royal ships, and whole fleets, at the mouths of cannon? The relative state of subjects, as to foreign nations, is that of their prince. It is a misdemeanour of a very high nature to carry on commerce with the enemies of the crown and kingdom. Confiscation here is one of the civil consequences of such a conduct. Metaphysical refinements about *bellum justum, perfectum, legitimum* are ridiculous. If learned authorities are to be quoted, Bynkershoek has a whole chapter to prove, from the history of Europe, that a lawful and perfect state of war may exist without proclamation. But it is said that this covered trade is politically useful for England and its manufactures, and the balance as favourable as insuring. I do not sit here to judge of political systems, or commercial ones, upon the subject of the greater or less degrees of possible profit and loss to the community. It is said that the returns will be made in French goods; that is, they will be smuggled into England; but at all events, between the trade of England and France, in the commutation of commodities, the balance is known to be greatly against England. In regard to insuring (and I do not wonder at this argument coming from insurers), I have a clear opinion, that as the insuring of his Majesty's life is not to be permitted, because it may be a temptation to some one to take it away, so insuring against the arms of the British nation is an inducement perpetually to betray them; it is an aiding, abetting, and comforting of the king's enemies, a discovery of the national councils, and a

1779 Jan. 11. THE MARIA MAGDALENA. Sir J. Marriott.

prolonging of the war, to the oppression, taxation, and ruin of millions of subjects, and instead of a great balance of profit in favour of the whole community, it is a less balance turned into the narrow channel of the pockets of a few private men, who often, without property, prey and grow great upon the public vitals. There seems little or no doubt but the claimants are insurers; not the ultimate owners, at all events; and the affidavit of one of the claimants clearly shows how the bargains are made between the shipper here by commission, and the consignee in France, as to the risk on the sea and on the land. How any man can swear (and *one only* has ventured to swear so, besides the variations of his dates) "that the goods, if they had been landed in France, would have continued his property," is astonishing: for it is clear that if they were English property, and had arrived in France, they would have been condemned; if they were to be free, they must be French. So that the fact either way stares the affidavit in the face. And these are merchants! Not indeed true Englishmen; for better would it be for England, that Englishmen to Frenchmen should set foot to foot, than thus to protract a war with all the subtleties of mercantile negotiation and every refinement. What is this but *cauponantes bellum?—carrying on war by retail?* I own I am shocked when I see the names of the claimants, and observe by the affidavits how little *attention* is paid to truth, and to the bond of all duties, public and private, the solemnity of an oath. Is the faith of a broker, and his report to his principals, or even his oath at a Custom-house, to heal over the conscience of his employer? But these are merchants!

Remitters, agents by commission, insurers of all things certain and uncertain, and the greatest enemies of this country and happy constitution, are found too often blended together in the general class of the denomination of merchants, assumed by men who are either born, or are dwelling, and growing rich under the laws, liberties, and protection of Great Britain, without affection or attachment to it.

The true merchant, importer and exporter, for his own account and risk, is a great character, and to be revered by all mankind, whose necessities are supplied by him, and the horrors even of war diminished. Such there still are, and who are men of the greatest probity, and worthy of the confidence of Sovereigns and of nations. I feel the utmost pain in this cause. I have a personal respect for some of the names I see in the claims and affidavits annexed, and am willing to be persuaded, that in the immense hurry of other business, or by the dissipation of the pleasures of the times, they have been led into a most dangerous error, in imagining that affidavits are nothing but forms, to be left to be settled by an attorney, a proctor, a clerk in office, or a counting-house; they are made with levity, and sworn to with rashness. If such affidavits had appeared in any other Court in this kingdom, the claimants would have been too sensible of the consequences of falsifications. Warned of their mistake and inattention here, they ought to be thankful for what is now said, to put them upon their guard from showing too much zeal for their correspondents in an enemy's country hereafter. The goods must be condemned, and the freight and costs on all sides paid by the claimants. No contract appears with the neutral carrier; they best know what it was, and for whom it was made. It is very reasonable that the master should pay the man.

1779 Jan. 11.

THE MARIA MAGDALENA.

Sir J. Marriott.

The proctor for the claimants protested of a grievance and appealing; but the appeal has since been withdrawn.

THE CONCORDIA AFFINITATIS.

[Hay & Marriott, 289.]

Practice—Affidavits—Proof of Neutral's Property—Cargo.

Affidavits in proof of neutral property in a cargo should be unequivocal, and should go to the property in the goods when they were first laden, when taken, and when finally landed.

THIS was a Swedish ship, bound from Hamburgh to Rochelle. Upon the 27th of November last the ship was restored with freight and the master's expenses charged upon the cargo. The hemp and copper sheets were ordered to be sold to the Commissioners of his Majesty's Navy, the money to be brought into the Registry, for the use of those who shall be entitled thereto; and the claimants of the cargo in general (the property not being verified by the master, or fully set forth in the bills of lading) were ordered to

1779 Feb. 8.

1779 Feb. 8.

THE CONCORDIA AFFINITATIS.

prove their property. The captors consented to accept of affidavits as proof, without going into pleadings. A great number of affidavits were accordingly brought in. Out of fourteen there were but three numbers which were unequivocal and direct. The Court restored the contents of these three bills of lading, and ordered that the claimants should give fuller proof of the property of all the rest.

The objections taken by the counsel for the captors were, that many of the affidavits were only in the present tense, viz., that the goods claimed *are* solely and wholly the property of claimants, and that no other person *hath* any share or interest therein: whereas it ought to have been sworn, not only that the goods were their entire and sole property at the time of lading, at the time of their being taken as prize, and are so at the present time, but also *will remain* so in case the ship shall arrive at the place of her original destination. One of the claimants swore that the hemp *does go over the sea* for his account and risk. Another swore that the goods are insured at Hamburgh and Amsterdam, and *thus* (drawing an inference) subjects of neutral states actually run the risk thereof. The case of *Charles Havernerswerth*, in 1741, was quoted. That was a Swedish ship, which had taken in goods upon general freight at Hambro' for Alicant, Cadiz, and Marseilles, by the bills of lading, to be delivered to the persons to whom the goods were consigned. There were attestations on board the ship concerning the property, and to them exceptions were taken as in the present, that they related to the property at the time of shipping only. The Court ordered fuller proof, and the mode of making it to be settled and agreed by the advocates on all sides by reference: Dr. Paul, the King's Advocate (Sir George Lee), Sir Ed. Simpson, Dr. Pinfold, Sir George Hay, Dr. Jenner, and the rest of the bar of civilians. They upon reference reported that affidavits should be made by the claimants that the goods were their sole and entire property at the time of their shipping, continued to be so at the time of the capture, and would continue so until the goods should be sold by their agents in France and Spain for their account. This form was exactly corresponding to the latter part of the twelfth of the standing interrogatories. It was urged, that affidavits being now made and insufficient, the Court should condemn.

1779 *Feb.* 8.

THE CONCORDIA AFFINITATIS.

Sir J. Marriott.

JUDGMENT:

The judge [Sir J. Marriott] observed that the affidavits were made, and bore date in November previous to his decree on the 27th; that although it was true that a line must be drawn in every cause after a certain period to exclude all further proof, otherwise causes would be immortal, yet he would allow further time to the claimants to make affidavits in proper form, as they made these before they knew what forms were required of them; that it would be very dangerous to admit such general affidavits, and that it was a very suspicious circumstance, that the same notary who had drawn the affidavits for the goods in the bills of lading, C. G. N., which *were sufficiently full* (and so it was clear therefore, from them, that he knew the forms that were proper), was the drawer of the eleven affidavits, one of which only spoke to the property of the goods while going over the sea, thereby raising an implication that they were the enemy's when they should arrive at land; or arguing, that by the insurers being neutrals they were therefore for neutral risk. This shows the propriety of the words account and risk, and the wisdom of the twelfth interrogatory; for goods may, especially since policies of insurance have become general, be for one man's account that are not for his risk, or for a man's risk which are not for his account. The very idea of complete and perfect property is perpetuity; that what was mine yesterday is mine to-day, and will be so to-morrow, and every day until I assign it over, or make delivery of it for some due consideration to another person. The word *proprius*, in the classics, means perpetual; thus in Terence, "*ut haec mihi propria fit felicitas:*" may this happiness continue mine, that is, long and lasting. It was not until the case of the *Charles Havernerswerth*, that the affidavits were ever admitted by the practice of the Admiralty Court, but as *semiplena probatio* only, and then they were admitted as sufficient by consent.

The claimants used to go into further pleadings and proofs, and the captors had liberty to plead in contradiction, and to have cross-examinations. The same distress and difficulty dwelt on the mind of the judge then as it does now. The going into pleadings and proofs is one of the most difficult points of adjudication in causes of prize. He felt the great inconvenience, expense and delay of

1779 *Feb.* 8.

THE CONCORDIA AFFINITATIS.

Sir J. Marriott.

this proceeding; but it is easier often to see an evil in the practice of a Court, than to find a remedy that has no objection, or may not lead to worse consequences. With respect to great names that have done honour to their profession, it must be observed that it would be dangerous to point out too exactly and invariably the forms of affidavits. Invariable forms are advantageous instruments for fraud to make use of. It will be sufficient to say that wherever further proof is indulged to claimants upon affidavits, those attestations must be without equivocality, and they must go to the property of goods at the periods when first laden, when taken, and when finally landed; and they ought to be negative as well as affirmative, that no enemies of the Crown of Great Britain, or its subjects trading with its enemies, had, have, or will have, at any of those times, any right, share, title, or interest therein, directly or indirectly, without fraud, collusion, equivocation, or mental reservation. The claimants on the whole are recommended to consider well what they can truly swear to, and advise with their advocates as to the forms of their affidavits and proofs.

[3 C. Rob. 300, note.]

THE SALLY.

Before the Lords Commissioners of Appeals (*a*).

Cargo—Neutral—Consignment to Enemy—Concealed Letter—Capture in transitu.

Property shipped by a neutral and consigned to a hostile port, and to become the property of the enemy on arrival, if captured *in transitu*, is liable to condemnation.

1795 *Dec.* 12.

THIS was a case of a cargo of corn shipped March, 1793, by Steward and Plunket, of Baltimore, ostensibly for the account and risk of Conyngham, Nesbit & Co., of Philadelphia, and consigned to them or their assigns:—By an endorsement on the bill of lading, it was further agreed that the ship should proceed to Havre de Grace, and there wait such time as might be necessary the orders of the *consignee* of the said cargo (the Mayor of Havre), either to deliver the same at the port of Havre, or proceed therewith to any one port without the Mediterranean, on freight at the rate of 5*s.*

(*a*) Present: Earl of Mansfield, Sir R. P. Arden, M. R., Sir W. Wynne.

per barrel on delivery at Havre, and 5*s*. 6*d*. at a second port; the freight to be settled by the shippers in America according to agreement.

Amongst the papers was a concealed letter from Jean Ternant, the Minister of the French Republic to the United States, in which he informs the Minister of Foreign Affairs in France, "The house of Conyngham & Co., already known to the Ministers by their former operations for France, is charged by me to procure without delay a consignment of 22,000 bushels of wheat, 8,000 barrels of fine flour, 900 barrels of salted beef from New England. The conditions stipulated are the same as those of the contract of 2nd November, 1792, with the American citizens Swan & Co. for a like supply to be made to the Antilles, namely, that the grain, flour, and beef are to be paid at the current price of the markets at the time of their being shipped; that the freights shall be at the lowest course in the ports; that an insurance should be on the whole; and that a commission of five per cent. shall be allowed for all the merchants' expenses and fees. It has been moreover agreed, considering the actual reports of war, that the whole shall be sent as American property to Havre and to Nantes, with power to our government of sending the ships to other ports conditional on the usual freight. As you have not signified to me to whom these cargoes ought to be delivered in our ports, I shall provide each captain with a letter to the mayor of the place."

There was also a letter from J. Ternant to the mayor of the municipality of Havre: "Our government having ordered me to send supplies of provisions to your port, I inform you that the bearer of this, commanding the American ship the *Sally*, is laden with a cargo of wheat, of which he will deliver you the bill of lading."

To the 12th and 20th interrogatories the master deposed, "that he believes the flour was the property of the French Government, and on being unladen, would have immediately become the property of the French Government."

In the argument it was insisted, on the part of the claimants, that the cargo was to be considered as the property of the American merchants; that it had been ordered of them, to be supplied and delivered at a certain place; and that under the general principle of law, property was not considered to be divested between the vendor and vendee till actual delivery. It was contended, that the contract remained executory till the completion by delivery in Europe; that the payment was contingent on the completion of the contract in this form, and that no money had passed, nor any compensation or agreement had intervened to produce an absolute conversion of the property; and it was prayed that the Court would admit farther proof to ascertain that circumstance.

On the part of the captors it was replied, that the general rule of law subsisting between vendor and vendee in a commercial transaction, referring only to the contracting parties, and not affecting the rights of third persons, could not apply to contracts made in time of war, or in contemplation of war, where the rights of a belligerent nation intervened; that the effect of such a contract as the present would be to protect the trade of the contracting belligerent from his enemy; and that if it could be allowed, it would put an end to all capture. It was said to be a known principle of the Prize Court, that neutral property must be proved to be neutral at all periods from the time of shipment, without intermission, to the arrival and subsequent sale in the port of the enemy; that the 12th and 20th interrogatories were framed with this view to inquire, "whether on its arrival, &c. it shall and will belong to the same owner and no other, &c.," and a reference was made to the case of the *Charles Havernerswerth* in 1741, in which the form of attestation was directed to be prepared by the whole bar, and was established in the present form to ascertain the property at the several periods of shipment, and arrival in the enemy's ports,—in cases where affidavits were to be received to supply the defects of the original evidence, in the place of plea and proof.

JUDGMENT:

The Court said—It has always been the rule of the Prize Courts, that property going to be delivered in the enemy's country, and under a contract to become the property of the enemy immediately on arrival, if taken *in transitu*, is to be considered as enemies' property. When the contract is made in time of peace or without any contemplation of a war, no such rule exists. But in a case like the present, where the form of the contract was framed directly for the purpose of obviating the danger apprehended from approaching hostilities, it is a rule which unavoidably must take place. The bill of lading expresses account and risk of the American merchant; but papers alone make no proof, unless supported by the depositions of the master. Instead of supporting the contents of his papers, the master deposes, "that on arrival the goods would become the property of the French Government," and all the concealed papers strongly support him in this testimony. The *evidentia rei* is too strong to admit farther proof. Supposing that it was to become the property of the enemy on delivery, *capture* is considered as *delivery*. The captors, by the rights of war, stand in the place of the enemy, and are entitled to a condemnation of goods passing under such a contract, as of enemy's property. On every principle on which Prize Courts can proceed, this cargo must be considered as enemy's property. Condemned (*a*).

1795 *Dec.* 12.

THE SALLY.

THE VIGILANTIA. THE EMBDEN.

[1 C. Rob. 1.]

Capture—National Character of Ship—Place of Residence of Owner—Nationality of Master.

The national character of a ship is generally determined by the place of residence of the owner, but special circumstances may negative the general rule, such as the traffic in which a ship is engaged, from which her national character may be presumed.—A master who serves on a foreign ship for many years is thereby divested of his national character.

THIS was a case of a ship sailing under Prussian colours, and taken on a voyage from Amstersdam to Greenland, laden with stores and other necessary articles for the Greenland fishery.

1798 *Nov.* 6.

A claim was given for Mr. Brower, a merchant of Embden.

SIR W. SCOTT.—This was a ship sailing under Prussian colours, and taken on the 4th of May, 1798, on a voyage from Amsterdam

(*a*) In the *Atlas* (May 21st, 1801), Sir W. Scott said: "I do not see how this case can be distinguished from the *Sally*. I must pronounce this cargo liable to condemnation, on the ground that it is taken whilst going to an enemy's port, to be delivered there to an enemy, and to be paid for by him. It came from America, as American property, but it was sold at Vigo to the Spanish Government, and went from thence to Seville as Spanish property. [It was captured on the voyage from V. to S.] The contract under which it went was absolute." Cargo condemned, ship restored. [3 C. Rob. 300.]

1798 *Nov.* 6.

THE VIGILANTIA. THE EMBDEN.

Sir W. Scott.

to Greenland: there was no cargo on board, but the vessel was fitted out with stores necessary for the Greenland fishery. The claimant is Mr. Peter Brower, of Embden; and the cause comes on to be decided by me, on the only evidence that can regularly be produced in the first instance, on the ship's papers, and the preparatory examinations.

[The Court first minutely examined the evidence and concluded.]

Looking, then, at these papers, and the conduct of the parties, I feel no scruple in pronouncing, that this ship still continues *de facto* the property of the former Dutch owner, and is, as such, subject to condemnation.

But I will go farther, and for the convenience of applying a ruling principle to some other cases which I am informed bear a strong affinity to the circumstances of the present case, I will express my opinion on the abstract question of law. I desire to state my opinion, then, subject to the correction of a Superior Court, that supposing Mr. Brower to be the actual proprietor of this vessel, and resident at Embden, yet this vessel and her concerns (however it may be with respect to other ships, and other concerns in which this gentleman may be engaged) are liable to be treated and considered as Dutch property.—In the first place, she is a Dutch-built vessel, a Dutch fishing vessel, that went from Amsterdam regularly, and habitually, to Greenland, and to return to Amsterdam, there to deliver her cargo: she is purchased in Holland, she is purchased avowedly for the purpose of pursuing the same course of commerce, the fishing trade of Holland: she is purchased at a time when, it is said, there was a defect of conveniences for carrying on this trade at Embden; but I am satisfied it was the intention of the parties to carry on this trade to and from Amsterdam. Now, I ask upon what grounds is it that this vessel, so purchased and so employed, is to be considered merely as a Prussian vessel? Here is a ship as thoroughly engaged and incorporated in Dutch commerce as a ship can possibly be; she is fitted out uniformly from Amsterdam; she is fitted out with Dutch manufacture, she is fitted out for Dutch importation, in all these respects employing and feeding the industry of that country; she is managed by a Dutch ship's husband, and

1798 *Nov.* 6.

THE VIGILANTIA. THE EMBDEN.

Sir W. Scott.

finding occupation for the commercial knowledge and industry of the subjects of that country; she is commanded by a Dutch captain; she is manned by a Dutch crew, and brings back the produce of her voyage for the purpose of Dutch consumption and Dutch revenue. If to this you add that the vessel is transferred by the Dutch because they themselves are unable to carry on the trade avowedly in their own persons, it is truly a Dutch commerce in a very eminent degree, not only in its essence, but for the very hostile purpose of rescuing and protecting the Dutch from the naval superiority of their British enemy. In my apprehension, unless it could be maintained as a rule, without any exception whatever, that the domicil of the proprietor constitutes the national character of the vessel, this ship must be condemned, even if she had been really transferred.

Now on that point, I conceive the rule to be, that where there is nothing particular or special in the conduct of the vessel itself, the national character is determined by the residence of the owner; but there may be circumstances arising from that conduct which will lead to a contrary conclusion. It is a known and established rule with respect to a vessel, that if she is navigating under the pass of a foreign country, she is considered as bearing the national character of that nation under whose pass she sails: she makes a part of its navigation, and is in every respect liable to be considered as a vessel of that country. In like manner, and upon similar principles, if a vessel purchased in the enemy's country is, by constant and habitual occupation, continually employed in the trade of that country, commencing with the war, continuing during the war, and evidently on account of the war, on what ground is it to be asserted, that vessel is not to be deemed a ship of the country from which she is so navigating, in the same manner as if she evidently belonged to the inhabitants of it?

Suppose the naval arms of France had been triumphant in her present contest with Great Britain; and that all the British Greenland ships could no longer have been navigated as such from British ports;—suppose a neutral country should offer her charitable assistance, and her merchants should say, we will purchase your vessels, but they shall still navigate to Greenland; they shall still continue under your management, and be fitted out in your

1798 *Nov.* 6. THE VIGILANTIA. THE EMBDEN. Sir W. Scott.

ports; they shall still contribute to the industry of your artificers; they shall be conducted by the skill of your own navigators, by the attention of your merchants, and they shall supply your manufactures and revenue: in my apprehension the enemy would be justified in saying, "you the neutrals are in this transaction mere merchants of Great Britain, your traffic is the traffic of Englishmen; with respect to this commerce it has all the marks of English commerce upon it, and as English commerce it shall be considered and treated by us." But farther, in considering this case as the case of a Dutch ship, I think I am strongly warranted from higher authority, by the judgment of the Lords of Appeal in a case which is well known in this Court, the case of *Zacharia Coopman & Co.* [*sub nom.* the *Nancy*, Lords, April 9, 1798].

There had been a determination last war, in the case [the *Jacobus Johannes*, Lords, Feb. 10, 1785] of two persons, one resident at Saint Eustatius, the other in Denmark, who were partners in a house of trade at Saint Eustatius—the one who resided there, forwarded the cargoes to Europe; the other received them in Amsterdam, disposed of them there, and then returned to Denmark. It was decided in that case, that the share of the person resident in Saint Eustatius was liable to condemnation, as the property of a domiciled Dutchman; and that the share of the other partner should be restored, as the property of a neutral. There was also a case [the *Osprey*, Lords, March 28, 1795] in this war, of some persons, who migrated from Nantucket to France, and there carried on a fishery very beneficial to the French; in that case, the property of a partner domiciled in France was condemned; whilst the property of another partner resident in America was restored. From these two cases a notion had been adopted, that the domicil of the parties was that alone, to which the Court had a right to resort; but the case of *Coopman* was lately decided on very different principles. It was then said by the Lords, that the former cases were cases merely at the commencement of a war; that in the case of a person carrying on trade habitually in the country of the enemy, though not resident there, he should have time to withdraw himself from that commerce; and that it would press too heavily on neutrals, to say, that immediately on the first breaking out of a war, their goods should become subject to confiscation; but it was then expressly laid down, that if a person entered into a house of trade in the enemy's country in time of war, or continued that connection during the war, he should not protect himself by mere residence in a neutral country. That decision instructs me in this doctrine, a doctrine supported by strong principles of equity and propriety: "that there is a traffic which stamps a national character on the individual, independent of that character, which mere personal residence may give him." In the present case I am clearly of opinion, that this is altogether a Dutch traffic; and that a ship, so employed as this ship appears to have been, is in every respect to be considered as a vessel of that country; in whose navigation, under all these circumstances, she was habitually employed. This is a determination which I shall certainly apply to the decision of all those cases which come before me under similar circumstances. If my opinion is erroneous, I am happy to think it will be set right by a much higher authority; but I feel no diffidence in the decision which I have now pronounced.

THE EMBDEN.

[1 C. Rob. 16.]

This was a case of a ship transferred in Holland under circumstances similar to the preceding case, and taken on a voyage from Amsterdam to Greenland.

A claim was given for Mr. Bowerman of *Embden*.

The points taken to distinguish this case from the *Vigilantia* are not material except as regards the position of the master.

For the claimant, *Laurence* and *Swabey*. This case is distinguishable from the last in the point: the master is a Prussian by birth.

For the captors, the *King's Advocate*.

SIR W. SCOTT.—The question which I am to consider is whether the distinctions which have been pointed out are sufficient to take this vessel out of the law which has been laid down in the preceding case.

The first distinction is taken from the master's national character, but I think he has scarcely a right to be considered as a Prussian subject; he is a single man who has established no domicil by family connections, and in his own person he has been employed constantly for ten years in trading from Amsterdam to Greenland. By such an occupation he is divested of his national character, and becomes, by adoption, a perfect Dutchman. . . . .

[1 C. Rob. 22.]

THE ENDRAUGHT.

Contraband—Ship Timber—Practice—Reference to Experts.

By treaty it was agreed that "all articles which serve directly for the building of ships, unwrought iron and fir planks excepted, shall be deemed contraband." A vessel to which this treaty applied having been seized with a cargo of timber, the Court referred the question as to whether such timber was ship timber to experts to report thereon.

1798 *Nov.* 19. THIS was a case of a ship taken on her voyage from Narva to Dort, in Holland, with a cargo of balks, fir-planks, battens, and firewood.

A claim was given for the ship and cargo, as the property of Danish subjects. [This case is of importance only for the point of practice.]

For the captors, the *King's Advocate* [Sir John Nicholl].

For the claimant, *Lawrence.*

SIR W. SCOTT.—There is a preliminary question which may make this discussion of property unnecessary; the nature of the cargo may perhaps decide this case: it is asserted to be "a cargo of ship timber going to an enemy's port of naval equipment"; and under this description to come under the character of contraband. This I consider to be the correct law of nations, notwithstanding some relaxations which may occasionally have been allowed.

But besides the general law of nations, there is an express treaty between this country and Denmark, which declares, "that ship timber, fir planks excepted, shall be deemed contraband." With respect to the true character of this timber, and the fair application of it, I do not seem to be in possession of sufficient facts to govern my decision; I shall therefore refer it to the principal persons employed in making repairs for ships or vessels belonging to Government at Yarmouth, where this cargo lies, to certify their opinion whether this is properly ship timber; if there are no such persons at Yarmouth, the opinions of respectable shipwrights there must be taken upon it; and the Court will judge upon their report of its nature and quality.

THE STAADT EMBDEN. [1 C. Rob. 26.]

Contraband—Masts—Produce of Shipper's Country—Non-contraband Goods Part of Cargo.

A cargo of masts exported from Russia destined for Holland: *Held* to be contraband. *Held*, also, that non-contraband goods, part of the same cargo and the property of the same owner, must be condemned.

1798 Nov. 19.

This was a case of a ship which had been a prize ship taken from the English, and carried into Christiansund. A pretended sale had passed there, and the vessel was retaken on a voyage from Riga to Amsterdam, laden with deals and masts.

A claim was given for the ship, as the property of Mr. Bowerman, of Embden; and for the cargo, as the property of merchants of Riga.

For the captor, the *King's Advocate* and *Croke.*

For the claimant of the cargo, *Arnold.*

Sir W. Scott.—This is a British vessel, carried as prize by the enemy to Norway, and purchased, as it was pretended, on behalf of Mr. Bowerman.

[The Court then examined the facts, and held that there had not been a *boná fide* sale, and condemned the ship.]

With respect to the cargo, there is no sufficient proof that it belongs to the Russians, for whom it is claimed; but if it did, it is contended to be of the nature of contraband; and most clearly the masts are liable to be so considered, in the judgment even of the most zealous advocates of neutral commerce. As to the relaxation in favour of the export of native produce, said to have been sanctioned by a determination upon Prussian hemp, in the case of *Jonge Pieter*, I am by no means disposed to consider that case as laying down any such universal principle.

There have been many cases in which native articles, going to the enemy's ports on the account of inhabitants of the country which produced them, have been treated as contraband. In the famous case of the *Med Guds Hielpe* (a), a cargo of pitch and tar, going on Swedish account from Stockholm to Port Louis, was condemned; that condemnation was afterwards confirmed by

(a) *Ante*, p. 1.

1798 Nov. 19. The Staadt Embden. Sir W. Scott.

a solemn judgment of the Lords, and the MS. note which I have of that case, expressly states it to have been condemned by the Lords of Appeal, on the ground of contraband (*a*).

It certainly does not aid the Russian claimant in this case, that the cargo is going to a country against which his sovereign is exercising hostility: that Russia is in a state of war with Holland, is more than I can venture to assert, no declaration to that effect having formally announced it; and therefore, if this was a cargo of a perfectly inoffensive nature, on the account of a Russian, it might perhaps be too much for this Court to confiscate it upon the ground of a trading with the enemy of his sovereign: at the same time it is to be remarked, that Russia is the declared public enemy of the French Republic, the patroness and ally of the present government of Holland; that the fleet of Russia is immediately co-operating with the fleet of Great Britain in the blockade of Amsterdam; and, though an auxiliary fleet is not of itself sufficient to make its government a principal in a war, yet where captures are made and prizes are claimed by that auxiliary force, as taken from a common enemy, which has been repeatedly done in the present Dutch hostilities, it is not easy to discover the grounds on which the government to which the auxiliary fleet belongs can be considered as entirely neutral.

Adverting therefore to all circumstances, considering that this is a shipment of naval stores to a port of naval equipment under possession of the French, and that Russia is engaged in declared hostilities against France, I shall condemn this cargo as contraband, and I shall make no distinction. The statement of the King's Advocate is in my opinion the law of nations, upon this point. To escape from the contagion of contraband, the innocent articles must be the property of a different owner.

I shall therefore condemn the whole cargo.

[(*a*) In the MS. note of Sir George Lee, *ante*, p. 3, the grounds of the decision on appeal are not stated.]

THE SANTA CRUZ.

[1 C. Rob. 50.]

Recapture — Condemnation — Restitution — Property of Allies — Reciprocity — Divestment of Property of Original Owner.

When a ship owned by a subject of an ally, has been recaptured by a British ship, the Court will apply the rule acted on in the Prize Court of Great Britain in regard to the recapture of British vessels, namely, to restore on payment of salvage, unless the rule of the Prize Court of the ally is less liberal than that of Great Britain, when on the principle of reciprocity the rule of the ally will be adopted. Per Sir W. Scott:— Probably the rule is, that in order to divest the owner of his property, the vessel after capture must have been brought *infra præsidia* (*a*).

Onus on claimant to prove law of his country after adverse *primâ facie* evidence of captors.

THIS was a case of some Portuguese vessels taken by the French, and retaken by English cruisers. 1798 *Dec.* 7.

For the captors, the *King's Advocate* and *Lawrence*.

For the claimant, *Arnold* and *Sewell*.

SIR W. SCOTT.—These are cases of Portuguese ships or cargoes, eight in number, which have been recaptured at different times by British cruisers.

As far as the dates of the recaptures are material, they are to be distinguished under three periods:—The first vessel was recaptured before the month of December, 1796, when an ordinance on the subject of recapture passed in Portugal: the second was retaken between the months of December, 1796, and May, 1797, when another ordinance took place, more expressly respecting the property of allies recaptured from the enemy: the rest may be stated generally, without further distinction, to have been taken subsequently to the 9th of May, 1797. It is necessary to distinguish these dates, as it is said the difference of date may affect the application of the general principle, whatever that may be, to the particular cases.

They are cases of very considerable value, of much importance, and of no mean difficulty in many respects; under a choice of cases, they are not such as I should particularly wish to determine; but they devolve on me in the regular course of my duty; and I am bound to decide them according to my own best informed

(*a*) But see the *Flad Oyen*, *post*, p. 78.

1798 *Dec. 7.* — THE SANTA CRUZ. — Sir W. Scott.

apprehensions of law and justice, of the general law of nations, as it has been understood and administered in the British Courts of Admiralty.

In the arguments of the counsel, I have heard much of the rules which the law of nations prescribes on recapture, respecting the time when property vests in the captor; and it certainly is a question of much curiosity, to inquire what is the true rule on this subject; when I say the true rule, I mean only the rule to which civilized nations, attending to just principles, ought to adhere; for the moment you admit, as admitted it must be, that the practice of nations is various, you admit that there is no rule operating with the proper force and authority of a general law.

It may be fit there should be some rule, and it might be either the rule of immediate possession, or the rule of pernoctation and twenty-four hours' possession; or it might be the rule of bringing *infra præsidia;* or it might be a rule requiring an actual sentence of condemnation: either of these rules might be sufficient for general practical convenience, although in theory perhaps one might appear more just than another: but the fact is, there is no such rule of practice; nations concur in principle indeed, so far as to require firm and secure possession; but their rules of evidence respecting the possession are so discordant, and lead to such opposite conclusions, that the mere unity of principle forms no uniform rule to regulate the general practice. But were the public opinion of European States more distinctly agreed, on any principle, as fit to form the rule of the law of nations on this subject, it by no means follows that any one nation would lie under an obligation to observe it.

That obligation could arise only from a reciprocity of practice in other nations; for from the very circumstance of the prevalence of a different rule among other nations, it would become not only lawful, but necessary, to that one nation to pursue a different conduct: for instance, were there a rule prevailing among other nations, that the immediate possession and the very act of capture should divest the property from the first owner, it would be absurd in Great Britain to act towards them on a more extended principle; and to lay it down as a general rule, that a bringing *infra præsidia*, though probably the true rule, should in all cases of recapture be deemed necessary to divest the original proprietor of his right; for the effect of adhering to such a rule would be gross injustice to British subjects; and a rule, from which gross injustice must ensue in practice, can never be the true rule of law between independent nations; for it cannot be supposed to be the duty of any country to make itself a martyr to speculative propriety, were that established on clearer demonstration than such questions will generally admit. Where mere abstract propriety therefore is on one side, and real practical justice on the other, the rule of substantial justice must be held to be the true rule of the law of nations between independent States.

If I am asked, under the known diversity of practice on this subject, what is the proper rule for a State to apply to the recaptured property of its allies, I should answer, that the liberal and rational proceeding would be to apply in the first instance the rule of that country to which the recaptured property belongs. I admit the practice of nations is not so, but I think such a rule would be both liberal and just; to the recaptured it presents his own consent, bound up in the legislative wisdom of his own country; to the recaptor it cannot be considered as injurious. Where the rule of the recaptured would condemn, whilst the rule of the recaptor prevailing amongst his own countrymen would restore, it brings an obvious advantage; and even in the case of immediate restitution, under the rules of the recaptured, the recapturing country would rest secure in the reliance of receiving reciprocal justice in its turn.

It may be said, what if this reliance should be disappointed? Redress must then be sought from retaliation, which in the disputes of independent States is not to be considered as vindictive retaliation, but as the just and equal measure of civil retribution; this will be their ultimate security, and it is a security sufficient to warrant the trust. For the transactions of States cannot be balanced by minute arithmetic; something must on all occasions be hazarded on just and liberal presumptions.

Or it may be asked, what if there is no rule in the country of the recaptured? I answer, first, this is scarcely to be supposed; there may be no ordinance, no Prize Acts immediately applying to recapture; but there is a law of habit, a law of usage, a standing and

1798 *Dec. 7.* THE SANTA CRUZ. Sir W. Scott.

known principle on the subject in all civilized commercial countries. It is the common practice of European States in every war to issue proclamations and edicts on the subject of Prize; but till they appear Courts of Admiralty have a law and usage on which they proceed, from habit and ancient practice, as regularly as they afterwards conform to the express regulations of their Prize Acts. But, secondly, if there should exist a country in which no rule prevails, the recapturing country must then of necessity apply its own rule, and rest on the presumption that that rule will be adopted and administered in the future practice of its allies.

Again, it is said that a country applying to other countries their own respective rules will have a practice discordant and irregular. It may be so, but it will be a discordance proceeding from the most exact uniformity of principle; it will be *idem per diversa.* It is asked also, will you adopt the rules of Tunis and Algiers? If you take the people of Tunis and Algiers for your allies, undoubtedly you must; you must act towards them on the same rules of relative justice on which you conduct yourselves towards other nations. And upon the whole of these objections, it is to be observed, that a rule may bear marks of apparent inconsistency, and nevertheless contain much relative fitness and propriety; a regulation may be extremely unfit to be made, which, yet, shall be extremely fit, and shall indeed be the only fit rule to be observed towards other parties who have originally established it for themselves.

So much it might be necessary to explain myself on the mere question of propriety; but it is much more material to consider what is the actual rule of the maritime law of England on this subject. I understand it to be clearly this: that the maritime law of England having adopted a most liberal rule of restitution on salvage, with respect to the recaptured property of its own subjects, gives the benefit of that rule to its allies, till it appears that they act towards British property on a less liberal principle; in such a case it adopts their rule, and treats them according to their own measure of justice. This I consider to be the true statement of the law of England on this subject; it was clearly so recognized in the case of the *San Iago;* a case which was not, as it has been insinuated, decided on special circumstances, nor on novel principles, but on principles of established use and authority in the jurisprudence of this country. In the discussion of that case much attention was paid to an opinion found amongst the manuscript collections of a very experienced practitioner in this profession (Sir E. Simson), which records the practice and the rule as it was understood to prevail in his time. "The rule is: that England restores, on salvage, to its allies; but if instances can be given of British property retaken by them and condemned as prize, the Court of Admiralty will determine their cases according to their own rule."

I conceive this principle of reciprocity is by no means peculiar to cases of recapture; it is found also to operate in other cases of maritime law: at the breaking out of a war it is the constant practice of this country to condemn property seized before the war, if the enemy condemns, and to restore if the enemy restores.

It is a principle sanctioned by that great foundation of the law of England, Magna Charta itself (a); which prescribes that at the commencement of a war the enemy's merchants shall be kept and treated as our own merchants are treated in their country.

In recaptures, it is observable, the liberality of this country outsteps its caution; it restores on salvage without inquiry, till it appears that the ally pursues a different rule: it may be said there may be inequality and hazard in this prompt liberality; and we may restore while the ally condemns; and so the fact has been: for it is not to be denied that before the case of the *San Iago* (b) had introduced a more accurate knowledge of the Spanish law, restitutions of Spanish property on recapture had passed as of course; the more accurate rule, however, is that which I have laid down.

In the present state of hostility (if so it may be called) between America and France, the practice of this Court restores American property on its own rule, without inquiring into the practice of America: it acts on the same principle towards Danes, and Swedes

(a) Art. 41. Omnes mercatores, &c. Et si sint de terra contra nos gwerrina, et si tales inveniantur in terra nostra in principio gwerræ, attachientur sine dampno corporum et rerum, donec sciatur a nobis, vel capitali justiciario nostro quomodo mercatores terræ nostræ tractentur, qui tunc inveniantur in terra contra nos gwerrina; et si nostri salvi sint ibi, alii salvi sint in terra nostra. [Stubbs, *Select Charters*, p. 293.]

(b) Lords, Jan. 28, 1795.

1798 Dec. 7. THE SANTA CRUZ. Sir W. Scott.

and Hamburghers, in the ambiguous state in which the rapine of France has placed the subjects of these governments. Towards Portugal then undoubtedly a less liberal treatment would not be observed: connected by long alliance, by ancient treaties, by mutual interests and common dangers, if Portugal forfeits the benefit of a rule which has been before observed as a general rule, it can be only on this ground, that the Courts of that country have applied a different rule to the property of British subjects. The question then for the Court to determine will be simply this: Has Portugal applied a different rule to British property taken by the enemy, and coming out of their hands into the possession of Portuguese subjects?

But before I enter on this inquiry, it may be proper to consider the treaties that subsist between the two countries; because if they have prescribed a rule, it will render all further discussion unnecessary. A treaty, to which much reference has been made, thus strongly and emphatically expresses the terms of union between the two countries: "Neither of the confederates shall suffer the ships and goods of the other, or of the people of either, which shall at any time be taken by the enemies of the one and carried into the ports of the other, to be conveyed away from the owners or proprietors; but the same shall be restored to them or their attorneys, provided they claim them before they are sold or cleared, and prove their rights within three months, and pay the necessary expenses for preservation and custody." Now I have no scruple in saying, this is an article incapable of being carried into literal execution, according to the modern understanding of the law of nations; for no neutral country can interpose to wrest from a belligerent prizes lawfully taken (*a*); but I think it goes

(*a*) The notion of receiving restitution from a neutral power seems, soon after this treaty, to have been found to be inconsistent with the rights of belligerents, as acknowledged by the law of nations: between the years 1666 and 1670, there is this report, among the letters of Sir L. Jenkins:—

"The question in law is, Whether this *biscainer*, being brought into your majesty's port, ought not, on account of your majesty being in amity with the Catholic king, to be rescued from under the power and force of his enemy; and *jure postliminii* to be restored to his own. The law of nations, as it is at this day observed, seems not to pass any obligation on your majesty to impart

a great way to prove the spirit of the contracting parties: and I agree with Dr. Arnold that it goes the whole length of the present claim; for such a treaty of alliance is not a thing *stricti juris*, but ought to be interpreted with liberal explanations. And although it may seem to point more immediately to a state of things in which one of the contracting parties is neutral; yet it would be strange to say, that it binds the party to seize for the purpose of restitution, where there is no right of seizure; but that it shall not oblige him to restore, when he has a complete right of seizure, and has already acted on that right. The treaty does therefore in its spirit and meaning embrace the restitution of property.

But then again, I am to inquire whether Portugal has put the same interpretation upon it, for if that government has used a different interpretation, that forms the rule which I must follow: the case therefore upon the treaty comes exactly to the same question, as the case upon the law: what has Portugal done? what acts are there, from which we may collect the construction which Portugal puts upon the law, and upon this treaty?

I come then to this important question on the fact:—On the original papers and depositions nothing appeared; restitution therefore would have passed on salvage, according to what I have described to be the law of England; but the captors offered papers to show that a different rule had prevailed in Portugal with respect to British property: in this state of doubt, the Court ordered further information, and proof to be produced, respecting the law of Portugal on recapture, and by both parties. Now the first question is: Who is more particularly expected to produce this proof? And it has been much pressed by the counsel for the

your royal protection unto one friend to the prejudice of another; this captor being *jure belli*, which is a very good title, in full and quiet possession of his prize, and so he was for a fortnight together at Portsmouth before he was discovered, will take it for an act of partiality to have it now wrested out of his hands and given to his enemies: whereas no man's condition is to be made worse than another's, in a place that is reputed of common security upon the public faith. Besides, the French ordinances do expressly provide, that leave be given to all strangers to depart those ports with such prizes as they happen to bring in: it is the practice of Spain at this day, and of all other ports that I can learn anything of, in cases of neutrality." *Life of Sir L. Jenkins*, vol. ii. p. 732.

1798 *Dec.* 7

THE SANTA CRUZ.

Sir W. Scott.

claimant, that the *onus probandi* lies on the recaptors: it lies with them, it has been said, to show that Portugal uses a different rule; or at least to raise a strong presumption of that fact. But I am of opinion that the recaptors have sufficiently discharged their duty to the Court, by the papers which have been produced.

The *onus probandi* then shifts: and it becomes a duty on the claimants to exonerate themselves from the presumption raised against them, and to show that their law is not such as the *primâ facie* evidence of the recaptors represents it to be.

They have besides great advantages in this research: the law and the country are their own: access is easy to them to the best information. They have reason to expect all that the diligence, the acuteness, and the zeal of their countrymen can produce on their side; but the captors must hunt out a foreign law, through a foreign language, and with the assistance of professors not much disposed to promote their inquiries: the means are evidently unequal between the parties; and the means being unequal, the obligation is by no means equal: all defect of proof, therefore, must press principally on the claimants; from whom the Court is entitled to expect proof of the fullest and most satisfactory nature.

It has been asked, What proof must we produce? The question admits of an obvious answer: In the first place the Court will expect the text law, the existing ordinances; now I think it does appear, that there are ordinances on the subject which have not been produced: the ordinance of 1796 refers to an ordinance of the year 1704, as the basis on which it was framed; I have therefore a right to conclude, that this ordinance has formed the substance of the Portuguese prize-law for a century; but yet no notice has been taken of it. In the next place information would be required respecting the decisions which have passed on their own recaptures; and if none such can be found, a certificate to this effect should be exhibited; but there is no certificate. Besides, it is, I think, scarcely probable that there should not have passed some decisions on this subject previous to December, 1796; Portugal has been active in the war, and the enemy has been active on those coasts; recaptures must have occurred; they must also have been brought to adjudication, and the rule by which they have been decided would have been considered by me as the law of Portugal.

It might have been expected, also, that authorities even more immediately in point might have been produced from decisions respecting the recaptured property of allies; some instances cannot but have occurred previous to May, 1797, when an edict issued on that subject. Three cases have occurred within three months after the edict, and afterwards many more; and it is scarcely probable that so many should have happened after that time, and none before. It has been suggested that the records of Portugal are not so kept as to furnish a ready answer to such inquiries; but I cannot admit an excuse so dishonourable to the tribunals of that great country. There is, therefore, a defect of evidence, for which no sufficient reason has been given on the part of the claimants.

After this statement of the reasonable expectations of the Court, let us now see what evidence has been produced; it consists of many documents, of which some must immediately be dismissed as of no use or authority in this case: of these, the first is a certificate from the Portuguese minister plenipotentiary at this Court. As far as character truly honourable both in public and private life can give weight to an opinion; as far as a conviction, that the party delivering that opinion delivers the sincere and unbiassed persuasion of his own mind, can influence me to respect it; this opinion must command the greatest attention; but the whole weight of this opinion is confined to these considerations: for it is to be remembered that the Chevalier d'Almeida is not a professor of the law, but a diplomatic character; and therefore incompetent to instruct us in questions of law.

Another paper which I shall dismiss, also, is an opinion of Mr. Da Sylva Lisboa, described to be a lawyer of considerable eminence in his own country. Upon this opinion many observations have been made, and more particularly on the impropriety with which it undertakes to explain to us the British laws of recapture; whilst it almost pleads ignorance of the Portuguese laws on the same subject. It is scarcely necessary to observe that the representation which it gives of our law is erroneous; it is, besides, very deficient in the preliminary circumstance which can alone give credit to it, or even make it intelligible to us; for it is not accompanied by any statement of the questions that were addressed to this gentleman: he could scarcely have imagined that the British Court of

1798 *Dec. 7.* THE SANTA CRUZ. Sir W. Scott.

Admiralty would apply to Portuguese professors for information on British law; and we are at a loss to conjecture in what view he could suppose we should derive any knowledge of the law of Portugal from such an opinion. It would, perhaps, therefore, be but due civility to the reputation of this gentleman to consider it as an opinion hastily obtained, on an imperfect representation of the case; and under this character, as it can avail nothing in point of authority, I would recommend it to those who may have to argue this cause again, if it should go to an appeal, to dismiss this paper wholly from the case.

The last paper which I shall dismiss is the certificate of Mr. Nash, a reputable merchant of this town. This paper relates something of a transaction that has happened to Portuguese masters accepting from the enemy, by donations, ships taken from the Portuguese.

"The enemy had captured a number of vessels, some Portuguese, some English, and willing to disencumber themselves of their prisoners they gave to the Portuguese and English masters jointly one of the Portuguese ships. On carrying their present into Portugal these persons are represented to have been severely treated, and to have been imprisoned by the Government." I am at a loss to understand this account, when I recollect the cases of the *Anne* and the *Endeavour*, unless I am to suppose that this severity was practised on them subsequently to the last ordinance, which pronounced such donations null and void; for otherwise I must suppose that donations of Portuguese property were considered void, while similar donations of British property were held to be perfectly good and valid. The same paper informs us further, "that the Portuguese masters remitted to England, to the captains of the English vessels, a part of the proceeds of their share of the donation." I am sorry for it, because the property belonged not to either party but to the former Portuguese owners, and no interest could accrue to those masters, but an ordinary salvage on restitution to the original proprietors.

This certificate cites also, as a sort of precedent, the acceptance of four pipes of wine in the same manner by an English captain, Bennet. It would be ridiculous to treat the conduct of this man as an authority. It was an irregular proceeding, and as irrelevant to this case as the former parts of this certificate.

Laying aside, therefore, these several documents, I come now to examine those papers which may be considered as matter of evidence in the case. These are, on the part of the claimants, 1st, opinions of Portuguese lawyers; 2ndly, a certificate of the Judges of the Supreme Court of Admiralty in Portugal; 3rdly, the decree of the Queen of Portugal, Nov., 1797, in the case of the *Anne;* and 4thly, a certificate of the Foreign Secretary of State of that country, Mr. Pinto de Souza. But it is scarcely possible to consider the effect of these documents without bringing under our view those at the same time which have been brought in by the captors: these are the ordinances of Dec., 1796, and of May, 1797, and the proceedings relative to the British ships, the *Anne* and the *Endeavour*.

In the ordinance of December, 1796, no mention is made of the recaptured property of allies. The ninth article refers only to their own recaptures, but a reasonable presumption arises from it that they would apply the same law to their allies; for this principle is not only liberal and just, but it is actually observed in the practice of England, France, and Spain. A presumption therefore arises, that Portugal would pursue a similar rule: but I think there are two circumstances which convince me, beyond mere presumption, that Portugal did act on this principle, and did mean to apply its own rule to the cases of allies. In the case of the *Endeavour*, which concerned the property of an ally, the sentence was in these words: "Having heard what has been alleged concerning the rule of twenty-four hours, it appears to us that that rule serves only to regulate the right of actions arising on recapture." Now, certainly, if this rule on recapture did not apply to the property of allies, it would have been entirely irrelevant to discuss that rule in such a case. We may infer, therefore, I think, that the rule of twenty-four hours' possession was the rule of Portugal; and also that, had the case of the *Endeavour* been considered as a case of recapture, it must have been governed and decided by that rule. The manner in which Portugal has acted on the last ordinance confirms me also in supposing that it was the practice of Portugal to extend its own rule to the cases of allies. The salvage there ordained for Portuguese property is one-fifth, and this proportion has been observed also in subsequent cases of British property, although it is not

1798 Dec. 7. THE SANTA CRUZ. Sir W. Scott.

the proportion of salvage which our own law prescribes: I may therefore conclude it was the practice of Portugal to apply its own law to the case of an ally.

But, it is said, this rule of twenty-four hours' possession had not prevailed in Portugal before the ordinance of 1796: that ordinance, I must observe, professes to take for its basis the ancient ordinance of 1704; and, therefore, I may presume that ancient ordinance was fundamentally the same. Had there been a difference so material, it was the duty of the claimant to have produced that ordinance for the information of the Court, and to have convinced us that the modern practice was a change and alteration in the jurisprudence of Portugal. It cannot, indeed, be supposed that an alteration so monstrous, so gigantic, so opposite to the general course of the relaxations which have gradually taken place in the law of prize during this century, should have found its way into the Courts of Portugal, and have been adopted by them for the first time in 1796. We know it to have been the ancient law of Spain. The vicinity of the two countries, their affinity of habits, the resemblance of their legal institutions, still farther strengthen the probability that this rule had also been the ancient law, or at least the usage of Portugal on this subject.

I consider myself, therefore, justified to conclude that the law of Portugal established twenty-four hours' possession by the enemy to be a legal divestment of the property of the original owner; and also that it would have applied the same rule to the property of allies.

But I acknowledge it is not sufficient to say such a rule would have been applied. It is also necessary to show that there have been actual proceedings under it; and for that purpose two cases have been produced: the cases of the *Anne* and of the *Endeavour*.

The case of the *Endeavour* was, I believe, prior in time. It was the case of a British ship taken by the French on the 24th of January, 1796: the French captain gave it to the master of a Portuguese vessel, which he had also taken: the ship was carried into Portugal: the English master demanded restitution; but it was denied to him, not only by the individual, but also by the Courts of Justice of Portugal. The case of the *Anne* happened in September, 1796, and is in one respect still stronger than that of the *Endeavour;* as it was a ship given in the same manner by the French captor to the very man who had been the master of this vessel, the *Santa Cruz:* let us suppose the master had been also the owner of the *Santa Cruz:* by what justice could he have claimed to have his own property restored from British hands, at the same time that his own law confirmed him in his refusal to restore British property under circumstances precisely similar? But restitution, it seems, was refused, under a particular order of the State, which declared "the property of the English owner had been divested, and that the title of the Portuguese owner was good and valid."

Now these are two cases strongly in point; and unless they can be overthrown, they will, I think, sufficiently establish this fact: that it was the practice of the Courts of Portugal, either under ancient ordinances or under a silent, but prevailing usage, or under some recent edict, to confiscate the property of allies coming into the possession of Portuguese subjects from the hands of the enemy: it is immaterial under which of these authorities the practice prevailed. These decisions are represented to us to be the only decisions that have passed during the present war on that subject; and they, therefore, establish the law of Portugal, from whatever sources it might be derived.

But the force of these cases has been attacked in different ways. It is said, in the first place, that they were cases not of recapture, but of donation; and it has been attempted to raise distinctions between these titles: but in all legal considerations they are precisely the same; they are both equally matter of prize: donation between enemy and enemy cannot take effect. The very character of enemy at once extinguishes all civil intercourse, from which such a title could arise. So distinctly is this rule acknowledged to be the law of this country, that if a case should happen in which an enemy after capture had made a donation, as it is called, in this manner to the original owner, that vessel must be condemned as a droit or perquisite of Admiralty; and the original proprietor could acquire no interest but as salvor, or from the subsequent liberality of the Crown.

I think I have evidence also that this matter is so considered in Portugal.

1798 Dec. 7

THE SANTA CRUZ.

Sir W. Scott.

In the certificate of the Secretary, Mr. Pinto de Souza, he says, "the order given by him was not intended to suspend the suit of the English claimant, but only to dispose of that property which of right belonged to the Queen, as being acquired from the enemy without letters of marque." It is, then, under this description, only the case of prize taken by a non-commissioned captor: and in this Mr. Pinto de Souza seems to coincide exactly with us in the view in which we should have considered it here. It has been said, however, that the law of Portugal does distinguish between donations and recaptures; but it is sufficient to observe that no proof has been produced of this assertion; and besides, it is a distinction which cannot in the nature of things reasonably exist; nor indeed should I consider myself by any means bound to pursue a foreign law through a variety of minute and subtle distinctions, which at last perhaps might be found to exist only in theory. It would be sufficient for me to know that I understand the practice as it has been administered in the only cases that have occurred on this subject.

But, it is said, these cases were decided before an incompetent tribunal; although I believe this objection applies only to the *Endeavour*: this objection, however, does not appear to have been taken by the Portuguese lawyers. In the order of her sacred Majesty, it is said indeed, "the Council of Commerce had no jurisdiction to decide questions of this nature;" but the certificates of the judges speak a different language; they say, not that the jurisdiction was incompetent, but "that the sentence which had been given by the Board of Commerce was founded on frivolous and insufficient reasons, and that the party might have appealed." The terms used by them are just the terms which would be applied to cases proceeding in their due and ordinary course.

In the case of the *Anne*, it is not, I think, pretended that the Court before which it was brought had not a competent jurisdiction: but it is argued against the British claimant that he acquiesced in the decision when he might have appealed. But let us see what must have been his prospect of success. The hope which the Portuguese lawyers held out to him is not founded on any opinion on the merits of his case, but on a point of form, "because the order of Council had not been produced." Whilst the cause was under investigation, the supreme authority of the State interposed to inform the Court that the title of the Portuguese master was legal and valid. The Court of Justice assents to this authority, and decides accordingly; and it is against a decision so deliberately pronounced and so irregularly influenced by the supreme authority of the country that this foreign claimant, the master of a small English vessel, is required to persevere. I must think it could not be expected of him.

Such are the observations which I think myself justified in making on the proceedings in these two cases; and after the general view which I have taken of the whole of this subject, it may be unnecessary to dwell more particularly on the minute parts of the several papers. It is, I think, clearly proved that before the ordinance of May, 1797, the Courts of Portugal considered British property coming out of the hands of the enemy as subject to confiscation: in two instances such property was actually confiscated, not by remote and inferior jurisdictions, but in their highest Courts, in the capital of the empire, and under the direction of the State. The ordinance of 1797 cannot be applicable to pre-existing cases; I must determine all cases as if they had come before me at the time of capture. The two former cases, therefore, of this class can receive no protection from this ordinance.

Looking then to the conduct which Portugal had observed towards British property, and conceiving myself bound by the general law of this country, and more particularly by the authority of the case of the *San Iago*, to proceed on strict principles of reciprocity, I have no hesitation in pronouncing the first two cases subject to confiscation.

I now come to the consideration of the subsequent cases. It has already been laid down that the law of England restores on salvage, unless it is forced out of its natural course by the practice of its allies. In the preceding cases it has been reluctantly so diverted from its free course; but in May, 1797, it appears Portugal renounced the harsher principles and adopted a more liberal rule; upon what ground then can it be contended that this country must, in regard to those cases which have occurred subsequent to this ordinance, follow the harsh and antiquated in preference to the new and more lenient rule? It is said, Portugal is not at liberty to make such an alteration in time of war, and

1798 Dec. 7. — The Santa Cruz. — Sir W. Scott.

that those who have once established a rule must abide the consequences of it; but I confess I see no one reason on which this exercise of legislation can be denied to an independent State.

It is said, Portugal will then legislate for this country; and so must every country in some degree legislate for us, whilst Great Britain professes to act upon the old principle, and adopt the law of its ally. In peace it is allowed such an alteration might be made; and why not in a time of war? There are no depending interests to be affected by it: it was an alteration as harmless to the world as if it had been made in times of most profound peace: but it is said the law is not even now established on equal terms of reciprocity towards this country. The salvage which Portugal has decreed is one-fifth, whilst the law of this country restores on payment of a sixth only. Perhaps a rule more closely concurring with our own might have been more convenient; but the difference is not sufficient to justify this country in refusing Portuguese subjects the benefit of their alteration. In professing to act on the law of our ally, we must do it for better and for worse.

I therefore restore the several vessels that have been taken since the ordinance of May, 1797, on the salvage which Portugal has established, a salvage of one-eighth to ships of war and one-fifth to privateers.

In the condemned cases I order the expenses of the claimants to be defrayed out of the proceeds.

[1 C. Rob. 80.]

THE MERCURIUS.

Restitution—Second Seizure—Effective Blockade—Notification at Entrance of Port—Violation of Blockade—Liability of Cargo Owner.

Restitution by consent of the parties to the suit does not bar a second seizure, by other parties, either on the same or different evidence; but a second seizor may be ordered to pay costs and damages.

Warning on the spot is a sufficient notice of a blockade *de facto*. Violation of a blockade affects the ship but not the cargo, unless it is the property of the same owner, or unless the owner of the cargo is cognisant of the intended violation.

1798 Dec. 10.

This was a case of a ship taken on a voyage from Baltimore to Amsterdam: the ship was claimed for a merchant of Hamburg, and the cargo as the property of a citizen of the United States: on the first capture the vessel had been restored by consent, but the officers of the Admiralty instituted new proceedings, and the claimant now appeared under protest: Amsterdam was said to have been in a state of blockade, and it was contended that the ship and cargo were liable to confiscation for attempting to enter a blockaded port.

SIR W. SCOTT.—In this case three questions arise: 1st, Whether restitution by consent bars new proceedings? 2ndly, How far the ship is affected by an attempt to break a blockade? and 3rdly, How far such a conduct will affect the cargo?

On the first question, I must say, that in restoring by consent in the present case, I think the party committed an oversight. Such a consent judicially recorded would bar him from a second seizure: against other parties it could be no bar; but whoever ventures on a second seizure must make it under the peril of costs and damages. A monition calls upon all claimants; but it does not call upon other captors: nor could a second seizure be made: nor could other parties intervene, as on a fresh seizure, till the proceedings under the first libel had been determined.

The King in his office of Admiralty is the second seizor in this case; and it is said, that as the fountain of all prize, he is to be considered also as the original captor: but the King holds the office of Lord High Admiral in a capacity distinguishable from his regal character; besides, although he is undoubtedly the fountain of prize, he has conveyed away his interests in it to various persons: to the commanders and crews of his own ships; to his other subjects by letters of marque; and to the Lord High Admiral of England. It has been declared by high authority that the interest of prize is vested in the captor, and that captors may, against the wish of the Crown, proceed to adjudication.

The case of the *La Paix* (a) does, I think, sufficiently support

(a) This was a case of a ship carried into St. Kitt's, and restored; and immediately afterwards seized by another privateer, who followed her out of the harbour, took her to the island of Nevis, and there obtained a condemnation: the illegality of a second seizure, after restitution, was strongly argued, on appeal; but the Lords decided on the merits, saying,

1798 Dec. 10. — THE MERCURIUS. — Sir W. Scott.

the principle for which it has been cited. In that case new depositions were taken; but the second seizor might in that instance have proceeded, if he had thought proper, on the original evidence. It is said here that proceedings should have been by appeal instead of a second seizure, but there was nothing in the possession of the Court. The proceedings, therefore, by a second seizure were, in my opinion, not only regular but necessary, and the only means which could have been pursued; I therefore overrule the protest, and assign the claimant to appear absolutely.

On the second question, it is necessary to inquire, Was there an actual blockade? Was it notified? Was it violated? If all these points can be established confiscation must necessarily follow. It is the necessary consequence acknowledged in all books, and confirmed by the practice of all nations; nor is it even denied in theory to be a just penalty by those who have laboured to extend to the utmost the rights of neutral nations.

By the evidence, it appears that when the vessel approached the Texel, the master was warned by the officer who boarded her, that he must not go into the Texel. The officer wrote on the manifest, "*Hindered from going into the Texel.*" The inability of the master to proceed into the Texel, therefore, proves the blockade; for a blockade may exist without a public declaration, although a declaration unsupported by fact will not be sufficient to establish it.

It has been so determined by the Supreme Court during the present war. The West India islands were declared under blockade by Admiral Jarvis; but the Lords held, that as the fact did not support the declaration, a blockade could not be deemed legally to exist: but the fact, on the contrary, duly notified on the spot, is of itself sufficient; for public notifications between governments can be meant only for the information of individuals: but if the individual is personally informed, that purpose is still better obtained than by a public declaration. Allusion has been made to the notification given to the Swedish Government, but I think

"As the captors can only now contend for farther proof, we are of opinion *that* will not be sufficient in this stage, although if this case had been appealed from the first judgment, we should have been disposed to order farther proof." Costs were given against the captor for misconduct: Lords, July 30, 1796.

irrelevantly; for the only declaration to which the claimant can allude must be one that has been made to his own government.

Much has been said about the purposes of blockade, which I do not think material to the case; I shall therefore pass it over, and proceed to consider what the master himself understood by the notification which he received; and whether he really thought, that though he might not go into the Texel, he was at liberty to get to Amsterdam by any other course. It appears that he asked the officers who boarded him whether he might go to other Dutch ports; other, as must be understood, than the object of his destination. It was never inquired whether he might go to Amsterdam by any other course. The master pretended to be proceeding to Hamburg till he came to the passage into the Zuyder Zee, and then he attempted to enter it. How far the blockade might extend to all the ports in the Zuyder Zee I shall not now inquire, because I am sufficiently convinced that the intention of this master was to proceed to Amsterdam, in defiance of the prohibition, which he distinctly understood: perhaps the officer might have expressed himself more clearly than he did; but if there had been anything insidious in the manner of giving this intimation, I should have thought it my duty to protect the neutral from suffering loss or inconvenience under it.

It is said this passage to the Zuyder Zee was not in a state of blockade, but the ship was seized immediately on entering it; and I know not what else is necessary to constitute blockade. The powers who formed the armed neutrality in the last war understood blockade in this sense; and Russia, who was the principal party in that confederacy, described a place to be in a state of blockade, when it is dangerous to attempt to enter into it.

On the third point, to maintain that the conduct of the ship will affect the cargo, it will be necessary either to prove that the owners were, or might have been, cognisant of the blockade, before they sent their cargoes; or to show, that the act of the master of the ship personally binds them. In America there could not have been any knowledge of the blockade: the cargo is innocent in its nature, and sets out innocently; the master certainly is the agent of the owner of the vessel, and can bind him by his contract or his misconduct; but he is not the agent of the owners of the cargo,

1798 Dec. 10. — THE MERCURIUS. — Sir W. Scott.

unless expressly so constituted by them. In cases of insurance, and in revenue cases, where, it is said, the act of the master will affect the cargo, it is to be observed that the ground on which they stand is wholly different. In the former, it is in virtue of an express contract which governs the whole case; and in revenue cases it proceeds from positive laws and the necessary strictness of all fiscal regulations.

It is argued that to exempt the cargo from this responsibility will open the door to fraud, if neutrals are allowed to attempt to trade to blockaded ports with impunity, by throwing the blame upon the carrier master; but if such an artifice could be proved, it would establish that *mens rea* in the neutral merchant which would expose his property to confiscation, and it would at the same time be sufficient to cause the master to be considered in the character of agent as well for the cargo as for the ship.

Where a cargo is of a contraband nature it will perhaps justify greater severity, but in cases of contraband it is held that innocent parts of the cargo belonging to other owners shall not be infected. This is, I think, a parallel case. There is misconduct on the part of the owner of the vessel, but none in the owner of the cargo.

If the evidence of the property of the cargo was sufficient, I should restore that; but as the case now stands, if the captors demand farther proof on that point it must be supplied.

Ship condemned.

[1 C. Rob. 86.]

THE FREDERICK MOLKE (*a*).

Blockade—Capture—Egress from Blockaded Port.

A vessel coming out of a blockaded port with a cargo is *primâ facie* liable to seizure: if the cargo was taken on board after the commencement of the blockade, ship and cargo will be liable to condemnation.

A blockade may exist, notwithstanding an accidental absence of the blockading force.

1798 Dec. 10.

THIS was a case of a Danish vessel, taken coming out of Havre on the 18th of August, 1798, and bound on a voyage from Havre to the coast of Africa. The cargo was miscellaneous.

A claim has been given for the ship and cargo as the property of the same person, a Danish merchant of Christiania.

(*a*) See *post*, pp. 86, 89.

Sir W. Scott.—Several questions have been raised respecting the property, the previous conduct of the vessel, the legality of this sort of trade, and the actual violation of a blockade. I shall first consider the last question, because if that is determined against the claimant it will render a discussion of all other points unnecessary.

First, then, as to the blockade. These facts appear in the depositions of the master, "that on his former voyage he cleared out from Lisbon to Copenhagen, but was really destined to Havre if he could escape English cruisers; that he was warned by an English frigate, the *Diamond*, off Havre, not to go into Havre, as there were two or three ships that would stop him; but that he slipt in at night and delivered his cargo." It is therefore sufficiently proved that there were ships on that station to prevent ingress, and that the master knowingly evaded the blockade; for that a legal blockade did exist results necessarily from these facts, as nothing farther is necessary to constitute blockade than that there should be a force stationed to prevent communication, and a due notice or prohibition given to the party (*a*).

But it is still farther material that this blockade actually continued till the ship came out again. It is notorious indeed that Havre was blockaded for some time, and although the blockade varied occasionally it still continued; for it is not an accidental absence of the blockading force, nor the circumstance of being blown off by wind (if the suspension and the reason of the suspension are known), that will be sufficient in law to remove a blockade.

It is said this was a new transaction, and that we have no right to look back to the delinquency of the former voyage; and a reference is made on this point to the law of contraband, where the penalty does not attach on the returned voyage. But is there that analogy between the two cases which should make the law of one necessarily or in reason applicable to the other also? I cannot think there is such an affinity between them; there is this essential difference, that in contraband the offence is deposited with the cargo, whilst in such a case as this it is continued and renewed in the subsequent conduct of the ship.

(*a*) It has since appeared, that the blockade of Havre was notified to foreign Ministers on the 23rd of February, 1798.

1798 Dec. 10.

THE FREDERICK MOLKE.

Sir W. Scott.

For what is the object of blockade? Not merely to prevent an importation of supplies, but to prevent export as well as import, and to cut off all communication of commerce with the blockaded place. I must therefore consider the act of egress to be as culpable as the act of ingress, and the vessel on her return still liable to seizure and confiscation.

There may indeed be cases of innocent egress where vessels have gone in before the blockade, and under such circumstances it could not be maintained that they might not be at liberty to retire.

But even then a question might arise if it was attempted to carry out a cargo, for that would, as I have before stated, contravene one of the chief purposes of blockade.

A ship then, in all cases, coming out of a blockaded port, is in the first instance liable to seizure, and to obtain release the claimant will be required to give a very satisfactory proof of the innocency of his intention. In the present case the ingress was criminal and the egress was criminal, and I am decidedly of opinion that both ship and cargo, being the property of the same person, are subject to confiscation.

Condemned.

[1 C. Rob. 89.]

THE RINGENDE JACOB.

Contraband—Ship not affected by Character of Cargo—Hemp—Unwrought Iron.

Freighting a ship to the enemy is not the lending mentioned in the Swedish Treaty, October 21, 1666. A contraband cargo alone will not affect the ship being the property of a different owner, and is attended only with loss of freight. Hemp is contraband under the Danish Treaty, July 4, 1780. Unwrought iron is an article *promiscui usûs.*

1798 Dec. 11.

SIR W. SCOTT.—This is a case of a ship under Swedish colours, laden with iron, hemp, tobacco, and oak logs, and taken on a voyage from Riga to Amsterdam, on the 15th of August, 1798.

The ship is claimed as Swedish property, the iron for Russian merchants: the hemp appears to be the produce of Russia; but it is claimed for a Danish subject; and some parts of the cargo remain still unclaimed. Objections have been made against the proofs of property as standing chiefly on the evidence of the master, whose conduct, it is said, has shown him to be unworthy of credit; but I think the property is sufficiently proved.

Three other grounds, however, have been taken, on which it is contended that the vessel is liable to condemnation: 1st, on account of the use and occupation in which she was employed; 2ndly, on account of the contraband nature of the cargo; and 3rdly, for violating a blockade.

On the former point reference has been made to an ancient treaty [Oct. 21, 1666] between England and Sweden, which forbids the subjects of either power "to sell or lend their ships for the use and advantage of the enemies of the other:" and as this prohibition is connected in the same article with the subject of contraband, it is argued that the carrying of contraband articles in the present cargo is such a lending as comes within the meaning of the treaty; but I cannot agree to that interpretation. To let a ship on freight to go to the ports of the enemy cannot be termed lending, but in a very loose sense; and I apprehend the true meaning to have been that they should not give up the use and management of their ships directly to the enemy, or put them under his absolute power and direction. It is, besides, observable that there is no penalty annexed to this prohibition. I cannot think such a service as this is will make the vessel subject to confiscation.

But it is said there is a contraband cargo. That there are some contraband articles cannot be denied: hemp, the produce of Russia, exported by a Danish merchant, would be confiscable even under the relaxation, which allows neutrals to export that article only where it is of the growth of their own country; but to a Dane hemp is expressly enumerated among the articles of contraband in the Danish treaty [July 4, 1780]; and to say that a Dane might traffic in foreign hemp, whilst he is forbidden to export his own, would be to put a construction on that treaty perfectly nugatory. The hemp must certainly be condemned; but I do not know that under the present practice of the law of nations a contraband cargo can affect the ship.

By the ancient law of Europe such a consequence would have ensued; nor can it be said that such a penalty was unjust, or not supported by the general analogies of law; for the owner of the

1798 Dec. 11. THE RINGENDE JACOB. Sir W. Scott.

ship has engaged it in an unlawful commerce. But in the modern practice of the Courts of Admiralty of this country, and I believe of other nations also, a milder rule has been adopted; and the carrying of contraband articles is attended only with the loss of freight and expenses, except where the ship belongs to the owner of the contraband cargo, or where the simple misconduct of carrying a contraband cargo has been connected with other malignant and aggravating circumstances.

The case [the *Holz*, July 3, 1794] which has been cited by the King's Advocate by no means establishes the contrary: that was a case attended with particular circumstances of falsehood and fraud, both as to the papers and the destination of the voyage. It was attempted under colourable appearances to defeat our right of pre-emption; and under a view of all these circumstances together, the Court judged it to be subject to confiscation; but I am not disposed to consider that decision as a general authority, in other cases of cargoes, simply contraband.

On the question of blockade, a doubt arises whether the master had received due notice of it: there appears not to have been any previous admonition at the time of capture. The notice, therefore, if any, must have been under the public declaration. The vessel left Riga on the 2nd of July, 1798; the notification of the blockade of Amsterdam to the foreign Ministers was made here on the 11th of June; it might have reached Riga before this ship sailed, and I think the probability is on that side, but I cannot take it as an established fact; I shall therefore order affidavits to be produced on that point. With regard to the cargo, the hemp is undoubtedly contraband and subject to confiscation; but it is disputed whether iron in bars is to be considered as wrought or unwrought, or whether or not it is to be ranked amongst naval stores.

There is perhaps no article in nature that comes more exactly under the description of an article of promiscuous use than iron; it is a commodity subservient to the most infinite variety of human uses. As this cargo is going to a port of naval equipment, it would very probably be applied as a naval store; but it may be too much to decide merely on this inference that it is an article absolutely hostile; nor can I agree to another argument that has been advanced, that because unwrought iron is excepted, in some treaties, as not contraband, therefore, where no exception is expressed, it is to be considered as contraband. Enumeration takes place in treaties to prevent misunderstanding: it distinguishes what shall be contraband from what shall not; but the exception of particular articles is not to be there understood in the strict sense in which it is sometimes said, *exceptio confirmat legem.*

1798 *Dec.* 11.

THE RINGENDE JACOB.

Sir W. Scott.

There is besides a doubt in my mind what is at the present moment the relative situation of Russia and Holland: I do not know that Russia is so far engaged as a principal in hostility with Holland as to cut off all communication of trade between them. This is an important point which I shall reserve for farther inquiry and information. In the meantime it will be equally necessary that the owners of the cargo should prove themselves not to have received notice of the blockade. It will be proper also to refer the iron and the oak timber to the inspection of the officers of the King's yards, that we may be assisted by their certificate in determining whether they are to be considered as naval stores or not.

THE BETSEY (No. 1).

[1 C. Rob. 93.]

Blockade—Proclamation—No de facto *Investment—Capture—Recapture by Enemy—Liability of Captors for Restitution.*

A declaration of a blockade by a commander, without an actual investment, will not constitute a legal blockade.

In a case of neutral property captured by a British ship and recaptured by the French, compensation was sued from the original British captors, but refused, on the ground of a *bonâ fide* possession; irregularities to bind a former captor, being a *bonæ fidei* possessor, must be such as produce irreparable loss, or justly prevent restitution from the recaptors.

1798 *Dec.* 18; affirmed *July* 22, 1799.

THIS was a case of a ship and cargo, taken by the English at the capture of Guadaloupe, April the 13th, 1794, and retaken, together with that island, by the French in June following. The ship was claimed for Mr. Patterson, of Baltimore, and the cargo as American property. The captors, being served with a monition to proceed to adjudication, appeared under protest; and the cause now came on upon the question, Whether the claimants were entitled to demand of the first British captors restitution in value for the

1798 Dec. 18. THE BETSEY. property which had passed from them to the French recaptors? The first seizure was defended on a suggestion that the *Betsey* had broken the blockade at Guadaloupe.

SIR W. SCOTT.—This is a case which it will be proper to consider under two heads. I shall first dispose of the question of blockade, and then proceed to inquire on whom the loss of the recapture by the French ought to fall, under all the circumstances of the case.

On the question of blockade three things must be proved: 1st, the existence of an actual blockade; 2ndly, the knowledge of the party; and 3rdly, some act of violation, either by going in or by coming out with a cargo laden after the commencement of blockade. The time of shipment would on this last point be very material; for although it might be hard to refuse a neutral liberty to retire with a cargo already laden, and by that act already become neutral property; yet, after the commencement of a blockade, a neutral cannot, I conceive, be allowed to interpose in any way to assist the exportation of the property of the enemy. After the commencement of the blockade a neutral is no longer at liberty to make any purchase in that port.

It is necessary, however, that the evidence of a blockade should be clear and decisive. But in this case there is only an affidavit of one of the captors, and the account which is there given is, "that on the arrival of the British forces in the West Indies a proclamation issued, inviting the inhabitants of Martinique, St. Lucie, and Guadaloupe, to put themselves under the protection of the English; that on a refusal, hostile operations were commenced against them all." But it cannot be meant that they began immediately against all at once, for it is notorious that they were directed against them separately and in succession. It is farther stated, "that in January, 1794 (but without any more precise date), Guadaloupe was summoned, and was then put into a state of complete investment and blockade."

The word complete is a word of great energy; and we might expect from it to find that a number of vessels were stationed round the entrance of the port to cut off all communication: but from the protest I perceive that the captors entertained but a very loose notion of the true nature of a blockade; for it is there stated, "that on the 1st of January, after a general proclamation to the French islands, they were put into a state of *complete* blockade." It is a term, therefore, which was applied to all those islands at the same time, under the first proclamation.

1798 Dec. 18.

THE BETSEY.

Sir W. Scott.

The Lords of Appeal have determined that such a proclamation was not in itself sufficient to constitute a legal blockade; it is clear, indeed, that it could not in reason be sufficient to produce the effect which the captors erroneously ascribed to it: but from the misapplication of these phrases in one instance, I learn that we must not give too much weight to the use of them on this occasion; and from the generality of these expressions, I think we must infer that there was not that actual blockade which the law is now distinctly understood to require.

But it is attempted to raise other inferences on this point, from the manner in which the master speaks of the difficulty and danger of entering; and from the declaration of the Municipality of Guadaloupe, which states "the island to have been in a state of siege." It is evident that the American master speaks only of the difficulty of avoiding the English cruisers generally in those seas; and as to the other phrase, it is a term of the new jargon of France, which is sometimes applied to domestic disturbances; and certainly is not so intelligible as to justify me in concluding that the island was in that state of investment from a foreign enemy which we require to constitute blockade. I cannot, therefore, lay it down that a blockade did exist till the operations of the forces were actually directed against Guadaloupe in April.

It would be necessary for me, however, to go much further, and to say that I am satisfied also that the parties had knowledge of it: but this is expressly denied by the master. He went in without obstruction. Mr. Incledon's statement of his belief of the notoriety of the blockade is not such evidence as will alone be sufficient to convince me of it. With respect to the shipment of the cargo, it does not appear exactly under what circumstances or what time it was taken in: I shall therefore dismiss this part of the case.

The case being on the first point pronounced a case of restitution, a second point arises out of the recapture of the property by the French; and the question is, Whether the original captors are exonerated of their responsibility to the American claimants? It

1798 *Dec.* 18. THE BETSEY. Sir W. Scott.

is to be observed that at the time of recapture America was a neutral country, and in amity with France. I premise this fact as an important circumstance in one part of the case; but the principal points for our consideration are, Whether the possession of the original captors was in its commencement a legal *bonâ fide* possession? and, 2ndly, Whether such a possession, being just in its commencement, became afterwards, by any subsequent conduct of the captors, tortious and illegal? for on both these points the law is clear, "that a *bonâ fide* possessor is not responsible for casualties; but that he may, by subsequent misconduct, forfeit the protection of his fair title, and render himself liable to be considered as a trespasser from the beginning." This is the law, not of this Court only, but of all Courts, and one of the first principles of universal jurisprudence.

The cases in which it has been particularly applied in this Court have been cited in the arguments; and I will briefly advert to the circumstances of them, as they will afford much light to direct us in the present case. The *Nicolas and Jan* was one of several Dutch ships taken at St. Eustatius, and sent home under convoy to England for adjudication. In the mouth of the Channel they were retaken by the French fleet. There was much neutral property on board, sufficiently documented; and in that case a demand was made on behalf of a merchant of Hamburg, for restitution in value from the original captor. It was argued, I remember, that the captors had wilfully exposed the property to danger, by bringing it home whilst they might have resorted to the Admiralty Courts in the West Indies; and, therefore, that the claimants were entitled to demand indemnification from them: but on this point the Court was of opinion that, under the dubious circumstances in which those cases were involved, and under the great pressure of important concerns in which the commanders were engaged, they had not exceeded the discretion which is necessarily intrusted to them by the nature of their command.

It was urged also against the claimants in that case that, since the property had been retaken by their allies, they had a right to demand restitution in specie from them; and on these grounds our Courts rejected their claims.

In the *Hendrick and Jacob* (*a*), also, the case turned upon similar considerations of the nature of the possession. It was a case of a Hamburgese ship, taken erroneously as Dutch, and retaken by a French privateer. In going into Nantes the vessel foundered, and was lost. On demand for restitution against the original British captor, the Lords of Appeal decided that, as it was a seizure made on unjustifiable grounds, the owners were entitled to restitution from some quarter: that as the French recaptor had a justifiable possession under prize taken from his enemy, he was not responsible for the accident that had befallen the property in his hands: that if the property had been saved, indeed, the claimant must have looked for redress to the justice of his ally the French; but since that claim was absolutely extinguished by the loss of the goods, the proprietor was entitled to his indemnification from the original captor. Under a view of these precedents, we must inquire first into the nature of the original seizure in the present case: whether it was so wrongful as to bring upon the seizor all the consequences of that strict responsibility which attaches to a tortious and unjustifiable possession?

It has been rather insinuated, than affirmed openly in argument, that there was anything wrong or unjustifiable in the first capture; but it is said the great injustice arises from the detention, and from that irregularity of conduct in the captors which has put it out of the power of the claimants to support their claim, and obtain restitution from the French.

In respect to the first seizure, although it is admitted now that there was not a blockade, yet it must be allowed also, on the other side, that the island of Guadaloupe was at that time in a situation extremely ambiguous and critical. It could be no secret in America that the British forces were advancing against this island, and that the planters would be eager to avail themselves of the interference of neutral persons to screen and carry off their property. Under such a posture of affairs, therefore, ships found in the harbour of Guadaloupe must have fallen under very strong suspicions, and have become justly liable to very close examination. The suspicion besides would be still farther aggravated if it appeared, as in this case it did appear, that those for whom the ships were claimed kept

(*a*) Lords, July 21, 1798.

1798 Dec. 18. THE BETSEY. Sir W. Scott.

agents stationed on the island, and might, therefore, be supposed to be connected in character and interests with the commerce of the place. It is true, indeed, the Lords of Appeal have since pronounced the island to have been not under blockade, but it was a decision that depended upon a greater nicety of legal discrimination than could be required from military persons engaged in the command of an arduous enterprise.

The same considerations which justify the seizure apply also to the second charge of detention in this case, for under these suspicions and these doubts it was not a slight examination of formal papers that could be deemed sufficient. The captors were entitled to reserve the property so taken for legal adjudication, and as they could not erect a jurisdiction on the spot, so neither were they at leisure then to send the cases to distant Courts. The first capture was made April 13th, the recapture took place so early as the 2nd of June following; there was an interval but of six weeks. The French were, as the subsequent event proves, in great force in those parts; the commanders had much to occupy their attention; the number of vessels taken under these circumstances was very considerable, and therefore it is not to be mentioned as an injurious or unnecessary delay that in six weeks so employed no means were found to bring the ships to adjudication.

But, it is said, the irregular proceedings of the captors have rendered them liable to the strictest responsibility. Now on this point I must distinctly lay it down, that the irregularities to produce this effect must have been such as would *justly* prevent restitution by the French. If such a case could be supported, I will admit there might then be just grounds for resorting to the British captor for indemnification, but till this is proved the responsibility which lies on recaptors to restore the property of allies and neutrals will be held by these Courts to exonerate the original captors.

What, then, has been the nature of these irregularities? It is said that the masters and proprietors were sent away from their ships, and, therefore, that there was no one to apply for restitution at the time of recapture. But what was there to prevent them from making these applications afterwards? Are the French more than the English Courts exempted from making subsequent restitu-

1798 Dec. 18. THE BETSEY. Sir W. Scott.

tion? They hold, indeed, that possession of twenty-four hours will convert the property of prize; but this is not applicable to a neutral vessel. So strongly did the maritime jurisprudence of ancient France consider neutral property to be in a state of absolute inviolability, that no salvage was allowed on retaking neutral vessels, on the supposition that no service had been rendered to them. Such was the language of their law, and therefore no bar to restitution can have arisen from the impossibility of making immediate application.

It is said, further, that the papers were all thrown confusedly together, by which it was put out of the power of the claimants to produce that proof and those documents which the Courts of France require.

I know it was a maxim of the French law, and a maxim not deficient in justice, that if in time of war a ship is found sailing about the world without any credentials of character, she is liable to confiscation. But if a just reason could be given for this defect; if accident or force could be shown to have stripped her of these documents, can it be conceived that the general rule would be applied to such a case? Unless the Courts of France have renounced every principle of justice, such a consequence could not have ensued from the want of documents in these cases, and therefore it is not in reason to be presumed. Supposing these irregularities to have existed, and in the censurable degree which this argument imputes to them, they have not in any manner taken off the obligation which the French lie under to restore this property. I must determine that they would not, under any proceedings of justice, have prevented restitution from the French.

On no other ground can the proprietors be entitled to claim it from the British. If the neutral has sustained any injury, it proceeds not from the British but from the French; and there is no reason that British captors should pay for French injustice. I must pronounce the protest to be well founded, and the captors to be discharged from any further proceedings.

[1 C. Rob. 102.]

THE BERNON.

Capture—Neutral Ship—Purchase from Enemy in Time of War—Defect of Proof—Condemnation.

The purchase of an enemy's vessel in time of war is liable to great suspicion: the suspicion is increased when the asserted neutral purchaser appears to be personally residing in the enemy's country at the time of sale of ship. Condemned on want of proof.

1798 Dec. 19. THIS was a case of a ship and cargo ordered for further proof on a former day.

SIR W. SCOTT.—This is a ship asserted to have been purchased by an American in France during the war. Such purchases have been allowed to be legal, but they will always be open to much suspicion. The Court will always feel it to be its duty to look into them with great jealousy, and it will do this strictly, even in purchases made under commission for neutrals resident in their own country. But the suspicion will be still farther increased, and the Court will exert its utmost power of research, where it appears that the pretended neutral purchaser was a person then resident in France; for the Court cannot be ignorant of the necessity which the French have felt of covering their trade, nor of the system of collusion practised for that purpose. But still greater suspicion will arise if the ship so purchased immediately engages in the commerce of France, and continues in the hands of the French proprietors.

Attending to these considerations, let us examine this purchase, asserted to have been made at Bordeaux, in May, 1796, by a person then in France, by Mr. Dunn, the present master, and let us see what has been her employment. She had made one voyage before this, according to the master's account, from Bordeaux to Hamburg, with wines; a destination perfectly neutral, although not, as we might naturally have expected, to her own country. But is this true? All the other witnesses say, "they went from Bordeaux to Brest," and this account is also confirmed by what appears in a paper found on board.

Now, I ask, this fact being proved, that she was engaged in the navigation of France, to a port of naval equipment with supplies, to the nature of which I cannot be inattentive: what is the consequence? It leads immediately to this conclusion: that the master is a person discredited, and not entitled to any belief; for it is a point on which he could not err by mere mistake. It cannot be said here (as it is sometimes said) that he was ignorant of the language in which he was examined. English is his vernacular tongue; and when he swears that his last voyage was to Hamburg, he swears to that which he knows to be false.

The employment of a vessel is, *in limine*, a point very proper for inquiry; for it may impress a national character, and must at all events in such a case as this very much elucidate the transaction. As to the property,—one witness, Mr. Alliston, says, "he believes Chanon, a person at Bordeaux, to be the owner, because he came often on board, and acted as owner; and because, on the misbehaviour of a Lascar sailor, complaint was made to Mr. Chanon." Other witnesses "believe Dunn to have been the owner;" but they give no reason for their belief.

The documents were deficient, there was no bill of sale; the vessel had been a prize ship; yet there was no proof of condemnation. The only documentary evidence that was on board was a certificate of property, on oath, before the American Consul, Mr. Fenwick, a person whose office is highly respectable; but men in office must themselves respect the duties of that office, if they mean that it should entitle them to the respect of others; and it has appeared in some cases that Mr. Fenwick has not been always very correct in the recollection of this important truth. So circumstanced, the case originally stood very naked of proof; and the Court gave the parties an opportunity of bringing further evidence, both as to the national character and the property of the vessel.

Now, 1st, wherever it appears that the purchaser was in France, he must explain the circumstances of his residence there; the presumption arising from his residence is, that he is there *animo manendi*, and it lies on him to explain it; and 2ndly, to satisfy the Court fully on this business, the claimant ought to be prepared to meet the presumption which arises, as to the property, on the face of the transaction; and which is confirmed by the evidence of Mr. Alliston. This he was bound to accomplish. In what manner is it performed? He swears "that he resided at Boston fourteen

1798 Dec. 19. THE BERNON. Sir W. Scott.

years, when at home;" but he does not say how often he had been at home. He then states, "that being at Bordeaux in 1796," &c.; but he does not say how long he had been there: he might have lived there a long time. The *onus probandi*, I have said, lay upon him; and the presumption is not rebutted by the asserted residence of his wife and family at Boston. It is said, his wife lives in America; but he may have been in Europe during the war, engaged in the trade of France; and, if so, such an occupation would supersede his pretended neutral character.

The account then states "that part of the purchase-money was paid, and the rest was to be paid on his return from his first voyage." This is represented as an excuse for his return to Bordeaux, to which place he was to return whether he obtained a freight or not; but his return appears not to have been for *one time* singly, and, besides, it cannot account from his strange deviation from truth in his depositions. "On his return to Bordeaux he brought some papers on board from his lodgings," so that he appears to have had a continued residence there during the interval of his voyages. Under these circumstances, I cannot say I am satisfied. I do not mean to lay down so harsh a rule as that two voyages from France shall make a man a Frenchman. I do not say that. But this claimant being called upon for further proof, and having an opportunity given to him of making out his case in a satisfactory manner, I must say he has not done it.

With respect to the sale, the evidence produced consists only of a formal bill of sale, in which Chanon, the person mentioned by Mr. Alliston, is the vendor, and of a note given by the master to pay part on his return, and of a receipt. How are these verified? It is said, "by the signatures of American houses." All that they attest is that their signatures affixed are true; but as to the transaction, they do not take upon themselves to verify that. It is not my business to say what precise proof a man is to bring to verify a purchase; but it might have been some satisfaction if the American houses had certified their belief of a *bonâ fide* transaction. The claimant might have shown his funds. I do not know that the enemy vendor's attestation might not have been received, *valeat quantum valere potest*, or there might have been some negotiation shown. As it is, it all stands on Mr. Dunn's affidavit; and when I look back to his misstatement of the destination, I cannot say that he makes full faith for such a public instrument. 1798 *Dec.* 19. THE BERNON. Sir W. Scott.

I need not look to the other part of the case, to the employment of the vessel. I am disposed to give him the benefit of the admission that the employment of this vessel would not be sufficient to bind upon it a French character. What shall I do then? Shall I order further proof? It is enough to have permitted it once, the party having had a full opportunity of proving his claim; and having failed to satisfy the Court, it is time to shut the door.

With respect to the cargo the Court must have further satisfaction. In the original evidence there was a bill of lading expressing account and risk of the claimant. One witness says, "Peters of Bordeaux was the lader, and that the goods were to be delivered at Hamburg for his account and risk, as he believes. That Peters said to him, when he expressed fears that it might be French property, it was *his*, and he was as good a neutral as himself." This is the account of one witness, and there seems to be no reason to induce him to swear falsely. Another witness, Mr. Alliston, believes the cargo was to be delivered at St. Malo.

The proof now produced is such as, it is said, would be held good in ordinary cases. It consists of attestations, letters of orders and advice, invoices, and bills of lading, but in cases so particularly circumstanced something more must be required; it is possible that there might be such documents as these if the transaction was fictitious. There is a reference made to a letter of the 25th of June: I have a curiosity to see that. The insurance would throw some light on the destination: if there was none made, *that* may be certified.

Ship condemned. Further proof ordered of the cargo.

The *King's Advocate* prayed that there might be attestations of the confidential clerks.

Court.—I have no objection. It is a case loaded with suspicion.

[1 C. Rob. 107.]

THE DANCKEBAAR AFRICAAN.

Capture—Ship—Change of Character in transitu.

Property sent from a hostile colony cannot change its character *in transitu*, although the owners become British subjects by capitulation before capture.

1798 *Dec.* 19. THIS was a case of a Dutch ship bound from Batavia to Holland, and taken on the 16th of November, 1795. On coming to the Cape of Good Hope a claim was given on the part of Goetz and Vos, inhabitants of the Cape, who had then become subjects of the Crown of Great Britain. The cargo had been delivered to them on bail to answer adjudication.

For the captors, the *King's Advocate.*

For the claimant, *Laurence.*

SIR W. SCOTT.—I am of opinion that this is a decided case on the authority of the Supreme Court in the *Negotie en Zevaart* (*a*). I remember that case well, having been junior counsel in it, and having attended much to it, as there was much difference of opinion respecting it in the Court below.

It was the case of a ship sailing from Demerara to Middlebourg in Holland, on the 30th of January, 1781, about six weeks after the declaration of hostilities against Holland. Demerara surrendered to the British forces on the 14th of March, and the capture was made on the 25th.

The terms of capitulation were very favourable: "The inhabitants were to take the oath of allegiance; to be permitted to export their own property, and to be treated in all respects like British subjects, till his Majesty's pleasure could be known;" and although this was in the first instance only under the proclamation of the captor, still, that being accepted, it took complete effect. These terms were afterwards confirmed by the King. There was, therefore, in that case as strong a promise of protection as could be, and recognised and confirmed by the supreme authority of the State. Under these circumstances, the Judge of the Admiralty thought

(*a*) Lords, July 18, 1782.

the claim so strong that he actually restored: and it was not his opinion alone.

On appeal, however, the Lords were of opinion that property sailing after declaration of hostilities, but before a capitulation, and taken on the voyage, was not protected by the intermediate capitulation. It was not determined on any ground of illegal trade, nor on any surmise, that when the owners became British subjects the trade in which the property was embarked became, *ex post facto*, illegal; nor was it at all taken into consideration that Demerara had again become a Dutch colony at the time of adjudication. It was declared to be adjudged on the same principles as if the cause had come on at the time of capture. It was not on any of these grounds, but simply on the ground of Dutch property, that condemnation passed in that case. I remember a *dictum* of a great law Lord then present, Lord Camden, "that the ship, as Dutch, could not change her character *in transitu*."

This decision of the Supreme Court must be binding on me, unless there are in the present case any distinctions that take it out of the law of that decision. The distinctions made are: 1st, that the colony in this case was not hostile; and, 2ndly, that the ship was not going into the hands of the enemy, but that she was coming first to the Cape into the hands of the owners, now become British subjects, and that they would have altered the ulterior destination to Holland.

On the first point, that Holland was not hostile, it is enough that hostilities have since followed, and with a retrospective operation. The state of affairs was at that time at best but very doubtful; and all property taken during that doubtful state of things has been since condemned; but it is said that, although Holland has become hostile, the Cape has not. If it could be proved that the colony adhered to the old government, it might entitle them to be exempted from this hostile character; but that is not shown, and there is no reason to presume it. They surrendered as Dutch subjects, and, therefore, there is no pretence now to contend for a different character.

The other distinction is, that this property was coming to the hands of the owners, whilst in the Demerara case it was gone from them, and must have fallen into the possession of the

1798 *Dec.* 19. — The Danckebaar Africaan. — Sir W. Scott.

mother country; but there is no decided proof that this ship was coming to the Cape, and, if so, she is still to be considered as taken merely *in transitu* towards Holland, where the voyage was clearly to have ended; and in what character?—As a Dutch ship, in a Dutch port. If the vessel had arrived at the Cape, I will not say, that coming actually into the hands of the capitulants, she might not have been protected as property in possession; but being taken before she arrived there, as Dutch property, I am bound down by the decision of the Lords, and I think myself obliged to say that her character could not be changed *in transitu*, and that she must be condemned as Dutch property.

[1 C. Rob. 125.]

THE JUFFROUW ANNA.

Practice—Further Proof—Refusal—Evidence of Fraud.

Where further proof is necessary by the practice of the Court, it will not be allowed to persons convicted of fraudulent conduct, or departing from a fair neutral character.

1799 *Jan.* 10.

This was a case of a ship asserted to have been purchased in the enemy's country.

Sir W. Scott.—This is a ship which appears, by the depositions of the master, to have been an English prize, purchased in France.

There is no bill of sale on board: whoever the neutral claimant is, he must be subject, therefore, to further proof. A claim has been given for Mr. Escherausen, of Embden, but not till eight months had elapsed, which is an extraordinary circumstance, as he could not be so long ignorant of the capture; and although the Court cannot say the claimant is out of time, it has some right to inquire how it happens that there has been such neglect of ordinary diligence.

Mr. Escherausen claims simply for himself; but the pass, which is the only paper translated, describes the vessel to be the property of two persons: if that was the case the claim should have been specific. It is besides observable that it undertakes to describe the voyage, but runs only in this vague form: from

—— to ——. This is an omission which I hope I shall not see again, as the destination is a very material circumstance to be known.

1799 *Jan.* 10.

THE JUFFROUW ANNA.

Sir W. Scott.

These are unfavourable circumstances; but independent of these, it would be a case for further proof, as the papers are false. The master says, "he took possession of the ship at Dunkirk"; the master's residence was at Ostend, and all the crew were hired at Ostend. She sails to Nantes, and there takes in the cargo, which was on board at the time of capture. Now, what was the destination? It is represented by the master to have been alternative, and to have been left to his discretion to go either to Ostend or Hamburg; but the papers represent Hamburg as the sole destination. To make a voyage fairly alternative, it should appear on the papers to be so, for otherwise it must mislead the cruisers of the belligerent countries, and prevent them from forming a right judgment of their case. The orders were, it appears, "to go to Ostend, if not obstructed by British cruisers."

The master was to use his best endeavour to get to Ostend, and only to take another destination if he should be prevented from accomplishing the first. This is scarcely to be considered as an alternative destination; and besides, all the papers point to Hamburg only. I think, therefore, there is in all these circumstances a *mala fides* in this case; and if so, the rule which I have laid down must apply to it. The party cannot be allowed to go into further proof. It is scarcely possible that it should have been a fair transaction; a suspension of the claim for eight months, the false representation of the claimant, the direct employment of the vessel in the enemy's trade, and false papers, convince me it must be a fraudulent case; and therefore I feel no hesitation to condemn.

[1 C. Rob. 135.]

THE FLAD OYEN (*a*).

Recapture—Hostile Prize Court in Neutral Port—Condemnation—Invalidity of Proceedings.

An enemy cannot legally establish a Prize Court in neutral territory. Therefore, when an English ship was captured by the French and taken to Bergen, and condemned there by the French consul and sold, she was deemed not to have been legally condemned. The ship was on recapture restored to the former owner on payment of salvage.

1799 *Jan.* 16.

THIS was a case of an English prize ship carried into a neutral country, and there sold, under a sentence of condemnation by the French Consul.

The claim was given on behalf of the purchaser, a Danish merchant.

SIR W. SCOTT.—This is the case of a ship taken by a French privateer, and carried into the port of Bergen, in Norway, where it appears she underwent a sort of process, which terminated in a sentence of condemnation, pronounced by the French Consul; and under that sentence she is asserted to have been transferred to the present neutral proprietor.

[The Court found on the facts that there had been no actual transfer.]

But another question has arisen in this case, upon which a great deal of argument has been employed; namely, whether the sentence of condemnation which was pronounced by the French Consul is of such legal authority as to transfer the vessel, supposing the purchase to have been *bonâ fide* made? I directed the counsel for the claimants to begin; because, the sentence being of a species altogether new, it lay upon them to prove that it was nevertheless a legal one.

It has frequently been said that it is the peculiar doctrine of the law of England to require a sentence of condemnation as necessary to transfer the property of prize; and that according to the practice of some nations twenty-four hours, and according to the practice of others bringing *infra presidia*, is authority enough to

(*a*) This decision was followed in the *Perseverance*, Nov. 22, 1799, and in the *Kierligheit*, *post*, p. 258; reported on the question of amelioration.

convert the prize. I take that to be not quite correct, for I apprehend that by the general practice of the law of nations a sentence of condemnation is at present deemed generally necessáry; and that a neutral purchaser in Europe, during war, does look to the legal sentence of condemnation as one of the title deeds of the ship if he buys a prize vessel. I believe there is no instance in which a man having purchased a prize vessel of a belligerent has thought himself quite secure in making that purchase merely because the ship had been in the enemy's possession twenty-four hours, or carried *infra presidia;* the contrary has been more generally held, and the instrument of condemnation is amongst those documents which are most universally produced by a neutral purchaser; that if she has been taken as prize, it should appear also that she has been, in a proper judicial form, subjected to adjudication.

Now, in what form have these adjudications constantly appeared? They are the sentences of Courts acting and exercising their functions in the belligerent country; and it is for the very first time in the world, that in the year 1799 an attempt is made to impose upon the Court a sentence of a tribunal not existing in the belligerent country, but of a person pretending to be authorised within the dominions of a neutral country; in my opinion, if it could be shown that, regarding mere speculative general principles, such a condemnation ought to be deemed sufficient; that would not be enough, more must be proved; it must be shown that it is conformable to the usage and practice of nations.

A great part of the law of nations stands on no other foundation; it is introduced, indeed, by general principles; but it travels with those general principles only to a certain extent, and, if it stops there, you are not at liberty to go further, and to say that mere general speculations would bear you out in a further progress; thus, for instance, on mere general principles it is lawful to destroy your enemy, and mere general principles make no great difference as to the manner by which this is to be effected; but the conventional law of mankind, which is evidenced in their practice, does make a distinction, and allows some, and prohibits other, modes of destruction; and a belligerent is bound to confine himself to those modes which the common practice of mankind has employed, and to relinquish those which the same practice has not

1799 Jan. 16.

THE FLAD OYEN.

Sir W. Scott.

brought within the ordinary exercise of war, however sanctioned by its principles and purposes.

Now, it having been the constant usage that the tribunals of the law of nations in these matters shall exercise their functions within the belligerent country, if it was proved to me in the clearest manner that on mere general theory such a tribunal might act in the neutral country, I must take my stand on the ancient and universal practice of mankind, and say that as far as that practice has gone I am willing to go; and where it has thought proper to stop, there I must stop likewise.

It is my duty not to admit that because one nation has thought proper to depart from the common usage of the world, and to treat the notice of mankind in a new and unprecedented manner, that I am on that account under the necessity of acknowledging the efficacy of such a novel institution, merely because general theory might give it a degree of countenance independent of all practice from the earliest history of mankind. The institution must conform to the text law and likewise to the constant usage upon the matter; and when I am told that before the present war no sentence of this kind has ever been produced in the annals of mankind, and that it is produced by one nation only in this war, I require nothing more to satisfy me that it is the duty of this Court to reject such a sentence as inadmissible.

Having thus declared that there must be an antecedent usage upon the subject, I should think myself justified in dismissing this matter without entering into any further discussion. But even if we look further, I see no sufficient ground to say that on mere general principles such a sentence could be sustained. Proceedings upon prize are proceedings *in rem;* and it is presumed that the body and substance of the thing is in the country which has to exercise the jurisdiction. I have not heard any instances quoted to the contrary, excepting in a very few cases which have been urged, argumentatively, in the way which is technically called *ad hominem*, being cases of condemnations of British prizes carried into the ports of Lisbon and Leghorn; but in those the condemnations were pronounced by the High Court of Admiralty in England. The only cases are of two ships carried into foreign ports and condemned in England by this Court; the very infrequency of such a practice shows the irregularity of it. Upon cases in the practice of other nations antecedent to the present war the advocates have been silent.

Now, as to these condemnations of prizes carried to Lisbon and Leghorn, it has been said that if the Courts of Great Britain venture this degree of irregularity other countries have a right to go farther. That consequence I deny. The true mode of correcting the irregular practice of a nation is by protesting against it, and by inducing that country to reform it. It is monstrous to suppose that because one country has been guilty of an irregularity every other country is let loose from the law of nations, and is at liberty to assume as much as it thinks fit.

Upon these ports of Lisbon and Leghorn it is to be remarked that they have a peculiar and discriminate character, a character that to a certain degree assimilates them to British ports. The British exist there in a distinct character under the protection of peculiar treaties; and with respect to Portugal, those treaties go so far as to engage that if a ship belonging to one country shall be brought by its enemy into the ports of another, which happens to be at peace, this neutral country shall be bound to seize that ship and restore it to its ally. To be sure no covenant can have more than the effect of giving the ports of England and Portugal a reciprocal relation of a very peculiar sort—to make the British ports Portuguese ports, and the Portuguese ports British ports to a certain degree. Now, unless I am given to understand that peculiar treaties between France and Denmark have impressed such a distinctive character upon the port of Bergen, I cannot allow that it can be considered, on the mere footing of general neutrality, to be a French port, exactly in the same manner in which London may be considered as a Portuguese port or Lisbon as a British port.

But supposing this possible, still it would not follow that such condemnations could be pleaded as authorities in the present case; because, in the first place, the validity of such condemnations themselves may be the subject of reasonable doubt. For it by no means appears that the enemy or neutrals, who might have an interest in contesting them, have ever acknowledged their validity. Whoever purchases under such sentences must be content to

1799
Jan. 16.

THE FLAD OYEN.

Sir W. Scott.

purchase them subject to all the questions that may arise upon their sufficiency.

But, secondly, supposing that no doubts could be entertained respecting the sufficiency of such sentences, it by no means follows that the efficacy of the present sentence can be supported. There the tribunal is acting in the country to which it belongs, and with whose authority it is armed. Here a person, utterly naked of all authority except over the subjects of his own country, and possessing that merely by the indulgence of the country in which he resides, pretends to exercise a jurisdiction in a matter in which the subjects of many other States may be concerned. No such authority was ever conceded by any country to a foreign agent of any description residing within it; and least of all could such an authority be conceded in the matter of prize of war—a matter over which a neutral country has no cognizance whatever, except in the single case of an infringement of its own territory, and in which such a concession of authority cannot be made without departing from the duties, and losing the benefits, of its neutral character.

Mark the consequences which must follow from such a pretended concession. Observe in the present case how it would affect the neutral character of the ports in the north. If France can station a judge of the Admiralty at Bergen, and can station there its cruisers to carry in prizes for that judge to condemn, who can deny that to every purpose of hostile mischief against the commerce of England, Bergen will differ from Dunkirk in no other respect than this, that it is a port of the enemy to a much greater extent of practical mischief? To make the ports of Norway the seats of the French tribunals of war is to make the adjacent sea the theatre of French hostility.

It gives one belligerent the unfair advantage of a new station of war which does not properly belong to him, and it gives to the other the unfair disadvantage of an active enemy in a quarter where no enemy would naturally be found. The coasts of Norway could no longer be approached by the British merchant with safety, and a suspension of commerce would soon be followed by a suspension of amity.

Wisely, therefore, did the American Government defeat a similar attempt made on them at an earlier period of the war. They knew

1799 *Jan.* 16.

THE FLAD OYEN.

Sir W. Scott.

that to permit such an exercise of the rights of war within their cities would be to make their coasts a station of hostility.

Whether the government of Denmark has shown equal vigilance in observing, or equal indignation in repelling the attempt, is more than I am warranted to assert; but though the publicity of the transaction in the town of Bergen may subject the police of that place to some degree of observation, I see nothing in the papers which issue immediately from the royal authority that at all affects the government itself with the knowledge and approbation of the fact, and indeed it would be indecent to suppose that a country, standing upon the footing of ancient and friendly alliance to this country, could have given its sanction to a measure so full of hostility to its friend and of possible inconvenience to itself. I must, therefore, deem the act of this French consul a licentious attempt to exercise the rights of war within the bosom of a neutral country, where no such exercise has ever been authorized.

I am of opinion upon the whole that this ship must be restored to the British owners upon the usual salvage, and I dismiss the claim of Mr. Krohn upon both grounds, as well upon the legality of the sentence as upon the want of reality in the pretended transfer from the French captors; and I must add, that Mr. Krohn appearing to possess two characters, that of Danish subject and of French agent, the claim which he has brought forward favours much more of the latter character than of the former. It is beyond my belief that any man standing in the genuine and unmixed character of a Danish subject should entertain a wish to establish that sort of law for which this French agent has thought proper to contend.

[1 C. Rob. 146.]

THE HENRICK AND MARIA (No. 1).

Blockade—Notification—Specification of Port.

Notification of a blockade is an act of sovereignty, and cannot be extended by the commander of a blockading ship. A notice by the commander to a neutral vessel not to proceed to any Dutch port when, in fact, Amsterdam only was blockaded. *Held* invalid.

1799 *Jan.* 15.

THIS was a case of a Danish vessel taken on a voyage from Norway to Amsterdam, June 28th, 1798.

For the captor, the *King's Advocate* contended that the ship was liable to confiscation for breaking the blockade, as the master, on being warned not to go to any Dutch port, declared "he must proceed according to his bills of lading."

For the claimant, *Lawrence* argued that the notice of a blockade of all Dutch ports was at that time not true, and therefore it could not be made good by limitation or construction for Amsterdam, the only Dutch port which was then under blockade.

SIR W. SCOTT.—There are two objections taken in this case: 1st, that the notice of the captor was illegal; and 2ndly, that the master did not in fact proceed towards Amsterdam.

Now, the notice appears to have been "not to proceed to any Dutch port": to be sure that goes a great deal beyond anything which the captors had a right to prescribe, for they ought to have specified the ports to which the blockade was confined. The great point is, to understand what the master apprehended was the prohibition upon him, for certainly what is represented to have passed between him and the captor cannot be conclusive.

The master says, "he was captured on account of his destination to Amsterdam, and because he said he must proceed thither." This, it is contended, was merely a hasty declaration of the master, not carried into effect; and if the master had taken upon himself to say that upon this warning he did intend to change his course, but was seized immediately, it would be pressing the matter too hardly upon his owners not to allow him time to express his determination. But he says no such thing; and if his conduct amounts to an obstinate perseverance to go there, I should hold that a blockade may be broken by obstinacy, as well as by fraud; and if a master says *he will go, and he must go* there, in defiance of notice, his owners must take the consequences of his conduct.

It is a circumstance in favour of this man that the only ships in sight were two Danish merchantmen. The sight of one vessel would not certainly be sufficient notice of a blockade; and therefore it is necessary that it should be signified to me that there was a blockade, *de facto*, before that port.

The evidence is very imperfect on that point: I shall therefore require further information, and give both parties an opportunity of producing what they think favourable to them.

May 10th.—Further proof was given of the notice which the master had received of the blockage of the Vlie passage.

Sir W. Scott.—On the former hearing it appeared that some notice had been given, but I wished to obtain more particular information respecting it. The notice was written on the ship's papers to this effect: "This ship was boarded and warned not to proceed to any Dutch port": the master states, "that the ship was arrested because he said he must proceed according to the bill of lading."

It was open to both parties to have given explanatory affidavits, but the captors have offered none; therefore, unless it is shown that they have been prevented, by absence at sea or other just cause, I must take the claimant's affidavit to be true. The notice is, I think, in point of authority illegal; at the time when it was given there was no blockade which extended to all Dutch ports. A declaration of blockade is a high act of sovereignty, and a commander of a king's ship is not to extend it.

The notice is also, I think, as illegal in effect as in authority. It cannot be said that such a notice, though bad for other ports, is good for Amsterdam. It takes from the neutral all power of election as to what other port of Holland he should go, when he found the port of his destination under blockade. A commander of a ship must not reduce a neutral to this kind of distress; and I am of opinion that if the neutral had contravened the notice he would not have been subject to condemnation.

1799 Jan. 15. — The Henrick and Maria. — Sir W. Scott.

But that he did so rests only on verbal answers and conversation. I adhere to what I said before, that an obstinate adherence to a first intention would subject a ship to the penalty, and the owners must bear the consequences of the obstinacy of their master. But I think the conversation of this man was not an expression of final intention, but that of a man deliberating under difficulties in which he was unfairly placed. The captain of the King's ship asked the master if he knew that Holland was blockaded, and he answered "that he did not." This question agrees with the written notice, and shows how strange a misapprehension the commander had entertained of the nature of the blockade which he was employed to form.

The master said, "he could not answer it to his owners to go to any place but Holland." The commander does not point out to him any ports of Holland to which he might go, but tells him he might go to Bremen, Hamburg, or England; and adds, "as you must go to Holland you are my prize." I think the notice was erroneous, and besides not broken; and therefore I restore this ship.

Application was made for the claimant's expenses but refused, there being other grounds of justifiable seizure, independent of the question of blockade.

THE VROUW JUDITH.

[1 C. Rob. 150.]

Blockade—Egress—Cargo Laden before Commencement of Blockade—Notice—Liability of Owner for Act of Master.

A blockade is violated by egress as well as by ingress; therefore a neutral vessel may only depart from a blockaded port if her cargo has been *bonâ fide* shipped before the commencement of the blockade. Continued existence *de facto* of a blockade is sufficient notice to all vessels within the blockaded port. The owner is liable for the act of his master in attempting to break a blockade.

1799 Jan. 17.

This was a case of a vessel taken coming out of Havre, August 21, 1798.

For the captors, the *King's Advocate* contended that it fell under the law which had been laid down respecting a breach of blockade; that blockade (*a*) was broken by egress as well as by ingress.

(*a*) See the *Frederick Molke*, p. 58; the *Betsey*, p. 147.

For the claimant, *Laurence* argued that it was necessary to show there had been a declaration of this blockade; or, if it was only a blockade *de facto*, that it was permanently existing; for the seizure was made by one vessel only, and it did not appear that the others were not at a great distance.

SIR W. SCOTT.—This is a ship that was taken sailing under Prussian colours. A claim has been given for a person of Embden, but the evidence of property is admitted not to be complete.

She appears to have been a prize vessel taken by the French, but after that her history is no further detailed, nor does it appear whether she had continued to navigate from French ports or not. All the papers are silent on that point, and there is no bill of sale. At all events, therefore, it is a case which must have gone to further proof.

The cargo is claimed by the master, a young man of four-and-twenty, under the description of his private adventure; but it is far beyond the ordinary value of claims of that sort. It was paid for, according to his account, by bills drawn on the owner of the vessel, and therefore it would be natural to expect some communication between them; but it appears they held no such correspondence, which is, to be sure, a very singular circumstance, not very credible, and one that throws a strong degree of suspicion on his title to the cargo. The vessel was taken on the 21st of August coming out of Havre, and, as a blockade existed at the time, it is argued that that act subjects her to condemnation.

Taking the fact to be that there was a blockade, and that the cargo was put on board after the knowledge of the blockade, I should have no hesitation in saying what I have indeed before laid down, that the act of the master of the vessel binds the owner in respect to the conduct of the ship as much as if it was committed by the owner himself. There are powers with which the law invests him, and if he abuses his trust it is a matter to be settled between him and the person who constituted him master; but his act of violation is, as to the penal consequences, to be considered as the act of the owners (*a*).

Now, with respect to the matter of blockade, I must observe that a blockade is just as much violated by a vessel passing outwards as

(*a*) See the *Columbia*, *post*, p. 89.

1799 *Jan.* 17.

THE VROUW JUDITH.

Sir W. Scott.

inwards. A blockade is a sort of circumvallation round a place, by which all foreign connexion and correspondence is, as far as human force can effect it, to be entirely cut off. It is intended to suspend the entire commerce of that place, and a neutral is no more at liberty to assist the traffic of exportation than of importation. The utmost that can be allowed to a neutral vessel is, that having already taken on board a cargo before the blockade begins, she may be at liberty to retire with it. But it must be considered as a rule which this Court means to apply, that a neutral ship departing can only take away a cargo *bonâ fide*, purchased and delivered, before the commencement of the blockade; if she afterwards takes on board a cargo it is a fraudulent act and a violation of the blockade.

It is certainly necessary that a blockade should be intimated to neutral merchants in some way or other. It may be notified in a public and solemn manner by declaration to foreign governments, and this mode would always be most desirable, although it is sometimes omitted in practice; but it may commence also *de facto*, by a blockading force giving notice on the spot to those who come from a distance, and who may therefore be ignorant of the fact. Vessels going in are, in that case, entitled to a notice before they can be justly liable to the consequences of breaking a blockade. But I take it to be quite otherwise with vessels coming out of the port which is the object of blockade; there no notice is necessary after the blockade has existed *de facto* for any length of time; the continued fact is itself a sufficient notice. It is impossible for those within to be ignorant of the forcible suspension of their commerce; the notoriety of the thing supersedes the necessity of particular notice to each ship.

In respect to this port, there had been a blockade notoriously existing during a great part of the summer: a person breaking it is *primâ facie* a delinquent; and the Court will hold it to be incumbent on those who are seized in this act to prove the circumstances by which they hope to be exonerated from the delinquency imputed to them. Now, it being proved in this, and in other cases, that there was a blockade existing at the time of capture, what is there in this evidence to satisfy me that it was not existing, and notoriously existing, when the cargo was taken on board, and at the time when the vessel came out? The lading was taken in on the 10th of August, and the ship sailed on the 21st of August.

Was there any reason to believe the blockading force had retired at that time? I find the ordinary force, which is never large, stationed round at the time of capture; this vessel sallies out, and is immediately arrested. I think, then, there is proof of force sufficient to blockade this port, and evidence to satisfy me that it could not be unknown to the parties; I will further add, that the case is, in other respects, of a very unfavourable appearance.

1799 *Jan.* 17.

THE VROUW JUDITH.

Sir W. Scott.

There is strong reason to suppose the cargo and the vessel are neither of them the property of the claimants.

There are many circumstances that prevent the indulgence of further proof; and looking at the whole of this case together, I think myself warranted to reject these claims.

The claim being rejected, the ship was restored on salvage to the former British owner.

THE COLUMBIA.

[1 C. Rob. 154.]

Blockade—Notice—Knowledge of Blockade—Intention to break Blockade.

A vessel sailed from America for Amsterdam at a time when it was not known that Amsterdam was blockaded. The vessel called at Cuxhaven, where the master learned that Amsterdam was blockaded, but he nevertheless attempted to enter that port, and in such attempt the vessel was captured. *Held* that the vessel must be condemned, for the owners were bound by the act of their master, whose knowledge of the blockade was sufficient. Absence of notice of blockade is immaterial if knowledge of it is shown in fact. Sailing with the intention to break a blockade is an overt act constituting an offence.

THIS was a case of an American vessel taken on a voyage from Hamburg to Amsterdam, August 20th, 1798.

1799 *Jan.* 17; affirmed *Aug.* 12, 1801.

SIR W. SCOTT.—There is pretty clear proof of neutral property in this case, both of the ship and cargo; but the vessel was taken attempting to break a blockade.

It is unnecessary for me to observe that there is no rule of the law of nations more established than this: that the breach of a blockade subjects the property so employed to confiscation. Among all the contradictory positions that have been advanced on the law of nations this principle has never been disputed; it is to be found in all books of law and in all treaties; every man knows it; the

1799 Jan. 17.

THE COLUMBIA.

Sir W. Scott.

subjects of all States know it, as it is universally acknowledged by all governments who possess any degree of civil knowledge.

This vessel came from America (*a*), and, as it appears, with innocent intentions on the part of the American owners; for it was not known at that time in America that Amsterdam was in a state of investment; and therefore there is no proof immediately affecting the owners. But a person may be penally affected by the misconduct of his agents as well as by his own acts; and if he delegates general powers to others, and they misuse their trust, his remedy must be against them.

The master was by his instructions to go north about to Cuxhaven. This precaution is perhaps liable to some unfavourable interpretation. The counsel for the claimant have endeavoured to interpret it to their advantage, but at the best it can be but a matter of indifference. When he arrived at Cuxhaven he was to go immediately to Hamburg, and to put himself under the direction of Messrs. Boué and Company. They therefore were to have the entire dominion over this ship and cargo. It appears, however, they corresponded with persons at Amsterdam, to whom further confidential instruction had been given by the owners; and these orders are found in a letter from Messrs. Vos and Graves, of New York, to Boué and Company, informing them that the *Columbia* was intended for Amsterdam, consigned to the house of Crommelin, to whom Boué and Company are directed to send the vessel on "if the winds should continue unsteady, and keep the English cruisers off the Dutch coast"; if not, they were to unload the cargo and forward it by the interior navigation to Amsterdam. Boué and Company accordingly direct the master "to proceed to Amsterdam if the winds should be such as to keep the English at a distance." There is also a letter from the master to Boué from Cuxhaven, in which he says "Amsterdam is blockaded."

We have this fact then, that when the master sailed from Amsterdam (? Cuxhaven) the blockade was perfectly well known both to him and the consignees; but their design was to seize the opportunity of entering whilst the winds kept the blockading force at a distance. Now, under these circumstances, I have no hesitation in

(*a*) See the *Betsey*, *post*.

saying that the blockade was broken. The blockade was to be considered as legally existing, although the winds did occasionally blow off the blockading squadron. It was an accidental change which must take place in every blockade; but the blockade is not therefore suspended. The contrary is laid down in all books of authority, and the law considers an attempt to take advantage of such an accidental removal as an attempt to break the blockade and as a mere fraud.

1799 *Jan.* 17.

THE COLUMBIA.

Sir W. Scott.

But it has been said that by the American treaty there must be a previous warning. Certainly where vessels sail without a knowledge of the blockade a notice is necessary; but if you can affect them with the knowledge of that fact a warning then becomes an idle ceremony, of no use, and therefore not to be required. The master, the consignees, and all persons intrusted with the management of the vessel appear to have been sufficiently informed of this blockade, and therefore they are not in the situation which the treaty supposes.

It is said also that the vessel had not arrived; that the offence was not actually committed, but rested in intention only. On this point I am clearly of opinion that the sailing with an intention of evading the blockade of the Texel was beginning to execute that intention, and is an overt act constituting the offence. From that moment the blockade is fraudulently invaded. I am, therefore, on full conviction, of opinion that a breach of blockade has been committed in this case; that the act of the master will affect the owner to the extent of the whole of his property concerned in the transaction. The ship and cargo belong in this case to the same individuals, and therefore they must be both involved in the sentence of condemnation.

THE VROUW HERMINA.

[1 C. Rob. 163.]

Practice—Further Proof—Power of Court to review Decree.

Further proof is not granted in cases appearing incapable of fair explanation. A petition for a rehearing on account of the mistake of the agent was refused.

THIS was a case of a ship, formerly a Dutch vessel, but asserted to have been transferred to a neutral merchant.

1799 *Jan.* 27.

1799 Jan. 27. THE VROUW HERMINA.

SIR W. SCOTT.—This is a claim given for a ship as the property of a person of Weender, in East Friesland. It is admitted on the part of the claimant to be a case loaded with considerable difficulties, and the prayer is only that an opportunity may be given for explaining them by further proof.

The question for me, therefore, to consider is, Whether these difficulties are of such a nature as to admit of a fair and satisfactory explanation? because, if they are not, if they are out of the reach of any rational solution, further proof would be no benefit to the party praying it: it would be attended with much delay and expense to the captors, and I should therefore think it my duty to refuse it.

[The Court, on a consideration of the facts, decided that no satisfactory explanation could be given on further proof, and condemned the vessel.]

February 7th.—Mr. Fridag, finding that he had made a mistake in claiming the vessel as the sole property of Bracktezende, when his instructions represented it as belonging two-thirds to Bracktezende and the other third to the master, petitioned the Court to rehear this case.

Court.—This is an application to the Court, on behalf of Mr. Fridag, to rescind the conclusion of a cause, and rehear it on another statement of the claims; and the suggestion is that Mr. Fridag, as agent, had made a mistake in claiming for one proprietor only, when the papers and his instructions represented the ship to be the joint property of Mr. Bracktezende and the master.

I will not go so far as to lay it down universally that it is not in the power of the Court to reconsider its decrees on very particular occasions, because I do not think it is necessary to discuss that point at present: I consider the application to proceed from the feelings of an honourable mind, anxious to acknowledge and rectify its mistakes, and in that point of view it is highly creditable to Mr. Fridag; but I think it can have no legal effect. As a precedent it would be a practice highly dangerous, and the liberty of reviewing its decrees, if it exists, which I do not affirm, is a liberty which the Court would exercise with very great caution, because I foresee that were applications of this sort to be easily admitted they would be very frequently made on reasons much less sincere than those which are now offered to the Court.

In this petition a reason is assigned for the lateness of the claim, "that Mr. Fridag had some scruples about the credit of his employer, as he had been obliged to have recourse to law to enforce a just demand against him." With this I have nothing to do, but with respect to the lateness of the claim I will say, that was only *spinis e pluribus una*—it was but one circumstance out of many with which the case was oppressed.

Another circumstance which Mr. Fridag wishes to explain is his misstatement of the claim: he claimed the ship for Mr. Bracktezende only, instead of claiming it as the joint property of Mr. Bracktezende and the master, "as he should have done if he had had recourse to his papers."

I protest I think the case had as good a chance on a claim given at random as if it had been made on these papers, for it must be extremely difficult to construct any claim upon them: no two agree. In one the ship is represented as the property of the master, and that document purports to have been granted on the master's oath; but the master denies that he ever made such an oath. In his depositions he describes Mr. Bracktezende to be the sole proprietor, and now Mr. Bracktezende states himself to be owner of two-thirds only; so that I cannot think but that the accident which has given Mr. Fridag so much concern might have been fully as beneficial to the claimant as if the papers had been scrutinized with the greatest accuracy; there must have been great discordance under any arrangement. The cause has not, in my opinion, sustained any injury. Without discussing the power of reviewing a sentence, I think the reasons given do not sufficiently sustain the application, and therefore I reject it.

[1 C. Rob. 170.]

THE NEPTUNUS [No. 1].

Blockade—Notification—Continuance—Egress.

When a blockade is accompanied by a notification thereof to neutrals, it must be presumed to be in force till the notification is revoked.

1799 *Jan.* 28. THIS was a case of a ship taken coming out of the Texel, September 7th, 1798.

SIR W. SCOTT.—This case comes on now upon the ship only.

In the affidavit annexed to the claim it is said there is an authority given to claim the cargo, and that there are some facts which may take that part of the case out of the law which has been laid down respecting a breach of blockade. I shall therefore reserve that till a future day, saying at present only that I shall expect the claim to be very special, and the proof to be very satisfactory as to the time when the transaction took place.

There are two questions respecting the ship: a question of property, and a question arising on a breach of blockade. Now, as the Court has frequently decided that neutral vessels breaking a blockade are liable to confiscation, if I am satisfied that the ship has been guilty of that offence it may be unnecessary to enter into the former question, or to inquire whether the property belongs to the claimant or to those Dutch merchants, Messrs. De Sylva, who have, in a letter found on board, certainly expressed themselves very much with the anxiety and the authority of owners.

The capture was made on the 7th of September, off the Vlie passage, by two English armed ships, about seven miles from the Dutch coast. The Court has before laid down the rule that a blockade is broken as much by coming out with a cargo as by going in (*a*), and the only exception which the Court has noticed in laying down this rule is that of a cargo shipped or delivered to the master, for the use of his owner, before the commencement of the blockade.

There are two sorts of blockade, one by the simple fact only, the other by a notification accompanied with the fact. In the former

(*a*) The *Frederick Molke*, *ante*, p. 58.

1799 *Jan.* 28.

THE NEPTUNUS (No. 1).

Sir W. Scott.

case, when the fact ceases (otherwise than by accident or the shifting of the wind) there is immediately an end of the blockade; but where the fact is accompanied by a public notification from the government of a belligerent country to neutral governments, I apprehend, *primâ facie*, the blockade must be supposed to exist till it has been publicly repealed. It is the duty undoubtedly of a belligerent country, which has made the notification of blockade, to notify in the same way, and immediately, the discontinuance of it. To suffer the fact to cease, and to apply the notification again at a distant time, would be a fraud on neutral nations, and a conduct which we are not to suppose any country would pursue. I do not say that a blockade of this sort may not in any possible case expire *de facto*, but I say such a conduct is not hastily to be presumed against any nation; and, therefore, till such a case is clearly made out, I shall hold that a blockade by notification is, *primâ facie*, to be presumed to continue till the notification is revoked.

The notification of the blockade of this port was made on the 11th of June, 1798. The ship was in the Texel at the time, the owner was at Embden, and the blockade must have been perfectly well known there by the latter end of the month. Her duty was to have retired; but it is said the cargo was Portuguese property, and purchased before the notification. Perhaps it might be so, but there could be no obligation on this Prussian vessel to take it away. Instead of pursuing the prudent conduct of withdrawing just after the blockade began, in the months of July and August, this ship is employed in taking a cargo on board.

That it should be done with an intention of continuing there till the blockade ceased is not probable. The presumption is that it must have been done with a fraudulent design of slipping out if any accident should afford an opportunity of escaping. In the month of September she sails, and is immediately stopped by these two armed vessels. But it is said there was no blockade *de facto*, and that this small number of vessels only is a proof that there was no efficient actual blockade. I am quite of a contrary opinion, for surely it is not necessary that the whole blockading force should lie in the same tier, nor is it material that a vessel had escaped the rest. These ships were in the exterior line, as I understand it; and if there had been only these I should have held them

1799 Jan. 28. THE NEPTUNUS (No. 1). Sir W. Scott.

to be quite sufficient. It is unnecessary for me to consider, however, whether the blockade was continued by these ships or not, as the presumption being raised by the notification, it rests on the other side to prove the contrary.

[1 C. Rob. 175.]

THE MENTOR.

Enemy Ship—Liability of Belligerent Officers.

The owner of a ship alleged to have been wrongfully destroyed is only entitled to proceed against the officer immediately responsible (*a*).

1799 Feb. 5.

THIS was a case of an American ship destroyed by his Majesty's ships the *Centurion* and *Vulture* (part of Admiral Digby's squadron), cruising off the Delaware in the year 1783, after the cessation of hostilities, but before that fact had come to the knowledge of either of the parties. [The facts of the case are stated in the judgment, p. 98.]

SIR W. SCOTT.—In this case, which comes before me for judgment, the loss which the claimant has sustained is extremely to be lamented; but it has been well observed by the counsel that it must be on legal grounds only that I can give him redress; and if there are legal grounds that impose upon the Court an incapacity of affording redress, I may lament it, but I cannot give relief upon mere grounds of humanity; humanity is only the second virtue of Courts; justice is unquestionably the first: and justice would be grossly violated by providing a relief for one innocent man at the expense of another, who is not legally subject thereto.

The case, I have said, is an unfortunate one. It is likewise a case extremely peculiar in its circumstances; and the first peculiarity I shall notice is the commencement of such a suit at the distance of near seventeen years from the transaction.

It is not within my recollection that a case of such antiquity has ever been suffered to originate in the Court; I do not say that the statute of limitations extends to prize causes; it certainly does not; but every man must see that the equity of the principle of

(*a*) See the *Ostsee*, Vol. II. p. 432.

that statute in some degree reaches the proceedings of this Court; and that it is extremely fit that there should be some rule of limitation provided by the discretion of the Court, attending only to the nature and form of the process conducted here, by which captors or other persons should be protected against antiquated complaints. And if there is any case of remote antiquity which ought not to be entertained, undoubtedly that would be one in which it clearly appeared that the party complaining had been fully apprised of the nature of his injury and of the mode of redress which he ought to have pursued.

That brings me to the second peculiarity in this case, which is, that there was a suit in this very Court upon this very subject ten years ago, not indeed against the same party, but instituted by the same party who now complains, and who was as perfectly in possession of all the facts of his case at that time as he is at this present moment.

The third peculiarity, I must notice, is an entire novelty in a prize cause, viz., that it is a proceeding for calling to adjudication, not the immediate alleged wrongdoer, but a person who was neither present at nor cognisant of the transaction; and who is to be affected in responsibility merely on this ground, that the person alleged to have done the injury was acting under his general authority; for as to particular orders applying to this transaction it is not pretended that any were given or could be given; he was only the admiral on the general station, and the ships which committed the alleged outrage were under his general command, but at a great distance from him.

Now, really it appears to me that it is the very first time that the attempt has been made in a prize cause to pass over the person from whom the alleged injury has been received, and to fix it on another person on the ground of a remote and consequential responsibility; and I call upon the experience of persons attending in this Court to state whether there is an instance of that kind to be found in the annals of the Court.

The actual wrongdoer is the man to answer in judgment; to him responsibility is attached in this Court. He may have other persons responsible over to him, and that responsibility may be enforced; as, for instance, if a captain made a wrong seizure,

1799 Feb. 5. — THE MENTOR. — Sir W. Scott.

under the express orders of an admiral, that admiral may be made answerable in the damages occasioned to the captain by that improper act. But it is the constant practice of this Court to have the actual wrongdoer the party before the Court, and every man must see the propriety of that practice; because if the Court was once to open the door to complaints founded on a remote and consequential responsibility, where is it to stop? If a monition is to go against the admiral for not issuing his revocatory orders, a monition might in like manner go against the Lords of the Admiralty for a similar neglect, or against the Secretary of State for not issuing similar directions to the Lords of the Admiralty; and these persons might be made parties in a prize cause, and called upon to proceed to adjudication.

If the legal responsibility is to be shifted from the actual captor, to whom is the claimant to look? Where is he to find the responsibility in the chain of persons who may be somehow or other involved in the different stages of the transaction? Where is he to find his wrongdoer, if you once take off that character from the person who immediately commits the injury? Where is he to resort if you take from him that easy and direct resort with which, in the present understanding of the law, he is provided? I am most clearly, on this ground, of opinion that Admiral Digby alone cannot be compelled to proceed to adjudication under this monition.

The circumstances of the case, as far as it is necessary to state them, are these: The ship, being American property, was on a voyage from the Havannah to Philadelphia; off the Delaware she was pursued by his Majesty's ships the *Centurion* and the *Vulture*, then cruising off that river, under the command of the admiral on that station, Admiral Digby. All parties were in complete ignorance of the cessation of hostilities; not only the persons on board the King's ships, but the Americans, as well those on the shore as those on board the vessel. In the pursuit shots were fired on both sides, and it is alleged on the part of the British that the ship was set on fire by her own crew, who took to the shore.

Now, I incline to assent to Dr. Lawrence's position, that if an act of mischief was done by the King's officers, though through ignorance, in a place where no act of hostility ought to have been exercised, it does not necessarily follow that mere ignorance of that fact would protect the officers from civil responsibility. If by articles a place or district was put under the King's peace, and an act of hostility was afterwards committed therein, the injured party might have a right to resort to a Court of Prize, to show that he had been injured by this breach of the peace, and was entitled to compensation; and if the officer acted through ignorance his own government must protect him, for it is the duty of government, if they put a certain district within the King's peace, to take care that due notice shall be given to those persons by whose conduct that peace is to be maintained; and if no such notice has been given, nor due diligence used to give it, and a breach of the peace is committed through the ignorance of those persons, they are to be borne harmless at the expense of that government whose duty it was to have given that notice.

I am therefore inclined to think that the determination of the judge in the former case did not turn upon the mere circumstance of ignorance on the part of the King's ships, but that, looking at all the circumstances under which the event took place, and considering their just and legal effect, he was of opinion upon the whole result that the protest on the part of the captors was well sustained. If that opinion of the judge was erroneous an appeal ought to have been prosecuted. No appeal was prosecuted, though such a purpose was formally declared and a protocol entered, but no further proceedings were pursued thereon.

Mr. Wilson states in his affidavit "that distress of fortune prevented him from proceeding further." I have to lament that, as well as many other circumstances that accompany the case, but Courts of Justice must pursue the legal modes; they cannot bend to the private distresses of individuals. If an appeal is not prosecuted the conclusion of law is that the party acquiesces in the decision.

Now, what did the judge determine? He determined this: that the act of destruction which took place took place under such circumstances that the captor was not compellable to proceed to adjudication upon it. And shall I, at the distance of ten years after he has determined that the actual captors were subject to no responsibility at all, determine that Admiral Digby, a person totally ignorant of the whole transaction, at the distance of thirty leagues

1799 *Feb. 5.* THE MENTOR. Sir W. Scott. from the place where it passed, and utterly unprovided with all the means of defence which either a knowledge of the fact or the possession of evidence can supply, is liable after a lapse of seventeen years to be called upon to proceed to adjudication, or, in other words, to justify the destruction of this vessel, or, failing therein, to be answerable in damages? Surely such a determination could be founded on nothing but a determined opposition to every principle of law and justice by which the proceedings of this Court have been directed ever since it bore the shape of an established Court of Justice.

Having said this, I shall decline to enter minutely into the circumstances of the case, which have been rather alluded to than particularly discussed by the counsel. I feel for the misfortunes of the claimant; he has applied to this Court, and he was judicially informed ten years ago that the loss he has sustained was not of that nature which would entitle him to support an action for damages against the persons whom he considered as the immediate wrongdoers; still less can he be entitled to support it against the person who is the object of the present suit; and I therefore, with the fullest conviction of mind, discharge Admiral Digby from the effect of the present monition.

[1 C. Rob. 189.]

THE JONGE MARGARETHA.

Contraband—Condemnation—Articles ancipitis usûs — Provisions — Cheese— Release of Ship.

The final use of an article *ancipitis usûs* is to be deduced from its destination. A cargo of cheeses, not the product of the country from which they were exported, and destined for a port of naval equipment, *Held* to be contraband. In extenuating circumstances the ship was not confiscated with the cargo.

1799 *Feb. 5.* THIS was a case of a Papenberg ship taken on a voyage from Amsterdam to Brest, with a cargo of cheese.

For the captors, the *King's Advocate.*

For the claimant, *Arnold* and *Swabey.*

SIR W. SCOTT.—There is little reason to doubt the property in this case, and therefore, passing over the observations which have been made on that part of the subject, I shall confine myself to the single question: Is this a legal transaction in a neutral, being the transaction of a Papenberg ship carrying Dutch cheeses from Amsterdam to Brest or Morlaix (it is said), but certainly to Brest? or, as it may be otherwise described, the transaction of a neutral carrying a cargo of provisions not the product and manufacture of his own country, but of the enemy's ally in the war—of provisions which are a capital ship's store—and to the great port of the naval equipment of the enemy?

If I adverted to the state of Brest at this time, it might be no unfair addition to the terms of the description if I noticed, what was notorious to all Europe at this time, that there was in that port a considerable French fleet in a state of preparation for sallying forth on a hostile expedition, its motions at that time watched with great anxiety by a British fleet which lay off the harbour for the purpose of defeating its designs. Is the carriage of such a supply, to such a place, and on such an occasion, a traffic so purely neutral as to subject the neutral trader to no inconvenience?

If it could be laid down as a general position, in the manner in which it has been argued, that cheese being a provision is universally contraband, the question would be readily answered; but the Court lays down no such position. The catalogue of contraband has varied very much, and sometimes in such a manner as to make it very difficult to assign the reason of the variations, owing to particular circumstances, the history of which has not accompanied the history of the decisions. In 1673, when many unwarrantable rules were laid down by public authority respecting contraband, it was expressly asserted by Sir R. Wiseman, the then King's Advocate, upon a formal reference made to him, that by the practice of the English Admiralty, corn, wine, and oil were liable to be deemed contraband. "I do agree," says he, reprobating the regulations that had been published, and observing that rules are not to be so hardly laid down as to press upon neutrals, "that corn, wine, and oil will be deemed contraband."

These articles of provisions, then, were at that time confiscable, according to the judgment of a person of great knowledge and experience in the practice of this Court. In much later times many other sorts of provisions have been condemned as contraband. In

1799 *Feb. 5.*

THE JONGE MARGARETHA.

Sir W. Scott.

1747, in the *Jonge Andreas*, butter, going to Rochelle, was condemned; how it happened that cheese at the same time was more favourably considered, according to the case cited by Dr. Swabey, I don't exactly know. The distinction appears nice; in all probability the cheeses were not of the species which is intended for ship's use. Salted cod and salmon were condemned in the *Jonge Frederick*, going to Rochelle, in the same year. In 1748, in the *Joannes*, rice and salted herrings were condemned as contraband. These instances show that articles of human food have been so considered, at least where it was probable that they were intended for naval or military use.

I am aware of the favourable positions laid down upon this matter by Wolfius and Vattel, and other writers of the Continent, although Vattel expressly admits that provisions may, under circumstances, be treated as contraband. And I take the modern established rule to be this, that generally they are not contraband, but may become so under circumstances arising out of the particular situation of the war or the condition of the parties engaged in it. The Court must therefore look to the circumstances under which this supply was sent.

Among the circumstances which tend to preserve provisions from being liable to be treated as contraband one is, that they are of the growth of the country which exports them. In the present case they are the product of another country, and that a hostile country; and the claimant has not only gone out of his way for the supply of the enemy, but he has assisted the enemy's ally in the war by taking off his surplus commodities.

Another circumstance to which some indulgence, by the practice of nations, is shown is when the articles are in their native and unmanufactured state. Thus iron is treated with indulgence, though anchors and other instruments fabricated out of it are directly contraband. Hemp is more favourably considered than cordage; and wheat is not considered as so noxious a commodity as any of the final preparations of it for human use. In the present case the article falls under this unfavourable consideration, being a manufacture prepared for immediate use.

But the most important distinction is whether the articles were intended for the ordinary use of life or even for mercantile ships' use, or whethey they were going with a highly probable destination to military use. Of the matter of fact on which the distinction is to be applied, the nature and quality of the port to which the articles were going is not an irrational test. If the port is a general commercial port it shall be understood that the articles were going for civil use, although occasionally a frigate or other ships of war may be constructed in that port. *Contra*, if the great predominant character of a port be that of a port of naval military equipment, it shall be intended that the articles were going for military use, although merchant ships resort to the same place, and although it is possible that the articles might have been applied to civil consumption; for it being impossible to ascertain the final use of an article *ancipitis usûs*, it is not an injurious rule which deduces both ways the final use from the immediate destination; and the presumption of a hostile use, founded on its destination to a military port, is very much inflamed if at the time when the articles were going a considerable armament was notoriously preparing, to which a supply of those articles would be eminently useful.

1799
Feb. 5.

THE JONGE MARGARETHA.

Sir W. Scott.

In the case of the *Eendraght*, cited for the claimant, the destination was to Bordeaux, and though smaller vessels of war may be occasionally built and fitted out there, it is by no means a port of naval military equipment in its principal occupation (*a*) in the same manner as Brest is universally known to be.

The Court, however, was unwilling, in the present case, to conclude the claimant on the mere point of destination, it being alleged that the cheeses were not fit for naval use, but were merely luxuries for the use of domestic tables. It therefore permitted both parties to exhibit affidavits as to their nature and quality. The claimant has exhibited none; but here are authentic certificates from persons of integrity and knowledge, that they are exactly such cheeses as are used in British ships when foreign cheeses are used at all, and that they are exclusively used in French ships of war.

Attending to all these circumstances, I think myself warranted

(*a*) Agreeably to this distinction Dutch cheeses going from Amsterdam to Bordeaux, on account of a merchant of Altona, were restored on further proof. The *Welvaart Kwest*, Aug. 27th, 1799.

1799 Feb. 5. — THE JONGE MARGARETHA. — Sir W. Scott.

to pronounce these cheeses to be contraband, and condemn them as such. As, however, the party has acted without dissimulation in the case, and may have been misled by an inattention to circumstances, to which in strictness he ought to have adverted, as well as by something like an irregular indulgence on which he has relied, I shall content myself with pronouncing the cargo to be contraband without enforcing the usual penalty of the confiscation of the ship belonging to the same proprietor.

[1 C. Rob. 196.]

THE HOOP.

Trade with Enemy—British Merchants—Exceptional Circumstances—Condemnation.

Trading with the public enemy is interdicted, and subjects the property of a person so trading to condemnation, unless it is done with the permission of the sovereign.

British merchants shipped a cargo of goods on a neutral vessel bound from Holland for Great Britain, having previously asked the Commissioners of Customs at Glasgow whether a licence to trade was necessary, and having been told that it was not. *Held*, that though the owners of the cargo had acted *bonâ fide*, such cargo must be condemned.

The course of judicial decisions *considered*.

1799 Feb. 13.

THIS was a case of a claim of several British merchants for goods purchased on their account in Holland, and shipped on board a neutral vessel.

The affidavit annexed to the claim set forth that Mr. Malcolm, of Glasgow, and several other merchants of North Britain had, long prior to hostilities, been used to trade extensively with Holland in the importation of various articles of the produce of Holland, which were particularly wanted for the use of Glasgow, and essentially necessary to the agriculture and manufacture of that part of the kingdom; that, after the irruption of the French into Holland, they had constantly applied for and obtained special orders of his Majesty in council, permitting them to continue that trade; that after the passing of the Acts of Parliament (35 Geo. 3, c. 15, s. 80; 36 Geo. 3, c. 76; 37 Geo. 3, c. 12) confirming and continuing the orders of council of the 16th and 21st of January, it was apprehended in that part of Great Britain that by these Acts the importation of such goods was made legal: but for the greater security they still made application to the Commissioners of Customs at Glasgow to know what they considered to be the interpretation of the said Acts, and whether his Majesty's licence was still necessary; and that in answer to such application the merchants were informed, under the opinion of the law advisers of the said Commissioners, that no such orders of council were necessary, and that all goods brought from the United Provinces would in future be entered without them; and that in consequence of such information they had caused the goods in question to be shipped at Rotterdam for their account, ostensibly documented for Bergen to avoid the enemy's cruisers.

SIR W. SCOTT.—This is the case of a ship laden with flax, madder, geneva, and cheese, and bound from Rotterdam ostensibly to Bergen; but she was in truth coming to a British port, and took a destination to Bergen to deceive French cruisers, and, as the claim discloses (of which I see no reason to doubt the truth), the goods were to be imported on account of British merchants, being most of them articles of considerable use in the manufactures and commerce of this country, and being brought under an assurance from the Commissioners of the Customs in Scotland that they might be lawfully imported without any licence by virtue of the statute 35 Geo. 3, c. 15, s. 80.

It is said that these circumstances compose a case entitled to great indulgence, and I do not deny it. But if there is a rule of law on the subject binding the Court I must follow where that rule leads me, though it leads to consequences which I may privately regret when I look to the particular intentions of the parties.

In my opinion there exists such a general rule in the maritime jurisprudence of this country, by which all trading with the public enemy, unless with the permission of the sovereign, is interdicted. It is not a principle peculiar to the maritime law of this country; it is laid down by Bynkershoek as an universal principle of law—*Ex naturâ belli commercia inter hostes cessare non est dubitandum. Quamvis nulla specialis sit commerciorum prohibitio, ipso tamen jure belli commercia esse vetita, ipsæ indictiones bellorum satis declarant,* &c. He proceeds to observe that the interests of trade, and the

1799. Feb. 13.

THE HOOP.

Sir W. Scott.

necessity of obtaining certain commodities, have sometimes so far overpowered this rule that different species of traffic have been permitted, *prout e re suâ, subditorumque suorum esse censent principes* (a). But it is in all cases the act and permission of the sovereign. Wherever that is permitted it is a suspension of the state of war *quoad hoc.* It is, as he expresses it, *pro parte sic bellum, pro parte pax inter subditos utriusque principis.* It appears from these passages to have been the law of Holland. Valin, l. iii., tit. 6, art. 3, states it to have been the law of France, whether the trade was attempted to be carried on in national or in neutral vessels; it will appear from a case which I shall have occasion to mention (the *Fortuna*) to have been the law of Spain; and it may, I think, without rashness be affirmed to have been a general principle of law in most of the countries of Europe.

By the law and constitution of this country the sovereign alone has the power of declaring war and peace. He alone, therefore, who has the power of entirely removing the state of war, has the power of removing it in part, by permitting, where he sees proper, that commercial intercourse which is a partial suspension of the war. There may be occasions on which such an intercourse may be highly expedient. But it is not for individuals to determine on the expediency of such occasions on their own notions of commerce, and of commerce merely, and possibly on grounds of private advantage not very reconcileable with the general interest of the State. It is for the State alone, on more enlarged views of policy, and of all circumstances that may be connected with such an intercourse, to determine when it shall be permitted and under what regulations. In my opinion, no principle ought to be held more sacred than that this intercourse cannot subsist on any other footing than that of the direct permission of the State. Who can be insensible to the consequences that might follow if every person in time of war had a right to carry on a commercial intercourse with the enemy, and under colour of that had the means of carrying on any other species of intercourse he might think fit? The inconvenience to the public might be extreme; and where is the inconvenience on the other side, that the merchant should be com-

(a) Bynk. Q. J. P. book i. c. 3.

pelled in such a situation of the two countries to carry on his trade between them (if necessary) under the eye and control of the government charged with the care of the public safety?

Another principle of law, of a less politic nature, but equally general in its reception and direct in its application, forbids this sort of communication as fundamentally inconsistent with the relation at that time existing between the two countries, and that is, the total inability to sustain any contract by an appeal to the tribunals of the one country on the part of the subjects of the other. In the law of almost every country, the character of alien enemy carries with it a disability to sue, or to sustain in the language of the civilians *a persona standi in judicio*. The peculiar law of our own country applies this principle with great rigour. The same principle is received in our Courts of the law of nations. They are so far British Courts that no man can sue therein who is a subject of the enemy, unless under particular circumstances that *pro hâc vice* discharge him from the character of an enemy, such as his coming under a flag of truce, a cartel, a pass, or some other act of public authority that puts him in the King's peace *pro hâc vice*. But otherwise he is totally *ex lege*. Even in the case of ransoms which were contracts, but contracts arising *ex jure belli*, and tolerated as such, the enemy was not permitted to sue in his own proper person for the payment of the ransom bill, but the payment was enforced by an action brought by the imprisoned hostage in the Courts of his own country for the recovery of his freedom. A state in which contracts cannot be enforced cannot be a state of legal commerce. If the parties who are to contract have no right to compel the performance of the contract, nor even to appear in a court of justice for that purpose, can there be a stronger proof that the law imposes a legal inability to contract? To such transactions it gives no sanction; they have no legal existence, and the whole of such commerce is attempted without its protection and against its authority. Bynkershoek expresses himself with great force upon this argument in his first book, chapter 7, where he lays down that the legality of commerce and the mutual use of courts of justice are inseparable. He says that cases of commerce are indistinguishable from cases of any other species in this respect: *Si hosti semel permittas actiones exercere, difficile est distinguere ex quâ*

1799 Feb. 13. THE HOOP. Sir W. Scott.

causâ oriantur, nec potui animadvertere illam distinctionem unquam usu fuisse servatam.

Upon these and similar grounds it has been the established rule of the law of this Court, confirmed by the judgment of the Supreme Court, that a trading with the enemy, except under a royal licence, subjects the property to confiscation, and the most eminent persons of the law sitting in the Supreme Courts have uniformly sustained such judgments.

In the *Ringende Jacob*, 1747, a Swede, which went from London to Bordeaux in ballast, there took in seventy-one tuns of wine for Mr. Minet, Mr. Challie, and Mr. Fetherstonhagh, to be delivered at Guernsey, but with false clearances at Bordeaux to deceive the enemy; condemned by the Lords of Appeal 7th Feb., 1750, in affirmance of the judgment of the Admiralty.

In the *Lady Jane*, a Hamburg ship laden at Malaga with mountain wine. Cargo claimed by English merchants as the produce of goods sent to Spain before the war; condemned 13th April, 1749. Present: Lord President, Archbishop of York, and Baron Clerke.

In the *Deergarden*, of Stockholm. Woollen goods shipped ostensibly at Lisbon, voyage in fact to the enemy's port at Bilboa, but on British account; cargo condemned 15th March, 1747.

In the *Elizabeth*, of Ostend. Cargo the property of British subjects coming from an enemy's port; condemned 27th Jan. 1749. Present: Duke of Dorset, Earl of Pembroke, Right Honourable W. Pitt, Mr. Justice Dennison, Mr. Justice Clive; *held*, "that a British subject cannot trade with the enemy, but that the only punishment which the Admiralty can inflict was confiscation of the goods."

In the *Juffrouw Louisa Margaretha*, Lords, April 3, 1781, a case of a claim of Messrs. Escott and Read, of London, for wines and other articles shipped on board a Dutch ship, April 7, 1780, at Malaga, for their account.

The affidavit of claim stated: That Mr. Escott was one of a house of trade known by the name of Escott and Read, of London; that they had for twenty years immediately preceding hostilities between Great Britain and Spain carried on considerable trade to and from Malaga, and had an established house of trade at Malaga, where

Mr. Escott had resided about thirty years preceding, excepting the last ten months, when he had left that place, and had since resided in England. It further stated that considerable quantities of wine and other merchandize belonging to the said house (deposited in vaults and warehouses set apart for the same) had been left at Malaga under the care of Mr. Grivegnee, a Fleming by birth, brought up in that house, who was suffered to remain to preserve the said goods during hostilities, unless a favourable opportunity should offer of sending them to London. It stated the destination to have been to Ostend, and the property to have been described for neutral account and risk, to avoid the enemy's cruisers; and claimed the whole as the entire property of the house of London, out of which Mr. Grivegnee was to receive 14 per cent. but no other emolument whatever.

The judgment of the Court of Admiralty rejecting the claim of Mr. Escott was affirmed. Present: the Earls of Bathurst, Sandwich, Marchmont, Hillsborough, Clarendon, Viscount Stormont, Lord Grantham, Lord Loughborough (Chief Justice of the Common Pleas), Sir Richard Worsley, Sir J. Goodricke, Sir J. Eardley Wilmot.

In the *St. Louis*, alias *El Allessandro*, Lords, July 18, 1781, the case of a claim of Messrs. Morgan and Mather for certain peltries shipped by them on board a vessel of New Orleans, bound to Bordeaux and consigned to merchants there, on the proper account and risk of the shippers.

The affidavit stated the history of Mr. Morgan from the year 1764, when he left England to settle in West Florida, and his subsequent transactions from 1774 on the river Mississipi; where, finding no troops nor any sort of protection granted by the British Government to those settled on the British part of the banks of that river, he had kept a ship as a floating storehouse, living himself at New Orleans by permission of the governor, under an express condition that he should not land any sort of goods in any part of the Spanish dominions. It then stated: That in 1779, finding the American troops in such force all over the river as to prevent any English ship from coming up the river, and that it was impossible to make any remittances to England but by hiring neutral vessels, he shipped the goods in question on board the *St. Louis*, belonging

1799 *Feb.* 13. THE HOOP. Sir W. Scott.

to inhabitants of New Orleans, at that time neutral subjects, that being the only vessel at New Orleans bound to any port of Europe; that they were consigned to merchants at Bordeaux, to be there sold and the proceeds remitted to Mr. Mather in London; that he was obliged to resort to this mode of remittance that the goods might not perish on his hands.

Annexed to the affidavit was a certificate of Colonel Dickson, the British commander in those parts, certifying that Mr. Morgan (*a*), a British subject, had received permission, under the 12th article of the capitulation of Baton Rouge, to convey himself and family to London under a passport from the Spanish Governor.

The sentence of the Court of Admiralty, condemning the ship and cargo as enemy's property, or otherwise liable to confiscation, was affirmed. Present: Earl of Bathurst, Earl of Clarendon, Lord Loughborough (Chief Justice of the Court of Common Pleas).

In the *Compte de Wohronzoff*, Lords, July 19, 1781, a case of a claim of Mr. Daly, Mr. G. Byrne, and other Irish merchants, for the ship and certain quantities of French wines shipped at Bordeaux, May, 1780, on their account, with ostensible papers for Russia, it was stated, in support of their claim, that during the whole of the war the Commissioners of his Majesty's Revenue and Excise in Ireland had constantly permitted trade to be carried on from Bordeaux to Dublin in the same manner as it was before hostilities commenced, and all ships belonging to British owners, navigated according to law, with cargoes the property of British owners, coming immediately and openly from Bordeaux, had been and still were admitted to enter and invoice their cargoes from thence, and that on all cargoes so entered the regular duties had been paid.

An Act of Parliament was recited, passed in Ireland in the nineteenth and twentieth of his present Majesty, by which it is enacted that from the 24th of June, 1780, till the 25th of December, 1781, there should be paid an additional duty of 10*l.* 7*s.* per tun on all French wines imported into the kingdom of

(*a*) In the *Victoria*, Lords, July 20, 1781, the property of this gentleman in the ship and goods sent from New Orleans, April, 1779, and consigned to London was restored.

Ireland during the said period. The practice of admitting such cargo to an entry was proved by an extract from the Entries Office, by which it appeared that several cargoes of a similar nature had been permitted to enter; and it was contended that the Act of the Irish Legislature was decisive, as far as it was competent for them to decide, being made long after the commencement of hostilities, as it could not be imagined that they would be inattentive to public affairs, or propose to draw a revenue from a trade prohibited and illegal.

The judgment of the Court of Admiralty, condemning the ship and cargo as good and lawful prize, was affirmed, and the appellant was condemned in the costs of the appeal. Present: Earl of Bathurst, Earl of Hillsborough, Earl of Clarendon, Lord Loughborough (Chief Justice of the Common Pleas).

In the *Expedite van Roterdam*, Lords, July 18, 1782, a case of the claim of Messrs. Gregory & Turnbull, of London, for a quantity of wine and other articles shipped on board a Dutch ship December 20th, 1780, at Malaga for them, though ostensibly for the account and risk of Mr. Carl Thomasze, of Amsterdam, their agent, Holland being then at peace with this country.

The affidavit of the claimant recited an Act, passed in the twentieth year of his Majesty's reign, to permit goods the product or manufacture of certain places within the Levant or Mediterranean seas to be imported into Great Britain or Ireland in British or foreign vessels from any place whatsoever, enacting that from the 1st of January, 1780, any goods which had been usually imported from any port or place in Europe within the Straits of Gibraltar (with an exception respecting the dominions of the Grand Signior), should and might, during the continuance of the said Act, be imported and brought by any person or persons whatsoever into Great Britain or Ireland in any ship belonging to any State in amity with his Majesty. The affidavit stated that the importation had been in every respect conformable to the said Act, and that the said goods were coming for the sole account, risk, and benefit of their house, being described in the bill of lading to be at the account and risk of Carl Thomasze, only to avoid the enemy's cruisers.

The judgment of the Court of Admiralty condemning these

1799 Feb. 13. goods was affirmed. Present: Lord Camden, Earl of Effingham, and Lord Ashburton.

THE HOOP. Sir W. Scott. In the *Bella Guidita*, Lords, July 20, 1785, a case of a claim of Mr. Vaughan and other British merchants, sending a cargo of provisions on board a Venetian vessel from Ireland to Grenada, one of the islands then lately taken by the French.

"The affidavit of claim set forth the particular situation of that and the other islands, since they had fallen into the possession of the French; that they were not considered by the French Government as entirely French islands; that by a certain ordinance of the French king it was ordained that the merchants and inhabitants of all or most of the conquered islands should, as to their trade and commerce, be upon the same terms and footing as the British merchants and inhabitants of the Island of Dominica; that by the 17th Article of the Capitulation of the Island of Dominica in 1778, it was permitted to the merchants of the said island, until peace, to receive vessels (except English) to their address from all parts of the world without their being confiscated; that before Dutch hostilities broke out the trade between the conquered islands and Great Britain had been carried on through the Island of St. Eustatius, under the sanction of British Acts of Parliament, for the purpose of supplying the islands with provisions absolutely necessary for their subsistence, and of taking off the produce in payment to British merchants, as the only means of keeping down the interests due to them on mortgage on the plantations."

"That after the Dutch hostilities, it became notorious to the British Government that the obstruction of this trade would be attended with very serious consequences to the British interests in the said islands; and under these considerations an Act was passed in the 20th Geo. 3, reciting that during the said hostilities the Islands of Grenada and the Grenadines had been taken by the French king, but it was just and expedient to give every relief to the proprietors of estates in the said islands, and enacting that no goods or merchandise of the growth, produce, or manufacture of the said islands on board neutral vessels, going to neutral ports, should be liable to condemnation as prize.

"That under this view of the necessitous situation of the said island, and of the favourable manner in which it was considered by the Government of this country the claimants chartered this ship to carry out a cargo of provisions to Grenada, and bring back in return a cargo of the produce of that island; that there was an ostensible destination to St. Thomas merely for the purpose of avoiding the enemy's cruisers."

"The judgment of the Vice-Admiralty Court of Barbadoes, condemning the cargo as French property, was affirmed, and the appellant condemned in the costs of appeal. Present: Lord Camden (President of the Council), Earl of Effingham, Marquis of Caermarthen, Viscount Howe, and Lord Sydney."

In the *Eenigheid*, Lords, 21st of March, 1795: a case of a claim of Mr. Hankey of London and of Mr. Alphen of Rotterdam for a quantity of corn shipped on board a Lubeck ship in December, 1792, from Rotterdam to Nantes.

It appeared from the evidence that the ship was chartered for this voyage on the 6th of December, 1792, and that the cargo was actually laden in the same month, but by various accidental delays the ship was prevented from putting to sea till the 9th of February. Hostilities were declared by the ruling powers of France against England and Holland on the 1st of February, 1793.

It was contended for the captors that hostilities having been declared by the ruling powers of France against England and Holland on the 1st of February, 1793, no cargo (much less a cargo so essential to the French as wheat) could lawfully be sent from Holland for France, on account of British and Dutch subjects, on the 9th of the same month; subsequent to which, this ship, with the cargo of wheat in question on board, set sail from Helvoetsluys for Nantes; and having been captured in such voyage on the 26th of that month, the cargo was rightly, justly, and lawfully condemned as prize to the British captors.

The sentence of the Court of Admiralty, condemning the whole cargo, was affirmed. Present: Earl of Mansfield (President of the Council), Lord Auckland, Sir Richard Pepper Arden (Master of the Rolls), Sir J. Eyre (Chief Justice of the Common Pleas), Sir W. Wynne, Charles Greville, Esq.

In the *Fortuna*, Lords, 27th of June, 1795: a case of a claim of Messrs. Tupper and Drake, British merchants carrying on trade at Barcelona, for a quantity of wine shipped on board a

1799 *Feb.* 13. — THE HOOP. — Sir W. Scott.

Swedish vessel at Barcelona, January, 1793, and destined to Calais.

It appeared in evidence that the ship was chartered for this voyage on the 11th of January, 1793, that she sailed to Tarragona and Saloe (in which latter port she arrived on the 15th of February), and completed her cargo, and sailed on her voyage to Calais on the 21st of March; the ship was taken on the 8th of April by a Spanish frigate, and released under this sentence of the Spanish Court of Admiralty:—That considering the vessel is under neutral colours; that the cargo does not consist of contraband goods; that the concerned do not appear other than merchants resident in Spain; *that the war was not declared against* France neither when she was laden or when she was detained, because it was on the 20th of March, and the last bill of lading appears dated at Saloe on the 15th of the said month, from whence she sailed on the 21st, they ought and did command the said brig to be set at liberty.

For the captors, it was contended that the ship was liable to confiscation because she sailed from Spain to Calais many months subsequent to the commencement of hostilities by the French against this country and against Spain, and because it was incumbent on the proprietors to have prevented the sailing of this ship from Spain for Calais, or to have shown that every endeavour had been used for that purpose.

The sentence of the High Court of Admiralty, condemning the cargo, was affirmed. Present: Earl of Mansfield, Lord St. Helens, Sir W. Wynne, Sylvester Douglas, Esq.

In the *Freeden*, Lords, July 4th, 1795: a case of a claim of Messrs. Herries, Keith, and Stembor, of Barcelona, merchants, for a quantity of brandies shipped on board a Swedish ship at different Spanish ports, in the months of March and April, 1793.

It appeared in evidence that the firm consisted of Sir Robert Herries and Charles Herries, resident in London; Alexander Keith, a British subject resident at Barcelona; George Keith, a British subject resident at Ostend; and Frederick Stembor, a Dutch subject resident at Barcelona. The vessel was chartered on the 7th of March for Ostend. On the 14th of March she sailed from Barcelona to Terrendembarra, and from thence on the 23rd of March for Terragona where the cargo in question was completed.

She sailed from thence on the 3rd of April, and put into Malaga on the 6th of May, and proceeding on her voyage was taken on the 2nd of June by a French privateer, and retaken on the 23rd by the respondents.

1799 *Feb.* 13.

THE HOOP.

Sir W. Scott.

On the former hearing, leave was given to Sir Robert Herries, resident in London, to give proof that on the breaking out of hostilities they had taken means to prevent their being implicated in the consequences of an illicit commerce. A letter was accordingly brought in, written on the 12th of Feb., 1793, in which was this passage: "We have learnt with certainty the declaration of war in France against this country and Holland, as well as the actual commencement of hostilities by the capture of several of our trading vessels; in consequence of which letters of marque and general reprisals are granted here against all ships and goods belonging to France, or to any persons being subjects of France or inhabiting within any of the territories of France."

The judgment of the High Court of Admiralty, condemning the cargo, was affirmed. Present: Earl of Mansfield (Lord President of the Council), Sir Richard Pepper Arden, Sir W. Wynne, Sylvester Douglas, and Charles Greville, Esqrs.

In the *William*, Lords, Dec. 19th, 1795: a case of a claim of Messrs. Munro, Macfarlane & Co., of Grenada, for a quantity of sugars shipped on their account at Guadaloupe, in June, 1793.

It appeared from the claimants' affidavit that for some years prior to the war a trade had been carried on by the merchants of the British islands supplying the French islands with slaves, on credit, to receive payment in sugars of the ensuing year. That there was, on that account, always a considerable debt due to them from the French merchants. That the sugar in question had actually been received at Guadaloupe by the agent of the claimants for slaves sold on their account prior to the war.

The judgment of the Vice-Admiralty Court of St. Christopher, condemning the ship and cargo, was affirmed. Present: Earl of Mansfield (President of the Council), Lord St. Helens, Sir Richard Pepper Arden (Master of the Rolls), and Sir W. Wynne.

I omit many other cases of the last and the present war merely on this ground, that the rule is so firmly established that no one case exists which has been permitted to contravene it. For I take

1799 Feb. 13. — THE HOOP. — Sir W. Scott.

upon me to aver that all cases of this kind which have come before that tribunal have received an uniform determination. The cases which I have produced prove that the rule has been rigidly enforced—where Acts of Parliament have on different occasions been made to relax the navigation law and other revenue acts; where the Government has authorized, under the sanction of an Act of Parliament, a homeward trade from the enemy's possessions, but has not specifically protected an outward trade to the same, though intimately connected with that homeward trade, and almost necessary to its existence; that it has been enforced where strong claims, not merely of convenience but of necessity, excused it on behalf of the individual; that it has been enforced where cargoes have been laden before the war, but where the parties have not used all possible diligence to countermand the voyage after the first notice of hostilities; and that it has been enforced not only against the subjects of the Crown, but likewise against those of its allies in the war, upon the supposition that the rule was founded on a strong and universal principle which allied states in war had a right to notice and apply mutually to each other's subjects. Indeed, it is the less necessary to produce these cases, because it is expressly laid down by Lord Mansfield, as I understand him, that such is the maritime law of England (*a*); and he who for so long a time assisted at the decisions of that Court, at that period could hardly have been ignorant of the rule of decision on this important subject; though none of the instances which I happen to possess prove him to have been personally present at those particular judgments. What is meant by the addition "but this does not extend to a neutral vessel," it is extremely difficult to conjecture, because no man was more perfectly apprised that the neutral bottom gives, in no case, any sort of protection to a cargo that is otherwise liable to confiscation; and therefore I cannot but conclude that the words of that great person must have been received with some slight degree of misapprehension.

What the common law of England may be it is not necessary, nor perhaps proper, for me to inquire; but it is difficult to conceive that it can by any possibility be otherwise, for the rule in no degree

(*a*) *Gist* v. *Mason*, 1 T. R. 85.

arises from the transaction being upon the water, but from principles of public policy and of public law, which are just as weighty on the one element as on the other, and of which the cases have happened more frequently upon the water, merely in consequence of the insular situation of this country. But when an enemy existed in the other part of the island (the only instance in which it would occur upon the land), it appears, from the case referred to by that noble person, to have been deemed equally criminal in the jurisprudence of this country.

The general rule of law being in my apprehension clear, it is only to be inquired whether there are any distinctions which take this case out of the application; and I need not add that these must be legal distinctions and not such as present mere considerations of indulgence and compassion, or mere considerations of the utility of the particular commerce; for to these the Court has no power to give way. A reference has been made to the statutes. It is not argued that the statutes will, in the just apprehension of them, authorise such a trade, but that they might have led to an innocent mistake on the subject. These statutes, it is admitted, were made to apply only to the property of persons in Holland while hostilities were impending. It was necessary that some provisions should be made for the security of the loyal Dutchmen who might migrate to this country. It was found necessary on this account to relax the navigation laws; and for this purpose an Order of Council first issued, which was afterwards confirmed by these Acts as necessary to support the Order and protect those who acted under it, but merely with respect to property so circumstanced. These were mere Custom House regulations, and nothing else; and it is impossible to entertain a doubt respecting the interpretation of them.

It appears that these parties had before applied to the council for special orders, and had always obtained them. It is much to be regretted that they had not applied again to the same source of information; instead of doing so, they consulted the Commissioners of the Customs, very proper judges, to ascertain what goods might be imported under the revenue laws; but this is a matter of general law, on which they are not the persons best qualified to give information or advice. The intention of the

1799 *Feb.* 13. The Hoop. Sir W. Scott.

parties might be perfectly innocent, but there is still the fact against them of that actual contravention of the law which no innocence of intention can do away. The same pleas were urged, and with equal reason, for Mr. Escott, and in many other cases; but it has been decided by a Court which has much greater power of construction that such pleas could not be sustained. I may feel greatly for the individuals who, I have reason to presume, acted ignorantly under advice that they thought safe; but the Court has no power to depart from the law which has been laid down, and I am under the necessity of rejecting the claims.

Freight and expenses were given to the master.

On application that the Court would decree the expenses of the claims to be paid out of the cargo, it was contended that there was no instance in which the Court had done this but in cases of recapture.

The *Court* directed the expenses to be paid.

[1 C. Rob. 227.]

THE REBECKAH.

Capture—Prize or Droit of Admiralty—Naval Station.

A vessel was captured by a boat's crew from a naval station. Such vessel was previously fired at from this station, and struck her flag. At this station there was no military establishment, and it was used solely by the crews of ships of war lying in the vicinity. *Held*, that the vessel was not a droit of Admiralty, but lawful maritime prize.

1799 *Feb.* 26.

This was a question of interest on the capture of a vessel made from the island of St. Marcou, whether it should be condemned as a droit of Admiralty or to the captor.

For the Admiralty, the *Advocate of the Admiralty* and *Laurence*. The circumstances of the capture are that this vessel, on putting into St. Marcou for safety, was fired at from the fort, and immediately struck her colours; that she continued to ride there a whole day before possession was taken; that it was at last taken by a boat's crew coming off from the fort.

These facts, it is presumed, are sufficient to establish the claim of the Admiralty, as the law gives the benefit of all captures made in roadsteads, creeks or havens, and on anchorage ground, to the Lord High Admiral as his *peculium.*

The case of the *Trautmansdorff* (Lords, Aug. 1, 1795), in which the Lords decided against the claims of the Admiralty, differs materially from the present, as that capture was made in the open sea off the bold shore of St. Helena. It was, besides, doubtful in what manner possession was first taken, whether by a boat from the *Powerful* or by the act of firing a shot from the fort. In this case it is not disputed that the surrender was made to the fort long before any boat went off to take possession. In a case of a capture made by the garrison of Gibraltar, the *Nostra Signora del Carmen* (*a*), it was condemned as a droit of Admiralty. In this case it is an additional circumstance in favour of the claim of the Admiralty that the island of St. Marcou is certified to be peculiarly under the direction of the Admiralty. On these grounds, it is submitted, the prize is to be condemned as a droit of Admiralty.

For the captors, the *King's Advocate* and *Arnold.* In this case there had been a mistake in praying condemnation to the Crown, but it has been rectified, and the individual captors are now the parties before the Court. Against either the Admiralty can have no claim. The capture was made by naval officers in their naval character, and therefore, *primâ facie,* it is acquired to the King, and through him to the actual captors. The proof, therefore, must lie with the Admiralty to take this case out of the general rule. But the asserted facts are not established by the evidence. It is by no means proved that the vessel was at anchor at the time of capture, as it is rather intimated by the expressions of the witnesses, that she struck her colours before she came to an anchor. If there was, however, proof of that fact, it by no means follows that this

(*a*) The *Nostra Signora del Carmen,* Bregnante, master, laden with wine and oil, seized in the harbour of Gibraltar by order of Colonel Roger Elliot, lieutenant-governor; "ship and cargo condemned to the Lord High Admiral as perquisites of Admiralty:" Adm., June 25th, 1708.

capture would be to be considered as a droit of Admiralty. There is no pretence to say that the place of capture was a port or haven; it is merely a strait running between the island and the French coast: is rather an anchorage-ground off the island of St. Marcou, than a port or haven within its limits. By the decision of the *Trautmansdorff* it is clearly settled that an intention to come in is not sufficient; there must be an actual coming in to support the claim of the Admiralty. No such thing is proved in this case, and, therefore, the condemnation must pass in favour of the actual captors.

SIR W. SCOTT.—The general question arises upon the capture of a vessel at the isle of Marcou, effected with considerable exertions of gallantry and perseverance by the crews of the *Sand Fly* and *Badger*, stationed in and near that little island; and it is a question of interest between the Lord High Admiral or, as in modern times it is more usually expressed, the King in his office of Admiralty representing that great officer, and the naval captors standing upon the general claim of prize under the Proclamation and the Prize Acts of Parliament.

The rights of the Lord High Admiral are of great antiquity and splendour, and are entitled to great attention and respect, and certainly to full as much in this Court as in any other place where they can possibly come under consideration. At the same time, it is not to be understood that an extension of these rights beyond their absolute limits is to be favoured by construction. They are parts and parcels of the ancient rights of the Crown, communicated by former grants to that great officer, under a very different state and administration of his office from that which now exists in practice.

All grants of the Crown are to be strictly construed against the grantee, contrary to the usual policy of the law in the consideration of grants; and upon this just ground, that the prerogatives and rights and emoluments of the Crown being conferred upon it for great purposes and for the public use, it shall not be intended that such prerogatives, rights and emoluments, are diminished by any grant beyond what such grant by necessary and unavoidable construction shall take away. It is not improper for me to add that the particular circumstances of the present case, which imply great merit of active exertion on the part of the captors, would certainly not dispose the Court to lose sight of this general rule in considering this question of interest.

The grant to the Lord High Admiral (evidenced as it is by the Orders in Council of 1665 (*a*), and by the subsisting practice,) gives him the benefit of all captures by whomsoever made, whether commissioned or non-commissioned persons, under certain circumstances of situation and locality, that is, "*of all ships and goods coming into ports, creeks, or roads of England or Ireland, unless they come in*

(*a*) The following is a correct copy of those orders:—

At a council held at Worcester House the 6th of March, 1665-6—PRESENT: The King's Most Excellent Majesty; His Royal Highness the Duke of York; His Highness Prince Rupert; Lord Chancellor; Duke of Albemarle; Earl of Lauderdale; Lord Fitzharding; Lord Arlington; Lord Berkeley; Lord Ashley; Mr. Secretary Morice; Sir William Coventry.

Whereas through the long intermission of any war at sea by his Majesty's authority, several doubts have arisen concerning certain rights of the Lord High Admiral in time of hostility, the determination whereof appearing very necessary for the direction as well of his Majesty's officers as of those of the Lord High Admiral; upon full hearing and debate of the particulars hereafter mentioned, the King's counsel, learned in the common law, and likewise the judge of the High Court of Admiralty, and those of his Majesty's and his Royal Highness the Lord High Admiral's counsel in the said High Court of Admiralty, being present his Majesty, present in council, was pleased to declare:

1st. That all ships and goods belonging to enemies coming into any port, creek, or road, of this his Majesty's kingdom of England or of Ireland, by stress of weather or other accident, or by mistake of port, or by ignorance, not knowing of the war, do belong to the Lord High Admiral; but such as shall voluntarily come in, either men of war or merchantmen, upon revolt from the enemy, and such as shall be driven in, and forced into port by the King's men-of-war, and also such ships as shall be seized in any of the ports, creeks, or roads, of this kingdom, or of Ireland, before any declaration of war or reprizals by his Majesty, do belong unto his Majesty.

2nd. That all enemies' ships and goods casually met at sea, and seized by any vessel not commissionated, do belong to the Lord High Admiral.

3rd. That salvage belongs to the Lord High Admiral for all ships rescued.

4th. That all ships forsaken by the company belonging to them are the Lord High Admiral's, unless a ship commissionated have given the occasion to such dereliction, and the ship so left be seized by such ship pursuing, or by some other ship commissionated, then in the same company, and in pursuit of the enemy; and the like is to be understood of any goods thrown out of any ship pursued.

1799 *Feb. 26.*

THE REBECKAH.

Sir W. Scott.

voluntarily upon revolt, or are driven in by the King's cruisers." Usage hath construed this to include ships and goods already come into ports, creeks, or roads, and these not only of England and Ireland, but of all the dominions thereunto belonging. But I can by no means agree to the position that has been laid down, that wherever a ship can find anchorage-ground, there is a road or roadstead within the meaning of this grant. For if that were so, the Lord High Admiral would be entitled to all captures made within a moderate distance of most parts of the coasts of England and Ireland, and the foreign dominions belonging to them, which assuredly is not the case, for who would say that if a ship at anchor in the channel of Dover is seized by a commissioned cruiser, the admiral is entitled? Every anchorage-ground is not a roadstead; a roadstead is a known general station for ships (*statio tutissima nautis*), notoriously used as such, and distinguished by the name, and not every spot where an anchor will find bottom and fix itself. The very expression of "coming into a road" shows that by road is meant something much beyond mere anchorage-ground on an open coast. When it was laid down in the *Trautmansdorff* (Lords, Aug. 1, 1795) that it was not necessary that the ship should be actually entered, and that it was enough if she was *in ipsis faucibus* of the port, creek, or road, it is evident that the words "ports, creeks, or roads" have a signification intimating certain known receptacles of ships, more or less protected by points and headlands, and marked out by limits, and resorted to as places of safety.

How far St. Marcou has a road that will at all satisfy this description may be questioned. The witnesses talk of a road, it is true; but it should seem that these small and barren rocks enclose no portion of the sea that can be strictly so considered. It is a pretty open strait running between them and the coast of France, where ships may ride as they may do in other open parts of the French coast. It might likewise admit of a question how far such a mere naval station, without inhabitants and without government, either civil or military, as in truth it is, and merely occupied for the temporary convenience of these gun vessels and their crews, is so far a recognised possession of the Crown of England as to come within the intention of the grant, which, according to the letter and my apprehension of its meaning, cannot travel beyond the ports, creeks, and roads of England and Ireland, and the dominions thereunto belonging.

Laying these questions, however, out of the case, the first question that will occur applies to the time of the capture, whether that is to be dated from the actual taking possession or the previous striking of the colours; and I think that the striking of the colours is to be deemed the real *deditio*. If the French had succeeded in their attempt to defeat that surrender, then the actual final taking of possession must have been alone considered. But as that attempt failed, I am of opinion that the act of formal submission having never been effectively discontinued, must be deemed the consummation of the capture; and if so, the next question will be, Where the vessel was at the time that this act took place? And this is proved to have been "when she was about to go into the road to anchor there," for such is the expression of the witness upon the third interrogatory, which points more immediately to the place of capture; although on the 29th, which is pointed only to the general course of the vessel upon her voyage, he says, "She put into the road there." The second witness describes her merely "as passing by the Isle of Marcou at the time"; and the third says, in the language of the first, that "she was about to go into the road to anchor there." Clearly, by all their descriptions, she had not entered the road, and she was under sail at the time she struck her colours. In point of locality, then, the claim of the admiral is not founded, for she was not *in ipsis faucibus;* she was *about to enter*, but was not actually entering, and that is the point at which the Admiralty-right commences.

The claim, therefore, of the Admiralty must be supported, if at all, upon the other ground, viz., that this was a capture made from the land, and by a land force, and therefore not a maritime capture by persons commissioned to take for their own benefit—and I think it is proved that the striking of the colours was compelled by a firing from the shore, and that a boat was sent from thence to take possession. Now upon this subject I entirely accede to what has been laid down, that a capture at sea made by a force upon the land (which is a case certainly possible, though not frequent) is considered generally as a non-commissioned capture, and enures to the benefit of the Lord High Admiral. Thus, if a

1799 *Feb.* 26. THE REBECKAH. Sir W. Scott.

ship of the enemy was compelled to strike by a firing from the castle of Dover, or other garrisoned fortress upon the land, that ship would be a Droit of Admiralty, and the garrison must be content to take a reward from the bounty of the Admiralty, and not a prize-interest under the King's proclamation. All title to sea-prize must be derived from commissions under the Admiralty, which is the great fountain of maritime authority; and a military force upon the land is not invested with any commission so derived, impressing upon them a maritime character, and authorizing them to take upon that element for their own benefit. I likewise think cases may occur in which naval persons having a real authority to take upon the sea for their own advantage, might yet entitle the Admiralty, and not themselves, by a capture made upon the sea by the use of a force stationed upon the land. Suppose the crew, or part of the crew, of a man of war were landed, and descried a ship of the enemy at sea, and that they took possession of any battery or fort upon the shore, such as may be met with in many parts of the coast, and by means of such battery or fort compelled such a ship to strike; I have no doubt that such a capture, though made by persons having naval commissions, yet being made by means of a force upon the land which they employed accidentally, and without any right under their commission, would be a Droit of Admiralty, and nothing more; and therefore I do not think it quite enough to say that the persons here were naval commissioned persons, and consequently entitled to the benefit of all property taken upon the sea. But I think that the peculiar nature and quality of the place where the capture was effected is to be added to the consideration. What is St. Marcou? It is styled a garrison and a fort by one or two witnesses, but inaccurately; for it is certified by the commander-in-chief, that there is no garrison nor any military establishment whatever—it is a mere naval station used for the temporary accommodation of the crews of these ships of war. There is not a person upon it who is not borne upon the ships' books, and who is not a part of their crews—they have the ship's pay, the ship's victuals, and the ship's officers to command them; the blockhouses which they have constructed are mounted with their own ship-guns, with the addition of a few spare guns otherwise procured. The whole force, such as it is, upon this little spot, is entirely subservient to these vessels, and for their use, and for no other purpose, as the certificates declare. Such a place, so selected and so employed, is hardly to be considered as anything else than as a part or appendage of the naval force; it is a fort of stationary tender, rather attached to and dependent upon these vessels, than having the vessels attached to and dependent upon it. This peculiar character of the place distinguishes it most essentially from the case of a land fortress possessed by a military garrison. The capture then was effected by naval commissioned persons using a force immediately subject to their use; and from its peculiar circumstances sufficiently naval in itself to be distinguished from an ordinary land force, subject to military persons. It is a maritime capture, effected regularly by a maritime force, and in a spot where the right of the Admiralty had not yet commenced upon the thing itself at the time of the surrender. And upon these grounds I shall pronounce for the claim of prize under the King's proclamation and the Prize Acts.

1799 *Feb.* 26.

THE REBECKAH.

Sir W. Scott.

THE SARAH CHRISTINA.

[1 C. Rob. 237.]

Contraband—Pitch and Tar—Pre-emption—Condemnation—Restoration of Ship—Forfeiture of Freight.

Pitch and tar destined for a hostile port are contraband of war, unless they are the produce of the shippers' country, but in such case they are subject to pre-emption. But if there is a want of *bona fides* on the part of the shipper as in ostensibly shipping these articles to a neutral port, they may be condemned.

THIS was the case of a Swedish vessel going to France with contraband articles, and sailing under a colourable destination to a neutral port.

1799 *March* 6.

SIR W. SCOTT.—This is a case of a Swedish ship laden with tar, pitch (*a*), iron hoops, and bars, and bound ostensibly to Cagliari.

The ship and cargo are claimed for the same person. The ship appears clearly to be Swedish property. But there are considerable doubts on the property of the cargo.

[The Court then examined the facts as to the cargo.]

(*a*) See the *Maria*, *post*, p. 152.

1799 *March* 6.

THE SARAH CHRISTINA.

Sir W. Scott.

I consider this, then, as the case of a Swedish ship carrying pitch and tar to a French port, under a pretended neutral destination. What will be the effect of such conduct? Pitch and tar are now become generally contraband in a maritime war: they have been condemned as such by the highest authority in this country (*a*). In the practice of this Court there is a relaxation, which allows the carrying of these articles, being the produce of the claimant's country; as it has been deemed a harsh exercise of a belligerent right to prohibit the carrying of these articles, which constitute so considerable a part of its native produce and ordinary commerce. But in the same practice this relaxation is understood with a condition that it may be brought in, not for confiscation, but for pre-emption—no unfair compromise, as it should seem, between the belligerent's rights, founded on the necessities of self-defence, and the claims of the neutral to export his native commodities, though immediately subservient to the purposes of hostility. To entitle the party to the benefit of this rule a perfect *bona fides* on his part is required.

It is asked, why should a real destination to French ports be concealed if the neutral has a right to carry these avowedly? Clearly to give the French market a greater security. If pitch and tar are going avowedly to the enemy, they may be brought in for pre-emption; but if papers, holding out a neutral destination, are put on board, this right is eluded, and the enemy is commodiously and securely provided with the instruments of war. The cruiser can only examine to satisfy himself of the fact of the destination; but he cannot detain without a responsibility in damages. The false representation, therefore, is not useless for the purposes of mischief: it is the passport and convoy for noxious articles to the ports of the enemy.

I am of opinion, then, that this cargo, consisting of some articles contraband in their own nature, and going to the enemy's port under a total absence of that fair conduct which ought to have been maintained in order to entitle it to the benefit of the more favourable rule, is subject to condemnation. With respect to the

(*a*) In the *Twee Juffrowen* (*post*, p. 384), a cargo of pitch and tar carried in a Prussian ship, bound from Embden to Dieppe, such cargo not proved to be the produce of Prussia, was condemned. See also *ante*, p. 1.

ship: if I was satisfied that the ship and cargo belonged to the same person, I must condemn that also, upon the ordinary rule which extends the penalty of contraband to all the property of the same owner involved in the same unlawful transaction (*a*). But I shall restore it under the strong doubt which I entertain, whether the cargo is not, in fact, the property of other persons, I mean French agents, for I suspect it, on the grounds mentioned above, to have been a French speculation throughout. In giving the owner of the ship any benefit from these doubts, I am, perhaps, practising a lenity which would require more apology than, upon strict principle, I might find easy to furnish; but I shall content myself with the restitution of the ship, withholding, as usual on the carriage of contraband, the allowance of freight and expenses (*b*).

1799 *March* 6.

THE SARAH CHRISTINA.

Sir W. Scott.

THE ODIN (No. 1).

[1 C. Rob. 248.]

*Capture—Neutral Ship—*De facto *British—Fraudulent Transfer—Condemnation.*

A British ship, ostensibly transferred to a Dane, captured while trading with the enemy, condemned with her cargo, involved in the same claim.

THIS was a case of a ship ostensibly transferred from a British subject to a Dane, and taken trading with the enemy.

1799 *March* 15.

SIR W. SCOTT.—This is a case of very considerable property, the ship and cargo, both of which are involved, being described to be of the value of 150,000*l.* Being of this value, it is of course a case of proportionable importance, and I feel the caution with which a judicial determination upon interests of such an extent ought to be framed and delivered. At the same time it is unnecessary to observe that the *quantum* of the property can have no influence upon the legal merits of the questions which I have to

(*a*) In the *America*, Sir W. Scott said: "It is not a new rule that if a ship is going with false papers the owner shall lose his freight. I do not say that if an owner makes out a clear case that he has been duped by the fraud of the master, the Court would in all cases press the rule to the utmost rigor against him." The Court then held that such a case had not been made out. [3 C. Rob. 36.]

(*b*) See the *Franklin*, *post*, p. 298.

1799 March 15. THE ODIN. Sir W. Scott.

examine. The same principles apply to a case of 150*l.* (all other circumstances being equal), which must be applied to this case of 150,000*l.*, and the same general duty lies upon the Court to proceed with all the tenderness which is due to property, however small, and with all the firmness which it is bound to exercise, be the property ever so large.

The claim given is for the ship and cargo, as the property of Mr. Jacob Krefting, described to be a Norwegian by birth, resident and carrying on his business at Fredericksnagore, a Danish establishment near Calcutta, in which he is second in council. It appears that the ship went with a cargo from the river Hooghley to Batavia; part of that cargo she disposed of there, and took another cargo destined to Copenhagen, and in the prosecution of her voyage was seized and taken by a British ship of war. And if this had been the whole of the case the consequence must have been an immediate restitution, because this Court has not taken upon itself to lay down that a Danish merchant at Fredericksnagore, a Danish settlement, may not send a cargo of his own in his own ship to Batavia, there dispose of that cargo and purchase another, and bring it to his own country in Europe. But a fact appears in the case, a fundamental fact, which gives rise to the whole of the present inquiry, namely, that this ship had been, a very short time before this voyage, the property of Messrs. Lambert & Ross, British subjects, residing at Calcutta. This fact leads to the question whether this ship had been actually and *bonâ fide* transferred from them to this Danish merchant? For if not, if she continued the property of these British merchants, going on their commercial errands to Batavia, then a port of the public enemies of his Majesty, she is going illegally, and illegally so as to subject her to confiscation, there being no maxim better or more firmly established in the maritime law of this country than this, that no subject of the King can trade directly with the public enemy but under a licence authorising him so to do, and that if he does presume to trade otherwise his property so employed is liable to confiscation. If this should turn out to be the case respecting the ship it will dispose of all British interests in her. The cargo, it is to be observed, is claimed for the same person and in the same claim. If the claim is deemed fraudulent, as it respects the property of the ship, it will, I think, be entitled to little regard as it respects the property of the cargo claimed for the same proprietor, and appearing evidently to be concerned in one and the same original adventure. I am not aware of the obligation that lies upon the Court, in the case of such a claim, to separate its sound from its diseased parts for the benefit of a claimant detected in the falsehood of a considerable portion of his claim. He has no right to insist that a discrimination shall be made in the property which, if any part be his own, he has fraudulently and with corrupt views mixed up with the property of others. But in this particular case it does not rest upon that general principle, because much of the evidence (at least arising from general circumstances) which applies to the property of the ship applies with equal force to that of the cargo.

It is not to be denied that the ship had been very recently the property of these British merchants, navigated by John Elmore; but here is a bill of sale regularly executed under their hands, by which she is transferred to Mr. Krefting; and the benefit of the general presumption has been claimed for this transfer, that every act must be presumed a *bonâ fide* and a real act, to which may be added the other general presumption that the acts of men must be taken *primâ facie* to be innocent; whereas if this transfer is fictitious, here is a criminal transaction of a direct trading with the enemy. Other more particular presumptions have been called in aid. It was said that it was highly improbable that British merchants should send their property of immense value to an enemy's port, where it would run the hazard of confiscation.

[The Court then examined the evidence at great length and condemned ship and cargo, on the ground that, on the evidence, the claimant was not the real owner of the ship.]

[1 C. Rob. 271.]

THE TWO FRIENDS.

Recapture—British Sailors on Foreign Ship—Right to claim in British Prize Court—Lien on Recaptured Goods landed.

An American ship with a crew partly British was captured by the French, between whom and the Americans there were *de facto* hostilities, and was recaptured by her crew. Proceedings were brought by the British seamen in England in respect of such recapture. Part of the salved cargo had been landed before the institution of the suit. *Held*, that the Court had jurisdiction in respect of the recapture of a ship belonging to a friendly power between whom and France there were *de facto* hostilities. *Held* also, that the salved goods when landed could be followed by the process of the Court.

1799 *March* 19. THIS was a case of salvage on recapture of an American ship by the crew, part of whom being British seamen, and praying to be rewarded, the cause now came on to be heard on protest against the jurisdiction of the Court over an American ship.

In support of the protest, the *King's Advocate* and *Sewell.*

Against the protest, *Lawrence* and *Swabey.*

SIR W. SCOTT.—This is a case of an American ship taken by the French on a voyage from Philadelphia to London, and afterwards rescued by her crew.

It is allowed to have been a rescue very much to the advantage of the owners, as a considerable reward has been already paid to the master by the underwriters. I shall not now, however, enter into a discussion of the facts for the purpose of settling the total of the reward, or the proportions to be assigned to the particular actors in the service, because a previous question has been started respecting the jurisdiction of the Court. It appears that there has been an arrest, by process, of the ship and of such goods as had not been delivered on shore; but that some goods had been landed and delivered whilst a negotiation was going on between the parties to settle the reward. An appearance has been given under protest as to the goods landed, but that cannot by any possibility legally avail, except as to those goods so landed on shore, so far as it is founded on the mere circumstance of locality.

For the rest an appearance has been given generally. But still I am willing to say that if there was a well founded objection to the jurisdiction of the Court in general, I should not think it right to hold the parties either to their general appearance or to the mere grounds of their partial protest.

It has been slightly questioned in the act of Court (which contains the exposition of facts given in by both parties), whether there was such a state of hostilities between America and France as to raise a title to salvage for American goods retaken from the French. But this point has not been pursued in argument; and, indeed, I should wonder if it had, after the determinations of this Court, which have, in various instances, decreed salvage in similar cases. It is not for me to say whether America is at war with France or not; but the conduct of France towards America has been such *de facto*, as to induce American owners to acknowledge the services by which they have recovered their ships and cargoes out of the hands of French cruisers by force of arms. In this very instance it seems to have been so understood, for the underwriters, representing the owners, have rewarded the master of this vessel for an act which would, on any other supposition than that of subsisting hostilities, have been reprehensible. For although it is meritorious to rescue by force of arms from an enemy, it is quite the reverse to rescue from a neutral, from whom the owner would have a right to claim costs and damages for an unjust seizure and detention. If, instead of this, a rescue by force is attempted, and the party takes the law into his own hands, it becomes a breach of the law of nations, which would endanger the ship and cargo if that attempt should be disappointed; if, therefore, the French seizors were to be considered as neutrals, the owners would have reason to complain that this rescue had exposed their property to unnecessary hazard instead of preserving it. These owners are therefore barred by their own act from objecting against the necessity and the legality of salvage, whatever may be the present situation of affairs between America and France.

This being disposed of, I come now to a second position, that every person assisting in rescue has a lien on the thing saved. He has, as it has been argued, an action *in personam* also; but his first and his proper remedy is *in rem*, and his having the one is no

1799 *March* 19. — THE TWO FRIENDS. — Sir W. Scott.

argument against his title to the other. Then where is this lien to be demanded? It should seem that that was an unnecessary question to be proposed, when the goods were admitted to be in England; but, strange as it may appear, it is argued that this claim is to be enforced in America, because the ship is an American ship, and the parties are American sailors. In the first place, I am satisfied that these persons are not to be considered as American sailors—they are British-born subjects returning to their own country, without any engagement or intention to go back to America, and without having any domicile there, and merely working their passage homeward on board this ship. They are, then, not at all in the condition of American subjects, neither are they so to be considered in this act, even if hired as mariners on board this American vessel; for this act was no part of their general duty as seamen: they were not bound by their general duty as mariners to attempt a rescue, nor would they have been guilty of a desertion of their duty in that capacity if they had declined it. It is a meritorious act to join in such attempts, and if there are persons who entertain any doubts whether it ought to be so regarded, I desire not to be considered as one of the persons who entertain any such doubts. But it is an act perfectly voluntary, in which each individual is a volunteer, and is not acting as a part of the crew of the ship in discharge of any official duty, either ordinary or extraordinary. The opposition, therefore, to the jurisdiction of the Court fails in its foundation of fact that these are American seamen. But it is asked, if they were American seamen, would this Court hold plea of their demands? It may be time enough to answer this question whenever the fact occurs. In the meantime I will say without scruple that I can see no inconvenience that would arise if a British Court of Justice was to hold plea in such a case, or conversely, if American Courts were to hold pleas of this nature respecting the merits of British seamen on such occasions; for salvage is a question of the *jus gentium*, and materially different from the question of a mariner's contract, which is a creature of the particular institutions of each country, to be applied, and construed, and explained by its own particular rules. There might be good reason, therefore, for this Court to decline to interfere in such cases, and to remit them to their own domestic forum; but this is a general claim upon the general ground of *quantum meruit*, to be governed by a sound discretion, acting on general principles; and I can see no reason why one country should be afraid to trust to the equity of the Courts of another on such a question, of such a nature, so to be determined.

It is said different countries may have different proportions of salvage, and, therefore, an inconvenience may arise from such interference. But I do not know that there exists any rule on this matter beyond that which subjects such matters to a sound discretion, distributing the reward according to the value of the services that have been performed. There is no rule prescribed in the English law, nor do I know of any in the codes of France or Spain, applying to the cases of foreign property rescued. In cases of *rescue* between English subjects this Court usually adopts the proportion of *recapture;* but it is not bound to do so, and in respect to foreigners there is no rule but that of the *quantum meruit* Indeed, I believe this is, perhaps, the first case in which a foreign rescue has been made by British assistance. As to the case which has been put, of a rescue by a crew, of which nineteen should be English and one a Spaniard, I cannot see that any great difficulty would ensue. The case of recapture is provided for by the regulations of Spain, but I do not recollect that the case of rescue is so; but supposing that it is, and that it gives the entire benefit of the rescued property to the rescuers, and that it was necessary, or at all proper, to decide such a mixed case with any attention to that rule, the whole effect, and, therefore, the whole inconvenience would be, that one-twentieth part of the property would be condemned to that Spaniard; for there is no pretence to say that the nineteen Englishmen would be entitled to any benefit from such a rule.

These considerations, therefore, found no solid objections against the exercise of the jurisdiction; but I go further and say that I think there is great reason for it, because it is the only way of enforcing the best security—that of the lien on the property itself. Between parties who were all Americans, if there was the slightest disinclination to submit to the jurisdiction of this Court, I should certainly not incline to interfere; for this Court is not hungry after jurisdiction, where the exercise of it is not felt to be beneficial

1799 *March* 19.

THE TWO FRIENDS.

Sir W. Scott.

to the parties between whom it is to operate. At the same time, I desire to be understood to deliver no decided opinion, whether American seamen rescuing an American ship and cargo brought into this country might not maintain an action *in rem* in this Court of the law of nations. But if there was British property on board, and American seamen were to proceed here against that, I should think it a criminal desertion of my duty if I did not support their claim.

In the present case no American seaman has appeared, nor is it proved that there was any British property on board. But as to these British seamen holding no connection with America, and having rescued foreign property, I have no doubt that they are entitled to have their services rewarded here; for it would be but a mere mockery, and a derision of their claims, to send them back to America to hunt out their redress against each individual owner of separate bales of goods. It were better to inform them that they were entitled to nothing than to remit them on such a wild pursuit. I should therefore think it a reproach to the Courts of this country if they were not open to lend their assistance in such a case.

I must do the owners themselves the justice to observe that they seem to have been so sensible of the impropriety of such a proceeding that they have referred the matter to the insurers here in this country; and it has been said that the insurers are the proper persons to distribute the reward. It might happen that property was not insured. What is to be done in such a case? I know of no necessity that exists for an arbitration on such a matter. If the parties agree and the arbitrators offer such terms, from equity and liberality, as induce them to abide by their arbitration, there can be no objection to that. But to say that the claimants are of right to abide by any arbitration, and that they are compelled to an arbitration when they have a legal right to a legal decision, is not a very reasonable expectation.

I think I might say without just offence that insurers, if arbitrations were necessary, are not the fittest persons to be resorted to as arbiters, for this simple reason: that they, being generally the persons who are to pay, are not exactly the persons whom a considerate man would select to determine the quantum of payment. On a question between those who are to pay and those who are to receive, either of those classes of men are but ill prepared to decide. It will not be understood to be any reflection on the known liberality of British insurers when I observe that one great end of the institution of civil society is to prevent men from being judges in cases wherein they are concerned, and to remit the decision of adverse interests to those who can have no interest whatever in the determination of any such cases. I am of opinion, therefore, that the jurisdiction of the Court is well founded, and that the parties had a right to resort to it; that the circumstance of the ship and cargo being American property will not exclude the jurisdiction where there are any British subjects concerned, and where the goods are within its jurisdiction.

But another question arises, whether the jurisdiction is ousted by the landing of the goods, so far as relates to that quantity landed. I confess I see no great advantage likely to accrue to the American owners from this objection, because if they take the case from this Court on such a ground they must go to another; and if their objection is to a British judicature, as I collect from the argument, much is not gained from going to a British Court of common law; it would be but to change postures on an uneasy bed. But let us see how far this objection can avail. It is said that the goods being on shore are out of the jurisdiction of the Court of Admiralty. With regard to the Instance Court, that may be true. In cases of wreck and derelict I have known many instances of great hardship, and I will add, of crying injustice; where salvors have been amused with negotiations till the goods were landed, and then the authority of this Court has been defied, and the just demands of the claimants laughed to scorn. How far such a proceeding would be sustained by a Court of common law is more than it would be proper for me to conjecture; further than that it seems matter of reasonable doubt how far a change of locality so effected would be permitted to defeat the claims of substantial justice.

There is no reason to surmise such an intention in these parties, although it does not appear that the goods were landed after notice that proceedings had been instituted here.

But whatever may be the law as to wreck and derelict, I conceive it does not apply to these goods, which I consider to be goods

1799 March 19.

THE TWO FRIENDS.

Sir W. Scott.

of prize; for I know no other definition of prize-goods than that they are goods taken on the high seas, *jure belli*, out of the hands of the enemy; and there is no axiom more clear than that such goods, when they come on shore, may be followed by the process of this Court. In such cases the common law courts hold they have no jurisdiction, and are even anxious to disclaim it. The case of the *Ooster Eems*, which has been alluded to, was very different from this. In that case there was a material distinction as to the origin of the subject-matter, for it was there expressly said by the great person who then presided, "that those goods had never been taken on the high seas, they had only passed in the way of civil bailment on delivery into civil hands, and were afterwards arrested on shore as prize. It was held, that there was no act of capture on the high seas, and therefore that they were not to be considered as prize (*a*).

But the present case is radically bottomed in prize; and if so, all the consequences of prize will follow. If the goods are removed before proceedings are commenced they are still liable to be called in by a monition. A different way has been taken in this case by a personal monition, as more convenient to the parties proceeded against. On the whole, I am of opinion that the English seamen are entitled to redress here; that these goods being matter of prize, even that part which had been landed, are subject to the jurisdiction of this Court, and I shall therefore overrule the protest. That is all that I can do at present.

(*a*) The *Ooster Eems* was the case of a ship stranded on the Goodwin Sands, on a voyage from the Texel to the East Indies. The cargo was sent on shore, and amongst the rest some boxes of silver were deposited with the Prussian Consul. The warden of the Cinque Ports claimed the cargo as the property of enemies, being become a perquisite of Admiralty within that jurisdiction. The master obtained a monition from the High Court of Admiralty to arrest the goods and remove the cause from the Cinque Ports to the Prize Court, where he gave a claim for the cargo as Prussian property. The cargo was condemned, but on appeal that sentence was reversed; and the Lords pronounced, "that the High Court of Admiralty had not a jurisdiction over the goods seized and proceeded against; and they reversed the decree appealed from for want of jurisdiction:" Lords, July 14th, 1784.

Present, Lord Thurlow, Lord High Chancellor of Great Britain; Earl Gower, Lord President of the Council; Marquis of Caermarthen; Sir Lloyd Kenyon, Master of the Rolls.

On the 16th of May the cause came on to be heard as to the merits of the parties. 1799 *March* 19.

THE TWO FRIENDS.

NOTE.—10th May, 1799.—In the *Good Intent*, Humphies, an English vessel recaptured from the French, by an American armed ship, the American salvors appeared praying salvage. *Court:* This is an amicable case; there is no opposition to the jurisdiction of this Court. There seems to have been no extraordinary merit, as the American ship was a ship of force, and no resistance was made. I shall therefore direct the usual salvage of a sixth.

THE CORIER MARITIMO.

[1 C. Rob. 289.]

Practice—Capture—Delay in Proceedings—Demurrage.

A vessel was captured on November 13th, and a claim for its restoration was made by the owners on December 23rd, but no appearance was entered by the captors till February 26th following. *Held,* that the claimants were entitled to recover demurrage from the captors, to be assessed by the registrar and merchants.

THIS was a case of a ship captured on the 13th of November, 1796, and carried into Shields. 1799 *April* 9.

The claim was given on the 23rd of December, and no proceedings having been instituted by the captors, the claimants took out a monition against the captors to proceed to adjudication, on suggestion that there was an intention of removing the vessel from Shields to Scotland.

No appearance was given for the captors till the 26th of February, when they consented to restitution. An application was now made that the claimants might be allowed demurrage.

Court: Demurrage is clearly due. The captor has not only neglected his duty, but there appears to have been an intention of violating it still further by carrying the vessel into another port out of the jurisdiction of this Court. On the part of the claimants there has been no precipitation, nor any attempt to throw odium on the captor. They waited nearly two months; and I must not suffer them to be prejudiced by that forbearance.

No appearance is now given for the captors. There has been some misconduct for which they are responsible, and perhaps it

1799 April 9. THE CORIER MARITIMO.

ought to call for more than a mere reparation in damage. I shall grant demurrage, referring it to the registrar and merchants to fix the proportion.

Demurrage assessed on 180 tons for three months and twenty days—330*l.*

[1 C. Rob. 288.]

THE COPENHAGEN.

Capture—Interruption of Voyage—Transhipment of Cargo—Right of Shipowner to Freight.

A neutral ship, driven in by stress of weather, and in need of repairs, was seized with her cargo in a British port. The cargo was restored and transhipped. Afterwards the ship was restored. *Held,* in the circumstances, that *pro ratâ* freight was due to the shipowner from the owners of cargo. Capture being considered as delivery, the captors of enemy's goods in a neutral ship are generally liable for the freight, provided that the voyage has been interrupted solely by the capture.

1799 April 9, 12.

PETITION to the Court for the settlement of freight for transhipment of prize goods, between the ship, cargo, and transhippers.

SIR W. SCOTT.—This is a ship not captured at sea, but seized in a British port, into which she had been driven by stress of weather, as it has been asserted "merely on account of the cargo, the ship being duly documented." Duly documented is altogether a relative term, for a vessel may be duly documented in one case by papers which would not be sufficient documents in another. Thus in ordinary cases a Danish ship would be duly documented by a Danish pass and other papers; but if she appeared to have been bought in the enemy's country during the war a bill of sale would be necessary, and that duly verified and supported. In the present case the Court ordered further proof as well of the *ship* as of the *cargo.* The latter was restored on the 1st of August, 1797, but the original hearing of the ship not coming on till the 20th of August, 1797, the ship was not restored on further proof till the 28th of May, 1798. The ship having come in originally in distress and wanting repairs, it became necessary to take out the cargo, and there being no warehouses at hand it was put on board three other vessels, which very reluctantly engaged in the service, and were finally induced to do so by a written contract with the master; and as the cargo consisted of commodities brought from Smyrna these ships were obliged to submit to perform quarantine, and the commodities being damaged these vessels sustained some actual injury by having them on board. As the *Copenhagen* was still further detained after the cargo was restored, and was therefore unable to prosecute her original voyage, part of the cargo was sent to London and part was put on board other ships to go on to the original destination.

On these facts four questions have arisen: 1st, Whether demurrage is due for the detention of the ship? and this question lies between the owners of the ship and the owners of the cargo, for there is no application for demurrage against the seizors nor any ground for it; 2ndly, Whether freight is due for the whole voyage or only *pro ratâ?* for that some freight is due is not denied, and this also is a question between the owners of the ship and the owners of the cargo; 3rdly, What sum of money is due to the owners of the three ships? 4thly, the last question arises in some measure out of the preceding one: Whether the owners of the *Copenhagen* or the owners of the cargo are responsible for this sum of money, and also for the expenses of the repairs of the ship and other charges?

The proprietors of the ship assert that the whole is a matter of simple or particular average on the cargo only, and the owners of the cargo contend that the expenses of transhipment are a matter of general average, falling on all parties, and affecting the ship in common with the cargo, but that the ship alone must bear the expenses of her own repairs.

In the first place the ship was not brought in by seizure; there was no bringing into port by capture. I think it is perfectly clear that she wanted repair; and that she stayed in Milford Haven for that purpose, as well as for the purpose of proving her neutral character. It appears also that the proof of the character of the ship took up more time than that of the cargo. Under these circumstances there cannot be the slightest pretence for a claim of demurrage against the cargo on any ground whatever.

Secondly. With respect to the freight, some is admitted to be due; as the ship has brought her cargo from Smyrna through much the most considerable part of the voyage. But it is said that, in matters of prize, the whole freight is always given; and for this

1799 April 9, 12.

THE COPENHAGEN.

Sir W. Scott.

reason, because capture is considered as delivery, and a captured vessel earns her whole freight. I have already said that this is not merely or originally a matter of prize; the ship was not brought in as such; she came in first from distress, and was afterwards put upon the proof of her character; it is a case of a mixed nature; and the maxim that capture is delivery is not to be taken in the general way in which it has been laid down. It is by no means true, except where the captor succeeds fully to the rights of the enemy, and represents him as to those rights. If a neutral vessel, having enemy's goods, is taken, the captor pays the whole freight because he represents the enemy by possessing himself of the enemy's goods *jure belli;* and although the whole freight has not been earned by the completion of the voyage, yet, as the captor by his act of seizure has prevented its completion, his seizure shall operate to the same effect as an actual delivery of the goods to the consignee, and shall subject him to the payment of the full freight. But if ship and cargo being both neutral are restored, the consequence is only that the ship must proceed on and complete her voyage before she can demand her freight. If the cargo is restored whilst the ship continues under detention, still less reason is there to contend that she has earned her whole freight. Such is the present case in which the ship has failed in her contract, and this not owing to the cargo in any manner, but to her own state of distress originally, and afterwards to her dubious character. Under these circumstances it is impossible to say that she has earned more than a freight *pro ratâ itineris*, which therefore the registrar and merchants must ascertain in the usual manner.

[The *Court* then dealt with the *quantum* of the demand of the owners of the three vessels, and with the rights of the owners of ship and cargo *inter se* for repairs to the ship, and the cost of the transhipment of the cargo.]

THE EMANUEL.

[1 C. Rob. 296.]

Capture—Enemy Goods—Neutral Ship—Right to Freight.

The general principle is that when enemy goods are captured on a neutral ship, the owner of such ship has the same right against the captors for freight as against the enemy. But *held* not to apply where a neutral ship was engaged in the coasting trade of an enemy.

1799 *April* 9.

THIS was a case respecting the allowance of freight and expenses to a neutral ship taken carrying on the coasting trade of the enemy.

SIR W. SCOTT.—This is the case of a ship sailing under Danish colours, and taken with a cargo of salt on a voyage from Cadiz to Castropel, in Galicia. The ship has been restored, reserving the question of freight and expenses. The cargo has been condemned as the property of the King of Spain, and the question now is, under these circumstances, whether freight and expenses shall be allowed in this case?

I shall first consider this case upon principle; and, secondly, upon the foundation of authorities.

First, where a capture is made of a cargo the property of an enemy carried in a neutral ship, the neutral shipowner obtains against the captor those rights which he had against the enemy. At the same time this principle is not so universal as not to be liable to some exceptions, as, for instance, in the known case of contraband goods. If an enemy puts on board a neutral vessel a cargo belonging to himself, which is a contraband cargo, and that cargo is taken, it is condemnable to the captor; but the Court will not consider itself as bound to enforce the payment of freight against the captors, although at the same time the neutral shipowner might have just reason to demand it from the enemy, with respect to whom his contract has been performed, as far as he had not been disabled from fulfilling it by the very circumstance of the other contracting party having put a cargo of that species on board, and consequently exposed the vessel to hostile seizure. And the Court may, in like manner, not conceive itself under any obligation to say, in other instances, that the captors are liable to the charge

1799 April 9. THE EMANUEL. Sir W. Scott.

of freight, although it may be a good and valid demand against the owner, which the parties must settle elsewhere.

Now the ground upon which it is contended that the freight is not due to the proprietors of this vessel is that she is a Danish ship employed in the transmission of Spanish goods from one Spanish port to another, and so carrying on the coasting-trade of that country. In our own country it has long been the system that the coasting-trade shall only be carried on by our own navigation. I observe, that in all the rage of novel experiment that has dictated the commercial regulations of France in its new condition, this policy is held sacred. It stands enacted by a decree, 21st September, 1793, that no goods, the growth or manufacture of France, shall be carried from one French port to another in foreign ships under pain of confiscation. The same policy has directed the commercial system of other European countries. In the ordinary state of affairs no indulgence is generally permitted to the ships of most other countries to carry on the coasting-trade. I think, therefore, the *onus probandi* does at least lie on that side, and always makes it necessary to be shown by the claimants that such a trade was not a mere indulgence and a temporary relaxation of the coasting system of the state in question, but that it was a common and ordinary trade, open to the ships of any country whatever.

Applying that principle to the present case (if I am right in the presumption), I am to infer that this vessel is carrying on a commerce which, according to the general trading system of Spain, she could not pursue, in consequence of the pressure to which the commerce of Spain has been reduced by the arms of this country. If so, upon what ground is it that she claims freight against the captor on a voyage undertaken for the peculiar accommodation and relief of the enemy, under the distress to which the successful hostilities of the captor's country had reduced him? Is there nothing like a departure from the strict duties imposed by a neutral character and situation, in stepping in to the aid of the depressed party and taking up a commerce which so peculiarly belonged to himself, and to extinguish which was one of the principal objects and proposed fruits of victory? Is not this, by a new act and by an interposition neither known nor permitted by that enemy in the ordinary state of his affairs, to give a direct opposition to the efforts of the conqueror, and to take off that pressure which it is the very purpose of war to inflict, in order to compel the conquered to a due sense and observance of justice? Is this so clearly within the limits of impartial and indifferent conduct, that if a neutral ship is taken in an office of this kind she is entitled to claim against the captor, whom she is thus counteracting and almost defrauding, the very same rights which she possessed against the claimant, to whom she is giving this extraordinary and irregular assistance?

It is said in argument that this principle, which applied likewise to the colonial trade between the mother countries and their plantations in the West Indies (that being equally a trade guarded by a monopoly in time of peace, and having been likewise occasionally relaxed under the pressure of a war), has been in a good measure abandoned in the decisions of the Lords Commissioners of Appeal. I am not acquainted with any decision to that effect, and I doubt very much whether any decision yet made has given even an indirect countenance to this supposed dereliction of a principle apparently rational in itself, and conformable to all general reasoning on the subject. It is certainly true that in the last war many decisions took place which then pronounced that such a trade between France and her colonies was not considered as an unneutral commerce; but under what circumstances? It was understood that France, in opening her colonies during the war, declared that this was not done with a temporary view relative to the war, but on a general and permanent purpose of altering her colonial system, and of admitting foreign vessels universally and at all times to a participation of that commerce. Taking that to be the fact (however suspicious its commencement might be during the actual existence of a war), there was no ground to say that neutrals were not carrying on a commerce as ordinary as any other in which they could be engaged; and therefore, in the case of the *Verwagtig* (*a*) and in many other succeeding cases, the Lords decreed payment of freight to the neutral shipowner. It is fit to be remembered on this occasion that the conduct of France evinced

(*a*) This was a Danish vessel bound from Marseilles to Martinique, and back to Europe, and taken on the outward voyage; the Vice-Admiralty Court of Antigua had given half freight; on appeal, the Lords gave the whole.

1799 *April* 9. — THE EMANUEL. — Sir W. Scott.

how little dependence can be placed upon explanations of measures adopted during the pressure of a war, for hardly was the ratification of the peace signed, when she returned to her ancient system of colonial monopoly. In the present war I am not aware that any judgments of the Supreme Court yet pronounced have receded from the principle, except in cases, and under circumstances in which a respect to public stipulations and treaties required that the application should be limited; the general principle I take to be entire and untouched, as far as it relates to that trade of the colonies.

As to the coasting trade (supposing it to be a trade not usually opened to foreign vessels), can there be described a more effective accommodation that can be given to an enemy during a war than to undertake it for him during his own disability? Is it nothing that the commodities of an extensive empire are conveyed from the parts where they grow and are manufactured to other parts where they are wanted for use? It is said that this is not importing any thing new into the country, and it certainly is not; but has it not all the effects of such an importation? Supposing that the French navy had a decided ascendant, and had cut off all British communication between the northern and southern parts of this island, and that neutrals interposed to bring the coals of the north for the supply of the manufactures and for the necessities of domestic life in this metropolis; is it possible to describe a more direct and a more effectual opposition to the success of French hostility short of an actual military assistance in the war? What is the present case? It is still more; it is the direct conveyance of a commodity belonging immediately to the King of Spain for the purpose of public revenue; the vessel is employed not merely in the private traffic of individuals, but in the revenue service of the state. The King of Spain, disabled from employing Spanish vessels in the collection of his revenues, enlists foreign vessels under this necessity. Salt is a royal monopoly in Spain, as it formerly was in France, and it is distributed on the Government account to the various provinces. This foreign ship is employed in the distribution, and by the employment becomes an actual revenue cutter of the King of Spain. It should seem to be no very harsh treatment of such a vessel if, on the capture, she is restored, and is only left to pursue her demand of freight against her original employers.

With respect to authorities, it has been much urged that in three cases this war the Court of Admiralty has decreed payment of freight to vessels so employed, and I believe that such cases *did* pass under an intimation of the opinion of the very learned person who preceded me, in which the parties acquiesced without resorting to the authority of a higher tribunal. But a case before the Lords seems to convey a different opinion upon this subject of the coasting trade of the enemy—the case of the *Mercurius* (*a*), in which freight was refused. The cargo was lawful under the Danish treaty, to the benefit of which the party was entitled as *bonâ fide* domiciled in Denmark, although a native subject of Great Britain. I am not able to say precisely how far the circumstance of his birth was an ingredient in the determination of the case, but the general rule is that a person living *bonâ fide* in a neutral country is fully entitled to carry on a trade to the same extent as the native merchants of the country in which he resides, provided it is not inconsistent with his native allegiance. It is conformable to more ancient judgments upon the subject, which have pronounced that "Neutrals are not to trade on freight between the ports of the enemy" (*b*). To this principle I shall adhere in the present case, leaving the party to such remedy for his demand of freight as he may think fit to pursue, either against the captor by appeal in this country, or against his freighter in the country where he was employed.

(*a*) This was a Danish vessel carrying a cargo of wheat from Dunkirk to Bordeaux, and restored by consent, reserving the question of freight; the sentence of the Court of Admiralty refusing freight was affirmed.

(*b*) See the *Immanuel*, *post*, p. 218.

[1 C. Rob. 329.]

THE JONGE TOBIAS.

Contraband—Tar—Interest of Cargo Owner in Ship—Liability to Condemnation.

Tar is liable to condemnation as contraband. If the owner of a contraband cargo has an interest in the ship, such interest is liable to condemnation. When the shipowner has no interest, freight only is liable to forfeiture.

1799 *May* 10. THIS was a case of a ship taken on a voyage from Bremen to Rochelle laden with tar. The ship was claimed for Mr. Schrœder and others; the tar remained unclaimed. The King's Advocate and Croke contended that the cargo was undoubtedly subject to condemnation as contraband; that the ship's papers all described the cargo to be the property of Mr. Schrœder, the principal claimant of the ship; that the master stated "Mr. Schrœder to be the lader and the owner;" and that there was a bill of lading and certificate of property on oath to the same effect; that on these grounds there was sufficient proof of the property of Mr. Schrœder, although he had withheld his claim, knowing it would affect the ship; that notwithstanding this artifice the same consequence would follow, as there was sufficient proof of property; and that the whole was liable to condemnation—his own share as being connected with his other property employed in contraband trade, and the shares of his co-partners as affected by the act of their partner and agent; the passport particularly purporting to have been obtained by Mr. Schrœder on oath that the cargo contained no contraband goods.

SIR W. SCOTT.—There can be no doubt in this case but that the tar is liable to condemnation as unclaimed, and also as contraband, being taken going from a port of the country of which it could not be the produce. Formerly, according to the old practice, this cargo would have carried with it the condemnation of the ship, but in later times this practice has been relaxed, and an alteration has been introduced which allows the ship to go free, but subject to the forfeiture of freight on the part of the neutral owner. This applies only to cases where the owners of the ship and cargo are different persons. Where the owner of the cargo has any interest in the ship the whole of his property will be involved in the same sentence of condemnation; for where a man is concerned in an illegal transaction the whole of his property embarked in that transaction is liable to confiscation. The proofs are very strong that Mr. Schrœder is the owner of the cargo, although it is not claimed: there is the sworn certificate of the man himself; and all that is said on the other side is that there is no claim. There may be cases in which the conduct of a man may prevail against the evidence of the ship's papers; but there is here only a continuance of the same fraudulent discretion which has guided his conduct throughout, as he must be aware that an acknowledgment of the fact by claiming would involve the ship. His share must be subject to condemnation.

1799 *May* 10.

THE JONGE TOBIAS.

Sir W. Scott.

The only question is, whether there is proof that there are more owners of the ship than one. I think it does appear that there are other persons concerned in the ship, although they do not appear to be affected with a knowledge of the cargo; the presumption is against them certainly, but that is not sufficient to induce me to go the length of condemning their shares. What I shall do will be to condemn Mr. Schrœder's share; and require an attestation of the other part-owners that they had no knowledge of the contraband goods, for being only part-owners of the ship, and not general partners with Mr. Schrœder, I shall not hold them to be necessarily affected by his criminal acts.

THE BETSEY (No. 2).

[1 C. Rob. 332.]

Blockade—Neutral—Inquiry.

A shipowner who, when his ship sails, is not in a position to know if a blockade previously notified still exists, may send her to the proximity of the blockaded port in order to inquire if the blockade still exists.

THIS was a case of an American ship taken by the French on a voyage from America to Amsterdam, retaken by the English, and proceeded against for an intentional breach of the blockade of Amsterdam.

1799 *May* 24.

For the captors, the *King's Advocate.*

For the claimants, *Laurence.*

1799 *May* 24.

THE BETSEY (No. 2).

Sir W. Scott.

SIR W. SCOTT.—I hardly think that there is sufficient evidence in this case to affect the parties with an intention of fraud. The ship sailed in January last, when the owners were certainly informed of the blockade, but the distance of their country is a material circumstance in their favour. I certainly cannot admit that Americans are to be exempted from the common effect of a notification of a blockade existing in Europe. But I think it is not unfair to say that, lying at such a distance, where they cannot have constant information of the state of the blockade, whether it continues or is relaxed, it is not unnatural that they should send their ships conjecturally, upon the expectation of finding the blockade broken up after it had existed for a considerable time. A very great disadvantage indeed would be imposed upon them if they were bound rigidly by the rule which justly obtains in Europe, that the blockade must be conceived to exist till the revocation of it is actually notified. For if this rule is rigidly applied, the effect of the blockade could last two months longer upon them than on the trading nations of Europe, by whom intelligence is received almost as soon as it is issued. That the Americans should therefore send their ships upon a fair conjecture that the blockade had, after a long continuance, determined, and for the purpose of making fair inquiry whether it had so determined or not, is, I think, not exceptionable; though I certainly agree that this inquiry should be made not in the very mouth of the river or estuary from the blockading vessels, but in the ports that lie in the way, and which can furnish information without furnishing opportunities of fraud. In the present case the blockade had been understood in America to have existed the whole winter, and therefore it was not unreasonable to suppose that by that time it had ceased.

The papers all bear an avowed destination to Amsterdam, which I think a favourable circumstance, and, in some degree, destroys the suspicion of fraud. If there had been a fraudulent intention Amsterdam would not have stood so prominent to observation. The directions certainly contain some expressions which are rather awkward: "If you should not be so fortunate as to get into Amsterdam." This is rather an alarming expression, but perhaps it may be a criterion of a fair case: a designing man would have been more cautious in the choice of his expression. The master was directed to inquire of the blockading frigates—I have already said that he ought to have been directed to inquire elsewhere—in the ports of the Channel. But, on the whole, as the property is not disputed, and as the papers all speak openly, I do not think there is anything to affect the owners with a fraudulent intention, and therefore I shall restore (*a*).

1799 *May* 24.

THE BETSEY (No. 2).

Sir W. Scott.

THE VROW MARGARETHA.

[1 C. Rob. 336.]

Capture—Cargo—Transfer in transitu—*War not Imminent.*

The rule of the Prize Court that property in goods is considered to be in the shipper until delivery, and that a transfer *in transitu* is invalid, does not apply unless at the time of such transfer war is existing or is imminent.

1799 *June* 6.

THIS was a case of a cargo of brandies, shipped by Spanish merchants in Spain in May, 1794, before Spanish hostilities, and transferred to Mr. Berkeymyer at Hamburg, during their voyage to Holland.

For the captors, the *King's Advocate* and *Sewel* contended that the property of these goods was to be considered under the original shipment as belonging either to the shippers in Spain or to the consignees in Holland; that in either case, in consequence of what had taken place between the two countries subsequent to hostilities, they would be subject to condemnation; that it had been the invariable practice of the Prize Court to look only to the time of shipment, and that there was no instance of a claim being sustained for goods purchased of the enemy *in transitu*.

For the claimants, the *Advocate of the Admiralty* and *Laurence* contended that the rule relied on might be true in shipments made

(*a*) In a later case, the *Posten*, 8th August, 1799, a Danish ship from Drontheim to Amsterdam, taken off the Texel, and proceeded against for a breach of the blockade of Amsterdam. The same excuse was made that they expected to receive information on the spot; and the *Betsey* was cited. The Court said, "Ships must call somewhere to obtain information, for the Court will not allow the information to be obtained at the mouth of the blockaded port."

1799 *June* 6. THE VROW MARGARETHA.

in an enemy's country in time of war, but that it could not apply to a case like this, in which shipment, being previous to hostilities (and before they could be in any way foreseen), furnished a just exception to the rule; and was also a sufficient answer to any suspicion of a fraudulent or collusive transfer.

SIR W. SCOTT.—This is a claim of Mr. Berkeymyer, of Hamburg, for some parcels of wine which were seized on board three Dutch vessels detained by order of government in 1795. The ships have been since condemned; the cargoes were described in the ship's papers, as far as the property was expressed, as belonging to Spanish merchants. It is material, in this case, to consider the relative situation of the countries from which and to which these cargoes were going. Spain and Holland were then in alliance with this country, and at war with France; it might, therefore, be an inducement with a Spanish merchant to conceal the property of his goods, although it does not appear to have existed in any great degree, as the goods were coming under an English convoy, and as they were shipped "as Spanish wines," and destined, avowedly, to Holland; there was, therefore, nothing in this part of the case to mislead our cruisers. Mr. Berkeymyer is allowed to be an inhabitant of Hamburg, although he had made a journey, a short time previous to the shipment of these cargoes, to Spain (where he had resided some years before), to settle his affairs, and bring off the property which he had left behind him. He had quitted Spain, however, previous to the breaking out of Spanish hostilities, and had resumed his original character of a merchant of Hamburg. The account which he gives of his transactions in Spain, as far as they regard this case, is that he entered into a contract with two Spanish houses for some wines which were at the time actually shipped and *in itinere* towards Holland. The first objection that has been taken is that such a transfer is invalid, and cannot be set up in a Prize Court, where the property is always considered to remain in the same character in which it was shipped till the delivery. If that could be maintained, there would be an end of the question, because it has been admitted that these wines were shipped as Spanish property, and that Spanish property is now become liable to condemnation. But I apprehend it is a position which cannot be maintained in that extent. In the ordinary course of things in time of peace—for it is not denied that such a contract may be made, and effectually made (according to the usage of merchants)—such a transfer *in transitu* might certainly be made. It has even been contended that a mere delivering of the bill of lading is a transfer of the property. But it might be more correctly expressed, perhaps, if said that it transfers only the right of delivery; but that a transfer of the bill of lading, with a contract of sale accompanying it, may transfer the property in the ordinary course of things, so as effectually to bind the parties, and all others, cannot well be doubted. When war intervenes, another rule is set up by Courts of Admiralty which interferes with the ordinary practice. In a state of war, existing or *imminent*, it is held that the property shall be deemed to continue as it was at the time of shipment till the actual delivery; this arises out of the state of war which gives a belligerent a right to stop the goods of his enemy. If such a rule did not exist, all goods shipped in the enemy's country would be protected by transfers which it would be impossible to detect. It is on that principle held, I believe, as a general rule, that property cannot be converted *in transitu*, and in that sense I recognize it as the rule of this Court. But this arises, as I have said, out of a state of war, which creates new rights in other parties, and cannot be applied to transactions originating, like this, in a time of peace. The transfer, therefore, must be considered as not invalid in point of law at the time of the contract, and being made before the war it must be judged according to the ordinary rules of commerce.

It has been further objected to the validity of this contract that a part of the wines did actually reach Holland, where they were sold, and the money was detained by the consignees in payment of the advances which they had made. It is said that this annuls the contract; to the extent of that part it may do so, and the deficiency must be made up to the purchaser by other means; but it appears that it has been actually supplied by bills of exchange and an assignment of other wines sent to Petersburg. It is not for me to set aside the whole contract on that partial ground, or to construe the defect in the execution of the contract so rigorously as to extend it to those wines which never went to Holland, and which

1799 June 6. — THE VROW MARGARETHA. — Sir W. Scott.

never became *de facto* subject to be detained by the consignees. They are free for the contract to act upon; and if the parties are desirous of adhering to their contract in its whole extent it does not become other persons to obstruct them.

It comes then to a question of fact, whether it was a *bonâ fide* transfer or not. I think the time is a strong circumstance to prove the fairness of the transaction. Had it happened three months later there might have been reason to alarm the prudence of Spanish merchants and induce them to resort to the expedient of covering their property. But at the time of the contract there seems to have been no reason for apprehension, and therefore there is nothing to raise any suspicion on that point.

The instruments of sale have been produced, and no observation has been made upon them. The correspondence has been exhibited, and there is certainly some confusion in the dates. Explanations have been given which are probable enough; still they are but conjectural. If the counsel for the captors require it I will order the original documents in proof of these explanations to be produced, although I must say, at the same time, that the impression upon my mind is that it is a fair transaction.

The originals decreed to be produced.

Jan. 15th, 1800. The captors being satisfied with the further proof produced, Mr. Berkeymyer's claims were restored without opposition.

[1 C. Rob. 340.]

THE MARIA (No. 1).

Search—Neutral Ship—Right of Belligerent—Contraband—Tar, Pitch, Hemp.

A belligerent cruiser has the right to search neutral vessels even if convoyed by a ship of war of a neutral State, and a deliberate and continued refusal of a neutral ship to permit a search by a duly commissioned cruiser causes such neutral ship to be liable to condemnation.

Tar, pitch and hemp destined for a hostile port are contraband, unless they are the produce of the shipper's own country, but in such case they are subject to pre-emption.

1799 June 11; affirmed July 2, 1802.

THIS was the leading case of a fleet of Swedish merchantmen, carrying pitch, tar, hemp, deals, and iron, to several ports of France, Portugal, and the Mediterranean, and taken, January, 1798, sailing under convoy of a ship of war; and proceeded against for resistance of visitation and search by British cruisers. 1799 *June* 11.

THE MARIA.

In December, 1798, this case coming on to be argued on the original evidence, the Court directed further information by both parties.

On a subsequent day this information being produced, it was again argued at much length.

For the captors, the *King's Advocate* and *Arnold*.

For the claimants, *Laurence* and *Swabey*.

SIR W. SCOTT.—This ship was taken in the British Channel in company with several other Swedish vessels sailing under convoy of a Swedish frigate, having cargoes of naval stores and other produce of Sweden on board, by a British squadron under the command of Commodore Lawford.

The facts attending the capture did not sufficiently appear to the Court upon the original evidence; it therefore directed further information to be supplied, and by both parties.

The additional information now brought in consists of several attestations made on the part of the captors, and of a copy of the instructions under which the Swedish frigate sailed, transmitted to the King's Proctor from the office of the British Secretary of State for the Foreign Department. On the part of the Swedes some attestations and certificates have been introduced, but all of them applying to collateral matter, none relating immediately to the facts of the capture. On this evidence the Court has to determine this most important question; for its importance is very sensibly felt by the Court.

In forming that judgment, I trust that it has not escaped my anxious recollection for one moment what it is that the duty of my station calls for from me—namely, to consider myself as stationed here, not to deliver occasional and shifting opinions to serve present purposes of particular national interest, but to administer with indifference that justice which the law of nations holds out without distinction to independent States, some happening to be neutral and some to be belligerent. The seat of judicial authority is,

1799 *June* 11. THE MARIA. Sir W. Scott.

indeed, locally here, in the belligerent country, according to the known law and practice of nations, but the law itself has no locality. It is the duty of the person who sits here to determine this question exactly as he would determine the same question if sitting at Stockholm: to assert no pretensions on the part of Great Britain which he would not allow to Sweden in the same circumstances, and to impose no duties on Sweden, as a neutral country, which he would not admit to belong to Great Britain in the same character. If, therefore, I mistake the law in this matter, I mistake that which I consider, and which I mean should be considered, as the universal law upon the question—a question regarding one of the most important rights of belligerent nations relatively to neutrals.

The only special consideration which I shall notice in favour of Great Britain (and which I am entirely desirous of allowing to Sweden in the same or similar circumstances) is, that the nature of the present war does give this country the rights of war, relatively to neutral States, in as large a measure as they have been regularly and legally exercised at any period of modern and civilized times. Whether I estimate the nature of the war justly, I leave to the judgment of Europe, when I declare that I consider this as a war in which neutral States themselves have an interest much more direct and substantial than they have in the ordinary, limited, and private quarrels (if I may so call them) of Great Britain and its great public enemy. That I have a right to advert to such considerations, provided it be done with sobriety and truth, cannot, I think, reasonably be doubted—and if authority is required, I have authority—and not the less weighty in this question for being Swedish authority—I mean the opinion of that distinguished person, one of the most distinguished which that country (fertile as it has been of eminent men) has ever produced, I mean Baron Puffendorff. The passage to which I allude is to be found in a note of Barbeyrac's, on his larger work, L. viii. c. 6, s. 8. Puffendorff had been consulted in the beginning of the present century, when England and other States were engaged in the confederacy against Louis XIV., by a lawyer upon the Continent, Groningius, who was desirous of supporting the claims of neutral commerce in a treatise which he was then projecting. Puffendorff concludes his answer to him in these words:—

"I am not surprised that the northern Powers should consult

the general interests of all Europe without regard to the complaints of some greedy merchants, who care not how things go, provided they can but satisfy their thirst of gain. Those princes wisely judge that it would not become them to take precipitate measures whilst other nations are combining their whole force to reduce within bounds an insolent and exorbitant Power which threatens Europe with slavery and the Protestant religion with destruction. This being the interest of the northern Crowns themselves, it is neither just nor necessary that, for the present advantage, they should interrupt so salutary a design, especially as they are at no expense in the affair, and run no hazard." In the opinion, then, of this wise and virtuous Swede, the nature and purpose of a war was not entirely to be omitted in the consideration of the warrantable exercise of its rights relatively to neutral States. His words are memorable: I do not over-rate their importance when I pronounce them to be well entitled to the attention of his country.

It might likewise be improper for me to pass entirely without notice, as another preliminary observation (though without meaning to lay any particular stress upon it), that the transaction in question took place in the British Channel, close upon the British coast, a station over which the Crown of England has from pretty remote antiquity always asserted something of that special jurisdiction which the sovereigns of other countries have claimed and exercised over certain parts of the seas adjoining to their coasts.

In considering the case, I think it will be advisable for me, first, to state the facts as they appear in the evidence; secondly, to lay down the principles of law which apply generally to such a state of facts; thirdly, to examine whether any special circumstances attended the transaction in any part of it which ought in any manner or degree to affect the application of these principles.

[Sir W. Scott having referred to the facts at length, then summarized them.]

That a large number of vessels, connected all together with each other, and with a frigate which convoyed them, being bound to different ports in the Mediterranean, some declared to be enemy's

1799 June 11. — THE MARIA. — Sir W. Scott.

ports and others not, with cargoes consisting, amongst other things, of naval stores, were met with, close upon the British coast, by his Britannic Majesty's cruisers; that a continued resistance was given by the frigate to the act of boarding any of these vessels by the British cruisers, and that extreme violence was threatened in order to prevent it, and that the violence was prevented from proceeding to extremities only by the superior British force which overawed it; that the act being effected in the night, by the prudence of the British commander, the purpose of hostile resistance, so far from being disavowed, was maintained to the last, and complaint made that it had been eluded by a stratagem of the night; that a forcible recapture of one vessel took place, and a forcible capture and detention of one British officer who was on board her, and who, as I understand the evidence, was not released till the superiority of the British force had awed this Swedish frigate into something of a stipulated submission.

This being the actual state of the facts, it is proper for me to examine, secondly, what is their legal state, or, in other words, to what considerations they are justly subject according to the law of nations; for which purpose I state a few principles of that system of law which I take to be incontrovertible.

First, that the right of visiting and searching merchant ships upon the high seas, whatever be the ships, whatever be the cargoes, whatever be the destinations, is an incontestible right of the lawfully commissioned cruisers of a belligerent nation. I say, be the ships, the cargoes, and the destinations what they may because, till they are visited and searched, it does not appear what the ships, or the cargoes, or the destinations are; and it is for the purpose of ascertaining these points that the necessity of this right of visitation and search exists. This right is so clear in principle that no man can deny it who admits the legality of maritime capture; because if you are not at liberty to ascertain by sufficient inquiry whether there is property that can legally be captured it is impossible to capture. Even those who contend for the inadmissible rule, that *free ships make free goods*, must admit the exercise of this right at least for the purpose of ascertaining whether the ships are free ships or not. The right is equally clear in practice, for practice is uniform and universal upon the subject. The many European treaties which refer to this right refer to it as pre-existing, and merely regulate the exercise of it. All writers upon the law of nations unanimously acknowledge it, without the exception even of Hubner himself, the great champion of neutral privileges. In short, no man in the least degree conversant in subjects of this kind has ever, that I know of, breathed a doubt upon it. The right must unquestionably be exercised with as little of personal harshness and of vexation in the mode as possible; but soften it as much as you can, it is still a right of force, though of lawful force —something in the nature of civil process where force is employed, but a lawful force which cannot lawfully be resisted. For it is a wild conceit that wherever force is used it may be forcibly resisted; a lawful force cannot lawfully be resisted. The only case where it can be so in matters of this nature is in the state of war and conflict between two countries, where one party has a perfect right to attack by force and the other has an equally perfect right to repel by force. But in the relative situation of two countries at peace with each other no such conflicting rights can possibly co-exist.

Secondly, that the authority of the sovereign of the neutral country being interposed in any manner of mere force cannot legally vary the rights of a lawfully commissioned belligerent cruiser. I say legally, because what may be given, or be fit to be given, in the administration of this species of law to considerations of comity or of national policy are views of the matter which, sitting in this Court, I have no right to entertain. All that I assert is that legally it cannot be maintained; that if a Swedish commissioned cruiser, during the wars of his own country, has a right by the law of nations to visit and examine neutral ships, the King of England, being neutral to Sweden, is not authorized by that law to obstruct the exercise of that right with respect to the merchant ships of his country. I add this, that I cannot but think that if he obstructed it by force it would very much resemble (with all due reverence be it spoken) an opposition of illegal violence to legal right. Two sovereigns may unquestionably agree, if they think fit (as in some late instances they have agreed) (*a*), by special

(*a*) It is made an article of treaty between America and Holland, *an.* 1782: Article 10, Mart. Tr. vol. ii. p. 255.

1799 June 11. THE MARIA. Sir W. Scott.

covenant, that the presence of one of their armed ships along with their merchant ships shall be mutually understood to imply that nothing is to be found in that convoy of merchant ships inconsistent with amity or neutrality; and if they consent to accept this pledge, no third party has a right to quarrel with it any more than with any other pledge which they may agree mutually to accept. But surely no sovereign can legally compel the acceptance of such a security by mere force. The only security known to the law of nations upon this subject, independent of all special covenant, is the right of personal visitation and search, to be exercised by those who have the interest in making it. I am not ignorant that amongst the loose doctrines which modern fancy, under the various denominations of philosophy and philanthropy, and I know not what, have thrown upon the world, it has been within these few years advanced, or, rather, insinuated, that it might possibly be well if such a security were accepted. Upon such unauthorized speculations it is not necessary for me to descant. The law and practice of nations (I include particularly the practice of Sweden when it happens to be belligerent) give them no sort of countenance, and until that law and practice are new-modelled in such a way as may surrender the known and ancient rights of some nations to the present convenience of other nations (which nations may perhaps remember to forget them when they happen to be themselves belligerent), no reverence is due to them; they are the elements of that system which, if it is consistent, has for its real purpose an entire abolition of capture in war—that is, in other words, to change the nature of hostility as it has ever existed amongst mankind, and to introduce a state of things not yet seen in the world, that of a military war and a commercial peace. If it were fit that such a state should be introduced, it is at least necessary that it should be introduced in an avowed and intelligible manner, and not in a way which, professing gravely to adhere to that system which has for centuries prevailed among civilized States, and urging at the same time a pretension utterly inconsistent with all its known principles, delivers over the whole matter at once to eternal controversy and conflict, at the expense of the constant hazard of the harmony of States and of the lives and safeties of innocent individuals.

Thirdly, that the penalty for the violent contravention of this right is the confiscation of the property so withheld from visitation and search. For the proof of this I need only refer to Vattel, one of the most correct and certainly not the least indulgent of modern professors of public law. In Book III. c. vii. sect. 114, he expresses himself thus: "On ne peut empecher le transport des effets de contrebande, si l'on ne visite pas les vaisseaux neutres que l'on rencontre en mer. On est donc en droit de les visiter. Quelques nations puissantes ont refusé en différents tems de se soumettre à cette visite; *aujourd'hui un vaisseau neutre, qui refuseroit de souffrir la visite, se feroit condamner par cela seul, comme étant de bonne prise.*" Vattel is here to be considered not as a lawyer merely delivering an opinion, but as a witness asserting the fact—the fact that such is the existing practice of modern Europe. And to be sure, the only marvel in the case is that he should mention it as a law merely modern, when it is remembered that it is a principle not only of the civil law (on which great part of the law of nations is founded), but of the private jurisprudence of most countries in Europe, that a contumacious refusal to submit to fair inquiry infers all the penalties of convicted guilt. Conformably to this principle, we find in the celebrated French Ordinance of 1681, now in force, Article 12, "*That every vessel shall be good prize in case of resistance and combat;*" and Valin, in his smaller Commentary, p. 81, says expressly that although the expression is in the conjunctive, yet that the *resistance alone is sufficient.* He refers to the Spanish Ordinance, 1718, evidently copied from it, in which it is expressed in the disjunctive, "*in case of resistance or combat.*" And recent instances are at hand and within view, in which it appears that Spain continues to act upon this principle. The first time in which it occurs to my notice on the inquiries I have been able to make in the Institutes of our own country respecting matters of this nature, excepting what occurs in the Black Book of the Admiralty (*a*), is in the Order of Council, 1664, Article 12, which directs, "That when any ship, met withal by the Royal Navy or other ship commissionated, shall

[(*a*) No. B.: "Instructions what the Lord Admiral is to doe at sea and on land in tyme of warr:" sec. 7, Black Book of the Admiralty (Rolls Series), vol. i. p. 28.]

1799 June 11. — THE MARIA. — Sir W. Scott.

fight or make resistance, the said ship and goods shall be adjudged lawful prize." A similar article occurs in the Proclamation of 1672. I am aware that in those orders and proclamations are to be found some articles not very consistent with the law of nations as understood now, or indeed at that time, for they are expressly censured by Lord Clarendon (*a*). But the article I refer to is not of those he reprehends; and it is observable that Sir Robert Wiseman, then the King's Advocate General, who reported upon the Articles in 1673, and expresses a disapprobation of some of them as harsh and novel, does not mark this article with any observation of censure. I am therefore warranted in saying that it was the rule, and the undisputed rule, of the British Admiralty. I will not say that that rule may not have been broken in upon in some instances by considerations of comity or of policy, by which it may be fit that the administration of this species of law should be tempered in the hands of those tribunals which have a right to entertain and apply them; for no man can deny that a State may recede from its extreme rights, and that its supreme councils are authorized to determine in what cases it may be fit to do so, the particular captor having in no case any other right and title than what the State itself would possess under the same facts of capture. But I stand with confidence upon all fair principles of reason—upon the distinct authority of Vattel; upon the Institutes of other great maritime countries, as well as those of our own country—when I venture to lay it down, that by the law of nations, as now understood, a deliberate and continued resistance to search on the part of a neutral vessel to a lawful cruiser is followed by the legal consequence of confiscation.

3. The third proposed inquiry was, whether any special circumstances preceded, accompanied, or followed the transaction which ought in any manner or degree to affect the application of the general principles?

The first ground of exemption stated on the part of the claimants is the treaty with Sweden, 1661, Article 12; and it was insisted by Dr. Laurence that although the belligerent country is authorized by the treaty to exercise rights of inquiry in the first instance, yet

(*a*) Lord Clarendon's Life, p. 242.

that these rights were not exercised in the manner therein prescribed. It is an obvious answer to that observation that this treaty never had in its contemplation the extraordinary case of an armed vessel sent in company with merchantmen for the very purpose of beating off all inquiry and search. On the contrary, it supposes an inquiry for certain papers, and if they are not exhibited, or "there is any other just and strong cause of suspicion," then the ship is to undergo search. The treaty, therefore, recognizes the rights of inquiry and search, and the violation of those rights is not less a violation of the treaty than it is of the general law of nations. It is said that the demand ought first to have been made upon the frigate. I know of no other rule but that of mere courtesy which requires this; for this extraordinary case of an armed ship travelling along with merchant ships is not a *casus fœderis* that is at all so provided for in the treaty. However, if it is a rule, it was complied with in the present instance, and the answer returned was, that "they were Swedish ships bound to various ports in the Mediterranean, laden with iron, hemp, pitch, and tar." The question then comes, What rights accrued upon the receipt of this answer? I say, first, that a right accrued of sending on board each particular ship for their several papers; for each particular ship, without doubt, had its own papers. The frigate could not have them; and the captors had a right to send on board them to demand those papers, as well under the treaty as under the general law. A second right that accrued upon the receiving of this answer was a right of detaining such vessels as were carrying cargoes so composed, either wholly or in part, to any ports of the enemies of this country; for that tar, pitch (*a*), and hemp going to the enemy's use are liable to be seized as contraband in their own nature cannot, I conceive, be doubted under the modern law of nations, though formerly, when the hostilities of Europe were less naval than they have since become, they were of a disputable nature, and perhaps continued so at the time of making that treaty, or at least at the time of making *that* treaty which is the basis of it—I mean the treaty in which Whitlock was employed in the year 1656; for I conceive that Valin expresses the truth of this

1799 *June* 11.

THE MARIA.

Sir W. Scott.

(*a*) The *Sarah Christina*, *ante*, p. 125.

1799 June 11. — THE MARIA. — Sir W. Scott.

matter when he says (p. 68), "*De droit* ces choses" (speaking of naval stores) "sont de contrebande *aujourd'hui* et depuis le commencement de ce siècle, ce qui n'étoit pas autrefois néanmoins"; and Vattel, the best recent writer upon these matters, explicitly admits amongst positive contraband "les bois et tout ce qui sert à la construction et à l'armement de vaisseaux de guerre." Upon this principle was founded the modern explanatory article of the Danish treaty, entered into in 1780, on the part of Great Britain, by a noble lord (*a*), then Secretary of State, whose attention had been peculiarly turned to subjects of this nature. I am therefore of opinion, that although it might be shown that the nature of these commodities had been subject to some controversy in the time of Whitlock, when the fundamental treaty was constructed, and that therefore a discreet silence was observed respecting them in the composition of that treaty and of the latter treaty derived from it, yet that the exposition which the later judgment and practice of Europe has given upon this subject would in some degree affect and apply what the treaties had been content to leave on that indefinite and disputable footing on which the notions then more generally prevailing in Europe had placed it. Certain it is, that in the year 1750 the Lords of Appeal in this country declared pitch and tar, the produce of Sweden, and on board a Swedish ship bound to a French port, to be contraband, and subject to confiscation, in the memorable case of the *Med Guds Hielpe* (*b*). In the more modern understanding of this matter, goods of this nature being the produce of Sweden, and the actual property of Swedes, and conveyed by their own navigation, have been deemed, in British Courts of Admiralty, upon a principle of indulgence to the native products and ordinary commerce of that country, subject only to the milder rights of pre-occupancy and pre-emption; or to the rights of preventing the goods from being carried to the enemy, and of applying them to your own use, making a just pecuniary compensation for them. But to these rights, being bound to an enemy's port, they are clearly subject, and may be detained without any violation of national or individual justice. Thirdly: another right accrued, that of bringing

(*a*) The Earl of Mansfield. (*b*) *Ante*, p. 1.

in for a more deliberate inquiry than could possibly be conducted at sea upon such a number of vessels, even those which professed to carry cargoes with a neutral destination. Was there or was there not the just and grave suspicion which the treaty refers to, excited by the circumstances of such a number of vessels with such cargoes intended to sail all along the extended coasts of the several public enemies of this kingdom, under the protection of an armed frigate associated with them for the very purpose of beating off by force all particular inquiry? But supposing even that there was not, is this the manner in which the observance of the treaty or of the law of nations is to be enforced? Certainly not by the treaty itself; for the remedy for infraction is provided in compensations to be levied, and punishments to be inflicted upon delinquents by their own respective sovereigns: Article 12. How stands it by the general law? I don't say that cases may not occur in which a ship may be authorized by the natural rights of self-preservation to defend itself against extreme violence threatened by a cruiser grossly abusing his commission; but where the utmost injury threatened is the being carried in for inquiry into the nearest port, subject to a full responsibility in costs and damages if this is done vexatiously and without just cause, a merchant vessel has not a right to say for itself (and an armed vessel has not a right to say for it), "I will submit to no such inquiry, but I will take the law into my own hands by force." What is to be the issue if each neutral vessel has a right to judge for itself in the first instance, whether *it* is rightly detained, and to act upon that judgment to the extent of using force?—surely nothing but battle and bloodshed as often as there is anything like an equality of force or an equality of spirit. For how often will the case occur in which a neutral vessel will judge itself to be rightly detained? How far the peace of the world will be benefited by taking the matter from off its present footing and putting it upon this is for the advocates of such a measure to explain. I take the rule of law to be that the vessel shall submit to the inquiry proposed, looking with confidence to those tribunals whose noblest office (and I hope not the least acceptable to them) is to relieve by compensation inconveniences of this kind where they have happened through accident

1799 *June* 11. — THE MARIA. — Sir W. Scott.

or error, and to redress by compensation and punishment injuries that have been committed by design.

The second special ground taken on the part of the claimants was that the intention was never carried into act. And I agree with Dr. Laurence that if the intention was voluntarily and clearly abandoned, an intention so abandoned, or even a slight hesitation about it, would not constitute a violation of right. But how stands the fact in the present case? The intention gives way, so far as it *does* give way, only to a superior force. It is for those who give such instructions to recollect that the averment of an abandonment of intention cannot possibly be set up, because the instructions are delivered to persons who are bound to obey them, and who have no authority to vary. The intention is necessarily unchangeable, and being so, I do not see the person who could fairly contradict me if I was to assert that the delivery and acceptance of such instructions, and the sailing under them, were sufficient to complete the act of hostility. However that might be, the present fact is that the commander sails with instructions to prevent inquiry and search by force, which instructions he is bound to obey, and which he is prevented from acting upon to their utmost extent only by an irresistible force. Under such circumstances how does the presumption of abandonment arise? If it does, mark the consequences. If he meets with a superior force he abandons his hostile purpose; if he meets with an inferior force he carries it into complete effect. How much is this short of the ordinary state of actual hostility? What is hostility? It is violence where you can use violence with success; and where you cannot it is submission and striking your colours. Nothing can be more clear, upon the perusal of these attestations, than that this gentleman abandoned his purpose merely as a subdued person in an unequal contest. The resistance is carried on as far as it can be, and when it can maintain itself no longer, *fugit indignata.*

3. It is said that the papers were not immediately taken possession of, nor proceedings instituted till long after the arrival in port. These are unquestionably irregularities; but I agree with the King's Advocate in maintaining that they are not such irregularities as will destroy the captor's right of proceeding, for the claimant had his remedy in the way of a monition. How these

delays were occasioned, whether in consequence of pending negotiations (as has been repeatedly asserted in the course of the argument), I am not judicially informed. If such negotiations ever existed, I may have reason personally to lament that they have proved ineffectual. But the legal consequence of that inefficiency undoubtedly is that the question of law remains the same as if no such negotiation had ever been thought of.

4. It is lastly said that they have proceeded only against the merchant vessels, and not against the frigate, the principal wrongdoer. On what grounds this was done—whether on that sort of comity and respect which is not unusually shown to the immediate property of great and august sovereigns, or how otherwise—I am again not judicially informed; but it can be no legal bar to the right of a plaintiff to proceed that he has, for some reason or other, declined to proceed against another party against whom he had an equal or possibly a superior title. And as to the particular case of one vessel which had obtained her release and a re-delivery of her papers, the act of the captors may perhaps furnish a reasonable ground of distinction with respect to her own special case; but its effect, be it what it may, is confined to herself, and can be extended no further.

I am of opinion, therefore, that special circumstances do not exist which can take the case out of the rule which is generally applicable to such a state of facts; and I have already stated that rule to be the confiscation of all the property forcibly withheld from inquiry and search. It may be fitting (for anything that I know) that other considerations should be interposed to soften the severity of the rule, if the rule can be justly taxed with severity; but I have neither the knowledge of any such considerations nor authority to apply them. If any negotiations have pledged (as has been intimated) the honour and good faith of the country, I can only say that it has been much the habit of this country to redeem pledges of so sacred a nature. But my business is merely to decide whether, in a Court of the law of nations, a pretension can be legally maintained which has for its purpose neither more nor less than to extinguish the right of maritime capture in war; and to do this, how?—by the direct use of hostile force on the part of a neutral State. It is high time that the legal merit of such a

1799 June 11. THE MARIA. Sir W. Scott.

pretension should be disposed of one way or other. It has been for some few years past preparing in Europe. It is extremely fit that it should be brought to the test of a judicial decision, for a worse state of things cannot exist than that of an undetermined conflict between the ancient law of nations, as understood and practised for centuries by civilized nations, and a modern project of innovation utterly inconsistent with it; and in my apprehension not more inconsistent with it than with the amity of neighbouring States and the personal safety of their respective subjects.

The only remaining question which I have to consider is the matter of expenses, and this I think myself bound to dispose of with as much tenderness as I can use in favour of individuals. It is to be observed that the question itself was of an importance and delicacy somewhat beyond the powers of decision belonging to such persons. The authority of their country has been in some degree surprised in this matter. The captors have been extremely tardy in proceeding to adjudication. Attending to all these considerations I think the claimants are clearly entitled to have their expenses charged upon the value of the property up to the time of the order for further proof. From that time the property might have been withdrawn upon bail, and it is no answer to the Court to say that this gentleman or another gentleman did not think it advisable to commit their private fortunes in the extent of the security required. It is the business of foreign owners who have brought their ships and cargoes into such situations of difficulty to find the means of relieving them when the opportunity can be used. I go sufficient lengths in allowing expenses for the further time in which orders could have been obtained from Sweden, and I fix this at the distance of two months from the order of further proof; and, condemning the ship and cargo, I direct all private adventures to be restored.

This is the substance of what I have to pronounce judicially on this case, after weighing with the most anxious care the several facts and the learned arguments which have been applied to them. I deliver it to my country, and to foreign countries, with little diffidence in the rectitude of the judgment itself. I have still more satisfaction in feeling an entire confidence in the rectitude of the considerations under which it has been formed.

THE ELSABE.

[4 C. Rob. 408.] 1803 *November* 28.

Sir W. Scott thus referred to the judgment of the Court of Appeal in the *Maria*:—

"How far the appellate judgment has confirmed all the principles that are there laid down has been questioned in argument. It is a question, however, into which I do not feel myself disposed, or called upon, to enter very minutely, for the reason already given, that if they are not positively disclaimed by the Court above they continue to bind the legal conscience of the Court below. At the same time, I think it hardly possible to avoid two observations. First, that if the principles had been such as that Court disapproved it could not but have felt the obligation of disclaiming them. They are principles of considerable extent—operating on great subjects—and leading to great consequences; they are not indifferent in their nature, and if erroneous, it should rather seem that public interests called forcibly for a public disavowal of them. Secondly, that although it is not to be supposed that every incidental expression of opinion is confirmed by that judgment (for this Court is not wild enough to attribute such effect to any appellate judgment, or even to conceive itself bound by such *obiter* intimations), it seems, *ex vi necessitatis*, that the leading and fundamental positions must be considered as affirmed. For instance, it must be taken to be affirmed that the Court of Prize has cognizance of such a matter; that it is competent to entertain the question; that it is not bound to leave it to the chance of force in this particular instance, or to the chance of negotiations afterwards, between two countries, neutral in law, but hostile in disposition in consequence of such an unnatural occurrence of hostility, to the chance of negotiations, I say, which might continue, whilst the same occurrence takes place again, as it would have done in this very instance. In the next place, it must, I think, be taken, *ex vi necessitatis*, as affirmed that resistance to search is penal, and that the penalty is confiscation; thirdly, that *that* resistance, being directed to be given by the sovereign of the State, affords no protection; fourthly, that the resistance of the convoying ship is the resistance of the whole convoy; and fifthly, that the resistance given in that particular case was the criminal

1803 November 28. — THE ELSABE. — Sir W. Scott.

act which led to the penal consequence. All these positions are not only unshaken, but they are, in my apprehension, bound up in the judgment of the Court of Appeal, and substantially affirmed by it; and if there are any persons who dispute the affirmance on these grounds, they are at least called upon to show on what other grounds *it was* or *could be* affirmed; or how it was possible to arrive at the same conclusion, on any other principles, than those laid down as the foundation of that sentence in the Court below. On the fundamental positions of that sentence, then, by which the justice of the decision must be tried, I do not feel myself disposed to doubt, either from anything that I have heard or from anything which further reflection has suggested to me, or from the manner in which the opinion of the Superior Court has been expressed upon it."

[The Court then proceeded to apply the principles of the *Maria* to the facts before it.]

[2 C. Rob. 1.]

THE EENROM.

Cargo—Property of Neutral—Property of Enemy—Liability of Neutral.

When a cargo on a neutral vessel consisted partly of goods the property of a neutral, and partly of goods the property of an enemy, and the whole cargo was described as belonging to a neutral, this will excuse the condemnation of the entire cargo.

1799 *May* 21; affirmed *March* 27, 1802.

THIS was a case of a ship and cargo taken on a voyage from Batavia to Copenhagen, December 27th, 1798, by his Majesty's ship the *Brilliant*.

SIR W. SCOTT.—In this case the ship is claimed as the entire property of Messrs. Fabritius and Wever, of Copenhagen, and half the cargo also is claimed as belonging to them by Mr. Fabritius, the son, being employed as supercargo on board this vessel.

The Court directed that this gentleman should give some account of the property of the remainder of the cargo; it being claimed "as the undivided property of Fabritius and others," he was called upon to specify who were the co-partners. The Court was more particularly induced to make this order by the special application which had been made on the part of the claimant to allow this very gentleman to be examined, as a person who was acquainted with every particle of the transaction, and who could give the Court the most satisfactory information upon every circumstance belonging to it. To the surprise of the Court, this gentleman has now said in his affidavit "that he cannot set forth the specific interests, except as hereafter mentioned, as he was sick and confined at Batavia, and obliged to intrust the actual shipment of the cargo to Mr. Inglehart, with whom he had not come to any final settlement before he left that place." It is worthy of notice that, although Mr. Inglehart was the actual shipper, his name does not appear in any one of the ship's papers, although it has happened to peep out since in several other cases. It is, I think, on the face of this excuse, an extraordinary circumstance that a person employed as supercargo in a foreign country (who must necessarily be required to give an account of all his transactions to his principals), falling, from illness, under the necessity of executing his trust by an agent, should not, immediately on his recovery, put himself in possession of everything that had been done for him by his substituted agent during his confinement. This is surely no more than what every agent, in such a situation, would naturally have done. Mr. Fabritius says "he did not," "but, knowing that the funds arising from the outward cargo of this vessel, and from the profits of her voyage to China, as far as they were applied to the present cargo, were not equal to more than a moiety, and also learning in England that Messrs. Fabritius and Wever had caused insurance to be made here to the amount of about half of this cargo, he is led to believe that not more than a moiety belongs to these gentlemen." The Court cannot forget that in a very late case, the *Denmark*, this very outward cargo of the *Eenrom* was represented as overflowing the capacity of her return, and as being employed in purchasing a large ship over and above that returned cargo. It now, however, appears that it was not equal to a moiety of the returned cargo; the other moiety, Mr. Fabritius says, "he supposes to have belonged to Mr. Inglehart, or to some person for whom he acted." He says, indeed, that Mr. Inglehart told him it belonged to him, but whether in his own right or as

1799 May 21. — THE EENROM. — Sir W. Scott.

agent he cannot say; "but from hearing on his return to England that Marshall Blucker had caused an insurance to be made here on a part distinct from Messrs. Fabritius and Wever, he is induced to think that some part belongs to him."

This leads me to dispose of this part of the case, the interest of Mr. Blucker, first. Mr. Cowie states in his affidavit "that he received orders (he does not say from whom) in May, 1798, to insure for Marshall Blucker, in the *Eenrom*, one thousand two hundred pounds on ship and cargo, and that he believes him to be interested to that amount." It appeared to the Court to be an extraordinary circumstance that the insurance should be made in these terms, on ship and cargo, for a person who was not suggested to have any interest in the ship, and the explanation was that Marshall Blucker, not being a mercantile man, might have fallen into this error inadvertently. I should rather have thought that such an expression, deviating from common speech, was more like the phrase of a person speaking in technical language than of a person ignorant of trade and writing simply from his own apprehension of his own concerns; and more especially since I learn, on reference to the merchants, that it is mercantile language, and that such an insurance, though including ship and cargo, is allowed to apply solely to an interest of that amount in the cargo, if the party had an interest in the cargo to that amount and no interest in the ship. Mr. Cowie states further, "that he has written for instructions," but does not say when. This ship was brought in, in January, 1799. As a careful and diligent agent he must have taken the first opportunity of giving intelligence of the capture. But it is not said what answer was received, nor is it even said that Mr. Cowie expects directions to claim; no paper on board expresses the name of Mr. Blucker, and he is perfectly quiescent and, as far as appears, ignorant of the matter; therefore, on the whole, I think this is not such a claim as I can admit under the circumstances in which it is introduced. If Marshall Blucker has any real interest in this cargo he may still claim it elsewhere, in the Court of Appeal.

There is another claim that I will also dispose of before I come to the consideration of the ship and cargo. It is a claim of Mr. Fabritius, the supercargo, for some bills of exchange asserted to have been given for money borrowed for the repairs of the ship, and purchased afterwards on his own account from the person in whose favour he had originally drawn them; these are pressed as regular bottomry bonds. It is not a little extraordinary that Mr. Fabritius, having such full power over the whole concern as supercargo, should resort to this mode of raising money; but it is only necessary to look at the papers produced to see whether they are of that species of instruments which, in maritime law, will constitute a lien on the ship. If I should think that they are not of that description it will not be necessary to enter into the question whether a claim can be given on account of a mere lien on a captured ship, though I am of opinion, for the moment, that it is not such an interest as is regarded and protected by the prize law. Now, looking at these bills, I am rather inclined to think that they are not of that kind which the maritime law supports as hypothecation bonds; there is no binding of the vessel, no hypothecation whatever; they are mere bills of exchange, stating something about repairs, indeed, but in no sense bearing the binding force of bottomry bonds. In the most liberal way in which they can be considered, and with the least scrupulous adherence to form that is consistent with substantial reasoning, I cannot hold them to be maritime bottomry bonds, and I reject the claim founded on them.

I come now to the consideration of the ship and cargo; or rather, I shall invert the order, and consider the cargo first. The outward cargo of this voyage consisted of tar, sheathing copper, sail cloth, and other articles, which by treaty this country and Denmark are expressly forbidden to carry to the enemy of the other; it sets out therefore with a violation of public treaties, and of the private law of Denmark, because every treaty is a part of the private law of the country which has entered into that treaty, and is as binding on the subjects as any part of their municipal laws. The clearance was general to the East Indies, though in some papers a destination to Fredericksnagore is held out; with respect to these general clearances to the East or West Indies, I cannot say that they are absolutely and necessarily illegal, although they are certainly inconvenient to all parties, by throwing a great uncertainty on the nature of the intended voyage. If neutral

1799 May 21.

THE EENROM.

Sir W. Scott.

governments permit these indefinite clearances which seem to allow a destination to the ports of a belligerent (if such belligerent has any ports in the East or West Indies), it seems proper at least that the nature of the cargo should correspond, and care should be taken that the cargo should be such as their subjects are allowed to carry to an enemy's port; there should be an affidavit, as in voyages to an enemy's port, that the cargo contains no prohibited goods; for without some precaution of this kind great frauds may be committed against the public treaties of the country, and the country may be involved in the consequences of such frauds. There seems to have been no such security taken in this case, and therefore I am inclined to think that there must have been some understanding on this subject at Copenhagen, that the voyage was to be to their own ports, or to neutral ports only; for it is not to be imagined that such a general clearance could have been obtained for articles of this description, being understood to have a liberty of going to an enemy's port; such a thing cannot be supposed, without imputing to the Danish Government such a connivance at the irregular and illegal conduct of its subjects, as I am in no degree disposed to surmise. The fact, however, is asserted to be that this vessel left Copenhagen with these noxious articles on board, and with full liberty of going to any port; that there was any other destination than to Batavia is not suggested by any one circumstance in the cause; therefore we may describe it to have been a voyage not contingent, nor left optional, but clear and certain, and definite, in direct violation of public treaties, and of the law of Denmark founded on those treaties.

These are circumstances *in limine*, and this is the manner in which the voyage sets out. The next circumstance on which I shall observe is, that the management of this whole affair seems to have been committed to Mr. Fabritius, jun., and that he acted with unlimited control, although he is scarcely mentioned in the papers; only in a corner of the instructions given to the master, who was to conduct everything: Mr. Ponsaing, who was master of the outward voyage, is directed to go to Fredericksnagore and manage everything; but in a note, "*Ponsaing and the supercargo* are directed to dispose of the cargo and to invest another in the best manner they might be able." This is the only manner in which Mr. Fabritius is mentioned, in a character merely *assistendo*, although he now appears to have been intrusted with unlimited power over the whole business.

The instructions further direct, "that if the cargo should not be sufficient for the returned voyage, other goods might be taken on freight, with a condition that they should be consigned to Messrs. Fabritius and Wever." This is not like an authority to buy a cargo in undivided moieties for these gentlemen and other persons; there are no directions for a partnership. When I see how these instructions are executed and by whom, in a manner totally different from what they purport, I am strongly induced to suspect that they are merely colourable instructions, and that the real history of this transaction is connected with previous arrangements in Batavia between Messrs. Fabritius and Wever and Mr. Inglehart, the person actually employed in putting this cargo on board.

The cargo is put on board by him, and it is a very material question on which the fate of the cargo and of the ship likewise may depend: Whether it was the intention of the supercargo, in this part of the transaction, to mislead the British Courts of Justice, and British cruisers, as to the property of the cargo? For I am of opinion that, if such an intention can be proved in the agent, let the interests of his employers in Denmark be what they may, they must be affected by his conduct, and the consequence will attach on them to confiscate their property so engaged. This is no ordinary supercargo; he is the son of his employer, and appears to have been delegated with greater powers than supercargoes usually enjoy; his conduct must in point of law and conscience, and under the most lenient considerations of equity, be held to bind his principal with peculiar force. In strict law every supercargo will bind his employer; and although where law is administered with great indulgence, cases may arise in which the Court will not implicate the owner, as in some cases where supercargoes have appeared, taking in small parcels of goods in contradiction to the orders of their employers, the Court has thought it hard to involve the interests of the owners, though perhaps strictly responsible. Yet this is not a case entitled to any such favourable treatment: this is not the case of a small portion of a cargo taken in

1799 May 21. THE EENROM. Sir W. Scott.

from false compassion to others, or from corrupt views of private interest: the fraud, if any, in this instance must be that of a deliberate interfering in the war, to mask and withdraw from the rights of a belligerent the property of his enemy, to the amount of one-half of a most valuable cargo. It is not the case of an ordinary supercargo: the person delegated is intrusted with the fullest powers, and if he has abused his powers so largely conferred, it is to him that the owners must look for redress.

The regular penalty of such a proceeding must be confiscation; for it is a rule of this Court, which I shall ever hold till I am better instructed by the Superior Court, that if a neutral will weave a web of fraud of this sort, this Court will not take the trouble of picking out the threads for him in order to distinguish the sound from the unsound; if he is detected in fraud he will be involved *in toto*. A neutral surely cannot be permitted to say, "I have endeavoured to protect the whole, but this part is *really* my property; take the rest, and let me go with my own." If he will engage in fraudulent concerns with other persons, they must all stand or fall together. Let us see, then, if there is not reason not only to suspect, but to conclude, that there was a design to represent the cargo, which appears to have belonged in great part to Inglehart, the Dutchman, as the entire property of Fabritius and Wever. In the first place, Mr. Inglehart was the shipper, yet his name is not once mentioned in the papers. In no one place does his name occur, which cannot be an accidental omission, since it is according to the most ordinary course of business that the name of the shipper should be specified. I must therefore consider this suppression as a studied contrivance to withdraw from the notice of the Court every connection that Mr. Inglehart has had with this transaction. The master and the mate describe Fabritius and Wever as the entire proprietors, and Mr. Fabritius, jun., as the shipper. They were examined as soon as the ship was brought in, and, as we may presume, before they were apprised of the existence of other papers; they agree with the formal papers in keeping out of sight the name of Inglehart, and never once make mention of him. This is an extraordinary circumstance, for the master is in this case not a common carrier-master: he is a confidential manager of the business, according to the instructions, yet so much is he kept in the dark, or keeps himself so, that he represents Fabritius and Wever as the entire proprietors of the cargo. It is said, as an excuse for this man, that he was affected with an almost total derangement of mind whilst he was at Batavia, owing to the climate, and that he came home perfectly ignorant of the transaction; but there is no mention of this malady in his deposition, nor are there any signs of it; he gives a cool and rational recital of facts, and shows at least *a method in his madness* in every part of his conduct that presents itself to our view. He was appointed joint agent with Fabritius, yet he was left under the delusion that the whole cargo, of which only half is now claimed, belonged to Messrs. Fabritius and Wever. If he was deceived, it serves to establish the imposition on the part of others; if he joined in the deceit, it still further fortifies the suspicion of a general combination of fraud. Mr. Fronier, who was the master substituted in his place for the return voyage, lies under the same mistake; he describes the cargo as the entire property of Fabritius and Wever. I do not say that this Court will lay down a rule so harsh as to require that every carrier-master should know the property of every part of her cargo; yet in time of war it cannot be unknown to neutrals that the master is expected to speak to the property of his cargo; more especially in a case like this, where the property is so great as one-half, and where the master is a confidential person, and where there is a son of his employer in the character of a supercargo on board, total ignorance can scarcely happen to such a master; and where it is pretended, it strongly rivets on the mind of the Court a suspicion (by which I always mean a legal suspicion) that there is something behind which it is for the interest of the parties to conceal. But the matter does not end here: there is no mention of any distinction of property in the papers. The invoice describes the whole cargo as the property of Fabritius and Wever; and this paper is signed not by the master but by the supercargo. It is said that the invoice is not a paper of consequence, that the bill of lading is the document to which reference is usually made; but this is both: it is a bill of lading as well as an invoice. Then how came this on board? It is said that Mr. Fabritius was ill, that the lading was conducted for him, and that he signed the paper

1799 May 21. THE EENROM. Sir W. Scott.

without attention to its contents. How can I accede to such an explanation? Is it credible that a man, intrusted with the management of so large a concern, should fall into such a misapprehension as to sign a solemn paper asserting the whole property to belong to his employer, when he well knew that it did not? or can it be believed that on his recovery he should not have made himself acquainted with everything that had been done for him? To act otherwise would be so monstrous, that no pretence of illness is sufficient to apologise for it.

But it is said Mr. Fabritius has since his arrival in England disclosed the truth and given in his claim for only one-half, and much credit is assumed for this instance of fair and ingenuous conduct. Allowing all the merit that is due to such a recantation, I do not know that it can be of any avail to protect this case from the penalties attaching on the former part of the transaction; for if the Court is satisfied that the intention was to hold out to British cruisers a *noli me tangere* as to the whole on an appearance of its being Danish property—although a *locus penitentiæ* is to be allowed to all men, I cannot but think that it comes a little too late, under the circumstances of the present case. Shall a deceit be allowed during the whole of such a voyage; and after it has had a great part of its effect in deceiving our cruisers, shall it be done away by this late confession? If the representation of the papers, and the master, and the substituted master had been believed, the whole of this cargo would have been long ago safe in Copenhagen or America. But what is more material, it is to be remembered that, before the present claim was given, a disclosure of evidence had been obtained from the papers of some other cases. In the *Nancy*, which was a ship under the management of the same parties, it had come to light that Mr. Inglehart was concerned in the cargo of the *Eenrom*, and in the exact proportion which squares with Mr. Fabritius's amended claim. This circumstance very much detracts from the merit of the confession, there being every reason to presume that no such claim would have been given if the evidence already exhibited in that case had not shown that a claim for the whole would be completely falsified. If so, the purpose of fraud is abandoned, merely because it can no longer be maintained.

Is the Court, then, to believe that Mr. Fabritius came into this country with an intention of making this disclosure, and of making the claim as it now stands, or that he meant to hold out the property to be as the formal papers represent? When I look to the other steps leading to this fraud, when I find all the papers on board in this tenor, and see the master and the displaced master using the same language in their depositions, even after their arrival in this country, it would be a strain of charity much beyond what is consistent with justice if I did not say that it was an intention, carried into effect, to cover the whole cargo as the property of Fabritius and Wever by persons knowing the contrary, and whose acts will legally affect their employers. What, in my judgment, decisively proves that such was the determined purpose of the parties is the fact that appears, that this ship was first carried into Lisbon, and that an inquiry was there instituted respecting the property of this ship and cargo. It has been pressed upon the Court by the captors to receive the depositions there made by Mr. Fabritius and others, but the Court has declined to receive those depositions as irregularly taken, and therefore cannot advert to them. How Mr. Fabritius swore upon that occasion with respect to this cargo I cannot say, but I cannot think it otherwise than highly probable that he represented the property as entirely belonging to the house of Fabritius and Wever, because I think it impossible that after such an inquiry had been pursued at Lisbon the master and the displaced master should have continued in the error (if it is a mere error) that has led them to depose here to the same effect, unless he had so held it out, as well in those depositions as in the conversations which he must since have had with them prior to their examinations here. And when I recollect his extreme eagerness to be examined here upon his arrival, I cannot but think that he was at that time fully prepared to support upon oath the same representation, and that nothing but the subsequent information he received, that the secrets had already been betrayed by the papers of the *Nancy*, prevented him from so doing.

With respect to the ship, is the property in that so proved as to support a claim for restitution without further proof? If that could be maintained, I might perhaps allow it to be distinguished from the other part of the case. But if further proof is necessary,

1799 May 21. THE EENROM. Sir W. Scott.

it comes to this question: Are persons so convicted of an attempt to impose on the Court entitled to the privilege of giving further proof? The ship was built at Batavia, and has been constantly trading from Batavia. It must have been the property of Dutchmen, and therefore under any circumstances a bill of sale would be necessary, and under the particular circumstances which I have pointed out a bill of sale could hardly be deemed sufficient. But a thicker cloud is raised over this part of the case from what appears from a paper in the *Nancy*, which is signed by Inglehart, and states, "I shall accompany this with the accounts of the *Eenrom*, of which Messrs. Fabritius and Wever are sharers." It is said that this applies to the cargo only; it may be so, it is a possible explanation; but how can this be proved? It can be only by further proof. Again, there are many passages in which Mr. Inglehart seems to assume great authority over the conduct of the vessel. It is said that this was in consequence of a charter-party, by which he had chartered the vessel. It may be so; but this is matter of explanation only and of further proof, as it is left at present, on the face of it, very ambiguous. There being the necessity of further proof, have the parties placed themselves in a situation in which they are entitled to a privilege of this kind? It is a rule that I shall uniformly adhere to, till I am better instructed, that where a party has been convicted of an attempt to impose on the Court in the same transaction, the privilege of further proof shall be denied him as a privilege which is justly forfeited by deception and fraud. I shall therefore pronounce both the ship and cargo subject to condemnation.

THE VRYHEID (No. 2). [2 C. Rob. 16.]

Capture—Right to share Prize—Common Enterprise—Contribution of Endeavour —Sight.

To entitle a ship of war to share in the proceeds of a prize, it is not sufficient that such ship be engaged in a common enterprise with other vessels which have actually taken the prize, but there must be some actual contribution of endeavour by such ship. Sight before a chase begins is not sufficient ground to allow a claim for joint capture (a).

THIS was a case of an allegation of joint capture on behalf of the *Vestal* frigate, in the capture of the Dutch fleet under the command of Admiral De Winter, October 11th, 1798. The substance of the allegation is recited in the judgment. 1799 *June* 19.

Against the allegation, the *King's Advocate* and *Laurence.*

In support of the allegation, the *Advocate of the Admiralty* and *Arnold.*

SIR W. SCOTT.—This is a contest between two bodies of persons, all deserving most highly of the public, and therefore as far as individual merit can go all equally entitled to every attention; it is a case of joint capture, and the Court has to lament that cases of this nature are in general attended with much difficulty, as they depend frequently on very minute facts on which the Court has to decide between contradictory representations; and it is to be regretted that the decisions of the Courts on this subject have not always been so uniform as it is highly desirable they should be. It would be a very great satisfaction to me, if, with the assistance which I may hope to receive from the gentlemen of the Bar, it should fall within my power to establish a settled and intelligible system, on principles that may become in future easily applicable to the various cases that may arise.

The Act of Parliament and the Proclamation give the benefit of prize "to the takers," by which term are naturally to be understood those who actually take possession, or those affording an actual

(a) See the *Forsigheid*, *post*, p. 314.

1799 June 19. — THE VRYHEID. — Sir W. Scott.

contribution of endeavour to that event. Either of these persons are naturally included under the denomination of "takers;" but the Courts of Law have gone further, and have extended the term "taker" to another description of persons—to those who, not having contributed actual service, are still supposed to have rendered a constructive assistance, either by conveying encouragement to the captor, or intimidation to the enemy.

Capture has therefore been divided into capture *de facto*, and capture by construction. I need not say that the construction must be such as the Courts of Law have already recognized, and not a new, unauthorized construction; for as the word has already travelled a considerable way beyond the meaning of the Act of Parliament, the disposition of the Court will lean, not to extend it still further, but to narrow it, and bring it nearer to the terms of the Act than has been done in some former cases. The case of the *Mars* (a) is a strong authority on this point, in which the claim of joint capture was disallowed to ships not in company, but stationed at different outlets to catch the enemy, who were known to be under the necessity of passing through one of them; and it was in that case intimated to be the opinion of the judges of the Common Law (as I have had means of knowing) that the Court ought to come nearer home, and conform more strictly to the precise words of the Act of Parliament.

In all cases the *onus probandi* lies on those setting up the construction, because they are not persons strictly within the words of the Act, but let in only by the interpretation of those acting under a competent authority to interpret it; it lies with the claimants in joint capture, therefore, either to allege some cases in which their construction has been admitted in former instances, or to show some principle in their favour so clearly recognized and established as to have become almost a first principle in cases of this nature. The being in sight generally, and with some few

(a) This was a case of a French ship taken by one of three King's ships; which, being apprised of the design of the enemy to escape from Port au Prince, had taken their station at different outlets to intercept them. The capture was made by one ship. A claim was given on behalf of the other two to share as joint captors, though not present at the capture; but it was rejected.

exceptions, has been so often held to be sufficient to entitle parties to be admitted joint captors, that where that fact is alleged we do not call for particular cases to authorize the claim; but where that circumstance is wanting, it is incumbent on the party to make out his claim by an appeal to decided cases, or at least to principles, which are fairly to be extracted from those cases.

The facts of this case come before the Court at present on the admission of the allegation—a very convenient mode, surely, of taking the opinion of the Court in the first instance; for, if the facts stated would not in the judgment of the Court be sufficient to sustain the claim, admitting them to be proved, it would only be attended with unnecessary expense and delay to the parties to permit them to enter into proof; it would be more convenient to resort in the first instance to higher authority. The allegation is therefore very properly examinable on its first admission; it is also very desirable that all the facts should be stated at once, and that the allegation should not be sent to be amended (as it was necessary to do in this instance, to show the Court in what manner Mr. Trollop composed a part of Admiral Duncan's fleet), for a repetition of argument on these facts begets expense and other consequences very incommodious to the parties and to the Court. All the particulars are, however, now before the Court, and if I should be of opinion that they are not sufficient to sustain the claim, I cannot see what service I should do the parties by admitting them to proof; and therefore I should hold it better in all respects to send them to take the opinion of a superior Court in the first instance. The allegation states "that the *Vestal* received orders from the Admiralty to join Admiral Duncan; that she accordingly did join him, and formed one of the fleet under his command, and received directions from him to cruise off the Texel, to reconnoitre and obtain intelligence of the Dutch fleet, which he did; that Admiral Duncan cruised till the latter end of September, and then returned to Yarmouth, ordering Captain Trollop to sail with two or three vessels to watch the motions of the enemy, and leaving directions for the *Vestal* to put herself under the command of Captain Trollop; that the *Vestal* accordingly did join Captain Trollop, and made one of the ships under his command, being part of Admiral Duncan's fleet; and on falling in with the Dutch fleet on the 8th of October, was sent by Captain

1799 June 19. THE VRYHEID. Sir W. Scott.

Trollop to reconnoitre them; that on the next day Captain Trollop gave the *Vestal* a written order to sail immediately for the first port in England, using her utmost endeavours to fall in with Admiral Duncan on the way, to send an express to the Admiralty, and then to use his best endeavours immediately to fall in with Admiral Duncan wherever he was, and acquaint him with the situation of the Dutch fleet; that in pursuance of these orders she sailed to England, landed the despatches, and again returned and actually joined Admiral Duncan on the 13th of October; that after the *Vestal* was so detached, Captain Trollop, with his Majesty's ships cruising with him, joined Admiral Duncan, and never lost sight of the Dutch fleet from the time the *Vestal* was so detached to the time of the capture of the ship proceeded against; that at the time of capture the *Vestal* belonged to and composed a part of Admiral Duncan's fleet, and was aiding and assisting in the capture, and afterwards, with his Majesty's ships the *Endymion* and *Ethalion*, assisted in bringing into the Humber two of the Dutch fleet captured in that engagement."

Now on these facts, and having stated the *onus probandi* to lie on the persons setting up the construction, I am to inquire on what authority this claim is to be sustained. There are no cases cited as being directly in point, but the case of the *Signior San Joseph* (a) has been alluded to; that is a case which I perfectly recollect, having been concerned in arguing it, but it was in its principal circumstances entirely different from the present case. That was a case of two vessels detached from the fleet under the command of Admiral Pigot in the West Indies, to chase two strange ships appearing in sight, the fleet bearing up all the time as fast as possible to support them; the chasing vessels took the two ships first appearing, and also a third, on which the dispute arose. There was much contrariety of evidence whether the fleet (which was continuing to sail in the same direction) was not up and in sight, and the chief doubt arose owing to the night coming on, for if it had been day the fleet would clearly have been in sight, and it was at all events well known to be at hand and ready to have given any support that might be wanting. Under these circumstances the Court of Appeal affirmed the sentence of the Court below pronouncing for

(a) Lords, May 4th, 1784.

joint capture; and in that sentence it is, I believe, true, as it has been stated by the counsel, that some mention was made of the words "joint enterprise"; but taking the case altogether, it can by no means be said to go the length of the present claim.

As far as cases go, then, there is an entire failure of authority on the part of the *Vestal;* but the usage of the Navy has been resorted to, and a case has been cited of the *Audacious*, one of the fleet under the command of Lord Howe, being permitted to share in the victory of the 1st of June, 1794. It is admitted, and it is certainly true, that the practice of the Navy, in opposition to the words of the Act of Parliament, or a Proclamation, or to the established practice of law, cannot weigh or be of any authority; at the same time, the Court would be extremely unwilling to break in on any settled and received notions of the Navy, or to disturb a practice generally prevailing among themselves. But I agree with the King's Advocate that the case cited is different from the present. In that case the *Audacious* had actually engaged the enemy's fleet, and had separated only in chase of one of their ships. The *Canada*, another case which has been mentioned, chased from the fleet by signal on the prize coming in sight; and the *Lowestoff*, which is another case, stated to have happened in the Mediterranean, was not detached from the Mediterranean fleet till after the chase had actually begun. These circumstances therefore materially distinguish these cases from the present, and I am at liberty to say that no case in point, no authority has been produced. Is there, then, any admitted principle? The gentlemen have resorted to the general principle of *common enterprise*, and it has been contended that where ships are associated in a common enterprise that circumstance is sufficient to entitle them to share equally and alike in the prizes that are made. But certainly this cannot be maintained to the full extent of these terms; many cases might be stated in which ships so associated would *not* share. Suppose a case that ships going out on the same enterprise, and using all their endeavours to effectuate their purpose, should be separated by storm or otherwise: no one would contend that they should share in each other's captures. There is no case in which such persons have been allowed to share after separation, being not in sight at the time of chasing. It cannot

1799 June 19. THE VRYHEID. Sir W. Scott.

be laid down to that extent, and indeed it would be extremely incommodious that it should; nothing is more difficult than to say precisely where a common enterprise begins. In a more enlarged sense, the whole navy of England may be said to be contributing in the joint enterprise of annoying the enemy. In particular expeditions every service has its divisions and subdivisions; operations are to be begun and conducted at different places. In the attack of an island there may be different ports, and different fortresses, and different ships of the enemy lying before them; it may be necessary to make the attack on the opposite side of the island, or to associate other neighbouring islands as objects of the same attack; the difficulty is to say where the joint enterprise actually begins. Again, is it every remote contribution, given with intention or without intention, that can be sufficient? I apprehend that is not to be maintained; an actual service may be done without intention, or there may be a general intention to assist, and yet no actual assistance given. Can anybody say that a mere intention to assist, without actual assistance, though acted upon with the most prompt activity, would in all cases be sufficient? If persons under such claims could share, there would be no end to dispute; no captor would know what he was about, whether in every prize he made there might not be some one fifty leagues distant working very hard to come up, and even acting under the authority of the Admiralty to co-operate with him; in serving his country every captor would be left in uncertainty whether some person whom he never saw, and whom the enemy never saw, might not be entitled to share with him in the rewards of his labour. The great intent of prize is to stimulate the present contest and to encourage men to encounter present fatigue and present danger, an effect which would be infinitely weakened if it were known that there might be those not present, and not concerned in the danger, who could entitle themselves to share.

On these considerations I must ever hold that the principle of mere common enterprise alone will not be sufficient; it is not sufficiently specific: it must be more limited, and a limitation is here attempted. It is said that the *Vestal* was detached on a service immediately connected with the object of capture. This would have been much stronger if the primary intention on which this ship was detached had been absolutely to join Admiral Duncan; but looking at the letter of Captain Trollop, I find the directions were, "you are to proceed to the first port of England if you do not meet Admiral Duncan, which you are to use your best endeavours to do on your way, &c." By fair construction, then, she was not to go out of her way, she was to go to England, that was the mission, the other purpose was secondary and collateral, and I cannot think that this ship is to be considered as so much connected with Admiral Duncan as she would have been if she had been sent immediately to join him. But I would ask again, is there any authority from adjudged cases, or from principles sufficiently established, to show that ships detached from the squadron on views immediately connected with the main enterprise are entitled to share? Many cases might be put in which that position could not be maintained. Suppose a fleet going to besiege a place, and one ship detached to procure provisions and stores, which does not come up and join the fleet till the place is taken; it would be very strong to maintain that such a vessel, neither present at the commencement nor at the conclusion of the enterprise, could be entitled to share; it has, I apprehend, been decided in practice that she would not; and the distinction taken was this: that if the ship was sent off for common necessaries after the operations had begun, or if she returned before the object was accomplished, she should be permitted to share, and not otherwise, though her absence was occasioned solely for the purpose of procuring necessaries for the service. Then the limitation ingrafted on the first principle, namely, that the detachment is made for an object immediately connected with the service is not sufficient; something more must be added, and that must be the being in sight.

Then the whole turns on this question, whether the being in sight at the beginning of the chase, in the manner in which that fact is alleged in this case, and in addition to the other circumstance, of being detached on a necessary service, will be sufficient to entitle the parties as joint captors? I must inquire then, what being in sight is necessary? for it is perfectly clear that being in sight in all cases is not sufficient. What is the real and true criterion? The being in sight, or seeing the enemy's fleet accidentally a day or two before will not be sufficient; it must be at

1799 June 19. THE VRYHEID. Sir W. Scott.

the commencement of the engagement, either in the act of chasing or in preparation for chase, or afterwards during its continuance. If a ship was detached in sight of the enemy, and under preparations for chase, I should have no hesitation in saying that she ought to share; but if she was sent away after the enemy had been descried, but before any preparations for chase, or any hostile movements had taken place, I think it would be otherwise; there must be some actual contribution of endeavour as well as a general intention. Then the question comes to this: was the *Vestal* in sight at the commencement of the chase before she separated? If so, it will clearly do; if not, I think as clearly it will not do. On this point, I am of opinion that it cannot be considered as a chase till Admiral Duncan's fleet came up; Captain Trollop dogged the enemy for the purpose of reconnoitring, but he is to be considered rather as the party chased, than as the chaser; with all the gallantry that is to be ascribed to him and the other gentlemen with him, he could not be expected to cope with the whole Dutch fleet and engage in such an unequal contest. When Admiral Duncan came up with the body of the British fleet, then the chase began, and that is in my estimation to be considered as the true point of commencement of actual engagement in this case. Here, then, is only a *general intention* on the part of the *Vestal;* she conveyed no terror to the enemy, nor encouragement to the friend at the time when the rival fleets must be said to have first met each other. It is said the Court will not judge by events, but I think the events of a case like this are the facts of the case; the facts of this case in my apprehension prove that the *Vestal* was not in sight at the time of the commencement of the chase, and therefore that she is not in law entitled to share in this capture (*a*).

[Acton, 211 (239).] [(*a*) In the *Le Bon Adventure*, Feb. 24th, 1810, the Court of Appeal stated, on a point raised, but which was not that on which the Court decided the appeal, which was a question of fact, "upon the principle thus advanced, it is necessary to inquire, under the circumstances of the present case, whether a vessel commencing a second chase in sight of a fleet, of which she had constituted a part before she had been detached by signal upon a former chase, and capturing the second chase at any distance from such a fleet, would necessarily, upon this principle, be compelled to let in the claim of a whole fleet to share in a prize so made, notwithstanding such fleet afforded no assistance or co-operation

THE DORDRECHT. [2 C. Rob. 55.]

Joint Capture—Army and Navy.

To entitle soldiers to share in the proceeds of a prize directly captured by the navy, there must be evidence of actual co-operation with the navy of a material kind.

THIS was the flagship of a Dutch squadron, captured by Admiral Elphinstone, in Saldanah Bay, August 17th, 1796. The cause came on to determine the question of joint capture between the British fleet and the land forces from the Cape of Good Hope, asserting to have co-operated in the capture.

1799 *July* 9.

[The Court dealt at great length with the facts, but in the course of the judgment laid down the following principles.]

SIR W. SCOTT.—I have now heard the evidence in this case, and the question is, whether such a case has been made out, on the part of the army, as will support their claim to be considered as joint captors? In the first place, it is not pretended that it is a case which comes within the provisions of the Act of Parliament (*a*) which directs the army to share, in some cases, in conjunction with the fleet. There are, it is well known, several descriptions of such cases, which I need not now advert to, as it is not pretended that this case comes under any one of them. In the next place, it is not argued that this is a case of concerted operations. That the army and navy might have similar views is not contested, but whatever was done was done separately and without concert or communication. Thirdly, it cannot be denied that it lies upon the army to make out a case of joint capture, and to show a co-operation on their part, assisting to produce the surrender; for the surrender was made to the fleet alone; possession was taken by the fleet; the army could not take it: therefore the *onus probandi* lies on them, to prove that there was an actual co-operation on

in the capture, but actually bore away from the captor in another track. No such principle has ever been recognized, nor do the cases cited (*Vryheid* and *Forsigheid*) support any such construction of the term 'association.'"]

(*a*) Prize Act, 33 Geo. 3, c. 66, s. 3.

1799 July 9.

THE DORDRECHT.

Sir W. Scott.

their part; for it is, I think, established by decided authority, and particularly in the late case of *Jaggernaickporam*, before the Lords of Appeal, that much more is necessary than a mere being in sight, to entitle an army to share jointly with the navy in the capture of an enemy's fleet. The mere presence, or being in sight of different parties of naval forces, is, with few exceptions, sufficient to entitle them to be joint captors; because they are always conceived to have that privity of purpose which may constitute a community of interests; but between land and sea forces, acting independently of each other, and for different purposes, there can be no such privity presumed; and therefore, to establish a claim of joint capture between them, there must be a contribution of actual assistance, and the mere presence, or being in sight, will not be sufficient. Fourthly, I am strongly inclined to hold that when there is no pre-concert it must be not a slight service, nor an assistance merely rendering the capture more easy or convenient, but some very *material service*, that will be deemed necessary to entitle an army to the benefit of joint capture. Where there is pre-concert it is not of so much consequence that the service should be material, because then each party performs the service that is previously assigned to him, and whether that is important or not it is not so material—the part is performed, and that is all that was expected. But where there is no such privity of design, and where one of the parties is of force equal to the work and does not ask assistance, it is not the interposing of a slight aid, insignificant perhaps, and not necessary, that will entitle another party to share. Suppose an engagement at sea, in which a part of the enemy's crews being disposed to fly to shore should be prevented from landing by an armed force, and should therefore be induced to surrender with the main fleet, or suppose this body of armed men on shore should have prevented the fleet from obtaining supplies two or three days previous to the action; these would be very remote services, and such as would not induce me to pronounce for a joint capture. The services which I should require must be such as were directly or materially influencing the capture, so that the capture could not have been made without such assistance, or, at least, *not certainly* and without great hazard. It is further expected that the evidence by which such a claim is supported should be clear and consistent, because it lies on those setting up an interest of joint capture to make out their case; the presumption is on the side of the actual captor. Their evidence, therefore, must be satisfactory, for if not, or if it is left at all doubtful, it is the duty of the Court to adhere to the interests of the actual captor.

1799 *July* 9.

THE DORDRECHT.

Sir W. Scott.

These being the principles, let us see what are the facts of the present case and the amount of the claim grounded upon them. . . .

THE WALSINGHAM PACKET.

[2 C. Rob. 77.]

Prize—Jurisdiction—Municipal Law.

The British Prize Court is a Court of the Law of Nations only, but it is bound to take notice of the municipal law of England. *Held*, therefore, that a British ship which had been engaged in an unlawful trade when captured by the enemy and had been recaptured, could not be restored.

1799 *July* 10.

THIS was a case of a British packet, retaken from the enemy, in which a claim was given for the cargo as the property of British and Portuguese merchants, and resisted on the part of the captors on the ground that the carriage of any cargo by the packet was illegal under the statute 13 & 14 Ch. 2, c. 11, s. 22.

For the captors, the *King's Advocate* and *Laurence.*

The Court suggesting that in a question of this nature it would be proper that some appearance should be given for the Crown,

The *King's Proctor* appeared, and prayed that the question of law, as to the interest in the penalty, might be reserved.

For the claim, the *Advocate of the Admiralty* and *Sewell;* for other parties, *Arnold* and *Croke.*

SIR W. SCOTT.—This is a case, as it has been truly observed, of a very different complexion from those which generally occupy the attention of this Court; it turns upon a principle which the Court of Appeals has sanctioned in respect to the power of a Court of this nature, to take cognizance indirectly of breaches of the municipal law of this country. This Court is properly and directly a Court of the law of nations, and I am not aware that

1799 *July* 10.

THE WALSINGHAM PACKET.

Sir W. Scott.

any case had occurred, before the present war, in which the Court had acted on the principle on which it certainly did act in the case alluded to; I mean the case of the *Eliza* (*a*). It was the case of a ship and cargo, in which the claimant being a British subject appeared to have been engaged in trafficking with that cargo in direct violation of British Acts of Parliament. It occurred to those who were entrusted with the concerns of the captor, that a resistance to such a claim might be sustained upon a ground which had not been occupied in any other case that had occurred, viz.: That although this Court is properly and directly a Court of the law of nations only, and not intended to carry into effect the municipal laws of this or any other country, and although it was in the habit of declining to take notice of the private laws of other countries; yet it was an inquiry worth pursuing: whether a British Court of Admiralty, sitting here, armed with its power from this country, and carrying all its process into effect by the authority of the British Parliament, was not so far a British Court as to be bound to take notice of British Acts of Parliament and the flagrant breach of our municipal laws with respect to the transactions of our own subjects coming incidentally before it. In that case the Court of Admiralty did not sustain the objection to the extent in which I have now stated it. My predecessor condemned the cargo, but generally as French property. The cause went up to the superior Court, where it was most elaborately argued; perhaps no case ever underwent a fuller discussion. There the principle was affirmed and established that a British Court of Admiralty was bound to take notice of a violation of an Act of Parliament appearing on the face of the claim, and that a British claimant could not entitle himself in such a Court to a restitution of that property, happening to fall by accident into the hands of a British captor, which by his own showing appeared to have been employed in an illegal trade.

That this decision has removed all difficulties on this question I will not assert. It is a good moral and legal principle, unquestionably, that a man must come into a Court of Justice with clean hands, and that the law will not lend its aid to persons setting up a violation of law on the face of his claim. It is a sound maxim,

(*a*) Admiralty, Feb. 6th, 1794; Lords, July 13th, 1798.

to which the Courts of the law of the land have always attended, and whether the penalty is great or small, or whether there be no penalty at all, yet, if the act is reprobated, a man will not be allowed to claim a right founded on it. But cases had not occurred in which the Court of Admiralty had met with occasion to apply such a principle, except in cases of British property taken in a trade with the King's enemies; but in such cases the exception is not to be considered as arising from municipal law, but from the principle of allegiance, which is a general principle of the law of nations. It was in the case of the *Eliza* that it was first decided that the Court of Admiralty was bound to take notice of an illegal practice, evidently appearing in the conduct of a British subject, though the illegality arose from a violation of some law merely municipal, and that it was bound to reject the claim of any British subject, whose property had found its way into the hands of a British captor, if the transaction in which that property had been employed was a transaction contrary to British law. The question is still not relieved from all its difficulties, and the observations which have been made to-day only revive the objections which were made before. It was said (and cannot be denied) that such a practice might carry the interest in a very different course from what the Act of Parliament which had been violated directs. In the *Eliza*, which was a case of traffic illegally carried on in violation of the charter of the East India Company, the interest has gone to the private captor, whilst the penalty by the Act of Parliament is given to the Company as a compensation for the damages arising to them from such illegal trade. In the *Enterprise* the course has been the same; but in the *Etrusco*, a later case, it has been questioned whether those decisions were right as to the conveyance of the forfeiture, and whether the penalty should not go to the King as the person injured by every violation of the law, where no specific appropriation of the property was directed; and this question still remains subject to further deliberation. On that part of the case, therefore, I shall not think of deciding till that question is disposed of.

As to the facts of this case they are pretty clear: the vessel is a British packet, and by the statute 13 & 14 Ch. 2, c. 11, s. 22, the carrying of all merchandise on board a packet is prohibited except

1799 July 10.

THE WALSINGHAM PACKET.

Sir W. Scott.

under special allowance there described. The amount of the articles is immaterial, except in a very minute degree, which the revenue laws themselves have specified. The quality also is altogether immaterial; neither does it make any difference whether the owners are on board or not, or whether the lading is called a cargo or a private adventure: the prohibition is general against the carrying any merchandise. With the policy of the Act I have nothing to do, as the law has determined it; but the reasons pointed out by the King's Advocate are obvious that a cargo must be a hindrance and obstruction to dispatch and expedition; and if it is said the crew would defend themselves, and fight the better for a cargo, it is to be remembered, at the same time, that it holds out a greater lure to the enemy. These goods are admitted to have been put on board for Lisbon for the purposes of trade, and the only question is, whether they come under the allowance of the Act of Parliament? The exception is, "unless it be in such cases as shall be allowed by the said person or persons which are or shall be appointed to manage his Majesty's Customs or officers aforesaid." Then who are the persons invested with this discretion? I think, by fair construction of the Act, they must be those mentioned in the clause immediately preceding, in the 21st section—the Collector and the Comptroller of the Customs. On any other explanation every tide-waiter would be competent to grant this indulgence, which is an interpretation the Court would not willingly admit unless absolutely forced upon it. In the next place, what sort of allowance would be held sufficient? It has been argued that a tacit permission would be sufficient: that it would be enough if a practice had grown up by connivance; but I cannot accede to that argument, nor can I consider that to be the permission which the statute recognises: it must be a full, distinct allowance, and expressed in such a manner as to be capable of proof. If it were proved to have been practised in twenty instances it would avail nothing; it would only show that the due vigilance had been laid asleep. But it could amount to nothing as a legal dispensation, nor be considered as any legal allowance which the Court can receive. Then how stand the facts? The claimants appear before the Court as persons trading contrary to law: it is said there can be no seizure but by the Custom-house officer. I admit it; but this is not a case of seizure. It is said that no forfeiture can attach but in a particular manner directed by the statute, and it is true; but this is not a forfeiture, although to the parties it has certainly much the same effect. The question is, what will be the effect in a Court of Prize? Whether a party can be admitted in this Court to say, "True it is I have been engaged in an illegal trade, but the property is mine; give it me, and let me go"? It has been decided by the Superior Court that he shall not. In the Exchequer, the seizing officer is put to make out his case; but here it is different, the claimant must support his title, and if the Court of Appeal has determined that such a person is stopped *in limine*, it matters not to him what becomes of the property; he can have no right to moot difficulties in this Court, as to the final disposition of it. Looking on the decisions of the Lords on this point as undisturbed decisions, I must apply the principle to this case, which, I am of opinion, comes fairly within it; but as I am aware of the doubts which have arisen on the judgment of the Lords of Appeal in the case of the *Etrusco*, and as I know that the Court feels it to be a question of weight, I shall direct this case to stand over as to that point to await their final decision. A mistake has run through the whole of this argument; the gentlemen have argued to bind me down to this particular Act, and then the difficulties arising from it are pointed out; but that is not the state of the case. The question is, whether I am to apply the general principle? The Act of Parliament is used only as a medium of proof, to show that what has been done is illegal, and then the principle applies as a great moral and legal principle, adopted in a very great extent in the jurisprudence of this country, and particularly sanctioned and introduced into the practice of this Court by those decisions to which I have alluded (*a*).

1799 *July* 10.

THE WALSINGHAM PACKET.

Sir W. Scott.

(*a*) In the *Fortuna* (March 12th, 1811), Sir W. Scott followed this decision, and further, condemned a neutral ship brought in as prize for an infraction of the Slave Trade Acts. "It has been established that the Court of Prize, though properly purely a Court of the Law of Nations, has a right to notice the municipal law of this country in the case of a British vessel which, in the course of prize proceedings, appears to have been trading in violation of that law, and to reject a claim for her on that account. A late decision [the *Amedie*] seems to have gone the length of establishing a principle that any trade contrary to the general law of nations, although not tending to or accompanied with any infraction of [1 Dods. 81.]

Claim rejected. Question reserved—To whom the property is to be condemned? (b)

[2 C. Rob. 109.]

THE VROW JOHANNA (No. 1).

Blockade—Revocation—Notification.

Until notice of a blockade is revoked, such blockade must be presumed to be in existence.

1799 *July* 18.

This was a case of a ship taken December 16th, 1799, and proceeded against for a breach of the blockade of Amsterdam, having sailed from Petersburg for that port, November 6th, 1798.

Court.—The cases alluded to of the blockade, set up by the Dutch in the wars of the last century, have no immediate application to this case. That was a blockade of the whole coast of their enemy; the present case stands on the question of a blockade of Amsterdam, and not of the coast. It is not denied that if a vessel sail for a blockaded port after having received notification of the blockade, the act of sailing is to be considered as a breach of the blockade. The only question is then, whether the blockade notified on the 11th June, and not revoked, is to be considered as continuing at this time? She sailed on the 6th of November. Am I to presume that the blockade so notified did not exist? I cannot presume it, nor could those concerned in despatching the ship have entertained such a presumption. I hold it to be the duty of a country notifying a blockade to notify the revocation also; there had been no such revocation notified, and therefore I must presume that it was still existing. I hold that a ship and cargo sailing for Amsterdam at that time are liable to condemnation (c).

Condemned.

the belligerent rights of that country, whose tribunals are called upon to consider it, may subject the vessel employed in that trade to confiscation. . . . The principle laid down in that case appears to be that the slave trade carried on by a vessel belonging to a subject of the United States is a trade which, being unprotected by the domestic regulations of their legislature and government, subjects the vessel engaged in it to condemnation." On the evidence the Court held the *Fortuna* to be an American vessel, and engaged in the slave trade, and condemned her.

(b) In the *Etrusco*, Lords, Aug. 11th, 1803, it was held that, under the above circumstances, the property should be condemned to the Crown.

(c) See the *Betsey* (No. 2), *ante*, p. 147.

THE NEPTUNUS (No. 2). [2 C. Rob. 110.]

*Blockade—Notification—*Bonâ fide *Mistake.*

As it is the duty of a foreign government, to which a blockade has been notified, to communicate such notice to its subjects, a neutral master cannot validly plead ignorance of the blockade. But if he is informed by a belligerent cruiser that the blockade does not in fact exist, the vessel of which he is master will not be condemned for attempting to break the blockade.

The offence of breaking a blockade is complete when the vessel commences her voyage for the blockaded port.

1799 *July* 18.

THIS was a case of a vessel sailing on a voyage from Dantzic to Havre, October 26th, 1798, and taken in attempting to enter that port on November 26th.

SIR W. SCOTT.—This is a case of a ship and cargo seized in the act of entering the port of Havre in pursuance of the original intention under which the voyage began. The notification of the blockade of that port was made on the 23rd of February, 1798, and this transaction happened in November in that year; the effect of a notification to any foreign government (*a*) would clearly

(*a*) Respecting the effect of notification as to the subjects of those states to whom it was not directly made:

August 22nd, 1799. In the case of the *Adelaide*, a Bremen ship, which had sailed into Amsterdam from America, September, 1798, and was captured in her voyage outward in April, 1799, it was contended that the penalty did not attach; that by the master's evidence it appeared that he was ignorant of the fact; that he sailed in September from a distant country, without seeing any blockading force; that at the time of sailing outward he met with only that one ship, which seized him; that no notification had been made to the Hanse towns, and therefore as to them it was a blockade existing *de facto* only, of which the master might be allowed to plead his ignorance; that the penal consequences of a notification given *to one power* did not affect the subjects of another State that had not received any notification; it was prayed that the claimant might be allowed to prove the *bonâ fide* ignorance of the master, and that no notification had been made of the blockade of Amsterdam to the Hanse towns.

Court.—This ship is proceeded against on account of having broken the blockade of Amsterdam. The Court has often decided that egress is as much a breach of blockade as ingress, if it be done fraudulently. The notification was made to different governments of Europe on the 11th of June, 1798; this ship sailed in from America, in September of that year, ignorant of the fact; but it by no means follows from that circumstance that the blockade was raised, as it might be suspended by accidents

1799 July 18.

THE NEPTUNUS.

Sir W. Scott.

be to include all the individuals of that nation; it would be the most nugatory thing in the world if individuals were allowed to

which would not make it legally cease to exist. She proceeded to take in a cargo in the months of November and December, and sailed on the 24th of April, 1799; the offence is, therefore, in the egress. That no notification was made to the Hanse towns is a suggestion of counsel which makes no part of the affidavit. I will go so far as to accede to the position that the notification would not affect such a case from the same time, and in the same manner as it would affect the subjects of those States to whom it was directly made. But that it does not affect at any time is going too far, because, if a notification is made to the principal States of Europe, I think a time would come when it would affect the rest; not so much *proprio vigore*, or by virtue of the direct act, as in the way of evidence. It is the duty of a State to make the notification as general as possible. But I must think that a time would come when a notification to neighbouring powers would affect those to whom it was not directly made; from the moment that a notification is made to a government, it binds the subjects of that State, because it is supposed to circulate through the whole country. But suppose a notification is made to Sweden and Denmark, it would become the general topic of conversation, and it would be scarcely possible that it should not have travelled to the ears of a Bremen man; and although it might not be so early known to him as to the subjects of the States to which it was immediately addressed, yet, in process of time, it must reach him, and must be considered to impose the same observance of it on him; it would strongly affect him with the knowledge of *the fact* that the blockade was *de facto* existing; therefore, on these grounds, I should hold that although a notification does not *proprio vigore* bind any country but that to which it is addressed, yet, in a reasonable time, it must affect neighbouring States with knowledge as a reasonable ground of evidence; and I think I do not strain the matter in laying down this rule. As to the circumstances of this particular case at Amsterdam, it must have been a subject of general notoriety that the port was legally considered by the English in a state of blockade; and it is impossible that it should not have come to the knowledge of this man after he came in; it is not to be said by any person "although I know a blockade exists, yet, because it has not been notified to my Court, I will carry out a cargo." I cannot but think that it would have been a very fraudulent omission to take no notice of what was a subject of general notoriety in the place. If it was known to every Dane and Swede, it is impossible that it should not be known to this man. It is not more likely to have been unknown to this vessel, from the circumstance of its being a Bremen ship, when we consider the particular relation which Bremen bears to the sovereign of this country. As to the affidavit of the master, I should receive that with great distrust. Masters have a direct interest to raise the blockade as soon as possible, therefore their affidavits come with a dead weight about them that must very much sink their credit whenever they are produced. I hold that the master must have known of

plead their ignorance of it; it is the duty of foreign governments to communicate the information to their subjects, whose interests they are bound to protect. I shall hold, therefore, that a neutral master can never be heard to aver against a notification of blockade that he is ignorant of it. If he is really ignorant of it, it may be a subject of representation to his own government, and may raise a claim of compensation from them, but it can be no plea in the Court of a belligerent. In the case of a blockade *de facto* only, it may be otherwise, but this is the case of a blockade by notification; another distinction between a notified blockade and a blockade existing *de facto* only, is that in the former the act of sailing to a blockaded place is sufficient to constitute the offence. It is to be presumed that the notification will be formally revoked, and that due notice will be given of it; till that is done, the port is to be considered as closed up, and from the moment of quitting port to sail on such a destination the offence of violating the blockade is complete, and the property engaged in it subject to confiscation: it may be different in a blockade existing *de facto* only; there no presumption arises as to the continuance, and the ignorance of the party may be admitted as an excuse for sailing on a doubtful and provisional destination. But this is a case of a vessel from Dantzic after the notification, and the master cannot be heard to aver his ignorance of it. He fails. Till the moment of meeting Admiral Duncan's fleet, I should have no hesitation in saying, that, if he had been taken, he would have been taken *in delicto*, and have subjected his vessel to confiscation; but he meets Admiral Duncan's fleet, and is examined and liberated by the captain of an English frigate belonging to that fleet, who told him that he might proceed on his destination, and who, on being asked whether Havre was under a blockade, said "It was not blockaded," and wished him a good voyage. The question is, in what light he is to be considered after receiving this information? That it was *bonâ fide* given cannot be doubted, as they would otherwise have seized the vessel; the fleet must have been ignorant of the fact; and I have to

the blockade, notwithstanding he and his men swear they did not; and therefore that the ship is penally liable to confiscation.

Ship condemned. Cargo ordered to stand over. Master's private adventure restored.

1799 *July* 18. — THE NEPTUNUS. — Sir W. Scott.

lament that they were so. When a blockade is laid on it ought by some kind of communication to be made known not only to foreign governments but to the King's subjects, and particularly to the King's cruisers, not only to those stationed at the blockaded port, but to others, and especially considerable fleets, that are stationed *in itinere* to such a port from the different trading countries that may be supposed to have an intercourse with it. Perhaps it would have been safer in the English captain to have answered that he could not say anything of the situation of Havre; but the fact is (and it has not been contradicted) that the British officer told the master "that Havre was not blockaded." Under these circumstances, I think that after this information he is not taken *in delicto.* I do not mean to say that the fleet could give the man any authority to go to a blockaded port; it is not set up as an authority, but as intelligence affording a reasonable ground of belief, as it could not be supposed that such a fleet as that was would be ignorant of the fact.

From that time I consider that a state of innocence commences; the man was not only in ignorance, but had received positive information that Havre was not blockaded. Under these circumstances, I think it would be a little too hard to press the former offence against him. It would be to press a pretty strong principle rather too strongly. I think I cannot look retrospectively to the state in which he stood before the meeting with the British fleet, and therefore I shall direct this vessel *and* cargo to be restored.

[2 C. Rob. 116.]

THE JUNO (No. 1).

Licence—Neutral Ship—Permission to Enter Blockaded Port—Presumption of Right to leave it.

Where a licence was granted to a neutral ship to enter a blockaded port—*Held*, that such licence gave an implied permission to take a cargo from such port.

1799 *July* 18.

THIS was a case respecting the meaning and effect of a licence granted to an American ship to go to the ports of the Vlie.

Sir W. Scott.—This is a case arising out of the blockade of Amsterdam; it is a case of an American vessel coming from America without any knowledge of the blockade of Amsterdam, and bringing a cargo for that port. She came to Falmouth, and then, finding that the port of Amsterdam was under blockade, she petitioned for a licence, and obtained one from this government, and, as I understand the master through the whole of his depositions, "a licence to go to Amsterdam." This he states in stating his difficulties, and the means he took to relieve himself. The application was "for leave to export to the Vlie, Embden, or Rotterdam"; but the terms of the permission are an enlargement of his petition, for they are "to the ports of the Vlie, Embden, Rotterdam, *or elsewhere*." Whether the petition was an imposition, and framed with a design of deceiving government, will appear on the inquiry which has been directed to be made. If the petition was in the usual form, and if the licence was understood by those who granted it to permit exportation to Amsterdam, it will clear up that part of the case. As to any opinion that I can form, I own that although the licence is expressed in this general way, "the ports of the Vlie," I cannot but think that it must have included Amsterdam, which is one of those ports; for it is not to be supposed but that they would intend to grant the licence in a natural and intelligible form, and not so as to keep the parties in the dark as to its extent. But it is argued that, allowing it to have been properly obtained it was not properly used, because it was at any rate a licence to go to Amsterdam through the Vlie passage, whereas this vessel was taken entering the Texel, and that there might be many reasons for making the distinction in the licence, and therefore that it ought to be strictly observed. Now, having heard it constantly argued, and having myself adopted the interpretation, that the blockade extended to one passage as well as to the other, and that the whole Zuyder Zee was shut up, I shall not go back again and restrict this interpretation and say it is confined to one passage only. I shall hold *e converso*, that if a licence is given to go through the Vlie it is not substantially violated by going through another passage, unless it is shown to me that it contained some specific prohibition as to other passages. Supposing it to have been honestly obtained for Amsterdam through

1799 July 18. — The Juno. — Sir W. Scott.

the Vlie, I shall not hold it to have been a material deviation to go another way, unless some special prohibition or unless some special inconvenience is shown, which the party was bound to take notice of.

It has been truly said that a licence is a thing *stricti juris*, a *privilegium* which a man does not possess by his own right, but that it is conceded to him as an indulgence, and, therefore, that it is to be strictly observed. At the same time, I am to remember that this is a licence to relax a right which bears pretty hardly, though justly, on other countries. To shut up the ports of a country and exclude neutrals from all commerce with it is a great inconvenience upon them, although it is one to which they are bound to submit, for there is no one principle of the law of nations better established than that a belligerent has a right to impose a blockade on the ports of his enemy; it may be incommodious to others, but if there is any such thing as a law of nations I hold this principle to be as firmly established from the earliest times, and by the general practice of mankind, as any one law whatever. It is, however, a harsh right, and though a licence is a privilege, I am not disposed to apply that exposition in the strictest manner to a blockade, but rather think that licences in such a case are to be favourably regarded, and that it imports the good faith and honour of the government which grants them not to press the letter too rigorously. I will go further, and say that if I was convinced that there had been an honest mistake on such a matter, if there appeared nothing insidious, nothing more than a misapprehension on the part of the neutral master, I should not apply too strictly the maxim *ignorantia juris non excusat* against a foreigner mistaking the exact meaning of a licence of another country, and in so doing should persuade myself that I did no more than what an equitable regard to the honour of the country which granted such a licence must be supposed to require.

The licence is, "To carry a cargo to the ports of the Vlie or elsewhere," with several provisions, amongst which there certainly is no proviso that she shall come out again; but that is a benefit incidental to the licence and inseparable from it, for it cannot be imagined that she was to go there and be shut up and incarcerated, and become herself an object of the blockade. A ship that has entered previous to the blockade may retire in ballast, or taking a cargo that had been put on board before the blockade. This is the distinction which I have held, and shall hold, till I am corrected by a Superior Court. The licence is silent on that point; but having said that if I was convinced the party acted under an honest application of his licence, though erroneously, I should think him entitled to the most liberal interpretation, it will be proper for me to consider what the man did, that I may see, supposing that there has been a mistake, whether it was a mistake of honest conduct, purely erroneous and innocent, thinking that, if it is so, it would be sufficient for the present case. The master takes the returned cargo on board, and comes to a port of this kingdom, and solicits the protection of a convoy, acting as openly and with as little concealment as possible. There is nothing in the *res gesta* on which the imputation of fraud can be fixed. Is there anything in the licence to instruct him that he was not at liberty to take a cargo, or to act as if the blockade was, in regard to him, entirely relaxed? If so, he would be bound to take notice of it. But I see this distinction, which might reasonably affect the mind of a man going in under such a licence: he goes in under the direct authority of the belligerent, and might suppose his privilege more extensive than that of a neutral vessel previously there. A neutral has no right to say, 'I am here accidentally, and therefore I have a right to take out a cargo, notwithstanding the blockade.' But this man goes in with a permission, which takes off, as to him, the first and primary object of the blockade—the prohibition of taking in a cargo; and I think he might conceive himself to be entitled to be distinguished from the ordinary case of other neutrals previously there. If any inconvenience is likely to arise from this, if government did not mean that his licence should have this effect, it might have been distinctly expressed; the proviso might have been inserted that he should not bring a cargo away, and then all persons would see a clear path before them, and know how to conduct themselves in this very delicate situation.

On the legal effect of such a licence it is not necessary for me to determine. I see no fraud in the interpretation of this licence, and if it turns out that this was the form in which licences were usually granted I shall not think myself warranted to say that this

1799 July 18. — THE JUNO. — Sir W. Scott.

man was guilty (if guilty at all) of anything more than an innocent misapprehension, and in a matter in which I shall hold such a misapprehension to carry no consequences of penalty after it.

July 24th, 1799.—This case having stood for inquiry as to the usual form of granting licences, the King's Advocate said he had obtained no particular information, but that after what had fallen from the Court he did not mean to press the matter any further.

Ship restored.

THE JUNO (No. 2).

Practice—Cargo—Property—Verification of Papers by Master of Ship—Affidavit of Belief.

A master must depose as to his belief that the cargo is as claimed. Freight and expenses allowed as a charge upon the cargo.

1799 July 25.

On the hearing as to the cargo, 25th of July, 1799, the King's Advocate contended—That it must go to further proof, unless all the rules of practice were broken down, that goods shipped in the enemy's country were to be considered *primâ facie* as the property of the enemy, and could only be taken out of that presumption by fair and unbiassed evidence, and not from evidence supplied only from the enemy; that the bills of lading and attestation in this case were of the latter description put on board by the enemy shipper; whilst the master, who was always expected to verify his papers, to the 12th Interrogatory says only, "that the laders of the cargo were Hollanders, and further he cannot depose."

On the part of the claimant, Laurence argued, that if further proof was to be required in this case, it would be impossible for owners of cargoes put on board carrier ships to obtain restitution in any case on the original evidence; as a carrier-master could not be so particularly acquainted with the several owners, or know anything of their course of trading so as to enable him to swear to their property; that the bill of lading expressed account and risk, and there was an attestation of property on board, and that the master swearing to the 13th and 27th Interrogatories "that all his papers were true, and that he knew of nothing to affect their credit," did in effect afford a sufficient verification.

SIR W. SCOTT.—The present application to the Court is to dismiss a cargo taken on board in Holland, on the ground that the proof in the case is sufficient according to the practice, or what ought to be the practice, of this Court. I presume it will not be contended that no proof is necessary in the case of a cargo taken on board in the enemy's country; and where there is *no* proof arising from the documents or the depositions, the Court is not to consider so much what that proof ought to be as what is required by the practice of the Court; for I sit here not as a legislator, but to administer the law that I find existing. If a reform is necessary, it must be sought elsewhere. The Court is neither to make law nor apologise for it.

The rule is, as I have always understood it in the Court of Admiralty, that papers by themselves prove nothing—they are a mere dead letter if they are not supported by the oaths of persons in a situation to give them validity. Those who look back to the elaborate exposition of the proceedings of our Courts of Admiralty in the answer to the Prussian Memorial will find this to have been laid down as a fundamental position, "that the master must verify his papers." It is true that in the case of a carrier-master it may be expected that the verification should be less positive than where he is himself the agent; but this is expected that he should depose at least that he believes the cargo to be as asserted in the claim; less than that I never remember to have been accepted in any case, and if it were necessary for me to apologise for the rules which I find established in this Court, I think this might be vindicated on every principle of reason and justice. When a cargo is taken on board in an enemy's port, and that port blockaded (which is a circumstance of some weight as affording a greater temptation to fraud), if the master is not required to say even that he believes the property to be as claimed, it would open the door to every sort of abuse; but it is said the master does go this length, in swearing "that all the papers are true," and that this amounts to a verification of the property. So he does, if you take that part of his deposition substantively, and apart from the rest; but looking to other parts, and finding that when he is asked on the 12th Interrogatory what he knows or believes (for he is examined to his belief) he can depose nothing, and that he has no

1799 July 25. — THE JUNO. — Sir W. Scott.

belief, it is impossible to say that this man's deposition confirms the papers in the manner in which it is necessary that they should be supported. It is said there are other papers which supply this defect—the attestations of the laders before the American Consul. What authority has an American Consul to administer an oath to Dutch subjects? Such papers can hardly be taken as sworn documents, or if they were, they come only from the Dutch shippers, the very persons who, if there is any fraud, have been the contrivers of it. Under such circumstances can it be reasonably or candidly addressed to the Court to restore this cargo immediately and without further proof? This ship goes under licence to a blockaded port with a cargo addressed to one set of merchants only: here are various parcels for a variety of different persons, the master evidently knowing nothing of the matter, and there being no proof but from the Dutch laders. I must say that I am not satisfied; the rules of the Court require further proof, and I feel that it is a rule which I could not relax without relaxing the essential demands of justice.

Arnold prayed freight and expenses for the ship to be a charge on the cargo.

Court.—I am of opinion that the master is entitled to his freight and expenses on two grounds: if he had taken no cargo he would not have been liable to be stopped; and, secondly, having received this cargo so improperly documented on board, he would have been liable to have been stopped on that account, although he had not been coming from a blockaded port.

Freight and expenses given, and to be a charge on the cargo.

THE HURTIGE HANE (No. 1).

[2 C. Rob. 124.]

Blockade—Breach—Inevitable Necessity.

A breach of a blockade can only be justified by an absolute and unavoidable necessity compelling a vessel to enter a blockaded port.

1799 *July* 19.

THIS was a case of a Danish ship taken in the act of entering the Texel, April, 1799, having sailed from a port in Barbary with an asserted original destination to Hamburg, February 15th, 1799.

It was prayed that the Court would permit a protest of the master to be read, in which it would appear that he was under the necessity of going into the Texel from distress and want of water; and that his crew rose upon him, and insisted that he should go into some Dutch port.

Court.—This ship was found in the act of entering the Texel, a fact by no means indifferent, but highly criminal, *primâ facie* at least, and requiring a very satisfactory explanation. It is usual to set up the want of water and provisions as an excuse; and if I was to admit pretences of this sort, a blockade would be nothing more than an idle ceremony. Such pretences are, in the first instance, extremely discredited on two grounds—that the fact is strongly against them, and that the explanation is always dubious, and liable to the imputation of coming from an interested quarter. I am not deaf to the fair pretensions of human testimony, but at the same time I cannot shut my senses against the ordinary course of human conduct; I will not say that cases of necessity may not occur that would afford a sufficient justification; and I add, that if the party can show that they were under any great necessity, and that, for four or five days before, they could get into no other port but the Texel, I would certainly admit such an excuse so supported. But if they cannot do this, and unless it is proved that in coming up the Channel there was no other port, either English or French, but the interdicted port of Amsterdam into which they could put, I shall reject the apology.

The protest of the master, the mate, and cook was admitted and read.

1799 July 19. THE HURTIGE HANE.

Court.—I have now heard the proof brought in, and I am to determine whether it comes up to the test which I have laid down, and to which I shall certainly adhere, that nothing but an *absolute and unavoidable necessity* will justify the attempt to enter a blockaded port; considerations of an inferior nature, such as the avoiding higher fees, or slight difficulties, will not be sufficient—nothing less than an unavoidable necessity which admits of no compromise, and cannot be resisted, will be held by me to be a justification of this offence.

The master sails under a knowledge of the blockade, being affected with the general notification of the preceding year; on the 28th of March they passed Dover, on the 2nd of April they were off Yarmouth; but although the protest is made to justify the master from barratry and the crew from mutiny, and does therefore, I must presume, contain all facts necessary for that purpose, I do not see that it is stated that they were going into Yarmouth. If on the 3rd of April there is so much want of water and provisions as to compel them to go into the interdicted ports of the Texel, why not go to the open and permitted port of Yarmouth on the 2nd of April? It is not alleged that the discovery of such a want was first made on the 3rd—on the next day, the weather becoming more violent, the crew came to the master and insisted on going into the nearest port on account of want of water and provisions; a third excuse is thrown in, that the ship wanted repair; but this is not mentioned in the depositions, and it appears not to have been a very pressing want, as the ship came afterwards back to England without difficulty; they insisted on going into the nearest port, saying that they would otherwise take the command from him. It does not appear where this happened, nor is it stated that the crew insisted on going to Amsterdam. The master should have said, "the Texel is shut up, I will go to any other port." He does not seem to have felt this necessity in an equal degree with the rest of the crew, as he represents himself "to have been forced in reluctantly." What was there then to carry him to this one interdicted port only, or what reason was there that he could find no other than this, either a little to the north or south? Is there that inevitable necessity which is required? If such pretences as this were to be admitted, I know very well that no one case would come unprovided with an excuse. I shall condemn this vessel; if the parties think themselves aggrieved, they must take the benefit of another Court. 1799 *July* 19. THE HURTIGE HANE.

Ship condemned.

THE WELVAART VAN PILLAW. [2 C. Rob. 128.]

Blockade—Capture on Voyage.

A vessel which has broken a blockade is liable to capture until the termination of her voyage.

THIS was a case of a Prussian ship, taken April, 1799, off Dungeness, and proceeded against for a breach of the blockade of Amsterdam, having sailed thence with a cargo in March. 1799 *July* 19.

SIR W. SCOTT.—There seem to be two grounds on which something of an indulgence is claimed in the present case. It is said that it was not a matter of notoriety in Amsterdam that the blockade was still continued; that a notification is addressed to neutral States, and therefore that a ship in the blockaded port may plead ignorance. But I am to remember that this is not a Dutch ship but a Prussian ship, and that it was the duty of the Prussian Government, having received the public notification many months before, to have communicated it to their subjects in different ports. Another circumstance on which exemption is prayed, is, that she had escaped the interior circumvallation, if I may so call it, that she had advanced some way on her voyage, and therefore that she had in some degree made her escape from the penalties. I cannot accede to that argument; if the principle is found that a neutral vessel is not at liberty to come out of a blockaded port with a cargo, I know no other natural termination of the offence but the end of that voyage. It would be ridiculous to say, "if you can but get past the blockading force you are free"—this would be a most absurd application of the principle. If that is found, it must be carried to the extent that I have mentioned; for I see no other point at which it can be terminated. (*Vide* Bynkershoek, Q. J. P. lib. i. ch. 11.) Being of opinion that the principle is found, I shall hold that if a ship that has broken a blockade is taken in any part of that voyage, she is taken *in delicto*, and subject to confiscation.

[2 C. Rob. 131.]

THE JONGE PETRONELLA.

Blockade—Notice—One Week.

A week's notice held not to be sufficient to affect parties with legal knowledge of a blockade.

1799 *July* 19.

THIS was a case of a Danish ship which had sailed from Rotterdam on the 28th of March, 1799, and was proceeded against for a breach of the blockade of the ports of the United Provinces, notified to foreign ministers on the 21st of March, and inserted in the Gazette on the 26th of March, 1799.

Court.—There seems to be no question made as to the property of the ship. I do not think a week is sufficient time to affect the parties with a knowledge of this blockade; I shall therefore restore this vessel.

Cargo reserved.

[2 C. Rob. 132.]

THE TWO SUSANNAHS.

Capture—Cargo—Sale—Restitution—Damages for Loss by Sale.

A captured cargo was properly sold, but the proceeds were less than its value. An order for its restoration was made. *Held*, that the captors were not liable for damages, no irregularity or *mala fides* having been proved against them.

1799 *July* 23.

THIS was a case on a prayer for compensation in value, for a cargo taken on board a Danish ship, restored on further proof, July 17th, 1799, on a suggestion that the amount of the proceeds was considerably less than the original value.

Court.—This is an unfortunate case; the Court is very desirous that full justice should be done to the claimants, but the cargo is not equal to it; there is no question about the seizure—that is justified by the order for further proof. The question is then, whether the captors have acted so irregularly as to make themselves liable? It is said that it was very desirable that the cargo should be brought here, and that it has been exposed to accidents by carrying it elsewhere. It was, however, carried to Leghorn, where there is a standing commission of the Admiralty Court. It is said that loss has been occasioned by selling it too early. Perhaps it might have been better if they had waited; but there is no suggestion that the sale was made for any sinister purposes, or in any manner injurious to the property. Under these circumstances, I cannot think that the captors are answerable for more than the proceeds, it not being shown that they have conducted themselves otherwise than with fair intentions.

1799 *July* 23.

THE TWO SUSANNAHS.

THE PACKET DE BILBOA.

[2 C. Rob. 133.]

Cargo—Shipment before War—Property in Goods.

In time of war goods shipped at risk of a neutral consignor to an enemy consignee are liable to capture and condemnation; but goods so shipped before war or prospect of war are not liable to condemnation.

THIS was a case of a claim of an English house for goods shipped on board a Spanish vessel, by the order of Spanish merchants, before hostilities with Spain, and captured December, 1796, on a voyage from London to Corunna.

1799 *August* 6.

SIR W. SCOTT.—This is a claim of a peculiar nature for goods sent by British subjects to Spain, shipped before hostilities, during the time of that situation of the two countries of which it was unknown, even to our Government, what would be the issue between them. There appears to be no ground to say that this contract was influenced by speculations on the prospect of a war, or that anything has been specially done to avoid the risks of war. It is sworn in the affidavit of the claimant, "That this is the constant habit and practice of this trade"; whether it is the practice of the Spanish trade generally, or only the particular mode of these individuals in carrying on commerce together, is not material, as the latter would be quite sufficient to raise the subject of this claim. The question is, in whom is the legal title? Because if I should find that the interest was in the Spanish consignee I must then condemn, and leave the British party to apply to the Crown for that grace and favour which it is always ready to show,

1799 *August* 6.

THE PACKET DE BILBOA.

Sir W. Scott.

the property being condemnable to the Crown as taken before hostilities.

The statement of the claim sets forth that these goods have not been paid for by the Spaniard; that would go but little way; that alone would not do. There must be many cases in which British merchants suffer from capture, by our own cruisers, of goods shipped for foreign account before the breaking out of hostilities. It goes on to state, "that, according to the custom of the trade, a credit of six, nine, or twelve months is usually given, and that it is not the custom to draw on the consignee till the arrival of the goods; that the sea risk in peace as well as war is on the consignor, that he insures, and has no remedy against the consignee for any accident that happens during the voyage." Under these circumstances, in whom does the property reside? The ordinary state of commerce is that goods ordered and delivered to the master are considered as delivered to the consignee, whose agent the master is in this respect, but that general contract of the law may be varied by special agreement, or by a particular prevailing practice that presupposes an agreement amongst such a description of merchants. In time of profound peace, when there is no prospect of approaching war, there would unquestionably be nothing illegal in contracting that the whole risk should fall on the consignor till the goods came into possession of the consignee. In time of peace they may divide their risk as they please, and nobody has a right to say they shall not; it would not be at all illegal that goods not shipped in time of war or in contemplation of war should be at the risk of the shipper. In time of war this cannot be permitted, for it would at once put an end to all captures at sea; the risk would in all cases be laid on the consignor where it suited the purpose of protection. On every contemplation of a war this contrivance would be practised in all consignments from neutral ports to the enemy's country, to the manifest defrauding of all rights of capture. It is therefore considered to be an invalid contract in time of war, or, to express it more accurately, it is a contract which, if made in war, has this effect: that the captor has a right to seize it and convert the property to his own use, for he, having all the rights that belong to his enemy, is authorised to have his taking possession considered as equivalent to an actual delivery to his enemy, and the shipper who put it on board during a time of war must be presumed to know the rule, and to secure himself in his agreement with the consignee against the contingency of any loss to himself that can arise from capture. In other words, he is a mere insurer against sea risk, and he has nothing to do with the case of capture, the loss of which falls entirely on the consignee. If the consignee refuses payment, and throws it upon the shipper, the shipper must be supposed to have guarded his own interests against that hazard, or he has acted improvidently and without caution.

1799 *August* 6.

THE PACKET DE BILBOA.

Sir W. Scott.

The present contract is not of this sort; it stands as a lawful agreement, being made whilst there was neither war nor prospect of war. The goods are sent at the risk of the shipper. If they had been lost, on whom would the loss have fallen but on him? What surer test of property can there be than this? It is the true criterion of property that, if you are the person on whom the loss will fall, you are to be considered as the proprietor. The bill of lading very much favours this account. The master binds himself to the shipper "to deliver for you and in your name," by which it is to be understood that the delivery had not been made to the master for the consignee, but that he was to make the delivery in the name of the shipper to the consignee, till which time the inference is that they were to remain the property of the shipper. As to the payment of freight, that is not material, as in the end the purchaser must necessarily pay the carriage. The other consideration—Who bears the loss?—much outweighs that; neither does the case put show the contrary. The case put is, supposing Spain and England both neutral, and that these goods had been taken by the French and sold to great profit, to whose advantage would it have been? The answer is, if the goods were to continue the property of the shipper till delivery it must have enured to *his* benefit, and not that of the consignee. To make the loss fall upon the shipper in the case of the present shipment would be harsh in the extreme. He ships his goods in the ordinary course of traffic by an agreement mutually understood between the parties, and in nowise injurious to the rights of any third party; an event subsequently happens which he could in no degree provide against. If he is to be the sufferer, he is a sufferer without notice and without

1799 *August* 6.

THE PACKET DE BILBOA.

Sir W. Scott.

the means of securing himself; he was not called upon to know that the injustice of the other party would produce a war before the delivery of his goods. The consignee may refuse payment, referring to the terms of the contract which was made when it was perfectly lawful; and under what circumstances and on what principles the shipper could ever enforce payment against the consignee is not easy to discover. The goods have never been delivered in Spain; they were to have been at the risk of the shipper till delivery, and this under a perfectly fair contract. I must consider the property to reside still in the English merchant; it is a case altogether different from other cases which have happened on this subject *flagrante bello.* I am of opinion that, on all just considerations of ownership, the legal property is in the British merchant, that the loss must have fallen on the shipper, and the delivery was not to have been made till the last stage of the business, till they had actually arrived in Spain, and had been put into the hands of the consignee; and therefore I shall decree restitution of the goods to the shipper.

[2 C. Rob. 174.]

THE HAABET (No. 1).

Cargo—Pre-emption—Premium of Insurance—Report of Registrar and Merchants.

A cargo of provisions was captured, and ordered to be sold to the Government, the price to be fixed by the Registrar and Merchants. Such cargo was uninsured, and the Registrar and Merchants disallowed a claim for a sum equal to premiums of insurance which it was alleged represented the risk taken by the cargo owner himself. *Held*, on objection to the report, that the decision of the Registrar and Merchants was right.

1800 *August* 30; affirmed *August* 16, 1803.

THIS was a case arising on an objection to a report of the Registrar and Merchants respecting the allowance of insurance as part of the price of a cargo of wheat going from Altona to Cadiz, but seized and brought into this country, and bought by government. The demand of the claimant, Mr. Peschie, of Copenhagen, had been disallowed in the report on the ground that the insurance had not actually been made.

For the petition, *Laurence* and *Swabey*.

Against the demand, the *King's Advocate* and the *Advocate of the Admiralty*.

1800 August 30.

THE HAABET.

Sir W. Scott.

Sir W. Scott.—This is a question on a report of the Registrar and merchants respecting an allowance of insurance on a cargo of corn seized and brought into this country. The cargo was decreed to be restored, and the Registrar and merchants were directed to make a report on the value due to the claimant. Such reports are in their nature partly legal and partly mercantile. It is a report proceeding from persons qualified in both these respects to form a sound judgment on the subject before them, one of them being, from his connection with Courts of Justice, supposed capable of forming his own opinion and of assisting his associates on all questions of law, in the first instance, subject to the inspection and correction of the Court; whilst the other part of this domestic forum, as I may call it, consists of persons acquainted with trade, and exercising their judgment on matters relative to commerce. It is from the report of a commission so constituted that the question is now brought before the Court on a subject partly legal and partly mercantile. Another report has been brought before me to-day from other persons, of whom it is impossible for me to speak with too much respect, attending either to the extent of their information or to their known probity and honour; but they have, I think, a little mistaken their function in delivering their judgment upon the question proposed to them. They are persons of great experience in mercantile affairs, and from whom the Court, upon subjects purely of that kind, would gladly receive any information which they could conveniently impart. If the Court had desired to know whether it was the practice of merchants, in the ordinary course of commerce, usually to charge and allow insurance, though the insurance has never actually been made, their answer to such a question would have satisfied its conscience upon a matter of usage best known to themselves, and requiring nothing on their part but a fair communication of their own experience and practice. But the question on which an opinion has here been obtained from them is this, "Whether, if a neutral cargo is seized by a belligerent during war, the belligerent is in all cases bound in compensation for this cargo (supposing it not liable to confiscation) to pay such an insurance, no insurance having been paid by the shipper?" That is not a question merely of the law merchant, it is a question which may embrace other considerations, and those

1800 *August* 30. THE HAABET. Sir W. Scott.

belonging to the general law of nations; in truth, it is the very question in the cause now submitted to my decision, and if I regard this opinion so given as an authority there is an end of any duty which I have to perform, for here is an actual decision upon the whole law and fact of the present case. They will acquit me, I am sure, of any incivility, when I venture to say that the labour of giving such a decision is not legally imposed upon *them*, and therefore that this private report so introduced does not come with any just credentials of authority.

The question is, whether there is any reasonable ground for me to pronounce that the Registrar and merchants have disallowed a just demand in disallowing a charge of insurance which had not been made? It has been argued that this charge ought to have been allowed, because it is usually so allowed in the dealings of merchants with each other. I am not clear that this is a necessary consequence, for it is surely no certain rule that in *all cases* where a cargo is taken *jure belli* but for the mere purpose of pre-emption, that it is to receive a price calculated exactly in the same manner and amounting precisely to the same value as it would have done if it had arrived at its port of destination in the ordinary course of trade.

The right of taking possession of cargoes of this description, *Commeatus or Provisions*, going to the enemy's ports, is no peculiar claim of this country; it belongs generally to belligerent nations. The ancient practice of Europe, or at least of several maritime States of Europe, was to confiscate them entirely; a century has not elapsed since this claim has been asserted by some of them. A more mitigated practice has prevailed in later times of holding such cargoes subject only to a right of pre-emption, that is, to a right of purchase upon a reasonable compensation, to the individual whose property is thus diverted. I have never understood that on the side of the belligerent this claim goes beyond the case of cargoes avowedly bound to the enemy's port, or suspected on just grounds to have a concealed destination of that kind; or that on the side of the neutral the same exact compensation is to be expected which he might have demanded from the enemy in his own port. The enemy may be distressed by famine, and may be driven by his necessities to pay a famine price for the commodity if it gets there; it does not follow that acting upon my rights of war in intercepting such supplies I am under the obligation of paying that price of distress. It is a mitigated exercise of war on which my purchase is made, and no rule has established that such a purchase shall be regulated exactly upon the same terms of profit which would have followed the adventure if no such exercise of war had intervened; it is a reasonable indemnification and a fair profit on the commodity that is due, reference being had to the original price actually paid by the exporter, and the expenses which he has incurred. As to what is to be deemed a reasonable indemnification and profit, I hope and trust that this country will never be found backward in giving a liberal interpretation to these terms; but certainly the capturing nation does not always take these cargoes on the same terms on which an enemy would be content to purchase them; much less are cases of this kind to be considered as cases of costs and damages, in which all loss of possible profit is to be laid upon unjust captors; for these are not unjust captures, but authorised exercises of the rights of war.

Two or three considerations have been urged which may, with all propriety, be dismissed: one is, that it was understood between the King's government and the parties that this charge should be allowed. Certainly, if it were made out by any credible proof that the faith of government had been in the slightest manner pledged to such an understanding, there is no principle which this Court would hold more sacred than that the faith of government should be held inviolate in transactions of this kind; but no sort of proof is offered of this, and the fact has in no way come to my knowledge. It is said, likewise, that in the cases of this kind which occurred last war, and which were then settled by the Navy Board, the charge of insurance was allowed; but the policy of insurance was never called for. How this practice came to prevail there, whether under a notion that the insurances had been really made whenever they were charged, whether under any order of government or how otherwise, I am not informed. The persons who had to settle those accounts were not mercantile men, and might be led by the charge to suppose that it had actually been incurred. Under whatever circumstances such a practice grew up, if it did obtain, it is no binding rule upon the Registrar and merchants

1800 *August* 30. here; it might be simple mistake, and at best it is no deciding authority.

THE HAABET. Sir W. Scott. I have already said that the expected payment at the port of delivery is not the necessary measure of compensation at the port of the belligerent. It is not so with reference to any constituent of price; with respect to insurance, considered as such, it would be peculiarly improper. It is reasonably to be charged at the port of delivery, although it has never been paid, because the merchant has stood his own risk, and has purchased the insurance at the expense of his own danger. But is that the case where the voyage has been interrupted almost in its commencement, where the cargo has been carried into a neighbouring port? In the present case the voyage was from Altona to Cadiz, from the north to the south of Europe, and the cargo is seized upon its entrance into the British Channel very soon after quitting its port. Most of the cargoes taken have a similar destination, and are taken under similar circumstances. What pretence is there to say that all risks of the voyage have been incurred? The utmost that could be claimed is an insurance *pro ratâ itineris peracti*, amounting to a very small proportion of the whole, hardly deserving a particular consideration. As to what is said, that in the case of capture of ships you allow the full freight of the whole voyage; that allowance is made on another account; you take the ship in that case on account, not of itself, but of its cargo; you interrupt its occupation which was legal and innocent, and it is therefore not unjust to allow it the benefit of its original contract, which you alone have prevented from being carried into execution. Very different is the consideration of risk, respecting a cargo, which has never been incurred, and of a payment which is due only on the event of that risk having been actually incurred—no contract subsisting, and the cargo being in its own nature liable to this species of interception.

Upon the whole, I see no sufficient reason to pronounce that the Registrar and merchants have adopted a wrong measure of value in disallowing the charge of insurance; they have allowed what, upon their own experience, they pronounce to be a reasonable indemnification and profit, and I do not understand that the sufficiency of this indemnification and profit is impeached on any other ground than that an insurance would have been added in the ordinary course of a mercantile account if the cargo had reached its intended destination. Being of opinion that the ordinary terms of a mercantile account, to be settled on the completion of the voyage, do not furnish (all circumstances being duly weighed) the necessary or just measure of value to be applied in transactions of this kind, I do not find myself enabled to sustain the objection. If, as it has been repeatedly urged, an undertaking to a different effect has subsisted between the King's government and the parties, there can be no doubt that on their resort to a superior tribunal, better acquainted with any communication that may have passed upon the subject, they will have the full benefit of any such engagement.

1800 *August* 30. THE HAABET. Sir W. Scott.

Report confirmed.

THE IMMANUEL.

[2 C. Rob. 186.]

Neutral—Trade between Enemy Port in Mother Country and Enemy Colony—Carrying Ship—Restoration—Forfeiture of Freight.

Neutral goods captured in direct transit from the mother country of the enemy to a colony of the enemy are liable to capture and condemnation. The ship in which such goods were carried restored, but the freight forfeited.

1799 *November* 7.

THIS was the case of an asserted Hamburg ship, taken 14th of August, 1799, on a voyage from Hamburg to St. Domingo, having in her voyage touched at Bordeaux, where she sold part of the goods brought from Hamburg, and took a quantity of iron stores and other articles for St. Domingo. A question was first raised as to the property of the ship and cargo; and, 2ndly, supposing it to be neutral property, whether a trade from the mother country of France to St. Domingo, a French colony, was not an illegal trade, and such as would render the property of neutrals engaged in it liable to be considered as the property of enemies, and subject to confiscation? It was denied that St. Domingo was to be considered in its present state as a French colony. After various observations on these points, further proof was directed to be made of the property; and permission was given to both parties to

1799 *November* 7. produce information as to the state and condition of St. Domingo at that time.

THE IMMANUEL.

On the 15th of August, 1800, the cause was heard on further proof.

For the captors, *King's Advocate* and *Laurence.*

For the claimant, *Arnold* and *Sewell.*

[The Court dealt first with the question whether St. Domingo was to be considered as a French colony, and found that St. Domingo continues a French colony, and proceeded :]

1800 *August* 15.

SIR W. SCOTT.—Upon the mere question of property, as it respects all the goods as well as the ship, I see no reason to entertain a legal doubt. Considering them as neutral property, I shall proceed to the principal question in the case, viz., whether neutral property engaged in a direct traffic between the enemy and his colonies is to be considered by this Court as liable to confiscation? And first with respect to the goods.

Upon the breaking out of a war, it is the right of neutrals to carry on their accustomed trade, with an exception of the particular cases of a trade to blockaded places, or in contraband articles (in both which cases their property is liable to be condemned), and of their ships being liable to visitation and search; in which case, however, they are entitled to freight and expenses. I do not mean to say that in the accidents of a war the property of neutrals may not be variously entangled and endangered. In the nature of human connections, it is hardly possible that inconveniences of this kind should be altogether avoided. Some neutrals will be unjustly engaged in covering the goods of the enemy, and others will be unjustly suspected of doing it. These inconveniences are more than fully balanced by the enlargement of their commerce; the trade of the belligerents is usually interrupted in a great degree, and falls in the same degree into the lap of neutrals. But without reference to accidents of one kind or other, the general rule is, that the neutral has a right to carry on, in time of war, his accustomed trade to the utmost extent of which that accustomed trade is capable. Very different is the case of a trade which the neutral has never possessed, which he holds by no title of use and habit in times of peace, and which, in fact, can obtain in war by no other title than by the success of the one belligerent against the other, and at the expense of that very belligerent under whose success he sets up his title; and such I take to be the colonial trade, generally speaking.

What is the colonial trade, generally speaking? It is a trade generally shut up to the exclusive use of the mother country to which the colony belongs, and this to a double use: that of supplying a market for the consumption of native commodities, and the other of furnishing to the mother country the peculiar commodities of the colonial regions; to these two purposes of the mother country, the general policy respecting colonies belonging to the states of Europe has restricted them. With respect to other countries, generally speaking, the colony has no existence; it is possible that indirectly and remotely such colonies may affect the commerce of other countries. The manufactures of Germany may find their way into Jamaica or Guadaloupe, and the sugar of Jamaica or Guadaloupe into the interior parts of Germany; but as to any direct communication or advantage resulting therefrom, Guadaloupe and Jamaica are no more to Germany than if they were settlements in the mountains of the moon; to commercial purposes they are not in the same planet. If they were annihilated it would make no chasm in the commercial map of Hamburg. If Guadaloupe could be sunk in the sea by the effect of hostility at the beginning of a war, it would be a mighty loss to France, as Jamaica would be to England, if it could be made the subject of a similar act of violence. But such events would find their way into the chronicles of other countries as events of disinterested curiosity, and nothing more.

Upon the interruption of a war, what are the rights of belligerents and neutrals respectively regarding such places? It is an indubitable right of the belligerent to possess himself of such places, as of any other possession of his enemy. This is his common right, but he has the certain means of carrying such a right into effect if he has a decided superiority at sea. Such colonies are dependent for their existence, as colonies, on

1800 *August* 15. THE IMMANUEL. Sir W. Scott.

foreign supplies; if they cannot be supplied and defended they must fall to the belligerent of course; and if the belligerent chooses to apply his means to such an object, what right has a third party, perfectly neutral, to step in and prevent the execution? No existing interest of his is affected by it; he can have no right to apply to his own use the beneficial consequences of the mere act of the belligerent, and to say, "True it is, you have by force of arms forced such places out of the exclusive possession of the enemy, but I will share the benefit of the conquest, and by sharing its benefits prevent its progress. You have in effect, and by lawful means, turned the enemy out of the possession which he had exclusively maintained against the whole world, and with whom we had never presumed to interfere; but we will interpose to prevent his absolute surrender by the means of that very opening which the prevalence of your arms alone has affected. Supplies shall be sent and their products shall be exported. You have lawfully destroyed his monopoly, but you shall not be permitted to possess it yourself. We insist to share the fruits of your victories, and your blood and treasure have been expended, not for your own interest, but for the common benefit of others."

Upon these grounds, it cannot be contended to be a right of neutrals to intrude into a commerce which had been uniformly shut against them, and which is now forced open merely by the pressure of war; for when the enemy, under an entire inability to supply his colonies and to export their products, affects to open them to neutrals, it is not his will but his necessity that changes his system; that change is the direct and unavoidable consequence of the compulsion of war—it is a measure not of French councils, but of British force.

Upon these and other grounds, which I shall not at present enumerate, an instruction issued at an early period for the purpose of preventing the communication of neutrals with the colonies of the enemy, intended, I presume, to be carried into effect on the same footing on which the prohibition had been legally enforced in the war of 1756, a period when, Mr. Justice Blackstone observes, the decisions on the law of nations proceeding from the Court of Appeals were known and revered by every State in Europe.

Upon further inquiry it turned out that one favoured nation, the Americans, had in times of peace been permitted, by special convention, to exercise a certain very limited commerce with those colonies of the French, and it consisted with justice that that case should be specially provided for; but no justice required that the provision should extend beyond the necessities of that case. Whatever goes beyond is not given to the demands of strict justice, but is matter of relaxation and concession.

Different degrees of relaxation have been expressed in different instructions issued at various times during the existence of the war. It is admitted that no such relaxation has gone the length of authorising a direct commerce of neutrals between the mother country of the enemy and its colonies, because such a commerce could not be admitted without a total surrender of the principle; for allow such a commerce to neutrals, and the mother country of the enemy recovers, with some increase of expense, the direct market of the colonies and the direct influx of their productions; it enjoys as before the duties of import and export, the same facilities of sale and supply, and the mass of public inconvenience is very slightly diminished. Even supposing that this trade is carried on with integrity (which it is difficult to hope under all the temptations and opportunities of fraud which a direct intercourse will supply), there is every reason to believe that the ancient monopoly will, in effect, revive itself without the aid of exclusive prohibitions. The force of long established connection, and of ancient habits of trade, would in a great measure preserve for a time to the mother country its ancient exclusive commerce with colonies, although the communication might be legally open to the merchants of other countries.

Much argument has been employed on grounds of commercial analogy: *this trade* is allowed; that trade is not more injurious; *why not that* to be considered *as* equally permitted? The obvious answer is, that the true rule to this Court is the text of the instructions. What is not found therein permitted is understood to be prohibited, upon this plain principle: that the colony trade is generally prohibited, and that whatever is not specially relaxed continues in a state of interdiction. The utmost that could be contended would be that a commerce exactly *ejusdem generis et gradûs* would be entitled to the favour of the permission; but the relaxation is not to be extended by construction, particularly where

1800 *August* 15.

THE IMMANUEL.

Sir W. Scott.

authority has been gradual in its relaxation. Where it has distinguished and stopped short in several stages, individuals have no right to go further, upon a private speculation of their own, that authority might as well have gone further. It is argued that the neutral can import the manufactures of France to his own country and from thence directly to the French colony. Why not immediately from France, since the same purpose is effected? It is to be answered that it is effected in a manner more consistent with the general rights of neutrals, and less subservient to the special convenience of the enemy. If a Hamburg merchant imports the manufactures of France into his own country (which he will rarely do if he has like manufactures of his own, but which in all cases he has an uncontrollable right to do), and exports them afterwards to the French colony, which he does not in their original French character, but as goods which, by importation, had become a part of the national stock of his own neutral country, they come to that colony with all the inconvenience of aggravated delay and expense; so if he imports from the colony to Hamburg, and afterwards to France, the commodities of the colony, they come to the mother country under a proportionable disadvantage; in short, the rule presses upon the supply at both extremities, and therefore, if any considerations of advantage may influence the judgment of a belligerent country in the enforcement of the right which upon principle it possesses, to interfere with its enemy's colonial trade, it is in that shape of this trade that considerations of this nature have their chief and most effective operation.

It is an argument rather of a more legal nature than any derived from these general topics of commercial policy that variations are made in the commercial systems of every country in wars and on account of wars, by means of which neutrals are admitted and invited into different kinds of trade, for which they stand usually excluded, and if so, no one belligerent country has a right to interfere with neutrals for acting under variations of a like kind made for similar reasons in the commercial policy of its enemy. And certainly if this proposition could be maintained without any limitation, that wherever any variation whatever is made during a war and on account of the state of war, the party who makes it binds himself in all the variations to which the necessities of the

1800 *August* 15.

THE IMMANUEL.

Sir W. Scott.

enemy can compel him, the whole colony trade of the enemy is legalised; and the instructions which are directed against any part are equally unjust and impertinent; for it is not denied that some such variations may be found in the commercial policy of this country itself, although some that have been cited are not exactly of that nature. The opening of free ports is not necessarily a measure arising from the demands of war; it is frequently a peace measure in the colonial system of every country. There are others which more directly arise out of the necessities of war: the admission of foreigners into the merchant service, as well as into the military service of this country; the permission given to vessels to import commodities not the growth, produce, and manufacture of the country to which they belong, and other relaxations of the act of navigation and other regulations founded thereon. These, it is true, take place in war, and arise out of a state of war; but then they do not arise out of the predominance of the enemy's force, or out of any necessity resulting therefrom; and that I take to be the true foundation of the principle. It is not every convenience or even every necessity arising out of a state of war, but that necessity which arises out of the impossibility of otherwise providing against the urgency of distress inflicted by the hand of a superior enemy, that can be admitted to produce such an effect. Thus, in time of war every country admits foreigners into its general service—every country obtains, by the means of neutral vessels, those products of the enemy's country which it cannot possibly receive either by means of *his* navigation or its own. These are ordinary measures to which every country has resort in every war, whether prosperous or adverse. They arise, it is true, out of a state of war, but are totally independent of its events, and have therefore no common origin with these compelled relaxations of the colonial monopoly; these are acts of distress, signals of defeat and depression; they are no better than partial surrenders to the force of the enemy, for the mere purpose of preventing a total dispossession. I omit other observations which have been urged and have their force; it is sufficient that the variations alluded to stand upon grounds of a most distinguishable nature.

Upon the whole view of the case as it concerns the goods shipped at Bordeaux, I am of opinion that they are liable to confiscation.

1800 August 15. — The Immanuel. — Sir W. Scott.

I do not know that any decision has yet been pronounced upon this subject; but till I am better instructed by the judgment of a superior tribunal I shall continue to hold that I am not authorised, either by general legal principles applying to this commerce or by the letter of the King's instructions, to restore goods, although neutral property, passing in direct voyages between the mother country of the enemy and its colonies. I see no favourable distinction between an outward voyage and a return voyage. I consider the intent of the instruction to apply equally to both communications, though the return voyage is the only one specifically mentioned.

The only remaining question respects the ship; it belongs to the same proprietors, and if the goods could be considered as properly contraband, would on that account be liable to confiscation, for in the case of clear contraband this is the clear rule. I incline to apply a more favourable one in the present case. It is a case in which a neutral might more easily misapprehend the extent of his own rights; it is a case of less simplicity, and in which he acted without the notice of former decisions upon the subject. The ship came from Hamburg in the commencement of the voyage; she was not picked up for this particular occasion, but was intended to be employed in her owner's general commerce. Attending to these considerations, I shall go no further than to pronounce for a forfeiture of freight and expenses, with a restitution of the vessel.

Cargo, taken in at Bordeaux, condemned; ship restored, without freight (*a*).

(*a*) On the same day, in the case of the *Rose*, which was a case of an American ship going from Amsterdam to Guadaloupe, with an assorted cargo, claimed on behalf of American merchants.

The Court: With respect to this case it differs only from the last, in this circumstance: that it is the case of a voyage from one enemy colony to the colony of another enemy allied in the war. I am of opinion that this does not form a solid distinction. On the principles which I have laid down, I think it would be impossible to maintain the rule of law without applying it also in this extent.

Sentence the same.

THE CHRISTOPHER.

[2 C. Rob. 210.]

Condemnation—Enemy Prize Court—Captured Ship in Port of Ally.

A sentence of an enemy Prize Court in relation to a captured ship then lying in the port of an ally is valid.

1799 *November* 18.

THIS was a case of a British prize ship taken by the French and carried into the Spanish port of St. Sebastian, from whence the ship's papers were transmitted to France, and a sentence of condemnation passed at Bayonne, May 9th, the ship still lying in the Spanish port. The ship was then sold to the present claimant, a merchant of Altona, and was sailing at the time of capture (July, 1799) in ballast from St. Sebastian to Altona.

SIR W. SCOTT.—This is a case materially differing from those in which condemnation has passed on ships carried into a neutral country. Those proceedings have been held illegal, principally because it was not to be presumed that a neutral government would so far depart from the duties of neutrality as to permit the exercise of that last and crowning act of hostility, if I may so express myself: the condemnation of the property of one belligerent to the other, thereby confirming and securing him in the acquisition of his enemy's property by hostile means. But this will not hold good with respect to condemnations passed on ships brought into the ports of an ally in the war. In such cases there is nothing to prevent the government from proceeding to that last act of hostility; there is a common interest between them on the subject, and both governments may be presumed to authorize any measures conducing to give effect to their arms, and to consider each other's ports as mutually subservient. I am, therefore, inclined to hold such a condemnation sufficient in regard to property taken in the course of the operations of a common war.

As the facts of purchase appear to be sufficiently proved on the further proof that has been exhibited, I shall decree restitution of this ship for the claimants.

Ship restored.

[2 C. Rob. 239.]

THE PERSEVERANCE.

Restitution—British Ship—Wrongful Sale to Neutral—Repairs—Amelioration.

Ship purchased by a neutral under illegal condemnation in Norway restored to original owner: allowance made under special circumstances for sum expended by purchaser on repairs.

1799 *November* 22; affirmed *Aug.* 10, 1803.

THIS was a case of a ship that had been a British prize, sold under a sentence of condemnation in Norway to a Swedish merchant, and was seized on coming to the Isle of Guernsey on the part of the former owner. An appearance being given for the neutral purchaser, it was submitted, on his part, that if the vessel was to be restored to the former owner under the authority of the *Flad Oyen* (a), it was still but reasonable that some compensation should be made for considerable repairs which the ship had undergone, in the possession of the Swedish purchaser, to the amount of 205*l.*

SIR W. SCOTT.—It is a general rule, undoubtedly, that whoever purchases under an illegal title does it at his own peril, and must take the consequence (both in his purchase and in his own subsequent expenditure upon it) of his inattention to his own security; but I think this was not a title so notoriously bad, at the time when this purchase was made, as to bring it fairly under the application of the general rule to its utmost extent.

The Court has had occasion to inquire into the validity of such purchases, and has, upon a regular discussion, pronounced them invalid; and if, henceforth, neutrals shall continue to purchase under such flimsy titles, they must take the consequences of their own imprudence. But it may be too much to apply this maxim without any alleviation to a person who has heretofore bought under a practice, which, though illegal, was too prevalent in some ports of the north of Europe. It appears that a sum of money has been expended on the repairs of this vessel by which the claimant will be benefited, though not to the amount of the sum laid out. Something must be allowed for wear and tear; and

(a) *Ante*, p. 78.

besides, the party who has expended this sum has had the use of the vessel in the meantime. I shall therefore not allow the whole sum, but I shall take a moiety; and I shall allow that in consideration of the benefit which the original owners are likely to receive from the amelioration.

1799 *November* 22.

THE PERSEVERANCE.

Sir W. Scott.

Sum claimed, 205*l.*
Decreed, 102*l.* 10*s.*

Ship restored to the former owner on salvage.

THE CAPE OF GOOD HOPE

[2 C. Rob. 274.]

AND ITS DEPENDENCIES.

Prize—Transports—Right to Share—Military Character.

Transports are not primarily entitled to share in a prize taken by a squadron to which they are attached. But they may acquire an interest in a prize if they have been given a military character, and become associated with a fighting squadron with an *animus capiendi.*

1799 *December* 10; affirmed *May* 24, 1802.

THIS was a case of an allegation given on the part of the Admiralty, claiming an interest in the capture of the *Cape of Good Hope*, in virtue of several non-commissioned East India ships, asserted to have assisted in that enterprise.

SIR W. SCOTT.—This question arises on the claim of certain East India ships, or rather of the Admiralty on their behalf, to share in the capture made at the Cape of Good Hope. It appears by reference to the gazettes, and in the allegation, and in all the evidence, as far as it is necessary for me to state it, that these ships were employed to carry a number of troops to the Cape of Good Hope. The greatest part of the naval operations necessary for the reduction of that colony had been performed before the arrival of these ships; and there appears to have been only one particular piece of military service performed on the part of the navy after their arrival, and on which only one of these ships was employed: that vessel will undoubtedly be allowed to share. As to the rest, although it must be admitted on all sides that the East India Company have performed services in respect to this expedition which may entitle them to the thanks of their country, yet

1799 December 10. THE CAPE OF GOOD HOPE. Sir W. Scott.

the question of legal merit, whether they will be entitled to share in the proceeds of this prize, will depend on very different considerations.

It is not stated in what way the agreement was made with these ships, whether it was to act in a military capacity or not; if it was to act in a military character, that might nearly decide the question. But nothing is said on this subject in the plea, and therefore I must infer that no such ground of pretension could be sustained. All that is said is "that they carried out General Clarke and his troops." It is perfectly clear that, at the time of leaving the coasts of Brazil, it was perfectly unknown to these ships for what attack these troops were conveying; whether, by virtue of their contract, they were to stay at any place, or come away after the troops were landed at such place, is wrapped in complete silence; and therefore, for want of any more particular description, I can look only to their general character, which is that of merchant vessels commissioned against the French, but having no commission against that enemy who was the particular object of this expedition. Whatever their force may have been, I do not see that they can be considered in their original character as more than transport vessels, liable to be called upon occasionally to act with alacrity and vigour (for British vessels of any character are liable to be so called upon on extraordinary occasions of public necessity), but not deriving from that circumstance, as far as this expedition was concerned, any title to invest them with a military character, for the mere conveyance of troops would have no such effect. At the same time, it is true that a military character might be afterwards impressed upon them by the nature and course of their subsequent employment. If they have been associated to act in conjunction with the King's fleet, and did so act, they may acquire an interest which, on proper application, will be sure to meet with due attention. The question for me to consider, then, will be whether they have acquired that military character or not. Their pretensions have been put on several grounds. It is first said that they were associated with the fleet; mere association will not do. The plea must go further and show in what capacity they were associated, and that capacity must be directly military. Transports are associated with fleets and armies for various purposes connected with or subservient to the military uses of those fleets and armies. But if they are transports merely, and as such are employed simply in the transportation of stores or men, they do not rise above their proper mercantile character in consequence of such an employment. The employment must be that of an immediate application to the purposes of direct military operations in which they are to take a part.

It is next placed on the ground of intimidation, and it is said that when the enemy is *proved* to have been intimidated, where it is not matter of inference but of *actual proof*, the assistance arising from intimidation is not to be considered as constructive merely, but an actual and effective co-operation. But I take that not to be quite correct, for a hundred instances might be mentioned in which actual intimidation might be produced without any co-operation having been given. Suppose the case of a small frigate going to attack an enemy's vessel, and four or five large merchant ships, unconscious of the transaction, should appear in sight. They might be objects of terror to the enemy, but no one would say that such a terror would entitle them to share; though the fact of terror was ever so strongly proved, there would not be that co-operation, nor that active assistance, which the law requires to entitle non-commissioned vessels to be considered as joint captors. What is the intimidation alleged? "That the Dutch forces were about to make an attack on the British army, but on the appearance of these fourteen ships desisted." This was an intimidation, of which the ships were totally unconscious, and which would have been just as effectually produced by a fleet of mere transports; and I see no principle on which I could pronounce these ships entitled on which I should not be also obliged to pronounce any fleet of merchantmen entitled in a similar situation, for any number of large ships, known to be British and not known to be merchantmen, would have produced the same effect. The intimidation was entirely passive; there was no *animus* nor design on their part, nor even knowledge of the fact, for it was not till the next day, when their commodore returned from Lord Keith, that they knew anything of the matter, or ever thought of the terror that they had assisted in exciting. I take it to be incontrovertibly true, that no case can be alleged in which a terror so excited has been held to enure to the benefit

1799 *December* 10. — THE CAPE OF GOOD HOPE. — Sir W. Scott.

of a non-commissioned vessel. Another ground on which it is put, and which it may be proper for me to advert to, is the ground of analogy. That it is a case of assistance, analogous to that of joint chasing, on which it is said to be sufficient if the non-commissioned ship puts itself in motion; and the cases of the *Twee Gesuster* (*a*) in the last war, and the *Le*

(*a*) This was a case of a Dutch ship taken 31st December, 1780.

The circumstances of the case were that on the morning of the 31st the prize in question of 300 tons and 16 men was discovered by two armed cruisers, the *Providence* and *Spitfire*, each manned with 16 men (the *Providence* being commissioned, and the *Spitfire* not commissioned, against the Dutch), when they immediately chased; the *Providence* first reached the prize; the *Spitfire* being then distant about one English mile soon afterwards came up, and immediately afterwards the prize was seized by the *Providence* and the *Spitfire*, her prisoners and papers secured, some in the *Providence*, and some in the *Spitfire*, and the master of the *Spitfire* was put on board the prize with several men, and the *Providence* left the prize with the *Spitfire* to convey her to Dartmouth.

These facts were acknowledged, and the *Spitfire* was allowed to have been a joint chaser by the *Providence*.

The sentence of the Judge of the High Court of Admiralty, 21st June, 1783, pronounced the *Providence* to be *the captor*, but that the *Spitfire was aiding and abetting*, and decreed the *Spitfire* to take half the share she would have been entitled to had she had a commission against the Dutch.

This part of the sentence being appealed from on the part of the *Providence*, the Proctor of the Admiralty intervened, 15th February, 1785, and prayed that such part of the prize as the *Spitfire* would have been entitled to, if commissioned, might be condemned as a droit of Admiralty.

On the 8th of March, 1785, the Lords of Appeal pronounced for the interest of the King, in his office of Admiral, and that such proportion of the prize as would have belonged to the *Spitfire*, if commissioned, was liable to confiscation as a droit and perquisite of Admiralty, and condemned the prize "*as taken by the private ship of war the Providence, and the non-commissioned ship the Spitfire*," and directed the same to be shared in proportion accordingly. Present: Lord Camden, Lord Grantly, Sir Joseph Yorke, Sir Lloyd Kenyon (Master of the Rolls).

A circumstance not unworthy of notice in this case, though not affecting the judgment, was that it was stated on the part of the *Spitfire*, "that on the commencement of hostilities against the Dutch, the owners of the *Spitfire*, fitted her out as a private ship of war, sent her on a cruise against his Majesty's enemies, and applied for letters of marque; that the Commissioners of the Admiralty granted a warrant to the judge of the Admiralty to issue letters of marque and general reprisal against the Dutch, to Tessier, the master of the *Spitfire*, on the 29th of December, 1780; but by reason of the then great flood of business in the Admiralty Court, the

Franc (a), have been relied upon. I see no ground on which the analogy can be supported; the cases cited were of a very different

letters of marque could not be obtained under seal, till the 1st day of January, 1781, and that this capture was made on the 31st December."

This was stated among other points in the *præsertim* of appeal, but the claim of the non-commissioned captor was not allowed. From which it appears that the endeavours of the party to obtain his commission, aided even by the warrant of the Lords of the Admiralty for its passing, will not be sufficient to vest any interest on intermediate captures till the commission is actually issued.

(a) The *Le Franc.*

This was a French East India ship taken by several vessels composing part of a British East India fleet, 24th June, 1793.

Of the ships in question, the *Glatton*, Captain Drummond, had not taken out a letter of marque; the others were commissioned as private ships of war.

On the part of the *Glatton* an appearance was given, praying a decision on the interests on the question of law. The facts being admitted on all sides "that she was not a commissioned ship, and that she was materially instrumental to the capture," the Proctor of the Admiralty appeared for the King in his office of Admiralty, praying that such proportion of the prize in question as would have been condemned to the *Glatton*, if she had been a commissioned ship, might be pronounced liable to confiscation to the King in his office of Admiralty as a droit and perquisite of Admiralty.

The sentence of the High Court of Admiralty condemned the prize as taken by six private ships of war, and the *Glatton*, but condemned the *Glatton's* share as a droit and perquisite of Admiralty.

The facts as to the situation and merits of the *Glatton* are thus represented in the words of the certificate of the commanders of the six private ships of war presented to the Lords of the Admiralty annexed to the memorial on the part of the *Glatton*, praying to be rewarded:—

"We, the subscribed commanders of the six duly commissioned private ships of war, which with the non-commissioned ship *Glatton*, Charles Drummond, commander, captured the French prize *Le Franc*, do hereby certify, that at daylight on the 24th of June, 1793, the *Glatton* was from 10 to 15 miles to windward of our ships, and at the same time the prize was upon the *Glatton's* weather quarter, distant about three miles steering to the northward; Captain Drummond thereupon (supposing her to be an enemy) kept the wind until he found the *Glatton* could weather her, and then wore and chased the prize until she was brought to by the *Ceres*, and some of the other ships. And we do further certify, that had the *Glatton* not been to windward, it would have been impossible for the other ships to have come up with the prize, as when she had discovered the ships to leeward, she might have kept to windward and got off had she not been prevented by the *Glatton*. Witness our hands the 25th day of March, 1795."

In the same case a claim was given for the *Barwel*, and several other ships of this fleet, stating, "that they sailed as an *associated* and *confederated* fleet for mutual defence by particular

1799 December 10.

THE CAPE OF GOOD HOPE.

Sir W. Scott.

nature; in both of them the non-commissioned ships chased *animo capiendi*, and contributed materially, in the case of the *Le Franc*, directly and immediately, to the act of capture. In the present case these ships approached, it is true, the coast of the Cape of Good Hope, but with no *animus capiendi*, with no hostile purpose entertained by themselves; for they were totally ignorant of the objects of the expedition. It is, moreover, obvious to remark, that all cases of joint chasing at sea differ so materially from the cases of conjunct operations at land, that they are with great danger of inaccuracy applied to illustrate each other. In joint chasing at sea there is the overt act of pursuing, by which the design and actual purpose of the party may be ascertained, and much intimidation may be produced; but in cases of conjunct operations at land, it is not the mere intrusion even of a commissioned ship that would entitle parties to share. The words of the Act of Parliament direct, "That in all conjoint expeditions of the navy and army against any fortress upon the land directed by instructions from his Majesty, the flag and general officers, and commanders, and other officers, seamen, marines and soldiers, shall have such proportionable interest and property as his Majesty under his sign manual shall think fit to order and direct." The interest of the prize is given to the fleet and army, and it would not be the mere voluntary interposition of a privateer that would entitle her to share. It would be a very inconvenient doctrine that private ships of war, by watching an opportunity and intruding themselves into an expedition, which the public authority had in no degree committed to them, should be at liberty to say, "we *will* co-operate;" and that they should be permitted to derive an interest from such a spontaneous act to the disadvantage of those to whom the service was originally entrusted. Expeditions of this kind, designed by

direction of the East India Company; that they were all together on the evening of the 23rd June, 1793; that during the night some of the ships had separated; that on the morning of the 24th, about six o'clock, the *Barwel* perceived one of the said ships to the eastward; that the commodore made signal to the *Barwel* to chase; that after chasing three hours she came completely in sight of the said ships that had separated, and when she came up with them, &c., she found they had taken the prize in question."

The claim on the part of these ships was rejected.

1799 *December* 10.

THE CAPE OF GOOD HOPE.

Sir W. Scott.

the immediate authority of the state, belong exclusively to its own instruments whom it has selected for the purpose; and it might be attended with very grave obstruction to the public service of the country if private individuals could intrude themselves into such undertakings uninvited and under colour of their letter of marque. I think, therefore, that the cases of chasing at sea and of conjunct operations at land stand on different principles, and that there is little analogy which can make them clearly applicable to each other. It is next said that they were directed to hoist pennants; and that it was the opinion of a very high military (*a*) officer in a former case that the permission to wear the pennant did give the character of a King's ship; but the decision, in the very case in which that opinion was offered (in the capture of *Negapatam*), held that a ship, which in that case had worn a pennant, was not to be considered in a military character, but as a transport; the mere circumstance, therefore, that these ships, which were large ships, and had before carried pennants, and had taken them down only out of respect to the King's ships, and were desired to hoist them again, I cannot hold to be a sufficient proof that they were by that act taken and adopted into the military character. I can attribute no such effect to a mere act of civility and condescension.

In the next place, it is argued that these ships were actually employed in military service, although there is no such averment in the plea. It comes out in evidence only (by which I must observe the other party is deprived of the opportunity of counter-pleading) that their boats were employed in carrying provisions and military stores on shore; that was a service certainly, but not a service beyond the common extent of transport duty. They landed them, probably at the same time with the troops for whose use they were intended; and if not at the same time, still it is no more than what they were bound to do with the stores and provisions they carried.

It is likewise said that they received military orders, and if that

(*a*) The Advocate of the Admiralty had said, during the cause, that in the case of *Negapatam*, he had waited on Lord Hood, and had received his lordship's authority to state it, as his opinion, "that the permission of the admiral of the fleet to merchant vessels to wear pennants was considered as an act adopting them into the King's service for that occasion."

1799 December 10.

THE CAPE OF GOOD HOPE.

Sir W. Scott.

fact was sufficiently proved it might be material; but it is observable that not a single order is pleaded in the allegation except in respect to the *Bombay Castle.* That vessel, it appears, was sent under military orders to create a diversion; and I think I do not give too much to that ship when I say that this circumstance was sufficient to clothe her with a military character, being engaged in a military employment and exposed to danger: but it is argued that because orders were given to man this ship by detachments from the rest, that it will make the whole fleet entitled to be considered as acting likewise in a military capacity. Taking it upon the argument that this was done by orders directly from Lord Keith, I cannot think it would have that effect; for, in the first place, can it be denied that a commander-in-chief might exercise a power of impressing a number of their crews without giving to those ships anything of a military character? It is within the power of commanders on maritime expeditions to press persons of that description to assist in any particular service in such a case of public emergency. But no such orders are pleaded, nor by any means proved to have been given. The communication was carried on between Lord Keith and one particular person, Captain Rees, in the same manner as it would have been done if they had been mere transport vessels; and the only order mentioned was that the crew of the *Bombay Castle* should be increased.

The next military orders that are relied on are those for a draft of twenty men from each ship, for the purpose of drawing the artillery, &c., and I think the same observation would apply to these also; for I have no hesitation in saying that in a remote expedition like this the commanders of his Majesty's forces have a right to call into their service for such purpose the assistance of British mariners, and I hope and trust the time will never come when British mariners will think they are called beyond the line of their duty when they receive an order to that effect. The fact is that it was done rather by invitation, as a better mode of doing it, and the words of Captain Rees' deposition describe it as an address for volunteers rather than as an exercise of authority and command. These are the whole military services with the exception of those indefinite services on which much argument has been bestowed; I mean those referred to in Lord Keith's letter, in which Lord Keith acknowledges that these transports had contributed to the surrender. In the first place, a letter of that kind, written in the moment of victory, should not be too strictly interpreted as conveying any opinion of the writer on the minute parts of the transaction. Taking it, however, to be as argued, that it does show his sentiments at that moment on the matter, it is by no means conclusive upon the question. It might be erroneous in fact; much less can it be considered as conclusive in point of law. Lord Keith is not the only party. On the facts, it is not conclusive against others; and on the law, it is not conclusive against himself; for if he should be found to be mistaken as to the legal effect of such services, who would say that he would be concluded by this admission? However, looking at the letter carefully, I do not see that Lord Keith might not have written just in the same manner to a fleet of transports doing their duty with alacrity and zeal, as a general expression of thanks for the performance of those services in which they had been respectively employed.

1799 *December* 10.

THE CAPE OF GOOD HOPE.

Sir W. Scott.

Upon the whole of these facts, I feel myself obliged to pronounce that it has not been shown that these ships set out in an original military character, or that any military character has been subsequently impressed upon them by the nature and course of their employment; and therefore, however meritorious their services may have been, and however entitled they may be to the gratitude of their country, it will not entitle them to share in this valuable capture.

THE FRAU MARIA.

[2 C. Rob. 292.]

Practice—Marshal's Expenses—Commission of Appraisement—Liability of Captor.

A commission of appraisement and sale is an instrument, in the first instance, taken out by captors, and they primarily are answerable for the expense of the same.

1799 *December* 16.

THIS was a motion for a new commission of appraisement on the part of the claimant, on suggestion that the former commission had not been executed by the Marshal, as he had refused to return the commission till his expenses were paid. It was said that the commission of appraisement was an instrument taken out by the captors, and therefore that the expenses ought to

1799 *December* 16. THE FRAU MARIA.

be paid, in the first instance, by them; that the cause of this delay had been unknown to the claimants; that they would have been ready at all times to advance the expenses to have prevented the delay, by which the cargo had sustained a deterioration of 40 per cent.

The *King's Advocate* resisted the motion, saying that the delay complained of could not have happened but by the laches of the claimants, who were the persons to look to the due execution of commission.

Court.—It must be allowed, I think, that the parties in this case are *in pari delicto:* but I am desirous of laying down some rule to prevent the same inconvenience from happening in future. I am of opinion that the captor is the person who is to make the payment in the first instance. He is the person who puts the commission into the hands of the officer, and desires him to execute it. By whom are the other fees of office paid?

Registrar.—By the captor.

Court.—Then what ground is there to pretend that there should be any distinction? That the claimant may be ultimately interested is a matter of future consideration. It may be proper that the captor should be indemnified; but I am of opinion that the captor is answerable in the first instance, and I cannot conceive that the Marshal is bound to look elsewhere. Where it is done for the accommodation of the claimant, that will be a matter to be settled between them; but I shall certainly hold that the captor is liable for the expenses in the first instance, though they may be ultimately to be divided between both parties. I shall direct a new appraisement in this case, and, as the commission is prayed by the claimant in this instance, it must be at his expense; but in future cases it must be as I have intimated.

THE SPECULATION. [2 C. Rob. 293.]

Capture—Adjudication—Irregularity of Procedure—Captors deprived of Costs.

Irregularity in bringing evidence before the Court is ground for depriving captors of costs.

THIS was a case of a Danish vessel, taken on a voyage from Dunkirk to Bordeaux, 13th June, 1799, and claimed, together with the cargo, for —— Lund, described in some of the papers as master of the vessel. 1799 *December* 16.

During the argument.

Court.—I perceive these examinations are taken at Jersey. The commissioners must understand that this is not the proper mode of proceeding. After the depositions have been taken and transmitted, the commissioners are not to go on examining afterwards; neither is it proper that the captor should take out the whole of the crew, and then come in afterwards with a subsequent examination. I shall pay no attention to this man's evidence.

[After dealing with the facts, the Court proceeded.]

The third deposition is stated to have been taken at the instance of the captors, and it now appears that they took out all but two persons from the captured ship. I cannot help thinking that to leave only two persons has the appearance of something very like a management and a tampering with the evidence. From the return of the commission it does not appear that there might not have been more than two on board, therefore it remains wholly unexplained how this evidence has been taken and introduced out of due time. I desire it may be intimated to the commissioners that they have not acted regularly, and that in future they are not to show so much facility to captors if such a thing should ever be required of them again. After this view of the case I am not disposed to aid the captors more than I am compelled to do. As far as the Court has any discretion they shall have no favour; the attempt to introduce evidence irregularly taken and liable to the suspicion of being unduly obtained will always work that conse-

1799 December 16. The Speculation.

quence at least. As to the property of the ship no doubt is raised, and the cargo does not appear liable to any solid objection. I am not disposed, therefore, to order further proof; and I am further of opinion that the captors are not entitled to that protection which the Court would otherwise have given them on a seizure of this nature, by directing the claimant to pay their costs.

[2 C. Rob. 298.]

THE CALYPSO.

Blockade—Notification—Loading of Cargo—Condemnation.

The continued loading of cargo after notice of a blockade may be presumed to have come to the knowledge of the master or agent of the ship renders her liable to condemnation.

1799 December 19.

THIS was a case arising on the blockade of the United Provinces, respecting the time allowed for the communication of intelligence and the consequence of taking in a cargo after due notice of the blockade. It appeared that the ship sailed from Rotterdam on the 4th of May, that the cargo had been begun to be laden on the 4th of April, and that remaining parts were taken in so late as the 20th.

SIR W. SCOTT.—I think I am under the necessity of saying that the notification of the blockade must have been known at Rotterdam on the 15th of April, as it has appeared in evidence in another cause that it was known to the Prussian Consul at Amsterdam on the 12th. I am therefore compelled to say that the continuing to take in a cargo after the time when the party was bound to take notice of the notification of blockade will be sufficient to render the ship liable to condemnation. This is the determination which I am bound to make in conformity to the principles which I have before laid down on the subject of blockade.

THE WAR ONSKAN.

[2 C. Rob. 299.]

Recapture—Neutral Property—Salvage.

Salvage, not formerly given on recapture of neutral property, given, owing to the rapacious proceedings of French cruisers and French Courts of prize.

1799 December 19.

THIS was a case of a Swedish ship, taken by the French on a voyage to Oporto, and retaken by a British cruiser, October 26th, 1799.

In opposition to the demand of salvage, which had been allowed in various instances during the present war, it was said, that it had not been the practice of former wars to grant salvage on the recapture of neutral property; that in the present case there was the less reason for it, as the vessel was seized only on account of the cargo, which, according to the French laws, would be a cause of inquiry only and not of condemnation; and that the French prize master had expressly engaged that the vessel should be restored.

SIR W. SCOTT.—I do not mean to lay down any general rule on this subject, nor am I so fond of doing that as gentlemen may be ready to propose it. It has certainly been the practice of this Court lately to grant salvage on recapture of neutral property out of the hands of the French; and I see no reason at the present moment to depart from it. I know perfectly well that it is not the modern practice of the law of nations (*a*) to grant salvage on

(*a*) In the early periods of English history (and perhaps much later) there are to be found traces of a pretension to appropriate to the captor the ships and goods of neutral merchants that were taken by one belligerent out of the hands of his enemy. *Litera ad Regem Portugalliæ, super bonis de guerra lucratis responsiva*, 31 Ed. 3, A.D. 1357; Rym. Fœd. vol. vi. p. 14; and again, an. 2 H. 4, Rym. Fœd. vol. viii. p. 203. To the master of the *Teutonic* Order of Prussia. In the former instance a strong remonstrance had been made on the part of Portugal, and the answer, asserting the property to be legally acquired to the captors, is very full and explicit. In the latter instance an embargo had been laid on British property, on account of the detention by the captors; and this fact of recapture from the enemy was deemed a sufficient justification on the part of the English monarch to found a demand that the embargo should be taken off. In later times a more

1799 *December* 19.

THE WAR ONSKAN.

Sir W. Scott.

recapture of neutral vessels; and upon this plain principle, that the liberation of a clear neutral from the hand of the enemy is no essential service rendered to him, inasmuch as that same enemy would be compelled by the tribunals of his own country, after he had carried the neutral into port, to release him with costs and damages for the injurious seizure and detention. This proceeds upon the supposition that those tribunals would duly respect the obligations of the law of nations—a presumption which, in the wars of civilized states, each belligerent is bound to entertain in their respective dealings with neutrals. But it being notorious to all Europe, in the present war, that there has been a constant struggle maintained between the governing powers of France, for the time being, and its maritime tribunals, which should most outrage the rights of neutral property: the one by its decrees, or the other by its decisions; the liberation of neutral property out of their possession has been deemed, not only in the judgment of our Courts, but in that of neutrals themselves, a most substantial benefit conferred upon them in a delivery from danger, against which no clearness and innocence of conduct could afford any protection; and a salvage for such service has not only been decreed, but thankfully paid, ever since these wild hostilities have been declared and practised by France, against all acknowledged principles of the law of nations and of natural justice. When these lawless and irregular practices are shown to have ceased, the

equitable practice has prevailed, and neutral vessels, taken out of possession of the enemy, have been restored, even without salvage, both in our Prize Courts and in France, provided the property was affected by no circumstances that would have incurred condemnation in the Court of the enemy.

Such was the limitation expressed in the ordonnances of France, Code des Prises, an 1784: "Sa Majesté a jugé pendant la dernière guerre, que la reprise du navire neutre faite par un corsaire *François* (*lorsque le navire neutre n'étoit pas chargé de marchandises prohibées, ni dans le cas d'être confisqué par l'ennemi*) étoit nulle." See various decisions, Cons. des Prises, 1784, vol. ii. pp. 725, 1024 and 1049.

Whether the dangers to which neutral property has been exposed from French Courts and French cruisers during this war have been sufficient to form an exception from the old rule, the reader will, in some degree, be able to judge for himself, by a summary view of their edicts, and the general character of their cruisers, according to the estimation of their own writers.

rule of paying salvage for the liberation of neutral property must cease likewise. But of that fact no evidence whatever is offered, excepting that the French prize-master said, "That the vessel would not be prize, only the cargo." A thousand motives might extract such a declaration as this from him, very little connected with its truth. It might be only to conciliate the master, and purchase from him a corrupt testimony respecting the cargo. When the ship was once within the grip of a French Admiralty Court, it was much beyond the power (supposing it within the inclination) of that master to say with certainty that she would ever find her way out of it. No proof is offered that the maritime tribunals of France have in any degree corrected either the spirit or the form of their proceedings respecting neutral property generally; and therefore I shall not think myself authorised to depart from the practice that has been pursued of awarding a salvage to the captors.

1799 *December* 19.

THE WAR ONSKAN.

Sir W. Scott.

THE HARMONY.

[2 C. Rob. 322.]

National Character—Domicil—Time of Stay in Foreign Country.

The length of time for which a person remains in a country is the chief test of his domicil, and if a person visits a foreign country for a special purpose, the length of time during which he remains in it may negative the inference to be drawn from the temporary character of the stay in the first instance.

1800 *January* 16; affirmed *July* 11, 1803.

THIS was one of several American vessels in which a claim had been reserved for part of the cargo, on further proof to be made of the national character of G. W. Murray, who appeared in the original case as a partner of a house of trade in America, but personally resident in France. Restitution had been decreed in the several claims to the house of trade in America, with a reservation of the share of this partner. The case was argued on this day, and again, on production of further affidavits, at several times.

Judgment pronounced November 19th, 1800.

SIR W. SCOTT.—This is a question which arises on several parcels of property claimed on behalf of G. W. Murray, and it is in all of

1800 January 16. — THE HARMONY. — Sir W. Scott.

them a question of residence or domicil, which, I have often had occasion to observe, is in itself a question of considerable difficulty, depending on a great variety of circumstances, hardly capable of being defined by any general precise rules. The active spirit of commerce now abroad in the world still further increases this difficulty by increasing the variety of local situations, in which the same individual is to be found at no great distance of time, and by that sort of extended circulation, if I may so call it, by which the same transaction communicates with different countries, as in the present cases, in which the same trading adventures have their origin (perhaps) in America, travel to France, from France to England, from England back to America again, without enabling us to assign accurately the exact legal effect of the local character of every particular portion of this divided transaction.

In deciding such cases the necessary freedom of commerce imposes likewise the duty of a particular attention and delicacy, and strict principle of law must not be pressed too eagerly against it; and I have before had occasion to remark that the particular situation of America, in respect to distance, seems still more particularly to entitle the merchants of that country to some favourable distinctions. They live at a great distance from Europe; they have not the same open and ready and constant correspondence with individuals of the several nations of Europe that these persons have with each other; they are on that very account more likely to have their mercantile confidence in Europe abused, and therefore to have more frequent calls for a personal attendance to their own concerns, and it is to be expected that when the necessity of their affairs calls them across the Atlantic, they should make rather a longer stay in the country where they are called than foreign merchants who step from a neighbouring country in Europe, to which every day offers a convenient opportunity of return.

In considering this particular case, it may not be improper to remark that circumstances occur in the evidence that address themselves forcibly to private commiseration, remarking, however, at the same time, that public duty can allow only a very limited effect to such considerations, and still less to another that has been pressed upon me, that the money, if restored, is to go in payment of debts due to British creditors from the bankrupt estate of this unfortunate person. My business is to inquire whether he is entitled to recover it, without regard to the probable application of it, if it finds its way again into his possession.

Of the few principles that can be laid down generally, I may venture to hold that time is the grand ingredient in constituting domicil. I think that hardly enough is attributed to its effects; in most cases it is unavoidably conclusive. It is not infrequently said, that if a person comes only for a special purpose that shall not fix a domicil. This is not to be taken in an unqualified latitude and without some respect had to the time which such a purpose may or shall occupy, for if the purpose be of a nature that may, probably, or does, actually detain the person for a great length of time, I cannot but think that a general residence might grow upon the special purpose. A special purpose may lead a man to a country where it shall detain him the whole of his life. A man comes here to follow a law suit; it may happen—and, indeed, is often used as a ground of vulgar and unfounded reproach (unfounded as a matter of just reproach, though the fact may be true) on the laws of this country—that it may last as long as himself. Some suits are famous in our judicial history for having even outlived generations of suitors. I cannot but think that against such a long residence the plea of an original special purpose could not be averred. It must be inferred in such a case that other purposes forced themselves upon him and mixed themselves with his original design, and impressed upon him the character of the country where he resided. Suppose a man comes into a belligerent country at or before the beginning of a war, it is certainly reasonable not to bind him too soon to an acquired character, and to allow him a fair time to disengage himself; but if he continues to reside during a good part of the war, contributing, by payment of taxes and other means, to the strength of that country, I am of opinion that he could not plead his special purpose with any effect against the rights of hostility. If he could, there would be no sufficient guard against the fraud and abuses of masked, pretended, original, and sole purposes of a long continued residence. There is a time which will estop such a plea; no rule can fix the time *à priori*, but such a time there *must* be.

1800 *January* 16.

THE HARMONY.

Sir W. Scott.

In proof of the efficacy of mere time, it is not impertinent to remark, that the same quantity of business, which would not fix a domicil in a certain space of time, would nevertheless have that effect if distributed over a larger space of time. Suppose an American comes to Europe with six contemporary cargoes, of which he had the present care and management, meaning to return to America immediately; they would form a different case from that of the same American, coming to any particular country of Europe, with one cargo, and fixing himself there to receive five remaining cargoes, one in each year successively. I repeat, that time is the great agent in this matter; it is to be taken in a compound ratio, of the time and the occupation, with a great preponderance on the article of time; be the occupation what it may, it cannot happen, but with few exceptions, that mere length of time shall not constitute a domicil.

[The Court then dealt with the facts of the case, and found that the claimant was domiciled in France. The point of decision was then summarised.]

When I find that he [the claimant] went there [France] as a mercantile man, that he stayed there four years, and that he was a man who came from America for the very purpose of mercantile operations in Europe, I feel a difficulty in saying that (exclusive of all trading) satisfactory reasons are assigned for it; or, supposing him to have gone to France for the purpose of obtaining payment, I should still find a difficulty in saying that the original purpose could privilege a residence of four years. Is it possible for me to say, then, that the explanation which is given in this affidavit is quite sufficient, supposing that no objection lay to the mode in which it is offered?

And I come now to observe, on what I consider as the fatal objection, that the whole depends on the single affidavit of Mr. Charles Murray, the brother. There is not one word coming from Mr. G. Murray himself to show what was the nature of his connection with France. Surely the information of Mr. Charles Murray is very incompetent. A striking instance of *his* incompetency is that he supposes his brother gone to America, when it appears that months after that time he was living in France. Can I suppose him sufficiently instructed as to all the courses of his brother's proceedings, to enable him to state satisfactorily to the Court the nature of his engagements in France? It is impossible that the Court can take the account of such a person that the residence of his brother in France was not connected with any mercantile engagements, unconfirmed as it is by the gentleman himself, who though at hand, as I may say, and in a neighbouring country, has not thought fit to give us any explanation. He knows the course and nature of his own transactions, and yet he expects restitution without taking the trouble of making so much as an affidavit for the purpose, after six years' residence (as I must deem it) in France, and with all possible opportunity allowed him for that purpose. From October, 1795, not a single word comes from him till the present day in November, 1799. I own I think it impossible that the Court can be expected to restore on this evidence. Taking it on the present evidence, as to the sufficiency of the explanation and the mode in which it is offered, it is impossible.

Then the only question is, whether I shall allow further opportunity to the party, and give time for further explanation? Considering the length of time which the cause has continued before the Court, with a degree of indulgence, perhaps open to some complaint on the other side, and the manner in which it has been put off from month to month, I do not think it any part of my public duty to allow such opportunity. I do not say that before another Court Mr. Murray may not supply the defects of his case, and by his own evidence; but, finding myself under the necessity of determining on the evidence now before the Court, which is, as I have before stated, that Mr. Murray has been in France four years at least, and that, connected with a former residence there, and that there is no direct proof that he has now quitted it, I feel myself under the necessity (which, if I might be allowed to speak as a private person, I should perhaps describe as a painful necessity) of condemning his share of the property in these several cargoes (*a*).

(*a*) See also *post*, p. 251.

[2 C. Rob. 343.]

THE ROSALIE AND BETTY.

Ship—Cargo—Circumstances of Fraud—Further Proof not Allowed—Condemnation.

When it is not proved that a ship and cargo are neutral property, and the circumstances of the case are covered with suspicion, further proof will not be allowed, and the ship and cargo will be condemned.

1800 *February* 5.

THIS was a case of a ship and cargo, taken on a voyage from the isle of France as asserted, to Hamburg, May 31st, 1799. The ship was claimed for Mr. Baurman, of Embden, and the cargo for Mr. Kaster, of Hamburg.

SIR W. SCOTT.—This is the case of a ship and cargo, taken on a voyage from the isle of France, as asserted, to Hamburg, and the question is, according to my view of it, a question of property; for I am of opinion that the question as to the legality of the trade does not arise, as the cargo, being intended for the port of the owners of the cargo, is entitled to the favourable construction of that Order of Council which permits the trade of neutral vessels from the colony of the enemy to *their own ports*. Till I am better instructed, I shall hold that the right to engage in such a trade is not vitiated on the part of neutral merchants by the circumstance of the cargo being put on board a neutral bottom of another country, and coming to the port of the claimant of the cargo. I have taken some time to consider this case, because it is a case of great value, and has been very laboriously argued; and because, as I understand, there are other cases of a similar nature which are likely to come before the Court; and it may save time to deliver the opinion of the Court on what will be the effect of similar evidence and similar circumstances in those cases also, if they occur.

[The Court then examined the evidence as to the property in the ship and cargo at great length, and concluded.]

With respect to the real foundation of this business, it is not, perhaps, very easy for me to develop it. If it is really a Danish ship, my own opinion is that it has been handed over for the purpose of carrying out contraband articles to the French settlement; and as to the cargo, when I see the outward cargo carried to a French settlement, and there delivered to Saulnier, who is the great agent of frauds there, and with much contrivance, connecting all the circumstances of French agency throughout the whole transaction, I cannot think that it is wholly unconnected with French interests. In what degree they are mixed in it I cannot say, but it is my comfort to think that it is not necessary for me to determine that point; for if Mr. Kaster has *any* property in this cargo, if he has mixed his interest in any proportion with the interest of the enemy, and resorts to modes of prevarication to conceal and protect the enemy's interest, such a conduct will affect his own share. If neutrals will not bring their claims fairly and ingenuously before the Court, but resort to such artifices to cover and protect the property of the enemy, it is a rule of the law of nations that they shall be concluded by the proof they bring. I shall therefore not decide this case in the affirmative on the ground that this ship and cargo are proved to belong to the enemy, but on the ground that the property in them is *not proved* to belong to the persons claiming them before this Court, and that, if it is their property, they have clothed it with such circumstances as justly exclude them from the opportunity of giving further proof. I wish neutrals to understand, that if they mean to avail themselves of the rights of neutrals, they must conduct themselves as such. It will then be the duty of this Court, and the ambition of it, to exert its utmost vigilance to give them the benefit of their neutrality. But on the other side, if they discredit their cases by a clothing of prevarication and falsehood, who is to blame for the inconvenience that may ensue? The rule of this Court is—and framed with as much moderation surely as the subject will admit—that if their proofs, dishonoured by such impure mixture, are nevertheless sufficient to establish the truth of their claim, it is well; but if they fall short of this (and it can hardly happen otherwise), they shall not be indulged with the means of supplying proofs from sources which have appeared to be corrupt.

Ship and cargo condemned.

[2 C. Rob. 361.]

THE POLLY.

Continuous Voyage—Importation—Neutral Territory—Subsequent Reloading.

Portions of a cargo were shipped at Havannah, unloaded in America, reshipped and captured on a voyage to Bilbao. *Held,* that under the circumstances there had been a *bonâ fide* importation into neutral territory, and that the capture was not made on a continuous voyage.

Cargo restored, but expenses of further proof allowed to captors.

1800 *February 5.*

THIS was a case of an American ship taken on a voyage from Marblehead to Bilbao, 16th October, 1799, with a cargo of fish, sugar and cocoa. The ship had been restored. With respect to the cargo, it was said on the part of the captor that it was a case of further proof, that it appeared from the deposition of the mate that the sugar and cocoa had been brought from the Havannah to America, and from thence sent on for Spain, from which a suspicion must necessarily arise of Spanish interest; that, if it was even neutral property, a question of law would arise whether such a trade was not to be considered as a direct trade between the colony of the enemy and the mother country (*a*). It was further said that the mate had deposed that the master had confessed to him that he had destroyed some papers, which of itself would subject the claimant to the necessity of making further proof.

On the part of the claimant, it was said . . . . in respect to the transhipment, to have been of but a small quantity of cocoa, that the sugar was part of a whole cargo which this vessel had brought on a former voyage from Havannah to Marblehead. . . . .

For the captors, the *King's Advocate* and *Arnold.*

SIR W. SCOTT.—This is the case of an American vessel taken on a voyage from Marblehead to Spain, with a cargo of a mixed nature, consisting of fish, sugar, and cocoa. The ship has been restored, therefore the only question that I have to consider is respecting the property of the cargo and the legality of the voyage. On the former hearing it appeared to be a case of further proof, as the cargo was the produce of a Spanish colony taken on a voyage to Old Spain, and as the master had withdrawn some of the

(*a*) See the *William, post.*

papers, and had, indeed, destroyed himself before his deposition was taken; it would therefore be a little extravagant to contend that such a case was not a case of further proof. I do not, however, impute it to the parties, as any diffidence in their own case, that they had sent for further proof before the cause came on. They might think that some difficulties would arise, and it was but a measure of prudence to be prepared with further proof. I am therefore not disposed to draw any inference disadvantageous to the claim from that circumstance: I am now to judge of the sufficiency of the proof brought in, and of the force of the different objections that have been made against it.

In respect to the fish, I do not think that there is anything that affects that part of the case. . . . .

Then there remains only the question of law, which has been raised, whether this is not such a trade as will fall under the principle that has been applied to the interposition of neutrals in the colonial trade of the enemy? on which it is said, that if an American is not allowed to carry on this trade directly, neither can he be allowed to do it circuitously. An American has undoubtedly a right to import the produce of the Spanish colonies for his own use; and after it is imported *bonâ fide* into his own country, he would be at liberty to carry them on to the general commerce of Europe. Very different would such a case be from the Dutch cases in which there was an original contract from the beginning, and under a special Dutch licence, to go from Holland to Surinam, and to return again to Holland with a cargo of colonial produce. It is not my business to say what is universally the test of a *bonâ fide* importation. It is argued that it would not be sufficient that the duties should be paid, and that the cargo should be landed. If these criteria are not to be resorted to, I should be at a loss to know what should be the test; and I am strongly disposed to hold that it would be sufficient that the goods should be landed and the duties paid.

If it appears to have been landed and warehoused for a considerable time, it does, I think, raise a forcible presumption on that side; and it throws it on the other party to show how this could be merely insidious and colourable. There is, I think, reason to believe that the sugar was *a part* and parcel of a cargo said to have been brought from a Spanish colony in this vessel; and, if so, the very distribution of the remainder is some proof that they were not bought with an intention only of sending them on. But I have besides positive proof in the affidavit of Mr. Asa Hooper, who swears (*a*) "that the duties had been paid for them." Then the only difficulty remains as to the cocoa; and it is said by one of the witnesses, and by one only, that it was tran-shipped from another vessel, and that it had been brought into America only ten days before; but although there is something of a difficulty arising on this small part of the cargo, yet upon the whole I cannot think it weighty enough to induce me to send the case across the Atlantic for still further proof as to the facts of this recent importation and transhipment, or of its having been trans-ferred to the present proprietors, or of its having been exported without a previous payment of import duties. If it had composed a larger part of the cargo, I might have deemed it reasonable to have had somewhat more of satisfaction on some of these points, which do not appear with sufficient certainty to found any legal conclusion against it. It appears by the collector's certificate that it had been entered (*b*) and imported; and I think that these words are sufficient to answer the fair demands of the Court.

Court.—I see nothing to affect the captors with misconduct; when the ship was brought in the claimant refused to accept the

(*a*) Affidavit of Asa Hooper, of Marblehead, master of the ship *Hope*, belonging to Boston, and now lying at Cowes, states, "that he had been acquainted with Mr. R. Hooper ever since he was a child; that he knows the brig *Polly*, and was at Marble-head when she sailed for Bilbao, and that he was informed by Captain Lasky and various other persons that the sugar, being part of the cargo, was a part of a much larger quantity, the whole of which had been im-ported, landed, and *the duties paid* at Marblehead by the said R. Hooper in the general course of trade, &c."

(*b*) The certificate of the collector stated, that in June the *Polly* entered at his office with a cargo of 590 boxes of sugars, the property of American citizens; that 17th August, the schooner *William* entered with 67 hogsheads, &c. of cocoa, and certified the clearing out of the *Polly*, &c. for Bilbao, with a cargo of 249 boxes of brown sugars *imported* in the said brig from the Havannah, on the 25th of June, and of 30 hogsheads, &c. of cocoa imported in the schooner *William*, from Laguira, with 1,800 quintals of fish. Be it known, &c., that this cargo of sugars, cocoa and fish, cleared out from this port for Bilbao, 27th August, 1799, is the property of citizens of America, &c.

restitution of the ship without the cargo, contending that it was not a case of further proof. The Court determined that it was; and it does not appear that any communication was made after the order for the captors to restrain them from proceeding to unlivery. The commission of unlivery passed as of course, and they proceeded in the execution of it till intimation was given on the part of the claimant, and on the first intimation the captors stopped their hand. I can impute no blame to the captors; and I shall give them what I was disposed to give them before the objection was taken: the expenses of further proof.

1800 *February* 5.

THE POLLY.

Sir W. Scott.

THE INDIAN CHIEF.

[3 C. Rob. 12.]

Ship—Owner—National Character—Change of Country.

The natural character gained by residence ceases with residence, and a character so gained ceases the moment a person *bonâ fide* sets himself to leave his place of residence.

1800 *February* 27.

THIS was a case of a ship and cargo seized in the harbour of Cowes, on a voyage from Batavia to Hamburg, in which two questions arose, respecting the national character of Mr. Johnson, claimant of the ship, and of Mr. Miller, claimant of the cargo.

SIR W. SCOTT.—This is the case of a ship seized in the port of Cowes, where she came to receive orders respecting the delivery of a cargo taken in at Batavia, with a professed original intention of proceeding to Hamburg; but on coming into this country for particular orders, the ship and cargo were seized in port. It does not appear clear to the Court that it might not be a cargo intended to be delivered in this country, as many such cargoes have been, under the Dutch Property Act. I mention this to meet an observation that has been thrown out, "that it is doubtful whether the ship might not be confiscable on the ground of being a neutral ship coming from the colony of the enemy, not to her own ports or to the ports of this country." I cannot assume it as a demonstrated fact in the case that the cargo was to be delivered at Hamburg. The vessel sailed in 1795, and as an American ship with an American pass and all American documents; but, never-

1800 *February* 27. THE INDIAN CHIEF. Sir W. Scott.

theless, if the owner really resided here, such papers could not protect his vessel. If the owner was resident in England, and the voyage such as an English merchant could not engage in, an American residing here and carrying on trade could not protect his ship merely by putting American documents on board; his interest must stand or fall according to the determination which the Court shall make on the national character of such a person.

There are two positions which are not to be controverted: that Mr. Johnson is an American generally by birth, which is the circumstance that first impresses itself on the mind of the Court; and also by the part which he took on the breaking out of the American War. He came hither when both countries were open to him, but on the breaking out of hostilities he made his election which country he would adhere to, and in consequence thereof went to France. As to the doubt that has been suggested whether he would be deemed an American, not having been personally there at the time of the declaration of the independence of that country, I think that is sufficiently cleared up by the circumstance of his being adopted as such by the act of the American Government declaring him and his family to be American subjects, and by the official character which that government has intrusted to him. I am of opinion, therefore, that he has not lost the benefit of his native American character. He came, however, to this country in 1783, and engaged in trade, and has resided in this country till 1797; during that time he was undoubtedly to be considered as an English trader, for no position is more established than this: that if a person goes into another country and engages in trade and resides there, he is by the law of nations to be considered as a merchant of that country. I should therefore have no doubt in pronouncing that Mr. Johnson was to be considered as a merchant of this country at the time of the sailing of this vessel on her outward voyage. That leads me to take a view of the circumstances of this case: the ship went out in 1795, with Mr. Hewlet on board, and Mr. Johnson says, "he sent out Mr. Hewlet as supercargo, and put the vessel under his control to take freight for America, but that his designs were frustrated by various circumstances;" and the ship actually went to Madeira, Madras,

Tranquebar, and Batavia, and from thence to Cowes, where she was arrested.

Now there can be no doubt that if Mr. Johnson had continued where he was at the time of sailing, if he had remained resident in England, it must be considered as a British transaction; and therefore a criminal transaction, on the common principle that it is illegal in any person owing an allegiance, though temporary, to trade with the public enemy. But it is pleaded that he had quitted this country before the capture, and that he had done this in consequence of an intention which he had formed of removing much earlier, but that he had been prevented by obstacles that obstructed his wish; to this effect the letter of March, 1797, is exhibited, which must have been preceded by private correspondence and application to some of his creditors. It does, I think, breathe strong expressions of intention and of an ardent desire to get over the restraint that alone detained him; and it affords conclusive reason to believe that if he had been a free man, and at liberty to go where he pleased, he would have removed long before; and that he was detained here as a hostage, as he describes himself, to his creditors, on motives of honour creditable to his character. On the 9th of September, 1797, he did actually retire; of the sincerity of his quitting this country there can hardly be a doubt entertained; it is almost impossible to represent stronger or more natural grounds for such a measure; and I do not think the Court runs any risk of encountering a fraudulent intention, put forward to meet the circumstances of the moment, without anything of an original and *bonâ fide* intention at the bottom of it.

The ship was sent out under the management of the supercargo, and it is said that Mr. Hewlet exceeded his commission. The affidavit does not go so far; it does not appear from that, that the agent had not the power to enter into such an engagement; but this, I think, appears clearly, that it was the understanding both of Mr. Johnson and of his agent, Mr. Hewlet, who had been his clerk, and to whom he refers for a confirmation of his avowed design of removing, that before the completion of such a voyage Mr. Johnson would be in America; therefore, if the illegality of the voyage must be supposed to have presented itself to their minds as a British transaction, owing to Mr. Johnson's residence

1800 *February* 27. — THE INDIAN CHIEF. — Sir W. Scott.

in England, there was reason enough for them to conclude that Mr. Johnson would be removed; and, on that view of the matter, although it is certain that an agent would bind his employer in such a case, there is ground sufficient to presume that the agent acted fairly and *bonâ fide*, and under the expectation that Mr. Johnson would be returned to America.

The ship arrives a few weeks after his departure; and taking it to be clear that the national character of Mr. Johnson as a British merchant was founded in residence only, that it was acquired by residence, and rested on that circumstance alone, it must be held that from the moment he turns his back on the country where he has resided, on his way to his own country, he was in the act of resuming his original character, and is to be considered as an American. The character that is gained by residence ceases by residence. It is an adventitious character which no longer adheres to him from the moment that he puts himself in motion, *bonâ fide*, to quit the country *sine animo revertendi* (*a*). The Courts that have to apply this principle have applied it both ways, unfavourably in some cases and favourably in others. This man had actually quitted the country. Stronger was the case of Mr. Curtissos: he was a British-born subject that had been resident in Surinam and St. Eustatius, and had left those settlements with an intention of returning to this country; but he had got no further than Holland, the mother country of those settlements, when the war broke out (*b*). It was determined by the Lords of Appeal that he was *in itinere*,

(*a*) In the *President* (*post*, p. 475), Sir W. Scott said: "A mere intention to remove has never been held sufficient without some overt act, being merely an intention, residing secretly and undistinguishably in the breast of the party, and liable to be revoked every hour. The expressions of the letter in which this intention is said to be found are very weak and general, of an intention merely *in futuro*. Were they even much stronger than they are, they would not be sufficient; something more than mere verbal declaration, some solid fact showing that the party is in the act of withdrawing, has always been held necessary in such cases."

(*b*) The order of reprisals against Holland, issued December, 1780. The *Snelle Zeylder* was captured 1st January, 1781. Mr. Curtissos had gone to Surinam in 1766, and from thence to St. Eustatius, where he stayed till 1776; from thence he went to Holland to settle his accounts, and with an intention, as was said, of returning afterwards to England to take up his final residence, but he did not return to England till 27th of April, 1781.

that he had put himself in motion, and was in pursuit of his native British character, and as such he was held to be entitled to the restitution of his property. So here, this gentleman was in the actual pursuit of his American character, and I think there can be no doubt that his native character was strongly and substantially revived, not occasionally, nor colourably, for the mere purposes of the present claim; and therefore I shall restore this ship.

1800 *February* 27.

THE INDIAN CHIEF.

Sir W. Scott.

THE SANTA BRIGADA.

[3 C. Rob. 52.]

Joint Capture—Private Ship of War—In Sight of Capture.

The fact that a private ship of war is in sight of the capture of an enemy vessel by a King's ship does not entitle such private ship to be considered a joint captor.

1800 *April* 8.

THIS was a case of an allegation of joint capture on the part of a private ship of war, asserted to have been in sight at the time of the capture of this valuable Spanish galleon by the *Triton* frigate, and to have put herself in motion in such a manner as *might have* been effectual in cutting off the retreat of the galleon into a Spanish port.

The act relied on in the allegation was stated in the 5th Article: "That on the evening of the 16th she plainly saw and discovered the Spanish frigate, and chased so as to keep in sight the whole night; on the morning she heard a firing, and about six o'clock perceived the engagement, and immediately sailed towards the Spanish coast among the rocks and lands, for the purpose of intercepting the escape of the Spanish frigate, and preventing her from getting into Vigo."

SIR W. SCOTT.—This is asserted to be a case of merit on the part of the private ship of war; and if so, it must certainly be considered as a case of diffident and modest merit, inasmuch as the parties have not thought proper to come forward and assert their pretensions till a very considerable time after the capture. I cannot help thinking that if they had felt much confidence in their case they would have thought it as good a cruise to pursue this prize into the Court of Admiralty as to have continued out on the cruise they were then engaged in; however, the matter is now

1800 *April* 8.

THE SANTA BRIGADA.

Sir W. Scott.

brought before the Court. The disparity of force that has been observed upon is certainly not conclusive, as we all remember instances of great merit in vessels of small force, especially that which has been mentioned in the case of the *Buen Consejo* (*a*), in which the annoyance given by a very small ship was the principal cause of the ultimate capture. But those are cases of a very different description from the present. The *being in sight only* will not be sufficient; it would open a door to very frequent and practicable frauds if, by the mere act of hanging on upon his Majesty's ships to pick up the crumbs of the captures, small privateers should be held to entitle themselves to an interest in the prize which the King's ships took. The sound doctrine of the Court has been that the being in sight with respect to these two descriptions of vessels is not sufficient to entitle the privateer to share. It is said, however, there was an actual assistance. The 5th Article states "that she made an attempt to get between the prize in question and the land, and would have pursued it, but that she herself became the object of chase to four other vessels that came out from the coast." Instead of the pursuer, she became the object of pursuit. It is the first instance, I believe, in which the character of a captor has been claimed by a flying vessel. *Lepus tute es et pulpamentum quæris.* It is argued, however, that she was eventually of service by diverting the attention of the four Spanish frigates from the transaction of this valuable capture, and it is not improbable. But mere diversion of attention has never been held a sufficient ground for a title of joint capture; it is a mere casualty, totally unconnected with all merit, actual or constructive. If she herself had been captured, it would have produced exactly the same effect in a still stronger degree, and yet it would have been perfectly ludicrous to have pronounced for

(*a*) This was a Spanish register ship of 800 tons and 26 guns, 12-pounders, taken 20th November, 1779, by the *Hussar*, Captain Salter. A claim of joint capture was given and allowed on the part of the *Resolution* privateer of 16 6-pounders, Captain Sladen, whose gallantry and perseverance appeared highly meritorious in keeping the prize in chase from the 5th November till the 20th, having fought her several times, notwithstanding the disparity of force, and having kept constantly up with her, burning false lights, &c. during the night, to attract the notice and assistance of some British cruiser.

her joint interest of capture under such circumstances. On the whole, I am of opinion that the articles of this allegation do not assert such a claim as can in law establish the parties to share as joint captors, if they are proved; and therefore I shall reject it.

THE CAREL AND MAGDALENA.

[3 C. Rob. 58.]

Capture—Sentence—Jurisdiction of Vice-Admiralty Court.

Vice-Admiralty Courts have as Prize Courts only local jurisdiction, unless an enlarged jurisdiction is given by statute.

1800 *April* 29.

THIS was a case respecting the power of the Vice-Admiralty Prize Courts to proceed to the adjudication of vessels not brought within their districts. It was a case of a Danish vessel taken at the capture of Demerara. The ship remained there, whilst the papers were sent to the island of Martinique, and proceedings were commenced in the Vice-Admiralty Court of that island, where the ship, with two others under similar circumstances, were condemned on the 20th September, 1797. A claim was given in the High Court of Admiralty for the ship, &c. on the part of a Danish merchant, and a monition was taken out against the captors to proceed to adjudication. The King's Proctor appeared for the captors under protest, and being assigned to extend his protest, the cause came before the Court on the following act on petition.

Heseltine, under his protest, alleged the said ship to have been taken possession of by his Majesty's sea and land forces at the island of Demerara, and to have been afterwards proceeded against and condemned as good and lawful prize in the Vice-Admiralty Court of the island of Martinique; and prayed the judge would be pleased to dismiss the captors from the monition served and returned in this cause. *Townley* dissenting, and alleging on the part of the claimants that such condemnation, if any such was pronounced, was illegal, inasmuch as the said ship was not carried to Martinique, and prayed the judge to over-rule the protest, and to assign the captor to appear absolutely.

1800 *April* 29. — THE CAREL AND MAGDALENA.

Court.—It can never be maintained that the sentence of the Court of Martinique, upon a prize not brought within the sphere of its jurisdiction, is a valid sentence. It is a known distinction between the Courts of Vice-Admiralty and the High Court of Admiralty, that the former have only a local jurisdiction, confined to the adjudication of property brought within their own limits (*a*), whilst the authority of the High Court of Admiralty in prize matters extends over the whole of his Majesty's dominions, and operates in every port belonging to them.

Protest overruled.

[3 C. Rob. 96.]

THE KIERLIGHETT.

Capture—Illegal Condemnation—Sale to Neutral—Recapture—Amelioration of Ship—Allowance to Neutral Purchaser.

A British ship was captured, illegally condemned and sold to a neutral purchaser. She was subsequently recaptured and restored by the Court to the original owner. *Held*, that the neutral owner, being a *bonâ fide* purchaser, was entitled to recover such sum as the registrar and merchants should consider reasonable for improvement made by him to the vessel.

1800 *May* 22.

THIS was a case of a British prize ship taken by the French and carried into Norway, and there sold, under a sentence of condemnation of the French Consul, to the present Danish claimant. It appeared that the ship had been afterwards, whilst in the possession of the purchaser, captured again by the French and carried into a Spanish port, and condemned there on that capture by the French Consul, notwithstanding the claim of the former purchaser. On appeal to the Superior Court of Prize in Paris, she was directed to be restored. After this restitution, the ship continuing to be navigated as the property of the Danish merchant, came to the port of Liverpool, where she was arrested on the part of the former British proprietor.

[The Court held that the vessel must be restored to the original British owner.]

(*a*) This applies to the extent of the late jurisdiction of the Vice-Admiralty Courts. By 41 Geo. 3, c. 99, this jurisdiction has been put on a new footing. [See now 27 & 28 Vict. c. 25, ss. 3 and 9.]

Sir W. Scott.—Among the many novelties that the French have introduced into the world, the condemnation of prize vessels in neutral ports, under the authority of Consular Courts sitting there, is not the least extraordinary. These condemnations, sustained by the tribunals of France, may be good and valid against French subjects on a second capture by French cruisers, or in any other way in which they may come before them in transactions amongst their own subjects, as considered by the law of their own country; but they are not binding on other countries. This Court, as representing this country in such matters, has already signified its opinion upon them.

This was a case of such a condemnation in the first instance, and if that had been all there could have been no question about it; but it appears that there has been a subsequent French capture, after a purchase made by a neutral subject, and that the vessel was then carried into a port of an ally of the war, which may, for the purpose of this argument, be considered as a French port. A second condemnation passed there; and on appeal, the Superior Court at Paris reversed that sentence, and decreed restitution to the Danish claimant. On what grounds either of these decrees passed we are not informed. The former of these sentences could not have been on any ground of defect in the condemnation in Norway, because condemnations of that species are sustained in France. It might be for want of requisite documents, or for having British goods on board, or on some of those arbitrary and fanciful regulations which the irregular policy of France has established as their expositions of the law of nations. There is nothing to show that the reversal of the second condemnation passed upon any ground that had a connection with the first condemnation in Norway, or that affirmed that sentence upon any view of its particular merits. If it affirmed it in any manner, I presume it would do so only on the general ground that these consular condemnations were to be sustained, in which it would be just as good as that condemnation, and no better. But in truth, I presume that it must have turned upon other questions totally foreign to it; it never could have been that the validity of such a condemnation had been disallowed by the inferior French Court so as to make it necessary for the superior tribunal to support it by a reversal. I

1800 May 22. — THE KIERLIGHETT. — Sir W. Scott.

think, therefore, that the second proceedings in France add nothing to the real authority of the first proceedings in Norway; and as those proceedings cannot sustain the title of the neutral purchaser, I must overrule his protest, and admit the claim of the original proprietor.

An absolute appearance being given for the Danish purchaser, *Arnold* prayed, on his behalf, that an allowance might be made to him for the amelioration which the ship had undergone in his service.

On the other side, *Swabey* said that in the *Constant Mary* (22nd August, 1696; on appeal, 31st December, 1697) the same demand was made, but rejected by the Court; that a purchaser under an illegal title must take the consequences of his own imprudence, and could support no claim to be indemnified for intermediate expenses.

Sir W. Scott.—I am obliged to Dr. Swabey for a case very much resembling the present—a case of great antiquity in this Court. In that case the demand for amelioration was refused, though not without a considerable difference of opinion between the delegates. Under the irregular practice which has prevailed, to a great extent, of carrying ships for condemnation into neutral ports, an individual might be led into an honest mistake. On this principle, in the *Perseverance* (a), I did decree something of an allowance to be made for amelioration. In the same manner I am not disposed to consider this purchaser as a person buying under a title notoriously bad at the time of purchase. In such a case, as a *malæ fidei* possessor, he must have taken the consequence of his own imprudence. As to ordinary repairs, the Court does not usually take any notice of them; the use of the ship must be set off against them.

It appears in this case that there is a person holding a bottomry bond incurred on the ship and cargo, though it does not appear in what proportion, or how far he has been indemnified out of the cargo. If the bond is for mere ordinary repairs, it must fall under

(a) November 22nd, 1799.

the considerations which I have first stated. The proper rule for the registrar and merchants to pursue will be to consider the *quantum* of the improved state in which the ship comes into the hands of the original proprietors. As to that part, it is not a restitution to them, but a new acquisition. This is the point to which I wish the registrar and merchants to apply their attention; and under this direction I shall refer it to them to report on the *quantum* of amelioration.

1800 *May* 22.

THE KIERLIGHETT.

Sir W. Scott.

Ship restored to the former owner.

THE RACEHORSE.

[3 C. Rob. 101.]

Recapture—Freight.

A vessel chartered from Liverpool to Lisbon, and thence to Ireland, was captured by a French privateer, on her homeward voyage, off Falmouth, and was subsequently recaptured and brought into Falmouth where the cargo was unladen. The ship was restored on 2nd July, but no claim was made in respect of the cargo till 17th July, and restitution was ordered on 16th November. *Held*, that the whole freight was payable by the cargo, less one-eighth deducted for salvage, and that the ship was not bound to wait adjudication on the cargo in order to carry it on.

1800 *June* 13.

This was a case of a British ship freighted from Liverpool in ballast to St. Martins and Lisbon, to bring a cargo of fruit to Dublin, taken on her return voyage by a French privateer off Falmouth, and afterwards recaptured and brought to Falmouth, where the cargo was unlivered. No application was made to the agent of the ship that the cargo should be carried on. The present question arose respecting the *quantum* of freight due from the cargo to the ship.

On the part of the owner of the cargo, the *King's Advocate*.

On the other side, *Robinson*.

Sir W. Scott.—This is a case originating in the misfortune of a capture by the enemy; which, however, a subsequent recapture and recovery must prevent the parties from considering as the grievance of a total loss and misadventure, notwithstanding that some delay and expense have arisen out of it.

It is much to be regretted that charter-parties do not contain provisions for the case of capture and recapture; it is an accident that frequently occurs, and it would have been extremely natural that some provision should be made for it; yet, in almost all the charter-parties that I have seen, it seems to have been as much out of the consideration of the parties, as if there had been no such thing as capture in the world.

This ship was chartered to go from Liverpool to St. Martins, and on to Lisbon, for a cargo of fruit; there, not finding a full lading of fruit, the master consented to take in wine, out of accommodation to the owner of the cargo, and was captured on her return voyage off Falmouth; a great part of her voyage was performed, the outward voyage entirely, and a great part of the returned voyage, and solely in the service of the freighters; the master, it appears, was taken out on the first capture, and owing to that circumstance no claim was immediately given for the cargo. The owner of the ship being dead, the care of the vessel devolved on his administrator; no blame is imputable to him that he did not interfere with respect to the cargo; his duties were duties of caution, he could not be expected to do all that the master or the owner himself might have done; it was natural for him to confine himself to the concern of the ship, and without intermeddling with the cargo, to act only in such a manner as seemed best for the interests of the estate of his party. The ship was restored by consent on the 2nd of July, whilst no claim was given for the cargo till the 17th of July, and restitution did not pass till the 16th of November. The case of the cargo was litigated—and is the Court to say that the ship was to stay and wait the result of the proceedings when she herself had been restored, whilst the cargo was contested and might be condemned, and whilst it was by no means clear that any cargo would remain to be carried on? This would be an unreasonable expectation. I do not say that a party is to act in a hasty manner, and to run away immediately on the restitution of his ship. Something is to be conceded in the way of accommodation; a reasonable time is to be allowed, and if it is not allowed, a proportion of the freight may be deducted. But I cannot say that a ship shall wait all this time for the mere chance of taking on the cargo, if eventually it should be restored. It is said that the contract was totally dissolved; but by whose means happened it that it was so dissolved? It was in no degree owing to the owner of the ship, who might have carried on the cargo, but that the owner of the cargo was not ready to proceed; though he acted as discharged from his contract, he is substantially entitled to the benefit of it. On these grounds I am of opinion that the ship is entitled to her whole freight (*a*).

(*a*) In the *Martha*, a similar question arose as to freight on an American ship from America to Amsterdam, captured in the Channel, 20th December, 1800, and brought in. The ship was restored, with freight, on the 10th of January. On the 15th of January a commission of unlivery passed, and on the 16th, one parcel of goods, for which a claim had been given, was restored. The unlivery was directed to be suspended as to those goods, but it being necessary to move them in order to get at the rest of the cargo, they were unlivered. On the part of the claimant of those goods, it was demanded of the master that he should take them on board again (the claimant offering to be at the charge of the reshipment), and carry them on upon the original freight. On the other side, it was contended that the master was entitled to have his whole freight pronounced due without being charged with any further services; that the ship had suffered a long demurrage, and some damage during that time; that the object of her returned voyage was frustrated by the delay, and that it would expose her to great inconvenience to go on with a part of her cargo only.

SIR W. SCOTT.—This is a case in which some loss must fall upon one of two innocent parties, both of whom, I fear, it will not be in the power of the Court to protect.. One is a carrier master, who is, if I may use the expression, a favourite with the Court; the other the owner of a cargo engaged in an innocent commerce. The ship has been released, and the cargo also; but it has happened that it became necessary to unliver the whole cargo, in order to get at a parcel of goods, for which no claim was given. After what I have said, I should have thought it my duty to look very particularly into all the circumstances attending this case, if I had not met with one determined by my predecessor, which comes so very near to the circumstances of this case that I can find no distinction between them. It is the case of the *Hamilton*, Rodman, Adm., 20th November, 1793, an American ship retaken from the French, and brought in, May, 1793, on a voyage from Lisbon to Petersburg. The ship was restored immediately, with some part of the cargo claimed for the owner of the ship; the remainder of the cargo was claimed on the 5th of June, and restored on the original evidence on the 9th of August. The cargo had been unloaded, but the ship was not gone away at the time of the restitution, and a demand was made upon the master to take the cargo on board again and proceed on his original voyage; but he refused, and went away with the ship, and the owners of the cargo were

1800 June 13. — The Racehorse. — Sir W. Scott.

It was prayed on the part of the owner of the cargo that one-eighth of the freight might be deducted for the salvage, which they had paid on the freight.

It was said on the other side that the owner of the ship had settled with the recaptors for salvage.

Court.—For the ship; but salvage is due for the ship, cargo, and freight.

Prayer granted.

[3 C. Rob. 108.]

THE NEPTUNUS (No. 3).

Contraband—Articles ancipitis usus—*Tallow.*

Tallow destined for Amsterdam: *Held* not liable to condemnation. Sail cloth: *Held* to be contraband, even when consigned to a port of mercantile and naval equipment.

1800 June 13.

This was a case of a miscellaneous cargo, taken June 12th, 1798, on a voyage from Cronstadt to Amsterdam. Further proof had been directed to be made on several claims for different parts of the cargo.

On a claim for a quantity of tallow, on the part of a merchant of Petersburg, the *King's Advocate* contended that tallow was to be considered as a naval store, liable to confiscation as contraband.

Court.—I am not disposed to consider it in that light, on a destination to such a port as Amsterdam; Amsterdam is a great mercantile port, as well as a port of naval equipment; if it had been taken going to Brest, I should have had little doubt about it.

Restored.

obliged to find another conveyance for their goods to Petersburg. On the 20th of November, 1793, the question as to the freight was brought before the Court, and it was objected that it was not due, as the ship had not performed her part of the contract; but the Court decreed the whole freight to be a charge on the cargo. This case is so exactly in point, that I can see no distinction between it and the present case. As long as that case stands uncorrected by the superior Court (if it requires any correction), I shall think myself bound to follow it, though I am sorry to say it may in particular instances fall with hardship on the owners of cargoes.

On a claim for 275 bundles of sail cloth, as the property of a merchant of Petersburg. 1800 *June* 13.

THE NEPTUNUS (No. 3).

Court.—That is universally contraband, even on a destination to ports of mere mercantile naval equipment; Amsterdam is a port both of great mercantile and military equipment.

Condemned.

On prayer for the freight and expenses of the ship, the *King's Advocate* contended that freight could not be given in a case of a contraband cargo.

Arnold and *Robinson.*—The Court will not think it necessary to apply that rule in its utmost rigour in such a case as the present, where the contraband articles are but in a small quantity, amongst a variety of other articles.

The Court acceded.

Freight and expenses given.

THE GRAAFF BERNSTORF.

[3 C. Rob. 109.]

Cargo—Property of Neutral—Property of Enemy—One Ship—Concealment of Enemy Interest by Neutral—National Character.

Where there has been a suppression of an enemy's interest in a cargo with a fraudulent intent by a neutral cargo owner, such neutral owner is not allowed to supply defects of proof as to his own part of the cargo.

THIS was a case of a valuable cargo taken on a voyage from Batavia to Copenhagen. The claim was given in the first instance for the whole cargo, as the property of the house of Black & Co., of Copenhagen; but after some circumstances respecting it had transpired, an amended claim was given, by leave of the Court, for the cargo, as the property of Black & Co. and a Mr. Van Tromp.

1800 *June* 17; affirmed *April* 23, 1803.

SIR W. SCOTT.—This cause now comes on upon a corrected claim given for Black & Co., of Copenhagen, and Mr. Van Tromp; the former claim was given for Black & Co. only, and all the papers concurred in representing the property in that manner: so it continued to be described till the time of hearing. Then, from

1800 June 17. — THE GRAAFF BERNSTORF. — Sir W. Scott.

papers that had come to light in other causes, it became a matter of almost unavoidable admission that another person had some interest in this cargo, and the Court called on the parties to explain that circumstance. The present claim is brought forward in an amended form, in obedience to that order, showing that Black & Co. are the owners of much the greater part of the cargo, but that Mr. Van Tromp is the owner of some portion of it. I shall first dispose of the claim for his share, which must depend entirely on his national character, on which I am clearly of opinion that he is to be considered as a Dutchman. He is a person born in Holland, and living there till the time of the commencement of this adventure, when he removes to Copenhagen and goes through the slight formalities of obtaining a burgher's brief—formalities on which, it is said, great importance is attached in Denmark, but on which other countries which have to consider its real nature and effect certainly can attach but little in the estimate of a real national character. He embarks immediately on an adventure to a Dutch settlement, under an intention, it is said, of returning to Europe, but is at the time of this capture left residing at Batavia. It appears from other papers that he considers himself as a Dutchman; he expresses a warm interest in the political events of Holland, as his own country, and evidently intends to return and end his days there. To say that his Dutch character is purged off by having made one voyage in a Danish ship, and under such circumstances accompanied with an actual employment in a Dutch settlement, and with an intention of perpetuating his connection with Holland by returning to end his days there, would be truly ridiculous. It is impossible to consider him as a Dane, or in any other light than in his original Dutch character (*a*). His share must be deemed liable to condemnation.

I come then to the question, in what manner the suppression of the interests of this person will affect the interests of others? It is a question on which great property depends, and therefore the Court is naturally disposed to consider it with that tender deliberation which objects of great value necessarily create; under these impressions, the Court would pass over nothing that could be urged with any effect for the claimants in such a case.

(*a*) See note, p. 270.

1800
June 17.

THE GRAAFF BERNSTORF.

Sir W. Scott.

It may not be immaterial to consider the origin of this transaction: it was a voyage to a Dutch settlement—from Copenhagen, indeed, but with a cargo procured in Holland. I do not say that a neutral merchant may not very lawfully carry on such a traffic, purchasing articles in Holland, and afterwards employing them as he pleases, when they have become *bonâ fide* his property, and have been *imported* into his own country. But certainly it is not too much, on the other side, to observe that the sending a cargo so purchased to a Dutch colony does necessarily afford a strong ground of suspicion that there are Dutch interests connected with it. It does not appear, I think, that there had been any orders sent from the house of Black & Co. for the purchase of the outward cargo. It was purchased by Dull & Co., of Amsterdam, but *for* Black & Co., as it is said; it does not, however, appear that the house in Amsterdam purchased under their directions, as their agents only, and as having no other connection with it. On the contrary, Mr. Van Tromp, the agent of Black & Co., writes to Dull & Co. about everything relating to the outward cargo; about the quality of the articles when sold; and likewise respecting the homeward voyage, and the ports of Europe to which it might be most advantageous for the ship to return. These gentlemen in Amsterdam appear to have been persons who had more interest in this transaction than as mere laders of the outward cargo. It is impossible, for persons dealing *fairly* in such a trade in an enemy's country, not to feel that they are exposed to suspicion; so as to excite in them a reasonable prudence as to the mode of conducting the transaction. It must occur, I think, to every person of ordinary prudence, that it would be extreme indiscretion in persons embarking in such a questionable commerce, to have the whole correspondence respecting it carried on, not immediately with themselves, but with the merchants in Holland, by their agent at Batavia. If any difficulty occurred, they, the neutrals, the real owners, were the persons to be consulted upon it. To see merchants in Holland interposed as a sort of middle men, or rather acting as the only European parties concerned, to see them conducting every part of the transaction, does unavoidably fix in the mind of the Court an impression that this is a transaction connected with other interests than such as are merely neutral; especially in a case that appears to have had its origin in Holland.

1800 June 17. — THE GRAAFF BERNSTORF. — Sir W. Scott.

There are other papers which point still further to some such complication of interests. At all events, it is a case of further proof, as the master cannot speak in verification of the property. The only question, therefore, is, whether it is such a case as can fairly be admitted to go to further proof. The general rule of the Court is certainly this, that where there has been a suppression of an enemy's interest with a fraudulent view, the party engaged in that fraud shall not be permitted to supply the defects of proof of his own property mixed up with it. It appears to be a rule perfectly reasonable in its principle, and one that this Court would find it necessary to support, even if the authority of the superior Court, which has adopted it, had not made it absolutely binding upon its practice. The question is, then, a question of fact: whether there is reason to suppose that these parties entertained a fraudulent intention of withdrawing this man from the view of the Court? whether this concealment was done in order to impart to him undue favour and protection, or from the more inoffensive causes suggested in the explanation? If I could be induced to believe it could be done from these suggested causes only, I should be unwilling to strain the rule of law to the disadvantage of these claimants; although they are persons who, from many cases that have appeared in this Court, cannot think themselves entitled to more attention than the demands of justice strictly require. On the other side, if the explanations are not satisfactory, I must pronounce that the imputation of fraud is not removed; and the consequence will be that under the rule which I have before stated, the parties cannot be allowed to sustain their interest by any further elucidation.

In this amended claim, it was to be expected that some account would have been given, as coming from the parties themselves, to explain how it happened that the original claim was framed in general terms.

[*Dr. Arnold.*—The parties were directed to amend the claim only; and it was apprehended that any explanation might have been considered as introducing further proof.]

I cannot but think such an explanation might have been given under the allowance of the Court to amend the claim; as it now stands, it is merely the explanation of counsel. It is said, however, in explanation, first, that the claim is to be considered as given for Black & Co., and that the addition of "& Co." implies that other persons were interested in the adventure; and that it is not necessary to specify the several shares. But can it be allowed that, if a neutral house of trade chooses to associate itself with an enemy, it is at liberty to cover his interests under a general claim so described? That never can be permitted; for, under such a claim, the interests of every subject of the enemy might be protected. It is said, further, that although Mr. Van Tromp is, under the circumstances now appearing in these papers, to be considered as a Dutchman by this Court; yet, in Denmark, he was considered as an adopted Dane; that therefore there could be no motive for dissimulation; and there being no motive for fraudulent concealment, no such concealment is to be imputed. Now, I am willing to say, that if in any one paper the name of Van Tromp had appeared, under the extreme disposition which I feel not to press the rule, where the facts will admit of an explanation that can justify a departure from it, I might accede to this reasoning; but when I see that it does not appear in *any one* paper, and that it comes out only accidentally at last from papers introduced from other ships by the fortunate diligence of the captors, the fact of dissembling his interests must, I think, be subject to the imputation fixed upon it—that it was done with a design of concealing his name from this Court, as a name that was not understood to be so clearly entitled to the rights of neutral character, as it is pretended to have been in Denmark.

1800 *June* 17.

THE GRAAFF BERNSTORF.

Sir W. Scott.

Again, if it could be shown that the concealment had been introduced only by the artifices of Van Tromp—although the principal is certainly in general to be held responsible for his agent—I should be unwilling to press the rigour of this rule, under such circumstances, against the neutral claimant. But how can this be understood? The original claim made no mention of such a person, or if the original claim was incorrectly formed under the original papers, how happened it that no application was made to reform it as erroneous till the secret had transpired from other quarters? On this view of the insufficiency of the explanation, and looking to the manner in which it is introduced, as the

1800 June 17. — The Graaff Bernstorf. — Sir W. Scott.

suggestion of counsel only, I am under the necessity of saying that a fraudulent purpose does lie at the bottom of this transaction; and I am therefore under the necessity of rejecting the application for further proof.

Arnold stated that the agent in London was under some anxiety lest blame might be imputed to him for not giving the explanation on the account of the widow Black & Co., with a specific declaration of their interests, as stated by them in a letter of 29th June, before the cause came on. He said that this had been omitted owing to an apprehension that had been entertained that the amended claim was only to state the specific interest; and therefore other points had been omitted, lest they might be thought to introduce further proof, without being authorized so to do.

Court.—I have not at this moment a very exact recollection of what passed, when the claim was ordered to be amended; but it having been agreed that the first claim was erroneous, I should not have thought the parties were wandering irregularly into further proof, if they had gone on to explain what circumstances had led to the inaccuracy of the former claim. I do not understand, that it is now asserted, that any notice was taken of Mr. Van Tromp's interest, or that the letters make this confession, before the discovery had been made of Van Tromp's interest: that being the case, it comes too late. The letters were not written till the 29th June—before the hearing indeed, but not before it was perfectly apparent that Van Tromp had this interest. I think this is not sufficient to exculpate the party. It may perhaps operate elsewhere, if the parties should incline, as they probably will in a question of such extent in point of value, to resort to other judgments; but it is not sufficient to induce me to alter the decree. It must be recollected that the decree is founded, not on this circumstance alone, but upon a view, collecting around it all other circumstances of suspicion with which the case abounds (*a*).

[4 C. Rob. 228.] (*a*) In the *Herman* (March 19th, 1802), Sir W. Scott, referring to the national character of a trader, said that where a person has a house of trade in a neutral country, and one in Great Britain "secondary to his house" in the neutral country, "that he may carry on trade with the enemy from his house at E. cannot be denied, provided it does not originate from his house in London, nor vest an interest in that house."

THE DER MOHR (No. 1). [3 C. Rob. 129.]

Capture—Prize—Loss—Negligence of Prize Master—Liability of Captor.

A captor is responsible for the act of his agent, and is therefore liable for the value of a prize lost through the negligence of a prize-master.

Refusal to take a pilot: *Held*, under the circumstances, to be an act of negligence.

THIS was a case of a ship and cargo taken September 10th, 1799, on a voyage from Surinam to Altona, but lost in coming through the Needles, owing to the ignorance and wilfulness of the prize-master put on board. The cause now came on, upon the claim of the owner of the ship for restitution in value. 1800 *June* 14.

For the claimant, *Swabey* and *Robinson*.

For the captor, the *King's Advocate* and *Arnold*.

SIR W. SCOTT.—This is certainly a very calamitous case—either to the neutral, whose property is destroyed; or to the officers of his Majesty's ship, the captor, if they are to answer for the loss which has been sustained out of their own private funds. What makes it more calamitous is, that the parties themselves, on both sides, appear to be entirely free from every imputation of blame; nothing could be more correct and meritorious than the conduct of the captors; at the same time, it is a principle too clear to be doubted, and too stubborn to be bent, that every principal is civilly answerable for the conduct of his agent. The original seizure was made on grounds which the Court has held to be justifiable; and the conduct of the parties themselves was perfectly unexceptionable; but under the principle that I have stated, the result of this application will depend on the manner in which their agent conducted himself, if the loss is immediately attributable to him.

It appears that the capture was made by two of his Majesty's ships; that the senior officer, Captain Church, committed the prize to the care of Captain Talbot, directing him to put a pilot on board, for the purpose of taking her through the Needles, and to accompany her to Spithead. These orders were most correctly obeyed by Captain Talbot; a pilot came up, and was sent on to the prize, which was at some small distance behind; indeed, it was not likely that it should be neglected, as Captain Talbot's own vessel

1800 June 14.

THE DER MOHR.

Sir W. Scott.

had herself been in some danger in getting through that passage. These gentlemen appear to have done everything that could be done on their part to exonerate them from this demand; but let us see how their inferior officer has conducted himself. The prize-master admits that a pilot came down and tendered himself as sent by one of the commanders to take charge of the vessel. The prize-master refused to admit him, but he insists "that the loss happened owing to the sudden shifting of the wind, and that no skill could have prevented it." What is the account given by the neutral master and the passengers on board? They say, "that the pilot came and told the prize-master that he was sent to take charge of the ship; but the prize-master declined to admit him, asserting that he was himself a pilot for the Needles, and wanted no assistance." How was he a pilot for the Needles? He was not, I presume, a licensed pilot for that navigation; he might be a good seaman, and equal to have taken the charge of the ship at sea, in an ordinary state of weather: but that will not be sufficient. It is clear that the captains of his Majesty's ships entertained a different opinion of his competency, for they directed a pilot to be taken on board; and if a pilot was to be had, he could not excuse himself for refusing to take his assistance. It is further stated that the neutral master, who knew this passage very well, warned him to brace his yards sharper, but he refused. Is it possible to see anything in this conduct but ignorance and obstinacy united? This account of the neutral master is fully confirmed by the affidavit (*a*) of a passenger on board, the widow of a British officer. She says, "that the prize-master refused to take the pilot on board, or to give the neutral master the management of the vessel, though he was repeatedly warned of his danger, and that she believes the vessel was lost through his want of skill, &c." These facts have not been in any manner denied, although ample time has been given to contradict them. Under these circumstances, it is impossible for me to say otherwise than that the ship was lost by the misconduct of the prize-master. It is undoubtedly a case of calamity, *miseranda vel hosti*, to be lamented by the claimant himself, if he considers himself as the enemy of his captors; but it is impossible for me to

(*a*) Affidavit of Mrs. Busch.

steer clear of the rule of law that a principal is civilly answerable for the conduct of his agent. I am under the necessity of pronouncing the neutral owner entitled to his property, and must direct restitution to be made in value of the ship.

1800 *June* 14. THE DER MOHR. Sir W. Scott.

With respect to the cargo, that is claimed for another person, a merchant of Hamburg; that may stand on other grounds. There appears to have been no cause of seizure of the ship, but for the purpose of bringing in the cargo, which was a cargo of West India produce going from the colony of the enemy. I should certainly hold there was justifiable cause of seizure as to the cargo, and as that may rest on other grounds, I shall direct that to stand over.

THE DAIFJIE.

[3 C. Rob. 139.]

Cartel Ship—Principle of Protection—Capture on Voyage to take up Cartel Duty.

Cartel ships are exempt from capture only when actually carrying prisoners or returning from the service. But when ships going in good faith to a port to become cartel ships were captured: *Held*, that under all the circumstances of the case an exception might be made to the general rule.

THIS was a question arising on two Dutch ships, taken 7th May, 1800, on a voyage from the Texel to Flushing, and claimed as being under the protection of a cartel, going to Flushing, for the purpose of taking on board some exchanged prisoners, to convey them to England.

1800 *July* 8.

SIR W. SCOTT.—These are two Dutch vessels, captured on the 7th May, and claimed as cartel ships. The question is, whether, from the circumstances under which they were taken, they are to be considered under the protection of that character or not? It is a practice of no very ancient introduction among the states of Europe to exchange prisoners of war in this manner; it has succeeded to the older practice of ransoming, which succeeded to the still more ancient practice of killing or carrying them into captivity. I say it is a practice of no remote antiquity, because, on looking into Grotius, I find not a word of exchange in the sense

1800 July 8. THE DAIFJIE. Sir W. Scott. in which we are now speaking of it. It is a practice, therefore, which, at least as far as his writings seem to indicate, was not of very familiar and general use in his time, though perhaps not altogether unknown; it is, however, of a nature highly deserving of every favourable consideration, upon the same principles as are all other *commercia belli*, by which the violence of war may be allayed as far as is consistent with its purposes, and by which something of a pacific intercourse may be kept up, which in time may lead to an adjustment of differences, and end ultimately in peace. At the same time it is highly proper that it should be conducted with very delicate honour on both sides, so as to leave no ground of suspicion that a practice introduced for the common benefit of mankind should be made a stratagem of war or become liable to fraudulent abuse. I presume the terms of cartel are usually settled by agreement between the two states. In the present instance we are not informed what those terms of agreement are; if they appeared, there might perhaps be no question left; perhaps the very letter of it might decide the present case; or, supposing it not to be within the letter, it might still be within the spirit of the agreement, liberally construed. Judging without such information, and on general principles, I must lay it down as clear that ships are to be protected in this office *ad eundum et redeundum*, both in carrying prisoners and returning from that service. Whether there is any stipulation usually made as to the species of ships to be employed does not appear; I should rather understand from the return made by the transport board that there is not any stipulation on this point, and perhaps it may be immaterial whether they are merchant ships or ships of war that are so employed. It may, indeed, be possible to put an extreme case, in which the nature of the ship might be material: as, if a fire-ship was to be sent on such service to Portsmouth or Plymouth, though she had prisoners on board, she would undoubtedly be an unwelcome visitor to a naval arsenal, and her particular character might fairly justify a refusal to admit her; but, in general, the nature of the vessel does not appear to be of consequence.

A particular circumstance in this case is, that these vessels were not actually employed as cartel ships nor taken *in trajectu* either way, either going or returning, between the ports of the two belligerents; they were not in the actual discharge of those functions, which would entitle them to protection *eundo et redeundo*, for they were going from the Texel to Flushing, there, as they say, to take the prisoners on board. It is the employment, and not the future intention, that protects; they ask protection, therefore, beyond the reach of the strict principle, which allows it only *eundo* and *redeundo*. I think, however, that the protection may be not improperly extended, if it appears that they had in any manner entered upon their functions by being put into a state of actual preparation and equipment for their employment. Suppose that such ships had been found in the Texel last year upon our expedition into Holland, actually fitted up for this use, and by being so fitted, unfitted for other uses: I think they would have claimed a favourable consideration, although they had not a prisoner on board. The passage of ships from one of their own ports to another is liable to more suspicion. If the protection of cartel were universally allowed in such cases, it would give the enemy the means of concentrating his force without molestation. It is said that this is a subject on which suspicions are not to be indulged, and that the strictest delicacy is to be observed on both sides: but such an employment of a vessel does in some degree necessarily beget suspicion; and the best way to avoid suspicion is to do nothing that excites it. If it is said that such a voyage as this between the ports of Holland is to be allowed, under the privileges of cartel, where are you to stop? I am informed a case has occurred in which an attempt was made by this very Dutch Government to get home their ships from Norway under a pretence of this same nature. May vessels be brought under this pretence from the East Indies, or where can the line be drawn? It is said that it was absolutely necessary, and that necessity justifies itself; but no such necessity is shown; it is hardly possible that there could have been any difficulty in finding shipping at Flushing. Necessity being out of the case, I will venture to lay it down that a ship going to be employed as a cartel ship is not protected by mere intention, on her way from one port to another of her own country, for the purpose of taking on herself that character when she arrives at the latter port. In some cases, perhaps, such a necessity may occur; but, then, what is the measure to be pur-

1800 July 8. THE DAIFJIE. Sir W. Scott.

sued? It is usual in such cases, and it is proper, to apply to the commissary of prisoners residing in the country of the enemy, and to obtain a pass from him. From this practice alone we may infer that it is not the employment that is held to convey a necessary protection in these cases, but that the security is derived from the special safe conduct, which would be unnecessary if the mere service were sufficient. It is a precaution most reasonable that such a safe conduct should be obtained, and I cannot consider it as depending on any particular adherence to form on the part of this country, nor as being peculiar to our government in any manner, to expect that such a caution should be observed.

At the same time, if these ships were going in perfect good faith on this service, and had ventured out to sea under a reliance of being protected by the nature of their service, though it must be considered to be a rash step, it would be too strict to hold them liable to the penalty of confiscation. The question, therefore, resolves itself into a question of fact, whether there was on the part of those intrusted with the management of this business an honest persuasion that in going to Flushing on this service they should be protected? If so, I should not be disposed to hold them liable to the penalty of confiscation. Then what are the particular circumstances of their situation? They have instructions on board from their own government, and they had an English ensign hoisted when they were addressed; so far they appear clothed with the usual marks of cartel ships, though the latter circumstance does not weigh much. The objections that have been taken are that they did not communicate with the adverse government to give notice that these ships were to be so employed. This, I have said, might be a rash and imprudent negligence on their part, but it is not decisive against them to show that they were acting fraudulently. It is, besides, stated to me that there is no English commissary residing in Holland, which takes off in some degree from the force of this objection. It is further urged that notice was not sent to their own agent here till after the capture, and perhaps till after the knowledge of it. The capture was made on the 7th May; the first letter that was written to him is of the 9th May, and the second of the 10th, both reaching him at the same time; but perhaps it was not thought necessary to write to him till the vessels were actually dispatched, when the functions of his office were to begin. It is said the size of the vessels is disproportionate to their employment, and that they were larger than such service required; but one is an old East Indiaman which had been lying some time in the Texel; and it is to be observed that the persons employed to navigate her were taken out of the military hospital, and might, on account of their health, require more than ordinary accommodation. It is to be considered also, that prisoners were to be brought back, and therefore perhaps the size might not be ill-adapted to all these circumstances. Again, it is objected that they had a quantity of shot on board, but as I understand, for the purpose of ballast only. The quantity is not large, not more than 12 tons out of 150; and it cannot be conceived that such an article might not be carried as conveniently, for any sinister purpose, from the Texel to Flushing, by their own inland navigation. As to the manner of stowing them in sand and gravel among the ballast, it is, I presume, the usual way of stowing such articles when they are not fastened down with cramps. It is said, the persons on board did not conduct themselves conformably to their instructions; they, however, appear to have done so sufficiently; or at least, if there was nothing indicative of a hostile intention, I should not be disposed to draw an unfavourable conclusion from slight circumstances of behaviour. It is said they had not their English colours flying, but they hoisted them on being addressed; it is said also, that they did not stop, on the inquiry of our cutter, to give an account of themselves. This again was an imprudence, as it might perhaps have prevented all this difficulty; but I do not think it amounts to anything more. These are the principal circumstances on which objections are raised, to show that they were not acting in a *bonâ fide* pursuit of the cartel character and office. There are, I think, on the other side, circumstances indicating a fair and honest intention. The quality of the ships is something; they appear to have been old East Indiamen, which had been laid up, and might be extremely fit for this service, and for hardly any other. In the next place, they were in some degree of preparation, and therefore entitled to the benefit of the principle, which I have thrown out on that point. Every gun was taken out; they showed no measure of offensive operations to the little English vessel that was hovering

1800 July 8. THE DAIFJIE. Sir W. Scott.

about them. I do not observe that it has been stated in argument that any particular view of hostility was to be answered by their repairing to Flushing. The officers on board positively swear "they were going as cartel ships." They must either be affected with ignorance or wilful fraud; credit must be given to their representations. The character of enemy does certainly admit of stratagem and artifice to a certain extent, yet not upon such occasions as these; on such occasions the most scrupulous attention to good faith has always been observed by the old governments of Europe, agreeably to the system on which the affairs of Europe have been happily conducted for a great length of time. There are, indeed, new governments that have omitted no opportunity of expressing themselves adversely to all rules on which the old system has been founded; and it may be doubtful how far they are disposed to conform in practice to those ancient principles: but they shall have an example at least to show them, that the ancient governments still adhere, with the most delicate attention, to all the principles on which the public affairs of Europe have hitherto been managed: they shall see that it is their interest to respect that system, whatever views they may have had in affecting to treat it with indignity and contempt.

These are the considerations on which I shall direct these vessels to be restored; at the same time, I must say that there has been much rashness and imprudence. The whole of the trouble and expense of these proceedings has been occasioned by the irregularity of their conduct. It is but fit that this expense should fall upon them; therefore I restore these vessels subject to the payment of the expenses of this suit (*a*).

[5 C. Rob. 192.] (*a*) In the *La Gloire*, December 2nd, 1803, the principle of this case was followed.

Court.—When this case came on before, the Court intimated a disposition to sustain the claim, if it should appear to have been the understanding of the parties, and particularly of the party granting the permission, that a ship sailing on this service under a flag of truce should be protected, though not strictly a cartel. Whether the British commander might have exceeded his powers, or have made an improvident concession, would not, I think, supersede the obligation which this Court would feel itself under to support the good faith of the agreement, on which the other party had acted with confidence. The prisoners were sent to Martinique, probably for mutual convenience. This contract was then entered into between the prefect of the government of that place and the master of this ship, under the direction of

THE JUFFROW MARIA SCHROEDER. [3 C. Rob. 147.]

Blockade—Non-effective Character—Ship Restored—Cargo Condemned.

When a neutral ship had been permitted to enter a blockaded port, and on coming out with a cargo there shipped had passed the blockading force, but was afterwards seized by a cruiser not engaged on the blockade: *Held*, that the blockade had been relaxed, and that under the circumstances the ship should be restored. The *Neptunus* (*No.* 2), *ante*, p. 195, followed. *Held* also, that the owners of the cargo had not brought themselves within the exception to the general rule, and that the cargo must be condemned.

THIS was the case of a Prussian vessel taken 14th June, 1799, on a voyage from Rouen to Altona, and proceeded against for a breach of the blockade of Havre. On a former hearing it had been contended on the part of the claimant that the blockade was to be considered as relaxed, and an application was directed to be made to the Admiralty for information respecting the continuance of the blockade of Havre. A certificate was now produced from the Admiralty in these words:—"Certifying to the Right Honourable Sir William Scott, Judge of the High Court of Admiralty of England, that the port of Havre de Grace in France, and the other ports of the Seine, were ordered to be blockaded by his Majesty's ships on the 28th of February, 1798; and that such blockade has not since that time been raised or relaxed by any orders from the Right Honourable the Lords Commissioners of the Admiralty to his Majesty's cruisers; but the said port has been, and still continues to be, in a state of blockade. July 4th, 1800." 1800 *July* 15.

the captain general. It is now certified not to have exceeded the intention of the British officer, under whose permission these prisoners were allowed to return to France; and that is the point to which I principally look, and which approaches to the foundation of the principle laid down by the Court in the case referred to. Something has been said of the bad faith which the Government of France has practised on some similar occasion in detaining a vessel sent regularly as a cartel ship from this country to a port of France. Such a behaviour would on no account be resorted to as a precedent, to which this Court would attend, in considering the proper effect of the proceedings of these parties in this transaction. I am of opinion that the representation of the claimant is substantially confirmed by the British officer, and I shall decree restitution, giving the captor the expenses of taking the depositions, and of the further proof that has been necessary to clear up this matter.

In the *Carolina*, the Court held as to contracts for cartel ships that "the actual existence of a war is not essentially necessary to give effect to them, but that it will be sufficient if they are entered into prospectively and in expectation of approaching war." [6 C. Rob. 336.]

1800 July 15. THE JUFFROW MARIA SCHROEDER. Sir W. Scott.

SIR W. SCOTT.—This is the case of a ship taken on a voyage from Havre to Altona. All the papers express that the ship came from Havre, and there is no dissimulation of that circumstance. The master, on his examination, says "that he does not know for what reason he was taken"; but it is not necessary that the captor should have assigned any reason at the time of capture: he takes at his own peril, and on his own responsibility, to answer in costs and damages for any wrongful exercise of the rights of capture. At the same time it may be a matter of convenience that some declaration should be made, because it is possible that if the grounds are stated it may be in the power of the neutral master to give such reasons as may explain away the suspicion that is suggested. It may therefore be convenient to both parties, but it is not absolutely necessary; it is not a duty incumbent on the captor to state his reasons; much less it is to be argued negatively, that because no mention was made of the blockade at the time of capture, it must necessarily have been unknown to both the parties.

In the depositions the neutral master swears very positively to his own ignorance of the fact of blockade, and states in a very ingenuous manner the course of his late voyages, "that he had been from Memel to Sandwich, that he sailed from thence for Embden, but was prevented by winds, and went to Bordeaux, from thence to Havre, and was now proceeding from Havre to Altona, having never broken a blockade nor received any notification;" and in this account he is supported by another witness. However, the fact turned out to be, and the captors had a perfect right to avail themselves of it, that Havre was in a state of blockade, and though this vessel had passed the blockading force, and was taken by a cruiser not employed on that service, yet it has been held by the Court (*a*), that where a ship has contracted the guilt by sailing with an intention of entering a blockaded port, or by sailing out, the offence is not purged away till the end of the voyage; till that period is completed, it is competent to any cruisers to seize and proceed against her for that offence. If, therefore, the fact is proved that the ship had violated a blockade, there can be no doubt but that this cutter will be entitled to the benefit of it against her.

(*a*) *Welvaart Van Pillaw*, *ante*, p. 207.

It is perfectly clear that a blockade had taken place some months before, and that the notification was communicated to the claimant's government not only that a blockade would be imposed, but of a most rigorous kind. A blockade may be more or less rigorous, either for the single purpose of watching the military operations of the enemy, and preventing the egress of their fleet, as at Cadiz; or, on a more extended scale, to cut off all access of neutral vessels to that interdicted place, which is strictly and properly a blockade, for the other is, in truth, no blockade at all as far as neutrals are concerned. It is an undoubted right of belligerents to impose such a blockade, though a severe right, and, as such, not to be extended by construction; it may operate as a grievance on neutrals, but it is one to which, by the law of nations, they are bound to submit. Being, however, a right of a severe nature, it is not to be aggravated by mere construction.

The notification in this instance declared that the blockade was to be of the most rigorous kind. The Seine was to be perfectly sealed up, no ingress or egress was to be allowed; the blockade was to be as complete as the blockading force could make it. This was the tenor of the notification given to foreign governments, and I cannot entertain the least doubt that the orders which were given to our Admiralty were conformable to it. It is impossible to suppose that the orders for carrying into effect a great measure so materially affecting other states would not be given by government with the utmost exactness. When such measures are imposed, it might be a matter of convenience if some notification was given to this Court, which is ultimately to decide on the consequences resulting from it. It might be desirable also that our fleets in other stations should be apprised of it. But these are considerations of convenience and practice, in no way interfering with the effect of the notification that has been made and the means that have been taken to carry it into execution. It is impossible to suppose that the communication so made by the government to the Board of Admiralty was not acted upon by the Admiralty with equal exactness; no one who knows the manner in which that Board has at all times been conducted, can doubt that the orders for carrying such a measure into effect were framed and delivered to our cruisers on that station with the utmost

1800 *July* 15. THE JUFFROW MARIA SCHROEDER. Sir W. Scott.

dispatch and precision. This fact I will venture to assume, that orders must have been given to these cruisers in the most regular manner; yet I cannot shut my eyes to a fact that presses upon the Court, that the blockade has not been duly carried into effect. A temporary and forced secession of the blockading force from the accidents of winds and storms would not be sufficient to constitute a legal relaxation; but here ships are stopped and examined and suffered to go in. The master of this particular vessel says, "that in coming out he saw no ships for forty-eight hours." That might be accidental; but when he entered they were on the station, yet no attempt was made to prevent him from going in. No contradiction is opposed to this account, though I have no doubt that a proper application has been made to the King's ships concerned. In other cases also, it appears that no force was applied for the purpose of enforcing the blockade; the same permission was given to go in. How this happened I cannot divine, for I find the orders of the Admiralty of the 27th August, 1799, were "to block up the port of Havre," and these seem to connect themselves with the former orders. There is, besides, a letter from Mr. Nepean to Captain Griffiths, in answer to a letter stating "that the *Fly* had examined a scow and suffered her to go in," in which Mr. Nepean writes, "I am commanded to acquaint you that you are not to suffer any vessel to enter, &c." There can be no doubt, then, of the intention of the Admiralty that neutral ships should not be permitted to go in, but the fact is that it was not in every instance carried into effect.

What is a blockade, but to prevent access by force? If the ships stationed on the spot to keep up the blockade will not use their force for that purpose, it is impossible for a Court of Justice to say there was a blockade actually existing at that time so as to bind this vessel. Then the only ground on which she could be affected would be that the whole voyage was criminal from the time of sailing from Bordeaux, without any reference to the conduct of the blockading force. In opposition to that, I am to consider that the ship was not coming from her own port. She had been some time absent from her own country; she had been in our ports, where it is possible the notification might not have reached her; she afterwards went to Bordeaux. During the time necessarily employed in two such voyages, if the master had been accidentally informed of the blockade before, it would be a little hard to say that he might not entertain a conjecture that the blockade had ceased. I fear that alone would not avail him; but coupling it with the fact that no force appeared to prevent him from going in, it would be a little rigorous to bind down the strict principle of law on him. I think these circumstances bring the case within the principle of the *Neptunus* (*a*), in which it appeared that the ship sailed with an intention of breaking the blockade of Havre, or, rather, under the chance of finding that the blockade had ceased. She met with Admiral Duncan's fleet, and was informed that Havre was open; and the Court held, that after that permission she was not to be considered as taken *in delicto*. In the present case the ship was permitted to go in with a cargo. Looking at the facts that she came from the south of Europe, and that she was actually permitted to enter, I think she brings herself within the scope of the favourable considerations applied to that former case. It is impossible for me to say this without observing, at the same time, on the great mischief that ensues from this sort of inattention practised by our cruisers. It is in vain for governments to impose blockades, if those employed on that service will not enforce them. The inconvenience is very great, and spreads far beyond the individual case: reports are eagerly circulated that the blockade is raised; foreigners take advantage of the information; the property of innocent persons is ensnared; and the honour of our own country is involved in the mistake.

Ship restored (*b*).

(*a*) *Ante*, p. 195.

(*b*) In the *Vrow Barbara*, which was a case of a ship taken on a voyage from Havre to Hamburg, 5th July, 1799, it appeared that she had been stopped and examined in going into Havre, and had been informed, on asking whether she might go in, "that on a particular signal (which was afterwards made) she might." The master in this case acknowledged "that he had known of the blockade, but understood that it had been relaxed."

For the claimant, *Laurence* said: It was a case in which all the favourable consideration applied to the *Neptunus* and the preceding case concurred; that on being warned off from the ports of Holland by the *Courier*, 26th April, 1799, the master of this vessel asked if she might go on to Havre: it was answered "she might;" she went on, and was

1801
June 24.

THE JUFFROW MARIA SCHROEDER.

THE question as to the cargo of the *Juffrow Maria* came before the Court on the 24th June, 1801, when affidavits were offered from several claimants, stating their ignorance of the blockade of Havre at the time of shipment; and it was contended that under the general relaxation of the blockade of Havre, which had appeared to have taken place during the winter, 1798, and the ensuing spring and summer, these persons had been led to suppose that it had altogether ceased; and therefore that orders given under that mistake were to be considered as given in a state of justifiable ignorance, and could not be imputed to them as a breach of the blockade of Havre.

SIR W. SCOTT.—The rule by which the Court has been induced to act towards certain vessels, in consequence of the relaxed manner in which the blockade of Havre appeared to have been enforced in those particular cases, by no means interferes with the general effect and operation of this blockade. On the contrary, the Court has held that there was no general relaxation, although particular

permitted to go in and come out, and was at last picked up by one of the same squadron with the *Courier*, who had warned her off from the ports of Holland, having at that time no intimation of the blockade of Havre.

The Court considered this to be a case still more strongly entitled to a favourable application of the principle.

Restored.

In the case of the *Henricus*, captured 8th September, 1799, on a voyage from Havre to Lisbon, a similar excuse prevailed. The master stated that he had received permission of the *Duchess of York* to go in with a cargo of coals, and was captured on his returned voyage. The Court held the permission to go in with a cargo included the permission to that ship to come out with a cargo.

Ship restored.

In the *Venscab*, taken 3rd October, 1799, going into Havre, the papers purported the voyage to be from St. Martin's to Copenhagen. To account for the deviation it was said that the ship had sustained damage, and was obliged to put in; that during the period in which the Court had determined there was no blockade existing, from November, 1798, to September, 1799, she had gone *in* and out without molestation.

The Court held this ship to be entitled to the same principle, but observed: "I beg it may be understood, that I hold the blockade to have existed generally, though individual ships, in some few instances, are entitled to an exemption from the penalty in consequence of the irregular indulgence shown to them by the blockading force. It *has never been held* by the Court that no blockade existed from November, 1798, to September, 1799."

vessels were considered to be protected by the loose manner in which the blockade was kept up towards them. The ship in the present case was restored on the ground that she had been allowed to go in with a cargo, and therefore might be understood to be at liberty to come out with a cargo. But the extent of that principle is to be confined to those who had been the objects of this improper indulgence. The ship was restored; but it by no means follows that the owners of the cargo stand on the same footing: that may have been shipped, in consequence of criminal orders, directing it to be sent on any opportunity of slipping out. It is therefore not to be argued that the release of the ship is any conclusive evidence respecting the cargo.

Then how stands this case as to the owners of the cargo? After the blockade had been notified, the most prudent conduct would have been to wait for a relaxation from the belligerent who imposed the blockade before they gave any orders. At any rate, it could go no further than this: that the orders should be provisional, directing shipments to be made when the blockade should be raised; as an absolute order during the continuance of a blockade, if executed, must be considered to be a breach of that blockade. Under any circumstances, such a provisional order would be attended with great hazard in respect to the good faith of the enemy shipper, who may be under a temptation to ship off his goods, without regard to the risk of his employer, and this risk persons giving such order must be content to take on themselves. The affidavit that has been introduced only states, "that he was ignorant at the time of shipment." That will not be sufficient; that will not purge away the offence at the time of giving the orders. The parties must either state themselves to have been ignorant of the blockade, at the time of ordering the goods, and show the grounds of their opinion arising out of any of these particular instances of relaxation to individual ships; or, at least, they must show that the orders were provisional. Under this affidavit they have not brought themselves within the limits of this indulgence, and I reject the application.

In some other claims, *Laurence* said there were several affidavits which had not been translated, and might prove orders given provisionally.

1801 June 24. — The Juffrow Maria Schroeder. — Sir W. Scott.

The Court was at first disposed to let them stand over. Afterwards, on consideration: I think the indulgence will not avail them; because, supposing they should make out that they gave a conditional order; still, I hold that the blockade did actually exist at the time when they were carried into execution, and they must take upon themselves to answer for the undue execution of those orders, and make the shippers answerable to them. If this rule was not adopted, there would be no end to shipments made during a blockade, whilst there would be nobody at all responsible for such acts of misconduct.

Cargo condemned.

[3 C. Rob. 162.]

TWEE GEBROEDERS (No. 1).

Capture—Neutral Territory.

When a ship lying in neutral territory sent out boats which captured an enemy ship outside the neutral territory: *Held*, that as an act of hostility must not take its commencement within neutral territory, the captured ship must be restored.

1800 July 29.

This was a case respecting four Dutch ships, taken in the Western Ems, in or near the Groningen Wat, by boats sent from the L'Espiegle, then lying in the Eastern Ems. The material point of the case turned on the question of territory. The Prussian consul claiming restitution (by the direction of the Chargé (*a*) des Affaires of Prussia), on a suggestion that it was a capture made within the protection of the Prussian territory.

Sir W. Scott.—This ship was taken on the 14th July, 1799, on a voyage from Embden to Amsterdam, which was then under blockade; a claim has been given by the Prussian Government, asserting the capture to have been made within the Prussian territory. In the course of the discussion which this suit has produced, it has been contended that although the act of capture itself

(*a*) In claims of this nature it has been held in the *Etrusco*, and in other cases, that a suggestion of neutral territory cannot be set up by an individual claimant, but that it must proceed from the government whose territory is asserted to have been violated.

might not take place within the neutral territory, yet that the ship to which the capturing boats belonged was actually lying within the neutral limits, and therefore, that wherever the place of capture might be, the station of the ship was in itself sufficient to affect the legality of the capture.

Upon the question so proposed, the first fact to be determined is the character of the place where the capturing ship lay, whether she was actually stationed within those portions of land and water, or of something between water and land, which are considered to be within the limits of the Prussian territory. On this point I am inclined to think, on an inspection of the charts, and on hearing what has been urged, that she was lying within the limits to which neutral immunity is usually conceded. She was lying in the eastern branch of the Ems, within what may, I think, be considered as a distance of three miles at most from East Friesland. An exact measurement cannot easily be obtained; but in a case of this nature, in which the Court would not willingly act with an unfavourable minuteness towards a neutral state, it will be disposed to calculate the distance very liberally, and more especially as the spot in question is a sand covered with water only on the flow of the tide, but immediately connected with the land of East Friesland, and when dry may be considered as making part of it. I am of opinion that the ship was lying within those limits, in which all direct hostile operations are by the law of nations forbidden to be exercised. That fact being assumed, I have only to inquire whether, the ship being so stationed, the capture which took place was made under such circumstances as oblige us to consider it as an act of violence, committed within the protection of a neutral territory.

It is said that the ship was in all respects observant of the peace of the neutral territory, that nothing was done by her which could affect the right of territory, or from which any inconvenience could arise to the country within whose limits she was lying, inasmuch as the hostile force which she employed was applied to the captured vessel lying out of the territory. But that is a doctrine that goes a great deal too far. I am of opinion that no use of a neutral territory for the purposes of war is to be permitted. I do not say remote uses, such as procuring provisions and refreshments, and

1800 July 29. TWEE GEBROEDERS. Sir W. Scott.

acts of that nature, which the law of nations universally tolerates; but that no proximate acts of war are in any manner to be allowed to originate on neutral grounds; and I cannot but think that such an act as this, that a ship should station herself on neutral territory, and send out her boats on hostile enterprises, is an act of hostility much too immediate to be permitted; for, suppose that even a direct hostile use should be required to bring it within the prohibition of the law of nations, nobody will say that the very act of sending out boats to effect a capture is not itself an act directly hostile—not complete, indeed, but inchoate, and clothed with all the characters of hostility. If this could be defended, it might as well be said that a ship lying in a neutral station might fire shot on a vessel lying out of the neutral territory. The injury in that case would not be consummated, nor received on neutral ground; but no one would say that such an act would not be an hostile act, immediately commenced within the neutral territory: and what does it signify to the nature of the act, considered for the present purpose, whether I send out a cannon-shot which shall compel the submission of a vessel lying at two miles distance, or whether I send out a boat armed and manned to effect the very same thing at the same distance? It is in both cases the direct act of the vessel lying in neutral ground; the act of hostility actually begins, in the latter case, with the launching and manning and arming the boat that is sent out on such an errand of force.

If it were necessary, therefore, to prove that a direct and immediate act of hostility had been committed, I should be disposed to hold that it was sufficiently made out by the facts of this case. But direct hostility appears not to be necessary, for whatever has an immediate connection with it is forbidden. You cannot, without leave, carry prisoners or booty into a neutral territory, there to be detained, because such an act is an immediate continuation of hostility. In the same manner, an act of hostility is not to take its commencement on neutral ground. It is not sufficient to say it is not completed there; you are not to take any measure there that shall lead to immediate violence; you are not to avail yourself of a station on neutral territory, making as it were a vantage ground of the neutral country, a country which is to carry itself with perfect equality between both belligerents, giving neither the one nor the other any advantage. Many instances have occurred in which such an irregular use of a neutral country has been warmly resented, and some during the present war. The practice which has been tolerated in the northern states of Europe of permitting French privateers to make stations of their ports, and to sally out to capture British vessels in that neighbourhood, is of that number. And yet even that practice, unfriendly and noxious as it is, is less than that complained of in the present instance, for here the ship without sallying out at all is to commit the hostile act. Every government is perfectly justified in interposing to discourage the commencement of such a practice, for the inconvenience to which the neutral territory will be exposed is obvious. If the respect due to it is violated by one party, it will soon provoke a similar treatment from the other also, till, instead of neutral ground, it will soon become the theatre of war. On these grounds I am of opinion that this capture cannot be maintained, and I direct these vessels to be restored.

1800 *July* 29.

TWEE GEBROEDERS.

Sir W. Scott.

[On prayer for costs and damages.]

Court.—With respect to that, I think the situation in which the vessels were stationed was too dubious to affect the parties with any intentional violation of neutral rights. The capture may have arisen from misapprehension and mistake. It is very different from a case of actual attack on clear neutral territory. There is no sufficient reason to induce me to give costs and damages against the captors.

THE IMINA.

[3 C. Rob. 167.]

Contraband Cargo—Destination—Neutral Port—Alteration of Destination.

A ship with a contraband cargo started on a voyage to a blockaded port. Such destination would have made the cargo contraband. The master, before reaching it, being apprised of the blockade, altered the voyage to a neutral port, but the ship was captured before reaching it. *Held*, that as the ship was captured after the alteration in her destination, the cargo should not be condemned, but that the captors should have their expenses (*a*).

THIS was a case of a cargo of ship timber which had sailed July, 1798, from Dantzic, originally for Amsterdam, but was going at

1800 *August* 1.

(*a*) See the *Minerva*, p. 301.

the time of capture to Embden, in consequence of information of the blockade of Amsterdam (*a*).

On the part of the claimant, it was said that it consisted of small pieces under 20 feet in length, and that it was fit only for making of masts, to which under the improved method of constructing masts almost any timber might be applied; that this was no criterion of its contraband quality. Another and more material question arose respecting the destination; as it appeared that the master, on hearing at Elsineur that Amsterdam was under blockade, had formed the design of changing his course for Embden, had entered his protest to that effect, and was at the time of capture sailing for Embden.

SIR W. SCOTT.—This is a claim for a ship taken, as it is admitted, at the time of capture sailing for Embden, a neutral port; a destination on which, if it is considered as the real destination, no question of contraband could arise, inasmuch as goods going to a neutral port cannot come under the description of contraband, all goods going there being equally lawful. It is contended, however, that they are of such a nature as to become contraband if taken on a destination to a hostile port. On this point some difference of opinion seems to have been entertained; and the papers which are brought in may be said to leave this important fact in some doubt. Taking it, however, that they are of such a nature as to be liable to be considered as contraband on a hostile destination, I cannot fix that character on them in the present voyage. The rule respecting contraband, as I have always understood it, is that the articles must be taken *in delicto*, in the actual prosecution of the voyage to an enemy's port. Under the present understanding of the law of nations, you cannot generally take the proceeds in the return voyage. From the moment of quitting port on a hostile destination, indeed, the offence is complete, and it is not necessary to wait till the goods are actually endeavouring to enter the enemy's port; but beyond that, if the

(*a*) The blockade of Amsterdam and of the ports of Holland was suspended by notification to the Foreign Minister, 27th November, 1799.

goods are not taken *in delicto*, and in the actual prosecution of such a voyage, the penalty is not now generally held to attach.

Some argument has been drawn in this case from the conduct of the owners. It is said "that they did not consider these articles as contraband; that they were sent openly, and without suppression or disguise;" perhaps that alone would not avail them. It appears, however, that Amsterdam was declared by this country to be in a state of blockade, a circumstance that would make it peculiarly criminal to attempt to carry a cargo of this nature to that port. The master receives information of this fact at Elsineur, and on consultation with the consul of the nation to which the cargo belonged, changed his purpose, and actually shaped his course for Embden, to which place he was sailing at the time of capture. I must ask them, was this property taken under such circumstances as make it subject to the penalty of contraband? Was it taken *in delicto*, in the prosecution of an intention of landing it at a hostile port? Clearly not; but it is said, that in the understanding and intention of the owner it was going to a hostile port; and that the intention on his part was complete from the moment when the ship sailed on that destination. Had it been taken at any period previous to the actual variation, there could be no question but that this intention would have been sufficient to subject the property to confiscation; but when the variation had actually taken place, however arising, the fact no longer existed. There is no *corpus delicti* existing at the time of capture. In this point of view, I think the case is very distinguishable from some other cases, in which, on the subject of deviation by the master into a blockaded port, the Court did not hold the cargo to be necessarily involved in the consequences of that act. It is argued, that as the criminal deviation of the master did not there immediately implicate the cargo; so here, the favourable alteration cannot protect it; and that the offence must, in both instances, be judged by the act and designs of the owner. But in those cases there was the guilty act really existing at the time of capture; both the ship and cargo were taken *in delicto;* and the only question was, to whom the *delictum* was to be imputed; if it was merely the offence of the master, it might bind the owner of the ship, whose agent he was; but the Court held that it would be

1800 August 1. THE IMINA. Sir W. Scott. hard to bind the owners of the cargo by acts of the master, who is not *de jure* their agent, unless so specially constituted by them. In the present instance there is no existing *delictum*. In those cases the criminal appearance which did exist was purged away by considering the owners of the cargo not to be necessarily responsible for the act of the master; but here there is nothing requiring any explanation. The cargo is taken on a voyage to a neutral port. To say that it is nevertheless exposed to condemnation, on account of the original destination as it stood in the mind of the owners, would be carrying the penalty of contraband further than it has been ever carried by this or the Superior Court. If the capture had been made a day before, that is, before the alteration of the course, it might have been different; but however the variation has happened, I am disposed to hold that the parties are entitled to the benefit of it; and that under that variation the question of contraband does not at all arise. I shall decree restitution; but as it was absolutely incumbent on the captors to bring the cause to adjudication from the circumstance of the apparent original destination, I think they are fairly entitled to their expenses.

Restitution. Captor's expenses decreed.

[3 C. Rob. 173.]

THE NEPTUNUS (No. 4).

Blockade—Neutral Cargo Owner—Liability for Act of Agent—Egress.

The stringency of the rule as to blockade may be relaxed in the case of a neutral cargo owner who is *bonâ fide* ignorant of the existence of a blockade.

1800 August 8. THIS was a case arising out of the blockade of Amsterdam, in respect to several parts of a cargo shipped in July and August, 1798, under the orders of neutral merchants of Hamburg and Portugal. The claims of several persons at Hamburg and other neighbouring ports were condemned under the general rule respecting shipments in a blockaded port after notification.

On behalf of claimants resident in Portugal, it was prayed that the Court would allow some indulgence in respect to the distance of their situation, and permit them to show that the shipments were made under orders given previous to the blockade.

1800
August 8.

THE NEPTUNUS.

Sir W. Scott.

Sir W. Scott.—It appears to me that this case is distinguishable from the case of the *Columbia* (a), and others (cited in the argument for the captors) in which the dominion and power over the ship and cargo were entrusted to the master and the agent of the claimants. It might be attended with great hardship to neutral merchants if a responsibility for the acts of agents in the enemy's country was to be bound down without any consideration on them, with the same strictness with which the law imputes the acts of agents in ordinary cases to their employers; it is obvious that such agents may have private interests in shipping off the merchandise of their ports whilst under blockade without attending sufficiently to the risk of their principals. I shall permit the orders to be produced, that it may be seen whether there has been time for counter-ordering the respective shipments after the notification of the blockade, and whether due diligence has been used to this effect on the part of the several claimants.

On a subsequent day the letters of orders were produced. In one claim a letter of orders was exhibited 17th October, 1797, "to send with all possible dispatch;" and a letter of advice of 19th July, 1798, giving information that the goods had *all* been put on board.

Sir W. Scott.—This is the case of goods put on board a vessel which, from the time of sailing, has been pronounced to have been guilty of a breach of the blockade of Amsterdam. *Primâ facie* certainly the cargo is to be considered as liable to the same judgment. It appears that the shipment was made between the 9th and 19th of July, the notification of the blockade of Amsterdam having been made on the 11th June, 1798. The first order that the Court made was for the production of the letters of orders, because, if it had appeared that they were given after the time when the notification could by a fair possibility be supposed to have been known to the person giving the orders, he would be

(a) *Ante*, p. 89.

1800 *August* 8. THE NEPTUNUS. Sir W. Scott.

bound directly by his own act, or, if they were sent *previous* to the notification, two questions might arise: 1st, whether sufficient time had intervened since the notification to have given him an opportunity of counter-ordering the shipment, for if so he would be legally answerable for the consequences of his own negligence; or, 2ndly, if sufficient time had not intervened, whether, though personally free from all imputation of offence, the claimant might not be bound by that powerful general principle of law which holds the employer responsible for the acts of his agent. The date of the order in this instance takes the party out of the first description, because it being given in October, 1797, long before the blockade *de facto* commenced, the parties are entirely exculpated from all offence in this stage of the transaction. But then the second question arises, whether there was not time to countermand?

On this point it would, perhaps, be holding the party too rigorously to the strict principle of law to say that he might have written with a hope, and under the chance of countermanding the order *in time;* the notification was made on the 11th of June; in all probability it was not known at Lisbon till the latter end of that month, as an interval of three weeks might not be too much to allow for the communication with that place. Supposing the notification to have been known there at that time, we must recollect that the party might naturally conceive from the time which had elapsed, and the particular directions which had been at first given to make the shipment "with all possible dispatch," that the order had been already executed, and that if he had written to counter-order, the letter would not have been received till the shipment had been actually carried into effect. The claimant stands, therefore, fully justified as far as his own personal act can be considered. But then it comes to this general question, which I am not aware that the Court has yet fully decided, whether the owners are in all cases bound merely by the act of their agents? the abstract rule is undoubtedly just, that persons are bound by their agents; but two or three considerations weigh much to induce me to limit the extent and application of this principle in these particular cases. In the first place, I cannot but recollect that the law of blockade is a thing rather out of the common course of mercantile experience; it is new to merchants, and not very familiar to lawyers themselves. It might be therefore a little too rigorous to expect, in the very first instance, an exact compliance with the strict rule of law. A second consideration is that the agents of foreign merchants in the enemy's country, that country being under blockade, do not stand in the same situation as other agents: they have not only a distinct, but even an opposite interest from that of their principal, to fulfil the commission at all risks as rapidly as possible for their own private advantage and for the public interest of their country, at that time under particular pressure as to the exportation of its produce. This may fairly be allowed to impose a strong obligation on the candour of the Court, not to hold an employer too strictly bound, on mere general principles, by an agent, who may be actuated by interests different from those of his principal.

[The Court directed the counsel to proceed on the other claims in the case.]

In a second claim, the letter of orders appeared to have been written 12th December, 1797, but renewed in a subsequent correspondence of the 19th June and 10th July, 1798 [and the Court held that the blockade must have been known at Lisbon on 10th July].

THE HIRAM.

[3 C. Rob. 180.]

Capture—Recapture—Freight.

A vessel was chartered from Liverpool to Halifax, then to the West Indies, and back to Liverpool. She was captured on her outward voyage, was recaptured and brought back to Plymouth. *Held*, that no freight was due.

1800 *October* 8.

THIS was an application for a freight *pro ratâ* for so much as had been performed, at the time of capture, of a voyage from Liverpool to Halifax and the West Indies and back. It appeared that the ship had been captured by the French, and afterwards recaptured and brought to Plymouth.

On the part of the ship, *Sewell*.

1800 October 8. THE HIRAM. Sir W. Scott.

SIR W. SCOTT.—This ship appears to have been chartered to go on a voyage from Liverpool to Halifax, from thence to one or more of the West India islands and back to Liverpool. The terms of the charter-party are "that she was to receive a freight of 210*l.* for each month: 500*l.* on delivery at Halifax, in bills of three months on London, and the remainder on the delivery of her returned cargo at Liverpool," with a proviso "that if the voyage was performed in less than six months freight should, notwithstanding, be paid for six months certain." This last circumstance tends strongly to show that it was not so much the time as the actual accomplishment of the voyage that was the material object in the contemplation of the contracting parties. To the same effect there is another clause respecting the returned voyage: "that if the ship should be lost or taken after sailing from Halifax no more freight should be due." The vessel took in her lading at Liverpool; whether she suffered by any delay or not does not appear; there is no complaint made that she was improperly detained, and indeed it is not likely that it should be so, as it must have been equally for the interest of the ship and cargo that everything should be forwarded with all possible dispatch.

The ship sailed and was taken, and afterwards retaken and brought back to a British port, which is in fair consideration of law to be taken as if she had been brought back to her own port; she was brought actually to Plymouth, the distance from which port to Liverpool is so short, in comparison of the whole projected voyage, that I may be justified in considering it in effect the same as if she had actually been brought back to Liverpool. That being the case, the question will be whether, under the general law or under the particular terms of this contract, any or what part of the freight becomes due? I am of opinion, that under either of these authorities no *part* is due. The case of *Luke* v. *Lyde* has been pressed upon the Court: that was a vessel chartered from Newfoundland to Lisbon, taken in a very late stage of her voyage, afterwards retaken and brought to Bideford. On these facts, Lord Mansfield held that a great part of the voyage had been accomplished, and that, agreeably to the old authorities, the ship was entitled to a freight *pro ratâ itineris peracti.* But, then, I am to consider that the ship was brought to Bideford, from which port to Lisbon the voyage is frequently not more than six or seven days; she had therefore almost arrived at the port of her original destination. To make that a parallel case with the present, we should inquire what would have been the opinion of that noble person if the ship had been carried back to Newfoundland? In such a case it would have been a complete defeasance of everything that the ship had done towards the accomplishment of the contract. It is said in the present case that the ship was not in fault; certainly not; neither was the cargo. If the cause of capture could be imputed as a fault, arising out of the national character, it was common to both; some of the consequences of this misfortune also are common to both, though there may be others peculiar to the several interests of the ship and cargo. It is said on the part of the ship, there is the wear and tear, the loss of time, and the consumption of provisions. But is there nothing of that sort falling on the cargo? Is there not leakage and ullage, and, besides, the peculiar loss of the particular market for which it was assorted?

On this view of the matter, considering it as the case of a ship brought to the *quasi* port of her departure, I am of opinion that the doctrine of freight *pro ratâ itineris peracti* cannot be maintained. The registrar has stated that it has not been usual in the practice of this Court to give freight in such cases, and therefore, on all general principle and practice, I should pronounce that the parties are not entitled. But still further, on the particular terms of the contract, I think this demand cannot be sustained. The charter-party stipulates "that the freighter shall not pay any part till the arrival at Halifax, where 500*l.* should be paid; and that if she arrives safe and shall be taken or lost afterwards, no more shall be paid or become due." It is said that the words "become due" are not in the former part of the instrument; but it is to be remembered that this is an instrument not usually drawn up with strict technical precision. The obvious meaning, according to common apprehension, must be that no part was to be paid unless the ship arrived at Halifax; that event was prevented by the accidents of war. I think, on the whole, that the Court cannot, without deviating not only from the settled principle and practice, but from the fair sense of the particular contract between the parties, order any part of the freight to be paid, and I reject the application.

[3 C. Rob. 217.]

THE FRANKLIN (No. 1).

Contraband—Enemy Port—Neutral Ship—Condemnation.

A ship was captured clearly bound for an enemy port under a false destination, carrying contraband. *Held*, that she must be condemned.

1801 *March* 6.

THIS was a case of a Prussian ship going with a cargo of hemp and iron from Lubeck, ostensibly to Lisbon, but actually, as it was inferred from the place of capture and course of the voyage, to Bilbao, and taken about three miles off St. Andero.

SIR W. SCOTT.—This is the case of a ship claimed as the property of Prussian subjects, and sufficiently proved to belong to them. The charter-party made with persons at Hamburg engages her to go from Lubeck to Lisbon. If that was the real destination, there could be no doubt that the owner would be entitled to a restitution. But a question has arisen on that fact from the nature of her cargo and the place in which she was taken. Her cargo consists of several articles directly contraband if going to the enemy, and not protected by the favourable considerations which are to a certain degree and in some known instances applied to the goods of persons exporting the native commodities of their country. The other articles, though not so distinctly contraband, are such as are of great use in naval equipment, and might subject the ship to some penal inconvenience if going to a hostile port.

The destination, therefore, is the principal fact in this case. The ship was taken out of her proper course, and in a direct course towards one of the Spanish ports in the Bay of Biscay, on this side of Cape Finisterre. I have had frequent occasion to observe that it is very difficult to detect a fraud of this species in the particular instances. Pretences and excuses are always resorted to, the fallacy of which can seldom be completely exposed; and therefore, without undertaking the task of exposing them in the particular case, the Court has been induced (and I hope not unwarrantably) to hold generally in each case that the certain fact shall prevail over the dubious explanations.

[The Court then examined the facts and concluded.]

I am satisfied, on the facts of this case, that it was the plan of this voyage to carry the ship fraudulently, under a false destination, into a Spanish port; no explanation having been offered, the present evidence must be taken to be conclusive. The consequence will be that this fraudulent conduct on the parts of those who are concerned in the ship will justly subject her to confiscation. Anciently, the carrying of contraband did in ordinary cases affect the ship, and although a relaxation has taken place, it is a relaxation the benefit of which can only be claimed by fair cases. The aggravation of fraud justifies additional penalties, and the right of pre-emption, which would otherwise be defeated, must be secured by them. This is the opinion which, on principle, I should entertain on this subject, but I wish to consider the authority of cases.

1801 *March* 6.

THE FRANKLIN.

Sir W. Scott.

10th March.

I have deliberated upon this case, and desire it to be considered as the settled rule of law received by this Court, that the carriage of contraband with a false destination will work a condemnation of the ship as well as the cargo. In the earlier case of the *Sarah Christina* (*a*), the Court, from a favourable regard to some particular circumstances, practised an indulgence in restoring the ship, but without freight and expenses, declaring it at the time to be an indulgence hardly reconcileable to just principle. Having now maturely and upon discussion considered the general point, I am decidedly of opinion that confiscation of the vessel is the legal result of the carriage of contraband under a false destination.

THE HELEN.

[3 C. Rob. 224.]

Recapture—Revenue Cutter—Amount of Salvage.

A revenue cutter, having recaptured a vessel, was held entitled to one-sixth salvage.

THIS was a question as to the *quantum* of salvage due on the recapture of a British ship and cargo by a revenue cutter having a letter of marque.

1801 *March* 12.

SIR W. SCOTT.—This is the case of a ship taken by the French and retaken by a revenue cutter. The question is, whether she is

(*a*) *Ante*, p. 125.

1801 March 12. THE HELEN. Sir W. Scott.

to pay a sixth for salvage, as to a private ship of war, or an eighth as to a King's ship? The question is, I say, to determine to which of these descriptions of vessels the recapturing ship belongs, as far as the necessity of the present case calls for a decision on that point, and no farther. We all know that in recapture no commission is necessary to vest a salvage interest in the recaptors. It is the duty of every subject of the King to assist his fellow subjects in war, and to retake their property in the possession of the enemy; no commission is necessary to give a person so employed a title to the reward which the policy of the law allots to that meritorious act of duty.

[The Court then read the Prize Act, 1793, by which prizes captured by private ships vested in the Crown. The question is now governed by 27 & 28 Vict. c. 25, s. 39.]

The recapturing ship is a revenue cutter, a custom house vessel, with a letter of marque.

So stands the matter with respect to prizes taken under their letter of marque; but it has been already observed that no letter of marque is required to enable a vessel to make a recapture or to entitle her to an interest of salvage. A recapture is not made at all under that authority, though they could not take a prize under any other. In the case of the *Robert*, the captor, being one of these ships, was considered on the footing of a private ship of war; and such appears to be their proper character, where they are not otherwise described by the Act of Parliament, and where the purpose of the Act does not interfere. The only point on which it does interfere is with respect to captures made under these cases. The provision of the Act is, that the ship's goods, the proceeds of merchandise so captured shall be reserved to his Majesty, &c. The Act does not necessarily extend to cases of recapture; and I am not disposed to carry the anomaly further than the words of the Act direct. For all the purposes of this transaction, these ships are to be considered as if no such Act had ever been made. If they would have been entitled to one-sixth, supposing the Act had never existed, I see nothing in it which should in any manner alter that proportion. It is true they are armed at the public expense, but for very different purposes, and no difference has been made in former wars on that account where these vessels are concerned. The interest which is reserved in the 10th section of the Prize Act is such as results from the commission, and not such as is in no way derived from it.

1801 *March* 12.

THE HELEN.

Sir W. Scott.

Salvage decreed, one-sixth.

THE MINERVA.

[3 C. Rob. 229.]

Neutral—Trade between Colony and Mother Country of Enemy—Interruption of Voyage—Nature of Original Voyage—Condemnation of Cargo—Forfeiture of Freight.

A ship was taken by the French on a voyage from a Spanish settlement to Corunna, and was subsequently captured by a British ship. *Held*, that having regard to the original destination of the ship, the cargo must be condemned and the freight forfeited.

1801 *March* 20.

THIS was a case of an American ship taken by the French on a voyage from Languera, a Spanish settlement, to Corunna, and afterwards retaken by a British cruiser, as the captors were carrying her to a French port. The ship and cargo were claimed for the same person.

On the part of the captors, the *King's Advocate*.

On the other side, *Laurence*.

SIR W. SCOTT.—I am of opinion that this case is to be determined by the nature of the original voyage. If the destination was diverted only in consequence of a *vis major*, which the party was unable to resist, I cannot consider it as a defeasance of the original illegality any more than if the diversion had been occasioned by the temporary fury of the elements. In both cases the original movement of the vessel must be considered; to which it must be presumed she would again immediately recur as soon as an opportunity presented itself. An allusion has been made to the case of the *Imina* (a), in which the Court allowed to a party the full benefit of a deviation voluntarily made by the master upon

(a) *Ante*, p. 289.

1801 *March* 20. THE MINERVA. Sir W. Scott.

receiving information in the course of his voyage that Amsterdam was in a state of blockade. There it was deemed not unreasonable to allow the act of the master in changing his course a favourable operation, respecting the cargo; considering that it was taken in a voyage no longer in the act of being prosecuted towards the enemy's country, according to the intention of him to whom it had been confided. The Court presumed favourably that the owners would have approved of this deviation. But it would be going a great deal further to say that the act of foreign necessity, to which this vessel and cargo were giving a temporary submission, no longer than whilst they were compelled so to do, was to be considered as a total discontinuance and abandonment of the intended voyage on the part of the owners. The voyage of the ship and cargo, when left to their own discretion, would have continued the same, and must therefore be considered to be still existing in law, though controlled in fact by that overbearing necessity for the moment.

But even giving the owners the benefit of a deviation compelled by the superior force of a party who stood in no relation of privity to them; yet this deviation being to a French port, it would be a voyage from the colony of one enemy to the mother country of an allied enemy, which I have before held is attended with undistinguishable consequences as to the cargo.

With respect to the ship, I could have wished there had been some case decided on this point by the Superior Court. The cases which have been mentioned were cases of more aggravated circumstances than the present. They were cases of false destinations, and attended with other circumstances of a closer and more incorporated adoption into the enemy's trade.

It is said that the principle on which trade with the enemy's colony is prohibited applies equally to the ship as to the cargo, and that the penalty ought reasonably to be the same; and it is impossible to deny it. There are, however, some other cases in which the penalty attaches in practice more strongly on the delinquent cargo than on the delinquent ship; though it is difficult to distinguish any degree in the delinquency. In cases of contraband, the offence of carrying the cargo is in its own nature as great as the offence of sending it: but yet a relaxation has in ordinary cases been introduced in favour of the ship, where the cargo is not the property of the same owner. Here the ship and cargo belong to the same person, and the offence being equally known, it would be impossible to find any distinction in principle why the same penalty would not attach on both; but as this whole subject has been attended with some fluctuation of practice, I am disposed to take the matter *in mitiorem partem;* and particularly adverting to the authority of the *Rebecca* (*a*), and to some prior cases determined by my predecessor, I shall restore the ship, but subject to a forfeiture of freight and expenses (*b*).

1801 *March* 20.

THE MINERVA.

Sir W. Scott.

THE HULDAH.

[3 C. Rob. 235.]

Practice—Claim—Time.

There is no fixed time within which a claimant may lodge a claim. So when a sentence of condemnation was passed by a Prize Court without jurisdiction, a claim was admitted a year and nine months after such illegal sentence.

1801 *April* 21.

THIS was one of several cases of ships and cargoes carried into St. Domingo, and proceeded against in a Court of Admiralty, which was held not to be vested with competent authority to proceed in prize causes. In consequence of that mistake, original proceedings were instituted afterwards in the High Court of Admiralty on the petition of the claimants by a monition calling on the captors to proceed to adjudication.

The claim in the present case was not given till a year and nine months after the sentence of condemnation passed in the Court of St. Domingo.

The captors appeared under protest.

(*a*) The *Rebecca.* Motion for an allowance of freight to a neutral (American) ship taken on a voyage from Surinam to Amsterdam, with a cargo of colonial produce. The motion was refused (12th July, 1799) without a formal judgment. [2 C. Rob. 101.]

(*b*) In the *Jonge Thomas,* Lords, November, 1801, which was the case of a ship going from Amsterdam to Surinam, the Court of Appeal considered the illegality to attach as strongly on the ship as on the cargo, and pronounced the ship subject to condemnation on the ground of the illegality of the trade between the mother country and the colony of the enemy.

1801
April 21.

THE HULDAH.

Sir W. Scott.

In support of the protest, the *King's Advocate* and *Arnold*.

On the other side, *Laurence* and *Swabey*.

SIR W. SCOTT.—This is a very hard case on the captors; but I do not think it is in my power to relieve them from the necessity of proceeding to adjudication. During the existence of the Prize Commission there is no fixed and definite time by which the party can be said to be legally barred from calling on the captor to proceed to adjudication, although it may be proper to hold that there *must* exist a time which would work such an effect; but I know of no prescribed limitation against the admission of a claim, nor of any other means by which the captor can protect himself, but by applying to a Court of competent jurisdiction. If he neglects to apply to any tribunal, he would be guilty of a great misdemeanour; if, through misapprehension, he applies to an improper tribunal, though he may defend himself against the charge of a misdemeanour, he cannot protect himself from the call of the claimant to proceed to adjudication before a competent tribunal. In this case there is no imputation of misconduct; the captor went to a Court which was sitting at St. Domingo, apparently with competent authority. In that Court he obtained a sentence of condemnation, and distribution has taken place in consequence of it. But that Court having no authority, those proceedings are null and of no legal effect whatever. On the other hand, it was the duty of the claimant to have brought this matter before the Court as soon as he could, as it is always in the power of the claimant to compel the captor to proceed, if he neglects to do so himself. It might, perhaps, appear to the claimant, who is not bound to look to the nature of the jurisdiction by an obligation equal to that of the captor, that the Court was not incompetent. It might be a common error. In that case it would be something to show that he had entered an appeal. The appeal, it is true, could not have been received, as it came from a Court which had no legal existence; but it would have proved the parties to have used diligence which might be material if questions of costs and damages should arise. There existed something of difficulty, a sort of cloud of uncertainty on the minds of persons as to the competency of the Court, which might account for some part of this delay. However, the claimant has now applied to this Court, and I am of opinion that the Court is under the legal duty of admitting the claim, and that it cannot relieve the captor from the obligation of proceeding to adjudication.

1801 *April* 21. THE HULDAH. Sir W. Scott.

Protest overruled.

An absolute appearance being given for the captors, the cause was heard on the merits, when the Court decreed restitution of the principal part of the cargo belonging to the owner of the ship.

THE DISPATCH.

[3 C. Rob. 278.]

Neutral Ship—Seizure—Rescue by Crew—Condemnation.

When a neutral ship is seized by a belligerent cruiser for inquiry into the character of herself and her cargo, it is an act of hostile opposition on the part of the crew to rescue such vessel, and it subjects the ship to condemnation.

1801 *December* 5.

THIS was a case of a Danish vessel which had been captured by an English cruiser, but had been rescued out of the hands of the prize-master by the former master and crew left on board. After the rescue she had been taken by a French privateer, and was again retaken by the original English captor and carried to St. Domingo.

SIR W. SCOTT.—It is admitted that a rescue had taken place, but it is now represented to have been a mere civil, peaceable rescue, by which it is attempted to be distinguished from a hostile rescue. I should very much like to be informed how a rescue can be anything else than, as the very term imports, a delivery from force by force. That there was this force in the present instance is evident from the depositions, and also from an affidavit to the same effect which has been brought in since, and which has not been contradicted.

Taking it to be, then, a case of a forcible rescue of a neutral ship from the hands of a lawful cruiser, the law is clear, and the principle of it is founded on the soundest maxims of justice and

1801 *December 5.* — The Dispatch. — Sir W. Scott.

humanity. If neutral crews may be allowed to resort to violence to withdraw themselves out of the possession taken by a lawful cruiser for the purpose of a legal inquiry, and may (as it has been termed) hustle them out of the command of the vessel, the whole business of the detention of neutral ships will become a scene of mutual hostility and contention; the crews of neutral ships must be guarded with all the severity and strictness practised upon actual prisoners of war, for the same measures of precaution and distrust will become equally necessary; the intercourse of nations, neutral and friendly towards each other, will be embittered by acts of hostility mutually committed by their subjects. At present, under the understanding of the law which now prevails, it is the duty of the cruiser to treat the crew of an apparently neutral ship, which he takes possession of for further inquiry into the real character of herself and her cargo, with all reasonable indulgence, and it is the duty of neutrals under that possession to take care that they do not put themselves in the condition of enemies by resorting to such conduct as can be justified only by the character of enemies. It is the law and not the force of the parties that must be looked to as the redresser of wrongs that may have been done by the one to the other. I have no hesitation in pronouncing this ship and cargo liable to condemnation, on the ground of the parties having declared themselves enemies by this act of hostile opposition to lawful inquiry.

[3 C. Rob. 281.]

THE ADELAIDE.

Property in Goods—Blockade—Capture—Knowledge of Blockade—Opportunity to Countermand—Liability of Principal for Act of Agent—Restitution.

A reasonable time must be allowed a neutral who has ordered goods from a port which is subsequently blockaded to countermand such order after the blockade has come to his knowledge, and the neutral will not be liable for the act of his agent in shipping such goods until such time has elapsed.

1801 *May 12.*

This was a case arising on the blockade of Amsterdam respecting the shipment of a cargo at Amsterdam for account of merchants in America, April and May, 1799.

Further proof had been directed to be made of the property, and the dates of the orders of the several claims.

On the first claim, it appeared that the original order had been given previous to the notification of the blockade in February and March, 1798. By a letter of the agent, reference was made to a later letter written by the owner to the agent in Amsterdam in December, 1798; but no letter of that date was produced.

SIR W. SCOTT.—The first question that arises on this claim is respecting the property, whether the goods are to be considered as the property of the merchants in America or of the Dutch shipper? The bill of lading expresses it to be the property of the American merchants; but the master being a carrier-master could not verify; and as it was a shipment made in an enemy's country, it became necessary to order further proof. The proof which has been brought in consists of the attestation of the owner and of the correspondence which passed between him and this agent in Amsterdam, the general tenor of it purporting that the goods were ordered for his account. If these orders were actually given, and the goods shipped in consequence of them, and for the account of this person, they do, according to our mode of considering the evidence of property, furnish a sufficient constat that they are the property of the person to whom they are going. There are some expressions in the letters of the agent at Amsterdam which seem to import the feelings of an owner; but perhaps they do not amount to more than an expression of uneasiness under some reproaches which had been thrown on him for delay by the second letter of his employer in America; they do not perhaps go much further than that; they by no means over-balance the proof that has been produced. One consideration, which very much weighs, is, that it would be highly improbable that the Dutchman should wish to ship off the goods as his own property during the blockade when he had an opportunity of shipping them for the account and risk of the person in America. I think on the whole the proof of property is sufficient.

Then comes the question as to the blockade, whether there was sufficient time for countermanding the orders that had been given for these goods, and whether the merchant is not bound by the act of his agent, and whether he himself appears to have used due diligence? The question as to the length of time proper to be

1801 *May* 12. — THE ADELAIDE. — Sir W. Scott.

allowed for notice must depend upon dates. It is a distinction of reasonable equity, and not of partiality or favour to a particular nation, to give rather a more liberal allowance of time for notice to persons in the situation of merchants in America. It is not, I think, to be taken merely on a calculation of the distance, but with reference also to the accidents by which the general intercourse, even after the allowance of distance, is liable to be retarded.

The first orders were given in February, and in March, 1798, there appears to have been a second letter of remonstrance against the tardy execution of the orders. It might be supposed by the merchant in America that this remonstrance would produce the effect of accelerating the shipment, and he might expect that the goods were actually *in transitu*. The notification was in June; the interval between that time and the shipment was not much more than is allowed in cases of further proof coming from America—nine months.

Under all these circumstances, it appears on the whole that there has not been time enough to affect the American merchant with culpable negligence; and therefore the only question will be, whether he can be held responsible, under these circumstances, for the act of his agent in Amsterdam? The rule which the Court has already laid down on this point is, that in cases of agency of persons in an enemy's country during a blockade, something more than the mere strict principle of law is necessary in order to bind employers by their acts. There must be time to give the principal an opportunity of countermanding. I have stated my reasons for thinking that there has not been sufficient time with respect to this claim, and therefore I must pronounce that the claimant is not, either in respect to proof of property nor on the ground of the blockade, incapacitated from receiving restitution.

THE NEUTRALITET (No. 1).

[3 C. Rob. 294.]

Contraband—Cargo—Ship—Same Owner—False Destination and Papers—Forfeiture of Freight.

If a ship carrying a contraband cargo is owned by the cargo owner, or is sailing under a false destination or with false papers, she is liable to condemnation.

Carriage of contraband is a cause of forfeiture of freight.

1801 *May* 16.

THIS was a case of a Danish ship taken with a cargo of tar on a voyage from Archangel to Dordrecht. The ship had been a Dutch vessel, and was asserted to have been purchased by Mr. Schultz, of Altona. She then went from Holland to Altona, and was from thence sent on to Archangel to carry a cargo to Dordrecht under a charter party made by the asserted owner.

SIR W. SCOTT.—The modern rule of the law of nations is, certainly, that the ship shall not be subject to condemnation for carrying contraband articles. The ancient practice was otherwise, and it cannot be denied that it was perfectly defensible on every principle of justice. If to supply the enemy with such articles is a noxious act with respect to the owner of the cargo, the vehicle which is instrumental in effecting that illegal purpose cannot be innocent. The policy of modern times has, however, introduced a relaxation on this point, and the general rule now is that the vessel does not become confiscable for that act. But this rule is liable to exceptions: Where a ship belongs to the owner of the cargo, or where the ship is going on such service under a false destination or false papers, these circumstances of aggravation have been held to constitute excepted cases out of the modern rule and to continue them under the ancient one. The circumstances of the present case compose a case of exception also, for it is a case of singular misconduct on the part of the asserted shipowners. They are subjects of Denmark, and as such are under the peculiar obligations of a treaty not to carry goods of this nature for the use of the enemies of Great Britain.

A reference has been made to ancient cases of Dantzic ships, which were restored, though taken carrying masts to Cadiz. The particulars of those cases are not very exactly stated, but they were clearly the cases of proprietors exporting the produce of their own

1801 *May* 16. — THE NEUTRALITET. — Sir W. Scott.

territory or of neighbouring parts without the breach of any obligation but such as the general law of nations imposed. In this instance the ship was freighted at Altona to go to Archangel for the purpose of carrying a cargo of tar to Holland, which is a commerce expressly prohibited by the Danish treaty. Tar is an article which a Danish ship cannot lawfully carry to an enemy's port, even when it is the produce and manufacture of Denmark. This ship goes to a foreign port to effect that which she is prohibited from doing, even for the produce of her own country—in this respect throwing off the character of a Danish ship by violating the treaties of her country; and all this is done with the full privity of the asserted owner, who is the person entering into the charter party. In such a case as the present, the known ground on which the relaxation was introduced, the supposition that freights of noxious or doubtful articles might be taken without the personal knowledge of the owner, entirely fails; and the active guilt of the parties is aggravated by the circumstances of its being a criminal traffic in foreign commodities, and in breach of explicit and special obligations. The confiscation of a ship so engaged will leave the general rule still untouched, that the carriage of contraband works a forfeiture of freight and expenses but not of the ship.

Ship condemned.

[3 C. Rob. 297.]

THE OCEAN.

Blockade—Port of Actual Shipment not Blockaded—Goods Ordered for Blockaded Port.

When goods were ordered for shipment from a blockaded port, but were actually shipped from a non-blockaded port—*Held*, that there had been no breach of blockade (*a*).

1801 *May* 16; affirmed *June* 24, 1807.

THIS was a question arising on the blockade of Amsterdam, respecting a cargo shipped for America at Rotterdam. It appeared that the persons ordering the shipment had ordered it of their agents at Amsterdam as a shipment to be made there, subsequent to the date of the blockade of that place, but previous to the blockade of the ports of Holland. It was argued that in the intention

(*a*) See the *Stert*, p. 348.

of the claimants it was to be an exportation actually from Amsterdam, and that in effect the trade was the same, as the goods were ordered and purchased at Amsterdam, and were to be considered as part of the commerce of that place. 1801 *May* 16. THE OCEAN.

SIR W. SCOTT.—I am inclined to consider this matter favourably, as an exportation from Rotterdam only, the place in which the cargo becomes first connected with the ship. In what course it had travelled before that time, whether from Amsterdam at all, and if from Amsterdam, whether by land carriage or by one of their inland navigations, Rotterdam being the port of actual shipment, I do not think it material to inquire. On this view of the case it would be a little too rigorous to say, that an order for a shipment to be made at Amsterdam should be construed to attach on the owner, although not carried into effect. It has been said from the letter of the correspondent at Amsterdam, that the agents there had informed their correspondents in America that the blockade was not intended to prevent exportation. The representation of the enemy shipper could not have availed to exonerate the neutral merchant, if otherwise liable. Were this to be allowed, it would be in the power of the enemy to put an end to the blockade as soon as he pleased. If the general law is, that egress as well as ingress is prohibited by blockade, the neutral merchant is bound to know it; and if he entertains any doubt, he must satisfy himself by applying to the country imposing the blockade, and not to the party who has an interest in breaking it.

It happens in this case that the intended exportation did not take place. The only criminal act, if any, must have been the conveyance from Amsterdam to Rotterdam. It would be a little too much to say that by that previous act the goods shipped at Rotterdam are affected. The legal consequences of a blockade must depend on the means of blockade. On the land side Amsterdam neither was nor could be affected by a blockading naval force. It could be applied only externally. The internal communications of the country were out of its reach, and in no way subject to its operation. If the exportation of goods from Rotterdam was at this time permitted, it could in no degree be vitiated by a previous inland transmission of them from Amsterdam.

[3 C. Rob. 305.]

THE EDWARD AND MARY.

Recapture—Salvage—Essentials of Capture—Prize Act—General Maritime Law.

In order to constitute a case of capture it is sufficient if a vessel become under the control of an enemy ship. The placing of a prize crew on board is not essential to constitute a capture.

For a vessel rescued but not actually "retaken," salvage awarded under the general maritime law.

1801 *June* 9.

THIS was a case of salvage on recapture of a British merchantman which had separated from her convoy during a storm, and had been brought to by a French lugger, which came up and told the master to stay by her till the storm moderated, when they would send a boat on board. The lugger continued alongside—sometimes ahead and sometimes astern, and sometimes to windward—for three or four hours. A British frigate, the *Arethusa*, coming in sight, chased the lugger and captured her, during which time the *Edward* made her escape, rejoined the convoy, and came into Pool, where her papers were some time afterwards demanded of her, by the agent of the *Arethusa*, for the purpose of instituting prize proceedings.

SIR W. SCOTT.—I entertain a different view of the cases that have been cited as cases in point. They were the cases of two colliers, that were from the first incapable of making any resistance: one was taken; the other appearing in sight, drew off the attention of the enemy, and during the chase the French ship blew up. There was not even the merit of intention in that case. Everything that was done was the mere effect of an independent casualty; there was nothing on which any plea of merit could be constructed. The present case is of a very different cast, for in this case the *Arethusa* came up for the very purpose of taking this French captor, if he is to be so considered, and actually took him; and it is owing to this act of the *Arethusa* that this vessel was rescued from his grasp. The master, I must observe, has given an improper deposition, and very ill according with the entries in his log-book. By that it appears that the French vessel brought him to, and declared herself a French privateer, and ordered him to lie to, but owing to the boisterous state of the weather she did not send a man on board. I can by no means agree to what has been advanced in argument, that it was on this account no capture. The sending of a prize master on board is a very natural overt act of possession, but by no means essential to constitute a capture. If the merchantman was obliged to lie to and obey the direction of the French lugger, and await her further orders, she was completely under the dominion of the enemy; there was no ability to resist, and no prospect of escape. The Frenchman who has been examined appears to have given the true account. He says "that he understood it to be a capture." There have been many instances of capture where no man has been put on board, as in ships driven on shore or into port. I remember particularly a famous case of a small British vessel armed with two swivels which took a French privateer row-boat from Dunkirk that had attacked her; the British vessel having only three men on board, and no arms but the swivels, was afraid to board the row-boat, which was full of men armed with muskets and cutlasses; but by the terror of her swivels she compelled their submission and obliged them to go into the port of Ostend, then the port of an ally, she following them all the way at a proper distance.

The only question will be, whether it is a case of salvage under the Act of Parliament on another ground, viz., that the vessel never came into the actual and bodily possession of the recaptor—I rather incline to think it is not. The terms of the Act of Parliament (*a*), "if at any time afterwards surprised and retaken by any of his Majesty's ships of war, &c.," seem to point to a case attended with the circumstance of an actual possession taken. But if it is not a case of recapture under the Act, it is however still a case of salvage under the general maritime law, and I shall give the same reward as if it had been under the Act of Parliament.

One-eighth salvage given.

(*a*) 33 Geo. 3, c. 66.

[3 C. Rob. 311.]

THE FORSIGHEID.

Joint Capture—Associated Service—Squadron not in Sight of Main Fleet—Sight—Detached Service.

Where a capture was made by several ships of a fleet which had been ordered to undertake a certain operation, and the main body of which, owing to a haze, was not in sight of the capture. *Held*, that as these ships were not detached on special service, but were acting in co-operation with the main body of the fleet, the latter were entitled to share in the capture (*a*).

1801 *June* 17

THIS was a case on the admission of an allegation of joint capture on the part of Admiral Dickson's fleet, claiming to share in a capture made by the *Director* and some other ships belonging to the same fleet, but sent to cruise at a certain distance by orders from the Admiral, with particular directions *not to be out of sight.* It was alleged that the distance of the place of capture was not above eight or nine miles from the fleet; but that owing to a fog or haziness that came on they were not in sight of the actual captors at the time of the capture.

For the actual captor, the *King's Advocate* and *Arnold.*

For the allegation, *Laurence* and *Swabey.*

SIR W. SCOTT.—This is undoubtedly a convenient method of taking the opinion of the Court on facts stated and admitted in the allegation, and on the arguments deducible from them, in order that it may be decided as expeditiously as possible whether the law arising upon the facts, if proved, would entitle the parties to the benefit they claim.

The facts stated on the part of the opponent to this allegation are that the ships making the actual capture composed part of a squadron employed in the blockade of the Texel; but that it appears, upon the showing of this very allegation, that at the time of the capture they were detached on a particular service, connected indeed with the main purpose of the blockade, and subordinate to

(*a*) See the *Vryheid*, p. 179.

it, but still a distinct and separate service, it is admitted that the capture was made *out of sight* of the fleet, and, what is more, without any concurrence in chasing—in fact, that the captured ships were not seen by the fleet till they were in the possession of the actual captor. The question is whether, on these facts, which seem to be mutually agreed, the fleet is entitled to share.

Undoubtedly different principles apply in cases where ships are associated by public authority on a common service, and where they are not so associated together. In the latter case, where a capture is made by ships not associated by public authority for a common service, it could not be maintained on any principle that the mere circumstance of being within such a distance as would bring them within sight in clear weather would entitle them to share, when in fact they *were not seen* at all. It would put this rule of law on a very uncertain footing indeed, unconnected with all rational principle, as well as incapable of all satisfactory proof, if the Court had to determine on the state of the atmosphere and on the loose conjectural evidence that might be applied to ascertain such a state, whether the distance was a proper distance for sight if the weather had been clear, and what under such a state could be the impression on the mind of the enemy or the friend. It is essentially necessary, in such cases, that the party should have *been in sight* at some part of the transaction, though it is not required that it should be at the moment of capture, because the impulse and impression on the mind of the enemy who is to be intimidated, or of the friend who is to be encouraged, may remain, notwithstanding the intervention of a headland or fog, and may therefore bring it within the reach of that principle of law on which constructive assistance is built. But in cases of ships associated together by public authority, the same principle does not necessarily apply. It will not be denied that if one ship of a squadron takes a prize in the night, unknown to the rest, it would entitle the whole fleet to share, although possibly the capture might have been made at a distance out of sight of most of the ships of war, even if it had been noonday; for the fleet so associated is considered as one body, unless detached by orders, or entirely separated by accident; and what is done by one continuing to compose *in fact* a part of that fleet, enures to the benefit of all.

1801 *June* 17. THE FORSIGHEID. Sir W. Scott.

In the present case no accidental separation is suggested. The only question is, whether or not the capture was made whilst those ships composed, *de facto*, a part of this fleet.

The whole case then is reduced to this point, whether these ships are to be considered as detached or not; *detached*, I mean, in the same manner as detachments are usually made, for some distinct and separate purpose, which, though possibly connected with the main service, carries them out of the scene of common operation for the time; or whether they were sent only on the look-out, to preserve their connection with the service of the fleet, and maintain their dependence on it? To determine this question, I must look to the orders that were given. They direct them "to watch well the motions of the enemy; to cruise between certain points, joining the fleet occasionally for communication." If they stopped here, I should be inclined to hold that it was a separate service, with orders to join again: but they go on—"directing them to avoid being at such a distance, as not to observe the signals that were made." It is impossible under these terms to say that it was a detached service. It is more like the stretching out of the arms of the fleet, without dissolving in any manner the connection between them and the main body. From this very circumstance, a presumption strongly arises, were it necessary to consider the probability of that fact, that the fleet would have been actually in sight, if an accidental haziness had not intervened. On the whole of the case contained in this allegation, I am of opinion that the fleet is entitled to share; and on the same principle by which it would have shared in a capture made by one of its own ships not sent off under such an order.

Allegation admitted.

THE HURTIGE HANE (No. 2).

[3 C. Rob. 324.]

Blockade—Non-European State.

The rules of the Law of Nations as to blockades are binding on merchants of non-European nations.

THIS was a case arising on the blockade of Amsterdam, respecting a cargo shipped at Saffee in Barbary for Amsterdam under a false destination to Hamburg.

1801 *June* 20.

On the part of the claimant, *Laurence* and *Sewell.*

SIR W. SCOTT.—This is the claim for the cargo of a ship which has already been determined to have been going into Amsterdam on the 8th April, 1799, a considerable time after the blockade of that port. It may be material in the present view of the matter as affecting the cargo to advert to the former judgment on the ship, and consider all the circumstances attending the capture. The master said " that his destination had always been for Hamburg till his crew compelled him to change his course for Amsterdam " ; so that almost up to the moment of capture the destination was held out to be to Hamburg. It now appears that the ship was freighted at Lisbon on a charter-party effected there on the 26th November, 1798, by Mr. Delamer, of that place, to go to Mr. Delamer at Saffee, and carry a cargo from thence, consigned to Mr. Delamer, of Amsterdam, these gentlemen being brothers and Jew merchants settled at different places, but keeping up a very intimate connection and correspondence with each other. It has been argued that it would be extremely hard on persons residing in the kingdom of Morocco if they should be held bound by all the rules of the law of nations as it is practised amongst European States. On many accounts undoubtedly they are not to be strictly considered on the same footing as European merchants; they may on some points of the law of nations be entitled to a very relaxed application of the principles established, by long usage, between the States of Europe, holding an intimate and constant intercourse with each other. It is a law made up of a good deal of complex reasoning, though derived from very simple rules, and

1801 June 20. THE HURTIGE HANE (No. 2). Sir W. Scott.

altogether composing a pretty artificial system, which is not familiar either to their knowledge or their observance. Upon such considerations the Court has, on some occasions, laid it down that the European law of nations is not to be applied in its full rigor to the transactions of persons of the description of the present claimants, and residing in that part of the world. But on a point like this, *the breach of a blockade*, one of the most universal and simple operations of war in all ages and countries excepting such as were merely savage, no such indulgence can be shown. It must not be understood by them that, if an European army or fleet is blockading a town or port, they are at liberty to trade with that port. If that could be maintained it would render the operation of a blockade perfectly nugatory. *They*, in common with all other nations, must be subject to this first and elementary principle of blockade, that persons are not to carry into the blockaded port supplies of any kind. It is not a new operation of war—it is almost as old and as general as war itself. The subjects of the Barbary States could not be ignorant of the general rules applying to a blockaded place so far as concerns the interests and duties of neutrals.

[3 C. Rob. 330.]

THE SARAH.

*Evidence—Further Proof—*Primâ facie *Neutral Cargo—Illegal Origin of Cargo—False Papers—Captors' Expenses.*

The Court will not, on an application for further proof, usually admit evidence not connected with the original evidence. Application for further proof to show an illegal course of trade, there being nothing in the original evidence pointing to such a suspicion, rejected, and the cargo restored.

The ship's papers being false, captors' expenses allowed.

1801 June 25.

THIS was a case of a cargo of Dutch butter shipped at Embden for the account of several persons in London. The orders had been taken from these persons by Mr. Foss, of London, and by him transmitted, as it was said on the part of the captor, to his agent or partner in Holland. The ship had sailed outward from London to Embden, and on that voyage had been stopped and searched, and a letter had been taken out by the cruising vessel. It was now prayed that the Court would admit this letter to be introduced on further proof, on a suggestion that it was written by

Mr. Foss to Mr. Harrison at Rotterdam, and would show this trade to have been carried on with the enemy's country by the mediation of agents in Embden, and that Mr. Foss had directed the person at Rotterdam to have a cargo ready for this ship.

SIR W. SCOTT.—This is an application on the part of the captor to introduce evidence on an order for further proof. That the Court does accede to applications of this nature, in certain cases, cannot be denied; but it is by no means the disposition of the Court to encourage them. It has seldom been done except in cases where there has appeared something in the original evidence which lays a suggestion for prosecuting the inquiry further. In such cases the Court has allowed it; but when the matter is foreign, and not connected with the original evidence of the cause, it must be under very particular circumstances indeed that the Court will be induced to accede to such an application; because, if remote suggestions were allowed, the practice of the Court would be led away from the simplicity of prize proceedings, and there would be no end to the accumulation of proof that would be introduced in order to support arbitrary suggestions. It appears that the goods were shipped at Embden. A reasonable presumption arising from that fact is, that they had fairly found their way thither. The Court is extremely disinclined to go out of the case that is immediately brought before it, and to mount up to the first possible terms of a transaction, although on some occasions it may be necessary to do so.

The cargo in question was coming from Embden, to be delivered in London, and documented as the property of persons at Embden; whether it does in reality belong to them or to persons in London, it will be equally a case for restitution. The papers represent it as the property of Abegg, of Embden, but it is claimed for persons in London; and it is said that the name of Abegg was used for the purpose of protecting it from the cruisers of the enemy: an artifice which this Court is not very scrupulous to detect where it does not appear that there is any sinister purpose concealed under that pretence, or that any enemy's interest is concerned. Further proof was necessary, however, to account for this variation between the shipment and the claim; it is now brought in, and I am disposed to think that it is sufficient.

1801
June 25.

THE SARAH.

Sir W. Scott.

But it is said the captors are in possession of evidence that would show the goods to have come in such a course, in an anterior stage of the transaction, as would make them subject to confiscation. I have already said that this Court is not inclined to go out of the limits of the present transaction, unless on some suggestion arising out of the original evidence. It has not been pointed out that there is any such foundation laid in this cause; all the papers and the depositions stop at Embden; and I do not perceive that there is anything that leads to a further inquiry. What would be the effect of the letter, if it was produced, I cannot say; but supposing it to be proved that the agent in London was in the general habit of procuring such articles from the enemy, I think there would be a defect of evidence to apply it to the present case. The circumstance of the intercepting these letters would, on the contrary, afford some ground of inference on the part of the claimant that this cargo did not arise out of such a course of trade.

It has been argued that if the matter were as it is suggested it would be hard to affect the actual proprietors of this cargo with confiscation, inasmuch as they knew nothing of the course in which their orders had been executed. How far they might be deemed answerable for the transaction of their agent, is a matter on which the Court need not give any opinion till the question comes necessarily before it. In the present case, supposing that they would be penally affected as to their property in the articles so procured, I am of opinion that the evidence is not offered upon such grounds as can entitle it to admission.

Cargo restored.

On the part of the captors, the *King's Advocate* prayed that they might be allowed their expenses.

Court.—If English merchants resort to the expedient of protecting their trade by these false papers, it leads captors into expenses for which these captors ought not to be answerable.

Captors' expenses granted.

THE COSMOPOLITE (No. 1).

[3 C. Rob. 333.]

Capture—Condemnation by French Consul in Spain—Bonâ fide *Purchaser—Restitution.*

An American ship was captured by the French, condemned in Spain, and purchased by a Danish merchant. On a subsequent capture by an English cruiser a claim was given for the Danish purchaser—and also for the former American proprietor, on the ground that the ship, having been condemned in a port neutral towards America, the condemnation was invalid. The Court declined to judge of the relation of foreign States, and ordered restitution to the Danish purchaser.

1801 *July* 1.

THIS was a case of an American ship, captured by the French, carried into Spain, there condemned by the French consul in a Spanish port, sold under that sentence, and afterwards transferred to the present master, a Danish subject, who, on the subsequent capture of the ship by a British cruiser, was the original claimant in this cause. A claim was likewise interposed on the part of the former American proprietor, on a suggestion that though France had been in some state of hostilities with America, Spain had not; that Spain was, in respect to America, a neutral port; and that a condemnation of American ships in a Spanish port was illegal, and the transfer under it invalid.

SIR W. SCOTT.—This is a question rather on the illegality than the fact of the transfer, which is asserted to have taken place. The vessel appears to have been an American ship, seized by the French and carried into the island of Teneriffe, where she was condemned under the authority of the French consul, and transferred subsequently to the present Danish possessor.

The objection that has been taken is, that as this was an American ship, and as Spain and America were in their political relations perfectly neutral, it must be considered as a condemnation in a neutral port, and subject to the same rule as the Court laid down in the *Flad Oyen*(*a*), with respect to the condemnation of British ships by the French consul in Norway. It is argued that the Court is, therefore, under the same obligations to restore this vessel to the original American proprietor: but that consequence will not, I think, necessarily follow, because, although this Court has interposed to entertain suits on the part of American subjects,

(*a*) *Ante*, p. 78; and see *post*, p. 339.

1801 July 1. THE COSMOPOLITE. Sir W. Scott.

in giving the same assistance to American salvors (*The Two Friends* (a)) as to British subjects; and in restoring American property retaken from the French by our cruisers, yet it has been only in cases of recapture during the same voyage where there had been no condemnation at all. There has been no case that I recollect in which this Court has proceeded to examine the legality of a condemnation passed on an American ship in consequence of capture by the French. It does so, it is true, with respect to captures made from this country by France. But the same rule of conduct does not apply to other countries, whose relations with France this Court cannot so well know nor so exactly estimate. The relative state of America and France has been so equivocal that it would be difficult for this Court to say distinctly whether it was a state of war or not, or whether it has been a state of peace, with many of the incidents of war attending it. Of the exact rights and duties arising from such an uncertain state it is not easy for this Court to determine, neither is the Court called upon by any duty to pass any judgment upon them. This Court is perfectly acquainted with the relations subsisting between our own country and Denmark. It can judge of the state of treaties (b) and amity under which the general principle has acquired additional strength, and by which the use of their respective ports is expressly prohibited to be granted to the cruisers of the enemy of the other party for the purposes of war. But can I pronounce with equal certainty in what manner Spain may lend out her ports to French captors relatively to Americans, or what understanding there may be on this subject between America and Spain? Under these considerations, I do not find myself authorized to say that this condemnation stands exactly on the same footing as the French condemnations of British property in Norway. The purchase appears to have been made fairly for a valuable consideration from the French possession. It does not appear to me that this Court is competent to examine and enforce the claim of the American owner, the justice of which depends upon political transactions and relations with which this Court is not judicially acquainted.

Restitution to the Danish claimant.

(a) *Ante*, p. 130. (b) A.D. 1489, 1523, 1661.

THE TWEE GEBROEDERS (No. 2). [3 C. Rob. 336.]

Capture—Passage of Captors through Territorial Waters—Validity of Capture.

A capture of an enemy vessel in non-territorial waters is not invalidated by the captors having passed through territorial waters to the place of capture.

THE case arose on the capture of vessels in the Groningen Watt, on a suggestion that they were bound from Hamburg to Amsterdam, then under blockade; and a claim was given under the authority of the Prussian Minister, averring the place in question to be within the territories of the King of Prussia. 1801 *November* 27.

SIR W. SCOTT.—This is the case of a ship and goods proceeded against for a breach of the blockade of Amsterdam; they are claimed as being taken on neutral territory, but it is denied on the part of the captors that they were so taken.

On the blockade of Amsterdam this Court has been inclined to hold, generally, that all sea passages to Amsterdam by that great body of waters, the Zuyder Zee, were blockaded, supposing those sea passages to be in the possession of the enemy. Such as were in the possession of neutrals, it was of opinion, were not included unless the blockading force could be applied at the interior extremity of their communication. Whether the present capture in question was made in a sea passage to the Zuyder Zee, belonging to the enemy or to a neutral power, will be decided by the considerations which are to be examined in the further pursuit of this question. Secondly, supposing that question determined against the immunity of the place of capture, another question is proposed, whether the belligerent party having passed over neutral territory, *animo capiendi*, to the place where his rights have been exercised, those rights of capture so exercised are not thereby invalidated.

[The Court then examined the evidence, and held that the captures had not been made on neutral territory.]

On this evidence, then, it is impossible for me to pronounce that these captures are invalidated by being actually made on Prussian

1801
November 27.

THE TWEE GEBROEDERS.

Sir W. Scott.

territory. There remains the other question, whether the captures are not vitiated by the capturing ship having passed over neutral territory to accomplish the capture—as it is alleged they passed up the Western Eems, and that the whole of that is Prussian territory. I have already intimated some doubts that might possibly be entertained upon the present evidence, whether the Western Eems is to be deemed at all times and in all parts of it clearly Prussian territory; but supposing it to be so, is it a violation of territory to have committed an act of capture after having passed over this territory to effect it? On this point there are some observations of law and some of fact that appear not unworthy of notice. In the first place, the place of capture is accessible by other passages not asserted to be neutral; it is not alleged that a hostile force might not have reached these ships by another route through the Lower Zee or other communications; it is not to be said that they were so inclosed and protected on all sides by neutral territory that you could not approach them without passing over it. In the next place, it is not the case of an internal passage into the heart of the country, into the Homegat, if I may adopt their own term; it is a passage over an external portion of water which you may prescribe for as territory, but not as inland river or as part of the internal territory; it is not an entrance of an armed force up an inward passage to reach an enemy lying in the interior of the land. Thirdly, it is an observation of law that the passage of ships over territorial portions of the sea or external water is a thing less guarded than the passage of armies over land, and for obvious reasons: an army in the strictest state of discipline can hardly pass into a country without great inconvenience to the inhabitants; roads are broken up, the price of provisions is raised, the sick are quartered on individuals, and a general uneasiness and terror is excited; but the passage of two or three vessels, or of a fleet, over external waters, may be neither felt nor perceived. For this reason, the act of inoffensively passing over such portions of water, without any violence committed there, is not considered as any violation of territory belonging to a neutral State; permission is not usually required. Such waters are considered as the common thoroughfare of nations, though they may be so far territory, as that any actual exercise of hostility is prohibited therein. Fourthly, it is to be observed that the right of refusal of passage, even upon land, is supposed to depend more on the inconvenience falling on the neutral State than on any injustice committed to the third party who is to be affected by the permission. Grotius and Vattel both agree that it is no ground of complaint nor cause of war against the intermediate neutral State if it grants passage to the troops of a belligerent, though inconvenience may ensue to the State beyond; the ground of the right of refusal being the inconvenience that such passages bring with them to the neutral State itself. This being the general state of the fact and of the law, it would be a proposition which could not be maintained in a full universal extent that the passing over water, claimed as neutral territory, would vitiate any ulterior capture made on a third party. Suppose the case of a war between England and Russia, and that the Sound was the pass in question, over which Denmark claims and exercises imperial rights on stronger grounds than can be maintained in support of this claim; or suppose a war between France and Russia, and the Dardanelles to be the pass in question; or suppose any two powers exercising hostilities in the Mediterranean, after having passed through the Straits of Gibraltar, occupied by an English fortress on one side and by Tangier on the other, formerly in possession of this country—could it be said in any of these cases that captures made beyond this point of passage over neutral water territory would be invalidated on any principle of the law of nations? Where a free passage is generally enjoyed, notwithstanding a claim of territory may exist for certain purposes, no violation of territory is committed if the party, after an inoffensive passage, conducted in the usual manner, begins an act of hostility in open ground. In order to have an invalidating effect it must at least be either an unpermitted passage, over territory where permission is regularly requested, or a passage under a permission obtained on false representation and suggestions of the purpose designed. In either of these cases there might be an original misfeasance, and trespass, that travelled throughout and contaminated the whole; but if nothing of this sort can be objected I am of opinion that a capture, otherwise legal, is in no degree affected by a passage over territory in itself otherwise legal and permitted.

1801 November 27. THE TWEE GEBROEDERS. Sir W. Scott.

Having before said that this act of capture was not exercised on neutral territory, as far as I am enabled to judge by the present evidence, I must pronounce that no sufficient objections are shown against the validity of these captures, and that the ships must be adjudged lawful prize to the captors, being bound to Amsterdam in breach of the blockade.

[4 C. Rob. 8.]

THE COSMOPOLITE (No. 2).

Licence—Enumeration of Articles—Construction of Licence—Alteration of Date.

A licence must be construed with the object of carrying out the intention of the grantor, and small deviations from the terms may be overlooked. But when a licence covers the export of certain enumerated kinds of goods, its protection will be confined to them only. Any alteration in the terms of a licence as to time must be clearly explained to give validity to such alteration.

1801 July 8.

THIS was a case respecting a licence granted to a British merchant to import certain specified articles from Spain. It appeared that the licence had been originally granted for three months from the date of the instrument, but that it had afterwards been altered to three months from the date of the bill of lading [and that articles of a different kind to those specified in the licence were on board at the time of capture].

On the part of the captors, the *King's Advocate*.

On the part of the claimant, *Laurence*.

SIR W. SCOTT.—This case arises on the construction of a licence granted to import from Teneriffe, during a war with Spain, goods of a specified description. It is perfectly well known that by war all communication between the subjects of the belligerent countries must be suspended, and that no intercourse can legally be carried on between the subjects of the hostile States but by the special licence of their respective governments. Under this view of the matter, it is clear that a licence is a high act of sovereignty, an act immediately proceeding from the sovereign authority of the State, which is alone competent to decide on all the considerations of commercial and political expediency, by which such an exception from the ordinary consequences of war must be controlled. Licences being then high acts of sovereignty, they are necessarily *stricti juris*, and must not be carried further than the intention of the great authority which grants them may be supposed to extend. I do not say that they are to be construed with pedantic accuracy, or that every small deviation should be held to vitiate the fair effect of them. An excess in the quantity of goods permitted might not be considered as noxious to any extent. A variation in the quality or substance of the goods might be more significant, because a liberty assumed of importing one species of goods under a licence granted to import another might lead to very dangerous abuses. In several cases of licences this Court has had occasion to observe that articles have been introduced which might interfere with our own manufactures, not merely raw materials for the necessary employment of the skill and labour of British artisans, but the finished productions of foreign industry and art, which might come in competition with those of our own; and it has been observed, not without surprise, that some licences themselves—I mean particularly those Irish ones which appeared in the case of the *Christina Sophia* (*a*)—have given a countenance to this practice. Where the licences have expressly permitted the introduction of such goods, this Court cannot take upon itself to withhold from the individual the benefit of such licences, however obtained, but it will always consider it to be its duty to look to the licence for the enumeration of the goods that are to be protected by it. In the present case it appears that the terms of the licence have not been followed in this respect. Here is a licence for barilla, wool, liquorice, orchilla wood, and dying wood, yet there are other articles, a considerable quantity of wine, and some hides on board. It is said that these, comparatively with the burthen of the vessel, form but a very trifling part of the cargo. Be the quantity what it may, it ought to have been provided for in the enumeration which the merchant submitted to the discretion of government when he applied for his licence. As it now stands, I must consider

(*a*) June 20th, 1801. The terms of the licence were general, "for articles for manufacture-use and agriculture," articles imported, "tobacco pipes, thread, bobbin, long holland, geneva, hops, &c."

1801
July 8.

THE COSMOPOLITE.

Sir W. Scott.

this part of the cargo as totally denuded of any authority under the licence, and therefore subject to condemnation. Another material circumstance in all licences is the limitation of time in which they are to be carried into effect; for, as it is within the view of government in granting these licences to combine all commercial and political considerations, a communication with the enemy might be very proper at one time, and at another very unfit and highly mischievous: it might be highly proper in 1799, and highly inexpedient in 1801. Time, therefore, appears to be a very important ingredient; if the party takes upon himself to extend the term of the licence in this respect, it would be, in my opinion, *licentia non sumpta pudenter*.

Two circumstances are required to give the due effect to a licence. First, that the intention of the grantor shall be pursued; and secondly, that there shall be an entire *bona fides* on the part of the user. It has been contended that the latter alone should be sufficient, and that a construction of the grant merely erroneous should not prejudice. This is, I think, laid down too loosely. It seems absolutely essential that that only shall be done which the grantor intended to permit; whatever he did not mean to permit is absolutely interdicted, and the party who uses the licence engages not only for fair intentions, but for an accurate interpretation and execution; when I say an accurate interpretation and execution, I do not mean to exclude such a latitude, as may be supposed to conform to the intentions of the grantor, liberally understood.

The present licence was first granted in 1799, for three months. At that time, as it stood, when coming out of the hands of the Sovereign of this country, and countersigned by the Secretary of State, it was a perfectly good licence for the articles enumerated and for the time therein specified. But I find a difficulty in holding that a licence so granted is a good licence for an importation in 1801. It appears on the face of the instrument that there has been an erasure, and that the words "three months" have been altered to "three months from the date of the bill of lading," extending it, not to this year, or to any other year, but to a time indefinite, whenever it might suit the convenience of the merchant to make use of it.

The question then is, whether the account given of this alteration is satisfactory? It may be so, as to one constituent part of a licence, and not as to another; it may be satisfactory as to the *bona fides* of the party obtaining it, but not as to its conformity with the intention of the grantor; and I have already said that it ought to combine both these properties. The affidavit states, "that the licence was originally made out for three months from the date of the said licence; but upon its being represented at the Council office by this deponent's said house, that owing to the jealousy of the Spanish Government, and the difficulty of communication with the said island of Teneriffe, and the secrecy necessary to be observed, the lives and property of the persons at Teneriffe being endangered by carrying on a trade with this country, if discovered, the said licence was altered at the Council office, to continue in force for three months from the date of the bills of lading."

Now it appears to me that this representation is not entirely satisfactory. As to exportation from Teneriffe and other parts of Spain, we have seen so many instances of it in neutral ships, that it is not very easy to understand how it could be exposed to so much jealousy on the part of the Spanish Government in the manner here described; or, if it were so, how happened it that this was a secret at the time of making the application? How came a licence to be taken restricted to three months if it was known that it could be carried into effect only by watching an opportunity of getting into Teneriffe, as it were by stealth, and by getting out in the same manner? If this fact had been mentioned, no doubt proper means would have been taken to provide for it under the very liberal attention which is, on all occasions, paid by government to the representation of merchants. If it was not known till afterwards, application should have been made, in the same manner as for the original licence, to the Secretary of State who countersigned the first instrument; whereas the affidavit only states, "that an application was made to the Council office," without mentioning *when*, or by whom, this alteration is supposed to have been made. From any observations of mine on the proceedings of the Council, I find a difficulty in supposing that any persons who compose that board would take upon themselves to alter a licence that had been sanctioned by the sign manual.

1801 *July* 8.

THE COSMOPOLITE.

Sir W. Scott.

Besides, how is it authenticated? The word of an inferior clerk of the Council cannot be received as a sufficient authentication; all instruments of this sort should be certified in some manner by the authority of the Council. It is too much for this Court to take it upon inferior authority, or on the mere representation of the party himself. After the alteration, the party carries it to the custom house (*a*), and there it is deposited, and filed, as a thing not immediately to be put in use. When it comes to be examined this erasure is perceived, and the custom office refuse to act upon it, and insist that before it shall be considered as an efficient licence it shall be re-signed. On this information, as the affidavit states, "the party sent his clerk to the Council office to get it re-signed." The more prudent measure would have been for the merchant to have applied himself to some person there of a more efficient character. It seems, however, that a clerk in the Council office told the merchant's clerk that nothing could be done in the business on account of the then existing embargo, as the vessel was a Swedish ship. In this answer the party imprudently acquiesced, and here the matter rested.

On this statement of the facts, I do not feel myself warranted to say that I can be satisfied with the authority of this licence; I think I shall administer the safest justice by referring the party to another Court, composed of members of the Privy Council, who are best capable of judging of the sufficiency of the authority under which the alteration was made, and of the validity of the licence so altered, applied as it has been to the present transaction.

(*a*) The affidavit stated, "that in December following the licence was deposited in the custom house in order that the customs might have notice of any cargo being imported *under* it. That in February, long before the knowledge of the capture, the deponent applied to the custom house to indorse the name of the ship on the licence; that a doubt was then expressed on the part of the custom house whether, in consequence of the alteration as to the time of the importation, they could with propriety act upon it. That the matter being referred to the board, and the same doubts being entertained by them, the licence was returned to the deponent that it might be *re-signed* by the Secretary of State, or *renewed;* that one of the clerks of the deponent was sent to make application to this effect, who addressing himself to Mr. E. S——, one of the clerks of the Council office, was informed by him that nothing could be done owing to the embargo which had lately taken place on Danish and Swedish ships, &c."

THE JEMMY. [4 C. Rob. 31.]

Ship—Transfer from Enemy to Neutral—Continuance of previous Management and Trade—Conclusive Presumption of Fictitious Transfer.

When an enemy ship has been transferred to a neutral owner, but is left under the same management and in the same trade as before the transfer, the conclusive presumption is raised that the transfer is not genuine.

THIS was a case of a ship asserted to have been purchased at Dunkirk by Mr. Schultz, of Altona. This cause now came on to be heard on further proof. 1801 July 17.

SIR W. SCOTT.—This case has been admitted to further proof owing entirely to the suppression of a circumstance which, if the Court had known, it would not have permitted further proof to have been introduced, namely, that the ship has been left in the trade and under the management of the former owner. Wherever that fact appears the Court will hold it to be conclusive, because, from the *evidentia rei*, the strongest presumption necessarily arises that it is merely a covered and pretended transfer. The presumption is so strong that scarcely any proof can avail against it. It is a rule which the Court finds itself under the absolute necessity of maintaining. If the enemy could be permitted to make a transfer of the ship and yet retain the management of it as a neutral vessel, it would be impossible for the Court to protect itself against frauds.

The positive objections which have been pointed out, on the fact of transfer, are also of considerable weight. The inadequacy of the price and the chasms appearing in the correspondence are circumstances inconsistent with the probability of ownership; there is also the course of trade, which has been entirely French without interruption, excepting in one voyage to Barcelona, but even in that instance the vessel returned again to a French port.

It would be impossible for the Court to admit further proof in such a case as this without exposing itself to continual imposition. I have no hesitation in condemning this vessel.

[4 C. Rob. 33.]

THE TWENDE BRODRE.

Contraband—Timber—Treaty with Denmark.

When a treaty stipulated that timber for the construction of ships should be regarded as contraband. *Held*, that if the character of the timber was ambiguous, its nature in reference to the treaty should be decided by reference to the character of the port of destination.

1801 *July* 17.

THIS was a case of a Danish ship, and cargo of fir timber, spars, balks, and deals, taken on a voyage "from Christiansand to Saint Maloes or Brest."

On the part of the captors, a certificate was produced from shipbuilders in his Majesty's yards at Plymouth, stating "that the cargo consisted of fir timber, hand-masts, deals, and spars; that the fir timber and masts were fit for naval purposes, and much wanted in his Majesty's service."

On the other side, an affidavit was exhibited from other shipwrights of Plymouth, stating the timber to be particularly sappy in its quality, and not fit for ship-building, and that no part could be considered as naval stores.

On the part of the captors, the *King's Advocate* contended that timber of this description was to be considered as contraband under the Danish treaty, in which it was expressly stipulated that timber, bois de construction, should be contraband, fir planks excepted. The exception proved that fir planks would have been contraband if not excepted; fir balks, not excepted, were *à fortiori* to be considered as contraband.

SIR W. SCOTT.—This is a ship which was taken on a voyage from Denmark to St. Maloes, as it appeared at the time of capture, having sailed originally on a destination to Havre, but having changed her course, in consequence of some obstacles, and under the direction of one of the owners of the cargo, for St. Maloes. It appears that she was first stopped by the *Juno*, and released, but afterwards stopped by the *Diana*, and brought into Jersey with a cargo of timber on board.

It being contended that the timber was of such a nature as to come under the prohibition of the Danish treaty, the Court directed it to be referred to the inspection of experienced persons in his Majesty's yards. A return is now made to that inquiry, on which I must say that it is not expressed in such specific terms as the Court might have expected to obtain from a reference to those gentlemen. They state "that they had taken a survey, and find it to consist of Dantzic fir timber very serviceable for his Majesty's yards," but without any specification of its dimensions, or any description of its fitness for particular uses, by which its general character might be ascertained. There is another phrase in the report, equally general, "that it is fit for naval purposes." What is that? It amounts to no information at all, since all timber is, I apprehend, fit for *some* naval purposes. There is another certificate, produced on the part of the claimants, from private unauthorized persons selected by the owners, which is rather more precise: it specifies the size of the timber, and states "that it is very sappy and not fit to be considered as naval stores." This is all the assistance that the Court has obtained to enable it to judge of the terms of the explanatory article which was made in the treaty of 1780 for the purpose of avoiding all disputes, and of settling a clear understanding on the subject between the two countries.

In delivering my opinion on the construction which is to be put upon this article, it may be proper to consider shortly the intention of the parties, the terms or expressions of the treaty, the decisions of our Courts, and the interpretation of practice.

With respect to the intention, it is to be remembered that there had been much contest on this matter; the belligerent, on one side, contending that the enemy should not be supplied with timber; the neutral country, on the other side, contending for the liberty of exporting its own produce, one of the great staples of the country. It is fair to presume, from this situation of the parties, that there was no intention on the part of Denmark to give up the timber trade, or to abridge the exercise of that species of commerce, further than the just demands of the belligerent might require. Denmark may be supposed to have agreed in these terms: "We are willing to give up the liberty of trading, as far as your interests are affected, but no further." The situation of the

1801 *July* 17 — THE TWENDE BRODRE. — Sir W. Scott.

contracting parties does not warrant me to imagine that there was any intention of giving up the entire benefit of the market of the other belligerent country for all other timber, but only for such as might materially affect the operations of war.

If a cargo of timber is carried to Rouen, or Havre, for the purpose of being sent to Paris for house-building, how is Great Britain injured by that? I am not to presume that there was any reason for demanding a sacrifice of such a trade, on one side, or that the other party would be willing to renounce a trade so beneficial to themselves and so innoxious to the interests of the belligerent. I must conclude from these considerations that it was only meant to prohibit the carrying of such timber as is fairly to be deemed ship timber.

The terms used in the treaty are, "Bois de construction;" but that must be understood, construction naval: it must be confined to purposes of naval equipment. The great difficulty will be to ascertain what is properly to be considered as ship timber. Timber has frequently, from particular circumstances, a definite and determinate character; it may be denoted by a particular form, as knee timber, which is crooked timber, peculiarly useful for the building of ships, or it may be distinguished by its dimensions of size; but as to other timber, generally, which is as much a thing of ambiguous use as anything can be, the fair criterion will be the nature of the port to which it is going. If it is going to Brest, the destination may be reasonably held to control and appropriate the dubious quality, and fix upon it the character of ship timber—if to other ports of a less military nature, though timber of the same species, it may be more favourably regarded. Then, as to the decisions of Courts of Justice, and the interpretation of practice, I do not know that any express decisions have taken place; and it would be a most desirable instruction to my judgment to have seen that of the Superior Court exercised upon this subject. But it is the everyday practice of this Court not to consider, as included within the prohibition, all that a more extended interpretation might justify: it restores spars and balks of ordinary magnitude, unless there is something special in the circumstances attending them, to show that they have a positive destination to naval purposes.

This then is the interpretation which I am inclined to put upon that treaty. With respect to such timber as is in its own nature ambiguous, I am disposed to look to the criterion of the destination, as an equitable rule of interpretation, taking a fair course between the rights of exportation of native produce, on the part of the neutral country, and the defensive rights of the belligerent. *Planches du sapin*, being expressly excepted in the treaty, may, I hold, be carried anywhere. In other timber, of an indeterminable nature, the judicial test is to be sought from the destination on which it is going. This being a case of timber going to St. Maloes—

[The *King's Advocate* stated some part of a letter to the master which indicated a destination to Brest: "You are to go to St. Maloes, but if the cargo will sell best at Brest, you are to ask a pilot if he cannot take you thither; you may escape the English by going between the shore and Ushant."

Laurence.—The original destination was certainly not to Brest; the ship went into Havre roads, and was then (after having been overhauled by a British cruiser) directed by one of the owners to proceed to St. Maloes.]

Judgment resumed.—If there had been a clear and determined destination to Brest, notwithstanding it might be lately taken up, it would, according to the interpretation I incline to adopt, subject every part of the cargo, except the fir planks, to confiscation; for it could never be permitted to be averred that a cargo of this sort might go on an innocent destination to St. Maloes, and then be sent on to Brest or Rochfort. If that were the case, it must be pronounced a case of condemnation; but the letter on which the captors rely does not show that the directions were absolute to that effect; the words, "if you resolve," indicate an ultimate discretion to have been reposed in the master. How does he execute it? He says, "that he was going to St. Maloes," not for the purpose of taking a pilot on board to carry him to Brest, but with a decided intention of making St. Maloes the ultimate port of his destination, and of discharging his lading there.

Upon the evidence I incline to hold that the conditional directions, which were given him to go to Brest, would not have been

1801 July 17. THE TWENDE BRODRE. Sir W. Scott.

carried into effect. I shall therefore restore this cargo, especially as I perceive that no small part of it consists of fir planks, which I have already said are specially protected; but in consequence of the expression of such an intention, I shall certainly hold that the captors are entitled to their expenses.

Registrar.—This is a cargo taken for the use of government; in such cases the ordinary expenses are paid by government. Is it the intention of the Court that the payment of the captor's expenses is to be included in those charges, or to be paid by the claimant?

Court.—I mean that they should be paid by the claimant; the liberty given by the owner to the master in the letter makes it not unfit that the expenses should fall on him.

[4 C. Rob. 39.]

THE CATHERINE AND ANNA.

Capture—Ship—Restitution—Captor's Expenses—Insurance.

Premiums of insurance on a ship paid by a captor, for his own security, are not chargeable against the owner on a decree for restitution of such ship on payment of the captor's expenses.

1801 July 22.

THIS was a case of a ship and cargo of very considerable value, which had been decreed to be restored on payment of the captor's expenses. In reporting those expenses, the registrar and merchants had refused to admit a charge of insurance against fire, which the captors had incurred to the amount of about 270*l*. Application was now made on the part of the captors to have the report re-committed, that the expense of insurance might be inserted.

The Court desired to know the grounds on which the charge had been disallowed.

Registrar.—It was on the ground that the claimant had before actually insured both ship and cargo, and could not have received any possible benefit under the insurance since effected by the captor.

The *King's Advocate* said that was a circumstance of which the captors were not apprised; that to insure was a reasonable precaution for them to take, who were answerable for the custody of so valuable a cargo, and therefore that they ought to be indemnified.

On the part of the claimants, *Arnold.*—Captors' expenses include only, as it is generally understood, necessary expenses, and not all that the captors may choose to incur on their own account. Insurance was not a necessary expense in the present case, inasmuch as the claimants had already insured. It is said the captors did not know this fact, but they might have informed themselves. They never apprised the agents of the claimants that they were going to insure.

Swabey said that the registrar and merchants had been in the habit of disallowing this charge in the last war.

SIR W. SCOTT.—The ship and cargo in this case have been ultimately restored; but the Court has decreed the captors' expenses to be paid—by expenses, meaning those expenses that are necessarily incurred by the act of capture to which the Court adverted in making the decree. The question is, whether this charge of insurance is such a necessary expense as the captors were bound to incur? Captors are generally bound for two things—for safe and fair custody, and if the property is lost or destroyed for want of that safe and fair custody, they are responsible for the loss. For these two things every captor is answerable; but if an accident, or mere casualty happens, against which no fair exertions of human diligence could protect, it must fall on the party to whom the property is ultimately adjudged. If to secure himself against the negligence of his own agents, or to secure his own responsibility, the captor chooses to make insurance, I understand the practice of the registrar and merchants has been not to allow it in their report, and I am not prepared to say upon any principle which occurs to me that such a disallowance is wrong. The security of the claimant must be considered as depending upon the obligation of safe custody, and personal responsibility in case of loss, on the part of the captors. The claimant is not bound to look further, nor to contribute to the expense which the captor, for

1801 *July* 22.

THE CATHERINE AND ANNA.

Sir W. Scott.

his own security, may choose to incur. It is said that insurance is an advantage to claimants, because it increases the responsibility of the captors—and so it does; but this is an advantage accidental and collateral. The captor who makes a seizure, engages for his own personal responsibility to the party whose property is seized; he seizes at the peril of making full restitution in case restitution is due, and he is to find the means of making that restitution. If the aid of insurers is requisite for such a purpose it may be very advisable for him to resort to it; but the claimant has nothing to do with that: he has a right to consider the captor as fully responsible, and is under no obligation to contribute to the expense of any additional security. The matter of insurance is *res inter alios acta;* I do not know that the captor is, in any event, compellable to assign to him the benefit of his policy. In the *St. Eustatius* cases (*a*), where ships and goods insured by the captors, on their voyage to Europe for adjudication, were taken by the enemy, I think the determination was that the claimants had nothing to do with the benefits of that insurance.

On these grounds I am disposed to hold that whatever means the captors may take to relieve themselves from their personal responsibility, it is a matter which is foreign to the claimant. Where the Court orders a removal, and a fresh risk is incurred, for which the Court directs an insurance, it may be subject to a different consideration. But this being a case in which no application had been made to the Court, where the captor has voluntarily taken the step for his own protection, and where he is not, as I conceive, compellable in any respect to make an assignment of his policy, I cannot think that it could, under any circumstances, be deemed a charge that ought to be thrown on the claim. But *where* the claimant himself has actually insured, the demand is utterly unsustainable. In such a case, to lay upon him the additional expenses which the captor incurred for his own security would be highly injurious. It was asserted before the registrar and merchants that such an insurance had been made by the claimants, and it was not questioned, as I understand, at that time.

(*a*) The Registrar had said that no instance had happened during the present war, but he thought in the *St. Eustatius* cases there was a question of a similar nature.

Further evidence might have been then demanded. It might have been required of them to produce the policies of insurance; nothing of the kind was then done. I shall not now direct them to be produced, but take the fact to be as it is asserted upon the admission of the captors at that time given.

1801 *July* 22.

THE CATHERINE AND ANNA.

Sir W. Scott.

On these grounds I am of opinion that the charge in question, being for insurance made for the benefit of the captor, without communication with the other party, and without any application to the Court, must be taken to be an expense incurred for his own security, and not chargeable on the claimant. Were it necessary, I should hardly hesitate in pronouncing for the justness, as well as for the application of the general rule, alleged to be observed by the registrar and merchants.

Report confirmed.

THE HENRICK AND MARIA (No. 2).

[4 C. Rob. 43.]

Capture—Condemnation—Vessel in Neutral Port—Sale—Title of Owner after Sale.

On principle, the condemnation of a vessel of a belligerent lying in a neutral port is invalid, and a sale arising out of such condemnation is also invalid. But, *held* by Sir William Scott, and by the Lords Commissioners of Appeal, that as the British Prize Court had condemned vessels in neutral ports, a title arising from a sale on a decree of a foreign Court as above, must be recognized as valid.

1799 *November* 26; affirmed *August* 7, 1807.

THIS was a case of a British vessel taken by a Dutch privateer 2nd October, 1795, and carried into Norway. It appeared that a sentence of condemnation had passed 24th March, 1796, at the Hague, before a Court styled "The Committee of the Affairs of the Marine of the Batavian Republic." On the 9th of June following the ship was sold at Christiansand to a Danish merchant, and was afterwards captured 21st June, 1796, with a cargo of fir timber, on a voyage to Amsterdam.

On the part of the captors, it was first contended that the ship was liable to condemnation on the ground of violating the blockade of Amsterdam (*ante*, p. 84). After the judgment of the Court on

1799 November 26. THE HENRICK AND MARIA.

that point, a further question was raised respecting the legality of a transfer of a prize ship not being carried into the port of the captor's country.

On the part of the Danish claimant, *Laurence* and *Croke.*

On the part of the captors, the *King's Advocate* and *Sewell.*

Judgment reserved.

SIR W. SCOTT.—This is a British vessel, captured by a Dutch privateer, carried into Norway, and sold there under a sentence of condemnation passed at the Hague. It has been contended that there is not enough to show that the vessel had not been actually removed to Holland at the time of the sentence; and an expression in the sentence, "brought to judgment," had been relied on as leading to a contrary conclusion, and as intimating that she was actually brought to Holland. I am satisfied, however, as to that fact; the term, "brought to judgment," is merely a figurative expression, signifying that the question respecting that ship was brought to judgment. The whole tenour of the instruments describe the ship herself as situate elsewhere. The bill of sale speaks of the ship as lying in Christiansand, where she was carried with several other English vessels which had been taken by Dutch privateers and put under the direction of the Dutch consul residing at that place; she is described as "to be sold in the condition in which she had been there lying for the inspection of purchasers." If she had been removed into Holland, the fact was perfectly capable of proof; but it is not even averred in the proofs that have been introduced on the part of the Danish purchaser. A claim has been given on behalf of the former British proprietor, and the question that arises is, whether the Danish purchaser can hold this vessel by the title of a condemnation passed upon her whilst lying in a neutral port, she having never been conducted into the country of the captor, nor into any port of an ally in the war? It has been contended that such a sentence is perfectly legal, both on principle and authority. It is said, that on principle the security and consummation of the capture is as complete in a neutral port as in the port of the belligerent himself. On the mere principle of security, it may, perhaps, be so; but it is to be remembered that this is a matter not to be governed by abstract principles alone. The use and practice of nations have intervened, and shifted the matter from its foundations of that species. The expression which Grotius uses on these occasions, "*placuit gentibus*," is, in my opinion, perfectly correct, intimating that there is a use and practice of nations to which we are now expected to conform.

Without entering into a discussion of the several opinions that have been thrown out on this subject, I think I may state the better opinion and practice to have been that a prize should be brought *infra præsidia* of the capturing country, where, by being so brought, it may be considered as incorporated into the mass of national stock. The greatest extension that has been allowed has not carried the rule beyond the ports or places of security belonging to some friend or ally in the war who has a common interest in defending the acquisitions of the belligerent, made from the common enemy of both.

In later times an additional formality has been required, that of a sentence of condemnation, in a competent Court, decreeing the capture to have been rightly made, *jure belli;* it not being thought fit, in civilised society, that property of this sort should be converted without the sentence of a competent Court pronouncing it to have been seized as the property of an enemy, and to be now become *jure belli* the property of the captor. The purposes of justice require that such exercises of war should be placed under public inspection; and therefore the mere *deductio infra præsidia* has not been deemed sufficient. No man buys under that title; he requires a sentence of condemnation as the foundation of the title of the seller; and when the transfer is accepted he is liable to have that document called for, as the foundation of his own. From the moment that a sentence of condemnation becomes necessary, it imposes an additional obligation for bringing the property, on which it is to pass, into the country of the captor; for a legal sentence must be the result of legal proceedings in a legitimate Court, armed with competent authority upon the subject-matter and upon the parties concerned—a Court which has the means of pursuing the proper inquiry and enforcing its decisions. These are principles of universal jurisprudence applicable to all Courts,

1799 November 26.

THE HENRICK AND MARIA.

Sir W. Scott.

and more peculiarly to those which by their constitution, in all countries, must act *in rem* upon the *corpus* or substance of the thing acquired and upon the parties, one of whom is not subject to other rights than those of war, and is amenable to no jurisdiction but such as belongs to those who possess the rights of war against him.

Upon principle, therefore, it is not to be asserted that a ship brought into a neutral port is with effect proceeded against in the belligerent country. The *res ipsa*, the *corpus*, is not within the possession of the Court; and possession, in such cases, founds the jurisdiction. What is the authority over the parties? Over the captors it is complete, on account of their personal relation to the belligerent country. The neutral government may be called upon, in the usual mode of requisition known to the law and practice of nations, to enforce upon them the orders and decrees of the State to which they belong. But how will it be maintainable over the other parties who are not subjects either of the neutral or belligerent State, and are, in respect to the point in issue, only subject to a jurisdiction of war? The belligerent State itself has not the means of exercising the rights of war over them directly. Can it call on the neutral State by requisition so to do? Most clearly not. The neutral State has nothing to do with the rights of force possessed by the one belligerent against the other; it has nothing to do with the enforcement or consummation of such rights; it owes to both parties the simple rights of hospitality, and even these are very limited in the practice of most civilised States. By the regulations of France, foreign ships are forbidden to enter with prizes into a port of France except in cases of distress, and then they are permitted to stay no longer than their necessity exists. Valin observes on this article that it cannot be doubted that such a rule is exactly conformable to the laws of neutrality, and Hübner admits that a wise hospitality will not be exercised beyond this. At any rate, the neutral State can have no compulsory jurisdiction to exercise upon either party upon questions of war depending between them, nor can any such jurisdiction be conveyed to it by the authority of one of them. Its own duties of neutrality prevent the acceptance of any belligerent rights; it cannot be called upon by requisition to give any facility or convenience to the one party to the prejudice of the other, much less to apply modes of compulsion to the one to serve the hostile purposes of the other.

In the administration of a jurisdiction of this kind the enemy who is vanquished is not only a necessary party, but likewise a necessary witness, according to the proceedings of all countries. Prisoners are necessary witnesses to be examined; according to our instructions they are the only witnesses. The French regulations (*a*) admit the evidence of the captor, but hold at the same time that natural justice requires the crew of the captured vessel should be examined touching the rights in question. How are they liable to be compelled to undergo such examination? No force can be applied in the way of strict or continued imprisonment to compel their answers to interrogatories. Their refusal would carry no consequence of legal contumacy with it, for legal contumacy can only exist where a legal jurisdiction has demanded a submission. From these considerations it should seem to result that in the case of a ship lying in a neutral country there is not only a want of original jurisdiction in the belligerent country from the want of possession, but that there is likewise a substantial defect of that authority, which is required for the attainment of justice, and which is essentially necessary to give effect to the ceremony of condemnation. Conformably to this view of the matter, all the more ancient instructions given to cruisers in almost every country require that prizes should be brought into the ports of the country to which the cruisers belong. In Denmark, so late as 1710, it is required under pain of death. In our own country the general instructions still in use are "to bring them into some ports of our dominions." In Holland, it appears in the instructions cited in the argument from Bynkershoek (*b*), that the States did not consider it sufficient for a prize to be brought into the ports of an ally in the war, for they require, in the terms of their judgment, that it should be brought into the ports of the captor. In France, where the practice of the Prize Courts has fluctuated

(*a*) The French practice has always admitted the depositions of the captors as well as the prisoners. Ord. 1400, Art. 6, Collectanea Maritima, p. 76. In this country the depositions of the captors are not received.

(*b*) Q. I. Pub. lib. i. ch. 5.

1799 November 26.

THE HENRICK AND MARIA.

Sir W. Scott.

more than in any other country, according to temporary views of convenience, no relaxation of the strict rule appears to have been introduced earlier than 1705; and it is worthy of observation, as an inconsistency and injustice of no small magnitude, that at the very time when their edicts forbade the cruisers of other countries to bring their prizes into the ports of France, they should authorise their cruisers to carry their prizes into the ports of other countries. That edict appears to have been revoked in 1759. Valin speaks of it rather as a recent and tolerated usage than as a legal practice in 1763. It was renewed at an early period of the present war, in 1793, and has since been largely indulged; but the editor of the new *Code des Prises*, I observe, speaks of it as an innovation, and in terms of considerable asperity. I am not aware that any instructions have issued from this Government during the present war permitting the carrying of prizes into other ports than those of allies. Some instructions have been alluded to as permitting in former wars (*a*) the carrying into Lisbon or Leghorn. I conceive, speaking without answering for the success that might attend a more persevering inquiry on such a subject, that such instructions have issued from this Government only when the Sovereigns of those ports, the Kings of Portugal and the Dukes of Tuscany, have been allies of Great Britain in the wars of Europe.

Some instructions have likewise been alluded to, authorising the cruisers to carry their prizes into the ports of Naples or Sicily (*b*), but I presume at no period in which the governing powers of those countries, or at least the parties in those countries whom we contended to be legally entitled to the government of them, were not engaged in some common confederacy with us.

If the practice of our Courts had conformed to instructions so restricted, the question would not have been subject to much difficulty, for it would still have remained within the pale of the principle which confines the jurisdiction of prize to the cases of prize brought to the ports of the capturing country or of an ally in the war, which, as to the operation of the common war, *unam con-*

(*a*) It had been said in the argument that the instructions of 1740 directed prizes to be carried into *those ports*.

(*b*) Instructions, 1694. England then confederate in the war with Spain.

stituunt civitatem with the belligerent. But it is not to be denied that the Court of Admiralty has gone further. It is now for a considerable time that this Court has been in the habit of condemning prizes carried to Lisbon and Leghorn, at times when I am not at liberty to say that the Sovereigns of those ports were engaged in a common war against the enemy of this country. The fact that the ships proceeded against *here were lying there* has not been dissembled. Such I take to have been the fact in the war called the American War, as well as the war preceding. In the war of 1756 I find commissions from this Court issued in that year to Madeira, to Leghorn, and to Lisbon, and in 1757 to Genoa, in 1758 to Messina, and in 1759 to Naples, for the examination of French prisoners of war carried into those ports; and these commissions were extended, on the breaking out of Spanish hostilities, to the examination of Spanish prisoners of war carried to the same ports. On the breaking out of the American War, in 1776, commissions were granted to Lisbon, Leghorn, and Oporto for the examination of American prisoners of war carried there; on the breaking out of French hostilities, the commissions for these places, with the addition of Naples, were enlarged for the examination of French prisoners, and in a following year or two of Spanish and Dutch prisoners, with the additions of the ports of Genoa and Nice. In the present hostilities commissions of a similar nature have issued to Civita Vecchia, Genoa, Leghorn, Lisbon, Nice, and the ports within that consulate, Naples and Oporto. Now, unless it can be shown that there is something in the nature of all these ports that essentially distinguishes them from the common character of neutral ports, not merely in certain other respects, but such as furnish a ground of solid distinction for purposes of this nature, I think it will be difficult to avoid the consequence, that whatever the correct principle may be, and however much it might import this country to respect and enforce this principle, this Court, *at least*, is bound against that principle by its own practice.

With respect to the characters of Lisbon, Oporto, and Leghorn, it is not to be denied that they are of a peculiar nature. The two first are cities, one of them the capital, of a State which has long maintained a singular relation of something more than amity to this country. The subjects of this country resident there are dis-

1799 November 26.

THE HENRICK AND MARIA.

Sir W. Scott.

tinguished by special privileges; they retain the British character in spite of the Portuguese domicile, even in the estimation of the enemy himself, and they exercise an active jurisdiction at least over their own countrymen established in those ports. The other port (Leghorn), though belonging to a Sovereign who is neutral, and singularly tenacious of that character, from circumstances peculiar to his policy, offers large and distinct privileges to British subjects, continues to them their British name and attributes, and authorizes them to exercise a large jurisdiction over their countrymen. These circumstances might naturally enough lead to the consequence which has taken place—that the British Courts of Admiralty have been in the habit of exercising, with the permission of those Governments (and without any remonstrance made to them on the part of the other belligerent), a prize jurisdiction over vessels captured and carried in there. But though the peculiar relation which these ports bear to this country may account historically for the introduction of such a jurisdiction (which may have since been carried to other ports, where the same foundation for it did not exist), yet even there it may be doubted whether it furnishes a solid ground on which such authority can be maintained. Supposing that there was authority enough existing to operate with legal effect upon the body of the thing, in what manner does it exist over the persons of the subjects of other countries carried prisoners there by a British cruiser? All the personal jurisdiction which the British establishments possess is over their own members; over the subjects of other countries, how is it communicated? They cannot be compelled to appear as parties or witnesses; and if in these ports any sufficient footing could be found for such an authority, its foundation would still be to look for, in some of these enumerated ports, which appear entitled to no such distinctive character.

I am of opinion on these grounds that this Court is bound, against the true principle, by the practice which it has not only admitted, but applied. The observation of Bynkershoek (*a*), "That, in the conduct of war, you must hold that to be lawful in your enemy which you practise yourselves," a rule true in all instances, is not

(*a*) *In jure belli, quod quis sibi sumit, hostibus tribuendum est.*

1799 *November* 26.

THE HENRICK AND MARIA.

Sir W. Scott.

more true in any instance than in one in which the rights and interests of other countries, being neutral, are so directly concerned.

How far the Superior Court will consider this question as concluded by the practice—even an inveterate practice—of this Court is more than I can say. It might be extremely proper that the opinion of that Court should be taken on this important question. It may deem it to be its duty, for anything I know (for it would be presumptuous in me to hazard a conjecture), to recall the practice of this Court to the proper purity of the principle. But sitting here and observing, as I am judicially bound to do, the course of judicial administration which has prevailed, I do not feel *myself* authorized to uphold the sentences which have passed in this Court over prizes carried into foreign ports, and disallow at the same time the validity of such as the enemy has pronounced, under circumstances so nearly similar, as not to afford ground of distinction between them, which appears, to my judgment, sufficiently solid.

The captors appealed.

Two other questions of the same kind were brought from Vice-Admiralty Courts in the cases of the *Gluclicke Peter* and the *Jonge Jan.*

On the 7th of August, 1807, the judgment of the Court of Appeal was delivered by the Master of the Rolls, Sir William Grant: [6 C. Rob. 138, n.]

"This case involves a question as to the validity of sentences of condemnation pronounced in a belligerent country on prizes carried into neutral ports. There was some difference of opinion among the members of the board before whom the case was originally argued. But it appeared to me that the acknowledged practice of this country must have the effect of making those sentences valid whilst that practice continued. For there could be no equity on which we could deny the validity of that title to neutrals purchasing of the enemy at the same time that they were invited to take them from ourselves."

The question is not altogether new. In the year 1761 a case occurred in which a British ship, captured by the French and carried to Christiansand, and condemned in the Courts in France, was sold to a merchant of Denmark, who sent the vessel in the course of her trade to a port in Scotland. The original proprietors arrested the vessel by precept from the Court of Admiralty on the ground of the invalidity of such a sentence to change the property. And the Judge of the Court of Admiralty sustained the objection, and decreed the vessel to belong to the original owners. An appeal was prosecuted to the Court of Sessions: *Benton* v. *Brink*, July 23rd, 1761; Dict. of Decis. vol. iii. p. 328; also Decis. Reported, from 1760 to 1764, vol. i. p. 104; and under the authority of that Court an inquiry was directed to be made into the practice of the High Court of Admiralty of England on this subject.

It was on that occasion certified to be the practice of the High Court of Admiralty to condemn vessels lying in neutral ports, and on that information the Court of Sessions reversed the judgment of the Court below, and decreed restitution to the Danish purchasers; and in that sentence the British owners acquiesced.

After this declaration of the practice of our own Courts, it would be a very great hardship on Danish merchants to expect that they should know the law better than the Courts of Scotland, or to require that they should abstain from purchases of this kind on a mere surmise that a different doctrine might be held forty years after. The equitable mode of correcting the principle of law, if it is wrong, would be to correct, in the first instance, the practice of our own Courts. If that is altered so as to be brought to the knowledge of neutral merchants, the question as to them will be materially changed. They will no longer be at liberty to stand on our practice and say the title is allowed to be good amongst yourselves. They must come forward and support their pretensions on other grounds, and then many of the considerations that were urged in argument at the hearing of this case will be deserving of very serious attention. It is not necessary to enter upon those topics now, because this Court is of opinion that neutrals are sufficiently confirmed in their title by the practice which has prevailed amongst ourselves. On these grounds the sentence of the High Court of Admiralty in the *Henrick and Maria* must be affirmed, and the sentences of the Vice-Admiralty Courts in the two other cases restoring such property to the former owners must be reversed (*a*).

[4 C. Rob. 65.]

THE STERT.

Blockade—Inland Navigation.

The blockade of a seaport does not make the ingress or egress of goods to or from such port by inland navigation illegal so as to subject them to condemnation if captured coming from another and unblockaded port.

1801 *August* 4.

THIS was a case of a cargo of butter and cheese, proceeded against on the ground of the blockade of Holland, and claimed for Prussian subjects. It appeared that letters of orders had been sent to the shippers in Edam directing them to ship the present cargo in a small vessel by the inland navigation to Embden, con-

(*a*) See *ante*, p. 321.

signed to Rudolff & Co., of that place, with orders to them to send it on to London.

1801 *August* 4.

THE STERT.

Sir W. Scott.

SIR W. SCOTT.—This is a question arising out of the blockade of Amsterdam, respecting goods put on board in a port of the Texel, for the very purpose of being sent to London, without any interruption of the voyage, but conveyed out of Holland to Embden, by the means of the canal navigation, as I understand it. The question is, whether this is to be considered as a breach of the blockade? A blockade may be of different descriptions. The blockade of Amsterdam, which was imposed on the part of this country, was, from the nature of our situation, a mere maritime blockade, effected by force operating only at sea. As far as that force could be applied, it was indubitably a good and legal blockade; but as to an interior navigation, how is it a blockade at all? Where is the blockading power? Let us suppose the case of the blockade of Havre. Can it be said that, by the maritime blockade of the Seine, the interior access to Havre is blockaded, so as that goods belonging to a neutral subject sent from Paris to Havre could be held subject to confiscation by virtue of the blockade? It is argued, that if this course of trade is allowed, the object of the blockade, which is to distress the trade of Holland, will be defeated. If that is the consequence, all that can be said is that it is an unavoidable consequence. It must be imputed to the nature of the thing, which will not admit of an effectual remedy of this species. This Court cannot, on that ground, take upon itself to say that a legal blockade exists, where no actual blockade can be applied. In the very notion of a complete blockade it is included that the besieging force can apply its power to every point of the blockaded State. If it cannot, it is no blockade of that quarter where its power cannot be brought to bear; and where such a partial blockade is undertaken, it must be presumed that this is no more than what was foreseen by the blockading State, which nevertheless thought proper to impose it to the extent to which it was practicable. The commerce, though partially open, is still subjected to a pressure of difficulties and inconvenience. To cut off the power of immediate export and import from the ports of Holland is of itself no insignificant operation, although it may not be possible to exclude them from the benefit of an inland communication. If the blockade be

1801 August 4. — THE STERT. — Sir W. Scott.

rendered imperfect by this construction, it must be ascribed to the physical impossibility of the measure by which the extent of its legal pretensions is unavoidably limited.

In laying down this rule as applicable to the present case, I proceed upon the supposition that this was a real inland navigation, and not a navigation over the Watt, the character of which might be subject to a different signification. Conceiving this to be a cargo which had gone to Embden on neutral account, by an internal canal navigation, where no blockade existed, I shall hold it free of all consequences of blockade, allowing the captors their necessary expenses upon the particular facts of the case (*a*).

[4 C. Rob. 68.]

THE EDWARD.

Contraband—Wines—Port of Naval Equipment—Destination Dissembled—Trinity Master Consulted.

Wines from one French port destined to another French port, being one of naval equipment. *Held* to be contraband.

When destination dissembled, ship condemned with cargo.

Trinity Master consulted as to inconsistency of ship's course with her alleged destination.

1801 August 7; affirmed November 28, 1804.

THIS was a case of a Prussian ship and a cargo of wines, claimed for Prussian subjects, taken June 16th, 1801, on a voyage from Bordeaux, ostensibly to Embden, but found so near to the Isle of Saints, and with such apparent contradictions in the log-book respecting the course the ship had held for two or three days before, that the King's Advocate, resting on that point chiefly, to prove a false destination, prayed the Court to request the attendance of one of the masters of the Trinity House.

On this day, Captain King, one of the Elder Brethren, attended at the request of the Court. It was argued, that, from the entries in the log-book, it was evident the ship was pursuing a course to Brest; that this suspicion was confirmed by the evidence of the mariners, who said the master stood in for the French coast at night, and particularly directed them to say they were going to Embden; that such a voyage with false papers would make it liable to be considered as a case of fraudulent contraband, affecting the ship as well as the cargo.

(*a*) See the *Ocean*, *ante*, p. 310.

The Court desired Captain King would state what impression the objections had made on him as to the course of navigation, and whether the ship appeared to be pursuing a *bonâ fide* course to Embden, or whether she was hugging or closing with the French coast, so as to make it highly probable that she was going into a French port.

Captain King stated that with respect to the entries of the log-book, nothing material occurred till the 10th of June, as the course would be nearly the same, whether for Brest or Embden; that on the 11th some inconsistencies appeared, but that from the 12th to the 15th the contradictions were such that they could not have been true entries in point of fact; that at the time when the ship was taken she was standing in for the Saints, which was so obviously out of her proper course that, unless the weather had been stormy, which was nowhere noticed, the master could not, as a man of ordinary skill, have been found in the situation in which he was taken if he had been pursuing a course to Embden.

SIR W. SCOTT.—That will be sufficient to found the judgment of the Court. After this representation the Court is under the necessity of inferring an intention of going into a French port. It appears that there was no reason why the vessel should have been found where she was described to be; on the contrary, that the ordinary rules of navigation required a different course. The ship had an opportunity of pursuing her voyage; the winds were rather favourable. Instead of pursuing her course she appears to have been hovering about and adhering to the French coast, for which no reason is assigned. There being no cause assigned, I am under the necessity of inferring that it was done without any justifiable cause, and with an intention of getting into a French port.

The consequences of this will be indubitable, for though wines are not an article generally contraband *per se*, yet in conjunction with all the circumstances of this voyage they are unquestionably to be considered as naval stores. It was a voyage to Brest, where there was notoriously a large armament lying, very much in want of articles of this kind, articles of an indispensable nature. If such articles had gone with an avowed destination to such a place and at such a conjuncture, the rule of pre-emption would have

1801 *August* 7. THE EDWARD. Sir W. Scott.

been a rule of excessive and undue indulgence to apply to such a case, but where the destination is dissembled confiscation is the clear and necessary consequence.

It has been said that this voyage, being a voyage from one port of the enemy to another, cannot be deemed a voyage of supply to him, but it is to be remembered that Brest is a port not situated within a wine province of that country, and must have its supplies by importation from other ports; and the rule has been already established that the transfer of contraband from one port of a country to another, where it is required for the purposes of war, is subject to be treated in the same manner as an original importation into the country itself. The vessel so employed can hardly be considered in any other character than that of a French victualler carrying to the place of naval equipment *munitions de bouche*, and this with a false representation of her voyage, in order to evade these rights of pre-emption or confiscation, whatever they might be, which would attach upon such a cargo visibly going upon such a destination.

Under such a state of facts the ship is involved in condemnation with her cargo.

[4 C. Rob. 78.]

THE TRITON.

Ship—Restoration—Costs and Damages.

When a ship is seized without reasonable cause, she will be restored with costs and damages.

1801 *October* 28.

THIS was a case of a Hamburg ship and a cargo belonging to merchants of St. Thomas, taken 13th June, 1798, on a voyage from St. Thomas to Altona.

SIR W. SCOTT.—This ship was coming on a voyage from St. Thomas to Altona, fully documented for such a voyage; the bill of lading did not express account and risk, but the other papers did; the depositions of the master and of the mate expressed the fullest belief of property. But the captors have picked up a Jew passenger, on whose evidence alone it is attempted to discredit this claim. These depositions seem, on the face of them, to have been strangely taken; without them the case would have been perfectly clear. It being a case of a voyage from St. Thomas to Altona, both neutral ports, without any doubt on the destination, and without any sufficient ground of seizure, I think the claimants are entitled to costs and damages (*a*).

1801 *October* 28.

THE TRITON.

Sir W. Scott.

A month's demurrage given to the ship.

THE JONGE PIETER.

[4 C. Rob. 79.]

Capture—Trade with Enemy—British Goods—Neutral Port—Ultimate Hostile Destination—Condemnation.

As a British subject may not trade with the enemy, British goods consigned to a neutral port to be transmitted thence to a hostile destination are liable to condemnation.

1801 *November* 13.

THIS was a case respecting the legal proprietary interest in certain articles purchased in England by Chr. Court & Co., and shipped by them for Embden, with directions that they should be sent on to Amsterdam. The goods were claimed as the property of J. Court, a merchant in America, and it was said that the transaction was conducted by Chr. Court & Co. in London, as agents for J. Court in America; that they had been in the habit of originating speculations of this sort, and of carrying the profit to the account of J. Court, to liquidate a debt due from him to the house in London.

On the part of the captors, the *King's Advocate* and *Sewell.*

On the part of the claimants, *Laurence* and *Swabey.*

SIR W. SCOTT.—These four cases stand on one common ground, being shipments of goods made in London for Embden, and, as it appears in the papers, with an ulterior purpose of sending them on to Amsterdam.

The whole case turns on the question of property. It is contended on the part of the captor that the property is either in the shipper or in the Dutch consignee. On the other side, it is insisted that the goods belong to J. Court, an American merchant, resident in America, for whom the claim is given. According as this point

(*a*) See the *Ostsee*, Vol. II. p. 432.

1801 *November* 13.

THE JONGE PIETER.

Sir W. Scott.

shall be determined, very different consequences will follow. If they could be shown to be the property of the enemy, they would be liable to confiscation on every ground, and without hesitation. But as that suggestion is principally founded on an expression in a letter, which is, I think, too equivocal to support such a conclusion, and as there are very strong circumstances in the further proof to show that the property is not to be assigned to the Dutch consignee, that supposition may be dismissed out of the cause. Then it comes to this question, Whether the property is to be taken as residing in the English shipper, or in the American merchant for whom it is claimed? If they are the goods of the American merchant, the only question will be, Whether Amsterdam, being under blockade, such a trade is not liable to the penal consequence of breaking the blockade? If they are the property of English subjects, the same question will arise; and also, an additional question, Whether, on their part, it is not such a circuitous trading with the enemy as will make the property on that ground liable to confiscation?

On the first point, supposing the cargo to be American property, I am not inclined to think that it would be affected by the blockade on the present voyage. The blockade of Amsterdam is, from the nature of the thing, a partial blockade—a blockade by sea; and if the goods were going to Embden, with an ulterior destination by land to Amsterdam, or by an interior canal navigation, it is not, according to my conception, a breach of the blockade (*a*). But in the case of a British subject shipping goods to go to the enemy through a neutral country, I am afraid the penalty would be incurred. Without the licence of government no communication, direct or indirect, can be carried on with the enemy. On the policy of that law, this is not the place to observe; it is the law of England; and if any considerations of mercantile policy interfere with it, the duty of the subject is to submit his case to that authority of the country which can legalise such a trade, looking to all the considerations, of political as well as commercial expediency, that are connected with it. But an individual cannot do this; he is not to say such a trade is convenient, and therefore legal; neither

(*a*) See the *Stert*, *ante*, p. 348.

can the Court exercise such a discretion. Where no rule of law exists, a sense or feeling of general expediency, which is, in other words, common sense, may fairly be applied; but where a rule of law interferes, these are considerations to which the Court is not at liberty to advert. In all the cases that have occurred on this question—and they are many—it has been held indubitably clear that a subject cannot trade with the enemy without the special licence of government. The interposition of a prior port makes no difference; all trade with the enemy is illegal (*a*); and the circumstance that the goods are to go first to a neutral port will not make it lawful. The trade is still liable to the same abuse, and to the same political danger, whatever that may be. I can have no hesitation in saying that during a war with Holland it is not competent to a British merchant to send goods to Embden, with a view of sending them forward on his own account to a Dutch port, consigned by him to persons there, as in the course of ordinary commerce.

1801 *November* 13.

THE JONGE PIETER.

Sir W. Scott.

The case is reduced then, to the simple question, Whether these goods are the property of the merchant in America, or of the British subject?

[The Court then examined the evidence and concluded.]

This being the state of the case, I feel myself under the necessity of saying that the property is not shown to have been legally divested out of the British house, and that, as their property, it is taken in a course of commerce which makes it liable to confiscation.

THE POTSDAM. [4 C. Rob. 89.]

Blockade—Transfer of Ship—Egress in Ballast.

A ship lawfully transferred from one neutral owner to another in a blockaded port may come out in ballast.

THIS was a case of a ship taken on a voyage from Cherburg to Caen, 27th August, 1801, and claimed for Mr. Abegg, of Embden.

1801 *October* 20.

(*a*) In the *Nancy*, a cargo was consigned "to Cowes or a market," and as by the evidence it appeared that the real destination was Amsterdam, the cargo was condemned. The case turned purely on the question of fact. [3 C. Rob. 32.]

1801 October 20. THE POTSDAM.

It appeared in the history of the ship that she had been transferred from another neutral merchant to the present claimant whilst lying in Havre, then under blockade, and that she had sailed out of the blockaded port in ballast.

It was argued that the claimant could not sustain a title derived under a purchase in a blockaded port.

SIR W. SCOTT.—It was a transfer from one neutral to another, in no manner connected with the commerce of the blockaded port. I am not disposed to think that circumstance will affect the title. The ship appears to have come out in ballast (*a*), and therefore I think the claimant's title stands clear of all objection on the ground of blockade.

Restored, paying captor's expenses.

[4 C. Rob. 90.]

THE BREMEN FLUGGE.

Capture—Neutral Vessel—Freight—Enemy Cargo—Right of Master—Expenses of Captors.

When a neutral vessel is restored, but the cargo is condemned, and freight is ordered to be paid by the captors, such decree does not give the master of the vessel the right to be paid his expenses in priority over the captors of the remaining proceeds of the cargo.

1801 November 7.

THIS was a question respecting the remaining proceeds of a cargo which had been condemned for want of further proof, the ship having been restored as a neutral ship, with freight and expenses, decreed to be a charge on the cargo. The sum of 1,050*l.* had been paid in discharge of the freight, and the question now

(*a*) So in the *Juffrow Maria Schroder*, a quantity of goods sent into Havre in 1797, before the blockade, for the purpose of being sent on to Paris, and sold for the account of the consignor, but re-shipped (as found unsaleable) by order of the neutral proprietor during the blockade, were restored, the Court saying: "As the truth of this representation is not impeached, these goods are, I think, entitled to restitution. The same rule which permits neutral merchants to withdraw their ships from a blockaded port extends also, with equal justice, to merchandise sent in before the blockade, and withdrawn *bonâ fide* by the neutral proprietor."

was whether the neutral master was entitled to the remaining sum, being not more than 50*l*. under the decree for his expenses; or whether the captor had not a prior claim to it, to defray the expenses which he had necessarily incurred.

1801
November 7.

THE BREMEN FLUGGE.

SIR W. SCOTT.—This is a question concerning a remnant of a cargo, left in the registry, which has been condemned for want of further proof, after the neutral owner of the ship had obtained a sentence of restitution of the vessel, with freight and expenses, decreed to be a charge on the cargo. It is true such a decree passed; but this decree of freight and expenses is not to be taken as exclusive of all further orders of the Court respecting the cargo, nor as giving a decided preference of payment, to the exclusion of other just claims upon it. if the fund should prove insufficient to satisfy all demands. On general principles, when condemnation has been obtained, the captor's claims appear to have rather the advantage. It has heretofore been a question of doubt whether the neutral vessel can lawfully carry the property of a belligerent at all. The modern rule, and indeed an ancient rule of this country, has been established on more liberal principles; and it is now held almost universally that the neutral has a right to carry the property of the enemy, but subject to the right of the belligerent to bring in the ship so employed, for the purpose of bringing the cargo to adjudication. It is now, I say, generally held that a neutral vessel so engaged is not exposed to any penalty at all, but that she is entitled to her freight as a lien attaching on the cargo. The captor takes *cum onere.* The freight attaches as a lien, which he must discharge by payment, provided, as it must always be understood, that there are no unneutral circumstances in the conduct of the ship to induce a forfeiture of this demand. But the expenses of the neutral master appear to me to stand on a somewhat different footing. As to them, this distinction seems to present itself, supposing the law to be that the neutral ship is liable to be brought in. If she can carry the property of the enemy lawfully, on that condition only, I do not know that she is entitled to the expenses incurred in consequence of being so brought in. Putting practice out of the question, which has established an indulgent rule, it does not appear that the neutral master would,

1801
November 7.

THE BREMEN FLUGGE.

Sir W. Scott.

on principle merely, be entitled to an indemnification for expenses so incurred. He is bound to know the condition annexed to his right, and to abide the consequences. A more favourable practice has obtained, under which his expenses are usually allowed; and this practice the Court will be disposed to sustain as far as it does not interfere with other rights equally protected by practice and more strongly protected by principle. But it is not a claim which the neutral master is entitled to urge against the captor as a right equally original and equally vested in him, and in the same manner as freight is vested, by the receipt of the cargo on board and the performance of the contract of conveyance. It is said that the cargo was condemned, not as enemy's property, but for want of further proof and the attestation of the asserted owner. Can that make any difference? The legal conclusion will be the same, that condemnation passed because it was not proved to be the property of the neutral claimant; the want of proof of neutral property induces the legal conclusion that it is the property of enemies. The captor is as much entitled as if the cargo had been condemned on affirmative grounds, and in the first instance on positive evidence, that it was the property of the enemy. On these considerations I think the captor is entitled to the priority (*a*).

[4 C. Rob. 93.]

THE ALEXANDER.

Blockade—Liability of Cargo Owner.

When a vessel is captured endeavouring to enter a blockaded port, the inference is that she is entering in the interests of the cargo, which, therefore, becomes liable to condemnation.

1801
November 13.

THIS was the case of a cargo, taken 3rd April, 1801, on a voyage from Lisbon, ostensibly to Altona, but actually going into Havre during the blockade under pretence of being in want of provisions. The goods were claimed for several persons, merchants of Lisbon. The ship had been condemned on a former day. It was argued now, on the part of the claimants of the cargo, that they were not

(*a*) See the *Vrow Henrica*, *post*, p. 399.

bound by the act of the master deviating into a blockaded port; and it was prayed that they might be permitted to give further proof.

SIR W. SCOTT.—I think this case is in effect decided by the decree which has pronounced the ship subject to condemnation for fraudulently attempting to go into a blockaded port; for when the Court decided that, it did in effect decide that the vessel was so going to dispose of this cargo, the inference in all cases being that a ship going into a blockaded port is going with an intention of disposing of the cargo. The Court has already decided that the ship was going in, and that the excuse assigned was a frivolous pretence. The master makes no distinction, nor asserts that he deviated under particular directions, applying to one part of the cargo only, or that when that part was delivered, under instructions unknown to the rest of the shippers, he was to go on to Altona with that part of the cargo which is the subject of the present claims. If that could have been made out, the Court might, perhaps, have given the claimants the benefit of that distinction. The same general cause is assigned for all, and I must suppose the whole cargo was to be there delivered. It is true that the owners of the cargo are not, in general cases, held to be affected by the act of the master, unless he is specially appointed their agent. But it would be impossible to maintain a blockade in cases of this nature, which is directed more against the cargo than against ships, if the Court did not draw the inference that a ship going in fraudulently is going in the service of the cargo, with the knowledge and by the direction of the owner. If any inconvenience arises to the claimants of the cargo from this necessary conclusion, the owners of the vessel or the master are the persons to whom they must look for indemnification.

Cargo condemned.

[4 C. Rob. 96.]

THE VRIENDSCHAP.

Licence—Enumerated Articles—Other Non-Licensed Articles on Board for Ulterior and Neutral Destination—Condemnation.

A licence was granted to convey to the port of the enemy enumerated articles. Other articles not inserted in the licence were sent at the same time, ostensibly destined to a neutral port, on the part of the British subject: *Held,* to be subject to condemnation.

1801 *November* 18.

THIS was a case respecting a quantity of barilla, sent from London to Rouen in the first instance, but with an asserted destination to Oporto, and claimed on behalf of a British merchant.

It appeared that the claimants had obtained a licence to export certain enumerated articles (*a*) to Rouen, but the barilla was not included in the licence. It was represented on their part that it was not the intention to unlade the barilla at Rouen, but that after the privileged part of the cargo had been delivered there, the ship was to go on with the barilla to Oporto.

On the other side, the *King's Advocate* and *Robinson* contended that there were several circumstances in the facts of this case which made the reality of such an intention liable to great suspicion and wholly incredible, but, further, that in point of law it was not competent to a British merchant to send goods unprotected by licence to an enemy's port, under a purpose of sending them on, upon an ulterior destination to a neutral port.

SIR W. SCOTT.—This question arises on a quantity of barilla, shipped at London and taken on a voyage, first to Rouen, but, as it is asserted, going ultimately to be delivered at Oporto, the other part of the cargo being to be delivered under the protection of a licence at Rouen. The first thing to be considered is whether it is satisfactorily proved that the barilla was actually to be delivered at Oporto. If not, the Court may require further elucidation, or it may think the contrary so clear that that question of law shall not arise. Upon the nature and quality of the goods, it must be allowed that the exportation of barilla to Oporto is liable to all

(*a*) These articles had been restored by consent.

the objections of incredibility that have been urged against it. Barilla is the produce of Spain, a country contiguous to Portugal, and on that account it is a commodity, which in the uninterrupted state of commerce that has subsisted between Spain and Portugal, might be expected to find its way to Oporto by a much more expeditious course than through this country. It is besides an article in great request in England and France, and much enhanced in price, owing to our hostilities with Spain; our own navigation laws have been relaxed to promote the importation of this very article, owing to the difficulty of obtaining it. This circumstance throws a great improbability on the fact; but considering the great flux and reflux of different articles in commerce, the Court would be unwilling to decide on the mere ground of improbability alone.

With respect to the other parts of the case, it appears there were two sets of papers on board: one expressing a destination from Hamburg to Rouen and Oporto, the other stating that the vessel was going to Harfleur. The account which the master gives of this contradiction is, "that he took the latter only for the purpose of deceiving French cruisers." It is impossible not to observe that this representation of the master is very inconsistent; for we should naturally have expected that if his account was true, he would, on being brought to, have presented this paper, since it appears that he was first impressed with a notion that he was stopped by a French privateer. But he acts quite otherwise; he gives up other papers but does not give up that paper; and when he finds that the ship which had brought him to was an English vessel, he still wishes to hold back this paper. The more material fact, however, is that he does not bring forward this paper, when only it could have been of use to him, according to his own account, to protect him against French cruisers. How could this inconsistency have proceeded from imprudence only? If it is mere imprudence it is an unfortunate imprudence, and leaves the fact very questionable as to a clear and fair intention of going to Oporto.

But supposing the ship was really going in this course of trade, a question arises whether it is such a course of trade as can be allowed. The shipper obtains a licence, which is a thing *stricti juris*, to be obtained by a fair and candid representation and to be fairly pursued. It is not pretended that any mention was made

1801 *November* 18. THE VRIENDSCHAP. Sir W. Scott.

of these articles in the application, or that it was at all presented to the view of the Council, that there was an intention of mixing up articles of this nature for a further destination to Oporto. It was stated to the Council that the ship was destined to Rouen. With the articles enumerated in the licence, would the Council have allowed such an article as this to have gone to Rouen, under a certainty of being put in requisition there, if wanted, notwithstanding the asserted purpose of the shipper to carry it on to Oporto? Then is this a fair execution of the licence? I cannot think that it is. I am disposed to refer it to the judgment of another Court, which will have the means of ascertaining what would have been the opinion of the Council on such a course of trade if it had been fairly disclosed to them.

It is certainly a good logical rule not to argue *ab abusu contra usum;* but if it is clear that the abuse would be certain and frequent, and impossible to be prevented in numerous cases which must occur, then the abuse so probable, certain, and so frequent is a fair argument against the allowance of the practice. If the Court is convinced that, out of a thousand instances, there would be nine hundred and ninety-nine of abuse in opposition to one fair and *bonâ fide* execution of such an intention as is here alleged, it is reasonable to conclude that such a practice would not be permitted. If this could be admitted, what has any British merchant to do but to put articles of any sort on board under such pretences; and how is it possible to prevent them from going, without molestation, into the hands of the enemy? I think the case alluded to is connected with this, though weaker, viz., that supposing a neutral ship going from London to an enemy's port, and on a further destination to a neutral port, it would not be competent to a British merchant to put goods on board under cover of that ulterior destination. In the case of a blockaded port, could permission be given to any neutral merchant to take goods there on an averment of an ulterior destination? I am of opinion that it would be impossible to prevent the perpetual abuse of such liberty as is here contended for, and, therefore, that the mere honesty of intention cannot be alleged as a justification in a course of transaction which, if allowed, would leave no means of preventing fraud in an infinite number of other cases.

Under these considerations, I am of opinion that the licence has not been fairly executed, and I shall refer it to another Court, who compose a part of the Council, to say whether it was the intention of those who granted this licence that under shelter of such protection a British merchant should be at liberty to put other articles on board, to go first to Rouen, under an averment that they were to be carried on to Oporto; more especially when it is notorious how much the manufactures of France have been in want of all articles, and to what violent modes the French Government has resorted, by seizing them whenever they came into their ports.

1801 *November* 18. THE VRIENDSCHAP. Sir W. Scott.

Condemned.

THE SECHS GESCHWISTERN.

[4 C. Rob. 100.]

Transfer—Cessation of Enemy Interest in Property—Effect of Restrictive Covenants on Transfer—Condemnation.

Property of an enemy may be transferred to a neutral, but such transfer is vitiated if any interest of the enemy remains in the transferred property. Restrictive covenants in a deed of transfer: *Held*, to invalidate it.

THIS was a case respecting a ship asserted to have been purchased in France by a neutral merchant, but not wholly transferred.

1801 *November* 19.

SIR W. SCOTT.—This is the case of a ship asserted to have been purchased of the enemy, a liberty which this country has not denied to neutral merchants, though by the regulation of France it is entirely forbidden. The rule which this country has been content to apply is that property so transferred must be *bonâ fide* and absolutely transferred; that there must be a sale divesting the enemy of all further interest in it; and that anything tending to continue his interest vitiates a contract of this description altogether. This is the rule which this country has always considered itself justified in enforcing; not forbidding the transfer as illegal, but prescribing such rules as reason and common sense suggest to guard against collusion and cover, and to enable it to ascertain, as much as possible, that the enemy's title is absolutely and completely divested.

In the present case there are covenants which preserve and retain the interest of the enemy seller. The formal instruments of

1801 *November* 19.

THE SECHS GESCH-WISTERN.

Sir W. Scott.

transfer rather import some such secret agreement; for in the account current, which bears date February, 1800, we find charges for neutral papers; and though the bill of exchange which is asserted to have been given in payment is produced, and bears the semblance of an actual bill of exchange, no notice is taken of it in this account. With respect to the balance of the account also, as it is termed, there is an agreement by which "the neutral purchaser mortgages the said brig, &c., to Citizen ——, deducting the sums received on account." But there are no such sums charged or entered as received; under these circumstances, the ship would stand bound for the whole amount, and it could not be said that the interest of the former owner is divested. But there is another condition of this contract which more directly points to the continuance of the enemy's interest. It recites that, "whereas the seller is bound in a penalty not to sell, unless under condition of restitution (*a*), at the end of the war, we bind ourselves to all suits to which the seller may become subject." It seems that it is the policy of the French Government not to allow sales of French vessels without this equity of redemption. From their inability to navigate their own ships during the war, they submit to a temporary transfer; but still keep their hand upon them, to enforce restitution on the return of peace. From this penalty the neutral purchaser undertakes to exonerate the vendor. It is impossible for him to do this, without making himself answerable for the money for which Citizen B. is bound; in which case, supposing that any adequate payment has been actually made, the neutral must be understood to undertake to pay a double price. Is there in this any sign of a *bonâ fide* transfer? Is not the hand of the French vendor still on the vessel? Looking to the control which the French Government and the vendor still retain over this property, it is impossible for me to hold that all the interest of the enemy is completely divested.

Ship condemned.

(*a*) Nemo potest videri eam rem vendidisse, de cujus dominio id agitur, ne ad emptorem transeat: Dig. de Cont. Emp. l. 80, § 3; Pothier Tr. des Oblig. vol. i. p. 6.

THE FRANKLIN (No. 2). [4 C. Rob. 147.]

Salvage—Cargo—Vessel for Enemy Port—Contingent Risk.

Military salvage, as for a rescue from the enemy, is not due unless the property at the time of the service is either in the possession of the enemy or inevitably within his power.

1801 *December* 18.

THIS was a case of a British ship and cargo, bound ostensibly on a voyage from Liverpool to Naples, but captured much out of that course whilst going actually into a Spanish port in the Bay of Biscay. Further proof had been directed to be made of the property and of the destination. Proof was now brought in, consisting of the affidavits of British merchants, asserting the destination of their goods to Naples. Their letters of orders and advice being also produced, the proof was held sufficient and the property was directed to be restored. To account for the deviation into a Spanish port, it was stated in an affidavit of the master "that he had met with bad weather, and that the ship becoming leaky he was compelled by his crew to make the nearest land." In opposition to this account it was stated on the other side, "that the ship was not in a bad condition, that she was after capture brought to Jersey without difficulty or danger."

The captors now claimed military, or in the alternative civil, salvage.

For the captors, the *King's Advocate* and *Robinson.*

For the claimants, *Arnold* and *Swabey.*

SIR W. SCOTT.—The first question now before the Court is, whether the captors of this ship and cargo can entitle themselves to be considered as salvors? On their part, two kinds of salvage are claimed. First, a military salvage, as it may be termed, in rescuing the property from the enemy; and secondly, a salvage in preserving it from distress and peril of the sea. The vessel had met with bad weather, and had sprung a leak, and was at the time of capture found very near St. Andero, intending to go into an enemy's port for the preservation of the lives of the crew. Whether the danger appeared so great to the privateer may be doubted, as it has turned out that, with the aid of a few more hands, they kept the ship eight days longer at sea, and at last brought her safely into a port of Jersey. There might therefore be a reason-

1801 December 18.

THE FRANKLIN.

Sir W. Scott.

able ground of inquiry, whether the distress alleged was a *bonâ fide* distress; and whether the ship and cargo were not actually going as the property of British subjects to trade with the enemy. These appearances did, in my apprehension, afford sufficient ground of a suspicion, and entirely remove all complaint against the privateers, "that they acted improperly in bringing her in for adjudication." Their conduct has already been justified by the order which has been made for further proof.

The next question that occurs is, whether military salvage is due as for a rescue from the enemy? I think it is not. No case has been cited, and I know of none in which military salvage has been given, where the property rescued was not in the possession of the enemy, or so nearly as to be certainly and inevitably under his grasp. There has been no case of salvage where the possession, if not absolute, was not almost indefeasible, as where the ship had struck, and was so near as to be virtually in the hands and grip of the enemy. In such cases, the same hazard is incurred by the salvor, and the same reason exists to hold out a stimulus to recaptors. But in this case there was no enemy to encounter. The danger to the parties was contingent only, and though probable to occur, had not actually occurred. The case which has been cited in argument, does in point of authority apply. It was the case of a Spanish ship coming from New Orleans, ignorant of hostilities, which had lately commenced, and going into the port of Bordeaux, where she would undoubtedly have been confiscated. A claim of salvage was set up on the part of a British cruiser; but the Court said, "No, the danger was something distant and eventual; you had no conflict to sustain; as well might you demand salvage for giving the first information of a war. On the same principle, a British man-of-war on the breaking out of hostilities might seize a whole fleet going, ignorant of the war, into an enemy's port, and set up a claim of salvage against them." On the authority of that judgment, the claim of military salvage cannot be sustained.

[The Court then dealt with the claim for civil salvage, and awarded 500*l*. (*a*).]

(*a*) Appraised value, 50,000*l*.

THE ELEONORA CATHARINA.

[4 C. Rob. 156.]

Neutral Property—Recapture—Salvage.

Neutral property taken out of the possession of a belligerent is not usually liable to salvage. *Held*, that there was an exception when the French Government condemned neutral property irregularly.

1802 *January* 12.

This was a case of a Russian ship, taken on a voyage from Archangel to London by a French privateer, and retaken by a British cruiser on the 7th December, 1800.

On behalf of a claimant of part of the cargo, *Robinson* contended that salvage on the recapture of neutral vessels had been allowed during this war on particular grounds only, and in deviation from the former practice. That the special reasons for this alteration, stated by the Court in the *War Onskan* (*a*), were the irregular and rapacious proceedings of the French cruisers and the French Courts of Prize, under which it was almost morally certain that every vessel would be condemned, without respect to the rights and privileges of a neutral character. That in this case the same reasons did not exist, since it had appeared that a more regular course of proceeding had been restored, and more especially since this capture was made subsequent to the convention between France and Russia, under which it could not be supposed but that the interests of the Russian merchant would be protected.

Sir W. Scott.—It is certainly true that the standing doctrine of the Court has been that neutral property, taken out of the possession of the enemy, is not liable to salvage. It is the doctrine to which the Court has invariably adhered, till it was forced out of its course by the notorious irregularities of the French cruisers and of the French Government, which proceeded without any pretence of sanction from the law of nations to condemn neutral property (*b*). On these grounds it was deemed not unreasonable by

(*a*) *Ante*, p. 239.

(*b*) In the *Carlotta*, December 13th, 1803, the Court refused to grant salvage on a neutral ship recaptured from a French cruiser, because the proceedings of the French Courts "have been conducted with more regularity," and there were no grounds for supposing that the ship in question would have been condemned by a French Court. [5 C. Rob. 55.]

1802 January 12. THE ELEONORA CATHARINA. Sir W. Scott.

neutrals themselves that salvage should be paid for a deliverance from French capture. The rule obtained early in the war, and has continued to the present time. It is said that a great alteration has taken place in the French proceedings, and that we are now to acknowledge a sort of return of "*Saturnia Regna.*" This Court is not informed in a satisfactory manner that any such beneficial change has taken place in the administration of Prize Law in the tribunals of France, and therefore it will continue to make the same decree till the instructions of the Superior Court shall establish a different rule. As little can the Court attend to the capricious and fleeting politics of Russia at that period, under which, it is said, this property would have been protected. They were probably unknown at the time, or, if known, it is not very likely that they would have availed the claimants, who were bringing a cargo of oil, tallow, and hemp to this country, which was then to be taken under such a situation of affairs as the common enemy of Russia and France. With respect to the oil, which is said to have been thrown overboard, it must be referred to the registrar and merchants to report whether any or what part of this oil was thrown out for the benefit of the ship and the rest of the cargo.

Salvage decreed.

[4 C. Rob. 158.]

THE APOLLO (No. 1).

Contraband—Hemp—Produce of Neutral Country—Ship of another Neutral Country.

A cargo of hemp, the produce of Russia, on a Prussian ship, was captured. *Held*, that it must be restored.

1802 January 15.

THIS was a question respecting a quantity of hemp, being the produce of Russia and the property of a Russian merchant, taken on board a Prussian ship on a voyage from Liebau, in Courland, to Amsterdam.

For the captors, the *King's Advocate* and *Robinson.*

On the other side, *Laurence* and *Swabey.*

1802 January 15. THE APOLLO. Sir W. Scott.

SIR W. SCOTT.—This is the case of hemp, being Russian property and produce, put on board the ship of another neutral country, and destined to Amsterdam. Hemp is certainly liable to be considered as generally contraband; but in relaxation of the strict principle, the general rule now prevailing is, that being the produce and property of the exporting country, and going in a vessel of that country, it is not liable to confiscation. The question is, whether, if it is put on board the ship of another country, that circumstance alone will defeat the relaxation, and leave it unprotected to the consequences of its general character? The treaty lately concluded with Russia must, I think, be laid out of the case. . . . .

The question, then, being abstracted from the treaty, is, whether hemp, being the produce and property of the country, but put on board the vessel of any other than the exporting country, is liable to confiscation? Reference has been made to the case of the *Jonge Pieter* (a), in which it was decided that this circumstance did not render it liable to be considered as contraband. In that case, hemp, being Prussian property, was put on board a Dutch ship and sent to Bordeaux. It did not appear of what country the hemp was, but it was strongly argued that, by the old rule, contraband affected the ship as well as the cargo; that the relaxation which had taken place was introduced in favour of the ship, and as a concession to the navigation of neutral countries when employed in the exportation of their own produce or manufactures; that cases which did not fall within the reach of this principle were still subject to condemnation under the old law; and on this point, three cases were relied on—the *Sanctissimo Sacramento* (b), the *Goede Vreede* (c), and the *Juffrow Wobetha* (d).

On the part of the claimants it was contended that the relaxation was not so restricted as was asserted on the other side; that the old rule was departed from, and, by the modern rule, neutral merchants were at liberty to export the produce of their own country on their own account; that this being allowed, there was no reason why it might not be in other ships as well as those of

(a) Adm. November 12th, 1781; Lords, April 24th, 1783.

(b) February 3rd, 1781.

(c) March 6th, 1780.

(d) August 8th, 1781; Lords, July 18th, 1782.

1802 January 15. — THE APOLLO. — Sir W. Scott.

their own country, it being equally in the course of their ordinary commerce so to do. Of the cases cited it was said that the first was a cargo of Bolognese produce, sold to a merchant of Genoa. It was therefore Bologna hemp going on Genoa account, and liable on that ground to confiscation. The second was a cargo of wheat, sent by a Swede, who is by treaty disabled from carrying wheat. A vehicle therefore was used which it was unlawful to use, and the total disability of the ship to carry such a cargo put the cargo into an unlawful state. The third was a cargo of timber from Dantzic, which could hardly be, and was proved not to be in strictness, the produce of the territory of Dantzic, but of the neighbouring kingdom of Poland (*a*). These are cases in which the unfavourable determination proceeded upon grounds that have nothing in common with the present case. But the case of the *Jonge Pieter* was exactly parallel, being the case of a cargo of hemp on board a foreign ship. On that occasion the Court thought there ought to have been stronger proof that it was Prussian produce, but decreed the cargo to be restored. That case went up to the Lords, where the sentence of the Court of Admiralty was affirmed. It is, therefore, a direct precedent binding on this Court, and in conformity to that authority I shall direct this cargo to be restored.

[4 C. Rob. 169.]

THE MADONNA DEL BURSO.

Seizure—Duty of Person Seizing—Restitution—Compensation.

A captor is bound to proceed to adjudication with reasonable expedition; where, therefore, it was proved that he did not do so: *Held*, that the owner of the ship which had been captured was entitled to compensation.

1802 March 18.

THIS was the case of a ship and cargo belonging to Greek merchants, seized November, 1797, in Dingle Bay, by Edward King Hill, commander of a revenue cutter, and proceeded

(*a*) In the Court of Admiralty, the cargo of the *Juffrow Wobetha* was condemned as contraband, August 8th, 1781. On appeal, that sentence was reversed, and the cargo decreed to be restored, July 18th, 1782; the Court of Appeal conceiving that Dantzic, though a free city, being within the immediate protection of Poland, was entitled to export such a commodity as one of its own products.

against, in the first instance, in the Court of Admiralty of Ireland as droits and perquisites of his Majesty in his Admiralty of Ireland, on a suggestion that the ship and cargo were bound to Amsterdam, in opposition to the ostensible documents representing a destination to Hamburg; that the master had been guilty of a suppression and spoliation of papers; and that the property actually belonged to enemies.

A claim was given for the ship by the master, and for the cargo by Mr. Barthold, the correspondent of the proprietor, on a supposition that the Court of Admiralty of Ireland was properly competent to entertain the question. But afterwards, on further consideration and advice, an exceptive issue was tendered, on the part of the claimant, objecting "that the Court of Admiralty of Ireland, as constituted under the Act of the 23rd and 24th of his present Majesty, had no power or jurisdiction to proceed on any manner of captures, seizures, prizes, or reprisals of any ships or goods that shall be taken in the ports or creeks of Ireland, &c." On these grounds a prohibition was obtained in the Court of Chancery of Ireland inhibiting the judge of the Court of Admiralty from proceeding further. A short time previous to the final order (*a*) of the Court of Chancery, making that rule absolute, the King's Advocate directed the proceedings in the Court of Admiralty of Ireland to be discontinued. After this discontinuance, further time was consumed in an action entered by the claimant of the cargo against the officers of the Court of Admiralty in the King's Bench of Ireland. That action was afterwards dropped; and in March, 1801, proceedings were instituted in the High Court of Admiralty of England by the Proctor of the Admiralty against the goods and merchandise laden on board the ship, but not against the ship herself. The libel against the ship had been withdrawn in the Court of Admiralty of Ireland, and she had been directed to be restored; but owing to the state in which she then was, the master declined to take possession.

SIR W. SCOTT.—This is the case of a ship which is unquestionably Ottoman. She is not at present proceeded against, as I

(*a*) April 23rd, 1799.

1802 *March* 18. THE MADONNA DEL BURSO. Sir W. Scott.

understand, in this Court; and though proceeded against in the Court of Admiralty of Ireland, yet she was directed to be restored upon the original proof. This ship, coming from the eastern part of Europe, was forced by stress of weather to put into Dingle Bay, in Ireland, and was there seized by the master of a custom-house cutter, Edward Hill, in November, 1797, the cargo being intended for Amsterdam, with an ostensible destination to Hamburg.

The Court has, upon a full inquiry into the proofs of property produced, weighing all the suspicions which the imprudence and improper conduct of the parties, and their agents, had thrown upon it, finally pronounced itself satisfied that the cargo belongs to the Greek merchants for whom it is claimed. The present question is upon the detention, and damages occasioned by the detention, of this ship and cargo.

It does not appear that any proceedings were commenced against this ship, or the valuable cargo which she contained, until the latter end of February, 1798, that is, for the space of about three months. However justifiable the seizure may have been, the first obligation which the seizor has to discharge is that of accounting why he did not institute proceedings against this vessel and cargo immediately; and unless he can exculpate himself with respect to delay in this matter, he is guilty of no inconsiderable breach of his duty. It would be highly injurious to the commerce of other countries, and disgraceful to the jurisprudence of our own, if any persons, commissioned or non-commissioned, could lay their hands upon valuable foreign ships and cargoes in our harbours, and keep their hands upon them, without bringing such an act to judicial notice in any manner for the space of three or four months. The complaints which such a conduct tolerated by this country would provoke against it from foreign countries are not to be described; and it is not very easy to suggest how the real honour of the country, connected as it is with its justice, could be defended against such complaints.

The general duty of attending to considerations of this nature becomes more peculiarly incumbent on the subjects of this country in respect to vessels sailing under the protection of the Ottoman Porte.

[The Court then dealt with the position of the Porte.]

1802 *March* 18.

THE MADONNA DEL BURSO.

Sir W. Scott.

These considerations should have imposed on the seizor a peculiar degree of caution; a caution which ought to have accompanied his proceedings in every subsequent stage, even if the original seizure had been ever so justifiable. Let us, then, see what case is set up for not having instituted any proceedings for considerably more than three months. All that I have heard is, that the seizure was made in Dingle Bay, and that this is a place very far from Dublin. How is this to excuse him? Suppose an English custom-house officer had made a like seizure in Polperry Bay, on the coast of Cornwall, or in Pulwhelly Bay, on the coast of Wales, much more remote from London than Dingle Bay is from Dublin, would this Court endure to hear him assign that distance as any excuse or justification for not proceeding for three or four months? What steps were taken to obtain legal advice? For it is the first and universal duty of those who do not know how to proceed to apply to those who do. Mr. Hill writes, it is said, to the Commissioners of the Customs to acquaint them with what he had done. I do not say that this was an improper step for a man to take who is answerable to his superiors for the propriety of his general conduct; but is this all that he ought to have done? Is it the most important part? Ought he not to have given immediate notice to the officers of the Admiralty that he had seized a ship and cargo as droits of Admiralty? The Commissioners of the Customs have nothing to do with such droits, as they very properly tell him in their answer. He might just as well suppose that he had satisfied his duty by writing upon such a matter to officers of any other description. I do not impute it to him that he did not write to this country, to the British Admiralty Court, or to any of its officers. It would be too much to expect that he should have taken upon him to decide upon a matter on which persons of learning may entertain different opinions. If he had applied to the eminent persons in the Court of Admiralty of Ireland in due time, he would have completely assoiled himself. What I impute to him as gross misconduct is, that he did not apply to them till after he had kept this Ottoman ship, with a cargo of great value, in this open bay during the extremity of the winter season, exposed in the manner that such a ship and cargo must be exposed—and all this upon his own private opinion, without putting himself in motion to obtain proper advice

1802 March 18. — THE MADONNA DEL BURSO. — Sir W. Scott.

till some time, according to his own account, in the month of February. I am surprised to hear of any defence that can be set up for such conduct. In truth, all the defence that I have heard is the words "Dingle Bay," and "that he did not know how to act in such a remote place." To which I have to answer that they who do not know how to act upon such seizures ought not to venture upon making such seizures. He ought to have kept his hands off, or resorted to good advice as soon as he laid them on. If he will not do the one or the other he must be the sufferer. I have no doubt in pronouncing a demurrage against him, for conduct utterly inexcusable, particularly connected as the case is with the national character of this vessel. In estimating the quantum of demurrage I shall allow him the benefit of so much time as would be necessary for transmitting the papers to Dublin and obtaining advice thereon. Recollecting how much those eminent persons are involved in business of various kinds, I shall allow him the benefit of full three weeks for these communications with Dublin. The allowance is, I think, liberal; for though I have heard much said of the distance of Dingle Bay, which I do not observe to be so very considerable, I cannot doubt that it has a very open and constant intercourse with the capital. Beyond these three weeks I hold Mr. Hill liable in demurrage.

It has been thrown out in argument that the same delay would have taken place, and therefore that the same harm would have happened, if the ship had been proceeded against here. This, if true, is small satisfaction to the claimant; but how could it have happened in fact unless the seizor was guilty of the same delay, in which case he would have been answerable in the same manner? Would this Court tolerate the act of a custom-house officer keeping a foreign valuable ship for such a length of time in such a situation without any proceeding? The very first step taken would have been to call upon him to justify his conduct, be the ship and cargo what they might. If such a seizure had been made here what would have followed? The depositions would have been immediately taken and sent up along with the ship's papers, or possibly the ship's papers alone, with some account of the circumstances of the behaviour of the captain, and these would have been immediately submitted by the Proctor of the Admiralty to the counsel for the Crown, in order to obtain their instructions. I cannot but think that the case would have immediately appeared to them a case for restitution of the ship, and a case of suspicion, of vehement suspicion, respecting the cargo, a suspicion principally excited by the behaviour of the master and the false representation of the voyage contained in the papers, but not amounting to a conclusive demonstration of the total falsehood of the claim. The effect of such misconduct would justly have operated to the forfeiture of freight and expenses on the part of the ship. But an order for further proof of the cargo would, I presume, have been consented to on the part of the Admiralty. If the master had taken this course a fortnight might have been sufficient for the dispatch of the business; the cargo would have been delivered upon bail to the claimant, or if he declined taking it would have been taken possession of by the Admiralty and have been brought to a port of security, perhaps in this same vessel, and there sold at a good market for the benefit of those who might be ultimately entitled. The ship might have gone about her business with her master and crew unbroken, with her stores unbroken, and with some little advance of money arising from the new freight for the necessity of her homeward voyage. All the inconvenience sustained would have been the delay of payment for the cargo, if proved to be neutral, and the forfeiture of the original freight for the ship—inconveniences not to be complained of by those who had brought them upon themselves, by prevaricating documents respecting the voyage and by the rash and intemperate conduct of the master entrusted with it. At any rate, the matter might have been dispatched within a time much short of that in which this ship and cargo lay, without being brought to the notice of any Court whatever.

This, I think, is the natural course which the matter, according to my apprehension, would have taken, because nobody has disputed anywhere, that I know of, the neutral ownership of the vessel; and nobody, that I know of, has contended anywhere seriously that the cargo was liable to absolute condemnation upon the original evidence, though liable to very malignant suspicion. But suppose that the counsel for the Crown had thought it their duty to take the opinion of the Court upon the cargo in the first

1802 *March* 18.

THE MADONNA DEL BURSO.

Sir W. Scott.

instance (as they might not improperly have done); in that case, it is said, "a delay must have taken place, because this Court would have felt great delicacy in proceeding upon a ship and cargo lying in a port of Ireland on account of the unsettled question of jurisdiction." Certainly nothing could be further from the inclination of this Court than to encounter the hazard of anything like a conflict with the sister jurisdiction of Ireland. But still the neutral is not to suffer on that account; he would have his claim upon the government of the two countries. A belligerent nation, which is in the exercise of these rights of war, is bound to find tribunals for the regulation of them—tribunals clear in their authority, as well as pure in their administration; and if from causes of private internal policy, arising out of the peculiar relation of the component parts of the belligerent State, difficulties arise, the neutral is not to be prejudiced on that account; he has a right to speedy and unobstructed justice, and has nothing to do with such difficulties created by questions of domestic constitution.

It is then said, "that the mass of business under which this Court was then labouring so choked up the avenues to justice that the cause, if entertained by the Court, could not have been heard for a considerable time." If it went upon an order for further proof by consent, there would have been no necessity for such a hearing; but if not, still it is no secret that this Court has never thought it a breach of that equal justice which it owes to all its suitors to suffer a cause to be interposed that, from its magnitude of interests, or other circumstances of just weight, had a peculiar claim to a pre-audience. By the counsel for the claimants, it has been asserted that an order was sent to the Court of Admiralty in Ireland by the government for the release of this ship and cargo, and that obedience to that order was declined by the Court upon an opinion that the Court itself had an interest in these droits. How these facts stood I am not sufficiently informed by these papers; it seems rather difficult to reconcile such an order from government with the prosecution at present maintained against this cargo; but if such an order had been sent to this Court, it certainly would have met with an instant obedience, because the Crown having the only beneficial interest in droits here (the seizor having nothing but a mere expectation of bounty), and the Crown having an undoubted right to exempt from the operations of war any individual subject of the enemy himself, this Court would, in pursuance of such an order, release the property, although it directly appeared to be an enemy's property. If the Court of Admiralty of Ireland had an interest of its own in such droits, which has been repeatedly thrown out in argument, that might properly produce a different conduct on the part of that Court. If it has such a right, it is, I presume, by virtue of some special grant; for this Court possesses no such interest, and is not aware of any possible ground on which a Court of Admiralty can, by virtue of its mere general constitution, claim it.

Respecting the next demand, the claim of actual damage done to the ship during the time she continued in Mr. Hill's possession, I have to lament that it is not brought before me in a more satisfactory manner. What the parties ought each to have done, for their own security, after the restitution, was to have had an accurate survey taken, and an authentic report made of her state and condition. But neither the one nor the other have done what might have been reasonably expected from both. That some damage was sustained before proceedings were commenced cannot be doubted upon the general face of the facts. Here is a valuable ship exposed in this bay, during the whole extremity of the winter season, in the neighbourhood of a country described to be semi-barbarous, her master turned out of possession, and the crew, a parcel of Greek sailors, without any superintendence! Is it to be supposed that, in such a state, there was no deterioration, no waste, no spoil, no embezzlement? I therefore pronounce for damage generally, referring to the Registrar and merchants to consider the *quantum*, as well as they can ascertain it by affidavits to be exhibited on either side, with liberty to resort to the Court on any matter of difficulty. So much for the claims or demurrage and damage against Mr. Hill personally, while the vessel continued under his hand, without the institution of any proceedings whatever. Of what passed afterwards, it is my inclination as it is my duty to speak with all delicacy and caution.

Proceedings were instituted against this property, as a droit of Admiralty, in the Court of Admiralty of Ireland. They depended long. I have not looked particularly into them, having no right

1802 *March* 18. THE MADONNA DEL BURSO. Sir W. Scott.

to exercise any particular judgment upon them. But I understand that the proceedings of the Court were finally inhibited by a judgment of the Court of Chancery in Ireland; and the fact is, that a proceeding *de novo* is commenced in this Court of Admiralty. The legal conclusion appears to be, that the proceeding in the Irish Court of Admiralty was *coram non judice;* for I must regard that judgment of the Court of Chancery as decisive upon this matter, as much as I should be bound to do a like judgment of inhibition of the Court of Chancery in England upon any proceedings of this Court, even if I should be presumptuous enough to entertain any lurking difference of private opinion upon the rectitude of that judgment. But supposing the proceedings to have been *coram non judice*, still I am far from insinuating that they were commenced from error on the part of those who advised them; knowing the high character of the persons concerned, I consider these proceedings as arising out of an unsettled state of things, in which these gentlemen could not consider themselves as conscientiously and honourably at liberty to abdicate their claim of jurisdiction in the first instance. But I must revert again to the principle I have laid down, that the neutral is not to be prejudiced by that; it is no business of his to settle the points of constitution, or fight the battles of conflicting jurisdictions; he is charged with having submitted to the jurisdiction, but how could he help following the proceeding into that Court? If he had even instituted the proceeding himself, I do not think that a foreigner applying to a Court of apparent competency which entertained the suit would have barred himself as an author of his own wrong. But he only followed where he was led; and if he has been put to expense in consequence of proceedings in a Court which could not do him justice, but which entertained the suit, not from any error imputable to the Court itself or its practices, but from the unsettled state of jurisdictions in the two countries, I will not call it a damage which he has sustained, but it is that for which he appears to have something like a conscientious demand against the government of one Court, or both.

In the course of this discussion it has been repeatedly asked, why did not this man take away this ship as soon as she was released? The situation of the man is itself an answer to the question. Here is a person, utterly unacquainted with the laws and language of the northern and western ports of Europe, detained in this remote bay of Ireland, without any agent to apply to (for Mr. Barthold was only the agent for the cargo, and all that he did for the ship could be mere charity or prudence), without a sixpence in his pocket, or credit upon the cargo, which was separated from the ship, and subjected to a proceeding. How was this Greek master in Ireland, in as helpless a state as a foreigner can be conceived to be placed in, to repair his ship after twelve months' detention, to victual her, to store her, to collect his dispersed crew, and to satisfy their pressing demands, and to set out on his return to Constantinople? It appears to me rather harsh language to say that he should have gone about his business, without pointing out the means by which he could do it. It is telling a man to walk without legs. The consequence has been that the ship has been lying rotting in Dingle Bay, and he himself lying rotting in a prison, and the ship has been finally sold for a mere nothing. In all this there is something which I will not call damage, but which founds a highly equitable claim of compensation.

Then as to the cargo; it has been sold to great disadvantage—it is said much below its original value. Something of damage must have taken place in respect to the cargo, which I refer generally to the Registrar and merchants. I observe that 4,000*l.* has been received in Ireland for duties, and is retained—a fact which I do not immediately know how to reconcile with the fact which has been repeatedly asserted, and not denied in this discussion, that the government of Ireland did, in an early period, issue an order for the release and restitution of the whole property.

It has been contended that all the loss and all the inconvenience has been produced by the misconduct of the parties themselves, by the bills of lading, which held out a false destination, and by the master's destruction of some papers. The practice of holding out a false destination (which in this case is sworn to have been done at the instance of the insurers) is unquestionably a bad practice, founded on a silly and dangerous policy, and penal to the party who employs it. But when I consider how familiar it is in the practice of other nations, and that even when it occurs there it is not held, absolutely and conclusively, to bar the admission of

1802 March 18. THE MADONNA DEL BURSO. Sir W. Scott.

further proof, unless the falsehood is supported by a concurrent falsehood of the depositions, or by other circumstances of grave suspicion—can I say that in this case, where the master avows, upon his deposition, the real voyage he was to pursue, that it is to have more than its ordinary effect, particularly connected with the habitual indulgence shown to the subjects of the Porte? Can it justify the detention for such a length of time without any proceeding, and all the expense of proceeding in a Court which eventually is declared to have no founded jurisdiction, and all the waste of property consequent upon both these causes? Again, the captain destroyed papers after the seizure—a most rash act. But what is the penalty? A forfeiture of his freight and expenses in ordinary cases, a diminution of his credit, greater or less, in proportion to the motives under which he appeared to have acted, and a necessity for further strict proof; not the destruction of the ship by a ruinous detention. The master swears that he destroyed these papers after the capture, which contained nothing of consequence more than the real destination, and that he did this in a fit of passion, for which he was condemned by his mate, upon the seizure. Agitated by the difficulty in which he was involved, conceiving himself to be oppressed, and subject to that irritability of temper to which the people of his country are peculiarly liable, he committed this rash act. In such a case, supposing the parties to be of the ordinary description, the Court would have punished the act by condemning him in all the expenses of the captors if the cargo was eventually restored, and by refusing him his freight and expenses if it was condemned, and there the matter would have ended.

Upon a full and deliberate investigation, conducted with the most jealous attention, I have finally restored the property of the cargo; and in the case of an ordinary European master, who had nothing to complain of, I should have followed that sentence by a sentence condemning him in the captor's costs. But I must consider here how much this man and his owners have already suffered beyond the extent of that penalty. That these acts of misconduct ought to entail on the parties all the accumulation of wretchedness which has been produced, I think it is impossible to maintain for a moment.

Upon these considerations I think there is much of what I shall not call damage, but a loss which calls for compensation. I shall refer it to the Registrar and merchants to consider what has been the undue diminution of the value; adverting likewise to the expense of proceeding in Ireland and to the payment of the duties. The distresses of the master render him a just object of the compassion of government. It has been repeatedly said by the officers of the Crown that government will very willingly attend to any recommendation from this Court, and I am happy to find that it will do so. At present it is not necessary for me to do more than to refer the *quantum* of loss to be ascertained by the Registrar and merchants. I am induced to hope from the declarations I have just alluded to that it will be unnecessary for me to advert to a question to which my attention has been repeatedly forced in the course of this discussion—how far the Crown, acting not upon its own prerogative rights but in the office of Admiralty, can be made at all answerable for damages accruing to property in the hands of its officers? I shall only say generally that I shall enter on such a question, if compelled, with all the reverence which is due to the rights and interests of the Crown, and with all the regard due to that justice which is demanded on the part of other governments and their subjects.

1802
March 18.

THE MADONNA DEL BURSO.

Sir W. Scott.

THE PEACOCK.

[4 C. Rob. 183.]

Neglect of Duty by Captor—Damages and Costs.

A neutral ship and cargo were taken by a British vessel, but were not brought direct to England: *Held*, that under the circumstances the claimants were entitled to damages and costs.

SIR W. SCOTT.—This was an American ship and cargo of wine, taken on a voyage from Cadiz to London on the 19th May, 1800, and carried into Lisbon, where they were detained a long time, though no proceedings were commenced till they were afterwards brought to Jersey. The capture was made in latitude 42, considerably to the north of Lisbon, the wind being then fair for England. It was the captors' duty to have brought the prize directly to England; for if the public instructions give to captors the power of coming to the most convenient ports, they do not

1802
February 5.

1802 February 5. THE PEACOCK. Sir W. Scott.

give them a wild and arbitrary discretion, but a discretion to be soundly exercised on a due consideration of their own convenience and of the interest of the neutral persons that may be concerned; instead of carrying the ship back to Lisbon, for which place the wind was then adverse, and from whence it would require several winds to bring her into the same situation again, they should have proceeded directly for England.

[The Court then examined the explanations offered by the captors.]

Under these circumstances, I feel it impossible not to pronounce that the privateer has acted improperly in carrying the vessel into Lisbon and keeping her there so long. I do not say that the original seizure was wrongful, or that the privateer would not have acted with perfect correctness if she had brought the ship to England and instituted proceedings here. The captors not having done that, but having carried her to Lisbon, and detained her there unnecessarily for such a length of time, I am of opinion that they are liable to costs and damages, deducting the expenses which would have been incurred by proceeding here, and also so much time as would have been necessary for that purpose.

[4 C. Rob. 195.]

THE OSTER RISOER.

Contraband—Freight—Ignorance of Master as to Character of Cargo.

The master of a ship on which contraband goods have been carried is not entitled to freight in respect of such goods, even if he is ignorant of their contraband character.

1802 February 11.

THIS was a case of a ship carrying sundry articles from Riga to Amsterdam; and, amongst the rest, a quantity of sail-cloth, described as linen. The innocent articles, belonging to proprietors not implicated in the contraband part of the cargo, were restored. The sail-cloth was condemned as contraband, and also some linseed included in the same claim.

On the question of freight, it was prayed that the master might be allowed his freight, even of the contraband articles, on a suggestion that he was totally ignorant of the contents of the packages described as linen, and that he was under a special agreement, endorsed on the bill of lading, "not to open the packages." 1802 *February* 11. THE OSTER RISOER.

On the other side, the *King's Advocate* and *Robinson* argued that the master was *de jure* the agent of the owners in respect to the ship, and capable of binding them by his conduct; that if the cargo was pronounced contraband, the privity and conusance of the master must be in law presumed, so as to affect the owners with the forfeiture of freight. That this being the rule of law, the master was not at liberty to bind himself to a voluntary ignorance, by which, if it could be allowed in one instance, the whole penalty of carrying contraband might be defeated. A master erring in judgment as to the nature of his cargo in not considering it as contraband, could not protect the ship from loss of freight, much less could such effect be allowed to a state of ignorance of the contents, voluntarily assumed under an agreement, which was itself sufficient to awaken his caution.

Judgment.—The Court held that the master could not be permitted to aver his ignorance; that he was bound, in time of war, to know the contents of his cargo. That if a different rule could be sustained, it might be applied to excuse the carrying of all contraband.

Freight for goods condemned refused; freight for the claims restored, allowed to be a charge upon that part of the cargo, the ship and goods having been separated.

THE WILLIAM (No. 1).

[4 C. Rob. 214.]

Capture—Failure to Proceed to Adjudication—Monition.

When a seizure has been made, and the captors have failed to take proceedings, they will be ordered to proceed to adjudication.

Court.—The monition that has issued against the captors is "to proceed to adjudication." They object that no claim has been given by the parties applying for the process of the Court. 1802 *February* 23.

1802
February 23.

THE WILLIAM.

Undoubtedly it is the usual practice for a party to give in his claim in the first instance; but it will not necessarily vitiate the process if there has been no claim. If it should in any manner come to the knowledge of the Court that a seizure had been made in the nature of prize, and that no proceedings had been instituted, it would be the duty of the Court to direct proceedings to be commenced. In common condemnations it is not necessary to wait for a claim. The captors, in this instance, admit all that is necessary to found the process of the Court, by the seizure and forcible possession; that is sufficient to oblige them to proceed to adjudication. Another ground that has been taken is, "that the captor is not liable to be called upon to proceed to adjudication, because he is not commissioned against the Dutch, and that the cargo was sent over here by the Court of Bermuda, under a suspicion that it was Dutch property, and on bail to answer all questions." The captor had taken out a commission against the French, at least; and *non constat*, that this cargo might not be French property. The Judge of the Court of Bermuda has determined nothing on that question, but rather remitted the cause, declining to decide upon it; but, if the captor had taken out no commission, is he to be at liberty to make a seizure, without being responsible to the neutral merchant, because he is non-commissioned, and cannot obtain condemnation to himself? I have no hesitation in overruling the protest, and with costs.

Captors directed to proceed to adjudication.

[4 C. Rob. 242.]

THE TWEE JUFFROWEN.

Contraband—Pitch and Tar.

Pitch and tar are contraband.

1802
March 26.

THIS was a case of a cargo of pitch and tar, taken in a Prussian ship on a voyage from Embden to Dieppe, and claimed as the property of a Prussian merchant.

SIR W. SCOTT.—I take it to be the established doctrine of this Court that pitch and tar are universally contraband (*a*) unless protected

(*a*) See *ante*, p. 1.

by treaty, or unless it is shown that they are the produce of the country from which they are exported, in which latter case they are considered on the more modern and lenient application of the rule as subject to pre-emption only. In certain instances, where they constitute the great staple commodity of the exporting country, as of Sweden, the presumption may be allowed in favour of the claimant without absolute proof; but in respect to East Friesland, or any part of Prussia, the same presumption does not arise. The fact is not proved in any manner by the claimant, and I am inclined to think that the presumption is on the other side.

1802 *March* 26.

THE TWEE JUFFROWEN.

Sir W. Scott.

With respect to what has been said of a different understanding prevailing in that country, I am afraid it is not the only instance in which our exposition of the law of nations differs from what they are inclined to hold upon the same article; but I must remember that it is my duty to adhere to what I understand to be the exposition authorized by the former decisions of this Court, founded on general and disinterested views of the subject.

Under that exposition I think myself bound to pronounce that this cargo is subject to condemnation as consisting of such articles as pitch and tar, which are not shown to be the produce of the exporting country.

THE CAROLINA.

[4 C. Rob. 256.]

Neutral Vessel—Employment by Belligerent—Carriage of Troops—Duress—Liability to Condemnation.

A neutral vessel employed against the will of the master by a belligerent is liable to condemnation even after the service has ceased, if still subservient to the purposes of the belligerent (*a*).

THIS was a case on petition respecting the loss of a Swedish vessel, captured at the taking of Alexandria and lost in the possession of the captors before she had been brought to adjudication.

1802 *April* 30.

On the part of the captors, the *King's Advocate*.

On the part of the claimants, *Laurence*.

(*a*) See the *Friendship*, *post*, p. 599.

1802 *April* 30.

THE CAROLINA.

Sir W. Scott.

SIR W. SCOTT.—This ship is stated by the master's account to be a Swedish ship, chartered by ———, of Leghorn, to go on a voyage to Civita Vecchia, with other common covenants not to go to a blockaded port or to carry contraband articles. The particulars of his representation are, "that on the 26th of March, 1798, his ship was chartered by P. Jaumer, a merchant of Leghorn, for four months, at 1,250 piastres per month, to go on a trading voyage between Leghorn, Civita Vecchia, and the adjacent ports, as the freighter should direct, with the exception of not going to French ports or ports that were blockaded, and also of not carrying contraband goods or stores; that he sailed accordingly from Leghorn to Civita Vecchia on the 9th of April, 1798, and on his arrival at the last-mentioned port was informed that an embargo had been laid upon all vessels in that port; that he was then summoned before the French agent of ———, who showed him a letter from ———, addressed to the said master, and informing him that Citizen D——— was to be the lader of the cargo in Civita Vecchia, and that he must hold his ship in readiness at the disposal of the French commissary." He then states, "that he went to Rome to solicit the interference of the Swedish consul, but could not find him, and when he returned he found his ship fitted up as a transport; that, being unable to avoid this service, he caused an insurance to be made for the benefit of his owner, and was ordered to victual his vessel for two months; that he took on board 150 dragoons and sailed with 57 other vessels, but he did not know on what destination; that on his arrival at Alexandria he applied for payment and for his discharge, but was put off." It does not appear that the master made any protest or remonstrance against this service; but rather in proof of his voluntary assent he proceeded to insure the vessel, and to provide the necessary provisions for the voyage. It is now, however, said that this was an act under duress, and that it is a by-gone transaction. On the former part of this representation my opinion is that a man cannot be permitted to aver that he was an involuntary agent in such a transaction. If an act of force, exercised by one belligerent on a neutral ship or person, is to be deemed a sufficient justification for any act done by him contrary to the known duties of the neutral character, there would be an end of any prohibition under the law of nations to carry contraband or to engage in any other hostile act. If any loss is sustained in such a service, the neutral yielding to such demands must seek redress against the government that has imposed the restraint upon him. He has no right to expect that the British Government should pay for the injustice of its public enemy. If this vessel had been taken *in delicto* I should have felt no hesitation in saying that she must have been subject to condemnation. Whether the troops were received on board voluntarily or involuntarily could make no difference.

Then as to its being a by-gone transaction; had she divested herself of the character of a French transport? Had she so receded from that character, as is represented? She was remaining under the power of the French military commander as much as ever. She had solicited leave to depart, but could not obtain it; and if the English fleet had not appeared, she might have been employed to carry on the dragoons to some other place, in the same manner as she had been employed before. I can by no means accede to the description given in argument, or consider her as having removed herself from all taint arising out of the preceding contract. When the British fleet appeared before Alexandria, the British commander did, with a tenderness to neutral commerce which is highly honourable to him, give liberty to neutral vessels to depart. But although this notice was given in general terms to neutral ships, it was not given absolutely to all that were neutral in build and property, but to such as were neutral likewise in their conduct and were acting fairly under that character. The very terms of the letter are, "to all such as are legally employed." This ship was still subservient to the purposes of the French commander, who refused to let her depart till the arrival of the British fleet rendered it impossible for him to make any further use of the vessel. Under these circumstances, what right or pretence had this vessel to claim the privileges which belonged only to those who had conducted themselves as neutral, or to claim the protection of that proclamation? On the first attempt to come out it appears she was taken, and under circumstances which do, in my opinion, fully justify the seizure. But, it is said, the captors were in fault for not proceeding immediately to adjudication. It must be conceded, I think, as a reasonable distinction, that commanders acting

1802
April 30.

THE CAROLINA.

Sir W. Scott.

in the management of great expeditions cannot be tied down exactly to the same rules by which individual cruisers are directed to proceed. If the vessel had been brought to adjudication, so far am I from thinking that it would have availed the claimants, that it rather appears to me there would have been strong grounds on which the captors might have been entitled to condemnation. It is said that the master was separated from his ship; but if we consider that he was a person who had appeared to engage his vessel voluntarily as a French transport, there might be very good reasons why it would not be improper to remove such a person. On the whole, I can by no means hold that this is a demand fit to be enforced in this Court.

It appears that there were on board some bills of exchange on the French Government, and it is made part of the prayer of the claimant that the Court will direct the captors to deliver them up. On what grounds can it be expected that this Court will busy itself to assist in enforcing a demand for what is to be considered as the *pretium læsæ fidei?* Is there a principle more universal than that Courts of Justice will not carry into effect an illegal contract? In some instances it may have been doubted whether the Court of Prize can properly take notice of a breach of our own municipal laws. But in respect to the law in question before us, can it be said that the Court of Admiralty shall lend its aid to carry into effect a contract which is in direct violation of the law of nations, that very law which it sits to administer? The parties must resort to the French Government, and settle their accounts with them as well as they can. I have no hesitation in rejecting the whole of this petition, with costs of the petition against the claimant (*a*).

(*a*) It has since been determined in several instances that a British subject cannot come before a Court of Prize to claim property taken in a course of trade which is forbidden by the laws of his country; and in the case of the *Etrusco*, Lords, August 11th, 1803, it was decided, after long deliberation, that property condemned in consequence of the inadmissibility of such a claim, is to be condemned not to the individual captor, but to the King.

THE THREE FRIENDS.

[4 C. Rob. 268.]

Re-capture—Salvage—Loss of Ship and Cargo by Accident—Incidence of Loss.

When a re-captured ship and cargo were accidentally destroyed by fire after a decree of restitution, the ship having been appraised but not the cargo. *Held, first,* that salvage on the ship should be decreed on the appraised value; *second,* that the owners of the cargo and the re-captors must bear the loss of the cargo.

THIS was a case respecting a ship and cargo re-captured from the enemy, and restored to the proprietor, on bail, to answer salvage, but destroyed by fire before the appraisement of the cargo had been completed. The question was, whether the re-captor was entitled to salvage according to the value before or after the accident.

1802 *May* 13, 19.

For the re-captors, the *King's Advocate* and *Sewell.*

On the other side, *Swabey.*

19th May.

SIR W. SCOTT.—This question arises on an accident, which carries with it neither censure nor penalty to the parties concerned. Owing to accident, more than to the fault of any party, the ship and cargo were consumed by fire in the harbour of Lisbon. As both ship and cargo were property taken out of the hand of the enemy, they were, though neutral property, to be restored on salvage, according to the usage of the present war. A commission was necessarily extracted for the valuation of the property. As to the ship, it had already been executed; but on the cargo it had only been begun, when a fire broke out on the 2nd of September, and consumed the whole property. The question is, by what valuation the salvage is to be decreed? Whether according to the value of what may be remaining, or according to the valuation of an appraisement, such as can now be made upon the original value of the property, unaffected by any such accident.

The Court had decreed restitution, and had issued a commission of appraisement, by which two shipwrights had been appointed to appraise the vessel, and two brokers to appraise the cargo. It is stated on one side in the act, "that the commissioners for the cargo went on board, and finding the prize-master absent returned back; that they went a second time, but did not proceed to business for the same reason, because the prize-master was not on board. On the same evening the fire broke out and consumed the remainder of the goods." It is, I perceive, represented a little differently on the other side. There it is alleged "that the prize-master was withdrawn, and that the ship and cargo had been put into the possession of the former master, for the account of the respective proprietors." With respect to the ship, it appears that the appraisement had been completed, and only waited to be confirmed by the Court. On that point, therefore, I have no hesitation in considering the appraisement as substantially executed, and the ship as restored to the possession of the owner. I shall therefore feel no difficulty in pronouncing for salvage, according to the entire value of the ship so ascertained by appraisement.

The difficulty arises as to the cargo. A case has been cited from the last war, which I remember perfectly well. It was the case of a ship (*a*) brought into the Thames, for the purpose of conveying the cargo to the London market. The Court in that case was of opinion, as I understood, that the removal took place under a joint speculation of advantage, as to the most beneficial manner of disposing of the cargo. The ship was considered as detained for the advantage of both, and consequently at the risk of both, and therefore the re-captors were to be affected with the loss *pro ratâ* upon an accident of the like nature which took place in the River Thames.

But is that decision a direct authority for the present case? I cannot think that it is; for here no agreement appears to have been entered into between the parties; the necessary measures were proceeding in the ordinary course of the practice of this Court, without being influenced in any manner by the agreement of the parties. A case depending on the agreement of the parties cannot, therefore, be cited as an absolute authority for a case proceeding only under the ordinary practice of the Court.

Then it comes to be a question what is the actual liability of the

(*a*) Creighton, Lords, 8th February, 1782.

cargo under such circumstances, independent of any agreement—I do not mean a penal liability, but a mere liability as to the extent of the salvage charged upon it, for no party is *in delicto* or answerable for any wrong imputed. That question must be determined by considering in whose custody the cargo then was; whether it was so completely restored to the exclusive possession of the claimants as that the Court and the other party had lost all power and control over it; or whether it was still in the possession of the Court by its commissioners or by the agents of the parties? For it makes no great difference, in my apprehension, whether the prize-master was still on board or was withdrawn with a view of accommodating the other party, if those who were put into his place are to be considered as being there by the consent of the recaptor, and *pro hac vice* as much his agents as agents of the claimants.

On this point I am disposed to think that the property was still in the possession of the commissioners of the Court, in order to ascertain the value before the claimant could be remitted into complete possession. The ship might have been taken away; but could the owner of the cargo have taken that away? Unquestionably not. The cargo was to remain till the value could be ascertained, and must during that time be considered to be in the custody of the Court. If the commissioners constituted the master of the ship to be keeper of the cargo whilst it was under their care and management, it does not divest them of the legal custody. With them the legal possession must remain till the purpose of the commission was executed, and whatever happens during that interval must be at the common risk of both parties. What is the fact during such a situation? The prize-master is usually continued on board, and if in one instance he is withdrawn, still the person to whom his possession has devolved must be taken to be substituted in his place. The property must still be considered as in the power of the Court, till the value is ascertained on which the decree is ultimately to be founded.

But there has been a return made since the accident of a valuation, which is in fact nothing less than an appraisement, estimated partly by conjecture and partly by the invoice charges, above twelve months after the property itself has been consumed. Who

1802 May 13, 19. THE THREE FRIENDS. Sir W. Scott.

can say that this is a fair mode of valuation, or that there had been neither deterioration nor embezzlement? If the invoice alone could be deemed conclusive as to value, all the purposes of a commission of appraisement would be entirely useless. The return of the commission itself states, "that some part of the flax had been damaged by water, and was on that account obliged to be unpacked"; from which it appears on the very face of this transaction that the invoice cannot be taken as a just measure of the real value.

On the whole circumstances of this unfortunate case, I am of opinion that till the valuation was taken the intervening accident must be held to be at the risk of the joint property remaining under the custody of the Court for the purposes of justice, and therefore that the loss must fall upon both parties in the proportion of their several interests.

[4 C. Rob. 278.]

THE FORTUNA (No. 1).

*Practice—Freight—*Caveat *against Payment Out—Capture—Right to Freight.*

After a decree of restitution, and whilst the proceeds are in Court, a party desiring to prevent payment out may lodge a *caveat*, but must also at once apply to the Court on the matter.

When captors had taken the ship to its destination, where the cargo was discharged: *Held,* that they were entitled to the freight due.

1802 June 24.

THIS was a case on petition of the captors, praying to be allowed freight for a cargo which had been restored as neutral property. The demand for freight was founded on a suggestion that the ship, which had been condemned, had actually performed the contract of the original affreightment by carrying the cargo to the place of its destination. It had been objected on a former day that as the decree of restitution had passed without any order respecting freight, it was not competent for the Court now to entertain a new suit on property which had actually been restored.

In answer to that objection, it was said that, although a decree of restitution had passed, the proceeds had not been paid out of the registry; that so long as they were in the custody of the Court, it was competent for the Court to make a new order respecting them. 1802 *June* 24.

THE FORTUNA.

It appeared that after the decree of restitution had passed, the proctor for the captor had entered a caveat in the registry warning the registrar not to pay out the proceeds, and then the demand for freight was instituted on the part of the captors. On the former day, when this was stated, the Court reserved the cause for further consideration on this part of the case.

On this day. *Court.*—I am of opinion that the cargo still remaining in the hands of the Court is subject to the order of the Court, notwithstanding the decree of restitution which has passed. It was the intention of the Court, not being apprised of any further demand, that the proceeds should be paid out; but that decree has not been carried into effect. I must observe, however, in reference to what has been done in this case, that when there is a decree of the Court for restitution it is not to be obstructed by the mere caveat of the party. Notice should be given to the Court, whose duty it is to look to the prompt execution of its decrees. If there is any delay interposed it should be notified to the Court.

[*Registrar.*—Parties enter their caveat, and warn me not to pay out the proceeds.]

I think the party has no absolute right to do that. He may enter it provisionally, and then come before the Court and state his reasons why the proceeds should not be paid out; but I cannot think that it is correct practice for the individual to stop the payment absolutely, and as long as he pleases, without the authority of this Court or of any other Court which may legally interfere. It may be a fit subject for a general rule. At present, in this particular case, as the cargo is still in the hands of the Court, I am of opinion that it is subject to the order of the Court, and that the question is fit to be entertained.

On the particular question in this cause, *Laurence* for the captors.

The *King's Advocate*, *contra.*

1802
June 24.

THE FORTUNA.

Sir W. Scott.

SIR W. SCOTT.—This is the case of a ship which had carried a cargo of corn to Lisbon, the original port of destination. In such a case I apprehend the rule to be that the captor is entitled to freight, and on the same principle on which he would be held not to be entitled where he does not proceed and perform the original voyage. The specific contract is performed in the one case, and not performed in the other. It is the rule of practice laid down in the case of the *Vryheid*, a case perfectly within my recollection as a case very deliberately considered at the cockpit (*a*). It is conformable to the text law, and the opinion of eminent jurists. "Quod additur de vecturæ pretiis solvendis (says *Bynkershoek*) (*b*), ejus juris rationem non adsequor. Satis intelligo, qui navem hostilem occupant, etiam occupasse omne jus quod navi, sive navarcho debebatur, ob merces translatas in portum destinatum. Proponitur autem, navem in ipso itinere fuisse captam. Eccur igitur capienti solvam mercedes? Si qui cepit navem, eam cum mercibus in locum destinatum perducere paratus sit, ejus juris rationem intelligerem, ceteroquin non intelligo (*c*)."

In the case of the *Vryheid* (*d*), all the considerations that could be applied to this question were fully canvassed, and it was then recognised as the true rule that the captor who has performed the contract of the vessel is, as a matter of right, and *de cursu*, entitled to freight, although, if he has done anything to the injury of the property, or has been guilty of any misconduct, he may remain answerable for the effect of such misconduct, or injury, in the way of a set-off against him.

The case then is reduced to a question, whether the captor, in this instance, has done anything to forfeit the right which, under the general rule, he had acquired? He had made a capture which is fully justified by the condemnation of the ship, and by the order for further proof as to the cargo. He carried the cargo to Lisbon, where the consignee was put into possession, though informally, and apparently without any shadow of right, by the hand of the Portuguese Government. Such interference was, however, given

(*a*) See the *Diana*, *post*, p. 425.

(*b*) Q. J. P. 1, ch. 13.

(*c*) Bynkershoek is, in this passage, discussing the propriety of the regulation of the Consolato, c. 273. See Collectanea Maritima, sections 6, 7, 8 of the 273rd chap.

(*d*) Lords, 23rd April, 1784.

at the suit of the consignee of the cargo, and by these means that consignee obtained possession of it. Being a cargo of corn, it was necessary that it should be sold. The sale was entrusted to Mr. Paxton by the agreement of both parties, and under a condition, as it is stated, that the proceeds should remain in his hands till a sentence of final adjudication could be obtained. This gentleman is therefore to be taken as the common depository of both parties. When it is said that the captor did not bring in the proceeds so soon as was required of him, we must consider whether it was in his power. The proceeds were left in the hands of this house at Lisbon, with the consent of the consignee, and they have not been transmitted. So that what has been brought in at last, is an advance made out of the private funds of the captor. If there has been any error in these proceedings, it has been the common error of both parties. Under the circumstances of this case, I am of opinion that the captor has not forfeited the interest which he had acquired.

1802 *June* 24.

THE FORTUNA.

Sir W. Scott.

Freight decreed to the captor.

THE DER MOHR (No. 2).

[4 C. Rob. 314.]

Freight—Vessel Lost through Negligence of Captor—Restitution.

When a vessel was lost through the negligence of the captor's agent, and a decree of restitution was made against the captor, he was held to be also liable for the freight.

1802 *December* 14.

This was a question respecting the freight of a ship lost by the negligence of the prize master. On the former hearing the ship had been decreed to be restored in value, with freight to be a charge on the cargo, which was ultimately condemned for want of further proof. The freight was reported by the registrar and merchants at the sum of 1,000*l.* The proceeds of that part of the cargo which had been saved amounted only to 600*l.*

On a motion now made for an attachment against the captor to pay the balance, the *King's Advocate* for the captor.

On the other side, *Swabey* and *Robinson*.

1802 December 14.

THE DER MOHR.

Sir W. Scott.

Sir W. Scott.—In an unfortunate case like the present, the Court would certainly be disposed to give the captor all possible relief; but I need not add that no relief is possible, which cannot be given consistently with the justice due to the claimant. The demand of freight is, I apprehend, an absolute demand in cases where the ship is pronounced to be innocently employed. This vessel was captured coming from an enemy's port, under a suspicion of having on board the property of the enemy; a cargo, nevertheless, which she had a perfect right to carry, provided it was not attended with any circumstances of ill faith or unneutral conduct. No imputation of fraud or improper conduct has been thrown upon her. On the other side it is to be observed that the seizure was perfectly justifiable; the ship was sent in under very proper orders from Captain Talbot, but unfortunately his orders were very improperly executed by the person to whom they were given.

On the principle of law, however, I am of opinion that the freight must be taken as having become as much the property of the neutral claimant as the ship itself. The captor took *cum onere*. If the loss had happened by accident only in bringing in, the captor, having made a justifiable seizure, would not have been liable to any restitution, either for the freight or for the ship; but the Court has already pronounced this loss not to have arisen from any casual misfortune. The freight is as much a part of the loss as the ship, for he was bound to answer equally for both. The captor has, by taking possession of the whole cargo, deprived the claimant of the fund to which his security was fixed. He was bound to bring in that cargo subject to the demand for freight. He was just as answerable for the freight of the voyage as for the ship which was to earn it, or which was rather to be considered as having already earned it. In the room of this fund the captor has substituted his own personal responsibility, for the loss accrues by the fault of his agent. I see no distinction under which I can pronounce that the claimant is not as much entitled to the freight as to the vessel.

With respect to the attachment that is prayed against Captain Talbot, as long as a hope is held out that the assistance of government may be obtained in aid of the actual captor it will be better to let this matter stand over. There must undoubtedly be a time when this forbearance must terminate, whatever the consequences may be; but at present I will content myself by pronouncing that the whole freight is due, in value, from the captor (*a*). 1802 *December* 14.

THE DER MOHR.

Sir W. Scott.

THE ODIN (No. 2).

Joint Capture—Constructive Co-operation—Boats. [4 C. Rob. 319.]

The principle of constructive joint capture by which a ship of war which is in sight at the time of the capture of an enemy ship is entitled to a share of the prize, does not apply to the case of a boat, or to the ship to which such boat belongs, by reason of such boat being in sight.

THIS was a question respecting a claim of joint capture, interposed on the part of the *Royal Admiral* to share in this prize, condemned. 1803 *April* 1.

SIR W. SCOTT.—This question arises on the admission of an allegation given on the part of the *Royal Admiral*, being a private ship of war, an East India ship duly commissioned by letter of marque, claiming to share in the capture of the *Odin*. . . . .

Then no effectual assistance having been shown, and the disinclination of the *Trusty* having been proved, the whole case is reduced to the question of law, whether in the case of a private ship of war, and a King's ship lying in harbour, and sending out their boats to make a capture, the boat of the private ship of war so sent out, but not coming up at the time of capture, can found a title to share in the capture made by the boat of the King's ship on the mere principle of being in sight? I know of no case that would sustain such a claim. The principle of constructive assistance has been altogether thought to have been carried somewhat far; and the later inclination of Courts of Justice has been rather to restrain than extend the rule. Between private ships of war and King's ships the rule of law has always been held more strictly, and it has not been the doctrine of the Admiralty to raise constructive assistance so easily between them as between King's ships. If the competition had been between two King's ships, it would, in my opinion, be highly questionable whether a boat so

(*a*) On a subsequent day it was stated to the Court that directions had been given by government for the payment of the amount of this restitution in aid of the captor.

1803 April 1. THE ODIN. Sir W. Scott.

sent out could support a title to share on the mere principle of being in sight.

There is, I think, a very solid ground of distinction between the claims of a boat in the different cases of an actual and a constructive capture. Where a boat actually takes, the ship to which it belongs has done by means of this boat all that it could have done by the direct use of its own force. In the case of mere constructive capture, the construction which is laid upon the supposed intimidation of the enemy, and the encouragement of the friend, from a ship of war being seen, or within sight of a capture, applies very weakly to the case of a boat—an object that attracts little notice upon the water, and whose character, even if discerned by either of the other parties, may be totally unknown to both. More unreasonable still would this be upon actual captors if the constructive co-operation of such an object would give an interest to the entire ship to which it belonged. Where a ship is in sight, she is conceived to co-operate in the proportion of her force. But what room is there for such a presumption where she co-operates only by the force of her boat?

I am not in possession of any case in which a boat, without any actual assistance or previous concert, has been held, from being in sight only, to be entitled to share as a joint captor, even to the extent of the persons actually composing the boat's crew, much less to establish a claim of joint capture for the whole ship to which the boat belongs. I have not been able to find any precedent to that effect; nor has any been produced by the counsel, in consequence of the inquiry which I directed to be made. Extremely different in principle is such a case from the case of two ships, on the grounds which I have already stated (*a*).

I am of opinion, both on principle and authority, that where no

[1 Dods. 18. (*a*) In the *La Belle Coquette*, February 12th, 1811, the Court decided this point in the following words: "There being a failure in the proof that the prize was seen from on board the *Tonnant*, her claim must necessarily depend upon the fact of the capture having been actually made by her boats. The first thing to be done then is to establish the interest of the boats. Constructive assistance by boats cannot entitle the ships to which they belong to share in the prize, though actual capture by the boats would be sufficient for that purpose, for they are a part of the force of the ship."

antecedent agreement is proved to have taken place, a vessel lying in harbour cannot be entitled to share in a capture made out of the harbour by the circumstance of her boat being merely in sight. I have already expressed my opinion that this was a capture made out of the harbour of St. Helena. I am therefore disposed to reject this allegation (*a*), in the first instance, as one that cannot benefit the parties if it is admitted to go to proof. It is a case, however, very proper to be brought before the Court, and one in which I think the parties may justly be allowed their expenses.

1803 *April* 1.

THE ODIN.

Sir W. Scott.

THE VROW HENRICA.

[4 C. Rob. 343.]

Capture—Neutral Ship—Condemnation of Cargo—Freight—Expenses.

When a neutral ship trading between the ports of two belligerents was captured and ordered to be restored, but the cargo was condemned. *Held*, that the proceeds of cargo being insufficient to pay the freight and the captor's expenses in full, the captor was entitled to his legal expenses as a first charge on the proceeds, and that the freight should rank next, and before other expenses.

1803 *May* 5.

THIS was a case of a Danish vessel, taken on a voyage from Valencia to London. The ship had been restored with freight to be a charge on the cargo, which was condemned, but the proceeds not being sufficient to pay the freight and the expenses of the captor, it was prayed on the part of the neutral ship that the priority of payment might be given to freight, on the authority of the *Bremen Flugge* (*b*).

The *King's Advocate* for the captors.

Laurence, contra.

(*a*) In the case of the *Nancy* (Lords, 1st December, 1803), this same question was brought to the decision of the Lords of Appeal in an allegation offered on the part of the *Royal Admiral* stating nearly the same facts as are set forth in the preceding recital—but concluding with an averment of rather a stronger case—that the boat's crew of the *Royal Admiral* came up very soon after the boat of the *Trusty*, and were admitted on board the *Nancy*, and did actually render assistance by navigating the ship into port, and bringing her to an anchor in the harbour of St. Helena; and further that the respective ships the *Royal Admiral* and the *Trusty* were lying at anchor at St. Helena, and were within sight, and seen by the officers and crew of the *Nancy* at the time of the capture. The Court of Appeal rejected the allegation as not sufficient in law to support the demand.

(*b*) See *ante*, p. 356.

1803 *May 5.*

THE VROW HENRICA.

Sir W. Scott.

Sir W. Scott.—I have considered the cases (*a*) which I directed to be looked up, and I see no reason to alter the opinion which I before expressed that freight is, in all ordinary cases, a lien which is to take place of all others. The captor takes *cum onere:* it is the allowed privilege of neutral trade to carry the property of the enemy, subject to its capture and to the temporary detention of his vessel; and if the party does not prevaricate, or conduct himself in any respect with ill-faith, he is entitled to his freight. This is the rule which I am disposed to apply in all cases of neutral ships carrying on their ordinary commerce. It is the general rule, which may nevertheless be liable to be altered by circumstances. There is one class of cases to which I think it ought not to be applied: I mean the case of ships carrying on a trade between ports of allied enemies—a trade which may be said to arise in a great measure out of the circumstances of the war, though not altogether. I say not altogether, because such a trade exists in a limited degree in times of peace.

In such a course of trade, although the Court has not altogether refused freight to the neutral ship, yet it may not think it unreasonable that the captor should, in preference, be entitled to his expenses, inasmuch as the nature of such a trade cannot but very much influence the judgment which he must unavoidably form of his duty to bring in the cargo for adjudication. In the present case the voyage is not between the ports of allied enemies, but between the ports of two belligerents, from Valencia to London; that constitutes, I think, a sort of middle case, with respect to the obligation by which the captor might conceive himself bound to bring the cargo to adjudication. There might be a presumption undoubtedly that the property belonged to the enemy exporter. But there is a foundation also for presuming that it might belong to the consignee, and that it would not have been sent on a destination to this country but under the protection of a licence.

It is therefore a case of a mixed nature, to which I shall apply a sort of a middle judgment. I will allow the captor his law expenses, and direct the other expenses to be postponed to the payment of freight.

(*a*) Not reported.

THE MARIA (No. 2). THE VROW JOHANNA (No. 2).

[4 C. Rob. 348.]

Captor—Liability for Loss of Goods without Negligence.

If a captor uses due diligence he is not liable for the loss of captured property. Therefore, *held*, that when a cargo ordered by the Court to be restored was stolen from a proper warehouse before restoration, the captor was not liable for such loss.

1803 *May* 21.

THIS was a question respecting the responsibility of the captors to account for certain goods which had been restored by a decree of the Court, but which had been stolen from the warehouses where they were deposited, under the joint locks of the officers of the Customs and the agents of the captor.

On the part of the claimant it was prayed that the captors might be decreed to make restitution in value.

For the captors, the *King's Advocate.*

On the other side, *Laurence.*

SIR W. SCOTT.—These two cases came before the Court on a former day, on a question of sufficient importance to induce the Court to pause for deliberation on the judgment which it should pronounce. The point is how far a captor is responsible for loss, alleged to be sustained under a commission of unlivery, which had been directed to him by the decree of the Court.

There has been some attempt to charge the captor with negligent keeping, but I think that charge is not substantiated. If it had been made out, there can be no doubt but that he would be answerable to the utmost; for though the original seizure might be justifiable, yet the captor holds but an imperfect right; the property may turn out to belong to others, and if the captor puts it into an improper place, or keeps it with too little attention, he must be liable to the consequences, if the goods are not kept with the same caution with which a prudent person would keep his own property. But there is no ground for any imputation of personal negligence in this case, because it appears that the loss happened by burglary, the warehouse having been broken open and the goods stolen.

1803 *May* 21.

THE MARIA. THE VROW JOHANNA.

Sir W. Scott.

This case has been assimilated in argument to the case of a common carrier or innkeeper, against whom the common law of this country does raise the presumption of an *assumpsit* for safe custody. But it is to be remembered that they receive a reward for their undertaking, and provide this custody only for a valuable consideration. Even the principle, as applied to them, is, I conceive, of the peculiar policy of our law. It is confined to persons of a particular description, and is not to be extended, as being the general law of bailment, to persons who receive no consideration for their care, and are only to be required to furnish such care and due diligence as they would apply to their own property.

The goods were taken *jure belli.* The captor had a right to bring them in, and if any accident had happened in so doing he would have been excusable, except for want of due care on the part of himself or his agents. When the goods were brought in they were placed under the custody of the law. It became necessary to take them out of the ship, and the captor obtained a commission of unlivery from the Court. They were put into warehouses, and nothing has been advanced to show that these warehouses were not proper places and sufficiently secure. The question comes forward, therefore, on the general principle, and on this point I am disposed to think that the captor is not responsible for a loss happening to goods whilst they were under the custody of the law.

But it is said "that such a rule will operate hardly against the foreign claimant, and that it is not reasonable to address to a subject of another country a justification arising out of the insufficiency of our own police." "When you take his property, it is said, you are bound to answer for secure keeping. However reasonably you might allege this excuse of robbery to persons living under the protection of the same law, foreigners have nothing to do with the defects of our law, or the execution of it." In my opinion this mode of reasoning is a little too rigorous upon all captors, and indeed upon all countries. In all countries, under whatever system of police, thieves break through and steal. It is the universal condition ascribed to things in this world in every part of it, and not peculiar to any one country, much less to our own. All nations stand in this respect on a common footing; the same thing might happen at Gluckstadt to English goods carried in as prize and deposited there, and in such a case, I apprehend, the Courts of Denmark would and ought to exonerate the Danish captor. In reciprocal and general justice that which may happen in any country under any system of police, is that from which innocent captors of all countries ought to be protected. *Veniam petimusque damusque vicissim* is the rule for such contingencies.

1803 *May* 21.

THE MARIA. THE VROW JOHANNA.

Sir W. Scott.

If the captor has used due diligence he is exonerated; it is necessary to show negligence on his part in order to fix a responsibility upon him.

THE VENUS.

[4 C. Rob. 355.]

Cartel Ship—Trade—Condemnation.

A cartel ship is not allowed to trade to the smallest extent with an enemy, and is liable to condemnation if she makes any attempt to trade.

1803 *June* 16.

THIS was a question respecting a British vessel which had gone to Marseilles under cartel, for the exchange of prisoners, and had there taken on board a cargo, and was stranded and captured on a voyage to Port Mahon.

On the part of the captor, the *King's Advocate* and *Parsons* contended that the ship was confiscable in consequence of the illegal trade in which she had been employed.

On the part of the owner of the ship, *Laurence*.

SIR W. SCOTT.—The question is respecting the restitution of the remaining proceeds of this vessel, which was wrecked on a voyage from Marseilles to Minorca, having gone to the port of the enemy as a cartel ship. Certain it is that the conduct of ships of this description cannot be too narrowly watched. The service on which they are sent is so highly important to the interests of humanity that it is peculiarly incumbent on all parties to take care that it should be conducted in such a manner as not to become a subject of jealousy and distrust between the two nations. It is not a

1803
June 16.

THE VENUS.

Sir W. Scott.

question of gain, but one on which depends the recovery of the liberty of individuals who may happen to have become prisoners of war; it is, therefore, a species of navigation which, on every consideration of humanity and policy, must be conducted with the most exact attention to the original purpose, and to the rules which have been built upon it, since, if such a mode of intercourse is broken off, it cannot but be followed by consequences extremely calamitous to individuals of both countries.

It is a species of navigation, therefore, as I have before observed, which more than any other requires to be most narrowly watched. There is no way by which this purity of conduct can be maintained but by considering the owner as answerable for the due execution of the service on which his vessel is employed. It is the very last description of cases in which the responsibility of the owner ought to be relaxed. At the same time, I will not say that if the master had taken on board a few articles for his own petty profit, such an act should, in all cases, subject the property of the owner of considerable value to confiscation; but where goods are not clandestinely taken on board, but in such quantities and in such a manner as to call for the remonstrance of the officers of the ship, as was the case in the present instance, it is, I think, too much to say that it is such petty malversation as shall be imputable only to the master.

Cartel ships are subject to a double obligation to both countries, not to trade. To engage in trade may be disadvantageous to the enemy, or to their own country; both countries are mutually engaged to permit no trade to be carried on under a fraudulent use of this intercourse; all trade must, therefore, be held to be prohibited, and it is not without the consent of both governments that vessels engaged on that service can be permitted to take in any goods whatever.

This vessel went to Marseilles, and discharged her prisoners, and then she ought to have gone away. Instead of pursuing this line of conduct, the master took on board three Jews, not merely with their pacotilles, but with goods, which are distinguished from pacotilles by this circumstance that they were made subject to a distinct freight; they were, besides, not taken on board in an obscure way, or clandestinely, but in such a manner as to draw upon the master the advice and remonstrance of his own officers, and of the masters of other neutral vessels, who must, therefore, have considered this transaction not as the mere taking in a few pacotilles, but as such an act of trading as might be expected to draw on it the confiscation of the property of his employer. Such a conduct was, in the first place, a direct breach of his obligation to the enemy; for I do not see that there was any licence, or permission, even on the part of the country where he was; it is also a breach of his obligation to his own country.

Then as to the consequences of such an act: it is not to be said that because the Lords of Appeal have restored some of the goods, the question as to the ship is necessarily superseded. It does not appear that this objection was taken in the Superior Court. What might have been the judgment of that Court upon it, if it had been brought into discussion, I cannot say. It does not seem necessarily to follow that because the claimant of the goods was innocent, being possibly ignorant of the condition of the vessel, the master's act in taking them on board was not a culpable act, to be visited by confiscation of the ship. It is said the amount of the goods restored was very small; but on this fact there is some disagreement in the representation of the different parties. The captors have made a distinct averment, by affidavit, that the property restored was only of the value of 49*l.*, whilst the claimants, who contend for a much larger quantity, have left it to be spelt out by bills of lading, and a reference to accounts which are not very intelligible. If it were necessary to determine on this fact, the affidavit of the captors appears to me to be entitled to the most credit; but on the principle of law, considering that the duty of the master bound him to abstain from all traffic whatever, and that the slightest deviation from this duty, especially if sanctioned by a judicial determination, might lead to the most calamitous consequences, I do not think myself justified to restore this property, and shall pronounce it subject to condemnation.

[4 C. Rob. 361.]

THE PICIMENTO.

Vice-Admiralty Court—Jurisdiction—High Court of Admiralty as Prize Court.

The Court of Admiralty as Prize Court can aid the process of a Vice-Admiralty Court.

1803 *June* 28.

THIS was a case of a Portuguese vessel, captured, and brought to adjudication in the Court of Vice-Admiralty at the Cape of Good Hope, where the Court pronounced a sentence of restitution with costs and damages.

From this sentence the captor appealed, but on the non-prosecution of his appeal, in the ordinary time, the Court of Appeal pronounced the appeal to be deserted, and remitted the cause.

Before the sentence of the Court, at the Cape of Good Hope, could be carried into execution, the settlement itself was given up, according to the Treaty of Amiens, and the Records of the Court of Vice-Admiralty were removed and deposited in the Registry of the High Court of Admiralty.

An application was now made on behalf of the claimant, praying that the High Court of Admiralty would carry into execution the decree of the Vice-Admiralty Court.

The captors appeared under protest, denying the jurisdiction of the Court.

Court.—I shall overrule the protest, and direct the process of this Court to issue as prayed. The Court of Admiralty appears to me to have general jurisdiction sufficient to aid the process of the Vice-Admiralty Court in order to prevent a total failure of justice (*a*).

(*a*) By the Naval Prize Act, 1864 (27 & 28 Vict. c. 25), s. 4, the High Court of Admiralty was given power to enforce a decree or order of a Vice-Admiralty Prize Court.

THE ORION.

[4 C. Rob. 362.]

Joint Capture—Right of Admiral to Share—Separate Service by Order of Admiralty.

The right of an admiral to a share in a capture by a ship of his squadron may be lost if such ship acts on a separate service by direction of the Admiralty.

1803 *August* 12; affirmed *March* 29, 1804.

THIS was a question respecting the right of Admiral Kingsmill, as admiral of the Irish station, to share in certain captures made by his Majesty's ship *Unicorn* in the Channel, September 24th, 1796. The point contested on the part of the *Unicorn* was, whether that ship was not to be considered as separated from the Irish station, by subsequent orders from the Admiralty, in such a manner as to supersede, or suspend, the authority of the admiral of the station at the time of capture, and defeat his claim to a flag-eighth.

SIR W. SCOTT.—This is a question on a claim for a flag-eighth, which is asserted by Admiral Kingsmill against Sir Thomas Williams on account of several ships taken by the *Unicorn* in the Channel, the 24th September, 1796. . . . .

The material facts are, first, an admitted fact that Sir Thomas Williams was at one time under the command of Admiral Kingsmill in such a manner as most clearly to entitle Admiral Kingsmill to the flag-eighth; the next material fact is one which is contested and is to be ascertained by evidence, it is this: whether any act was done that did totally supersede or suspend for a time this command, for I presume that a temporary suspension might be sufficient for this purpose—a total separation is not requisite—it is not necessary that there should be no prospect of a speedy revival of the command; it is enough if another competent authority, and still more if a paramount authority, had employed him on a clear, distinct, and separate service, although that service might in its own nature be very short, and the party be directed immediately after the performance of it to revert to his former relation of subjection.

I have said a separate service, because it would be too much to

1803 *August* 12. THE ORION. Sir W. Scott.

say that there may not be services so coincident as not to affect the relation. There may be duties which can hardly be considered as obstructing the execution of the original duties, mere incidents, and nothing more. It may, perhaps, be extremely difficult to distinguish in particular cases whether the new services are merely of this incidental nature; it may not be easy to lay down any general criterion that shall be sufficient for all cases. Courts must distinguish as well as they can when the cases arise, subject, undoubtedly, to a possibility of some misapprehension in a matter which, in the nature of it, admits of very thin partitions of very nice and slender gradations. One safe ground on which the discretion of a Court might perhaps venture to trust itself, would be if the new service imposed was of such a kind as necessarily to carry the party out of the direction and in a contrary direction to that in which the original service would have engaged him. If the service carries him merely on his road it may be too much to say that this is to be deemed a separate service, it produces no separation; but if it is that which by necessity carries him, or by probability may carry him, elsewhere, then I incline to think that it has something of the character of a separate service, and does *pro tempore* lay the original authority asleep till its functions are executed.

[The *Court* then examined the facts, and concluded.]

Upon the whole of the question, which I cannot but consider as one that is very open to discussion, I should have been extremely glad to have fortified my own judgment by the authority of decided cases; but neither the industry of the Bar, nor my own researches, can furnish me with any case on this particular point. I am therefore driven to decide it on principle. Upon principle, I am of opinion that those captures were made under the orders of the Admiralty, not confirmatory of, nor coincident with, the orders of Admiral Kingsmill, but suspending and annulling those orders for the time, and producing captures and events which would not otherwise have taken place. On these grounds I conceive myself bound to pronounce that Admiral Kingsmill's right to the flag-eighth does not exist. At the same time, considering it to be a question of mere right between the parties, fit to be contested and fairly and liberally conducted, I do not think that I shall incur the imputation of showing any improper indulgence to litigation, if, in adjudging the whole prize to Sir Thomas Williams, I nevertheless decree that Admiral Kingsmill is entitled to his expenses.

1803 *August* 12.

THE ORION.

Sir W. Scott.

THE VROW ELIZABETH.

[5 C. Rob. 4.]

Ship—Flag—Neutral Owner—National Character.

A ship under the colours and pass of a nation is to be considered as a ship of such nation to whatever nationality her actual owners may belong (*a*).

1803 *September* 6.

THIS was a case of a ship taken under a Dutch flag and pass, on a voyage from Surinam to Holland. A claim was given on the part of Mr. ———, a merchant of Bremen, stating "the ship to have been *bonâ fide* his property, though nominally transferred to a Dutch merchant, and placed under a Dutch flag and pass, for the purpose of enabling her to trade between the Dutch colonies and Holland."

SIR W. SCOTT.—This application appears to me to be against the evidence of fact, as well as against the settled principle of law. The vessel was sailing under Dutch colours from Surinam to Amsterdam, with a Dutch pass, and all other papers, representing her to be a Dutch ship; and this description is confirmed by the deposition of the master, who states her to be a Dutch ship, the property of Mr. Gildermester. The evidence on the fact then is that she is a Dutch ship; to this nothing is opposed but the account of two other persons, who, though competent witnesses, are certainly inferior to the master, both with regard to the credit due to them and to their opportunity of knowing the real fact. It would, I think, be extremely hazardous to admit a claim in opposition to this evidence. I will go further and say that I hold the claim to be also against the established rules of law, by which

(*a*) See the *Primus;* and the *Industrie*, Vol. II. p. 297.

1803 September 6.

THE VROW ELIZABETH.

Sir W. Scott.

it has been decided that a vessel sailing under the colours and pass of a nation is to be considered as clothed with the national character of that country. With goods it may be otherwise (*a*),

(*a*) In the case of the *Vreede Scholtys*, the claim of Mr. Dede for a share in the ship taken under a Dutch flag and pass was rejected. On the part of the captor it was further objected, as to the cargo, that the claim of the same gentleman for an undivided part of the cargo, documented as Dutch property, must be precluded also by the Dutch character, and by incorporation into Dutch commerce. The Court overruled this objection, observing: "A great distinction has been always made by the nations of Europe between ships and goods. Some countries have gone so far as to make the flag and pass of the ship conclusive on the cargo also, but this country has never carried the principle to that extent. It holds the ship bound by the character imposed upon it by the authority of the government from which all the documents issue. But goods which have no such dependence upon the authority of the State may be differently considered. Then comes the question whether the Court will make the separation. Generally, it cannot be doubted that such separation may be made. It is in every day's practice to make such distinctions. Are there, then, any particular circumstances to prevent the Court from doing it in the present instance? Has the claimant assumed the character of a Dutchman so as to render the property liable to be considered as Dutch property? I know of no case that has fixed such a consequence upon a transaction of this kind in time of peace. On the contrary, we all remember the cases of the Swiss who had shipped property from Curaçao under Dutch names to avoid the Alien Duties, and yet obtained restitution of their claims. Had the trade in the present instance been even an exclusive trade, it might have been questionable how far the party could have been held to the Dutch character merely on account of a false representation practised against the Dutch revenue laws—unless, indeed, it had appeared that there had been some pass or licence conferring on him the special privileges of a Dutch merchant, or unless it was a trade arising out of the circumstances of war, or the expectation of such an event. Here the party appears only to be availing himself of Dutch names in time of peace for the benefit of avoiding particular duties; in such a case it would be going further than the Court has hitherto gone to declare that the person is to be held to all the revolutions which may attend the Dutch character. In time of war a more strict principle may be necessary. But it is needless to decide what considerations might be fit to be applied to such a transaction in time of war, as this case arose altogether in time of peace, and without any expectation of war. I see nothing to prevent the Court from performing the office of separating this undivided share, and as the property is fully proved, I shall decree it to be restored."

So, in the *Broders Lust*, Mr. Richter, part owner of the ship, and supercargo on board the vessel, obtained restitution of his claim for parts of the cargo, though his claim as to the ship was rejected.

but ships have a peculiar character impressed upon them by the special nature of their documents, and have always been held to the character with which they are so invested, to the exclusion of any claims of interest that persons living in neutral countries may actually have in them. In the war before the last this principle was strongly recognized in the case of a ship taken on a voyage from Surinam to Amsterdam, and documented as a Dutch ship. Claims were given for specific shares on behalf of persons resident in Switzerland, and one claim was on behalf of a lady, to whom a share had devolved by inheritance, whether during hostilities or not I do not accurately remember, but if it was so she had done no act whatever with regard to that property, and it might be said to have dropped by mere accident into her lap. In that case, however, it was held that the fact of sailing under the Dutch flag and pass was decisive against the admission of any claim; and it was observed that as the vessel had been enjoying the privileges of a Dutch character, the parties could not expect to reap the advantages of such an employment without being subject at the same time to the inconveniences attaching on it. When I lay down this rule I do not say that there may not be cases of such particular circumstances as to raise a reasonable distinction. The Treaty of Amiens had stipulated for the liberty of withdrawing British property from the ceded and restored islands. But the Governments of France and Holland afterwards refused to suffer such property to be exported from these colonies otherwise than in ships of France or Holland, and on a destination to those countries. The difficulty which has arisen in the removal of British property for want of shipping may have induced our own Government to permit British ships to put themselves under Dutch flags for this particular purpose; and in such cases the particular situation of affairs arising out of this refusal to execute a treaty may have entitled such parties to a relaxation (*a*) of the general rule. But no ground

(*a*) In the *Onderneeming* a British subject obtained restitution of seven-eighths of the ship under a Dutch flag and pass. The King's instructions, 23rd July, 1803, direct "restitution of ships and cargoes *bonâ fide* belonging to British subjects sailing before the knowledge of hostilities, from the colonies of France and Holland, to whatever country they might be going."

1803 *September* 6. — THE VROW ELIZABETH. — Sir W. Scott.

of exemption whatever is stated in the present claim—nothing more than that the claimant found it convenient to place his vessel under the Dutch character; to which the answer is obvious, that with the convenience he must take also the inconvenience attending such an act. The case referred to in the argument has nothing in common with the present claim. In that case the ship had merely a colonial pass or licence, being in all other respects undoubtedly and avowedly an American ship, and described as such in the usual American documents. This ship has all the documents of a Dutch ship, and I have no hesitation in pronouncing her subject to condemnation.

[5 C. Rob. 15.]

THE VROW ANNA CATHARINA (No. 1).

Capture—Claim of Territory by Neutral—Evidence—Claim of Neutral Shipper in Opposition to Ship's Papers—Ante-War Purchase and Shipment.

The right of a belligerent to seize enemy's property being universal, a claim of territory in opposition thereto must be established by clear evidence. Though claims in opposition to the papers are not as a rule admitted, there is an exception in respect of property shipped and purchased in time of peace.

1803 *October* 7; affirmed *December* 15, 1805.

THIS was a case of a ship and cargo, documented as Dutch property, and captured on a voyage from Batavia to Amsterdam, near to the Island of Saint Michael. On a representation made to the Portuguese Government that the seizure took place within the road or harbour of Saint Michael, a claim of territory was interposed by the Portuguese Consul.

On the part of the captor, *Arnold.*

On the other side, the *King's Advocate* and *Laurence.*

SIR W. SCOTT.—The sanctity of a claim of territory is undoubtedly very high. The Court is at all times very much disposed to pay attention to claims of this species, and to none more readily than to those which concern the territorial rights of the State of Portugal. When the fact is established it overrules every other consideration. The capture is done away, the property must be restored notwithstanding that it may actually belong to the enemy, and if the captor should appear to have erred wilfully, and not merely through ignorance, he would be subject to further punishment.

It is to be remembered, however, at the same time, that it is a point on which foreign States are extremely liable to be misinformed and abused by the interested representations of those who are anxious to catch at their protection. The claim of territory is therefore to be taken as a matter *stricti juris*, and to be made out by clear and unimpeached evidence. The right of seizing the property of the enemy is a right which extends, generally speaking, universally wherever that property is found. The protection of neutral territory is an exception to the general rule only; it is not, therefore, to be considered as disrespectful to any government that the fact on which such claims are founded should be accurately examined.

[The Court then examined the evidence, and concluded :—]

Under these circumstances the claim of territory, being altogether contradicted by the preparatory evidence, must be rejected.

On the merits, it was contended that all the documents, as well as the depositions of the Dutch crew, described the cargo to belong to Dutch merchants, and it was prayed that the Court would condemn the ship and cargo as Dutch property.

On the other side, a claim was offered for A. B., a neutral merchant, setting forth his interest in the cargo under a sub-contract made to him by the Dutch merchant, who was the original purchaser in the contract with the Dutch East India Company; and it was contended that the rule of not admitting claims in opposition to the original papers and depositions was a rule arising out of the relations of war, and was not to be applied to a transaction which took place altogether in time of peace.

SIR W. SCOTT.—I have never understood that the rule against the admission of claims, which stand in entire opposition to the

1803
October 7.

THE VROW ANNA CATHARINA.

Sir W. Scott.

papers and to the preparatory examinations, was applicable to cases arising before the war. There may be private reasons to induce merchants to trade under borrowed names, and to suppress the exact representation of the property. In time of war the rule is certainly otherwise, as it would open a door to fraud in an incalculable extent if persons were not required to describe their property with perfect fairness. The interests of a third party interpose, and call upon them so to do. It is not any relaxation of the rule, therefore, to admit such a claim for property shipped and purchased, as it is asserted, in time of profound peace. In Mr. Allwood's (*a*) case the same distinction was recognized; and indeed the objection has never, to my knowledge, been held to be a decisive objection as applied to such cases. I shall admit the claim, and give the parties an opportunity of enabling me to form a better judgment of this transaction by showing what was the particular nature of this contract (*b*).

[5 C. Rob. 22.]

THE PLANTER'S WENSCH.

Licence—Peace—Subsequent War—Invalidity of Licence.

A licence granted before a peace has no validity after peace is signed, and in a subsequent war.

1803
December 13.

THIS was a case of a claim made for property, avowedly Dutch, by a person represented as an accredited agent of the Batavian Republic. The claim was given for the ship and for parts of the cargo, as sailing under a licence granted by the British Government, October, 1801.

On the part of the captors, the *King's Advocate* and *Robinson.*—This claim is given for a Dutch ship, sailing under Dutch colours, from Demerara to Amsterdam, and seized (May, 1803) prior to hostilities against Holland. It is claimed as protected generally by the Treaty of Amiens; and, secondly, in a more specific manner, by the licence which was on board. The licence is dated October,

(*a*) *Superb*, 6th August, 1800: Lords.

(*b*) This property was afterwards restored.

1801, and expresses a permission for this vessel to sail from Amsterdam to Demerara in the ensuing April, in pursuance of the preliminaries of peace. It was granted between the signing of the preliminary articles and the definitive treaty; and must, in its obvious intent, have been designed only to enable Dutch vessels to go to the Dutch settlements, whilst still under the dominion of this country, prior to the surrender that was expected to take place on the return of peace.

On the other side, *Laurence* and *Swabey.*

Sir W. Scott.—This claim is given by a Mr. Apostol, who is described as the commercial agent of the Batavian Republic, though it is not very easy to understand how that character, springing out of the pacific relations of the two countries, can now exist in a time of war. Waiving, however, all objection to the political description of this gentleman, I will consider the nature of the claim and the ground on which it is defended. It is represented as sustainable under the Treaty of Amiens, and on the special licence which has been produced. As to the Treaty of Amiens, the argument on that head would amount to this, that all property taken before the actual declaration of future hostilities should be protected by it—a position which it is, in my opinion, impossible to maintain. The second ground is that of the licence, a protection which, if it could be shown to apply to this class of cases, would be entitled to the greatest respect, and would certainly meet with every disposition on the part of the Court to give it due effect. The licence was granted in October, 1801, to empower this vessel, being a Dutch ship, to go to the colony of Demerara, then in British possession, but intended to be restored to the Batavian Republic under the treaty then in contemplation. Whilst the island was in British possession it was certainly an indulgence to allow Dutch vessels to sail with this destination, on which they could not have ventured without the special protection of a licence. It must be recollected also that it was granted during the pendency of the negotiation, whilst it was uncertain whether hostilities might not be renewed, and whilst it was probable that the cruisers then in commission might retain their legal authority to seize; and there-

1803 December 13. — THE PLANTER'S WENSCH. — Sir W. Scott.

fore the terms of the licence are, I think, to be referred to the state and condition of affairs as they were at that time existing. All those prospects of renewed hostility certainly ceased; and although the train of events has led to fresh hostilities, the Court cannot consider them as the revival of old hostilities, but as a war *de novo*. The former war was absolutely concluded by a total and entire peace, which was recognized by the Legislature, and by which I am bound to look upon that war as being as effectually, in all legal consideration, buried in oblivion and extinguished as any hostilities of any anterior times of the world. It does not become me to speculate upon the causes of the present war, nor to consider how far it may be supposed to originate out of the seeds of those hostilities, which had been formally terminated. Peace having been concluded, this licence was necessarily done away and destroyed, having no subject-matter to act upon. At the time of seizure, therefore, this vessel was to be considered on the ordinary footing of other Dutch ships.

This appears to me to be the legal view of the question. Whether anything has passed between the Government of this country and the Batavian Republic that should entitle the claimants to contend for restitution under a capture of the present war is for the consideration of those who have to advise his Majesty as to the political relations of the State. If any such pledge has been given it will, I doubt not, be redeemed with that good faith which has always marked the proceedings of the British Government. It is sufficient for me to say that nothing is produced to the view of this Court that can in fair legal interpretation have the effect of distinguishing this vessel from other Dutch property taken prior to hostilities, or that can protect it from the just effect of capture made in contemplation of the war which is now actually existing.

THE FORTUNA (No. 2). [5 C. Rob. 27.]

Blockade—Compulsion to Enter Port—Provisions.

An overruling compulsion being the only legal excuse for entering a blockaded port, mere want of provisions is rarely an excuse for so doing.

THIS was a case of a ship bound ostensibly from Stettin to Bremen, but seized and proceeded against for a violation of the blockade of the Weser. 1803 *November* 4.

SIR W. SCOTT.—In this case it is admitted that the master was apprised of the blockade. The excuse offered is that he had taken a pilot on board to carry him into the Eems, but that owing to want of provisions and a strong westerly wind he was compelled to make for the Weser. The want of provisions is an excuse which will not on light grounds be received, because an excuse to be admissible must show an imperative and overruling compulsion to enter the particular port under blockade, which can scarcely be said in any instance of mere want of provisions. It may induce the master to seek a neighbouring port, but it can hardly ever force a person to resort exclusively to the blockaded port. What is stated respecting the wind is of a different nature. . . . . I shall admit evidence to be introduced on this point.

This ship was finally restored.

THE ST. JUAN BAPTISTA. [5 C. Rob. 33.]
LA PURISSIMA CONCEPTION.

Capture—Imprisonment by Captors—Damages.

Captors are not justified in putting a captured crew under restraint, unless it is absolutely necessary for the security of the captors, and are liable in damages for so doing.

THESE were cases of Spanish ships detained under charges of resistance to search, but restored with demurrage and compensation to the crew for improper treatment received at the hands of the captors. 1803 *November* 22.

1803 *November* 22.

THE ST. JUAN BAPTISTA. LA PURISSIMA CONCEPTION.

[The first part of the judgment was concerned entirely with the question, whether upon the facts there had been a resistance to search, the Court holding that the master of the vessel had no reasonable ground for believing there was a state of war, and that he acted under "innocent misapprehension."]

SIR W. SCOTT.— . . . . There are besides two other parts of the charge to which it is necessary for me to advert. The first is the imputation of a practice, which, if proved to have existed in the extent alleged and without necessity, must be pronounced to be disgraceful to the character of the country, since no one who hears me will deny that to apply even to enemies modes of restraint that are unnecessary, and at the same time convey personal indignity and personal suffering, is highly dishonourable. It is alleged in this case that the Spanish crew, to the number of twenty-two persons, were put in irons. This is a fact which certainly requires much explanation, for I will not say that there may not be cases in which such restraint may be necessary, and therefore justifiable. But the necessity must be urgent and evident. The captor, when called upon for his explanation, has furnished no apology but what is suggested by his counsel, that these persons would naturally be regarded as bent on their original purpose of resistance, and might, in that view, be justly subjected to closer custody. The master acknowledges that he did handcuff some who were most outrageous, and menaced him and his officers. Admitting the motive to be truly stated, that this act was done for security, I am afraid it will not amount to a justification, because it was incumbent on the captor to pursue a proper purpose by proper means. It should be established to the satisfaction of the Court that this species of security alone would have been sufficient for his preservation. There might have been a separation of those who showed symptoms of violence, or there might have been a personal confinement of a slighter kind. Some such measures should have been resorted to, or it should have been shown that they would have been insufficient. As the case now stands, the party has not made out a sufficient justification. At the same time, I must say that the misconduct appears to have proceeded rather from an improper notion of security, than from any intention to inflict pain or personal indignity. If any such malignant motive had been proved, I should have thought it my duty to pursue this matter much further; but there is no decisive ground for such an imputation. I am of opinion, however, that the party has not justified his conduct, and that it is due to the honour of the country and to the injury the Spaniards have sustained that some civil compensation should be made; and with that view I decree 100*l.* to be distributed amongst the sufferers. Embezzlement is also charged; but it is said, on the other side, that some articles were withdrawn, only with a view to protect them from the eagerness of the crew, and that they will be forthcoming. Till I see how far this answer will satisfy the demands of the claimants, it will be impossible for me to pronounce upon this part of the case. I shall refer this matter to the Registrar and merchants to ascertain the fact and quantity of loss, and I shall reserve my judgment on this question till I receive their report.

1803 *November* 22.

THE ST. JUAN BAPTISTA. LA PURISSIMA CONCEPTION.

Two months' detention allowed.

THE MELOMANE.

[5 C. Rob. 41.]

Capture—Ship of War—Detached Boat.

In order to entitle a ship of war to share in a prize made by a boat, it must be proved that such boat is acting as the boat, at the time of the capture, of such ship of war.

A capture made by a cutter, not commissioned, but hired and manned by the commander of a ship of war, is liable to condemnation as a droit of Admiralty, not as a prize to the ship of war.

1803 *December* 8.

THIS was a case respecting a prize interest in a capture made by a boat hired by the captain of the King's ship the *Dragon*, and sent out, manned with part of the *Dragon's* crew, for the purpose of impressing mariners that were expected to arrive in the homeward-bound ships. The question was, whether a prize made by such a vessel was to be condemned as a droit of Admiralty or as prize to the *Dragon*.

SIR W. SCOTT.—This case comes on upon the claim of Captain Aylmer [of the *Dragon*], who is unquestionably a very meritorious officer, and, as it appears by his affidavit, commands a very meritorious crew. If considerations of this kind could supply a principle of judgment, the case might easily be decided; but that gentleman, as well as everyone else, must know that the Court can

1803 December 8. THE MELOMANE. Sir W. Scott.

only look to legal principles as the foundations of a legal decision; and that whatever the personal merits of the parties may be, they cannot in any degree influence the judgment of the Court, but must be left to seek their remuneration elsewhere. It is made a question in the act of Court, and in argument, whether the capture was effected by the *Assistance* cutter or by the boat of the *Dragon*, accompanied by the cutter. All the depositions represent the capture to have been made by the *Assistance* cutter, acting, as the French witnesses describe her, as a tender to the *Dragon*, though this is a fact which could not be a subject of observation at the time, and could be known to them only by the report of the boat's crew afterwards. The effect of this evidence only serves to show that the *Assistance* cutter was the actual captor. It is contended in argument, however, that the boat of the *Dragon* was sent out to take possession, and that such an act of seizure by the boat's crew of the *Dragon* will entitle the ship herself to the whole benefit of the prize. The Court would certainly be disposed to extend, as far as it could with propriety, to ships of war the benefit of captures made by their boats acting distinctly in that capacity. There must be situations in which the capture could not be made otherwise, and many considerations of convenience require that they should be allowed to take in whatever manner their judgment may deem most expedient, according to the circumstances of the case, either by their whole force or by a part detached on that particular service. The Court would therefore not be disposed to narrow the legal effect of the operations of their boat's crew. But in this particular case it remains to be considered, in the first place, whether the boat was acting as the boat of the *Dragon* or not. The tenor of all the evidence inclines me to think that she was not; that she had been detached from the *Dragon* and attached to the *Assistance* cutter, and that she was employed in performing the same services for the cutter as she would have performed for her own ship. If that is to be taken as a correct view of her situation, I cannot but accede to what has been said in argument, that a boat so detached from one and attached to another vessel must be taken as acting under the authority and for the benefit of the ship to which, at that time and in those operations, she more properly belongs. The fact appears to me to be, as it is described by the witnesses of the captured ship, "that the capture was actually and effectually made by the *Assistance* cutter, and that the boat was only used to perform such acts as would in the ordinary course of service have been performed by the cutter's own boat."

Taking the fact to be that the capture was made by the *Assistance* cutter, the Court has only to decide how far the act of the *Assistance* can enure to the benefit of the *Dragon*, on which she is represented as attendant. It is an elementary principle of Prize Law that all prize belongs to the State, in monarchies to the Sovereign. By modern policy this interest has been granted out to persons of certain descriptions, acting under the authority of public commissions. A very ancient grant has given to the Lord High Admiral the benefit of all prize taken by persons not commissioned, and it lies on the individual captor in every case to show the authority by which he is entitled to take for his own benefit. The title-deeds, on which only claims of this kind can be constructed, are the Prize Act and the Proclamation. The Proclamation confers the interest in prize "on our ships of war and those which have taken out letters of marque." The Prize Act is much to the same effect, adding only in the last Act, "mariners, &c. on board our hired armed ships." These descriptions of vessels are, with those acting under letter of marque, the only parties that can maintain a legal interest in prize. What are the circumstances of this case? Captain Aylmer's affidavit states that the cutter was hired at his expense, and stored and manned from the King's ship the *Dragon*. That commanding officers of his Majesty's ships may have a right to put their men, arms, and stores on board another vessel I shall not question in the present case. There may be circumstances that may render it fit, in many instances, that such a discretion should be exercised, subject to the responsibility that always attends them in the discharge of their public duty. But the question which I have to consider is whether, by so doing, an officer can be said to put that other vessel into commission, and entitle it to the privilege of being reckoned amongst the description of vessels to which the interest in prize is given by the Proclamation and the Prize Act. Indeed, I may observe that the very claim that is set up for the

1803 December 8.

THE MELOMANE.

Sir W. Scott.

Dragon contradicts the suggestion, because if this cutter, so employed, could be considered as commissioned to take for herself, she would become a constituent part of the navy, and the *Dragon* could have no interest to maintain. If, then, the cutter is not a commissioned vessel, the question must be whether, not being entitled to take for herself, she does, from being so fitted out, become a boat, or, in a legal point of view, a constituent part of the *Dragon's* force? What I have said of boats may in some degree apply to tenders. If a capture is made by a tender attached by the interposition of public authority, on every principle on which a capture by a boat would entitle its ship, a capture made by a tender specially employed in that capture by the ship of war to which she belonged might, perhaps, entitle that ship. But this is not a tender attached by any interposition of public authority, but by the private act of the officer hiring and manning her himself. Is a cutter so set forth recognized by the Admiralty in any capacity? Is she borne on the books, or considered as a part of the navy of England? I apprehend not; she is taken up by the gentleman himself, acting from his own discretion, for good purposes no doubt, but not in a manner that can give such a vessel any connection or incorporation with the navy of Great Britain. Surely it is not to be maintained that an officer, by putting his men on board, can constitute a ship to be a part of the navy of Great Britain. Such a character is not, in my opinion, to be impressed without the intervention of some public authority. If the contrary could be held this must follow: that an officer of a large ship might form out of these tenders as many ships of war as he pleased. He might compose a fleet. It is said that a similar practice has been not unfrequent in the West Indies. But everybody knows that in remote situations the principal persons in command must necessarily be intrusted with a greater latitude of discretion. In such a situation they must act as well as they can from their own judgment, not having an opportunity of referring immediately to the Board of Admiralty for instructions and authority suited to the various circumstances that may occur. They grant commissions, it is to be observed, for the same reason, and if these commissions are afterwards confirmed by the Admiralty they rank from the original date. If a case of this description was to come before the Court from any such remote station the Court would have to consider how far the particular circumstances would bear it out in point of validity. At home the case is very different. When an officer has it in his power to refer instantly to the Admiralty the same effect will not follow. Nor is it to be ascribed even to the acts of an admiral; for it appears to me that an admiral on the home station would have no more power than a captain of a single ship to constitute a tender to be part of the public navy, though all that is done by the admiral in this case is simply to give them leave to go out. A good deal has been said upon the consequences and general convenience of such a practice. It is impossible to attend much to such considerations. If I am to entertain them at all, I confess it appears to me that the inconvenience of such measures would very much preponderate. More captures, it is true, might be made, but what would be the general effect? If every merchant ship might sally out and take under the authority of ships of war, the number of captures might be greatly increased; but such a consequence, however lucrative to individuals, never could be admitted as a sufficient justification of such a principle in point of political expedience. It is of much more important expedience that it should be left to the State alone to judge, both of the extent and of the mode of hostility that is to be exercised. That is a principle which must never be lost sight of. Looking at this case, therefore, in every point of view, both on principle and expedience, I have a clear and decided opinion, on which I feel no hesitation to pronounce, that this capture was not made by persons legally commissioned to take for their own benefit, and consequently that the petition of Captain Aylmer must be rejected.

[5 C. Rob. 70.]

THE DIANA.

Capture—Ship—Cargo—Freight.

If goods are not carried to their destination freight is not due; if they are, the claimant is entitled to restitution with payment of freight to the captor.

1803 *December* 19.

SIR W. SCOTT.—This is a question of freight, in which I have to determine whether these cargoes, taken before hostilities and brought into this country, should pay freight, having been destined to another country under the original contract. . . . .

There are two rules on this subject equally general. The first is, that if goods are not carried to their original destination, within the intention of the contracting parties, freight shall not be due; and on this ground, that the contract not being completed, either in substance or form, the speculation of the party has not been productive. The benefit of the contract is lost, and the party has to provide another vehicle to carry on the goods to the port of their destination. In some cases, indeed, it may happen that the port to which the goods are brought may prove more beneficial, and afford a better market. But the Court does not enter into the minutiæ of such calculations, which would be attended with great trouble in the inquiry, and much uncertainty in the result. It takes the presumption arising from destination only, and founds upon it the general rule, that in such a case the claimant shall receive restitution of his goods without the burden of freight. The other rule equally general is, that when the contract is executed, by bringing the cargo to the place of destination, the captor, to whom the vessel is condemned, shall be entitled to the freight which has been earned. He stands in the place of the owner of the ship, and is held entitled to the price of the services which have been performed in the execution of the contract. In some instances it may prove disadvantageous to the claimant; and it is certainly a clear inconvenience in all cases to be obliged to receive the goods under the process of a Prize Court, subject to the expenses which may have been incurred, or to the delay of further proof, instead of taking them with more facility in the course of their original consignment. But on the same principle the Court declines, on this side also, to enter into a minute estimate of these circumstances, which must in every case branch out into particulars of infinite variety. It constructs a general rule on the same grounds of presumption which it assumes on the other side, and decrees freight to be paid to the captor, in the same manner as if the goods had been delivered under the original consignment. These are two classes of cases, and the question is, under which class the present case falls, or whether it may not form a third and distinct class, founded on peculiar circumstances, and requiring a rule not strictly applicable on the same precise ground to either of the other two. What are the facts? The claims were given by persons of this country, on a representation that these goods were going on a destination which was obtruded on them by the narrow policy of Holland; that having themselves elected this country as the most eligible country for importation, they were compelled to send their goods to Holland, though with the final intention on their own parts to have these goods remitted either in specie or in proceeds to this country, as the country to which they would immediately have consigned them if at liberty so to do. Now I cannot but think that this fact forms a material fundamental basis for the rule which is proper to be applied to such cases; for although the voyage has not been precisely that described in the contract, it is that which the parties themselves would have elected, if not prevented and diverted by the over-ruling policy of the foreign country. As to what is said of the disadvantages which the claimants may have sustained, the Court enters not into such considerations, and for the reasons described. It is not in the habit of doing it in cases falling under either of the general rules which I have mentioned. Indeed, the parties are in a great measure stopped from averring that the arrival in this country is not beneficial to them, by having framed their application on a previous averment of their wish and final determination to have brought the produce hither, if they had not been restrained. They must be presumed to have formed this determination on a view of all the advantages and disadvantages that were likely to proceed from it. At the same time, though I will not enter minutely into the question, I cannot but observe that they have received restitution in their own ports under their own eye, and where the delivery has been in London, in a port which has been the great depôt of articles of this kind for some years, and may be supposed therefore to be a port eminently beneficial. As to what is said of the delay or expense of obtaining possession through litigation, those inconveniences are not more than may be imputed to other cases falling under the old rules. Once for all on that subject, it cannot be expected that the merchant in time of war should obtain possession of his goods seized, with exactly the same convenience as he would have done under the original consignment in time of peace, and when none of the accidents of war had intervened to interrupt the delivery.

Looking at the substance of the case, and seeing that the parties have obtained restitution in their own country, and generally in the very port which they would have elected if they had not been diverted by over-ruling necessity, I think it may be considered as coming under the second rule, or, if not under that, under another resting on nearly the same principles. The case of the *Etrusco*, which has been cited, was a case of a ship that had come from the East Indies almost to the port of her destination, which was Ostend. The claimant was a Swiss gentleman, who was brought hither solely in consequence of the capture, and who was afterwards induced to settle in this country by circumstances of a private and domestic nature. That case therefore bears no real resemblance to this. It would have been precisely a parallel case if, by any physical possibility, the ship and goods could have gone to Switzerland; or if the parties could and would have sent them there, if not obstructed by the authority of a hostile power. If either of these cases could have happened, will anybody say that freight would not have been decreed? In that particular case, the Court of Appeal would not enter into the subsequent history of the claimant, though it is impossible not to remember that a good deal of commiseration mixed itself with the considerations on which that judgment was formed. On the reasons which I have stated, applying only to the circumstances of this class of cases, and not to be made a ground of experiment for similar demands in other cases not attended with the same original facts on which this case is to be decided—not because the result in coming to these ports may have been more beneficial to the parties, but because the intention of the parties, as they have themselves stated it, has been substantially fulfilled, and the goods have been delivered to their possession in the very country (*a*) to which they would have wished them to have come—I pronounce these to be cases in which freight is due.

1803 *December* 19.

THE DIANA.

Sir W. Scott.

THE SPES AND THE IRENE.

[5 C. Rob. 76.]

Blockade—Inquiries by Master of Neutral Vessel—Condemnation.

After notice of an existing blockade of a port, a master of a neutral vessel who takes her to the entrance of such port to obtain information renders his vessel liable to condemnation.

THIS was a case of two vessels proceeded against and condemned for a violation of the blockade of the Elbe (*b*).

1804 *January* 10; affirmed *July* 11, 1807.

On the part of the captors, the *King's Advocate.*

On the other side, *Laurence.*

SIR W. SCOTT.—These cases stand upon one ground, being the cases of ships belonging to the same owner going from Archangel with an avowed purpose of entering the Elbe. The master of the *Irene* had, as it appears, received a letter from his owner giving notice of the blockade, but expressing an opinion that it would not be of long continuance. Under this expectation he was directed to proceed on his intended destination, to come off the Elbe, and to inquire whether the river was then under blockade or not. It has been contended that the blockade of the Elbe is to be considered on different principles from those that are applied to other blockades, inasmuch as it is a blockade not imposed upon the

(*a*) On the claims restored to foreign merchants, no freight was paid—*Hoop*, June 15th. In the case of the *Vrouw Henrietta*, 23rd March, on the claim of Mr. Ancrum, a merchant of London, a distinction was taken that the goods were not brought to London, but were unlivered at Plymouth, and therefore that they had not been brought to the claimant's own port. The Court overruled the distinction, and held that parcel of goods to be equally subject to freight.

(*b*) The notification of the blockade of the Elbe appeared in the Gazette, 28th June, 1803: Weser, 26th July; Havre, 6th September.

1804 January 10.

THE SPES AND THE IRENE.

Sir W. Scott.

country, but on the enemy in the interior; that it was directed principally against the enemy, and that it is only incidentally and by unavoidable consequence that the trade of the neutral neighbourhood is made subject to it. This representation is to a great extent true, and may, under circumstances that admit of any latitude of interpretation, entitle the parties to all the indulgent considerations that can fairly be applied to their case. But all the general consequences of such a blockade must be supposed to have been duly considered by the Government imposing it, and when the measure is once applied the Court is under the necessity of enforcing it on the only principles on which any other blockade ever has been or can be established. Were the Court disposed to desert those principles and to wander into new speculations respecting blockades, I do not observe that the gentlemen have even suggested the new principles on which it could act. The Court is therefore under the necessity of applying the same general principles on which all former decisions on this right of war have been founded, though in so doing it would be disposed, undoubtedly, to apply them leniently, and with attention to every circumstance that could entitle the parties to favourable considerations. Then what are the facts? These ships had both received notice from the owner that the Elbe was at that time in a state of blockade. It has been said that no such intelligence had been received from the consul of the State of Hamburg, though I must presume it had, because as the notification was made to the consul here, it was his duty to make the communication to the consuls of his government in foreign ports. And as the information had arrived at Hamburg, and had been actually communicated from thence to Archangel by private channels, the same communication must be supposed to have been made from public authority to the public Minister; or, if not, if there had been any neglect, the consequence must be imputed only to the State and its officers, who are answerable to their subjects for the consequence of their neglect. It is said, indeed, that the masters received contrary information from their consul, and that they were told by him that the blockade was raised, though the averment does not, I perceive, distinctly state that, as appears by the evidence in this very case, but only that it would be raised before they arrived. Had the information been more positive it would be difficult to attribute to it any such effect as would serve to the indemnification of these parties. If this conjectural information at Archangel proved false, they must look for redress to their own government, or to those employed under it, who gave such erroneous intelligence. If the information of foreign ministers could be deemed sufficient to exempt a party from all penalty there would be no end of such excuses. Courts of justice are compelled, I think, to hold as a principle of necessary caution that the misinformation of a foreign minister cannot be received as a justification for failing in actual breach of an existing blockade. The letters of the owner inform the masters that the blockade would probably be at an end before they arrived, and direct them to proceed for the Elbe. Are these the orders which owners ought to have given? I think not. The neutral merchant is not to speculate on the greater or less probability of the termination of a blockade to send his vessels to the very mouth of the river and say: "If you do not meet with the blockading force, enter; if you do, ask a warning, and proceed elsewhere." Who does not at once perceive the frauds to which such a rule would be introductory? The true rule is, that after the knowledge of an existing blockade, you are not to go to the very station of blockade under pretence of inquiry. It is contended, however, on this point that the parties are entitled to the same equity as was allowed to American vessels during the last war (*a*). But what was that? That ships sailing from America, before the knowledge of the blockade had reached America, should be entitled to a notice, even at the blockaded port; and that ships sailing afterwards might sail on a contingent destination even to that port, with the purpose of calling at some British port, or at some neutral port, for information; and that they should be allowed the benefit of such a contingent destination to be ascertained and rendered definite by the information which they should receive in Europe. But in no case was it held that they might sail to the mouth of a blockaded port to inquire whether a blockade, of which they had received previous formal notice, was still in existence or not. If particular parties are

(*a*) See the *Betsey* (No. 2), *ante*, p. 147.

1804 January 10. — THE SPES AND THE IRENE. — Sir W. Scott.

innocent in their intention, it is still a measure of necessary caution, and of preventive legal policy, to hold the rule general against the liberty of inquiring at the very mouth of the blockaded port, which would amount in practice to a universal licence to attempt to enter, and, on being prevented, to claim the liberty of going elsewhere. It is next contended that the master on being brought to said that he was not going to a blockaded port, but that he would go, in obedience to his instructions, to a port in Norway, and therefore that the claimant is entitled to the benefit of a deviation. But this comes too late; he was taken in the act of going towards the blockaded port. The act is, in my opinion, to be taken as completed by the attempt. If the owners are innocent, they must, in law, be bound by the indiscretion of their agent. But this is not a case of persons suffering merely by the misconduct of their agents. The owners here are directly implicated by the instructions which they themselves have given. It may fall hardly upon them, but I feel myself obliged to pronounce that there would be no principle upon which a blockade could be enforced, if such excuses as these were to be admitted, and that these vessels are subject to condemnation.

[5 C. Rob. 82.]

THE TWILLING RIGET.

Ship—Restitution with Freight—Rate to be Allowed.

A decree was made that a ship should be restored with freight, and the amount to be paid was referred to the Registrar and merchants. *Held*, on objection to the report that though the Registrar and merchants should not, without good cause, depart from the rate of freight provided by the charter, they were not bound by such rate.

1804 January 11.

THIS was a case on objection to the Registrar's report, respecting the amount of freight that was to be paid to this vessel and several other ships under a decree of restitution with freight. They were ships that had been captured on a voyage from Batavia to Copenhagen, under an affreightment to Mr. De Coninck, and employed in transporting to Europe the quantity of Batavian produce which that gentleman had purchased under contract with the Dutch East India Company.

The Act of Court set forth, on the part of the owners, that the ship had been chartered at Copenhagen, in June, 1798, to perform a voyage to Batavia in ballast, and back to Copenhagen, with a cargo at the freight of 60,000 dollars, being equal to about 120 rix dollars per ton. In the report, the Registrar and merchants were disposed to consider this freight as above the just rate, and allowed only what other ships appeared to have contracted for, about the same time, 95 dollars per ton. The freight was calculated at that rate on the burthen of 365 tons, whereas it was stated as a material objection that the tonnage in the East India trade is not confined to the shipbuilder's measurement, but that there is an option allowed of taking either that measurement, or another known rule, according to the proportionate bulk and weight of certain articles.

SIR W. SCOTT.—It is agreed on all sides that these cases must go again before the Registrar and merchants to be reconsidered on the objections that are made to the mode of calculating the burthen. It will, therefore, not be necessary for me to say much on that point, or to give any precise judgment upon the case at large; because if it should happen that they see occasion to make a larger allowance on that score, it is probable that the difference between the parties may no longer be very material. At the same time I will say, that I perfectly accede to the principle that has been advanced, in support of the rule on which the Registrar and merchant have proceeded, that the charter party is not the measure by which the captor in all cases is bound, even where no fraud is imputed to the contract itself. When by the events of war navigation is rendered so hazardous as to raise the price of freight to an extraordinary height, captors are not necessarily bound to that inflamed rate of freight. When no such circumstance exists, when a ship is carrying on an ordinary trade, the charter party is undoubtedly the rule of valuation, unless impeached; the captor puts himself in the place of the owner of the cargo, and takes with that specific lien upon it. But a very different rule is to be applied when the trade is subjected to extraordinary risk and hazard from its connection with the events of war and the redoubled activity and success of the belligerent cruisers. It appears to me that this is a case of that kind; and it may not be improper to advert a

1804 January 11. THE TWILLING RIGET. Sir W. Scott.

little to the nature of the commerce in which the ship was engaged in the performance of a contract which has been deemed illegal, both in this Court and in the Court of Appeal. In such a service it could not but have been considered as an adventure of some hazard to send ships on a new and experimental trade, which was, in its effect, to put Mr. De Coninck into the place of the Dutch East India Company. The owners would naturally look for their indemnification in an advanced freight in terms which might not be in any degree unfair or unreasonable between the parties, considered as the premiums of a voyage eminently hazardous on account of its illegality, as against the rights of this country. Mr. De Coninck also might look for his indemnification to the Dutch East India Company in the price at which he had obtained this contract, in consequence of their distress. Considerations of this nature might render it a real and fair contract between the parties; but the freight, as a burthen upon the English captor, does not come loaded with all these considerations, none of which apply to him. The cases of the corn ships do, I think, bear a fair analogy to this case. I remember well that in those cases a paper was thrown on this table stating the price not to be unreasonable, under the opinion of some of the most respectable merchants of this town, that such would be the price paid by the French consignee under the then distressed state of the French market. But the Court said that they mistook the principle, and were deciding a question of law, viz., that the captor was in all cases bound to stand to the chartered price, if not impeached by the real prices of the market. The principle of that decision is not, in my opinion, improperly pressed into the present case, and it does sufficiently confirm the general position that captors are not in all cases bound by the terms of the charter party, though they may not be colourable or liable to any imputation of fraud. At the same time, the Registrar and merchants will not depart from the charter party without good cause, and without looking on all sides for information. Something has been thrown out in argument as if they had looked no further than to the two particular cases, in which a freight of ninety-five dollars per ton has appeared to have been the freight stipulated for a similar voyage in Copenhagen about the same time. I cannot suppose that to be the case; on the contrary, knowing their experience in matters of trade, their opportunities of information, and the strict sense which they entertain of their duty to the Court and to the public, I am to suppose that they look abroad on all sides to obtain all possible information that may enable them to do justice between the parties. I consider their report not as an opinion formed only with a reference to those two cases of Mr. De Coninck, but as the result of deliberate inquiries by which they were led to consider this allowance as an adequate freight for such a voyage under all the circumstances that were fairly applicable to it. Affirming the general principle, I shall refer the report back for their reconsideration.

1804 *January* 11.

THE TWILLING RIGET.

Sir W. Scott.

THE NOSTRA SIGNORA DE BEGONA. [5 C. Rob. 97.]

Contraband—Resin—Mercantile Port.

Resin consigned to a mercantile port *held* not contraband.

In this case a question arose respecting the contraband quality of resin going from St. Sebastian to the port of Nantes.

1804 *January* 31.

On the part of the captors the *King's Advocate* contended that it was an article much used as an ingredient in various military preparations, and that it was to be deemed contraband.

Sir W. Scott.—Are there any cases in which this article has been held to be contraband on a destination to a port merely mercantile? If it had been going to a military port of the enemy I should have had no hesitation, as there are many cases in which, under such circumstances, it has been deemed contraband. Going to a mercantile port (*a*), it is not, I think, so decidedly of a warlike nature as to be excluded from the favourable considerations that are applied to other articles *ancipitis usus*. I shall therefore decree restitution.

(*a*) *Santa Bona Ventura.* Resin on board a Portuguese ship to Nantes restored to the owner of the ship. December 12th, 1747. In the ship *Carpenter*, January 24th, 1810, a similar question arose as to brimstone, on appeal from the Vice-Admiralty Court of Malta. The judgment was: "It is not to be understood that brimstone cannot be contraband in any case, but merely that it is not under the circumstances of this case." [2 Acton, 11.]

[5 C. Rob. 128.]

THE JAN FREDERICK.

Capture—Enemy Cargo—Transfer in Contemplation of War—Condemnation.

A transfer of property *in transitu*, before a declaration of war, but in contemplation of war, is invalid (*a*).

1804 March 9. THIS was a question on the legality of a contract made for colonial produce, *in transitu* 10th May, 1803, before the war, but in avowed contemplation of war on the part of the contracting parties.

On the part of the capture, the *King's Advocate* and *Parsons.*—This question relates to a very considerable quantity of colonial produce, in this and in other vessels, shipped as Dutch property on board a Dutch vessel bound to Holland, but purchased *in itinere* by Mr. Jonassen, of Embden, under a contract of the 10th May, 1803.

On the other side, *Arnold* and *Laurence.*

SIR W. SCOTT.—This question arises on parts of several cargoes put on board Dutch ships in January and February, 1803, and brought in under the general embargo on Dutch property previous to hostilities in the month of May. The property is documented for the account and risk of certain estates in Surinam; and certainly, if it was not allowable under any considerations to aver against the evidence of the ships' documents, it must be subject to condemnation as Dutch property. But the Court has opened a door to such claims in opposition to the averment of the ships' papers; and it has done this on a consideration of the fair course of mercantile speculation in time of peace. It has even allowed a change of property *in transitu*, by the transfer of the bills of lading, where it had been done without any view of accommodation to relieve the seller from the pressure or prospect of war. In the present instance, there is no proof of any transfer of the bills of lading, except as to one or two parcels of goods belonging to the

(*a*) See the *Baltica*, Vol. II.

widow Noble, which do indeed bear an endorsement, but whether they were so endorsed before or after the war it does not appear. This alone would be sufficient to defeat the claim; since, till the bill of lading was so endorsed, the contract would, I apprehend, be a thing remaining in covenant only. It might subject the party to an action *damni dati*, but it would not amount to a transfer, being only an engagement that the goods should be transferred when they arrived. That a transfer may take place *in transitu* has, I have already observed, been decided in two or three cases where there had been no actual war, nor any prospect of war, mixing itself with the transaction of the parties. But in time of war this is prohibited as a vicious contract: being a fraud on belligerent rights, not only in the particular transaction, but in the great facility which it would necessarily introduce of evading those rights beyond the possibility of detection. It is a road that in time of war must be shut up; for although honest men might be induced to travel it with very innocent intentions, the far greater proportion of those who passed would use it only for sinister purposes, and with views of fraud on the rights of the belligerent. This, however, is not a contract made in time of war; and therefore an important question is raised, whether the contemplation of war would have the same effect in vitiating these contracts as actual war? It cannot be said that all engagements in the proximity of war, into which the speculation of war might enter, as, for instance, with regard to the price, would therefore be invalid. The contemplation of war is undoubtedly to be taken in a more restricted sense. But if the contemplation of war leads immediately to the transfer, and becomes the foundation of a contract that would not otherwise be entered into on the part of the seller, and this is known to be so done in the understanding of the purchaser, though on his part there may be other concurrent motives, as in the case of the *Rendsborg*, such a contract cannot be held good, on the same principle that applies to invalidate a transfer *in transitu* in time of actual war. The motive may indeed be difficult to be proved, but that will be the difficulty of particular cases. Supposing the fact to be established that it is a sale under an admitted necessity arising from a certain expectation of war, that it is a sale of goods not in the possession of the seller, and in a State where

1804 *March* 9.

THE JAN FREDERICK.

Sir W. Scott.

they could not during war be legally transferred on account of the fraud on belligerent rights, I cannot but think that the same fraud is committed against the belligerent—not, indeed, as an actual belligerent, but as one who was in the clear expectation of both the contracting parties likely to become a belligerent—before the arrival of the property which is made the subject of their agreement. The nature of both contracts is identically the same, being equally to protect the property from capture of war—not, indeed, in either case, from capture at the present moment when the contract is made, but from the danger of capture when it was likely to occur. The object is the same in both instances, to afford a guarantee against the same crisis. In other words, both are done for the purpose of eluding a belligerent right, either present or expected. Both contracts are framed with the same *animo fraudandi*, and are, in my opinion, justly subject to the same rule.

Upon the general ground, also, of guarding against fraud, it appears to me to be equally necessary to apply the same rule to antecedent contracts of this nature. The danger and extent of the mischief to be apprehended is perhaps greater, as it is the only method by which the accumulation of colonial produce could be brought home. It is to be observed also, that the destination is from the colony to the port of the mother country, in which, with the slightest management, a system of protecting the interests of the enemy might be constructed which no vigilance could detect. I am of opinion, therefore, that if the papers and letters which have been produced do sufficiently establish the purpose attributed to the contract—if it is proved to have been built immediately and fundamentally on the contemplation of war on the part of the seller, and that it would not otherwise have fallen into the hands of the purchaser—it is an illegal contract, and must so be held on every ground on which similar contracts in time of war have been held to be invalid.

It remains, then, only to consider the evidence of this fact, though perhaps a preliminary question might not unfairly be raised which would have excluded all other observations, viz., whether in truth this contract was a *bonâ fide* transfer.

[After an examination of the evidence the *Court* concluded.]

But taking it to be a *bonâ fide* contract, yet being formed *in transitu*, for the purpose of withdrawing the property from capture, it does intimately partake of the nature of those contracts which have, in the repeated decisions of this and of the Supreme Court, been pronounced null and invalid; and I pronounce this property subject to condemnation.

1804 *March* 9. THE JAN FREDERICK. Sir W. Scott.

THE WILHELMSBERG.

[5 C. Rob. 142.]

Capture—Prize Act—Duty of Captor—Convenient Port—Damages and Costs.

When a vessel is not taken to a convenient port for adjudication, the captor is liable to be condemned in damages and costs.

1804 *March* 16.

This was a question of costs and damages, owing to the neglect of the captor not bringing the vessel into what could be reasonably termed a convenient port under the Prize Act. (43 Geo. 3, c. 161 (*a*).)

Sir W. Scott.—This ship was seized on a voyage from Amsterdam to Archangel, under a suspicion, I presume, of Dutch property. She was going in ballast to bring a cargo to Amsterdam, and appears to have been very much in the habit of Dutch trade, particularly during the war. On these and other grounds, it could not be fairly denied that there were circumstances to justify the seizure; but the second act of sending the vessel to such a place as Shetland is not so defensible. The Prize Act undoubtedly gives the captor some latitude on this subject: he is directed generally "to send his prize to some convenient port." Shetland cannot, I think, be considered in any manner as such a port. It is a place where the captor cannot get advice; much less can the claimant learn in what manner to proceed, or where to resort for justice. The captor is certainly not justified under the Prize Act to select any port that he pleases. It must be a convenient port, and in that consideration the convenience of the claimant in proceeding to adjudication is among one of the first things to which the attention of the captor ought to be addressed. If the vessel had been sent, in the first instance, to Leith, or Berwick, or to any of the

(*a*) This point is no longer regulated by statute. See Naval Prize Manual, No. 654. (March, 1904, Art. 111.) See also *post*, p. 555.

1804 March 16. THE WILHELMSBERG. Sir W. Scott.

principal northern ports of this kingdom, the consequences that have arisen in this case could not have ensued. The papers were brought in on the 2nd of August, but nothing more was done till the 16th. In the meantime, the vessel was removed to Leith, and on the 23rd of August an offer was made to release. Surely it cannot be maintained that no damage had accrued at this time when the offer was made. The master swears that he could not obtain his papers, and that it was too late in the year to prosecute his voyage to Archangel. The offer, it seems, was rejected on this account, and because there was no reservation of costs and damages, which might very prudently and in most cases very safely be made. I cannot think that the neutral master acted in any manner improperly in declining such an offer, being only told to go about his business, and that he would hear no more of the matter. To release a vessel in this summary manner, without her consent, after she was once brought in, would be contrary to the directions of the Prize Act. Upon the whole, considering that the Court is called upon to beat down and discourage the notion that captors may carry their prize wherever they please, and that the injury sustained in this case has proceeded entirely from that mistake, I shall allow one month's demurrage and the expenses of the present hearing.

[5 C. Rob. 148.]

THE URANIA.

Salvage—Recapture—Non-Commissioned Vessel.

Salvage on recapture can be claimed by a non-commissioned vessel.

1804 May 1.

THIS was a case, on the admission of an allegation of joint recapture on the part of the King's ship, pleading the affidavits of some French sailors who were on board the recaptured ship. The recapture was made by a non-commissioned vessel, and proceedings were first instituted on the part of the Admiralty as for droits of Admiralty, but were discontinued. The *Loyal Briton* afterwards appeared, demanding salvage in her own right.

In support of the allegation, the *King's Advocate* and *Arnold.*—The first point, which appears one of considerable importance, is whether the non-commissioned vessel has any *persona standi* before the Court. In the case of an original capture she could not maintain an interest in prize. In recapture also, which partakes intimately of the nature of prize, the same principle seems equally to bar the non-commissioned person from maintaining a suit for salvage, and it is presumed that no instance can be produced in which such an interest has been pronounced for.

1804 *May* 1. THE URANIA.

Court.—Surely a distinction has been always held in cases of salvage. There must be many cases in which the claims of non-commissioned persons have been allowed for salvage on retaking property out of the hands of the enemy. The words of the Prize Act appear to me clearly to recognise such a practice, which direct salvage to be paid on recapture by his Majesty's ships of war, or any privateer, or other ship or vessel or boat under his Majesty's protection and obedience. Objection over-ruled.

THE ZACHEMAN.

[5 C. Rob. 152.]

Capture—Restitution—Pre-emption—Delay—Payment of Damages by British Government.

When a cargo should have been restored, but the British Government had a right to pre-emption, and delay occurred in the exercise of this right: *Held,* that his Majesty's Government should pay damages in the nature of demurrage.

THIS was a case on the detention of a Swedish ship with a cargo of iron and 1,200 barrels of tar, taken on a voyage from a Swedish port to Rochefort.

1804 *May* 1.

The *King's Advocate* stated that the ship had been offered to be restored, that the cargo being tar consigned to a port of the enemy had been detained for pre-emption, but that the offer was at last declined on the part of government.

On the part of the claimant, *Laurence* stated that the vessel had been taken so long ago as March, that compensation was due for the detention under the second and third articles of the late convention with Sweden.

1804 May 1.

THE ZACHEMAN.

In reply, the *King's Advocate* and *Robinson*.—The captor in this case has done nothing but what was perfectly justifiable. To detain and send in a cargo of tar bound to such a port as Rochefort was an act of duty which he was not at liberty to omit. The very Treaty (*a*) referred to seems to indemnify the captor in this instance, by the distinctions made in the second and third articles, between cargoes of this kind bound to neutral ports and those going to the port of the enemy. In the former case it is provided, "that if a cargo bound to a neutral port is brought in on suspicion of a destination to the port of an enemy, and it afterwards appears that the destination was actually to the neutral port, she shall be restored with compensation, &c." that is, as against the captor. In the next article, the case of such cargoes bound to the port of the enemy is provided for. It is there considered as a case of pre-emption, in the exercise of which the bringing in must be justified as a preparatory step, and if any delay takes place, it is obviously not to be imputed to the captor, who is by that very article of the Convention virtually authorised to bring in such a cargo.

Sir W. Scott.—I have no hesitation in pronouncing that the seizure in this case was perfectly justifiable. In the case of a ship carrying such a cargo as tar to one of the great naval arsenals of the enemy, it was not improper to bring in for inquiry as to the fact of property, whether it was going on the private account of the neutral merchant or under a contract with the government, by which those arsenals are more usually supplied. The captor had therefore a perfect right to have the formal papers verified. In bringing in and taking the depositions, the captors were in my opinion perfectly justifiable. That being done, the effect of this evidence ought to have induced them to consent to restitution. Then comes the question of pre-emption. In the Convention lately entered into, this country has been induced to waive its former right of forfeiture for that of pre-emption, which Sweden has admitted, and I think in terms which do warrant the construction put upon them, in argument, that they justify the bringing in. As to the exercise of the right of pre-emption, if particular orders from

(*a*) 25th July, 1803.

government are necessary, I apprehend that there is some mode in which those orders can be expeditiously obtained. The terms of the treaty seem to relate principally to the time taken in unlivery; but if the ship is detained as a warehouse, under any uncertainty as to the intention of government, the equity of the treaty will, I think, extend also to such detention. The ship was brought in on the 20th of March, the claim was given on the 27th, and on the 31st the offer of restitution was made. Since that time there seems to have been some delay. In the present case, which is perhaps the first that has arisen under the treaty, and one of not the most favourable complexion, I should be unwilling to press these considerations to the utmost; but I wish it to be understood that cases of this description must be conducted with great tenderness to the neutral interest, and that as little time as possible must be lost in deliberation. Some demurrage must be allowed, but not against the captors in this case. I shall allow three weeks demurrage to be paid by his Majesty's Government; and I wish that the Admiralty may be apprised that under the treaty which now exists, matters of this kind must not be kept subject to long negotiation, since it is not less expedient for the purposes of justice than for the interests of all parties concerned that a prompt answer should be returned as to the disposition of government to avail itself of the right of pre-emption.

1804 *May* 1. — THE ZACHEMAN. — Sir W. Scott.

THE ELSEBE.

[5 C. Rob. 173.]

Search—Convoy—Liability of Owner of Cargo on Convoyed Ship—Property of Neutral—Right of Crown to release before Adjudication—Non-consent of Captor.

A neutral owner of cargo is presumed to be bound by the act of the master of a ship who places his vessel under a convoy which subsequently resists search.

The Crown has a right to order the release of a captured vessel before adjudication, since prize is a creature of the Crown, and the captor derives his right by grant from the Crown.

1804 *December* 19.

THIS was a case of considerable importance and delicacy, arising on an order of government for the release of several vessels, being part of the second Swedish convoy, under particular circumstances.

1804 *December* 19. THE ELSEBE. The question made on the part of the captors was whether the Crown had such a power, or rather whether a right and interest in the thing taken did not vest in the captor at the time of seizure under the grant of prize made to captors by the Order of Council, the Proclamation, and the Prize Act, in such a manner as to entitle the captor to proceed to adjudication, notwithstanding an order of release on the part of government.

The question was argued by the *King's Advocate* and *Robinson* on the part of the Crown; by *Laurence* and *Swabey* on the part of the claimant; and by *Arnold* and *Burnaby* for the captor.

SIR W. SCOTT.—This question, which has been very elaborately argued, arises on several Swedish ships with their cargoes, belonging to subjects of other countries and cities, taken under the convoy of a Swedish man-of-war and proceeded against on that ground. Several points have been made on behalf of the owners of the ships and cargoes; one applying to the ships as well as to the cargoes, and two that are peculiar to the cargoes. With respect to them, it is first contended that they belong not to Swedes, but to subjects of the Hanse towns, and that they are not involved in the penalties of Swedish resistance, which was an act of the Swedish Government, and will not bind the subjects of other powers; that the proprietors of the cargoes were not privy to this fact; and that the masters of the vessels were not the agents of the cargoes so as to bind them. This is contended on the same principle that has been adopted by the Court in some blockade cases, where ships, sailing originally in ignorance of the war, and having been warned in their voyage, have nevertheless persisted obstinately in their original destination to the blockaded port. I am of opinion that this defence cannot be set up with effect, since in the only charter-party which has been produced, and which must be taken as produced by the claimants as representatives of the rest, there is an express stipulation that the ship should proceed under convoy. But I will take the case on a supposition that there was no such engagement. The master associates himself with a convoy, the instructions of which he must be supposed to know; he puts the goods under unlawful protection, and it must be presumed that this is done with due authority from the owners and for their benefit.

It is not the case of an unforeseen emergency, happening to the ship at sea, where the fact itself proves the owners to be ignorant and innocent, and where the Court has held, that being proved innocent by the very circumstances of the case, they shall not be bound by the mere principle of law which imposes on the employer a responsibility for the acts of his agent. On the contrary, it is a matter done antecedently to the voyage, and must therefore be presumed to be done on communication with the owners and with their consent; and the effect of this presumption is such that it cannot be permitted to be averred against; inasmuch as all the evidence must come from the suspected parties themselves, without affording a possibility of meeting it, however prepared. The Court has therefore thought it not unreasonable to apply the strict principle of law in a case not entitled to any favour, and holds, as it does in blockade cases of that description, that the master must be taken to be the authorised agent of the cargo, that he has acted under powers from his employer, and that, if he has exceeded his authority, it is barratry, for which he is personally answerable, and for which the owner must look to him for indemnification. I pass over many considerations which have been properly pressed in argument; but I cannot omit to observe that this is not merely a question arising on a single act of limited consequence, it is a pretension of infinite importance and of great extent, being nothing less than an opposition to the general law of search, by which, if it could in one instance be admitted, the whole provisions of the law of nations on that head might be effectually defied; for if this principle could be maintained, by an interchange of convoys the whole unlawful business might be carried on with security. To put the goods of one country on board the ships of another would be a complete recipe for the safety of the goods, with a trifling alteration, easily understood, and easily practised, whilst the mischief itself would exist in full force.

Secondly, it is contended that no grant of prize made by the Crown attaches upon such property as this, because the grant is of property of the King's enemies—that is, of the French and other nations with whom we are at war. But the grant is not so construed and applied. It is held in construction and practice to embrace all property liable to be condemned as prize, and not

1804 December 19. THE ELSEBE. Sir W. Scott.

particularly reserved by the rights of the Crown or of the Admiralty. By fiction, or rather by intendment of law, all property condemned is the property of enemies—that is, of persons so to be considered in the particular transaction; and half the business of this Court is exercised on such property, in determining whether it is not liable to be condemned as prize to the captors. It is therefore a position not seriously to be maintained that the captor's grant does not reach to this extent by the constant course of interpretation authorising such a construction.

These two points being disposed of, which are confined to the cargoes, another of much greater extent, as comprehending both ships and cargoes, and of still greater importance, is suggested to arise upon the facts of this case. As it was a point on which the rights of the Crown were directly involved, I felt it to be my indispensable duty to call on those who are specially entrusted with the defence of the interests of the Crown to assert and vindicate those rights, unless it was the intention either to disclaim them entirely, or at least to waive the exercise of them on the present occasion. When the rights of the Crown were brought forward by the claimant, in a way which it was impossible not to notice, the Court was bound, as every Court would be, to take care that justice was done to them. The rights of the Crown are public rights, conferred not merely for private purposes, or for personal splendour, but for the public service, and to answer the great exigencies of public interest and claims of public justice; as such they demand the active protection of every Court in which the occurrence of them is suggested to arise. The right which is asserted by the claimant, and is denied on the part of the captor, is that of releasing ships and goods that had been taken *jure belli*, before adjudication and without the consent of the captors. I say without consent, because I think I must hold, upon the present evidence, that the captors have not done any act by which they can be considered as communicating their consent.

Before such a question can with propriety be introduced, it must appear that the Crown has actually exercised the power, and that the party has not renounced the benefit of it. For, if the Crown has not exercised it, or if the party has renounced the benefit, the Court would, for obvious reasons, decline to entertain a question of this high nature, without an actual necessity calling for the discussion, and would be glad to dismiss it from further consideration. That the Crown has exercised the power in this instance, is, I think, sufficiently proved, by the solemn evidence of an official letter from the Secretary of State for the Foreign Department to the minister of that country whose subjects were principally interested in the question, informing him that the ships were released, and that orders were given by the Lords of the Admiralty for that purpose. This I apprehend is the regular mode of communication with the ministers of foreign powers; and it must be presumed that what is so communicated, unless disavowed, is the act of the State. It proceeds from those who are the organs of the State towards foreign powers and their representatives, and what they say binds the State unless disavowed. That the order was conveyed immediately through the Admiralty is no objection surely to the validity of the act. The conveyance of the orders is merely the subordinate and instrumental part of the business; and I take the Admiralty to be the proper channel through which the order for release should be transmitted to the captors. But even if there had been some little irregularity in the mode of transmitting such an order, an irregularity such as may and must sometimes occur in the shifting exigencies of the public service, it could in no degree have been considered as vitiating the substance and effect of the thing. Whether the communication had been made by this or that hand signifies nothing; whether it was in writing or in words signifies nothing. The question is, whether it was so directed by the proper authority of the State; had it the seal and impress of that original authority? Through what course that direction travelled, whether by one post or the other, is a matter of small moment, and perfectly immaterial, provided the fact is clear that it proceeded from the State. It is not suggested that the Admiralty did not issue the orders. They are averred to have been procured by the Secretary of State, and are not at this moment disavowed or in any manner receded from on the part of government after the call which the Court has made on the officers of the Crown, for the purpose of knowing in what light they are to be considered. I am bound, I think, to hold the order that has been called in question to have proceeded from sufficient authority, and to stand at this moment unrevoked.

1804 December 19. THE ELSEBE. Sir W. Scott.

The next ground that has been taken is, that the party had not accepted the release; and if this had been shown, it would, I think, have been sufficient to defeat the effect of the order. It would undoubtedly have been competent to the claimant to have said, "the restitution is defective; I will not accept it, but will go to the Courts of Justice to obtain a more ample compensation." Without imputing to the Crown an injustice, which is not to be imagined, it cannot be conceived that the party would have been denied his resort to a Court of Justice, which sits principally to enforce the rights arising from the law of nations. If he had appealed from the government to the Court of legal redress, the Court must have received the complaint and have proceeded to an ultimate determination on the quantum of the grievance alleged; and by such a conduct the party might fairly have been considered to have waived the benefit of a partial release. But I find nothing of the kind. The letter which the claimant wrote on the occasion has been very properly described to be written in most respectful terms. It is a letter of grateful acceptance, appealing only to the equitable consideration of government for some further compensation on grounds therein stated, but it contains no appeal to the Court, no declining of the offer made by government. On the contrary, it is rather to be taken as a total relinquishment of all legal remedy, as a statement of their case in a style of political negotiation merely, and containing nothing that can with any propriety be deemed a waiver of the release then offered. Something has been said of the lapse of time that had intervened before the papers were brought to the notice of the Court. It has been great; but I cannot blot out of my remembrance the important transactions to which this matter has, at least in some degree, given birth. Many years of negotiation—I am sorry to add, some months of actual hostility—passed before this question was happily adjusted by a convention. During that period nothing was done in this Court. When the general question was settled prospectively between the parties, the question came forward with respect to the fleet of which these vessels composed a part. Whilst the question respecting the whole fleet was under discussion, these ships had a right to stand on the general ground of defence as long as it might possibly be determined in their favour. They might feel it their duty so to do, in order that they might not prejudice the rights of the other ships associated with them. Having so done and failed, they have now a right to resort to the benefit of the order which applied to them exclusively, and to call upon the officers of the Crown either to admit and avow these papers or to contradict and renounce them. On this part of the case I feel myself bound to say that the order is sufficiently authenticated; that the Crown does not disavow it; and that I must consider the case as subject to the effect of the order, whatever that may legally be, for the release of this property.

The facts then being completely established, the question of right arises, how far the Crown can release at any time before adjudication without consent of the captors? It is an important question connected with most momentous consequences. No reflecting man can approach it without feeling that he has to weigh a matter of extreme delicacy, though perhaps not of equal difficulty. Be the delicacy or the difficulty what it may, however, it will be the duty of the Court to meet with firmness any exigencies which the administration of justice may impose upon it.

It is admitted on the part of the captors, whose interests have been argued with great force (and not the less effective, surely, for the extreme decorum with which that force has been tempered), that their claim rests wholly on the Order of Council, the Proclamation, and the Prize Act. It is not (as it cannot be) denied that, independent of these instruments, the whole subject-matter is in the hands of the Crown, as well in point of interest as in point of authority. Prize is altogether a creature of the Crown. No man has, or can have, any interest but what he takes as the mere gift of the Crown. Beyond the extent of that gift he has nothing. This is the principle of law on the subject, and founded on the wisest reasons. The right of making war and peace is exclusively in the Crown. The acquisitions of war belong to the Crown; and the disposal of these acquisitions may be of the utmost importance for the purposes both of war and peace. This is no peculiar doctrine of our constitution; it is universally received as a necessary principle of public jurisprudence by all writers on the subject, *bello parta cedunt reipublicæ*. It is not to be supposed that this wise attribute of sovereignty is conferred without reason; it is given for the purpose assigned, that the power to whom it belongs

1804 *December* 19. THE ELSEBE. Sir W. Scott.

to decide on peace or war may use it in the most beneficial manner for the purposes of both. A general presumption arising from these considerations is, that government does not mean to divest itself of this universal attribute of sovereignty, conferred for such purposes, unless it is so clearly and unequivocally expressed. In conjunction with this universal presumption must be taken also the wise policy of our own peculiar law, which interprets the grants of the Crown in this respect by other rules than those which are applied in the construction of the grants of individuals. Against an individual, it is presumed that he meant to convey a benefit with the utmost liberality that his words will bear. It is indifferent to the public in which person an interest remains, whether in the grantor or the taker. With regard to the grant of the sovereign it is far otherwise. It is not held by the sovereign himself as private property; and no alienation shall be presumed, except that which is clearly and indisputably expressed.

With these rules of interpretation the title deeds of the captors must be considered, to determine whether the Crown has in these deeds renounced that power, which in principle it possesses, and in practice has frequently exercised. If there is anything which can be supposed to produce that effect, it must be the conveyance of a right of some species or other to other persons, and these can be no other than the captors, in virtue of which they claim an indefeasible interest in prize once taken. The right contended for is a right to seize and bring to adjudication all ships of the enemy. Does the right to seize, thus generally given, alone bind the Crown, so as to bar it from any further exercise of its power with respect to seizures? Certainly not; for after that right is given to seize all ships of the enemy, the Crown can exempt as it sees fit. The Crown, which declares general hostilities, can limit their operation. It can except individuals; it grants particular passes; it exempts particular classes of the enemy's ships, notwithstanding the right thus given of seizing all ships. If, then, the right of seizing all ships thus generally given does not bind the Crown in its power of qualifying that right by subsequent modifications, on what ground is it contended that the exercise of its power with respect to proceeding to adjudication is barred by the mere act of seizure? The mere act of seizure surely cannot work any such effect; it is an act in itself in some degree always dubious till adjudication, and possibly erroneous; yet this dubious act is to convey to the party a right indefeasible to proceed to adjudication, when the very proceeding may be a further wrong done, an aggravation of costs and damages already occasioned by the improper seizure. I attended with great impatience to the able argument of Dr. Arnold to learn what was the specific nature of the right conferred on the captors by the act of seizure, to which the effect of barring the power of the Crown to release is to be attributed. It is admitted to be, in degree, an imperfect right. In species it was stated, if I understand the argument, to be a *jus persequendi*, a right of action, and no more; no right of interest, but a mere right of bringing to adjudication. Whatever is the nature of this right, it is conveyed only in the Order of Council, it is not given in the Proclamation or the Prize Act. It is indeed recited in both as a thing otherwise existing, but it makes no part of the powers conferred in either of those instruments. Now, according to the construction which is in my opinion to be put upon this matter, this *jus persequendi*, as it is called, is not a right conveyed, but a duty enjoined. Captors have generally a right to seize, subject to this duty of bringing to adjudication, a duty enjoined that they may not make seizures without bringing the ships and goods seized to the notice of the proper tribunal, in order to prevent the right of seizure from degenerating into piratical rapine. If the Crown imposes that obligation the Crown can release it. Supposing the Proclamation and Prize Act to be out of the way, and that the matter stood singly upon the Order of Council, there can be no doubt that the Crown could so release. The Crown imposed the obligation, and so far as the Order of Council alone is considered the Crown retains the whole interest. If the prize is condemned, it must be condemned to the Crown and for its interest, for the Order of Council gives no interest to captors. No doubt could exist, supposing the matter to stand on the Order of Council alone, that the Crown is completely *dominus litis*, and also *dominus rei litigatæ*, supposing there is no claim maintainable on the part of any neutral proprietor.

As far as any right to the extent contended for can be supposed to be vested in the captor, then it must be attributed to some enlargement of these rights given by the Order of Council, derived

1804 December 19. THE ELSEBE. Sir W. Scott.

from the Prize Act and Proclamation. Let us consider what this enlargement is. The Proclamation gives the whole property, but not till after adjudication; until that time, no beneficial interest attaches. So the Prize Act in like terms gives the whole interest or property, in opposition to that proportional and partial interest given by former Acts (*a*), but not till adjudication. In adverting to these instruments, it is impossible not to remark the very guarded terms in which the benefit is conferred. The Proclamation gives to privateers "after final adjudication, and not before;" not merely after adjudication, but superadding a negative pregnant, "and not before." With regard to King's ships, the grant is expressed with similar caution; it gives the neat produce of all such prizes taken, the right whereof is inherent in us and our Crown. And, again, "it directs that such prize may be lawfully sold or disposed of, by them and their agents, after the same shall have been to us finally adjudged lawful prize, and not otherwise." What is the use of these guarded expressions; surely, not merely the object of protecting the interests of the claimant till after adjudication? The Crown cannot be supposed to be anxious to make a reservation or exception of that which, without any such exception, would be perfectly safe; for no interest of the Crown or its grantee could divest the interest of the claimant. The reservation must, *ex necessitate rei, ex defectu alicujus alterius materiæ*, apply to rights over which the Crown has a dominion, and which, unless reserved, it might be supposed to have granted away. What are these rights? The right of controlling the whole proceeding till final adjudication; the right of declaring that the party shall not be further proceeded against as an enemy;

(*a*) Before the statute 6 Anne, c. 37, which first gave to the captors the whole or sole benefit, as it is there termed, and which has been continued in the several Prize Acts passed since that time, the statute 4 & 5 William & Mary had given to privateers four-fifths of the cargo, and the whole of the vessels; and to king's ships, one-third. This statute had regulated the practice till the conclusion of that war, which happened in 1697. On the breaking out of the ensuing war against France, a proclamation issued, 1st June, 1702, giving to her Majesty's ships half, and to privateers the whole benefit of prize; but no general parliamentary regulation during that war appears to have passed on the subject prior to the statute 6 Anne, in 1708.

the right of suspending hostility against him with regard to property which has been seized under the general order of reprisals. For such purposes, and such purposes only, it must be that the Crown has declared that, till after adjudication, the captor has no interest which the Court can properly notice for any legal effect whatsoever. In the case of captures made by the King's own ships, the authority of the Crown is most marked upon the face and in the substance of every part of the proceedings in the most emphatical manner. The Crown officers are the prosecutors, in the name of the Crown; the final adjudication, under the very terms of the Act, is a condemnation to the Crown, and most clearly the interest would vest in the Crown under that condemnation, if the Act had not expressly superadded that it should enure to the benefit of the captor. In seizures made by private ships of war, the hand of the sovereign authority is less visible in the mode and style of proceeding; but the right of the Crown is sufficiently guarded by the repeated declarations that the interest shall vest in such captors "after final adjudication," and not before.

So much upon principle! How stands the matter as to practice? The practice, I conceive, has been unquestioned, for the Crown to direct the release of ships before final adjudication. The instances are not, indeed, very numerous, because it is not to be supposed that the occasions for the exercise of such an act of authority would be very frequent. I cannot but think, however, that an expression which is reported to have fallen from Lord Mansfield in a case (*a*) relating to the insurable interest of captors (of which case I have been favoured with a note from a noble person, who was himself of counsel in the cause), namely, "that the Crown does not interfere," must have been founded in some error of the fact. Such instances will appear less numerous, because the fact that they have been so released is not necessarily, nor very distinctly, entered in the books. All that appears is, that the proctor then proceeding for the Crown, as he must do, declares that he proceeds no further; on which the Court issues an order of restitution as a matter of course and of necessity; for what party can interpose and pray a condemnation to the Crown when the Crown has

(*a*) *Lecras* v. *Hughes*.

1804 December 19. THE ELSEBE. Sir W. Scott.

declared that it prays no such a thing, but consents to the restitution. I take this, therefore, to be the first case in which the effect of such a consent on the part of the Crown has been called in question. I do not mean to intimate that it has been in any degree improper to take the opinion of the Court upon this question, more particularly in the very decorous manner in which the application has been urged. But I must say, that when it is alleged that all former cases have passed by consent, the fact itself, that the power was not questioned in these cases, affords a strong proof that the power was considered as unquestionable; and I must add, that though I have suffered a party to stand before the Court for the purpose of arguing the question, I do not know the party who can legally stand before it, praying a condemnation to the Crown which the Crown itself publicly renounces.

It will not be necessary for me to travel over instances (*a*); they have been cited in the argument; but I will appeal to the judgment

(*a*) Modern instances cited, as subsequent to the regular grant of the whole benefit of prize to the captor by Act of Parliament, in 1708, were the *Freya* (29th July, 1800), the leading case of a Danish convoy brought in, but restored by negotiation with government; the *St. Johannes*, one of the first Swedish (1798) convoy, released by the captor under an order from the Lords of the Admiralty; the *Edwin* (November, 1801), an American vessel which had sailed for the port of Havre with other American ships, in 1801, under some misunderstanding as to the blockade of Havre, and was released in consequence of a letter of 24th November, 1801, from Lord Hawkesbury, directed to the King's Advocate, "stating the special circumstances which had led to an ignorance of the blockade on the part of the Americans, and expressing his Majesty's pleasure that all the rights and interests which may belong to him in such captured vessels and cargoes, shall be given up and released."

More ancient instances, prior to the Prize Act of 1708, were an Order of Council, 1705, for the release of certain Dutch ships seized and brought in for trading with the common enemy. The *Salvador*, 31st August, 1704, on which there was an Order of Council addressed to her Majesty's Advocate for the release of certain Swedish ships which had been captured under a Swedish convoy after a contest between the Swedish man-of-war and Admiral Whetstone. 15th August, 1689, an Order of Council for the release of certain Danish ships. 23rd September, 1609, an order for the release of certain Portuguese ships. 27th July, 1589, an Order of Council communicated to the Court of Admiralty for its direction in proceeding against the ships and contraband cargoes of the Hanse towns going to Spain, and seized by Queen Elizabeth. (Collectanea Maritima, p. 163, note.)

of every person of any experience in these Courts, whether a doubt ever existed on the subject in any man's mind till it was excited by, I will not say a dictum, but by an interrogatory or question of a noble and reverend person in the argument upon the *St. Jago*. It will not be supposed that I mean to treat the memory of that eminent person with the slightest disrespect, when I say that it was an unexamined and unweighed dictum in that particular case, and upon a subject not generally familiar to his most excellent understanding. I cannot think that he himself would have regarded such an hasty excursion of his mind as that which he would deliberately have followed if he had been called upon to apply himself to the serious discussion of such a point. To this dictum, be its authority what it may, I must oppose that of his predecessor to which I have already adverted, "that the Crown does not interfere," because it would be nugatory to speak of not interfering if the right was altogether denied to exist. As to the practice of this Court, it has undoubtedly not been guided by the opinion intimated in that dictum of Lord Kenyon. On the contrary, the same measure has been adopted in the cases cited in argument, the *Johannes*, the *Freya*, and the *Havre* cases; in all which the Court conceived itself to be doing no more than its duty in obeying the order for release. It is true that the captors did not oppose in those instances; but I have already stated the grounds on which I conceive that they could not have been heard by the Court in an effectual support of any such opposition. There is, besides, one class of cases from which we may, I think, infer that such a power must be supposed to exist in the Crown, I mean cases (*a*) of restitution at the close of a war. It is a frequent practice to stipulate in the preliminary articles of peace for a cessation (*a*) of hostilities at certain times, in different latitudes, and for the restitution of property taken afterwards; and this as well within as beyond the period assigned for the ratification of the preliminary articles themselves. The same provision is after-

(*a*) *Adolphus Frederick*, captured 2nd May, 1748, proclamation, 5th May, announcing the cessation of hostilities in the Channel from twelve days after the 19th April, 1748, being the date of the signature of the preliminary articles of the peace of Aix la Chapelle—restored by decree of Court, 17th May, 1748.

1804 December 19. THE ELSEBE. Sir W. Scott.

wards inserted in the definitive treaty. In matters of treaty, it is true, the act of ratification may be said to operate with retrospective effect to confirm the terms of the treaty from the date of the preliminary articles. But it is not easy to conceive a power lodged in the prerogative of the Crown to secure that retrospective effect to the conclusion of a treaty, without supposing also a corresponding power over the acts of its own subjects to supersede the intermediate events of war, and to annul captures, rightly made, up to the moment of ratification under the only known rule of action then promulged and communicated to cruisers for the government of their conduct.

Something has been said of the hardship which captors may sustain if they are to be held liable to costs and damages, and are at the same time denied the power of proceeding to adjudication; and, to be sure, nothing could be more unjust than to leave the captor at the mercy of the claimant for costs and damages by taking from him the power of justifying the seizure. But to this objection I think two answers may be given, either of which removes the possibility of such injustice, even if the fact could be supposed (which cannot be supposed without the most extravagant indecency) that the Crown in the transaction had left its officer totally unprotected: first, that after acceptance of such an extra-judicial release, the claimant would no longer be competent to proceed against the captor, the act of acceptance would be considered as a waiver of his judicial remedy, as a total release on the one side and on the other; and if the captor was to appear under protest, alleging that the claimant had accepted such an extra-judicial release, I cannot but think that the Court would pronounce the protest to be well founded, and dismiss him from any further responsibility; or, secondly, if the Court did not overrule the protest, it surely would not deny the captor his right to proceed, not indeed for the adjudication of any prize interest under the seizure, but for all purposes of justification.

To considerations of public policy upon such a question I decline to advert at any length, for two reasons: one is, because my judgment must be formed on grounds of another species—on the legal construction of the Order of Council, the Proclamation, and the Act of Parliament. If those have in fact taken away the right of the Crown against the public interest, be the consequences ever so mischievous, the remedy must be sought not in erroneous judgments here, but in wise legislative provisions elsewhere. Another reason is, that the considerations of public policy are too vast and too obvious not to present themselves to every man's imagination. When I state the position contended for on the part of the captors to be in effect this, that it shall be in the power of every man who has made a capture, of the pettiest commander of the pettiest privateer, to force on, in spite of all the prudence of the Crown opposed to such an attempt, the discussion and decision of the most delicate questions, the discussion and decision of which may involve the country in the most ruinous hostilities, I state a proposition that must awaken the apprehension of every man who hears me as to the extent of the danger which would attend the establishment of such a principle. It has been stated, and truly stated, that great encouragement is due to the navy of this kingdom. I feel this, I hope, in its full extent, and I can have no doubt that it is still more sensibly felt by the government of this country; but I must presume that, in estimating duly the weight of that consideration in any particular cases, the government will likewise estimate the weight of other public considerations which in those particular cases may happen to be still more urgent and more important, high and important as that consideration unquestionably is.

On the whole case, I am of opinion that all principles of law, all forms of law, all considerations of public policy, concur to support the right of release prior to adjudication, which I must pronounce to be still inherent in the Crown. It is with peculiar satisfaction of mind that I reflect, that if I have erred in forming this opinion, the law has provided more ways than one in which the effect of the infirmity of my judgment may be repaired, to the relief of the parties who feel themselves aggrieved by it.

[5 C. Rob. 218.]

THE TOBAGO.

Bottomry—Enemy Ship—Capture—Restitution.

The Prize Court does not recognize liens on an enemy vessel, and therefore cannot decree restitution to a British holder of a bottomry bond on an enemy ship of his interest in such ship.

1804 *May* 30.

THIS was a case of a claim on behalf of A. B., a British merchant, for the interest of a bottomry bond executed to him by the master of the ship, being a French vessel, previous to hostilities.

Against the demand, the *King's Advocate* and *Robinson.*

On the other side, *Laurence* and *Adams.*

SIR W. SCOTT.—The integrity of this transaction is not impeached, but I am called upon to consider whether the Court can, consistently with the principles of law that govern its practice, afford relief. It is a case of a bottomry bond given fairly in time of peace, without any view of infringing the rights of war, to relieve a ship in distress—a contract certainly regarded with great attention and tenderness by this Court when brought immediately before it. But can the Court recognize bonds of this kind as titles of property, so as to give persons a right to stand in judgment, and demand restitution of such interests in a Court of Prize? The total silence of those who have argued for the claimant as to any precedents for this demand, strongly shows that it has not been the practice of the Court to consider such bonds as property entitled to its protection; and I think I may venture to say that there has been no such instance. The person advancing money on bonds of this nature acquires by that act no property in the vessel; he acquires the *jus in rem*, but not the *jus in re*, until it has been converted and appropriated by the final process of a court of justice. The property of the vessel continues in the former proprietor, who has given a right of action against it, but nothing more. If there is no change of property, there can be no change of national character. Those lending money on such security take this security subject to all the chances incident to it, and, amóngst the rest, the chances of war. But it is said that the captor takes *cum onere;* and therefore that this obligation would devolve upon him. That he is held to take *cum onere* is undoubtedly true, as a rule which is to be understood to apply where the onus is immediately and visibly incumbent upon it. A captor who takes the cargo of an enemy on board the ship of a friend, takes it liable to the freight due to the owner of the ship, because the owner of the ship has the cargo in his possession, subject to that demand by the general law, independent of all contract. By that law he is not bound to part with it but on payment of freight; he being in possession can detain it by his own authority, and wants not the aid of any Court for that purpose. These are all characters of the *jus in re*—of an interest directly and visibly residing in the substance of the thing itself. But it is a proposition of a much wider extent which affirms that a mere right of action is entitled to the same favourable consideration in its transfer from the neutral to a captor. It is very obvious that claims of such a nature may be so framed as that no powers belonging to this Court can enable it to examine them with effect. They are private contracts passing between parties who may have an interest in colluding; the captor has no access whatever to the original private understanding of the parties in forming such contracts, and it is therefore unfit that he should be affected by them. His rights of capture act upon the property, without regard to secret liens possessed by third parties. In like manner his rights operate on no such liens where the property itself is protected from capture; indeed it would be almost impossible for the captor to discover such liens in the possession of the enemy upon property belonging to a neutral. The consequence, therefore, of allowing generally the privilege here claimed would be that the captor would be subject to the disadvantage of having neutral liens set up to defeat his claims upon hostile property, whilst he could never entitle himself to any advantage from hostile liens upon neutral property. This Court therefore excludes all consideration of liens or incumbrances of this species. On the whole, I am of opinion that there is no instance in which the Court has recognized bonds of this kind as titles of property, and that they are not entitled to be recognized as such in the Prize Court, however much the Court of Admiralty may be disposed to uphold them in the other branch of its jurisdiction when they are brought directly before it.

[5 C. Rob. 232.]

THE CATHARINA ELIZABETH.

Rescue—Neutral or Belligerent Master—Effect on Cargo.

If a master of a neutral ship attempts a rescue, he thereby renders the cargo liable to condemnation. But it is otherwise in the case of a master of an enemy ship having on board a neutral cargo (*a*).

1804 *June* 12.

THIS was a case of a claim for goods as American property on board a French vessel, against which it had been contended, amongst other arguments on the proof of property, that there had been a resistance on the part of the master that would expose the whole cargo entrusted to his management to condemnation.

SIR W. SCOTT.—The circumstances of this case cannot, I think, be taken to raise the question respecting the rescue. The ship was a French vessel and the master a Frenchman, therefore be his conduct what it may, it would be the conduct of an enemy and not of a neutral master. The documents are in some parts defective, and may on that account justify a call for further proof; but beyond this, that there is any ground for condemnation of the cargo in the conduct of the master cannot be maintained. It could only be the hostile act of a hostile person who was prisoner of war, and who, unless under parole, had a perfect right to attempt to emancipate himself by seizing his own vessel. If a neutral master attempts a rescue he violates a duty which is imposed upon him by the law of nations, to submit to come in for inquiry as to the property of the ship or cargo, and if he violates that obligation by a recurrence to force the consequence will undoubtedly reach the property of his owner, and it would, I think, extend also to the confiscation of the whole cargo entrusted to his care and thus fraudulently attempted to be withdrawn from the rights of war. With an enemy master the case is very different. No duty is violated by such an act on his part—*lupum auribus teneo*, and if he can withdraw himself, he has a right so to do. But a material fact in this case is, that the master did not attempt to withdraw this property; he seized the ship of the captor, and not

(*a*) See the *Fanny*, Vol. II.

this vessel. The case being clear, then, of that question, as to the rescue, it is merely a case for further proof, and if the goods are shown to be American property, they must be restored. 1804 *June* 12. THE CATHARINA ELIZABETH. Sir W. Scott.

THE BOEDES LUST.

[5 C. Rob. 233.]

Embargo—Seizure—Retroactive Effect of Hostilities—Enemy a British Subject at Time of Adjudication—Condemnation.

An embargo is a provisional seizure, and if hostilities are declared after such seizure, enemy's property so seized is liable to condemnation even if at the time of adjudication such former enemy has become a British subject.

Possession of the soil impresses on the owner the character of the country.

THIS was the case of a claim given for property belonging to persons resident at Demerara, on a suggestion that they were at the time of seizure and of adjudication not enemies of the Crown of Great Britain. 1804 *July* 24.

This property was shipped in January and February, 1804, and was seized 19th May, 1804, after the order for the detention and seizure of all Dutch property, and a month before the declaration of war against Holland. At the time of adjudication the owners, as other inhabitants of Demerara, had become British subjects.

SIR W. SCOTT.—This case comes on upon the claims of persons resident in Demerara before the war, and at the time of capture, and I cannot but say that I am glad that the question has been raised, since it may have the effect of putting an end to much uncertainty on the part of persons who, on various grounds, may think themselves entitled to more favourable considerations than the rules of law prescribe for ordinary cases. The claim is given for several persons as inhabitants of Demerara, not settling there during the time of British possession, nor averring an intention of retiring when that possession ceased. They are therefore to be treated under this general view as Dutch subjects (*a*), unless it

(*a*) In the *Phœnix* (Nov. 2, 1803), a claim on behalf of neutrals for the produce of their property in the Dutch colony of Surinam, Lord Stowell said: "Nothing can be more decided and fixed as the principle of this Court, and of the Supreme Court, than that the possession of the soil does impress upon the owner the character of the country, as far as [5 C. Rob. 20.]

1804 *July* 24.

THE BOEDES LUST.

Sir W. Scott.

can be shown that there are any other circumstances by which they are protected. It is contended that the property was taken in a state of peace, and that the proprietors are now become British subjects, and consequently that this property could not be considered as the property of an enemy, either at the time of capture or adjudication. Now with respect to the first of these pleas, it must be admitted, that alone would not protect them, because the Court has, without any exception, condemned all other property of Dutchmen taken before the war, and upon what ground? That the declaration had a retroactive effect, applying to all property previously detained, and rendering it liable to be considered as the property of enemies taken in time of war. This property was seized provisionally, an act itself hostile enough in the mere execution, but equivocal as to the effect and liable to be varied by subsequent events, and by the conduct of the government of Holland. If that conduct had been such as to re-establish the relations of peace, then the seizure, although made with the character of a hostile seizure, would have proved in the event a mere embargo or temporary sequestration. The property would have been restored, as it is usual at the conclusion of embargoes—a process often resorted to in the practice of nations for various causes not immediately connected with any expectations of hostility. During the period that this embargo lasted, it is said that the Court might have restored, but I cannot assent to that observation, because, on due notice of embargoes, this Court is bound to enforce them. It would be a high misprision in this Court to break them by re-delivery of possession to the foreign owner of that property, which the Crown had directed to be seized and detained for further orders. The Court, acting in pursuance of the general orders of the State, and bound by those general orders, would be guilty of no denial of justice in refusing to decree restitution in such a case, for it has not the power to restore. Its functions are suspended by a binding authority, and if any injustice is done, that is an account to be settled between the States. The Court has no responsibility, for it has no ability to act.

the produce of that plantation is concerned, in its transportation to any other country, whatever the local residence of the owner may be. This has been so repeatedly decided, both in this and in the superior Court, that it is no longer open to discussion."

This was the state of the first seizure. It was at first equivocal, and if the matter in dispute had terminated in reconciliation, the seizure would have been converted into a mere civil embargo, so terminated. That would have been the retroactive effect of that course of circumstances. On the contrary, if the transactions end in hostility, the retroactive effect is directly the other way. It impresses the direct hostile character upon the original seizure. It is declared to be no embargo; it is no longer an equivocal act subject to two interpretations; there is a declaration of the *animus* by which it was done, that it was done *hostili animo*, and is to be considered as an hostile measure *ab initio*. The property taken is liable to be used as the property of persons trespassers *ab initio* and guilty of injuries, which they have refused to redeem by any amicable alteration of their measures. This is the necessary course, if no particular compact intervenes for the restitution of such property taken before a formal declaration of hostilities. No such convention is set up on either side, and the State, by directing proceedings against this property for condemnation, has signified a contrary intention. Accordingly the general mass of Dutch property has been condemned on this retroactive effect; and this property stands upon the same footing as to the seizure, for it was seized at the same time and with the same intent. There is no ground of distinguishing the time of seizure between these claims and former cases of a similar nature; it was a provisional seizure in all, declared to be hostile by subsequent events, acting in a reflex manner upon all the property then seized, and declaring it to be all enemy's property, unless some circumstances can be shown to take these particular claims out of the common operation.

At the time of the declaration of hostilities, then, this property stood exactly on the common footing; and the result of any proceeding then pronounced must have been a sentence of condemnation. It lay open to the same legal conclusion at that time, but the Settlement has since surrendered to the British arms, and the parties are become British subjects; and this, it is said, takes off the hostile effect, although it might have attached. This argument, to be effective, must be put in one of these two ways—either that the condemnation pronounced upon Dutch property went upon the ground that, though seized in time of neutrality, it could not be restored, only because the parties were not now in a condition to receive it; or else, that though seized at a time that may to some effects be considered as time of war, yet the subjects, having become friends, are entitled to restitution. This latter position cannot be maintained for a moment. It is contradicted by all experience and practice, even in the case of those who had an original British character. In the case of Mr. Whitehead, who had but just set his foot on the colony of an enemy for a few hours, but was proved to have gone there for the purpose of settling, his property was condemned, although at the time of adjudication he was again become a British subject, by the surrender of St. Eustatius to the British forces; and where property is taken in a state of hostility the universal practice has ever been to hold it subject to condemnation, although the claimants may have become friends and subjects prior to the adjudication. The plea of having again become British subjects, therefore, will not relieve them, and the other ground must be resorted to. That is equally untenable in point of fact; for the condemnation of the other Dutch property proceeded on no such ground as the mere incapacity of the proprietors to receive restitution. It proceeded on the other ground, which I have before mentioned, the retroactive effect of the declaration, which rendered their property liable to be treated as the property of enemies at the time of seizure. The reasonings of the Court have been founded upon that principle. Property is, indeed, frequently condemned upon the other ground of incapacity to claim, where it is accidentally found in British possession before the breaking out of hostilities; but where it is seized by an order of State, acting provisionally in contemplation of hostilities, the declaration produces something more than a prospective, future, personal incapacity to claim. It decides upon the character of the property already seized, and on the nature and quality of the seizure. I am of opinion, therefore, that when it is assumed that the capture is legally to be considered as made in time of peace, the argument legally fails, because in all legal view of the matter, it is taken in hostility; it is rendered enemy's property at the time of seizure by the necessary and general retroaction of the subsequent declaration of hostilities. The whole foundation of the argument, therefore, is defective in the fact. We distinguish, it is true, as between the different interests to which such prize enures, whether it is taken before or after the declaration. That is a matter of subsequent and domestic regulation, but not influencing the general question of prize. If I am right in this opinion, it is quite unnecessary to discuss many questions which have entered into the debate; whether the description of property comes within the periods of the test affidavit or not will be perfectly immaterial. Nothing is more clear to my apprehension than that the reference to those periods is not prescribed as the constituent and the distinguishing qualification of property, but merely for the purpose of ascertaining a clearer view of the general facts respecting that property. For instance, as to the first periods, the time of shipment, nobody can suppose that the time of shipment can be there introduced for any other purpose than that of bringing out the whole detail of facts, it being perfectly clear that it is in no degree necessary that it should be enemy's property at the time of shipment to subject it to condemnation. It is equally immaterial to look to the style of the sentence, for that has accommodated itself according to the discretion of the Court to correspond with the facts. The Court is under no necessity of referring to any period of time in the descriptive language applying to the property or to the parties. If the Court is legally satisfied that it is liable to be condemned as enemy's property, there is no occasion to express in the construction of the sentence the particular time at which the liability attached.

With as little effect can it be contended that a postliminium can be attributed to these parties. Here is no return to the original character, on which only a *jus postliminii* can be raised. The original character, at the time of seizure and immediately prior to the hostility which has intervened, was Dutch. The present character which the events of war have produced, is that of British subjects; and though the British subject might under circumstances acquire the *jus postliminii* upon the resumption of his native character, it never can be considered that the same privilege accrues upon the acquisition of a character totally new and foreign. As to more popular topics to which recourse has been had, I shall leave them to their operation in that quarter, where only they can have a proper effect. It is my duty, in the present case, to apply

1804 July 24. — The Boedes Lust. — Sir W. Scott.

the principles of a law not very lenient. How far it may be proper to relax the rigour of such an application will be best considered by those who have more latitude of judgment, as well as a wider sphere of political information and knowledge. It may be fit in that ultimate and superior consideration to refer still further back to the former condition of the claimants as British subjects during a considerable period of the late war, and down to a time but shortly antecedent to the shipment of these goods. It may be fit to look to the affections and dispositions of the colony, though every surrender of war must be legally considered as the effect of mere force. It may be fit to consider that the property belongs to those who are now entitled to the character of British subjects. These considerations may have their separate or their united influence upon that ultimate judgment to which the law refers the disposal of property captured prior to hostilities. They could only mislead me from the execution of my duty, which is simply to pronounce that the property at the time of the capture belonged to subjects of the Batavian Republic, and is as such, or otherwise, liable to confiscation.

[5 C. Rob. 251.]

THE ABBY.

Trade with Enemy—Act and Intention.

In order to constitute a trade with an enemy there must be an actual trading as well as an intention so to do; therefore when an enemy's colony became a British colony before the sailing of a ship which was captured on her voyage to such colony: *Held,* she was not liable to be condemned.

1804 July 26.

This was a case of a ship belonging to Mr. Dawson, a British subject, that had sailed from Liverpool to the coast of Africa on the 11th September, 1795, with an ulterior destination to the island of Demerara. On the voyage to the West Indies she was captured and carried into Martinique, and proceeded against, first in the Prize Court, but afterwards by libel in the Revenue Court of Admiralty for a violation of the Navigation Laws. On this proceeding the vessel was condemned. On appeal it was found that the Vice-Admiralty Court of Martinique had no jurisdiction over an offence committed in violation of the revenue laws in another island; but at the time when the cause would have been remitted to await the issue of the prize proceedings that had been instituted, the Vice-Admiralty Court of Martinique was abolished. The cause was now brought to the High Court of Admiralty on a suggestion that the ship was subject to condemnation in the Prize Court as a British ship taken in a trade with the colony of the enemy.

SIR W. SCOTT.—The question arises on the property of Mr. Dawson, who fitted out this vessel for a voyage to Africa, there to barter her cargo for slaves and then to carry them to the island of Demerara, at that time a Dutch colony. The vessel sailed on the 11th of September, 1795. At that time, and until the declaration of hostilities, which issued on the 16th of that month, Demerara could not be considered as the colony of the enemy; it would be impossible for me to say, therefore, that it was an illegal trade at that time as a trade to the colony of the enemy, because there was no state of hostility. The order for the detention of Dutch property had passed indeed, but that was an equivocal act which might terminate amicably, and cannot be taken as fixing on the party an intention of trading with a declared enemy. Soon after the sailing of the vessel, the declaration of hostilities took place, viz., on the 16th of September, 1795; and if the ship had been taken on a voyage to a colony now become an enemy, the Court would have required it to be shown that due diligence had been used to alter the voyage, and to exonerate the claimant from the charge of an illegal trading with the enemy. The vessel sailed from the coast of Africa in May, 1796, and was taken off the island of Demerara after the surrender of that island to the British forces, and carried to Martinique. There the proceedings were first instituted in the Prize Court, though it does not clearly appear on what grounds. During those proceedings a libel was given, as in a revenue cause, the prize suit was suspended, and the ship was condemned for a breach of the revenue laws. The case came up on appeal before the Privy Council, where it was found that the former proceedings in Martinique were a nullity, as the Vice-Admiralty Court of that island had no jurisdiction over a

1804 July 26. THE ABBY. Sir W. Scott.

breach of the revenue laws committed in another colony. The regular mode would then have been to have sent back the cause to the Prize Court where proceedings had first been instituted, but that Court was annihilated. The case was therefore brought before this Court, as it has been done in two or three instances (*a*) of a similar nature, where it has become necessary to carry into effect the proceedings of Vice-Admiralty Courts that have been abolished. It is now objected to the claim that the party has stated himself out of court on two grounds: first, on the ground of trading with the enemy if Demerara was a Dutch colony, and on the ground of an illegal importation, if that island was to be considered as a British settlement. With regard to the first objection, I conceive that there must be an act of trading to the enemy country, as well as the intention. There must be, if I may so speak, a legal as well as a moral illegality. If a man fires a gun at sea, intending to kill an Englishman, which would be legal murder, and by accident does not kill an Englishman, but an enemy, the moral guilt is the same, but the legal effect is different. The accident has turned up in his favour—the criminal act intended has not been committed, and the man is innocent of the legal offence. So, if the intent was to trade with an enemy (which, I have already observed, cannot be ascribed to the party at the commencement of the voyage, when hostilities were not yet declared), but at the time of carrying the design into effect the person is become not an enemy, the intention here wants the *corpus delicti*. No case has been produced in which a mere intention to trade with the enemy's country, contradicted by the fact of its not being an enemy's country, has enured to condemnation. Where a country is known to be hostile, the commencement of a voyage towards that country may be a sufficient act of illegality; but where the voyage is undertaken without that knowledge, the subsequent event of hostility will have no such effect. On principle, I am of opinion that the party is free from the charge of illegal trading.

(*a*) The *Picimento*, *ante*, p. 406.

THE ADONIS.

[5 C. Rob. 256.]

Blockade—Fraud of Master on Belligerent—Liability of Cargo Owner.

The conduct of a master in endeavouring to run a blockade presumptively binds the owner of cargo, and where a blockade was known to such owner at the time of shipment, the presumption was held to be conclusive.

1804 *September* 4, 6; affirmed *July* 11, 1807.

THIS was a case respecting a vessel captured on the 13th July, standing towards Havre, east south-east of Cape Barfleur, after having been warned by one of the blockading frigates that Havre was under blockade. The excuse offered on the part of the master was that the mate had asserted the land to be English land, that the master was doubtful as to that fact, and for the purpose of ascertaining it had continued his course towards the land.

The *Court* in the first instance gave judgment on the facts, concluding—The excuse set up is incredible in itself, and is practically inconsistent with the maintenance of the blockade, and I reject the claim.

On the cargo, which was re-claimed for other persons than the owner of the ship, the *King's Advocate* contended that the presumption from the conduct of the ship applied also to the cargo, since it was not to be supposed that the master could have had any view in the fraudulent deviation of which he now stood convicted but for the service of the owner of the cargo.

On the other side, *Laurence* and *Robinson* contended that the presumption, however strong, was only a presumption of evidence which might be counteracted by other proof; that the master was not *de jure* the agent for the owner of the cargo, and therefore that the Court could not find the same satisfaction in concluding the claim of the proprietor on the principle of legal responsibility, on which considerable stress had been laid in the sentence of the ship.

On the next day, Sept. 5th.

SIR W. SCOTT.—This is a case in which I have taken some short time to deliberate, being unwilling to press with any degree of

1804 *September* 4, 6. THE ADONIS. Sir W. Scott.

unnecessary severity the effect of presumption against this class of cases more especially, because it is one in which the principle of law, though unquestionably built upon the just rights of war, must be allowed to operate with some hardship upon neutral commerce; and because it is a class of cases on which the Court has little authority to resort to, but has to collect the law of nations from such sources as reason, supported in some slight degree by the practice of nations, may appear to point out. In the present case, it is now to be assumed that the ship was taken in a course to Havre. I collect that from the strange and incredible account of the master which, I have already said, in my opinion, cannot be true. It is to be inferred also, I think, that the master was induced to make this deviation from some sinister intention; and I may be warranted to presume that all this would not have been resorted to but in the service of the cargo. It has happened in other blockade cases that excuses have been set up from want of water and provisions or from other occasions; but when the Court pronounces these excuses to be not real, a presumption necessarily arises that it was for the delivery of the cargo that such a fraud had been attempted; since there is scarcely any other adequate motive which can be supposed to induce a master to hazard the interests of his vessel, the motives which he has assigned being demonstrated to be false. There is a presumption, also, in such cases, that this is done with the knowledge and at the instigation of the owner of the cargo; because, although it is not an impossible thing that masters may be guilty of barratry, it is not a natural conduct nor what is gratuitously to be supposed. These are, I think, just inferences; and the only question can be as to the effect of the presumption arising from them, whether it shall exclude all contrary averment or whether it shall operate only as matter of evidence, in concurrence with other proof, as to the guilt of the intention. It must undoubtedly bind the owner; but the question is, whether it shall do so presumptively, or conclusively, and whether the party shall be let in to prove a contrary intention. I am of opinion that he cannot. I will not say that the fact may not exist that a master should commit a barratry in a case of this kind, but I think myself justified in holding that the owner cannot be admitted to go into proof on this point on account of the fraudulent abuse to which such a liberty must inevitably lead, since it would be perfectly easy at any time to set up the pretence, and equally impossible on the other side to detect it. For what would be the ordinary test? Letters sent to correspondents elsewhere, and insurances—measures wholly in the power of the parties, and capable of being made at their pleasure a complete recipe for a safe traffic with a blockaded place. When this consequence is duly weighed on one side, and when it is considered on the other what few inducements a master can have to go to any other port than that at which his charter-party binds him to deliver his cargo, and particularly to a blockaded port, it appears to me that less injustice will be done by adopting this rule than by permitting the freighter to distinguish, by external and collateral evidence, the destination of his cargo from that of the master.

It has been argued that the master is not the representative of the owner of the cargo. Certainly he is not to that extent and in the same direct manner in which he is held to be the representative of the owner of the ship. On that account, in some cases where facts have shown that the intention of the owner was pure, the Court has given the party the benefit of this distinction; for instance, where the voyage began before the knowledge of the blockade, and where the master, on being warned, has appeared to have been actuated only by a personal obstinacy and perverseness in pursuing his course to the place of his original destination. That is a case where the intention of the owner is admitted to be pure, where nothing stands against it *in limine*, where there is no question of fact whether he was consentient to the fraud, and where, if he was affected at all, it could only be by the strict legal principle that affects the principal by the conduct of his agent. Here the blockade was perfectly well known to all parties at the time of shipment, and therefore the question is raised whether the owner was not consentient at first, and whether the conduct of the master is not demonstrative evidence that he was so. In my opinion the effect of all just presumption is against him, since there could scarcely be any inducement to lead the master to commit such a fraud contrary to the instructions and intention of the owner of the cargo. Considering the infinite danger of admitting

1804 September 4, 6. THE ADONIS. Sir W. Scott. the shippers to distinguish their purpose from that of the master, I feel myself obliged to hold that it is sufficiently proved that the ship was going to a blockaded port for the purpose of delivering the cargo, and with the knowledge of the proprietor, and that the cargo is legally involved in the same penalty as the ship.

[5 C. Rob. 262.]

THE SHEPHERDESS.

Blockade—False Papers—Intoxication of Master—Attempt to break Blockade.

A neutral ship was captured apparently intending a breach of a blockade; the master alleged that he was intoxicated, and the supercargo alleged that he would not have allowed the master to break the blockade. *Held*, that ship and cargo must be condemned.

1804 September 4. THIS was an American ship and cargo taken on a voyage from America to the port of Havre, in violation of the blockade of Havre.

SIR W. SCOTT.—This case sets off with some circumstances in the conduct of the claimant which are not entitled to the praise of a fair and ingenuous proceeding. It begins with this fact, that though the ship was intended to go to Havre, all the ostensible papers bear a destination for Embden, to which port the vessel was not to go in any event, unless all the ports of the Channel should be in a state of blockade. It is impossible to maintain that it is a just representation of such a voyage "to describe it to Embden and a market," when Embden was the very last port to which the vessel was to resort. Yet all the public papers are made out for Embden, and it is only in private letters that a destination to Havre is avowed; with regard to which, it is to be observed, that it depended very much on the discretion and good faith of the master whether the letters would be produced or not. In some cases it has appeared that the masters of American vessels have very improperly conceived themselves to be under no obligation to produce such papers, which they consider as private papers, and as not belonging to the ship. In all events it must have depended very much on the good faith of the master whether he would have produced these concealed papers or not, and there are, I think, circumstances that show it not to have been the disposition of the master to produce them in the present case.

It must be inferred, and indeed admitted, that the notification of the blockade of Havre had been received in America. To all the general rules of observance of a blockade duly imposed, the subjects of America are undoubtedly bound equally with those of other countries. At the same time, looking to the great distance at which they are placed, and being unwilling to press with any degree of hardship on the fair convenience of commerce, the Court has held, even where the blockade of a port in Europe has been notified in America, that the merchants of that country might still clear out conditionally for the blockaded port, on the supposition that before the arrival of the vessel a relaxation might have taken place. But as to the line of caution to be observed in this state of uncertainty, the Court has always expected that the inquiry should be made at some of the British ports in the Channel. It could not be that ships should be permitted to resort to the ports of the blockaded country for this information, since every one must perceive that such a liberty would place it in the power of the enemy to determine the continuance of the blockade. The ports of the blockading country are certainly the proper ports for inquiry; and it would not be too much to expect that this precaution should be noted in the papers, and that it should be most explicitly enjoined on the master and supercargo in their instructions to obtain the information that might be necessary to fix the destination at some of the British ports in the Channel. I must observe also, that there is less room for excuse in this instance, since it is stated to have been the universal impression in America at the time of sailing that Havre was under blockade. There could have been scarcely a doubt as to any relaxation of the blockade; and therefore it became incumbent on the parties to send out their vessel with more particular caution.

The ship sailed, and appears evidently to have pursued a voyage for Havre, not only by her course, but also by a letter put on board at sea by a French privateer, directed for Havre de Grace, a few days before the capture. She was coming up the Channel towards Havre, with no other port apparently in contemplation. Another fact which bears a strange and unfavourable appearance against

1804 September 4. — THE SHEPHERDESS. — Sir W. Scott.

the master is the representation which he has given of what passed between him and one of his Majesty's ships, "that on being hailed by a King's ship, he answered that he was cleared for Embden, but was going to Havre if not under blockade, and that he was permitted to proceed." Could this have been the whole of that conversation, or can this be a fair account of it? The King's ship, on being informed of an intention of going to Havre, would have immediately endorsed the usual prohibition on the papers. It is morally impossible that the conversation could have stopped short in this manner, or that the master should not have been warned against proceeding to Havre, and with very imperative effect. The other witnesses, who are the mate and the supercargo, make no mention of Havre in their representation of this conversation. According to them the answer was, "that they were bound to Embden." If their account is to be believed, it will very considerably affect the master as to his veracity, and will also fix upon him a material violation of his duty in not stating the whole truth of his destination. But does it not go further and involve these other witnesses also as parties to the fraud, if they heard this representation and did not correct it, more especially since one of them is the supercargo, the agent entrusted with the management of the cargo, and capable of affecting his employers with a legal responsibility for his acts? These witnesses are, I think, to be taken as privy to the fraud on the British cruiser, and as concurring in suppressing the true destination of the voyage. Then how can the Court give credit to the subsequent part of their representation, viz., that "they were afterwards met by another British cruiser, the *Pluto*, and were told 'that they must not go to Havre, but that they might go to Fecamp'; that the master, nevertheless, kept the ship's course to Havre, but that he was in a continued state of intoxication; and that it was the intention of the supercargo not to have permitted him to go into that port"?

The master himself says that he was intoxicated, but if such an excuse could be admitted there would be eternal carousings in every instance of violation of blockade. The master cannot, on any principle of law, be permitted to stultify himself in this manner by the pretended or even real use of strong liquors, of which, if it were a thing to be examined, the Court could in no instance ascertain the truth of the fact. The owners of the vessel have appointed him their agent, and they must in law be bound by his imprudence as well as by his fraud. As to the cargo, the supercargo says, "that he would not have suffered the master to go into Havre," but he had taken no steps to supersede him. It would be a dangerous doctrine to hold that a master in a state of intoxication might be permitted to go on for the blockaded port, and that the supercargo should lie by and then come and plead the intoxication of the master, and exculpate himself by stating a mere intention to dispossess him and to steer another course. It was the duty of the supercargo and of the officers concerned in the navigation of the ship to have dispossessed the master of the command in such critical circumstances. Here was a vessel duly warned not to go into Havre, yet the master, in a continued state of intoxication, refuses to alter his course. I cannot think that it would have amounted to any culpable act of disobedience, or to anything like mutiny, to have resisted the command of such a master in such a condition, and to have given a proper direction to the voyage. Instead of that, the supercargo suffers the vessel to proceed in this interdicted course, and relies only on a secret intention of his own mind to dispossess the master before he actually got into Havre, without being able to show any one step taken for that purpose. Looking at the whole case throughout, and recollecting always the fraudulent suppression of the original voyage, I am of opinion that if the instructions had been much more clear on the part of the owners than these are, they could not have been allowed to weigh against the actual conduct of the master. It would be the easiest thing in the world to put on board instructions perfectly smooth and unobjectionable. If they alone could be sufficient to exonerate the owner from the penalty attending the misconduct of the vessel, by imputing it to the mere barratry of the master, there would be an end to all means of enforcing a blockade. I am of opinion that the owners of the ship must be concluded by the conduct of the master; and I think that the interests of the cargo are also implicated in this act, and that the ship and cargo are subject to condemnation.

[5 C. Rob. 268.]

THE LA FLORE.

Joint Capture—King's Ship—In Sight of Capture—Presumption of Law.

If a King's ship is in sight at the time of a capture, it is a presumption of law that she is present *animo capiendi*, and she is, therefore, without further proof, entitled to be considered a joint captor. But otherwise in the case of a private vessel.

1804 *September* 6.

THIS was a case of joint capture, on evidence chiefly, but involving a question of law respecting the claim of a King's ship to share in a capture, made by the *Trimmer* privateer, on the ground of being in sight only, without an affirmative averment of the fact of joint chasing.

SIR W. SCOTT.—This case has been not improperly described to be a question of credit, a character which can by no means be said to be peculiar to the present case, since it belongs almost universally to the whole class. No class of cases is better supplied with witnesses on both sides, each set generally speaking up to the full exigencies of their case. We find them seeing not unfrequently over capes and headlands, and sometimes over whole islands, and speaking nevertheless to facts so seen by them with as much precision as if they were matters of the purest and most absolute demonstration. The Court has generally to perform the unpleasant task of discussing the credibility of such witnesses, and of deciding on which of the two accounts it can most safely rely. A question of law, however, has been introduced into the argument, on which it may not be improper for me, in the first place, to say a few words. It is observed that the claimants in joint capture have only pleaded the being in sight, without asserting that they were in chase; and it is contended that it is necessary to plead and prove that they were joint chasers as well as that they were in sight. The manner in which the facts are alleged would, I think, scarcely support this objection, because it is stated in the plea that they were in chase under the disadvantage of an almost entire calm, and a part of the evidence goes to support that fact. But I conceive that the law is not correctly laid down in this representation, as applying to the case of King's ships. They are under a constant obligation to attack the enemy wherever seen; a neglect of duty is not to be presumed, and therefore, from the mere circumstance of being in sight, a presumption is sufficiently raised that they are there *animo capiendi*. In the case of privateers the same obligation does not exist. The law, therefore, does not give them the benefit of the same presumption. Ships of this description go out very much on speculations of private advantage, which, combined with other considerations of public policy, are undoubtedly very allowable, but which do not lead to the same inference as that which the law constructs on the known duty imposed on King's ships. A privateer is under no obligation to attack all she meets, but acts altogether on views of private advantage. She may not be disposed to engage in every contest; and, therefore, the presumption does not arise, in any instance, that she is present *animo capiendi*. A contrary route, if proved, would defeat the claim even of a King's ship. But if nothing appears, on one side or the other, as to that fact, the mere presence would, I think, be sufficient to entitle the King's ship to the character of a constructive joint captor.

1804 *September* 6. THE LA FLORE. Sir W. Scott.

[The Court then proceeded to consider the evidence as to whether the claimant ship was in sight.]

THE PRESIDENT.

[5 C. Rob 277.]

National Character—Settlement in Foreign Country—Intention to Leave.

Evidence of an intention of a merchant settled for a long time in a foreign country to leave it, is not sufficient to divest him of the national character which he has obtained, without some overt act.

THIS was a case of a ship taken on a voyage from the Cape of Good Hope to Europe, and claimed for Mr. J. Elmslie, as a subject of America. It appeared that he had been a British-born subject who had gone to the Cape of Good Hope during the last war, and had been employed as American Consul at that place.

1804 *September* 8.

In support of the claim, *Laurence* and *Robinson* contended that the claimant was entitled to the most favourable construction of

1804 September 8. THE PRESIDENT.

his case that was consistent with the rules of law; that he was a British-born subject who had settled at the Cape, and though he had borne the character of an American Consul whilst that settlement was under British possession, it appeared that the Dutch Government had since refused to admit him in that character, from which it might be inferred that he was considered at the Cape rather in his hostile British character than as an incorporated Dutchman; that his vessel had been during the year preceding the present voyage hired by the East India Company to carry troops to India; that she had been in that employment recognized as an American vessel, and was now coming in that character, in the service of British merchants, under a licence from the British Government; that the claimant was, besides, entitled to be considered as a person settled there during British possession, and as affording evidence of an intention to remove, since there was a letter on board written to his correspondent at Embden, in which he directs him "to sell the ship and remit the proceeds to him in America, where he hoped to be in a few months." It was prayed on this point that proof might be permitted to be given of his removal.

On the other side, the *King's Advocate* contended that he could be no otherwise considered by the Court than as a resident merchant of a Dutch settlement. This ship sailed so late as March, 1804, nearly twelve months after the breaking out of the war, and left the owner still resident there in his Dutch character; that there was no case in which an intention to remove after a residence so long continued for nearly a whole year after the breaking out of the war had been allowed to be averred, and no overt act of removal was asserted to have taken place.

SIR W. SCOTT.—The Court must, I think, surrender every principle on which it has acted in considering the question of national character, if it was to restore this vessel. The claimant is described to have been for many years settled at the Cape, with an established house of trade, and as a merchant of that place, and must be taken as a subject of the enemy's country. The ship was purchased by him of an American owner, and still continued to be documented as an American vessel. It has appeared, I think, in other cases to be the disposition of the American Government to confer the privileges of American navigation on vessels occupied by their consuls in foreign States. That Government has, undoubtedly, a perfect right to grant such a privilege for the purposes of their own navigation, at the same time that this country is also at liberty to apply what we consider as the more correct principle of the law of nations, so far as third parties are concerned. Some stress has been laid on the services in which this vessel had been employed, and in which she was engaged at the time of capture, under a licence, which is said to amount to a recognition of her American character. Any description that is given of her in that licence must depend entirely on the representation of the parties, and if that is not true, it will not avail to affect the principle of law that would be otherwise applicable to the vessel in her proper character. Such a recognition, as it is called, has never been allowed to weigh in any case of vessels coming under a licence whenever a question has been raised as to the real character of the owner, or as to the fact of property. This circumstance, therefore, is immaterial. It is next said that the claimant is entitled to the benefit of an intention of removing to Philadelphia in a few months. A mere intention to remove has never been held sufficient without some overt act, being merely an intention, residing secretly and undistinguishably in the breast of the party, and liable to be revoked every hour. The expressions of the letter in which this intention is said to be found are, I observe, very weak and general, of an intention merely *in futuro*. Were they even much stronger than they are, they would not be sufficient. Something more than mere verbal declaration, some solid fact, showing that the party is in the act of withdrawing, has always been held necessary in such cases. Nothing of that sort is averred. The Court is therefore under the necessity of considering this gentleman as a merchant of the enemy's country, and of pronouncing the ship, as his property, liable to condemnation.

[5 C. Rob. 280.]

THE CHARLOTTE (No. 1).

Tender—Qualification—Right of Superior Ship to Share of Prize.

In order to entitle a ship of war to a share of a prize made by a vessel alleged to be her tender, it must be shown that the latter has been recognised as such by order of the Admiralty, or has been constantly employed as such.

1804 *April* 10.

THIS was a case of interest, asserted on the part of his Majesty's ship the *Euridice*, in a capture made by the hired armed revenue cutter the *Duke of York*, on a suggestion that the cutter was placed under the command of the *Euridice*, and was to be considered as a tender attached to that vessel.

SIR W. SCOTT.—The question which arises on the capture of this vessel is, viz., whether the actual captor can be considered as commissioned, and as commissioned in such a manner as to entitle the King's ship to take an interest in the prize. The capturing vessel was a revenue cutter, and, according to the practice of the present and last war, commissioned with a letter of marque. The policy of employing such vessels in this manner is, I believe, a modern usage, arising out of the exigency of the public service, which has particularly required the use of small vessels of this kind. They have been allowed to take out private commissions, and if those commissions are properly executed they will enure to the benefit of the parties till they are superseded; and I am not disposed to think that the employment of the vessel in the manner alleged would have the effect of superseding that commission. It happened that the master was not on board at the time of capture, and on that account no claim is made for the vessel herself, but for the *Euridice*, as the vessel to which she is represented to have been attached as a tender. It is said that she was commanded by a lieutenant of the *Euridice*, but by what reasoning that can be made out I am at a loss to conceive, since it appears that every order was addressed to the master, and there is no circumstance appearing that leads to a supposition that there was any such person as the lieutenant of the *Euridice* on board. The claim for the King's ship is given in virtue of a seizure said to be made by this vessel as a tender, and

1804 April 10. THE CHARLOTTE. Sir W. Scott.

in order to support that averment it must be shown either that there has been some express designation of her in that character by the orders of the Admiralty, or that there has been a constant employment and occupation, in a manner peculiar to tenders, equivalent to an express designation, and sufficient to impress that character upon her. The former species of proof would undoubtedly be most desirable, but no such description by the Admiralty is averred. She is not described anywhere as a tender *in terminis.* Then what is there in the mode of employment? I see nothing in the orders to distinguish her from any other small vessel that might be associated with a King's ship to act under superior command, but not as a tender. I am of opinion, therefore, that there is no sufficient foundation to induce the Court to consider her in the capacity of a tender. She is not so recognized in terms by any authority proceeding from the Admiralty; neither is the nature of the service imposed upon her such as to induce a supposition that she must have been so considered by the Admiralty. As the master was not on board, the legal interest in the capture will not enure to the private captors under their commission; but it must be condemned as a droit of Admiralty, taken by non-commissioned captors.

THE LIESBET VAN DEN TOLL.

[5 C. Rob. 283.]

Neutral—Fishing Vessel—Effect of Visiting Enemy Port for Bait.

A neutral fishing vessel sold its cargoes at sea, but resorted to enemy port for bait. *Held,* that this fact did not affect the vessel with an enemy character.

1804 October 10.

THIS was a question respecting the national character of a fishing adventure, carried on by a native Dutchman, who had become by domicile a subject of Prussia and had purchased the vessel, formerly a Dutch vessel, in February at Embden. It appeared that he had since been employed in fishing off the Dutch coast, having sold his cargoes to English ships and having once or twice resorted to Dutch ports, not for the purpose of selling his cargoes, but merely to procure bait.

1804 *October* 10.

THE LIESBET VAN DEN TOLL.

Sir W. Scott.

SIR W. SCOTT.—It appears to me that this case is very favourably distinguished from that (*a*) of yesterday, where there was reason to believe, from the evidence of the mate, that the master had delivered his cargoes in Dutch ports, although that circumstance was altogether suppressed by the master in his deposition. That fact, connected with the original character of the vessel and of the master, seemed to the Court to amount to a case of Dutch occupation, and the vessel was on that ground condemned. Here the occupation is certainly much slighter. It is not denied that a native Prussian might have engaged in such an adventure without drawing on himself the consequences of a Dutch character. He might unquestionably have resorted to the Dutch coast for the purpose of fishing, as it is indeed not unusual for fishermen to frequent very distant shores. Then the only question will be whether this man, being a native Dutchman and a Prussian subject by domicile only, but of seven years' continuance, and not having recently taken it up for any purposes connected with the present war, would be differently affected by this employment. I am disposed to hold that he would not. It was open to him to go to the coasts of Holland to carry on his fishery in his Prussian character. He was also at liberty to sell his cargoes at sea, as he appears to have done, in every instance, to British vessels, who have lately been very numerous on the coasts of Holland, and might be expected to furnish a good market for commodities of that kind. The only circumstance that can raise a doubt is, that he appears to have resorted to the Texel for bait. It is said that this, though in itself a slight circumstance, affords no immaterial indication of the Dutch character and of the Dutch origin of this employment. But I am not prepared to say that this circumstance alone, unconnected with any habits of delivering his cargoes in the Dutch ports, will be sufficient to affect him with a Dutch character. To hold otherwise would, I think, be to press the doctrine of occupation rather too rigidly against a class of cases which has usually been very favourably considered, and treated with peculiar lenity and forbearance.

(*a*) *Jonge Jeroem*, condemned 9th October, 1804 (not reported).

THE APOLLO (No. 2). [5 C. Rob. 286.]

Practice—Depositions—Affidavit—Blockade—Notice—Duty of Vessel Warned.

An affidavit by a person who has been examined on standing interrogatories, which contradict his depositions, cannot be received by the Court.

After receiving notice of a blockade of which he was ignorant, it is the master's duty to leave the locality of the blockaded port.

1804 *October* 11.

THIS was a case of a ship proceeded against for a breach of the blockade of Dieppe, after having had due warning noted on her papers. In the depositions, the master and all the other witnesses appeared to have said, "that the master, on being warned, declared that he was bound to Dieppe, and could not go anywhere else, and that if he could obtain a fair wind he should run into Dieppe"; and his conduct was represented as conformable to this declaration in hovering on the coast of Dieppe. An affidavit was now offered on the part of the master, complaining that his answer to the interrogatories had been incorrectly taken; and that he had never made such a declaration, or entertained an intention of going into Dieppe after the warning.

SIR W. SCOTT.—The first question which I have to determine is, how far the depositions can be taken to contain a true representation of the facts? If they cannot, the Court undoubtedly will be under the necessity of resorting to some other source of information. An affidavit has been offered on the part of the master, complaining that he has been very greatly misrepresented in these depositions; but I am of opinion that this complaint comes in a manner which does not entitle it to be received by the Court. It is a very lenient mode of administering justice that prevails in these Courts to take the evidence, in the first instance, only from the captured, who are produced, in the presence of the agents of the parties, before the commissioners and actuary, whose duty it is to superintend the regularity of the proceeding, and to protect the witnesses from surprise or misrepresentation. When the deposition is taken, each sheet is afterwards read over to the witness, and separately signed by him, and then becomes evidence common to both parties, it being very rarely permitted to the captor to produce any evidence. The principle

1804 October 11. THE APOLLO. Sir W. Scott.

therefore on which the evidence is conducted is as favourable to the claimant as it can possibly be. If any of these precautions are omitted, it would be competent to the party to complain immediately; and if such a complaint was regularly made, it would become a duty most pressing on the conscience of the Court to institute the most accurate inquiry into the grounds of such complaint. In this case nothing of the kind has been done; but when the cause is opened, and the depositions are read, then something is produced in the form of an affidavit, which is to have the effect of overruling all the evidence that has been taken in the solemn manner already described. I think I am bound to reject this affidavit *in toto*, and I cannot but consider it as an unjust imputation (*a*) on those who have the functions of the Court, for the purpose of taking the evidence, delegated to them. Then I am to consider the case on the representation which the master and the other witnesses have given. It appears that the vessel sailed ignorant of the blockade which had been imposed on the port of Dieppe (*b*), but she was duly warned, and the master does not say that he did not understand the warning. I accede to what has been observed on the part of the claimant, that such a warning might be allowed to be received at first with some hesitation, and that it would not be the disposition of the Court to take advantage of any hasty expressions used in the moment of surprise. If a foolish declara-

(*a*) On a subsequent day, in answer to the intimation which had been directed by the Court to be conveyed to the commissioners and actuary, before whom the depositions were taken, of the charge made against their proceedings in the master's affidavit, it was mentioned by the King's Advocate that the interpreter, Mr. Moses Hart, had made an affidavit, stating "that he had been twenty years employed as German interpreter under the commissioners of the Court at Portsmouth, and that he had possessed a competent knowledge of the German language from being born a Jew in Amsterdam, where the German language is usually spoken amongst Jews, and from a subsequent residence of many years as a printer in Berlin; that the depositions were taken with great caution, and carefully read over, and interpreted to the witness; that the account of the declaration therein contained was accurately taken down from the words of the master." The King's Advocate stated also that there were affidavits from the captain and officers of the blockading frigate representing the conduct of the ship to have been conformable to the declaration of the master as represented in his depositions.

(*b*) By notification, 9th August, 1804.

tion was made, apparently idle and without a persevering, obstinate intention of carrying it into execution, it would, I think, be a harsh exercise of the rights of war to press such a hasty declaration to the disadvantage of the master, and more especially to the forfeiture of the property of others entrusted in some measure to his discretion. But if such a declaration is made, and accompanied by such circumstances as impress on the mind of the Court a conviction that the master was persisting in a serious determination of acting agreeably to it, the captor is not bound to wait till he proceeds to carry his design into execution; it is sufficient that he had made a deliberate declaration, accompanied with such facts as induce the Court to believe that he really intended to carry it into effect. It is said that a master, in such a situation, would be under much distress and difficulty to determine where he should go. It may be so; but he could be under no doubt as to his negative duty, as it may be called, that he was not to go into the blockaded port. It must be clear and obvious to him that the neighbourhood of the blockaded port cannot be considered as the fit *locus deliberandi* for his future plans. If the Court was to admit that a master might lie to, and call a council of his own thoughts or of those of his crew in such a place, the rights of blockade could no longer exist to any purpose; he would stay in all cases until an opportunity offered of slipping into the interdicted port. It would be practically inconsistent with the exercise of this right of war to hold that the blockading force is bound to stay by him, and wait for the result of his deliberation in this suspected place. On the contrary, his first duty is obvious, *fuge litus;* that neighbourhood is at all events to be avoided. He is bound on the first notice to take himself out of an equivocal situation, and if he obstinately refuses and neglects so to do this Court will hold, till it is corrected by the judgment of the Superior Court, that such a conduct will amount to a breach of the blockade, and subject the vessel to condemnation. Then what is the fact? The master declared, according to the depositions of himself and of the other witnesses, not only "that he must go," which it is said would be the same expression in German as "that he ought to go," but also that "he will go" to Dieppe, and after due warning he is still found near the same place, with the ship's head towards Dieppe. Taking this

1804 *October* 11. — THE APOLLO. — Sir W. Scott.

representation to be true, as I am bound to do, it appears incredible to me, I confess, that he should, as he now asserts, have acted in this manner, without any intention of going into Dieppe. If, however, it is possible that this assertion can be true, I have only to lament, as I have abundant occasion to do, the folly and obstinacy of masters, who will place themselves in situations which it is impossible for the Court to admit to be innocent, without breaking down all the rules on which alone the principle of blockade can be sustained. On these grounds I feel myself obliged to pronounce this vessel guilty of a breach of the blockade, and consequently subject to condemnation.

[5 C. Rob. 295.]

THE BETSEY (No. 3).

Bail—Cargo—Claimant—Reduction in Value.

Where a claimant took his cargo at an agreed value on giving bail in such amount, and subsequently the cargo proved to be of less value. *Held*, that the amount of bail could not be reduced.

1804 *November* 22.

THIS was a case of an application made to the Court on the part of a claimant, who had taken the goods on bail at an admitted value, to have the bail reduced to the actual value of the goods, on a suggestion that the sale had not produced so much as the sum at which they had been appraised.

COURT.—There seems to be no pretence for this application. The party took the cargo not merely as a middle man, as he has been described in argument, who was to be employed to sell to the best advantage for the use of the *jus habentium*. It was to the claimant himself that the goods were delivered at his own desire, and at an agreed value, by which the amount of the interest in dispute was completely concluded. If the value had proved much greater than the appraised sum, the captor would have derived no benefit from the increase. The speculation in that event would have been advantageous to the claimant only; he would have brought in no more than the appraised value. The adventure being unfavourable, the same valuation must be adhered to, as equally binding against him. I have no hesitation in rejecting this prayer, and with costs (*a*). 1804 *November* 22.

THE BETSEY.

THE JONGE KLASSINA.

[5 C. Rob. 297.]

Licence to Import Goods from Enemy Country—Invalidity—Merchant Exporter in Enemy Country—National Character—Merchant in Two Countries.

A licence was granted "for the importation of goods from H. into this country." The licensee was proved to be likewise the exporter from H., and a merchant of H. *Held*, that the licence was thereby invalidated.

A merchant who habitually transacts business in two countries is liable to be considered as a subject of each.

THIS was a case on the national character of the claimant, under the particular circumstances of this transaction, and on the effect of a licence granted to Mr. Ravie, of Birmingham, "for the importation of certain goods from Holland into this country." The question was, whether it could operate to protect a shipment made by him in person, in Holland, and under papers describing the firm of his house as "Ravie and Co. of Amsterdam." 1804 *November* 30.

On the part of the captors, the *King's Advocate* and *Robinson*.

On the part of Mr. Ravie, *Laurence*.

(*a*) So, as to salvage cases, in the *Jonge Bashan*, 17th February, 1806, in which a proportional salvage had been decreed. The owners had taken the cargo on bail at an appraised value. An application was afterwards made to the Court to reduce the rate of salvage on a suggestion that it exceeded the net proceeds owing to the expenses attending the sale.

The Court rejected the petition.

So, in the *Graeff Bernstorff*, April 3rd, 1805. In respect to the expenses attending the sale of a cargo taken on bail by the claimant, and afterwards condemned, it was objected on the part of the claimant that the Registrar and merchants had refused to allow certain charges made for warehouse room, and expenses attending the conversion of the property. But the Court overruled the objection, observing, I can have no hesitation as to any expenses incurred after the property was taken on bail—the captor cannot be liable to any such charges. It was a free speculation on the part of the claimant to take the property at an appraised value with all the charges attending it. As it appears that a sum of 1,800*l*. has been retained in the hands of the claimant under the pretext of this objection, I shall overrule the objection, and decree interest to be paid for the money so detained.

1804 November 30.

THE JONGE KLASSINA.

Sir W. Scott.

SIR W. SCOTT.—This question arises on the claim of Mr. Ravie, describing himself as "Ravie of Birmingham," for certain goods coming to be imported into this kingdom from Holland under the authority of a licence. In all cases of this kind the terms of the licence must be considered, as the only authority under which the goods can be imported by a British subject from the enemy's country; and I may here observe that it would not be the disposition of the Court to narrow the operation of such a licence, more especially under the severe pressure which the commercial concerns of British merchants have sustained from the war. Mr. Ravie appears to be a person engaged very extensively in the manufactures of this country, in the employment of our artisans, and in the export and import trade of the country; and it will be to be lamented if exertions so laudable and so prosperous should meet with any check from the effects of war. But if such a misfortune should have befallen him, I need not say that it is out of the power of this Court to afford relief against the necessary conclusions of law. The province of this Court can extend no further than to pronounce whether the transaction comes fairly and adequately within the terms of the licence, under which alone it can be supported.

The licence was granted to Mr. Ravie to import certain goods, "being his property." On the question relating to the property, considering the terms on which the goods are now stated to have been shipped "for Mr. Berry, but at the risk of Mr. Ravie during the voyage," I am disposed to hold that this provision of the licence, which refers to the description of property, has been sufficiently complied with. But it appears that Mr. Ravie was not only the importer, but the exporter also; that he was personally present in Holland superintending the shipment according to the evidence, as it is now explained, in the same manner as any other merchant of that country would have done. So the master describes him in the additional affidavit which has been permitted to be introduced. What is it that the broker does on being employed by the master to procure a freight? He goes to Mr. Ravie, as a man would go to a known merchant of this place. Mr. Ravie appears to have been the shipper. He contracts with the broker, and is described in the charter-party as "Ravie and Co., merchants at Amsterdam." Am I then at liberty to say that this is a transaction which comes fairly within the terms of the licence, or that it is lawful for any individual to engraft the character of Dutch exporter on a licence granted to him as a British merchant to import? If it could be shown that there was any necessity, or any consideration of policy, that required such an indulgence, the proper mode would be that it should be presented to the view of the government at the time when the licence is obtained, and then permission to that extent might be inserted in the terms of the licence itself. Without such a declaration of the intention of government, for this Court to apply the licence to the protection of such a transaction as this is, would be, I think, to carry it far beyond the fair construction which the terms of the grant will bear. I am far from imputing to Mr. Ravie any improper motive in this affair. A breach of native allegiance it could not be, as Mr. Ravie does not appear to be a native subject of this country. I will go further and say, that there does not appear to have been an intention on his part of violating any duties which he owed to this country. The motive was, I dare say, merely commercial, and, perhaps, within his apprehension of what was permitted to him under the terms of his grant. But I fear that this is his exposition only, and not one which the law will allow me to entertain. If trade with the enemy is generally unlawful, it is not in the power of this Court to admit it, beyond the degree which is fairly described in the terms of the licence. The hardship of the case has been strongly pressed on a representation that Mr. Ravie went to Holland only for the purpose of collecting debts, and on his return from the fair at Frankfort. The Court has looked anxiously into the evidence to see on what ground such an assertion was founded; because if it had appeared that this was a solitary instance of engaging in Dutch commerce, the Court would be induced to strain hard to escape from the necessity of pronouncing the property subject to confiscation. Something of that kind does appear, indeed, in the affidavits; but of the persons who make those affidavits I must say that they seem to know more of Ravie's affairs than Mr. Ravie himself. I have looked into his affidavit, and can discover nothing respecting the particular purpose of collecting debts. All that he says is, "that after the

1804 November 30. — THE JONGE KLASSINA. — Sir W. Scott.

Frankfort fair he went to Holland to settle some mercantile concerns." Those concerns might be all future arrangements. Without assenting to the principle that a British merchant could, with strict propriety, go in any case into the enemy's country without the authority of the State, the Court might be disposed to exert the utmost indulgence that could be consistent with the rule of law for the relief of a person who had found himself in the enemy's country *in transitu* merely, and for occasional purposes only, not originally connected with this transaction. But when I look at Mr. Ravie's affidavit, I can find no grounds for considering his case as that of a man merely stepping over the line of demarcation, and making shipments only for the purpose of collecting his debts.

This brings me to the consideration of Mr. Ravie's national character. It is not said what is his native character, but it is much insisted on that he is settled in this country, and engaged in extensive manufactures here. Mr. Ravie must know, and those who have stated his case know perfectly well, that his meritorious establishment in this country, to the extent of which I have stated, cannot be permitted to affect this question. A man may have mercantile concerns in two countries, and if he acts as a merchant of both, he must be liable to be considered as a subject of both with regard to the transactions originating respectively in those countries. That he has no fixed compting-house in the enemy's country will not be decisive. How much of the great mercantile concerns of this kingdom is carried on in coffee-houses? A very considerable portion of the great insurance business is so conducted. It is indeed a vain idea that a compting-house or fixed establishment is necessary to make a man a merchant of any place. If he is there himself and acts as a merchant of that place it is sufficient, and the mere want of a fixed compting-house there will make no breach in the mercantile character, which may well exist without it. Mr. Ravie's own representation is, "that he went to Holland for the purpose of arranging his mercantile concerns, and that he has for a long time carried on trade and business at Birmingham." As to his business at Birmingham, I may dismiss the whole of that circumstance as what cannot admit of a doubt. The question will still remain, whether he is not also a merchant of Holland in this particular transaction? He says, "that he employs Mr. V. as his agent at Amsterdam to receive letters, and that letters are addressed to him there to Ravie and Co. at Amsterdam." This circumstance has been contended to be parallel with the case of Mr. Portalis, who had agents at Bordeaux and at various other places, whilst he himself was resident at Neuchatel. But there is this distinction, which has been overlooked, that Mr. Portalis did not appear to have been personally present at Bordeaux; he might have agents in different parts of the world, but he himself was resident at Neuchatel. If he had been himself at Bordeaux that fact might have made a very material difference in his case. What is the situation of Mr. Ravie in this respect? He says, "that he has employed agents at Amsterdam, except at those times when he finds it convenient to go there," which may be three or five times in a year. At such times I am to suppose that he did not employ agents, but transacted his own business. What is meant by a nominal firm at that place, which I perceive in several passages of these affidavits, I am at a loss to understand, since Mr. Ravie appears to have been as substantially employed in the trade of Amsterdam as any other mercantile firm of that place. The character in which he stands before the Court in this particular transaction corresponds exactly with this view of his general connection with that place. The charter-party is brought, not to Mr. V., his agent, but to himself, and he signs it as a merchant of Amsterdam. It would, I conceive, be too much for me to pronounce that this can legally be done, or, in effect, that a man may go to the enemy's country as often as he pleases, under the authority of a licence of this kind, and there act as a Dutch merchant carrying on the export trade of that country. I feel, I hope, as much as other persons, for the difficulties under which the commerce of this country and commercial men may be placed by the events of war, but it is not in my power to bend the principles of law for their relief. If it is fit that such relief should be afforded, it must be given elsewhere and by higher powers. This Court has no authority to exercise such a discretion, but is under the painful necessity of pronouncing this property subject to condemnation.

[5 C. Rob. 305.]

THE CHARLOTTE (No. 2).

Contraband—Masts.

Masts are absolutely contraband without reference to the port to which they are destined.

1804 *November* 16. THIS was a case of a cargo of masts and spars, taken in a Lübeck ship on a voyage from Riga to Nantes, being the produce of Russia, and claimed as the property of a merchant of that country.

For the captors, the *King's Advocate* and *Laurence.*

For the claimants, *Arnold* and *Robinson.*

SIR W. SCOTT.—This case has been argued much at length on the operation of the treaty and on the authority of former practice, and it certainly presents a question of considerable importance; but it will not be necessary or proper for me to travel much into the argument, because, if there is a decision of the Superior Court so recent as 1803 on a similar point, it will be conclusive upon my judgment, and I shall have only to follow the rule of law there laid down, and to act under the authority of that decision. Let us see, then, whether the cases are so far parallel cases as to be subject to an application of the same principle. The *Graeffen Van Gottland* (*a*) was a shipment of masts to Cadiz in a Swedish ship, and, as the master appears to have said in his depositions, "to be delivered to private consignment." This is a shipment of similar articles, going in a Lübeck ship to Nantes. The two cases have this circumstance in common, then, that the claimants are merchants of Russia, exporting articles of the same kind to the enemy, not in the vehicles of their own country. Unless there are other circumstances to distinguish the cases, the decision of the Lords upon the former case must be the guide, which this Court would be bound to follow. Then what are the distinctions pointed out? It is said that the claimant in that instance was the Swedish consul in Russia, but that circumstance could have made no difference, since it must have been familiar to all who had to judge of that case that

(*a*) August 19th, 1803.

his character of consul to a foreign nation could not vary the principle that was to be applied to it. As a person resident in Russia, he could be considered in no other light than other merchants of the country. It is then said that the cargo was going to the public arsenal of the enemy. It was going to Cadiz, which is a place of great military equipment, but it is a place of great mercantile equipment also; and it does not appear, I think, exactly as it has been represented that those articles were to be delivered to the public arsenal of the State. What has been said on the other side is, I think, true, that the nature of the port is not material, since masts, if they are to be considered as contraband, which they will be unless protected by treaty, are so, without reference to the nature of the port, and equally, whether bound to a mercantile port only or to a port of naval military equipment. The consequences of the supply may be nearly the same in either case. If sent to a mercantile port, they may be there applied to immediate use in the equipment of privateers, or they may be conveyed from Nantes to Brest, and there become subservient to every purpose to which they could have been applied if going directly to a port of military equipment. The only other distinction is that the decision alluded to, passed on a capture of the late war in 1797, when this country and Russia were bound by a particular convention to a stricter co-operation in the war against France; but the destination of the *Graeffen Van Gottland* was not to France, but to Spain, which country was by no manner affected by the convention of 1793. It has appeared, I think, in numerous instances that the commercial intercourse between Russia and Spain was not interrupted, but that there was a considerable trade going on between the two countries during the whole war. These distinctions, then, are insufficient to vary the principle of law, which I feel myself bound to apply under the authority of the Superior Court. Without going into the antecedent history of the law on this question, I must consider the authority of this recent case decided by the Superior Court as binding on me. That judgment must be supposed to have been formed with reference to former authorities; and it is not even now contended, on the part of the claimant, that the late treaty of 1801 puts the commerce of Russia with respect to these articles on a more favourable

1804 November 16. — THE CHARLOTTE. — Sir W. Scott.

footing than it was before. The effect of that decision is conclusive on me, and I have no hesitation in pronouncing this cargo subject to condemnation.

[5 C. Rob. 315.]

THE WIGHT.

Salvage—Recapture—Convoy—Hostile Possession of Captured Vessel.

A convoying vessel has a right to salvage for the recapture of a vessel under her charge, if such vessel has been in the effectual possession of an enemy. *Held, also,* that the Court will not entertain a charge of negligence against the convoy as a defence to such a claim. Such charge must be made to the Lords Commissioners of the Admiralty, and if substantiated before them, the Court will then act on their finding.

1804 November 30.

THIS was a case of salvage arising on the recapture of a vessel by a convoying ship within a short time after the capture, and before she had been carried out of sight. The facts of the case were, that the *Wight* was sailing under the convoy of the *Thisbe*, on a voyage from Zante to London; that in passing the narrow channel between Cephalonia and Ithaca the whole convoy was becalmed, and whilst in this situation a privateer rowed out from the land by means of sweeps and made a capture of the *Wight*. On signal being made, the *Thisbe* immediately put out her boats, which pursued the privateer, and within an hour or two retook the *Wight*, and also made a capture of the privateer, with the loss of one man.

On the part of the captor, the *King's Advocate* and *Arnold*.

On the part of the owners, *Laurence* and *Robinson*.

SIR W. SCOTT.—This case comes before me upon an alleged act of recapture performed by the *Thisbe*, who had a number of merchant vessels under her convoy. One was captured by the enemy and was afterwards retaken by the *Thisbe;* and for that service the *Thisbe* now stands before the Court, demanding the salvage which is allowed to King's ships on ordinary occasions by the Prize Act. The first question that arises is, whether a convoying ship may be entitled to salvage from ships under her protection? That question has, I think, been decided by the authority of the case of the *Hinchinbrook*, which is binding on me, because it was there laid down that the relation which had subsisted between the convoying ship and those under her care would not take the case out of the general provisions of the Prize Act. I consider that to have been the ancient doctrine of this Court; and it was, I think, recognized as such by the decisions of my predecessor, because he seemed to hold that the demand might generally be considered as fairly within the operation of the Act, although he determined that, under the particular circumstances of the case then before him, no salvage was due. He entered, I recollect, pretty fully into the circumstances of that case, and concluded that there had been some neglect on the part of the convoying ship, which would defeat the right of the salvors. The Court of Appeal was of opinion that no such imputation was raised against the convoying ship by the facts of the case; and further, that such a question, if it arose in fact, was a matter to be discussed in another form, and was not fit to be introduced in a civil cause of this nature, to repel a demand to which the recaptor would be entitled on the general principle of law. It would indeed, as it was then observed, be attended with very great injustice to the character of naval officers, if the propriety of their conduct on such occasions could be brought into discussion incidentally in this manner; and I advert to this consideration more particularly, because I perceive that an insinuation of improper conduct has also been introduced into the present case. But under the authority of the *Hinchinbrook*, I think myself warranted to consider it as a charge to which this Court will not attend till otherwise established. If a complaint was gravely preferred and substantiated elsewhere on a proper representation to the Lords of the Admiralty, it might be competent to this Court to say that no claim to reward should be grounded on an act, thus pronounced to be an act of misconduct by a tribunal properly qualified to decide upon it. But to admit such accusations in this form would be attended with great injustice to the naval officer whose character was implicated in the charge, and would be productive of great inconvenience to the Court. If I was to admit the insinuation in any degree, I must also receive exculpatory evidence on the other

1804 *November* 30. THE WIGHT. Sir W. Scott.

side, and that would be to let myself out to the practice of trying a criminal case throughout, which was so justly reprobated by the Superior Court on the former occasion. The only material question for me to consider, then, is, whether there was such a capture made by the enemy as would found a case of recapture? Many cases might be put of the effect of immediate acts of recapture, to show that it is by no means necessary that the possession by the enemy should be long maintained, or at any particular distance from the convoying ship. The question will always be, whether it was an effectual possession, and such as would suspend the relation of the convoying ship; not, whether it is a complete and firm possession, which, for some purposes, is, in contemplation of law, not held to be effected till the prize is carried *infra præsidia?* The rule of *infra præsidia*, however, is certainly not the measure to be applied to questions of this kind. The very clause of the Prize Act alludes to cases of salvage in which no such complete possession is supposed, since it speaks of vessels being recaptured and permitted to continue on their original voyage. As little can it be contended that the vessel should have been out of sight to found a case of recapture; it will be sufficient if there has been that complete and absolute possession which supersedes the authority of the convoying ship, and such a possession must have been maintained for some time in the present instance. Every act of possession was exercised; the master was taken out, the vessel was completely manned with as many of the captor's crew as were sufficient to overpower all resistance, and the vessel was taken in tow by the enemy. By these acts the former relation subsisting between this vessel and the convoying ship was necessarily suspended. A ship in possession of the enemy can obey no signal, nor support its former duties and subordination to the convoying ship. There might still remain an obligation on the part of the convoying ship to attempt the recapture, as far as it could be done consistently with the safety of the other vessels under her protection. Such a duty would result from the injunctions of the Prize Act, which provides a reward for the recaptor when the service is effected, and cannot therefore be intended to preclude the demand of salvage, though the service rendered to the individual by the recaptor may be no more than a sense of public duty would otherwise require from him. The capture is, I think, proved to have been sufficiently completed; and unless I could go to the length of holding that there must be a firm possession and a bringing *infra præsidia*, I must pronounce this vessel to have been recovered from a situation which has been decided to be sufficient to support the claim of salvage by the decision of the Superior Court.

1804 *November* 30.

THE WIGHT.

Sir W. Scott.

THE MARIA (No. 3) (*a*).

[5 C. Rob. 365.]

Continuous Voyage—Touching at Intermediate Port—Intention to Sell Cargo at Intermediate Port—Further Proof.

An American ship sailed from Havannah, thence to New Providence, where she remained from May 31st to July 20th, with a cargo of colonial produce, and thence, with part of the original cargo, to Amsterdam; she was captured between New Providence and Amsterdam. *Held*, that as the *terminus ad quem* was not a port of the mother country, and as there was only on board part of the original cargo, the owner of the ship was entitled to produce further evidence to prove that the ship sailed from the Havannah with the intention that all the cargo should be sold in America, and that the voyage was not continuous.

THIS was a case of an American ship which had come from the Havannah to New Providence with a cargo of colonial produce, and was proceeding, when taken, with a considerable part of that cargo on board to the port of Amsterdam.

1805 *September* 18.

For the captor, the *King's Advocate* and *Laurence*.

For the claimant, *Swabey* and *Adams*.

SIR W. SCOTT.—This question arises as to a vessel which had gone to the Havannah, and from thence to New Providence (*b*), where she was refitted, and took on board part of the same cargo, with other goods belonging to the same owner, and some other articles on freight, and was at the time of capture proceeding to Amsterdam. On these facts two questions have been made—First, whether the goods so going are not liable to condemnation? and secondly, whether the ship, as concerned in the same illegal trans-

(*a*) See the *William*, *post*, p. 505.

(*b*) She arrived on May 31st, and sailed on July 20th.

action, is not subject to the same penalty? It is certainly true that a continued voyage from the colony of the enemy to the mother country, or to any other ports but those of the country to which the vessel belongs, will subject the cargo to confiscation; and the only point which the Court has to decide is, whether the voyage in question is to be considered as a continued voyage or not? It is a question in its nature subject to very considerable difficulties in particular cases, and one on which the Court must exercise its judgment with great caution on the special circumstances which compose the substance of each case, and with great care not to attribute more weight to any particular fact than what it justly demands. In the case of the *Essex*, which was decided by the Court of Appeal, the principle of law, by which such cases are to be decided, was distinctly affirmed. It certainly is not a novel principle; and I cannot but express my surprise that it should be represented in any place, as I understand it has been, that the principle is new. On the contrary, it is an inherent and settled principle in all cases in which the same question can have come under discussion, that the mere touching at any port without importing the cargo into the common stock of the country will not alter the nature of the voyage, which continues the same in all respects, and must be considered as a voyage to the country to which the vessel is actually going for the purpose of delivering her cargo at the ultimate port. The *Essex* was in fact the first case which called for the direct decision of the Superior Court; but the same doctrine would have been held in any other case, if such a case had occurred at an earlier period; and cases had occurred before, very sufficient to convey a full admonition upon the subject. As the *Essex*, however, happened to be the leading case on the subject, it may not be improper that I should state what I conceive to be the substance of it. It was the case of an American vessel which had gone from America to Lisbon, where, finding the market bad, she went on to Barcelona, and there took on board a cargo of Spanish produce for the Havannah, under the direction of the agent in Europe, "that she should go to the Havannah, first touching at Salem, in America, where the owner (a)

(a) The claim was given by the master for the ship and cargo as the property of William Orne, of Salem.

resided, who adopted the plan and sent the vessel on." It appeared clearly to the Court that it was the intention, originating in the mind of an authorized agent, acting under full powers, that the vessel should go to the Havannah, and that this purpose was adopted by the owner; that it was in reality a continued voyage from Spain to the Havannah; that as to the intention, all doubt was done away with by the adoption on the part of the owner, who had the vessel in his own port, and was fully implicated in the engagement of sending her on, according to the projected voyage. That was the fundamental case, a case of a trade from the mother country to the colony, with full knowledge of the circumstances, and a distinct adoption of the purpose on the part of the owner. Other cases have occurred since in this Court, which have been determined on their own particular circumstances; as, indeed, all cases of this kind must be entertained on their own evidence, which may be slighter or stronger, according to the manner in which the transaction has been conducted. The first case that called for the decision of this Court was that of the *Enoch* (*a*), in which appeared one fact, which was in itself conclusive of the intention, viz., a charter-party, providing "for a voyage to the colony of the enemy and back to America, and from thence to the mother country in Europe," affording a complete demonstration of one entire voyage. It was not merely a circumstance, it was an absolute and conclusive fact, declaratory of the intention of sending on the cargo to Europe. The next case was the *Rowena* (*a*), which happened on the same day, and which the Court did not distinguish in judgment from the preceding case, though there was this difference between them, that it had not a charter-party linking together the two parts of the original voyage. But other circumstances occurred leading to the same conclusion, and the Court can only decide on circumstances. There were the former habits of the vessel, from which it appeared that she had been for a considerable number of voyages employed in the same course of trade in the hands of the same owner. The whole cargo had come from the colony of the enemy, and had lain in America only a very short time; just long enough for the purpose of being landed and

(*a*) Adm., 23rd July, 1805.

reshipped. Under these circumstances the Court thought itself bound to presume that the original intention of sending the cargo to Europe had actuated the whole adventure. Soon after came the case of the *Respect* (a), in which it was affirmed in the claim that the goods which composed part only of a former cargo were intended for sale in America. This averment was solemnly interposed on oath, and as the matter was dubious, the Court thought proper to admit the parties to establish their averment in proof. These are the principal cases which have occurred in this Court, without adverting to cases that have occurred in the Superior Court; and I now have to consider whether there was in those cases anything on which the Court relied, which binds me to conclude that the present voyage was a continued voyage, and that there could have been no real *bonâ fide* importation. There are no letters or writings as in the *Essex*, purporting an original intention to send on; there is no charter-party as in the *Enoch;* there are no instructions, disclosing a course of similar voyages to Amsterdam, as in the *Rowena.* The former voyages are clear of suspicion; and I think there is something in that fact, and that it is but just that the presumption from former habits, which weighs unfavourably in some cases, should have its due weight on the other side. It is, indeed, the very purpose of the seventh interrogatory to illustrate what is obscure in the transaction immediately before the Court by former habits. The present case is distinguishable also in another point of view, that the destination is not to the mother country of the colony. I do not say that the rule of law would be different on that account, but as evidence of intention it is something. When the *portus ad quem* is not a port of the country to which the colony belongs, and is itself a place of great general trade, there is not the same preponderance of evidence; the proof of intention is slighter—I will not say how much slighter—but it is a circumstance to be taken into consideration in forming a judgment on the whole case. It is something, also, that the goods are not the whole of the former cargo, since the inference of original intention is not so strong as to goods which compose a part only, though a large part of a miscellaneous cargo, picked up in different places and belong-

(a) Adm., August 1st, 1805.

ing to different proprietors. On these grounds it does appear to me that the present case is substantially distinguished from other cases determined by the Lords of Appeal, or in this Court, and that it has not the same proof to be collected from circumstances on which a judicial mind is bound to acquiesce. There is room to let in the supposition that there might be an intention of selling in America, and that in consequence of the failure of that prospect only, the design was taken up of sending on these goods to the European market. Without abandoning the principle, or being in the least disposed to let it out to a degree of laxity, which may endanger the stability and consistency of the general rule, I think that the claimant may in this case be admitted to prove the averment of an intention of selling in America, which is not shown to be incredible or inconsistent with any circumstance which is at present in evidence before me. As to the other parts of the cargo, on which no question is raised, they must be restored. The question as to the ship will stand over to wait the judgment which the Court may ultimately form on the real intention of the owner as to the cargo.

1805 *September* 18.

THE MARIA.

Sir W. Scott.

On the 22nd of April, 1806, this cause came on again upon further proof, when it was admitted on the part of the captor that the proofs were sufficient, and the Court decreed restitution.

THE ANNA.

Capture—Neutral Territory—Three Mile Limit—Uninhabited Island Adjacent to Mainland—Belligerent Cruisers Within Neutral Waters—Commencement of Capture—Duty of Captors—Convenient Port—Adjudication.

[5 C. Rob. 373.]

A vessel was captured within three miles from some uninhabited islands at the mouth of the Mississippi. *Held*, that the territorial limit was to be reckoned from these islands. *Held*, also, that if the chase of the captured vessel had begun at a greater distance than three miles from these islands the capture might, having regard to the fact that they were uninhabited, have been valid, but that in the present case it was invalid because the captors had behaved illegally in stationing their ships within the mouth of a neutral river.

It is the duty of a captor to take a prize to a convenient port for adjudication.

THIS was a case of a ship under American colours, with a cargo of logwood and about 13,000 dollars on board, bound from the

1805 *November* 6, 15, 20.

1805 November 6, 15, 20. — THE ANNA.

Spanish Main to New Orleans, and captured by the *Minerva* privateer near the mouth of the River Mississippi. A claim was given under the direction of the American Ambassador for the ship and cargo, "as taken within the territory of the United States, at the distance of a mile and a half from the western shore of the principal entrance of the Mississippi, and within view of a post protected by a gun, and where is stationed an officer of the United States."

For the captors, *Arnold* and *Robinson.*—The description which the commander of the privateer gave in his affidavit was that "about 5 p.m., 14th July, he discovered the *Anna* at the distance of about nine miles, steering north-west and by north; that he immediately gave chase, and about half-past six the *Anna* altered her course; that about three-quarters past six he ordered a gun to be fired; that no notice being taken he ordered another, when finding that the *Anna* instead of taking notice hoisted her staysail to favour her escape, he fired round and grape shot till she brought to; that the *Anna* was not within neutral territory, but two miles and a half from the bar of the river and five miles from Fort Balise, which is a small fort erected on made land, and is surrounded by water for many miles which never ebbs dry." The representation which the master of the captured ship gave was, "that the place where she was first fired upon is not more than two miles and a half off the shore, and the place where the ship was anchored when taken not more than one mile and a half, and both, he apprehends and believes, within the territory and jurisdiction of the United States; that the spots marked in the plan or chart as between the Balise or beacon and his ship are small islands, which are always dry and covered with reeds and small shrubs, where people go, and that he had been many times, to shoot wild fowl and procure eggs which are there found in great abundance; that the intervening parts are shallow water, in part filled up with timber which drifts down the river; that the Balise was, during the time of the possession of the Spaniards, a fort with small houses or cabins round the same, where cannon were mounted, and where a Governor resided with his wife and family, as also pilots for the navigation of the river and officers of the Customs, who used to visit all vessels at their entrance."

For the claimant, the *King's Advocate* and *Laurence*.

20th November.

[The Court first dealt with certain matters of fact as to the ship's papers and as to the port to which she was taken.]

SIR W. SCOTT.—The ship with this cargo on board was brought to England for adjudication; and it lies on the captor to exonerate himself from the impropriety of this act; because though the instructions to cruisers give something of a discretion to captors as to the port to which they are to bring their prize—to some convenient port—it is a discretion which must be cautiously exercised, and with sound reason, so as to be justified in the Court before which the case is brought. It would be cause of infinite vexation if neutral vessels taken on slight pretences at so great a distance as the coast of America were to be dragged across the Atlantic for adjudication; more especially when this country has established Courts in different islands in the West Indies, to prevent inconvenient recurrence to this Court and to provide for claimants in that part of the world justice at their own doors, that their commerce may be subject to as little interruption as possible from the exercise of the rights of war on the part of this country in those seas. At the same time there may be circumstances that would justify such a procedure: as if a King's ship bound on the public service makes a capture in her course, such a vessel cannot depart from her instructions, but must proceed upon her original destination. That would be a case of necessity, arising out of the public service, for which States must make allowance reciprocally. But with respect to privateers, I cannot think that any such circumstances as are here set up can be pleaded as a justifying excuse for such conduct on their part.

[The Court then dealt with the excuses put forward.]

When the ship was brought into this country a claim was given of a grave nature, alleging a violation of the territory of the United States of America. This great leading fact has very properly been made a matter of much discussion, and charts have been laid before the Court to show the place of capture, though with different representations from the adverse parties. The capture was made, it seems, at the mouth of the River Mississippi, and, as it is contended in the claim, within the boundaries of the United States. We all know that the rule of law on this subject is "*terræ dominium finitur, ubi finitur armorum vis*," and since the introduction of firearms that distance has usually been recognized to be about three miles from the shore. But it so happens in this case that a question arises as to what is to be deemed the shore, since there are a number of little mud islands composed of earth and trees drifted down by the river, which form a kind of portico to the mainland. It is contended that these are not to be considered as any part of the territory of America; that they are a sort of "no man's land," not of consistency enough to support the purposes of life, uninhabited, and resorted to only for shooting and taking birds' nests. It is argued that the line of territory is to be taken only from the Balise, which is a fort raised on made land by the former Spanish possessors. I am of a different opinion; I think that the protection of territory is to be reckoned from these islands, and that they are the natural appendages of the coast on which they border, and from which, indeed, they are formed. Their elements are derived immediately from the territory, and on the principle of alluvium and increment, on which so much is to be found in the books of law, *Quod vis fluminis de tuo prædio detraxerit, et vicino prædio attulerit, palam tuum remanet* (*a*), even if it had been carried over to an adjoining territory. Consider what the consequence would be if lands of this description were not considered as appendant to the mainland and as comprised within the bounds of territory. If they do not belong to the United States of America, any other Power might occupy them; they might be embanked and fortified. What a thorn this would be in the side of America! It is physically possible at least that they might be so occupied by European nations, and then the command of the river would be no longer in America but in such settlements. The possibility of such a consequence is enough to expose the fallacy of any arguments that are addressed to show that these islands are not to be considered as part of the territory of America.

(*a*) Inst. L. 2 Tit. 1, § 21.

Whether they are composed of earth or solid rock will not vary the right of dominion, for the right of dominion does not depend upon the texture of the soil.

I am of opinion that the right of territory is to be reckoned from those islands. That being established, it is not denied that the actual capture took place within the distance of three miles from the islands, and at the very threshold of the river. But it is said that the act of capture is to be carried back to the commencement of the pursuit, and that if a contest begins before, it is lawful for a belligerent cruiser to follow and to seize his prize within the territory of a neutral State. And the authority of Bynkershoek is cited on this point. True it is that that great man does intimate an opinion of his own to that effect, but with many qualifications, and as an opinion which he did not find to have been adopted by any other writers. I confess I should have been inclined to have gone along with him to this extent, that if a cruiser which had before acted in a manner entirely unexceptionable, and free from all violation of territory, had summoned a vessel to submit to examination and search, and that vessel had fled to such places as these, entirely uninhabited, and the cruiser had, without injury or annoyance to any person whatever, quietly taken possession of his prey, it would be stretching the point too hardly against the captor to say that on this account only it should be held an illegal capture. If nothing objectionable had appeared in the conduct of the captors before, the mere following to such a place as this is would, I think, not invalidate a seizure otherwise just and lawful.

But that brings me to a part of the case on which I am of opinion that the privateer has laid herself open to great reprehension. Captors must understand that they are not to station themselves in the mouth of a neutral river for the purpose of exercising the rights of war from that river, much less in the very river itself. It appears from the privateer's own log-book that this vessel has done both; and as to any attempt to shelter this conduct under the example of King's ships, which I do not believe, and which, if true, would be no justification to others, captors must, I say, be admonished that the practice is altogether indefensible, and that if King's ships should be guilty of such misconduct they would be as much subject to censure as other

1805 November 6, 15, 20.

THE ANNA.

Sir W. Scott.

cruisers. It is unnecessary to go over all the entries in the log. The captors appear by their own description to have been standing off and on, obtaining information at the Balise, overhauling vessels in their course down the river, and making the river as much subservient to the purposes of war as if it had been a river of their own country. This is an inconvenience which the States of America are called upon to resist, and which this Court is bound on every principle to discourage and correct. With respect to one vessel, it appears that the *Bilboa*, under Spanish colours, and an undoubted Spanish ship, had been captured and carried into the river; and it was stated in an affidavit, which was exhibited to account for the absence of the usual witnesses in that case, that the prisoners had escaped. The cause was brought on upon the evidence of the releasing witnesses under this representation. It now appears by an entry in this log "that the prisoners were set on shore," an act highly unjustifiable in its own nature, independent of the deception with which it has been accompanied. The prisoners are the King's prisoners, and captors are particularly enjoined by the instructions not to release any prisoners belonging to the ships of the enemy, and they violate their duty whenever they do. When I advert to the imposition that has been put upon the Court in that transaction, how can I trust myself to any representation coming from the same persons? Indeed I think I can perceive strong traits of bad faith running throughout the whole conduct of the captors in the present case. In answer to the complaint that has been made against the captors for bringing this prize to England, it was said that it was done at the desire of the master of the captured vessel; though in the affidavit of the master, which is not contradicted, it is sworn "that the captors offered to set him on shore, but that he refused to be separated from his cargo." The conduct of the captors has on all points been highly reprehensible. Looking to all the circumstances of previous misconduct, I feel myself bound to pronounce that there has been a violation of territory, and that as to the question of property there was not sufficient ground of seizure; and that these acts of misconduct have been further aggravated by bringing the vessel to England, without any necessity that can justify such a measure. In such a case it would be falling short of the justice due to the violated rights of America, and to the individuals who have sustained injury by such misconduct, if I did not follow up the restitution which has passed on the former day with a decree of costs and damages.

1805 *November* 6, 15, 20.

THE ANNA.

Sir W. Scott.

THE WILLIAM (No. 2) (*a*).

[5 C. Rob. 385.]

(*Before the Lords Commissioners of Appeal in Prize Causes.*)

Continuous Voyage—Deviation—Landing of Cargo—Actual Termination of Voyage—Evidence.

A deviation by the landing and reshipping of cargo will not break the continuity of a voyage. When, therefore, a vessel took on board a cargo at La Guira which was carried to Marblehead and unladen, and the import duties paid, and the greater part was taken on board after slight repairs to the ship, which sailed again for Bilbao and was captured before her arrival there: *Held*, that there had been no real importation of the cargo at Marblehead, and that the vessel was on a continuous voyage from La Guira to Bilbao.

1806 *March* 11.

THIS was a question on the continuity of a voyage in the colonial trade of the enemy, brought by appeal from the Vice-Admiralty Court of Halifax, where the ship and cargo, taken on a destination to Bilbao in Spain, and claimed on behalf of Messrs. W. and N. Hooper, of Marblehead, in the State of Massachusetts, had been condemned 17th July, 1800.

It appeared in evidence that the ship had gone to Martinique, where the outward cargo was disposed of; that she then proceeded to La Guira, and took on board a cargo of cocoa, the property of the owners, which was brought to Marblehead on the 29th May, and unladen; that the ship was then cleaned and slightly repaired, and again took on board the chief part of the former cargo, with some sugars brought from the Havannah in other ships, and purchased by the owners, and sailed on or before the 7th June upon a destination to Bilbao. Among the papers was a certificate from the collector of the customs "that this vessel had entered and landed a cargo of cocoa belonging to Messrs. W. and N. Hooper, and that the duties had been secured agreeable to law, and that

(*a*) See the *Maria*, *ante*, p. 495.

1806 *March* 11. THE WILLIAM.

the said cargo had been reshipped on board this vessel bound for Bilbao; and that her cargo, consisting of cocoa, sugar, and fish, was the property of the said W. and N. Hooper."

On the 7th May, 1804, the cause came on to be heard before the Lords of Appeal upon the original evidence, when the case was argued on the principle of continuity, and the application of that principle to the circumstances of the present case, by the King's Advocate and the Attorney-General on the part of the captor, and by Mr. Dallas and Dr. Arnold on the part of the appellant. The Lords "pronounced for the appeal, reversed the sentence appealed from, and retained the principal cause, therein admitted the claim for the ship and cargo, pronounced the said cargo, except 70 hogsheads of cocoa and five bags of cocoa, to have belonged as claimed, and dismissed the bail given in the Court below to answer the appeal in respect thereto; but directed further proof to be made of the importation of the said cocoa into, and exportation from, the port of Marblehead in America, and the payment of duties thereon within nine months."

In obedience to that decree further proof was exhibited, consisting of sundry documents.

On this proof the cause was further argued, and on the 11th March, 1806, the judgment of the Court of Appeal was delivered by the Right Honourable Sir William Grant, Master of the Rolls, in the following terms:—

SIR W. GRANT.—The question in this case is, whether that part of the cargo which has been the subject of further proof, and which, it is admitted, was at the time of the capture going to Spain, is to be considered as coming directly from La Guira within the meaning of his Majesty's instructions. According to our understanding of the law, it is only from those instructions that neutrals derive any right of carrying on with the colonies of our enemies, in time of war, a trade from which they were excluded in time of peace. The instructions had not permitted the direct trade between the hostile colony and its mother country, but had, on the contrary, ordered all vessels engaged in it to be brought in for lawful adjudication, and what the present claimants accordingly maintain is, not that they could carry the produce of La Guira directly to Spain, but that they were not so carrying the cargo in question, inasmuch as the voyage in which it was taken was a voyage from North America, and not directly from a colony of Spain.

What, then, with reference to this subject, is to be considered as a direct voyage from one place to another? Nobody has ever supposed that a mere deviation from the straightest and shortest course in which the voyage could be performed, would change its denomination and make it cease to be a direct one within the intendment of the instructions. Nothing can depend on the degree or the direction of the deviation, whether it be of more or fewer leagues, whether towards the coast of Africa or towards that of America. Neither will it be contended that the point from which the commencement of a voyage is to be reckoned changes as often as the ship stops in the course of it; nor will it the more change because a party may choose arbitrarily by the ship's papers, or otherwise, to give the name of a distinct voyage to each stage of a ship's progress. The act of shifting the cargo from the ship to the shore, and from the shore back again into the ship, does not necessarily amount to the termination of one voyage and the commencement of another. It may be wholly unconnected with any purpose of importation into the place where it is done. Supposing the landing to be merely for the purpose of airing or drying the goods, or of repairing the ship, would any man think of describing the voyage as beginning at the place where it happened to become necessary to go through such a process? Again, let it be supposed that the party has a motive for desiring to make the voyage appear to begin at some other place than that of the original lading, and that he therefore lands the cargo purely and solely for the purpose of enabling himself to affirm that it was at such other place that the goods were taken on board, would this contrivance at all alter the truth of the fact? Would not the real voyage still be from the place of the original shipment, notwithstanding the attempt to give it the appearance of having begun from a different place? The truth may not always be discernible, but when it is discovered, it is according to the truth and not according to the fiction that we are to give to the transaction its character and denomination. If the voyage from the place of lading

1806 *March* 11.

THE WILLIAM.

Sir W. Grant.

be not really ended, it matters not by what acts the party may have evinced his desire of making it appear to have been ended. That those acts have been attended with trouble and expense cannot alter their quality or their effect. The trouble and expense may weigh as circumstances of evidence to show the purpose for which the acts were done; but if the evasive purpose be admitted or proved, we can never be bound to accept as a substitute for the observance of the law, the means, however operose, which have been employed to cover a breach of it. Between the actual importation by which a voyage is really ended, and the colourable importation which is to give it the appearance of being ended, there must necessarily be a great resemblance. The acts to be done must be almost entirely the same; but there is this difference between them: the landing of the cargo, the entry at the custom house, and the payment of such duties as the law of the place requires, are necessary ingredients in a genuine importation; the true purpose of the owner cannot be effected without them. But in a fictitious importation they are mere voluntary ceremonies, which have no natural connection whatever with the purpose of sending on the cargo to another market, and which, therefore, would never be resorted to by a person entertaining that purpose, except with a view of giving to the voyage which he has resolved to continue the appearance of being broken by an importation, which he has resolved not really to make.

Now what is the case immediately before us? The cargo in question was taken on board at La Guira. It was at the time of the capture proceeding to Spain, but the ship had touched at an American port. The cargo was landed and entered at the custom house, and a bond was given for duties to the amount of 1,239 dollars. The cargo was re-shipped, and a debenture for 1,211 dollars by way of drawback was obtained. All this passed in the course of a few days. The vessel arrived at Marblehead on the 29th of May; on that day the bond for securing the duties was given. On the 30th and 31st the goods were landed, weighed and packed. The permit to ship them is dated the 1st of June, and on the 3rd of June the vessel is cleared out as laden and ready to proceed to sea. We are frequently obliged to collect the purpose from the circumstances of the transaction. The landing thus almost instantaneously followed by the re-shipment has little appearance of having been made with a view to actual importation; but it is not upon inference that the conclusion in this case is left to rest. The claimants, instead of showing that they really did import this cargo, have, in their attestation, stated the reasons which determined them not to import it. They say, indeed, that when they ordered it to be purchased "it was with the single view of bringing it to the United States, and that they then had no intention or expectation of exporting it in the said schooner to Spain." Supposing that from this somewhat ambiguous statement we are to collect that their original intention was to have imported this cargo from America, with a view only to the American market, yet their intention had been changed before the arrival of the vessel. For they state that in the beginning of May they had received accounts of the prices of cocoa in Spain, which satisfied them that it would sell much better there than in America, and that they had therefore determined to send it to the Spanish market. Nothing is alleged to have happened between the landing of the cargo and its re-shipment that could have the least influence on their determination. It was not in that short interval that American prices fell, or that information of the higher prices in Spain had been received. Knowing beforehand the comparative state of the two markets, they neither tried nor meant to try that of America, but proceeded with all possible expedition to go through the forms which have been before enumerated. If the continuity of the voyage remains unbroken, it is immaterial whether it be by the prosecution of an original purpose to continue it, as in the case of the *Essex*, or, as in this case, by the relinquishment of an original purpose to have brought it to a termination in America. It can never be contended that an intention to import once entertained is equivalent to importation; and it would be a contradiction in terms to say that by acts done after the original intention has been abandoned such original intention has been carried into execution. Why should a cargo, which there was to be no attempt to sell in America, have been entered at an American custom house, and voluntarily subjected to the payment of any, even the most trifling duty? Not because importation was, or in such a case could be intended, but because it was

1806 *March* 11. THE WILLIAM. Sir W. Grant.

thought expedient that something should be done, which in a British Prize Court might pass for importation. Indeed, the claimants seem to have conceived that the inquiry to be made here was not whether the importation was real or pretended, but whether the pretence had assumed a particular form, and was accompanied with certain circumstances which by some positive rule were, in all cases, to stand for importation, or to be conclusive evidence of it; and it has, I understand, been said that our departure from that supposed rule in the case of the *Essex* (*a*) was a surprise upon the merchants of America, who had by our former decisions been led to believe that proof of landing and payment of duties in America would in every case be held absolutely decisive of the legality of the voyage.

How far even that rule would have been departed from by the decision in the case of the *Essex* will hereafter be considered. But after having looked very attentively into all the cases in which, as far as I am aware, this sort of question has occurred, I conceive, not only that it will be impossible to point out a judgment in which any such unqualified doctrine has been laid down, but that the judgments antecedent to that in the *Essex* had clearly and unequivocally negatived the existence of the alleged rule of decision.

The first case of the kind, that of the *Polly*, occurred in the High Court of Admiralty, in February, 1800. The learned judge of that Court expressly disclaimed the attempt to define what should be deemed universally the test of a *bonâ fide* importation. He did, indeed, lay great and just stress on the payment of the American import duties, which was there sworn to have been actually made. But still it was as evidence of *bonâ fide* importation. The very statement that the thing in question was the *bona fides* of the importation did of necessity exclude the supposition that one uniform effect was in all cases to be ascribed to a given set of circumstances, without regard to the manner in which their effect as evidence might be varied by other circumstances with which, in different cases, they might be found contrasted or combined. The first case of this class which I believe came before this

(*a*) Lords, 22nd June, 1805.

board was that of the *Mercury*, in January, 1802. By all the documents found on board, the cargo appeared to have been laden at Charlestown; and among those documents there was an attestation sworn at the custom house that all the parts of the cargo which were of foreign growth or manufacture had been legally imported, and the duties thereon paid or secured. It came out, however, in the depositions of the witnesses examined on the standing interrogatories, that the cargo had been laden at the Havannah, and that it never had been landed at Charlestown, the place of the alleged shipment. It being evident that the touching at Charlestown was for the mere purpose of giving to the voyage the colour and appearance of having begun there, we affirmed the sentence of condemnation, without previously endeavouring to ascertain whether any duties had really been paid in America. The true nature of the transaction being clearly ascertained, it seemed immaterial to inquire whether the payment of duties had been one of the means employed to disguise it.

The next case which occurred was that of the *Eagle*, in May, 1803. By the original evidence it appeared that the cargo had come from Bilbao to Philadelphia, where it had been landed, and whence it was proceeding in the same vessel to the Havannah. The condemnation in the Court below had proceeded on the ground that the cargo was contraband of war. But the only question here was with regard to the continuity of the voyage. As to that, further proof was ordered. We had the landing at Philadelphia already in evidence; therefore, according to the supposed rule, the only other circumstance, with regard to which proof could be material, was the payment of duties: but we did not so limit our inquiry. In order to endeavour to discover the real purpose and intention of the owner, we called for the orders which he had given concerning the purchase and shipment of the cargo at Bilbao, and also for the insurances made from thence. Had it clearly appeared from those orders or insurances that the cargo was from the beginning destined for the Havannah, could it be supposed that we would pay no regard to that result of the inquiry which we had directed, but would ascribe to the payment of duties such a conclusive effect as would have rendered every other part of the inquiry perfectly nugatory? When the case came back on the further

1806 *March* 11. THE WILLIAM. Sir W. Grant.

proof, nothing appeared in the letters of orders to show a destination to the Havannah. No insurance had been effected on the first branch of the voyage. It was positively sworn that the import duties, amounting to 1,333 dollars, had been actually paid; also, that the cargo had been warehoused at Philadelphia and advertised and intended for sale there, but that not being able to obtain a price that would answer, the owner had resolved to ship it for the Havannah. Giving a credit to this evidence, which, it now appears, it did not deserve, we thought that a complete *bonâ fide* importation had taken place, and therefore decreed restitution of the ship and cargo.

The case of the schooner *Freeport*, and the original hearing of the *Essex*, came on in August, 1803. The *Freeport* had carried from Cadiz to Boston the cargo with which at the time of the capture it was proceeding to one of the Spanish colonies. The cargo had been landed and remained some time on shore; but the master, who was half owner of both ship and cargo, admitted in his claim that the cargo was intended for the Spanish West Indian market, and did not even assert any purpose of importation into America. We therefore affirmed the sentence of condemnation. The cargo having been landed, it might be taken for granted that whatever duties were payable had been paid. But, as the case stood, we thought that fact immaterial, and therefore directed no inquiry with regard to it.

In the case of the *Essex* the cargo had been brought from Barcelona to Salem, and after having been landed and re-shipped was proceeding to the Havannah. From the original evidence there was great reason to believe that the master had from the beginning destined the cargo for the Spanish colony; but as what had passed at Salem, or what had been the conduct of the owner after the ship's arrival there, did not distinctly appear, it was thought right to give him an opportunity of entering further proof of the alleged importation. It had never been denied that in a doubtful case payment of duties would have great weight, and therefore the further proof was particularly directed to that point. But it having been suggested that in these cases the duties charged on landing were almost entirely drawn back on the re-shipment, we also called for an account of the drawbacks, if any, which had been received. This additional enquiry sufficiently showed that the same effect would not be ascribed to a nominal as to an actual payment of import duties. With a view of further elucidating the transaction, the insurances made, if any, were directed to be produced. The final event of this case will be afterwards noticed.

The next case was that which is the immediate subject of the present judgment. It was first heard in May, 1804. By the original evidence the landing of the cargo at Marblehead was proved; it was also in proof that the duties had been secured according to law—so the owners swore, so the custom-house certified. It was to be supposed that duties which were secured were one day to be paid, and it was doubtless meant to be so understood here; for the fact was suppressed that at the moment when the certificate issued from the custom-house, and the oath was made by the owners, a debenture had been granted which in effect extinguished almost the whole of the duties that had been previously secured. Here was what is now said to have been by us held conclusive evidence of importation. But what did we determine? That the importation was not sufficiently proved, and therefore we directed further proof of it to be made. Could any American, who at all attended to the proceedings of this Court, be really surprised by our again deciding a twelvemonth afterwards that such evidence was not conclusive? Yet this effect, I mean of surprise, is ascribed to our decision in the *Essex*, in May, 1805. Upon the further proof, it appeared to us that no real importation into Salem had taken place, or had ever been in the contemplation of the parties to the transaction; the sentence of condemnation was therefore affirmed. As it is not the object of this review of the cases to discuss the merits of the particular judgments, but only to examine whether there be any inconsistency in their principles, it is unnecessary to advert to any other point in the last-mentioned decision than its alleged novelty in departing from the supposed principle of holding that landing and payment of duties in America did, absolutely and under all circumstances, legalise the subsequent voyage. I have shown that there was not one decision in which any such principle had been asserted or implied, and that there were at least two decisions which stood in direct contradiction to it, that in the *Freeport* in 1803, and that in the *William* in 1804.

1806 *March* 11. THE WILLIAM. Sir W. Grant.

But supposing that we had uniformly held that payment of the import duties furnished conclusive evidence of importation, would there have been any inconsistency or contradiction in holding that the mere act of giving a bond for an amount of duties, of which only a very insignificant part was ever to be paid, could not have the same effect as the actual payment of such amount? The further proof in the *Essex* first brought distinctly before us the real state of the fact in this particular. It has been already mentioned that we had called for an account of the drawbacks, if any, that had been received. This produced the information that although the duties secured amounted to 5,278 dollars, yet a debenture was immediately afterwards given for no less than 5,080 dollars, so that on that valuable cargo no more than 198 dollars would be ultimately payable, which sum is said to be more than compensated by the advantage arising from the negotiability of the debenture. In the case of the *Eagle*, immediately preceding, it had been sworn by the owner and certified by the custom-house that the duties amounting to 1,333 dollars, not an unsubstantial sum on the not very valuable cargo of a small vessel of 110 tons, had been actually paid. In the *Polly*, it was sworn generally that the duties were paid; in the *Mercury*, that they were paid or secured; in the *William*, that they were secured: not a word was said about drawbacks. It was therefore natural for us to understand American claimants, as they certainly wished we should understand them, to be speaking of the payment of such duties as were chargeable on importation into America, and of a security that would make the whole amount secured become payable at some future day. If we had ascribed to the fact, as we believed it to exist, ever so decisive an effect, I again ask where would be the inconsistency in denying the same effect to a fact of a totally different nature? It must not be supposed that we pretend to judge what duties it may be proper for the American Government to exact or to remit, neither do we contend that an importation cannot be genuine because a high duty has not been paid. All we say is, that in the nature of the thing, the payment of a slight duty does not tend in the same degree to establish the *bona fides* of an importation as the payment of a heavy duty would have done. We never held that either would necessarily outweigh all the evidence which could possibly be put into the opposite scale, but that the one has less weight than the other is obvious to every man's apprehension. 1806 *March* 11. THE WILLIAM. Sir W. Grant.

On the whole, I trust I have demonstrated that we did not in the case of the *Essex*, and that we do not in the case now before us, depart from any principle which we have ever adopted. The application to this case of the principles on which we really have proceeded has been already shown. The consequence is that the voyage was illegal, and that the sentence of condemnation must be affirmed.

THE LA FLORA.

[6 C. Rob. 1.]

Cargo—Voyage—Actual Destination of Ship—Ultimate Destination of Cargo.

By an Order in Council, Spanish wool consigned to a merchant of the United Kingdom was to be free from capture. A vessel was chartered for Embden to carry a cargo of Spanish wool which the consignees intended should be ultimately sent to the United Kingdom. The vessel and cargo were captured: *Held*, that as the immediate destination of the cargo must alone be regarded, the cargo in question was not exempted, under the Order in Council, from condemnation.

THIS was a case arising on a claim for a cargo of Spanish wool given by Mr. Lewis, of London, under the instructions of 4th of September, 1803 (*a*). 1805 *March* 14, 20.

The ship's papers expressed a destination to Embden, and the master and other witnesses examined in preparatory described the voyage to have been to Embden.

(*a*) "Whereas we have thought it expedient to protect from capture and condemnation wool, the growth and production of Spain, laden on board ships belonging to any State in amity with us, and coming consigned to any merchant of our United Kingdom: The commanders of our ships of war and privateers are hereby required and enjoined not to detain or molest any vessels belonging to any State in amity with us on account of their having on board any wool, the growth and production of Spain, and coming consigned to any merchant of our United Kingdom. And in case any such wool so laden and consigned shall be brought for adjudication before any of our Courts of Admiralty, we hereby direct that the same shall be forthwith liberated upon a claim being given for it by or on behalf of the merchant to whom it is consigned, notwithstanding the existing hostilities, or any other hostilities which may take place."

1805 *March* 14, 20.

THE LA FLORA.

On the 20th March this case came on again upon proof of the actual consignment, to be extracted from the correspondence of the Spanish shippers (*a*).

(*a*) 18th December, 1804. "We have only time to confirm to you our last of the 13th instant, whereof a copy accompanies this, and to inform you that in consequence of the declaration of war between the two powers, we shall be under the necessity of altering the destination of Captains E. Haseman and Olfert Olferts Klein, who will be documented as if they were bound to Embden, to the consignment and for account and risk of Mr. Louis Sethe, but their real destination will be to your place to your consignment, which you will communicate to the underwriters of our wools."

6th January, 1805. "The measures adopted by this Government in consequence of the declaration of war with your island, and the existing state of the commerce in this province which has plunged the merchants into the greatest distress, prevent the transactions of business with that confidence which took place during other wars, and which, in the present case, deprive us of the means hitherto resorted to for the exportation of wools. The Government, which has recently prohibited all direct and indirect commerce with your kingdom, and the vigilance of the royal judge invested with the execution of such order, involves us in the greatest confusion as to the destination of Captain Olfert Olferts Klein, of the Prussian vessel *Flora*.

"We chartered this vessel under a colourable destination for Embden, but actually for Southampton, agreeable to the constant practice, the separate obligations which the captains were in the habit of contracting constituting the security of real destination, but which it was not prudent to demand under the present rigorous circumstances, and which would inevitably expose us to danger.

"This extreme inconvenience has induced us to depart from the system adopted in other times, being obliged to leave to the courtesy and will of the captain the performance of the original simulated affreightment, or the performance of the one appearing by the ship's papers.

"Impressed with apprehension of such consequence, we told Captain Klein we were unable to furnish him with any other instructions, in the consequence of existing circumstances, than those of proceeding to his actual destination of Embden, but that he knew his primitive obligation, and that in the event of his putting into any of the ports of your island he should advise you. Our language on taking leave of Captain Klein, and he himself feeling the rigour with which he was treated, impressed upon the said captain the motives which compelled us to explain ourselves in that tone, without leaving him ignorant that our intentions were that he should put in at one of your ports. We know not whether this captain will perform his engagement or not as a man of honour, although it is to be apprehended that he will proceed direct to Embden, seeing himself without any signed obligation to the contrary; and should the same happen, we have this day written to Mr. Louis Sethe in order that he may immediately, on the receipt of the two hundred

For the claimant, *Laurence*. 1805 *March* 14, 20.

For the captor, the *King's Advocate* and *Robinson*. THE LA FLORA.

SIR W. SCOTT.—The Order of Council directs the restitution of Spanish wool "consigned to this country." But the fact now turns out to be that this cargo was consigned to Embden, not only ostensibly, but according to the private understanding of the shippers, who say "that they had given instructions to persons there to receive the cargo if it should actually arrive at Embden." The master also says absolutely "that he should have gone to Embden"; and unless I could hold to the extent contended in argument that a circuitous ulterior destination to this country, either in the same ship or in other ships, is to be considered in law as one identical consignment, I fear it is out of my power to bring the case within the provisions of the Order of Council. How far it may be proper to allow further relaxation, or what considerations may interfere with such an extension of the indulgence, is a question of policy which it may not be very easy to decide immediately, and which it would not become this Court to decide, or even entertain in the first instance. One consequence of such an extension may be easily foreseen, that if such a circuitous voyage was to be allowed, Spanish wools might with great security find their way into France and Holland for the supply of the manufactures of those countries. I cannot but think, therefore, that Government would pause in sanctioning such an interpretation till it had maturely weighed all the consequences that might be expected to result from it. It is my duty, however, to consider only whether the words of the Order can be supposed to embrace such a case, and my opinion is that they cannot. There is, I think, some force in the argument which has been drawn from the ordinary bearing of the navigation laws. An act of relaxation has, I know, passed for the importation of certain articles of Spanish produce from other ports, but whether wool is so admitted I cannot immediately take upon myself to determine. Looking to the whole circum-

and thirty-six bags on board the vessel under the command of Captain Klein, forward them to you under his neutrality, availing himself of the first vessel he may wish to carry them."

1805 March 14, 20. — THE LA FLORA. — Sir W. Scott.

stances of this case, I am induced to consider it as one which has not yet met the attention of Government, and which does not come under the Order of Council. Under that view I feel myself bound to reject this claim.

[6 C. Rob. 24.]

THE MARIANNA.

Enemy Ship—Transfer—Lien of Neutral.

When a ship has been legally transferred to a purchaser, the Prize Court will disregard liens arising out of the purchase, and will condemn the ship if it is *primâ facie* the property of an enemy, and also enemy cargo even if bound by a lien as between the shipowner and the vendor of the ship.

1805 April 30.

SIR W. SCOTT.—This ship appears to have been originally an American vessel, sold to a Spanish merchant at Buenos Ayres, and seized on a voyage to this country, documented as belonging to a Spanish merchant and sailing under the flag and pass of Spain. A claim is given on behalf of the former American proprietor in virtue of a lien which he is said to have retained on the property for the payment of the purchase money; but such an interest cannot, I conceive, be deemed sufficient to support a claim of property in a Court of Prize. Captors are supposed to lay their hands on the gross tangible property, on which there may be many just claims outstanding between other parties which can have no operation as to them. If such a rule did not exist it would be quite impossible for captors to know upon what grounds they were proceeding to make any seizure. The fairest, and most credible documents, declaring the property to belong to the enemy, would only serve to mislead them if such documents were liable to be overruled by liens which could not in any manner come to their knowledge. It would be equally impossible for the Court which has to decide upon the question of property to admit such considerations. The doctrine of liens depends very much on the particular rules of jurisprudence which prevail in different countries. To decide judicially on such claims would require of the Court a perfect knowledge of the law of covenant, and the application of that law in all countries, under all the diversities in which that law exists. From necessity, therefore, the Court would be obliged to shut the door against such discussions, and to decide on the simple title of property with scarcely any exceptions. Then what is the proprietor's character of the ship? She is described as the property of the Spanish merchant, Mr. Romero. She is sailing under the Spanish flag and is fully invested with the Spanish character, not ostensibly only, but actually, and in the real intention and understanding of the parties. She had been sold to Mr. Romero, but it is said that a part of the purchase money had not been paid. That objection can have little weight, since it is a matter solely for the consideration of the person who sells to judge what mode of payment he will accept. He may consent to take a bill of exchange, or he may rely on the promissory note of the purchaser, which may not come in payment for a considerable time, or may never be paid. The Court will not look to such contingencies. It will be sufficient that a legal transfer has been made, and that the mode of payment, whatever it is, has been accepted. Upon this view of the principle upon which the Prize Court has always acted, the ship must be considered to have been legally transferred, and must be pronounced subject to condemnation, as Spanish property, which will dispose of that part of the claim which prays for an indemnification to be allowed out of the freight. Then as to the title of property in the goods, which are said to have been going, as the funds out of which the payment for the ship was to have been made. That they were going for the payment of a debt will not alter the property—there must be something more. Even if bills of lading are delivered, that circumstance will not be sufficient, unless accompanied with an understanding that he who holds the bill of lading is to bear the risk of the goods as to the voyage and as to the market to which they are consigned; otherwise, though the security may avail *pro tanto*, it cannot be held to work any change in the property. It is said that the shipper had covenanted to pay 20,000 dollars in London, and that to supply the necessary funds he covenanted to ship, and did actually ship, these goods, consigned to the correspondent of the American merchant in London. That might be mere matter of arrangement as to the convenience of the

1805 *April* 30.

THE MARIANNA.

Sir W. Scott.

parties, but it can found no title to property, unless it was done with a full transfer of the account and risk at the same time. Who was the shipper?—not the American, but the Spanish merchant. He consigns the goods to the care of the house in London, and if they had been lost, the loss would have fallen upon him. The person in America could exercise no dominion over them—he could not direct the consignment to be made to the house in London. That the transaction was so conducted was mere matter of convenience and accommodation, but can make no difference as to the principle on which the question of property is to be considered. It is said also that the shipper had agreed to send the bills of lading to the person in America, that he might forward them to his correspondents in London, to enable them to receive the proceeds; and it is intimated that the goods were insured by the correspondents of the person in America, but it does not appear how, or in what character; it could not be as American property, I conceive, because it is quite clear that the risk of the market was to fall on the Spanish shipper. The merchant in London was to pay whatever might exceed the demand of the person in America to Mr. Romero, and not to the claimant in America—no title of property is conveyed to the American merchant but a mere interest in the goods in question, under the form in which the transaction then stood. Suppose that the shipper had thought proper to have paid for the vessel in any other manner, it was clearly in his power to have made such a provision; and it could not then have been maintained that the person in America would have retained any interest, much less any title of property in the goods. Upon this view of the claims, which have been given in the alternative, as to the amount of the purchase money of the ship, I am of opinion that the title of property in the ship had been effectually transferred, and that no title of property in the parcel of tallow had been acquired.

THE NEUTRALITET (No. 2). 6 C. Rob. 30.

Blockade—Proximity to Port of Neutral Ship—Presumption—Breach.

If a neutral vessel approaches a blockaded port so as to be in a position from which she can enter (per Sir W. Scott), there is a legal presumption that such vessel intends to break the blockade.

THIS was one of several ships with cargoes of wine and brandy, ostensibly described in the ship's papers to be bound from Bordeaux to Embden, but taken amongst the Flemish banks, under a suspicion that they were endeavouring to get into Ostend. As it was a question turning upon points of nautical judgment and experience, the Court was, at the request of the captors, attended by two gentlemen of the Trinity House. 1805 *May* 9.

[The case is of importance from the *obiter dictum* of Sir W. Scott as to the liability of a neutral vessel which approaches a blockaded port.]

On the part of the captors, the *King's Advocate* and *Arnold.*

On the part of the claimant, *Laurence.*

In reply, the *King's Advocate* said that the ship had anchored in a situation, where, at daylight, she would have been under the protection of the batteries.

SIR W. SCOTT.—This is the case of a ship taken on a professed destination to Embden; but the fact is that she was seized in Ostend roads. Every witness uses the same expression, "Ostend roads," and I understand the situation of the vessel to have been at no great distance from that port. The term roads, undoubtedly, is not a word of very definite meaning: there may be roads which have no immediate connection with any particular port, as the Downs; other roads are so connected with particular ports as almost to form part of them; and these two descriptions of roads may be subject to very different considerations. If a ship comes into the Downs, which is the common passage and highway to the German Ocean, and to different parts of Europe, it would not be

1805 May 9. The Neutralitet. Sir W. Scott.

at all just to infer from the mere coming there that she is necessarily coming to a British port. But if the roads are of the other species, there is then reason to conclude that a ship comes there with a view to some communication with that particular port.

From the description given of the roads of Ostend, they are, I think, to be taken as being of the latter species. The ship was lying within a sand, and within the protection of the batteries, and in a place, as I conceive, where ships of large burden are usually unlivered by lighters, as the more commodious method of delivering their cargoes at Ostend. If I am correct in that view, a ship going there must be considered as in the port of Ostend, since, for the purpose of enforcing a blockade, it is not necessary to restrict the meaning of the word port to the limits of the particular local port regulations, which may not extend beyond the pier-head. A belligerent is not bound to that restricted sense of the word. If the situation of the vessel is within the protection of the batteries, and in a place which vessels usually frequent for the purpose of unlivery, and from which importation into Ostend can safely be effected, and it is not unusually effected, it would not unreasonably be held to be a part of that port. But I will take the case as if the vessel was not in the port, but only near to it. It comes then to be considered how far a neutral ship has a right to anchor in such a spot, where she may have an opportunity of slipping into the blockaded port without molestation. It will not be necessary in the present case to lay down a general principle on this point, but I am disposed to agree to a position advanced in argument, that a belligerent is not called upon to admit that neutral ships can innocently place themselves in a situation where they may with impunity break the blockade whenever they please. If the belligerent country has a right to impose a blockade, it must be justified in the necessary means of enforcing that right; and if a vessel could, under the pretence of going farther, approach, *cy près*, close up to the blockaded port so as to be enabled to slip in without obstruction, it would be impossible that any blockade could be maintained. It would, I think, be no unfair rule of evidence to hold, as a presumption *de jure*, that she goes there with an intention of breaking the blockade; and if such an inference may possibly operate with severity in particular cases, where the parties are innocent in their intentions, it is a severity necessarily connected with the rules of evidence and essential to the effectual exercise of this right of war.

I do not, however, lay down the general rule on the present occasion, as I think it is not rendered necessary by the circumstances of the case. I will take it on the point contended for, that notwithstanding the suspicions arising from the nature of the situation, it might still be open to the parties to show the innocence of their intentions by clear and satisfactory evidence, and to exonerate themselves from the penalty of the law. We will suppose the question to be only as to the innocence of intention. To determine that, I must consider the motives assigned for the course which has been pursued. The voyage was originally to Embden; what produced the deviation? The master in his deposition states "that the ship's course was directed towards Embden till the 6th of February, when she spoke a small vessel, which informed them that the Eems was full of ice, which induced him to go to Ostend to get a pilot, as it was necessary on account of the water made by the ship that she should be taken into a place of safety." This necessity seems afterwards to be a little disclaimed, since in his affidavit he says "that he should have gone on to Embden but for the information received as to the state of the Eems"; and another witness, I observe, states "that they went to get a pilot for Flushing."

Now the first question which I wish to propose to these gentlemen is, whether this was natural conduct to be pursued by a person in such a situation? I confess it appears to me, from the little judgment which I can exercise on such subjects, that it was not. It might, I conceive, rather have been expected that the master would have gone on to some other ports, as to the Texel, where he might have waited till the Eems was open. It appears to me to be perfectly unnatural that he should have made choice of such a port as Flushing, which is of intricate navigation and not so accessible as the Texel, to which he might have gone through an open sea. The second question which I have to propose, not as a question of nice nautical skill, but as a point to be decided by the natural conduct of maritime men of ordinary prudence, is, whether it was a prudent and natural course that the master should have

1805 *May* 9. THE NEUTRALITET. Sir W. Scott.

resorted to such a port as Ostend for the mere purpose of obtaining a pilot for Flushing? And I must request you, gentlemen, to consider it with reference to everything which you may have read or heard in evidence, as arising from the state of the winds and the weather, and from other circumstances, with the effect of which I may be little acquainted, that might render it a measure to which a man of ordinary habits of prudence would be likely to resort.

The Trinity Masters reported it to be their opinion that a master ought not to have gone to Ostend for the purpose of taking a pilot to Flushing; that if there had been a leak, as was represented, he should not have stood in within the banks for a pilot.

THE COURT proceeded: That being the case, I am warranted to pronounce the excuse alleged not to be justifiable. It will be unnecessary for me to consider the other question, as I am of opinion that the ship had been brought into this situation, not with any honest intention, but for the purpose of importing her cargo into Ostend.

Ship and cargo condemned.

[6 C. Rob. 54.]

THE HAABET (No. 2).

Practice—Affidavit of Captor—Admissibility—Contradiction of Depositions of Crew of Captured Ship.

The Court, when on the depositions of the crew of a captured ship no doubt arises, will not permit such depositions to be contradicted by affidavits of the captors.

1805 *June* 20.

THIS was the case of a Danish vessel laden with spars and fir timber, taken near Dunkirk on a voyage from Frederickstadt to L'Orient, and proceeded against for a breach of the blockade of that port. The master had stated in his depositions "that he was twelve English miles from Dunkirk when he first made land; that he had shaped his course for the Channel, and was steering for L'Orient at the time of capture."

On this evidence, *Laurence* contended, on the part of the claimant, that it was a case of immediate restitution, and that there was nothing on the face of the transaction that could in any manner justify a demand for captors' expenses, which had been intimated on the other side.

On the part of the captors, the *King's Advocate* in reply pressed strongly upon the Court the hardships to which persons employed on the blockading service would feel themselves exposed, if the vessel was to be released immediately upon the representation of the neutral master, without affording the captors an opportunity of giving their statement of what passed at the time of capture, so far, at least, as to justify the seizure and to entitle them to their expenses.

SIR W. SCOTT.—This vessel was going from Frederickstadt, as it is asserted, to Port L'Orient with a cargo of timber. The first source of information to which the Court usually resorts is the evidence of the persons on board the captured ship. Among the interrogatories that are addressed to them are some from which the captors might be supposed to be equally qualified to supply information. The number of the crew, the place of capture, and many other circumstances which are included in the number of standing interrogatories are as much in the cognizance of the captors as of the other parties. The general rule of law, notwithstanding, is that on all points the evidence of the claimants alone shall be received in the first instance, and, if no doubt arises upon that view of the case, the Court is bound by the general law, as well as by the Act of the British Legislature, to take those points as fully demonstrated. It is a possible thing, indeed, that witnesses may be forsworn, and that much injustice may be done, as in all references to human testimony dangers of that kind may be to be encountered. Courts of justice must nevertheless proceed on general principles, though they will receive the evidence with caution, and weigh it against any test of credibility that can be collected from the nature and complexion of the whole case taken together. The rule by which this Court has always been guided

1805 June 20. — THE HAABET. Sir W. Scott.

is, I believe, conformable to the general practice of all the nations of Europe, which directs the evidence to be taken from the persons on board the captured ship. . . . . The rule being, then, to take the original evidence of the claimants as conclusive if not impeached, I feel myself bound to pronounce that the depositions in this particular case are as void of suspicion as any which the Court is in the habit of perusing. . . . . Under this defect of all circumstances of suspicion in the original evidence, the Court is called upon to admit the affidavits of the captors—first, for the purpose of working condemnation, or, if that fails, to save the captors from the payment of any expenses which they may have incurred. If I should accede to this demand, the consequence would be that I must do it upon a uniform principle of admitting affidavits universally and in all cases, though there should be nothing to excite suspicion in the original evidence, and though the language of all the witnesses is as precise as possible. I can come to no such conclusion. It would, I think, be productive of great mischief on all sides. It might throw into the way of captors a temptation to exceed the line of their duty, and the exact bounds of justice and of truth; and it could not fail to impose upon the Court a most unpleasant difficulty in the exercise of its judicial functions. For how could the Court decide? Counter affidavits must be introduced, which would necessarily be contradictory. Which should the Court believe? Can it be maintained that the preference should be given to the captors; and that in opposition to the general rule of law which has given the preference the other way, and which directs that the property of the neutral claimant shall not be condemned except on evidence coming out of his own mouth, or arising out of the clear circumstances of the transaction? If this rule is unsatisfactory to captors, it is nevertheless the rule which the law prescribes. It is my duty to take care that the rules of law are observed, and that the rights of war are not exceeded; and certainly in no cases more than in this particular branch of the law of nations, which must in its nature operate with severe restraint upon neutral commerce; and if, in discharging this duty, dissatisfactions are created, as has been intimated, I must endeavour to supply fortitude, to treat with proper disregard the unfavourable but unjust opinions that any persons may be disposed to entertain.

Looking to the depositions, I am obliged to hold that the affidavits of the captors cannot be admitted (*a*).

(*a*) The *Glierktigheit*, 25th of July, 1805. The Court had occasion to observe again upon the inconvenience of admitting affidavits to be introduced (*a*).

SIR W. SCOTT.—The imputation of breaking the blockade has already been pronounced, under the assistance of gentlemen of the Trinity House, not to be supported on a general view of the evidence and the situation of the vessel. The ship would therefore have been restored on the former hearing but for an averment on the part of the captors that a flag was flying for a pilot to carry her into Ostend, and that the master admitted in conversation that he was going to Ostend. Certainly if the captor's evidence could be taken alone it would be sufficient to substantiate this averment; but the Court is under the necessity of not taking their representation alone; and if that is positively contradicted, the Court finds itself under a dilemma to which it must always expect to be reduced by admitting such affidavits. When the facts are positively denied, and that denial cannot be invalidated by any adequate means of estimating the credit of the witnesses, there is no other way of proceeding but by laying out of the case all this extraneous matter, and by recurring to the original evidence. The Court cannot attach itself to personal considerations, and say, this is the affidavit of such a gentleman, and that of an ordinary person; it cannot decide on grounds so vague and unjudicial as those of mere rank and situation in life; those are grounds to which it is impossible for me, sitting here, to advert in any manner that can produce a conclusion. The imputation of direct interest is equal or perhaps stronger on the captor than on the witnesses from the captured ship. The master positively swears that he had not a flag flying; he admits that a flag had been flying at a particular time, and for another purpose, but not agreeing with the representation of the captors; and the two accounts can only be reconciled by supposing that there must have been some mistake as to the time. As to the declaration which is said to have been made of an intention of going to Ostend, the master denies it altogether. This is the state of the dilemma to which the Court is reduced, and it will, I hope, put it upon its guard against the admission of such affidavits in future cases. On a view of the whole evidence, I cannot say that the averment of the captors is established. I say no more, but that it is not established. That being laid out of the question, the case reverts to its former state, in which it would have been pronounced a case of restitution; I shall therefore now decree this ship and cargo to be restored.

(*a*) See the *Aline and Fanny*, Vol. II. p. 537.

[6 C. Rob. 61.]

THE GENERAL HAMILTON.

Blockade—Purchase of Ship in Blockaded Port—Termination of Voyage (*a*).

The purchase of a ship in a blockaded port is illegal, and after a ship has broken a blockade, entry into a port in distress will not be a termination of a voyage so as to take away her liability to condemnation.

1805 *July* 4.

THIS was the case of a ship which had been purchased in a blockaded port, and had sailed on a voyage from the Seine to New Orleans, and had been driven by stress of weather into a port of this kingdom, where she was seized. A claim was given for the vessel as the property of the purchaser, a merchant of America.

In support of the claim, *Laurence*.

On the part of the captor, the *King's Advocate*.

SIR W. SCOTT.—This is a vessel which has been purchased in a blockaded port; and therefore, unless any just grounds of distinction can be pointed out, it will come under the general rule which has been already applied to cases of that description. It is first said, that the vessel had been purchased out of the proceeds of the cargo of another vessel, but that circumstance cannot avail on a question of blockade. If the ship has been purchased in a blockaded port, that alone is the illegal act, and it is perfectly immaterial out of what funds the purchase was effected. Another distinction is, that the vessel had terminated her voyage, and therefore that the penalty would no longer attach. It is true that she had been driven into a port of this country by stress of weather; but that is not described by the master as forming any part of the original destination, which is represented to have been to New Orleans. It is impossible to consider this action as any discontinuance of the voyage or as a defeasance of the penalty which has been incurred.

Condemned.

(*a*) See the *Welvaart Van Pillaw*, *ante*, p. 207.

THE CLIO.

[6 C. Rob. 67.]

Licence—Leave to Obtain Vessel from Bankrupt Estate in Enemy Country—Bond to Restore.

A licence to purchase a vessel out of the hands of an enemy merchant with a view of recovering a bad debt is not vitiated by a bond to restore at the conclusion of the war, if the transaction is *bonâ fide* and in accordance with the intention of the licence (*a*).

1805 *July* 23.

THIS was the case of a ship taken on a voyage from Antwerp to London, and claimed by the house of Rucker, Lushington & Co. as property which had been accepted by Mr. Osy, their agent at Antwerp, for their account, in satisfaction of a debt due to them from the bankrupt estate of a merchant of that place, under a licence obtained by them for that purpose in February, 1805.

In objection to the claim, the *King's Advocate* relied on the *Sechs Geschwistern* (*b*).

In support of the claim, *Laurence*.

SIR W. SCOTT.—This case comes before the Court upon the construction of his Majesty's licence, granted to the house of Rucker & Lushington, to accept the assignment of the British ship, the *Clio*, which was to be made over to them as a satisfaction for a debt due to them before the war from a merchant at Antwerp; and as far as the parties themselves were concerned, the transaction appears to have passed in perfect conformity to the application. They employed Mr. Osy, of Antwerp, as their agent, and he acts for them throughout in recovering this property out of the wreck of a bankrupt estate. It appears, however, that he gave a bond to the French Government for the restitution of the ship at the conclusion of the war, and it is objected that this circumstance ought to have been disclosed to Government at the time of obtaining the licence. If known, certainly it ought. The exact state of the transaction ought to be fairly represented; but here is enough, I think, to exonerate the claimant from any charge of suppression, since the licence was obtained in February, and the first mention

(*a*) Cf. The *Sechs Geschwistern*, *ante*, p. 363.

(*b*) *Ante*, p. 363.

that occurs of the bond was not till the May following, which is sufficient to remove from them all suspicion of ill-faith in concealing this circumstance.

The whole foundation of the claim is that what has been done is agreeable to the intention of Government, and I am disposed to think that it is. The parties were not to purchase, but to take from a bankrupt's estate. When Government grants a licence, it must be supposed to grant all that is necessary to carry it into effect. The claimants could not go to Antwerp themselves; they were under the necessity of employing an agent: he, acting as their mandatory under the licence, might, I conceive, be entitled to recover (*a*) against them, though an alien enemy, a full indemnification for the terms of the assignment. They would be answerable to him if the bonds were put in suit, on their refusal to re-deliver the vessel.

Under these circumstances, it is altogether a case very different from that which has been cited, in which the Court did think itself warranted to hold a different rule against persons going into the enemy's country, and becoming the asserted purchasers of vessels, which the enemy is induced to make over, either really or ostensibly on account of the war. In that case, the fact itself suggested a strong ground of suspicion, and it became necessary, for the purpose of counteracting fraud, that the Court should set its face against such limitations in the pretended act of transfer. In the present instance, there is no reason to doubt the reality of the transfer. In acceding to the terms of the bond, the claimants would do no more than they were bound to do for the indemnification of their agent, and they are, I think, entitled, under the fair construction of the licence, to accept the ship upon these terms, as the only terms perhaps upon which it could be obtained.

(*a*) See *Kensington* v. *Inglis*, East's Rep. Vol. 8, pp. 273—287; *Wells* v. *Williams*, 1 Salk. 46, there cited.

THE JOHANNA THOLEN. [6 C. Rob. 78.]

Coasting Trade of Enemy—False Papers—Condemnation.

To carry on the coasting trade of an enemy with false papers is a ground of condemnation.

Sir W. Scott.—Upon the facts in this case there is no reasonable ground to doubt that the ship was engaged in carrying on the coasting trade of the enemy with false papers. All the documents purport a destination to Embden, but the ship is admitted to have been forcing her way to Antwerp, and for the purpose of delivering her cargo there. To allow that the parties could justify such a deviation by the pretence of a subsequent intention taken up at sea would enervate every rule that could be laid down respecting the coasting trade of the enemy. As to the principle itself, I confess that the impression on my mind has always been agreeable to what has been stated by the King's Advocate, "that the carrying on the coasting trade with false papers is a ground of condemnation, according to the established doctrine of this Court." I do not mean at present to enter into a discussion of the principle, which the Court has in many instances already applied. If there is any doubt upon the rectitude of that principle, it will be a great satisfaction to my mind to see it corrected by the decision of the Superior Court. Until that is done I shall not be disposed to depart from the rule upon which the Court has hitherto proceeded. With regard to the distinction that has been drawn from the character of the port at Antwerp, I see nothing in the peculiar regulations which the French Government may have wished to form for the commerce of that port that can extend to neutral ships the privilege of carrying on the coasting trade of France to that port, on any other footing relatively to foreign States, than to any other French ports, acknowledged as such and not distinguished by any singular regulation whatever.

1805 *July* 24.

Condemned.

[6 C. Rob. 93.]

THE ZELDEN RUST.

Contraband—Cheese—Commercial Port in same Bay as Port of Naval Equipment.

A cargo of cheese destined to C. was captured. C. was assumed to be an ordinary commercial port, but was in the same bay as F., a port of naval equipment. *Held*, that having regard to the proximity of the two ports, the cargo must be condemned.

1805 *July* 16.

THIS was the case of a cargo of Dutch cheese taken on an asserted destination from Amsterdam to Corunna.

SIR W. SCOTT.—It certainly has been held by the Court that cheese going to a place of naval equipment, and fit for naval use, is contraband. As to the quality of the cheese, in this instance, there is, I think, sufficient to satisfy the Court, from the representation given of it by a person conversant with this particular article in the way of his trade, and by another person who is employed in the capacity of storekeeper at Yarmouth. The quality may therefore be fairly assumed on the declaration of their judgment; and if going to a place of naval equipment it will fall under the rule of law that has been applied to other cases.

Corunna is, I believe, itself a place of naval equipment in some degree, and if not so exclusively and in its prominent character, yet from its vicinity to Ferrol it is almost identified with that port. These ports are situated in the same bay, and if the supply is permitted to be imported into the bay, it would, I conceive, be impossible to prevent it from going on immediately and in the same conveyance to Ferrol. There is in this respect a material difference between the present case and the case (*a*) which happened yesterday, of similar articles going to Quimper. That port, though in the vicinity of Brest, is situated on the opposite side of a projecting

[6 C. Rob. 92.] (*a*) The *Frau Margaretha*. The judgment was as follows:—

SIR W. SCOTT.—A destination to Quimper cannot, I think, be considered as such an identical destination, with a voyage to Brest, as to bring this cargo under the authority of the case [*Jonge Margaretha, ante*, p. 100] which has been relied on. I am not disposed to hold that these articles on this destination are so clearly contraband, though certainly very near it, as to preclude the claimant from giving further proof of the property.

Further proof ordered.

headland or promontory, so as not to admit of an immediate communication except by land carriage. Without meaning to interfere with the principle of that decision, I think myself warranted to consider this cargo on the present destination as contraband, and as such subject to condemnation.

1805 *July* 16.

THE ZELDEN RUST.

Sir W. Scott.

Condemned.

THE HOFFNUNG (No. 1).

[6 C. Rob. 112.]

Blockade—Interruption by Belligerent—Resumption—Notification to Neutrals.

When a blockade has been forcibly raised by the blockading ships being driven away by the belligerent forces, the original notification of the blockade becomes extinct, and a renewed blockade must be brought to the knowledge of neutrals in the same manner as the original blockade. *Held*, therefore, that the arrival of a blockading squadron off a port from which a squadron had been previously driven, was not sufficient to bind neutrals with notice of a blockade (*a*).

THIS was the case of a Swedish vessel, which had sailed on the 17th of July from Nantes with a cargo of corn or flour for the port of Seville, which was claimed under his Majesty's instructions, 1st February, 1805.

1805 *September* 11. 1806 *July* 24.

For the captors, the *King's Advocate* and *Adams*.—This vessel appears to have laid for some time under an embargo in the port of Nantes, and to have been liberated at last on the condition that she should take a cargo on board for Seville, notwithstanding the blockade of St. Lucar, which comprehends that port, and which had existed since the notification of the 25th of April. On a former (*b*) occasion a doubt was entertained whether the blockade of St. Lucar had been resumed after Sir John Orde was driven off. It now appears from a communication with the Admiralty, that immediately after the intelligence was received respecting Sir John Orde's squadron, directions were sent to Lord Collingwood to proceed to Cadiz, and that he had arrived on that station on the 8th of June. It cannot be doubted, therefore, that long before the date of this transaction it must have been perfectly notorious at Nantes that Cadiz and St. Lucar were in a state of blockade. It appears, indeed, from a correspondence which passed between

(*a*) But see the *Hare*, *post*, p. 579 (note).

(*b*) The *Triheten*, July 7th, 1805. See note, p. 534.

1805 *September* 11. 1806 *July* 24.

THE HOFFNUNG.

Lord Collingwood and the neutral consuls at Cadiz, on the 23rd July, that he had been before that port some time, and had given public intimation of his intention to enforce the blockade.

SIR W. SCOTT.—There had been a very humane order issued by the British Government, in consideration of the distress to which the Kingdom of Spain was reduced by famine, to permit cargoes of corn to be carried to that country, without exception as to the property, but with a reservation "that it should not be carried to blockaded ports." . . . .

It appears that the port of Cadiz and St. Lucar were put under blockade by a notification of the 25th of April; but it unfortunately happened that the notification issued at a time when it became equally notorious that no blockade actually existed, since the British squadron had been recently driven off by a superior force. In a former case (*a*), a question was raised whether the notification which had issued was not still operative, at least for the purpose of sustaining the effect of these instructions. But the Court was of opinion that it could not be so considered, and that a neutral power was not obliged under such circumstances to presume the continuance of a blockade, nor to act upon the supposition that the blockade would be resumed by any other competent force.

It was argued on that occasion that neutrals were bound to act upon such presumptions, and on the same principle on which it has been held that, when a blockading squadron is driven off by adverse winds, they are bound to presume that it will return, and that there is no discontinuance of the blockade. But certainly the two cases are very different. When a squadron is driven off by accidents of weather, which must have entered into the contemplation of the belligerent imposing the blockade, there is no reason

[6 C. Rob. 64.] (*a*) The *Triheten*. Judgment:—

SIR W. SCOTT.—If that is so, I must require the fact to be proved, because it certainly is notorious that the British squadron was driven off on the 10th of April by a superior force. It must be shown that the actual blockade was again resumed. Considering the circumstances of this case, and that the vessel was taken on the French coast so long ago as the 28th of May, I am not disposed to hold that the mere act of sailing for Seville or St. Lucar under the dubious representation which we have of the state of the actual blockade at that time is sufficient to fix upon this vessel the penalty of breaking the blockade.

Ship and cargo restored.

to suppose that such a circumstance would create a change of system, since it could not be expected that any blockade would continue many months without being liable to such temporary interruptions. But when a squadron is driven off by a superior force a new course of events arises, which may tend to a very different disposition of the blockading force, and which introduces, therefore, a very different train of presumptions, in favour of the ordinary freedom of commercial speculations. In such a case the neutral merchant is not bound to foresee or to conjecture that the blockade will be resumed; and therefore if it is to be renewed, it must proceed *de novo*, by the usual course, and without reference to the former state of facts, which has been so effectually interrupted. On this principle it was that the Court held the former blockade to have become extinct, and intimated an opinion that there should be a repetition of the same measures on its recommencement, to bring it to the knowledge of neutral States, either by public declaration or by the notoriety of the fact.

It is not now contended that any new declaration has issued, and the Court has already determined that the former notification had become extinct. It remains, therefore, to be considered whether there has been that notoriety of the fact, from the operation of time or from other circumstances, which must be taken to have brought the existence of the blockade to the knowledge of the parties.

Among other modes of ascertaining that fact, a prevailing consideration undoubtedly is the length of time in proportion to the distance of the country from which the vessel sails. What I have to lament in this instance is, that we labour under an ignorance of the true *terminus a quo*, not having the necessary information as to the time when Admiral Collingwood returned to that station. Although something is to be collected from the letters to which reference has been made, they do not, I think, supply sufficient information, or with such precision, as can enable me to found a judicial sentence upon it.

With regard to the ship I am bound to advert to the situation of hardship in which Swedish vessels were placed by the embargo which was imposed upon them in the ports of France. It was a material object with the French Government to have the ports of

1805 September 11. 1806 July 24.

THE HOFFNUNG.

Sir W. Scott.

Spain supplied with articles of provision. To effect this purpose it was not unlikely that means of imposition and force would be employed, more especially against Swedish vessels, who were in a particular manner *inopes consilii*, owing to the cessation of all diplomatic correspondence between their own Government and France. They had been put under an embargo and were released, it appears, for the purpose of being made the instruments of conveying these supplies to the ports of Spain. It is natural to suppose that any information that might have reached the Government of France as to the actual state of the ports of Spain would be withheld from them. Unless it is shown, therefore, in the clearest manner that the knowledge of the actual blockade of Cadiz and St. Lucar, which is said to have existed, had reached the masters of these vessels, I shall think myself bound to act towards them with great indulgence, and with due consideration of the difficulties under which they were placed.

Their case is very different from that of the proprietors of the cargo. For who are they? The Spanish Government, who were bound to observe the most perfect candour and good faith. They could not but know the fact, if Cadiz was actually blockaded. It was their duty to have transmitted the earliest information to their agents in France, and to have altered the destination of their cargoes to other ports to which they might go without infringing the instructions which had issued in their favour. There is, therefore, a material distinction between the ship and the cargo. Unless it is proved in the most unequivocal manner that the master was affected with a knowledge of the alleged blockade, I shall hold the vessel to be exonerated. With respect to the cargo, if it is shown that the blockade did exist, and that there had been time for communication from Spain, those interests will not be entitled to the same indulgence. I shall, therefore, at present make no other order, but to require the recommencement of the blockade to be distinctly ascertained, meaning to apply the inferences that may arise from the interval of time very differently to the case of the ship and of the cargo.

On a subsequent day (*a*) this case came before the Court again

(*a*) 24th July, 1806.

on the information required to be produced of the time when Lord Collingwood resumed the blockade of Cadiz. No further information was exhibited, but only the certificate of the Admiralty, stating "that Lord Collingwood arrived off Cadiz on the 8th of June." The cause was argued on the sufficiency of that act, and the inferences deducible from it, whether they were such as could be held to re-establish the blockade, so as to impose on the Government of Spain an obligation of counteracting this shipment, previous to the sailing of the vessel.

Sir W. Scott.—What the Court has already decided, on the best consideration, is, that the raising of the former blockade by a superior force was a total defeasance of that blockade and its operations. Whether that is a sound opinion or not must be left to the determination of the Superior Court. My persuasion is that there could not be a more effectual raising of the blockade, and that it should be renewed again by notification, before foreign nations could be affected with an obligation of observing it as a blockade of that species still existing. Under this view I have already intimated my opinion that the mere appearance of another squadron would not restore it, but that the same measures would be necessary for the recommencement that had been required for the original imposition of the blockade, and that foreign merchants were not bound to act on any presumption that it would be *de facto* resumed.

It became therefore very desirable that some account should be given of the manner in which the blockade was recommenced. Inquiries were directed to be made at the Admiralty, which have produced no other answer than this, "that Lord Collingwood had arrived off Cadiz on the 8th of June"; and a letter is produced from Lord Collingwood to the foreign consuls at Cadiz, of the 23rd of July, of which the Court was already in possession. This appears to me to be very unsatisfactory, since Lord Collingwood might arrive off Cadiz with very different intentions. He might go there with a fleet of observation merely, or for purposes of a qualified blockade.

The Court expressed a wish to be informed whether any orders had been sent to Lord Collingwood respecting the renewal of the

1805 September 11. 1806 July 24.

THE HOFFNUNG.

Sir W. Scott.

blockade, and whether it had been notified to the Spanish Government. In answer to these inquiries no further information is obtained than what relates to the arrival of Lord Collingwood and the letter of the 23rd of July. It is manifest, I think, that Lord Collingwood did connect the two blockades together, and that the same apprehension has been entertained since. But I am of opinion, as far as my opinion can have any weight, that this interpretation cannot be supported, but that it would be necessary that the same form of communication should be observed *de novo* that is required to establish an original blockade.

The question now is, whether, independent of any notification, the fact of Lord Collingwood's arrival and his subsequent conduct were such as would impress on foreign nations the obligation of knowing that there was a blockade *de facto*, and more particularly whether the Spanish Government ought to have taken notice of it so as to have communicated the intelligence to the shippers in France, and to have prevented the sailing of this cargo. On the former hearing I was of opinion that the Swedish vessel was clearly excused, although the Spanish Government might possibly be affected with the obligation of communicating advice to their agents. In the case of the *Falck*, it appeared that the violence of the French Government had actually forced that vessel out of port, and in defiance of the knowledge of the blockade, which the master admitted himself to have received, but at a later period than the date of this transaction. I am now to consider whether any evidence is produced that can fix upon the Spanish Government a knowledge of the blockade that should have prevented the sailing of this vessel, and that should affect them legally with the consequences of culpable negligence. I am of opinion that there is not. It appears from the letters of the 23rd and 25th July that the question was at that time dubious at Cadiz, and that some vessels had been suffered to pass. That the Spanish Government at Madrid should be impressed with a distinct knowledge of the fact that was rendered doubtful at Cadiz on the 23rd of July, so as to have prevented the sailing of this vessel from Bordeaux on the 13th of July, is, I think, out of all physical possibility. I must, therefore, make the same decree in this case as in other cases under the instructions.

Restored on payment of the captor's expenses.

THE FRANKLIN (No. 3). [6 C. Rob. 127.]

Trade with Enemy—British Merchant—Partnership in Neutral Country and Great Britain—Liability of British Partner.

A British merchant who is a partner in a firm in a neutral country is liable, if such firm trades with the enemy, to the forfeiture of his share of a cargo which has been captured.

1805 *September* 13. 1806 *February* 28.

THIS was the case of a ship claimed as the property of Mr. Ingals, an American merchant, and of a cargo of tobacco shipped in America for France, as the property of I. and W. Bell, partners in a house of trade in America, and also of a house in London, where Mr. W. Bell resided, but claimed as the sole property of I. Bell, of America.

SIR W. SCOTT. [The Court first dealt with the question of the property in the ship, and ordered further proof.]—Then as to the cargo, that has been claimed for Mr. I. Bell, of America, who is a partner in a house of trade in America, and also in a house in this town, under the firm of John and William Bell, of London. Some of the formal papers hold out the name of I. Bell only, but other documents, as the charter-party and the instructions, mention the interest of I. and W. Bell; and there are papers which point to directions which were to be received from Mr. W. Bell when the property came to Europe. It has been decided by an authority to which this Court must bow that even an inactive or sleeping partner (as it is termed) cannot receive restitution in a transaction in which he could not lawfully be engaged as a sole trader. I can have no doubt, therefore, that any share belonging to Mr. W. Bell, who is by no means an inactive partner, but appears rather to have been the person principally concerned in the management, if not in the interests of this transaction, will be subject to condemnation. The master says, to the 12th interrogatory, "that the cargo belongs jointly to I. and W. Bell, and that I. Bell told him so"; though in another place he says "that it is the sole property of the lader." It is a case, therefore, in which the papers are inconsistent, and the master's account is inconsistent even with itself. The fact of property is left in such obscurity as to create a necessity for further proof. Then, have the parties so conducted themselves as to forfeit this privilege? I do not think that they have. The master is

1805 September 13. 1806 February 28.

THE FRANKLIN.

Sir W. Scott.

charged with a suppression of papers, which is denied. It will be proper that he should give an explanation of his conduct in this respect, so as to exonerate those by whom he is employed. There must be also further proof to negative the interest of Mr. W. Bell. As that gentleman is in London, his testimony on that point might, perhaps, be most material; but the nature of the proof, which shall be exhibited, will more properly be left to the discretion of his legal advisers.

Further proof ordered of ship and cargo.

On a subsequent day (*a*) the cause came on again, to be heard upon the production of Mr. Bell's further proof, and upon the claims of the merchants in America who had used the name of Mr. Bell, in exporting sundry parcels of tobacco to France. The Court was of opinion that the letter of Mr. W. Bell, in which he had given notice that he could not be concerned during the war in any cargo sent to France, was not sufficiently corroborated by proof of the receipt of that letter, or of the manner in which it had been acted upon, and gave him an opportunity of producing still further proof. That being now exhibited—

(28th February, 1806.)

SIR W. SCOTT.—This is a claim for a quantity of tobacco shipped at Petersburg, in Virginia, for Bordeaux, by several planters exporting the produce of their own plantations, but documented in the formal papers as the property of Mr. I. Bell. A reason, however, is given for the misrepresentation, which is perfectly innocent, viz., "that intending to make use of Mr. Bell's correspondent in France as their consignee, they had shipped it in his name." There was no design to impose on British cruisers, nor has any such effect been produced, since it was a trade free from exception, whether going on their account or on account of Mr. Bell. It is now sufficiently shown from certificates of property and the correspondence of the parties that they are really the owners of the quantity claimed on their behalf; and though the proof is not of the most formal kind, I should think it an act of great oppression if, after being satisfied of the fact, I was to send these claims across the Atlantic, with all the delay that must

(*a*) 12th February, 1806.

inevitably ensue, to have the proof exhibited in a more formal manner from themselves. I shall therefore direct their property to be restored.

The principal question then remains, respecting the moiety of seventy hogsheads of tobacco which are claimed in the name of Mr. I. Bell. They are described in the general bill of lading "as for the account and risk of I. Bell," who was the general shipper of the whole cargo. But there was a particular bill of lading, also, for this parcel with the marks of I. and W. Bell; so that it is not correctly true that nothing arises on the face of the papers to attribute any share of the property to Mr. W. Bell. In addition to this suggestion arising out of the papers, the master says to the 12th interrogatory, "that it is the property of I. and W. Bell, and that I. Bell told him so." This is a direct declaration, and of no mean authority; though not absolutely conclusive, it affords ground of presumption unquestionably, more especially as the master is a cautious and discreet man, as far as I can collect, and is not very likely to have spoken lightly or loosely to the prejudice of his employers. In a subsequent part of his depositions he says, indeed, "that the property belongs to the lader," but that must be taken *referendo* to what he had before deposed, and as not excluding the joint interest of the brother in the transaction. When he comes to give in his claim, however, and perhaps after some instructions received here, he claims this parcel of tobacco as the sole property of Mr. I. Bell.

It might have been natural to expect that if it had been the sole property of that gentleman in America, he would have informed the master with particular precision that it belonged to him exclusively, and that W. Bell was to have no interest in it, and that he must understand it to be on his own separate account. It is clear, from the manner in which the master speaks to the 12th interrogatory, that no such communication could have passed. If in time of war, which necessarily requires particular precision, persons conduct their business in such a manner as furnishes no means of discrimination, they must not be surprised if the Court is unable to protect them from the inconvenience that must ensue from such a state of obscurity and doubt. There is no invoice; but the manifest describes I. Bell "as of the house of I. and W. Bell," which could not have been done with propriety if he had been acting only with relation to his own separate interest. It is impossible under these appearances not to say that further proof was necessary to discharge Mr. W. Bell of an interest in this shipment. Mr. W. Bell is a person who had come from America to settle here; but in so doing he can enjoy no greater privileges than other British merchants, who are prohibited in time of war from being concerned in any manner of commerce carried on with the enemy. It is admitted that I. and W. Bell are general partners, and that there has been no dissolution of the partnership; but that it does still, as it may legally, exist with regard to exportations to neutral countries. It is averred, however, that there has been a separation as to all shipments to France, and that W. Bell had written to his brother at the commencement of the war renouncing all concern in the trade to France. Mr. W. Bell has made an affidavit of this fact; he states also, "that he has not been interested, directly or indirectly, in any such shipments; that he has not considered himself as interested, nor has he been so considered by his brother, to the best of his knowledge and belief"; not absolutely, but only in this qualified manner, to the best of his knowledge and belief. . . .

It is admitted that this mode of separation would not be sufficient to discharge an interest in a ship; and with respect to the cargo it is impossible not to feel that, as it was a letter which was to draw the line of demarcation between the joint and separate concerns of two partners, we might expect that it would have received a particular answer. Mr. W. Bell presses the subject with particular earnestness on his attention: "Let nothing induce you to neglect this advice, for I will have nothing to do with any commerce to France till the war is over." It was an occurrence that would be likely to introduce no inconsiderable alteration in the manner in which the business of the house had been carried on; and it is quite impossible that it should not have required particular notice. The letter that was first produced as the answer is of the 10th of November, in which Mr. I. Bell writes, "yours and ——— letters from the 24th of August to the 6th of September are before me," but there is not a syllable relative to this separation. It does not, indeed, necessarily appear that the letter of the 6th of September was Mr. W. Bell's, or that it might not be a letter from the other gentleman who is included in the same paragraph. However that might be, there is no mention of any inconvenience that might be occasioned to the ordinary course of their business, nor of any remedy to be provided to obviate the difficulties produced by this separation.

The difficulty that might be likely to occur is obvious from this circumstance, that the vessels were to come in the first instance to Falmouth, and there to take their ulterior destination to France, or elsewhere, under the direction of Mr. W. Bell, according to the state of the markets in Europe. In America, then, it could not be known whether any particular shipment would be a separate or joint account, or to whom the cargo would belong, because it remained uncertain whether the vessel would proceed to France or not. It might be supposed that some expedient would have been necessary to obviate this inconvenience, yet no mention whatever is made of that necessary part of this subject.

When the cause came on before, the Court was anxious to give Mr. Bell further opportunity of elucidating these difficulties, which had not been satisfactorily removed. An additional affidavit has now been brought in, which states "the letter of the 10th November not to have been the immediate answer to Mr. Bell's renunciation of the partnership, and that there must have been some other letter, which either did not arrive, or which has been destroyed, as containing matters of private concern, as their letters frequently did, and were on that account not preserved in the counting-house." Taking it either way, if the letter did not arrive, can I suppose that there would not have been some other reference to the same subject, and that Mr. W. Bell would not have urged his former observations till there was a precise and distinct understanding between them? If it did arrive, is it a reason why the letter should be destroyed, because it contained some things that were not proper to be generally known in his counting-house? There are other modes very familiar in practice of preserving a correspondence of a particular nature; and it is not easy to conceive that such a letter would be destroyed on that account. The affidavit states, "that there has been no settlement of accounts between them, owing to the extensiveness of their engagements, and that Mr. W. B. has not considered himself, nor is he considered by his brother in America, to be interested in any shipments to France." That must be taken, I conceive, with reference to the manner in which it was before stated, "to the best of his knowledge and belief." This interest might still be a matter to be brought forward in account at the end of the war, a supposition which may not unfairly be entertained, and which does, I think, in an extraordinary manner harmonize with the loose manner in which the separation was first notified and received. There is one other letter produced from Mr. Bell, which was written after the capture, and in which he refers to this transaction in very general terms: "It was well known to me, and I supposed you equally informed, having regularly replied to your letter of the 6th September, that I considered you as not concerned in shipments to France." He does not say that he had acted upon it. It is not even confirmed by affidavit, and it is altogether a very loose and general letter on a subject of so much importance. All that remains is the affidavit of the clerk of Mr. W. Bell, who says, "that Mr. W. Bell has not charged the profits of such consignments to himself, but only the commission of agency, &c." This also is not inconsistent with the supposition that the real accounts, in which Mr. W. Bell's interest may stand prominent, are kept in America.

The Court concluded the hearing of the evidence, and found that, "having given Mr. W. Bell further opportunity of proving in a satisfactory manner the dissolution of partnership, which is suggested to have taken place, under a hope that he would have been able to effect this, I feel myself compelled to pronounce that he has failed to produce that conviction in my mind; consequently, a moiety of these goods must be condemned, as the property of a British merchant engaged in commerce with the enemy."

THE SCHOONE SOPHIE.

[6 C. Rob. 138.]

Capture—Condemnation by Foreign Prize Court—Title of Captor—Effect of Treaty of Peace.

When a British vessel has been condemned by a foreign Prize Court, and has been transferred to a foreign owner, the English Prize Court, after the conclusion of peace, will not, if the vessel has been recaptured, inquire into the title of the foreign owner, but will restore the vessel to him, or to his transferee if he has transferred the vessel.

1805 *September* 18.

This was a question as to the ship, reserved at the former hearing, on a claim given by the British proprietor, who stated her to have belonged to him, and to have been captured by the French, and carried into a port in Norway, and condemned by the French Consular Court in that country, 1799. It now appeared that other proceedings had been afterwards had on the former evidence in the regular Court of Prize in Paris, where a sentence of condemnation had been pronounced, professing to affirm the sentence of the Consular Court.

For the British owner, *Arnold.*

For the neutral claimant, *Laurence* and *Robinson.*

Sir W. Scott.—I am of opinion that the title of the former owner is completely barred by the intervention of peace, which has the effect of quieting all titles of possession arising from the war; and if the vessel has been transferred to the subject of another country, he also will be entitled to the same benefit from the treaty as the captor himself would have been if he had continued in possession. It is admitted that as to the enemy it would have this effect, and that it would not be lawful to look back beyond the general amnesty to examine the title of his possession. If his property is transferred the purchaser must also be entitled to the benefit of the same considerations, for otherwise it could not be said that the intervention of peace would have the effect of quieting the possession of the enemy, because if the neutral purchaser was to be dispossessed he would have a right to resort back to the belligerent seller and demand compensation from him. I

1805 *September* 18. — THE SCHOONE SOPHIE. — Sir W. Scott.

am of opinion, therefore, that the intervention of peace has put a total end to the claim of the British proprietor, and that it is no longer competent to him to look back to the enemy's title, either in his own possession or in the hands of neutral purchasers. As to any effect of the new war, though that may change the relation of those who are parties to it, it can have no effect on neutral purchasers, who stand in the same situation as before. Those purchasers, though no parties to the treaty, are entitled to the full benefit of it, because they derive their title from those who are (*a*).

Further proof of the property ordered. Finally restored, 27th September, 1806.

[6 C. Rob. 201.]

THE MARIA (No. 4).

Blockade—Goods brought out of Blockaded River in Lighters—Free City.

Goods were brought in lighters from the free city of Bremen on the Weser when such river was blockaded. Such goods were transhipped outside the river into a vessel which had gone out in ballast. *Held*, that as the River Weser was blockaded, it was illegal to bring goods from Bremen either in lighters or otherwise for exportation.

1805 *September* 20.

THIS was a case on the blockade of the Weser, relating to a cargo which had been sent from Bremen in lighters to the Jade, for the purpose of being shipped for America under a charter-party made at Bremen. The vessel had gone from the Weser to the Jade in ballast, and, having taken on board the cargo, sailed from thence on the 12th August, 1805, and was captured in the North Sea, 15th August.

For the captors, the *King's Advocate* and *Laurence*.

For the claimants, *Arnold* and *Robinson*.

SIR W. SCOTT.—This ship was taken on a voyage from Varel to America, having on board a cargo that had been sent from the Weser to the Jade in lighters, and there transhipped; and it is contended that this being the carrying of goods sent expressly

(*a*) See *ante*, p. 343.

from Bremen, for the purpose of being exported in the course of the foreign commerce of that port, would be a violation of the blockade which had been imposed on the River Weser. I have had frequent occasion to observe how severely the neutral cities connected with the Weser and the Elbe are pressed upon by the blockade of those rivers. At the same time it is my duty to apply to those operations of blockade the principles that belong to that branch of the law of nations generally, and by which only such measures can be maintained. The principles themselves cannot differ, although it will undoubtedly be the disposition of the Court to alleviate the situations of those towns as much as possible, by attending to any distinctions that can be advanced in their favour not inconsistent with the sound construction of the general principles of law. A blockade imposed on the Weser must in its nature be held to affect the commerce of Bremen, because if the commerce of all the towns situated on that river is allowed, it would be only to say in more indirect language that the blockade itself did not exist. It cannot be doubted, then, on general principles, that these goods would be subject to condemnation as having been conveyed through the Weser, and whether that was effected in large vessels or in small would be perfectly insignificant. That they were brought through the mouth of the blockaded river for the purpose of being shipped for exportation would subject them to be considered as taken on a continued voyage, and as liable to all the same principles that are applied to a direct voyage, of which the *terminus a quo* and the *terminus ad quem* are precisely the same as those of the more circuitous destination. The case (*a*) which has been referred to is, in this respect, very different, because there the communication had been by inland navigation, which was in no manner and in no part of it subject to the blockade. If, therefore, nothing had passed between the Government of this country and the city of Bremen, it appears to me that these goods would be subject to condemnation (*b*), and that I should be unable to distinguish the

(*a*) The *Ocean*, *ante*, p. 310.

(*b*) On this principle. In the *Charlotte Sophia*, ship and cargo condemned, 20th November, 1806. Voyage from Tonningen to Algesiras with goods shipped at Tonningen, but having been sent in lighters from Hamburg, under charter-party, with the ship proceeding also in

1805 September 20. port of Bremen from any other place liable to the general operations of a blockade.

THE MARIA. Sir W. Scott. But a communication has passed on this subject between the Government of this country and the city of Bremen, which may be of a nature to furnish the rule that is to govern this particular case and to supersede the general principle of law.

[The Court then examined the communication, and held that under it the claimants were justified in carrying on this particular trade.]

[6 C. Rob. 213.]

THE FREDERICK AND MARY ANN.

Capture—Prize Crew—Right of Crew of Capturing Vessel to Share in Further Prize.

Where a prize crew was put on board a prize from a privateer, and such crew subsequently made another prize. *Held*, that those on the privateer were entitled to share in the second prize.

1805 November 26. THIS was a case, on the claim of the ship's company of the *Ceres* privateer, to share in salvage decreed to be paid on the recapture of some British property on board this vessel, effected by Barnaby Vick and eight others of the crew of the *Ceres*, from on board a prize belonging to the privateer, which the said Vick was conducting into port in the capacity of prize master.

SIR W. SCOTT.—The facts of this case are generally admitted, and stand without controversy between the parties. It appears that the *Ceres* privateer, having a crew of 100 men, had recaptured an English vessel, the *Prince*, and had put a prize master and eight men on board, with orders to make Jersey or any port of England.

ballast from Hamburg, that they should be so shipped for Spain, &c. [1 Acton, 46.] Also in the *Sophia Elizabeth*, June 30th, 1809, the Lords Commissioners of Appeal held, on the authority of the *Maria*, that a vessel taking cargo from Tonningen, which had been sent there in lighters, was liable to condemnation unless protected by certain Orders in Council. The judgment turned solely on the construction of such orders.

In proceeding on that course they descried another vessel, which they considered from her appearance to be a prize in the possession of the French, and concerted a plan of recapture with so happy a mixture of address and gallantry, that what seemed an enterprise of apparent danger was accomplished without any loss. To all expressions of eulogium on the merit of these individuals I readily assent. But the question is, whether they are entitled to take the whole benefit to themselves. I have always understood it to be the general practice of the navy, as stated by his Majesty's Advocate, that prize interests acquired by a prize master on board a captured ship shall enure to the benefit of the whole ship's company. I am not aware of any instance in which this rule has been recognized or established by the decrees of this Court. It has prevailed, I conceive, without judicial authority, on the general notion which has been entertained of the intrinsic equity of such a communication of interest.

With respect to privateers, the shares of different persons concerned are regulated by articles of agreement, and when those articles are not literally applicable to the circumstances of the capture, their place must be supplied by the principles of natural equity and reason. . . . . .

On these grounds I am of opinion that the reward of salvage enures to the benefit of all united in the common cruise, as part of that undertaking; and that the principle of reciprocal equity applies to one description of capture as well as to another. It never could be the meaning of the articles that persons embarked on board a prize ship should share with the privateer in her captures, and that the privateer should not share with them in any captures which they might make.

[6 C. Rob. 231.]

THE HOFFNUNG (No. 2).

Capture—Unlivery of Cargo—Restitution of Ship and Cargo—Right of Cargo Owner to Demand Continuance of Voyage.

The act of unlivery by order of the Court dissolves the contract of carriage between the shipowner and the cargo owner. The shipowner is not bound to carry on the cargo.

1805 *December* 18, 19.

THIS was a question respecting freight decreed to be a charge on the cargo, which was ultimately restored.

On the part of the owners of the cargo, the *King's Advocate* and *Adams* referred to the *Martha* (*a*).

For the ship, *Laurence* and *Robinson*.—It will be material, in the first instance, to state the dates. It appears that the capture took place on the 18th August, off the Goodwin Sands. On the 1st September the sentence of restitution of the ship passed, and a commission of unlivery was taken out by the captor on the same day.

SIR W. SCOTT.—I have considered this case, and the cases which have been referred to, and I am of opinion that the owner of the cargo cannot come back on the vessel and demand to have the cargo taken on board again. The captor, who succeeded to the right of both, has invoked the authority of the Court to decree a separation, and the contract between them must be held to have ceased by the act of unlivery. At the moment of separation the vessel acquires a right to proceed, and it is by accident only that she continues here. That accident cannot, I think, have the effect of reviving the contract which had been before dissolved.

I am fully sensible that this rule may occasionally operate with considerable hardship on the owners of cargoes. But the proper remedy for that inconvenience will be to insert a special provision for such accidents in the charter-party (*b*). Rules of law being

(*a*) *Ante*, p. 263, note.

(*b*) In some cases, charter-parties have appeared containing a clause for the time which the vessel shall be bound to wait for the purpose of carrying on the cargo in case of capture and subsequent restitution.

in their nature general, must in particular instances sometimes operate with inconvenience. That inconvenience has been the cause of introducing many special covenants into bills of lading and other commercial instruments. I know of no other remedy that can be applied to hardships arising, in cases of this description, from the general principle of law, which I must pronounce to be that the act of unlivery is binding on the parties, and must be taken to be decisive in producing a complete dissolution of the contract.

1805 *December* 18, 19.

THE HOFFNUNG.

Sir W. Scott.

THE L'AMITIE.

[6 C. Rob. 261.]

Joint Capture—Privateer—Overt Act.

In order to entitle a vessel not a ship of war to share in a prize, there must be an *animus capiendi* proved by some overt act.

1806 *February* 21.

THIS was a case of joint capture on the claims of two privateers, the *Lark* and the *General Coote*, to share in the prize made by his Majesty's ship *Gannet*.

SIR W. SCOTT.—This is a claim on the part of two privateers to share in a prize which is admitted to have been actually taken by his Majesty's ship *Gannet*. The rule of law on this subject, which has been long established in this Court and the Court of Appeals, in various cases, is that it must be shown on the part of privateers that they were constructively assisting. The being in sight is not sufficient, with respect to them, to raise the presumption of co-operation in the capture. They clothe themselves with commissions of war from views of private advantage only. They are not bound to put their commissions in use on every discovery of an enemy. And therefore the law does not presume in their favour, from the mere circumstance of being in sight, that they were there with a design of contributing assistance and engaging in the contest. There must be the *animus capiendi* demonstrated by some overt act, by some variation of conduct, which would not have taken place, but with reference to that particular object, and if the intention of acting against the enemy had not been effectually entertained.

[6 C. Rob. 269.]

THE VROW ANNA CATHARINA (No. 2).

Capture—Ship and Cargo—Restoration of Cargo—Right of Captors to Freight.

A captor is only entitled to freight if he brings the cargo to the port of destination.

1806 *March* 20.

THIS was a case on the demand of the captors to have freight allowed to them for the cargo, or part of the cargo of coffee, claimed for merchants of Hamburg, and restored to them, and afterwards sold in this country under a licence from his Majesty's Government.

For the captors, *Arnold* and *Swabey*.

For the claimants, the *King's Advocate* and *Laurence*.

SIR W. SCOTT.—The Lords having permitted this application to be brought here, I shall not enter into the question of jurisdiction, but take it as granted that the jurisdiction of the Court is well founded. The claim is given for the freight of goods captured on a voyage from Batavia to Amsterdam, and carried to Liverpool, where they have been restored, and finally sold under the permission of a licence; and the demand is founded on a suggestion that they have been sold advantageously for the claimants in this country, and at their particular request.

The general rule is well known, being founded on very ancient principles of law, that whenever the captor brings the goods to the port of actual destination, he shall be entitled to the freight, on the ground that the contract has been fulfilled; but that in all other cases freight shall not be due, although the ship may have performed a very large part of her intended voyage, and so large a portion as to raise at first sight an appearance of hardship and injustice in the refusal of freight, and to suggest a doubt whether it might not be a better rule to allow a proportion of freight *pro ratâ itineris peracti*. But I am very certain that such a rule, if fully considered, would be found to be productive of much practical injustice, and would lead to endless litigation and uncertainty in the discussion of the particular circumstances that would be relied on in every case. The ancient rule of practice, therefore, is one to which the Court may be allowed to adhere with much rational bigotry. The only exception which has been admitted in this Court is that of the Dutch ships (a), in which the claimants, being British subjects, who were deeply engaged in bringing their effects from the Dutch islands, had made an affidavit, for the purpose of fortifying their claims, that it was their original wish and intention that the property should have been brought to this country, but that they had been compelled, by the policy of Holland, to accept a consignment to Dutch ports. In these cases the Court did not look so much to the advantage that the claimant had derived, though there might be reason to presume that the destination was not disadvantageous, as that the delivery was made ultimately in the port of their original election. In Mr. Constant's case there was no original intention to sell the goods here, but they were afterwards sold; and though he had himself fixed his residence in this country, the Court of Appeal did not think that circumstance sufficient to vary the application of the general rule.

In the present case there was no original wish to sell in this country. The cargo was brought in by force to Liverpool, and after restitution the claimants elected to sell there, combining many considerations of further difficulty and expense in hiring other vessels to carry it on to Holland. The possible advantage or disadvantage of such an interruption of the original voyage is but an accidental circumstance to which the Court will but slightly attend. It would introduce a labyrinth of minute considerations, through which the Court could not find its way. Sometimes the advantage would be on the side of the vessel and sometimes on that of the cargo. I see no sufficient ground of distinction to support this demand, and therefore I reject the prayer.

(a) The *Diana*, *ante*, p. 424.

[6 C. Rob. 273.]

THE GAGE.

Recapture—Derelict—Amount of Salvage.

If a British vessel in a derelict state is recaptured, the Court will award a larger amount of salvage than is presented by the Prize Act.

1806 *April* 16. 1807 *July* 14.

This was a question on the recovery of a British vessel, with a cargo of timber, &c. (*a*), which had been captured by a French privateer, but was found abandoned at sea, with a fire burning in her cabin, by the *Kite* sloop.

On the part of the recaptor, the *King's Advocate* contended that it was not merely a case of salvage on recapture, but that it approached rather to the nature of derelict, as the vessel was abandoned and left at the peril of perishing by fire as well as by the waves; that in such a case the Court would not consider itself restricted to the rate of salvage prescribed by the Prize Act, but would allow a larger reward.

On the part of the British owner, *Swabey* contended that it was to be considered only as a case of salvage on recapture.

Court.—What I shall do at present will be to pronounce for the rate of salvage due under the Act, since the salvors are unquestionably entitled to that. If, on further information, it can be shown to be distinguishable from other cases of recapture, I shall permit that question to come on again. If the case had rested upon the depositions alone, it would have borne the appearance of a case of derelict, because there is in them no mention of recapture. But the affidavit of the officer who brings in the papers describes it as a recapture, and in that view the recaptors will not be entitled to more than the war salvage.

(July 14th, 1807.)

This cause came before the Court again on the affidavit of the master of the *Gage*, made at Verdun, he being then a prisoner in France. The affidavit stated only that his vessel had been

(*a*) Value of ship and cargo as admitted, 1,002*l*. 10*s*.

captured, and that he had been taken on board the French privateer, and carried into Calais. It did not fix the time of abandonment, or establish the fact whether the enemy were on board when the British cruiser was first descried, so as to show that the prize had been abandoned on that account. On the contrary, in a letter from him of the 21st February, 1806, exhibited on the former hearing, he appeared to have been altogether ignorant of the fate of his vessel, stating, "I was taken on the 24th February by a lugger, but I believe the *Gage* was retaken and carried into Dover, but I cannot tell." Under these circumstances the Court held the case not to fall under the restrictions of the Prize Act, and allowed a salvage of one-fourth (*a*).

THE WASHINGTON.

[6 C. Rob. 275.]

Capture—Convenient Port—Duty of Captors—Damages.

Captors are bound to take a captured vessel to a convenient port. A port not of sufficient capacity to admit the captured vessel without unloading her cargo:—*Held*, not to be a convenient port, and that the captors were liable in costs and damages (*b*).

1806 April 18.

THIS was a case on a demand for costs and damages against the captors for losses sustained by the ship being carried to Jersey, a place, as suggested, not fit for the reception of vessels of that burthen.

SIR W. SCOTT.—This is a question of damage sustained by a vessel coming from Monte Video to London, as it turned out, with a large cargo, documented generally as belonging to persons in America, but of which a considerable part has been claimed for merchants in London. The vessel had sailed from the colony of the enemy after hostilities. Considering the general circumstances of the case, therefore, and that the property did not clearly appear,

(*a*) So in the case of the *Lambton*, 29th October, 1807, which was a case of a small British ship of 100 tons, found at sea by his Majesty's ship *Resistance*, without any cargo on board, and claimed on salvage as recaptured.

(*b*) See *ante*, p. 437.

1806 *April* 18.

THE WASHINGTON.

Sir W. Scott.

I am of opinion that the captors were justified in the act of seizure, and that it was not an unreasonable curiosity on their part to bring the question of property to judicial investigation, and to take the benefit of any question of law that might arise out of the facts. The original seizure, therefore, was, in my opinion, justifiable; and the question for the consideration of the Court now is, whether the vessel has been so treated in the custody of the captors as to exonerate them from subsequent responsibility.

The first duty of captors, according to the instructions, is to bring their prize "to some convenient port." Convenient is a large and general term, leaving a certain latitude of discretion, but a discretion to be cautiously exercised and with reference to the view which the Crown itself must be supposed to have entertained in issuing the instructions. Conveniences are of different kinds, some of a slighter nature, others almost indispensable. Among the most important must be considered that of bringing a vessel to a port where she may lie in safety, since that cannot unquestionably be deemed a convenient port which does not afford security and protection to the property that is brought in. An open road, for instance, where the ship may be occasionally exposed to the weather, cannot be a place of security. It is, therefore, quite impossible that it should be considered as a convenient port for the preservation of property.

Another material ingredient of convenience will be, that the port shall be of sufficient capacity to admit vessels to enter without unloading their cargoes, since it is the intention of the legislature that bulk shall not be broken. If there is not depth of water to allow the vessels to lie without taking out the cargo, *non erit his locus;* since captors are not to meddle with the cargo in any manner without the authority of the Court, which cannot be exercised until the vessel has been brought into port.

It is also highly desirable that the port should be a place which holds ready communication with the tribunals which have to decide on questions arising out of the capture, that the parties may have access to advice and may be enabled to obtain the necessary information, and that the directions of the Court of Admiralty may be carried into effect with dispatch. For all these purposes it cannot be supposed that Shetland, for instance, or St. Kilda, could be deemed convenient ports for vessels that have to wait for adjudication in the Admiralty Court of England. These are the leading points of consideration, and may be deemed indispensable.

On the other hand, there may be conveniences of a subordinate nature in favour of the captor, which may be also very deserving of attention when they do not interfere with those of higher moment. For instance, that owners of privateers may elect their own port is but a reasonable advantage in itself, when kept within proper limits and not suffered to predominate over the interests of other persons, and more especially over those general purposes of public justice, to which the Court is principally bound to attend. The privilege of electing their own ports is a convenience which may be allowed *cœteris paribus;* and it is one in which the Court will be disposed to support them, when it does not become the cause of greater inconvenience to others. But the just limits of this personal accommodation are to be distinctly observed; it is not an object to be pursued indiscriminately for the mere profit of agency and commission, in neglect of other considerations of higher or more general importance.

In the present case, the port to which the vessel was carried, which was that of Jersey, is not altogether without objection, arising from a want of opportunity of intercourse with this Court; which renders it, in that respect, not so convenient for the general dispatch of business as the out-ports of this kingdom. That inconvenience, however, if not increased by further neglect of due diligence and attention to the general interests concerned, is not so great as to induce the Court to overrule the indulgence which has usually been granted to the privateers of that island, and the neighbouring islands, of carrying their prizes to their own ports. They are places of great martial enterprise, and of important service to the State, from their local advantages and from their exertions in time of war. The privateers of these islands have in practice been always permitted to carry their prizes to their own ports, and therefore it is not to be said, generally, that it is not a proper exercise of the discretion reposed in them, or that they should be compelled in all cases to bring their prizes into the ports of this country.

But there is enough, on the captors' own showing, to convince

1806
April 18.

THE WASHINGTON.

Sir W. Scott.

the Court that the port of Jersey was on other grounds an improper port for a vessel of this description. It was a vessel of 900 tons, of a burthen beyond what that port was capable of receiving. It must have been obvious that such a vessel ought not to have been carried there, or, at least, that she should not have been detained there in opposition to the request so repeatedly made for her removal. She might have been taken to some port of England, or, what would have been most proper, on the information which was received she might have been sent to London, which has turned out to be the place of her actual destination. I do not say that a privateer is bound to rest entirely on the veracity of the neutral master, because, if ships were to be released immediately on the good faith of such representations, I am persuaded the sanctity of that faith would be very frequently violated. But the assertion of the actual destination to London might at least have suggested to the captors the propriety of making inquiries by their correspondents in London, and if by writing to London they had ascertained the truth of the asserted destination, it would have been expedient then to have acquiesced in the removal, on a just view of the convenience of all parties. For if such a state of facts had been presented to the notice of the Court, it would undoubtedly have held itself bound to order the removal for the general benefit of the property concerned.

[The Court then examined the facilities of Jersey for receiving this vessel in an inner harbour, and found that they were not such as were necessary for a vessel of the size of the *Washington*, and that she should have been taken to some other port, and concluded.]

From the neglect of due precaution in this respect, loss has been sustained, and therefore I shall refer the question of damage to the registrar and merchants under the observations which I have made.

THE MARIA FRANCOISE.

[6 C. Rob. 282.]

Capture—Droits of Admiralty—Right of Crown.

Enemy vessels which come into port from a cause other than one caused by war, and are seized in port, belong to the Lord High Admiral.

1806 *March* 20. *April* 22.

THIS was a question of droits of Admiralty, as to a French ship which had sailed from Europe to the Isle of France, prior to the declaration of hostilities in March, 1803, and had been captured off Pondicherry by the *Fox* cutter and carried to Negapatam, but had been released from capture there by an order from the English admiral of the station in those seas, and was lying in the road of Negapatam when a second seizure was made, 7th September, 1803, on the part of his Majesty's ship *Sheerness*, who brought the prize to England, and proceeded to adjudication. On these facts appearing in the depositions, a claim was directed to be interposed on the part of the Admiralty as for a droit of Admiralty seized in port subsequent to hostilities.

SIR W. SCOTT.—This ship was taken as an undoubted French ship and with a French cargo on board, and therefore both were unquestionably subject to condemnation. But when the case came before the Court in the first instance, something appeared in the depositions which showed that there might possibly be an interest accruing to the Admiralty from the circumstances attending the capture. The Court, therefore, conceived it to be its duty to condemn only generally, and directed notice to be given to the officers of the Admiralty, in order to afford them an opportunity of sustaining such an interest if it should appear advisable. It would, indeed, have been a gross dereliction of duty in the Court not to have used that precaution. Because it is the duty of every Court of Justice to take notice of all interests that appear to result from the evidence before it, and not to suffer any persons to be precluded from asserting their just demands from want of notice of any facts that may have transpired in the course of the proceedings, and may have come to the observation of the Court. If the original proceedings had been instituted on the part of the

1806 *March* 20. *April* 22.

THE MARIA FRANCOISE.

Sir W. Scott.

Admiralty, and it had appeared that the individual captor might be interested, it would have been equally the duty of the Court to have preserved his rights, and not to have shut him out from an opportunity of interposing his claim. It was a most extraordinary proceeding on the part of the actual captor, that because the registrar had entered the decree of condemnation, without noticing the direction which was afterwards given for suspending it, upon the notice taken of these circumstances so appearing, a complaint should be raised against the King's proctor, the officer of the Crown, that he did not take advantage of a sentence so passed, and make a dishonest use of a mere act of inadvertency in the officer of the Court. The King's proctor would have deserted his duty as a practiser in the Court if his conduct had not been exactly what it was; and the complaint against him is founded in a gross misconception of the nature of that duty (*a*).

We now come to the question of interest, whether this prize is to be condemned to the captor, or as a droit of office to the Lord High Admiral, or, as that office is now constituted in practice, to the King in his office of Admiralty. It is well known that formerly there was a Lord High Admiral, who now exists only in contemplation of law. All rights of prize belong originally to the Crown, and the beneficial interest derived to others can proceed only from the grant of the Crown. It was thought expedient to assign a certain portion of those rights to maintain the dignity of the Lord High Admiral; but during the civil wars, those ancient grants had grown into obscurity; and it is observed by Sir Leoline Jenkins, that it had been the policy of the usurper to expunge as much as possible from record the very name and office of Lord High Admiral (*b*), and all rights belonging to it. At the restora-

(*a*) These observations were thrown out in allusion to the former proceedings in this cause. On the facts above stated by the Court, the captor had considered himself aggrieved by not having the copy of the sentence delivered to him, and had directed an appearance to be given by his own proctor to assert his interest, in opposition to the King's proctor, in whose hands the care and management of the case was officially lodged. On a motion being made to that effect, the Court adverted to the circumstances of the case, and dismissed the application with strong disapprobation of the measures which had been pursued.

(*b*) The Earl of Warwick was appointed Lord High Admiral by the

tion, therefore, it became necessary to institute an inquiry into the nature of those rights, for the purpose of ascertaining their just limits. The discussion that took place respecting them is recorded in the works of Sir Leoline Jenkins; and I think it does appear from the history of that transaction, that the nature and distinction of those rights had been very much obliterated in the minds of those who might be expected to be best acquainted with them. For the opinions that are reported to have been held by persons of eminence in this profession at that time are in no trifling degree at variance with each other, and contradictory to the understanding which has now for a long time universally prevailed.

Very few passages from Sir Leoline Jenkins will be sufficient to justify this remark. In the first letter on this subject, the right of seizure in port is supposed not to belong to the Lord High Admiral, in prejudice of King's ships, though nothing is more established now than that such perquisites belong to the Lord High Admiral in exclusion of King's ships, as well as of others. It is said, also, "that this right in port does not appear to be in the Lord High Admiral, to the prejudice of the King's own ships, either by patent or prescription," which if taken separately might appear to impugn a principle now most clearly understood, that these claims of special privilege, on the part of the Lord High Admiral, can have no other legal origin than the grant of the Crown. The meaning, however, which the words of that learned person, as explained by subsequent passages, were intended to convey (*a*), is not chargeable with any inaccuracy on this point,

Parliament. He resigned under an ordinance that members should have no employments, April 15th, 1645; was appointed again by the Commons, 28th April, 1645; was deprived finally, 23rd February, 1648, under an ordinance that "that office and the wardenship of the Cinque Ports should be executed by the Council of State, appointed by the authority of Parliament": Scobel, February 23rd, 1648.

(*a*) Sir Leoline Jenkins is to be understood as saying, "that the patent granted only *bona casu fortuito reperta*," that the extending it to *bona inimicorum* was an extension of the grant by interpretation under the late regulations. In that sense he explains himself, "not by patent, for the words *bona inimicorum casu fortuito reperta* do refer as well to the open sea (and then the admiral claims not against the King's ships) as to the ports." "Not by prescription, for in the two precedents, which is all I yet find of enemies' goods seized in port and adjudged to the Lord

1806 *March* 20. *April* 22.

THE MARIA FRANCOISE.

Sir W. Scott.

and therefore I dwell on this observation no further than may be necessary to obviate the danger of misconception on a subject of public importance. In the account (*a*) of the discussion which afterwards took place, this eminent person has recorded the traces of other opinions, which it is not so easy to reconcile to the more correct view which is, I conceive, properly to be taken of this subject. He says, "We all agree that his Majesty has not any interests in such ships and goods belonging to enemies as are taken and brought in by any of his Majesty's subjects who are not employed in the King's ships or in private men-of-war."

But we differ only in this circumstance. Sir R. Wiseman is of opinion that such ships and goods ought to be condemned to the taker; Sir W. Turner and myself, "to the Lord High Admiral." Here, again, is an opinion wholly untenable in favour of non-commissioned captors; for that they should hold any interest to be vested in the taker, originally, and in opposition to the rights of the Crown, is so contrary to the true doctrine on this subject, that it shows, I think, most strongly that all legal consideration of these matters had gone much into a state of desuetude; and it is not easy to reconcile the opinions there stated with any view of the subject which we can now form, looking either to the general principles on which alone such rights could originally be founded, or to the opinions which have, in later times, been universally entertained respecting them.

It is stated also in another place, "We agree that enemies' ships that come in voluntarily to his Majesty's ports, or are driven in

Admiral, it does not appear by whom the seizure was made in the one at Swansea, and it is express the vice-admiral made the other in the Isle of Wight." So also in another place: his words are, "before this regulation be applied to the fact, it will, I suppose, be granted without difficulty, that there is nothing new granted to the admiral by this regulation, only his patent is explained, and his right, which was in part acknowledged in an Order of Council, December 14th, 1664, is more expressly declared as to *bona inimicorum*. The Lord High Admiral has *bona inimicorum pro derelictis habita seu casu fortuito reperta* within his jurisdiction granted to him by patent; and by the same regulation, March 6th, 1665, his right is declared to extend to enemies' ships coming into port by stress of weather or other accidents; so it is if they come in by mistake of port, or not knowing of the war": Sir Leoline Jenkins, vol. ii. p. 742.

(*a*) Page 767.

thither by stress of weather or other accidents, do belong to the Lord High Admiral, if his officers or those of the custom-house, or indeed any other, do seize them. This Sir R. Wiseman would have understood to be without prejudice to the King's men-of-war"; whereas it is not now pretended that they constitute any ground of exception whatever. He proceeds, "and Sir W. Turner is contented it should be so, provided the men-of-war make the first seizure in the pursuit of an enemy; and these restrictions, he says, I do also submit to as very reasonable in this case." Not as collecting the traces of former practice, but asserting only what appeared consonant to the reason and equity of the case.

On all these points, it is impossible not to observe that the opinions of those eminent persons, who are not to be named in this Court without great respect, are so inconsistent, so opposite to the Order made in Council, and the interpretation which that Order has always received, that we are induced to conclude that they were speaking on a subject which had gone into some disuse and consequent oblivion, and on which they had not refreshed their memories by recurring to any traces that then existed of the more ancient practice; that their opinions can afford but little light for our guide in the present times, and therefore that the true rule must now be taken from the Order of Council of 1665.

It appears to me, I confess, from the tenor of this Order, that the distinction between the Admiral and rights of the Crown is founded in this—that when vessels come in, not under any motive arising out of the occasions of war, but from distress of weather, or want of provisions, or from ignorance of war, and are seized in port, they belong to the Lord High Admiral; but where the hand of violence has been exercised upon them, where the impression arises from acts connected with war, from revolt of their own crew, or from being forced or driven in by the King's ships, they belong to the Crown. This is the broad distinction which is laid down in the Order of Council, and which has since been invariably observed.

It is an opinion which I have occasionally thrown out, that the rights of the Lord High Admiral, though they are to be duly supported, are not to be extended by construction; and for these reasons, that the grants of the Crown differ in this respect from other grants, that they are to be taken strictly, and are not to be

1806 *March* 20. *April* 22.

THE MARIA FRANCOISE.

Sir W. Scott.

interpreted to the benefit of the grantee; and secondly, that the rights of the Crown, being public rights, deposited there for great public purposes, are not to be alienated beyond the precise tenor of the grant. It is said that the captors are grantees also, and that their claims stand in that respect on the same footing with those of the Lord High Admiral; but that description of them is subject to an essential distinction. In the first place, it is to be recollected that the grant to the Lord High Admiral was made at a time when that office was on a footing which the present state of society and modern policy would scarcely suffer to exist. It is an establishment of ancient times, but little adapted to reasons of modern convenience. This at least we may presume, that if such an office was to be now instituted, some other mode of providing for its support would be resorted to than that of perquisites, which are so fluctuating in their own nature, which supply no regular fund for a permanent establishment, and are in no manner adapted to the exigencies of the public service. The grant, which is now made to those who by a commission execute that office, is accommodated to the necessities of the present times, and is directed under the view of the legislature attending to these present necessities, and to purposes of national concern.

Another distinction of rather a more legal nature is, that the grant to the Lord High Admiral, whatever it conveys, carries with it a total and perpetual alienation of the rights of the Crown. They are gone for ever, and separated from the Crown, and nothing short of an Act of Parliament can restore them; whereas the grant to captors is nothing more than a mere temporary transfer of the beneficial interest. The Crown would not be chargeable with a violation of any public law, if it did not issue the grant; and though the practice of issuing it after the commencement of every war has been so constant in later times as to authorize the expectation of the continuance, it still is to be considered as the occasional act of the Crown's bounty, by which not the right but the mere beneficial interest of prize is conveyed for a time; but to return to the Crown and there to remain till again conveyed by a fresh act of royal liberality. Against such captors standing on an interest of that species the construction is the same as it would be against the Crown itself; because they cannot be pronounced against without pronouncing, in effect, that a perpetual alienation of the Crown's right to prize taken under such circumstances had already been made to the Lord High Admiral.

Having premised these general observations, I come now to the matter of fact. It is not very distinctly ascertained where the capture was made, since there are not less than three or four representations which by no means agree with each other. One French witness deposes "that they were taken in port at Negapatam"; a second, "that they were taken at Negapatam"; the third states "that they had been seized and brought to Negapatam, where they were released, and that after twenty days they were captured, whilst lying in the road of Negapatam," that is, not in port, but in the road of Negapatam. Then comes the account contained in the affidavit of Captain Lind, the actual captor, "that she was seized three or four miles from the shore, and not within gunshot, and that the road is no other than the common anchorage ground, which extends along the coast of Coromandel for two or three hundred miles." These are four separate and contrary representations. On the question of locality, then, the description which is given of the place of capture is not so accurate as to enable the Court to draw any very satisfactory conclusions from it. With respect to captures in roads generally, it must be understood that to raise a question of this kind, a road must at least be so connected with the common uses of the port as to constitute a part of the port in which the capture is alleged to have been made. We all know that there are roads along many parts of the coast of this kingdom which make no part of any port. The port of Yarmouth is very different from the roads of Yarmouth; and I am not aware of any case in which a ship lying merely at anchor in a road, without being protected by points of lands, has been held to support a claim of this nature on the part of the Admiralty. It is not enough that ships should anchor there for a short stay. It must, I conceive, be the place where vessels not only arrive, but take up their station for the purpose of unlivering their cargoes in the ordinary course of commerce. If it were necessary to decide on this point I should be of opinion that the exact nature of the place of capture was not so defined as to enable the Court to pronounce

1806 *March* 20. *April* 22.

THE MARIA FRANCOISE.

Sir W. Scott.

for the claim of the Admiralty, in opposition to the general interest of the captor under the Prize Act.

Another topic which has been discussed is, whether this settlement could be considered as part of the British territories, being, as it is described, only a possession of the East India Company for the purposes of trade. On this point the inclination of my opinion is, that since the possessions of the East India Company have been so incorporated with the rights and interests of this kingdom, the claims of the Lord High Admiral would extend to them, and would attach on seizures made in that part of the world, as well as in other ports. This is a question, however, which has not been directly decided, nor, perhaps, ought it to be until some case occurs which may render it necessary to consider fully and with due deliberation all the consequences that may be involved in it. The only point which remains to be considered is that on which I have already made some observations, viz., that this ship did not come into port through ignorance, or under inducements unconnected with exertions of a military nature, but that she was driven or forced in by one of his Majesty's ships. This is what appears to me to be specially reserved in the Order of Council. It is the case of a ship not only driven in, but brought in, upon conjecture of war, when hostilities existed but were not certainly known. She was on that account released, and seized again within about twenty days, when the existence of hostilities was no longer a matter of conjecture. Under these circumstances, unless I could apply a more liberal interpretation of the Lord High Admiral's grant than I conceive myself warranted to do, I must hold the right of prize to be in the King. I am of opinion that it is a case not only not within the words of the grant to the Lord High Admiral, but that it is that which is specially reserved to the Crown, and consequently that the condemnation ought to pass to the captor.

THE NOSTRA SIGNORA DEL CARMEN.

[6 C. Rob. 302.]

Capture—Interest—Naval Officer on Board as Passenger.

A naval officer on board a ship of war as a passenger at the time of a capture is not entitled to a share of prize money even though he does work on the ship.

THIS was a question of interest, on the claim of Lieutenant Nicholas, of his Majesty's ship the *Niger*, to share in the prize captured by the *Tribune*. 1806 *May* 17.

SIR W. SCOTT.—This question arises on the claim of Lieutenant Nicholas to share as lieutenant of his Majesty's ship the *Tribune*, he being a lieutenant of his Majesty's ship the *Niger*, but on board the *Tribune* for the purpose of taking his passage home, and doing duty at the request of the commander when the prize was taken; and I must confess that, if it had not been pressed with great earnestness by persons to whose judgment I am always disposed to pay great respect, I should not have thought that there was any very serious question in the case. . . . .

The proclamation and the Prize Act lay down two requisites as necessary to entitle a person to share: that the officer should be not only on board, but that he shall be also an officer belonging to the ship. This is the obvious and likewise the decided meaning of the clause, and Lord Mansfield, in *Wemys* v. *Linzee* (*a*), states it to have been judicially determined "that the officers must not only be on board, but belonging to that ship"; and therefore the only question is, whether this gentleman could be considered as a lieutenant belonging to the *Tribune?* On what ground can it be contended that he was? . . . .

These are the observations which suggest themselves on the facts of the case, and I think they are fully supported by the doctrine of decided cases. In *Wemys* v. *Linzee* (*b*) the question is reported to have terminated finally in a verdict that the plaintiff had not acted in the capacity alleged. The duty had not been performed.

(*a*) 1 Douglas, p. 326.
(*b*) On a new trial, 1 Douglas, p. 328.

1806 May 17. — THE NOSTRA SIGNORA DEL CARMEN. — Sir W. Scott.

It will not follow, however, that if it had the demand could have been sustained. But the case of the *Cabadonga* (*a*) does, I think, furnish a complete decision on the general law, and is clearly applicable to this case. . . . . With the most perfect conviction of mind I decide against this claim, and must leave it to be corrected elsewhere, if the opinion which I have formed should be erroneous.

[6 C. Rob. 351.]

THE ROMEO.

Evidence—Document Seized in a Non-captured Ship—Admissibility of Document in Suit against a Captured Ship.

A letter was, on search, taken from the A., which was allowed to proceed on her voyage, which paper referred to the B., which had been captured. *Held*, that such letter was admissible in evidence on further proof against the B.

1806 October 29.

THIS was a question as to the admissibility, in a suit against the *Romeo*, of the evidence of a letter, applicable to this case, which had been taken out of an American vessel, the *Mary*, by Lieutenant Rigby, of his Majesty's gun brig *Urgent*, who had stopped that vessel and had examined her papers, and finding a letter which purported to disclose the real state of a transaction, which had been fraudulently concealed, had sent the paper in question to the King's proctor officially, but without detaining the ship in which it was found.

(*a*) The *Nostra Signora de Cabadonga* was a case of a prize taken by the *Centurion*, on board of which ship were several officers of his Majesty's ships the *Gloucester* and *Trial Prize*. These two ships had been associated with the *Centurion* in a voyage of discovery under Lord Anson, but had been destroyed during the voyage as no longer seaworthy. The decree of the Court of Admiralty had pronounced "that these officers were officers in his Majesty's service on board the *Centurion* at the time of capture, and adjudged them to share respectively according to their ranks with the officers of the *Centurion*": 8th March, 1745; Book 2, fo. 228.

On appeal this sentence was reversed, and it was decreed (Lords, 17th May, 1747), "that they were not commissioned or warrant officers of or belonging to the *Centurion*, nor in pay as such, nor aiding or assisting as officers of or belonging to the *Centurion* at the time of capture, and that they have not any right to share in the distribution of the prize money with the officers." See also 1 Douglas, p. 326, where the circumstances of this case are stated.

1806 *October* 29.

THE ROMEO.

For the captors, the *King's Advocate* and *Robinson*.

For the claimant, *Arnold* and *Laurence*.

SIR W. SCOTT.—A paper is offered to the Court as evidence in this cause, which, it is contended, cannot be received, as not having been found on board this or any other captured vessel, and as being on that account not within the regulations of the Prize Act. In the course which I mean to pursue it will not be necessary to enter into this discussion, because if there is a mode conformable to the Act of Parliament and the practice of the Court, the Court would naturally rather adopt that mode than be led unnecessarily into a consideration of the difficulties that have been stated.

The Act of Parliament ordains, that if any doubts arise the Court may direct further proof; but it has not limited the cause of doubt to evidence actually on board, nor could it with propriety have imposed any such restrictions. The Court itself might possess information that would completely falsify the claim. Could it be said in such a case that, because the depositions and the formal papers were consistent, there should be no means of extracting the real truth of the facts? Could it be expected that the Court should proceed to judgment on the mere formal evidence, in opposition to its own private conviction that the whole of what was there stated was false? It would be impossible to maintain that proposition to the utmost extent (*a*). It must be allowed, then, that there may be instances in which the Court has the power of calling for extraneous evidence. In acceding to any prayer, the Court will undoubtedly be much guided by the nature of the original evidence; but it cannot with propriety be maintained that the Court is absolutely concluded by it. When a case is perfectly clear and not liable to any just suspicion, the disposition of the Court will certainly lean strongly against the introduction of extraneous matter and against permitting the captors to enter upon further inquiries; but in the present instance the case is not free from objection on the original evidence.

The Court may also, I conceive, in the exercise of its discretion and under the grave responsibility which accompanies all its actions, be at liberty to consider a little the effect of the evidence

(*a*) But see Vol. II. p. 549.

1806 October 29. — THE ROMEO. — Sir W. Scott.

proposed to be introduced. If it is slight and vague in its nature, the Court will be less easily induced to depart from its usual course. But can it be said that the relevancy of the paper in question is not material? If there is no doubt that the paper offered was a ship's paper, though on board another vessel, which I think there is not, I am of opinion that it is competent to me, when the evidence is of so stringent a nature as that proposed, to admit it. I accede very much to what has been said as to the dependence which the credit of papers must have on the circumstances under which they are brought in. But that is an observation which affects the question of credibility. This is a paper apparently under the handwriting of Noble and Arbuthnot, who have been avowedly much engaged in the concerns of the vessel now before the Court; is not such a paper material? I am of opinion that the Court is at liberty to have doubts extrinsic of the evidence, and that this paper may be admitted on an order for further proof. What I shall do at present will be to make an order for further proof, giving the captors leave to introduce the paper in such a manner as they may be advised.

On a subsequent day (*a*), this cause came before the Court again on further proof, when no explanation being offered of this paper, which had been brought in by the King's proctor, duly verified by the affidavit of Lieutenant Rigby, the Court observed: This is a paper which stands entirely free from all suspicion of fabrication, since it had been sent in before the capture of this vessel; and, from the particular and circumstantial manner in which it refers to directions appearing to have been given in the charter-party, it is clear that it could not have been fabricated for unfair purposes by the captors. Under these circumstances, and especially when no notice is taken of it in the further proof, it is to be considered as a paper which verifies itself. All the other papers which have been introduced in further proof are mere formal papers, which would have been precisely the same if the transaction had passed in the manner described in this uncontradicted letter. There can be no doubt, in my opinion, that the transaction did pass in that

(*a*) May 3rd, 1808.

manner. Whether the property of this vessel belongs to persons at Antwerp or Papenburg does not perhaps distinctly appear; but as Papenburg was in a state of hostility at the time of capture, that circumstance is altogether immaterial.

1806 *October* 29.

THE ROMEO.

Sir W. Scott.

Claim rejected.

THE CONFERENZRATH.

[6 C. Rob. 362.]

Blockade—Intention to Break—Blockade Raised before Sailing—Neutral Cargo—Neutral and Enemy Ports Adjacent.

A vessel sailed intending to break a blockade, which was raised before she sailed, and was captured. *Held*, that she could not be condemned.

A neutral cargo was taken to Hamburg. *Held*, that Altona and Hamburg being closely adjacent and commercially connected ports, they could be considered as one, and the port of destination as though it were actually Altona.

1806 *December* 18.

THIS was a case of a Danish vessel belonging to Altona, which had sailed from Altona to Monte Video, and was captured on a return voyage to Hamburg, provided that port should not be under blockade, with an alternate destination to Frederickstadt.

SIR W. SCOTT.—This is clearly a Danish vessel. No objection has been raised against the property of the ship; but with respect to the cargo it is objected that, as there appears to have been no Spanish licence authorizing these persons to trade at Monte Video, it is reasonable to infer that the cargo must belong to Spanish merchants. But I think there is enough to be collected from the papers to show that persons introducing a cargo would be received, and allowed to export a cargo in return. It appears that the outward cargo produced more than was invested in the return cargo, and that some part of the money was left in that country. If the commerce of that place had been so far open that the parties would be at liberty to engage in subsequent adventures, it was not unnatural that the surplus of their funds should be left for another voyage. I am of opinion, therefore, that these objections are not sufficient to weigh against the general current of evidence, which represents the cargo to belong to merchants of Hamburg; and I shall, on that part of the case, have no hesitation in pronouncing it to be Hamburg property.

1806
December 18.

THE CONFERENZRATH.

Sir W. Scott.

But two questions of law are raised. It is objected that the ship had been guilty of a breach of blockade on the outward voyage, and the terms of the Order in Council of the present war do impose that limitation on the liberty of commerce to the colonies of the enemy. With respect to the intention of the parties, it does appear from the charter-party that there was a design to violate the blockade; but though there may have been the *mens rea*, the parties have had the benefit of extrinsic circumstances turning out in their favour. The blockade was raised before the vessel sailed; so that there is not the *corpus delicti* existing that would be necessary also to draw upon them the penalties of the law.

The second objection is, that the ship had gone to Buenos Ayres and had taken a cargo, with an intention of returning, according to the charter-party, to Hamburg; and it was only on the event of the renewal of the blockade that the ship was to go to Frederickstadt. It is, therefore, a Hamburg cargo on board a Danish ship, and going, not to a port of the country to which the ship belonged, but to Hamburg. It is true that the rule has been laid down with more precision and with greater strictness in this war than in the last. It is now restricted to the country of the ship, whereas the former rule extended to the country of the owner of the cargo also. It is not in my power, neither is it my inclination, to relax the strictness of the latter rule by interpretation. But when ports are so nearly conjoined as Hamburg and Altona, not merely by juxtaposition only, but by the closest connections of familiarity and commercial intercourse; when they use one common exchange, and when the merchants have their country houses on each side of the river indifferently, it would be pressing the rule too harshly on the merchants of Hamburg to hold that they should not be at liberty to enjoy the convenience which Altona affords for all the purposes of commerce. I am rather disposed to consider them, as far as the reasonable construction of this Order is concerned, as the same port. I shall therefore admit the claim, and pronounce this property to be Hamburg property.

THE ROLLA.

[6 C. Rob. 364.]

Blockade—Authority of Naval Commander to Establish Blockade—Ratification by Government—Notice to Neutrals—Subsequent Invalidation of Blockade.

A naval commander at a distance from his Government has authority to order a blockade of a port, and if such action is irregular, it can be ratified and thus made valid by the Government.

When notice of a blockade to neutral States is not possible, a *de facto* notice of a less formal kind which is brought to the notice of neutral shipmasters in the blockaded port is binding on them.

1807 *June 3.*

THIS was a case of an American ship and cargo, proceeded against for a breach of the blockade of Monte Video, as imposed by the British commander in the expedition to the River Plata, and notified at Monte Video by communication through the Spanish governor at Monte Video.

The case was argued much at length in several arguments. The points chiefly contended on the part of the claimant were:—That it was a blockade imposed without competent authority, having originated with Sir Home Popham only, and without any communication with his Government; that this defect was more conspicuous, from the manner in which the whole of that expedition had been undertaken without orders. Secondly, that the mode of notification resorted to, by communication through the enemy, was vicious in its nature, improperly thrown upon the enemy, and to which neutral nations were not bound to attend. Thirdly, that if the blockade could be held to have had a valid commencement, the fluctuating manner in which it had been from time to time relaxed by the British commander, would defeat the efficacy of the measure altogether, more especially as it was at most but a blockade *de facto* only, not aided by any of the presumptions which had been held to support the continuance of a blockade by notification, till the notification was regularly withdrawn. The blockade originated with Sir Home Popham, and therefore a relaxation admitted by him would justify a supposition that the measure was altogether abandoned.

SIR W. SCOTT.—This ship was taken with a cargo on board, off Monte Video, on the 20th November, 1806, and is proceeded

1807 June 3. THE ROLLA. Sir W. Scott.

against for a breach of the blockade of that port. When that ground is taken, it must be shown that there was a competent authority to impose a blockade; secondly, that it was in fact imposed; and thirdly, that it was maintained in such a manner as to lay upon the parties an obligation of attending to it. If these three points are established with respect to a ship coming out with a cargo taken on board subsequent to the blockade, the *onus probandi* is thrown on the party to prove that, though the blockade might exist, there were circumstances that would operate to the release of that particular vessel, exempting her from the penalty of the law.

On the former hearing it was contended that the power of imposing a blockade is altogether an act of sovereignty which cannot be assumed or exercised by a commander without special authority. But the Court then expressed its opinion that this was a position not maintainable to that extent, because a commander going out to a distant station may reasonably be supposed to carry with him such a portion of sovereign authority delegated to him as may be necessary to provide for the exigencies of the service on which he is employed. On stations in Europe, where Government is almost at hand to superintend and direct the course of operations, under which it may be expedient that particular hostilities should be carried on, it may be different. But in distant parts of the world it cannot be disputed, I conceive, that a commander must be held to carry with him sufficient authority to act, as well against the commerce of the enemy as against the enemy himself, for the more immediate purpose of reduction.

It has been also further contended that the commander, in this expedition particularly, did not possess this authority, because it has appeared from the result of a subsequent inquiry into his conduct that he had acted irregularly in entering upon it without orders. But however irregularly he may have acted towards his own Government, the subsequent conduct of Government in adopting that enterprise by directing a further extension of that conquest will have the effect of legitimating the acts done by him, so far at least as the subjects of other countries are concerned. The Government has not disclaimed the acquisitions as obtained wrongfully; on the contrary, it has recognized his acts by seizing

Maldonado, and by retaining the footing which had been acquired for them in that country, thereby expressing their recognition of the seizure as a seizure made by the forces of this country validly applied. I am therefore of opinion that the blockade is not to be impeached on the ground of want of regular authority, and I have no hesitation in pronouncing that, however irregularly Sir Home Popham may be deemed to have acted towards his own Government, it is that for which he is in no manner answerable to other States, and that it is not open to the individual subjects of other countries to dispute the validity of the blockade on that account.

The second question that arises is whether the blockade was imposed in a legal form. All that is necessary to make a notification effectual and valid is that it shall be communicated in a credible manner, because, though one mode may be more formal than another, yet any communication which brings it to the knowledge of the party in a way which could leave no doubt in his mind as to the authenticity of the information would be that which ought to govern his conduct and will be binding upon him. Sir Home Popham came before the place in June, and it appears by his letters that he considered the blockade to have been imposed in June, though not by notification. Why it was not accompanied with a notification at that time we are not informed. It would have been more regular, undoubtedly, as indeed it is at all times more convenient, that it should be declared in a public and distinct manner, instead of being left to creep out from the consequences produced by it. On the 23rd of September, however, it appears that a notification was sent into Monte Video. As to all that passed previous to that day, I shall consider it as that to which the Court is in no manner bound to attend, for I think it is evident from the letters of Sir Home Popham, which are produced by himself, that ships had been permitted to pass, and that the blockade, though intended to commence in June, had not been kept up with exactness and uniformity. The very expressions requesting the governor to make it known to neutral vessels do away the effect of all transactions antecedent to the 23rd September, and I look upon them as wholly unimportant to both parties (*a*). The

(*a*) It had been contended in argument that this particular vessel had run in, in breach of the blockade, and in defiance of the blockading ships.

notification is made on the 23rd of September. The usual mode of communicating such intelligence undoubtedly is not to the hostile Government, but to neutral States, and when the more regular form is practicable it is proper that it should be observed; but here it was not practicable. Sir Home Popham took the only method that could be adopted, by sending to the governor of the place and by desiring him to make it known to the subjects of neutral Powers who had no public agents or consuls resident there, to whom it could be more formally addressed. From papers exhibited in another case, it appears that the steps which the governor took were of the most formal and effectual kind. He summoned all the foreign shipmasters before him, and among them the master of this vessel. He communicated to them the letter which he had received, and told them that the port was under blockade, and that they must take notice of it at their peril. They were also required to sign a paper to the effect of that notice, but they refused—that they might not appear to bind themselves by their own voluntary act.

That this notification was sent and communicated is established beyond contradiction by every part of this large bundle of papers, so that it was quite impossible that any person in that port could pretend ignorance of the blockade. It is not without considerable surprise, therefore, that I see the manner in which the master of this vessel, and other persons who have joined in an affidavit with him, have expressed themselves. He says that some time in October a notice was communicated, as he had heard, when it is quite notorious that it was done two days after the notification was received, and in September. He says, also, that "they were allowed fourteen days to come out," whereas the notification says "seven," and "that he never saw the letter, and that it was not notified in such a manner as made them consider the place to be under blockade." In direct contradiction to all this, it is abundantly proved by the certificate of the Spanish officer, and by the petitions of different neutral masters, that they were convened for the purpose of hearing the letter read, and that the measure itself was perfectly understood by them, since it is recited in direct terms in several of their petitions. The manner in which the mate speaks also, who is the brother of the master, is still more extraordinary. He says, "that he first heard it mentioned on board the ship after their departure from Monte Video." This is perfectly incredible. Without observing further on these inconsistencies, I am of opinion that the notification was made in such a manner as would legally affect the master with an obligation of observing it.

But it is said that the terms of the notification are illegal, as containing an unwarrantable limitation of the general rule of law, in "requiring neutral vessels to come out in seven days in ballast, or with those cargoes only on board which they had carried in." It is objected that the neutral masters were abridged of some of their just rights, namely, that they might bring out also any cargo which had been taken on board previous to the notification; and it is contended that this will have the effect of invalidating the whole proceeding. In support of this argument, a reference has been made to a case in which a notice, irregularly given to a neutral vessel on the coast of Holland by one of his Majesty's officers, was held in this Court to have the effect of relieving that vessel from the penalty under which she had fallen. But no cases can be more distinguishable. That was the case of a vessel warned by a King's officer, off the coast of Holland, "that she was not to go into any of the ports of Holland," at a time when the port of Amsterdam alone was under blockade. Here there is a blockade, properly imposed by a person having authority, and rightly expressed as to the particular port. If there had been an irregularity leading to a mistake as to the port which was actually placed under blockade, there might have been some ground for expecting relief of the same kind from the Court. But the blockade is good *pro tanto;* and the Court will not vitiate the effect of it merely on account of the omission of one of the conditions under which vessels might be permitted to go out. In that case the irregularity proceeded from an erroneous construction put upon a public notification of Government by one of his Majesty's officers. Here it was a restriction imposed by the commander himself, who might possibly find himself under circumstances that would make such a restraint perfectly justifiable, though no such circumstances are stated. I am of opinion, therefore, that the notification was valid in authority, sufficiently notified, and not illegal.

1807 June 3. — THE ROLLA. — Sir W. Scott.

Then the question comes to this, whether the claimant can show any special circumstances that will take off his responsibility of observing it, and relieve him from the penalty of the law. The cargo was taken in after notice, which, under the general rules that have been laid down in this class of cases, is not permitted. But it is contended that, in the commerce with South America, a greater latitude must, in equity, be allowed from the nature of that trade; that the object of the voyage is principally to obtain a return cargo, and on that account a liberty to go in should imply a liberty to come out with a cargo; that the cargo consists chiefly of hides and tallow, and other articles of which, in warm climates, it would be necessary to defer the shipment till the last moment for their better preservation; that the return being in goods of that description, a possession in warehouses as to them should be taken as equivalent to the possession by shipment, to which the Court has confined the liberty of coming out with a cargo in other cases. I do not feel myself warranted to accede to the consequences of this mode of reasoning. The trade to the colony of the enemy is not one that is entitled to considerations of peculiar indulgence. It is one not ordinarily open, but allowed only by the enemy, as a relaxation for the relief of their distresses proceeding from the war. It is a trade, therefore, which persons resorting to it for their own extraordinary profit and advantage must be content to take with all the consequences attending it. I do not feel that there is any just call upon me to distinguish in their favour, or to depart in this particular case from those rules which the Court has felt itself under the necessity of laying down, to prevent the continual danger of being imposed upon by particular evidence, if it was to permit the exemption to be carried further than to a delivery on board the ship, or in lighters. I must therefore reject that plea.

It is then said that there are other circumstances that will defeat the operation of the penalty, namely, that the blockade was irregularly maintained by the blockading force, in suffering some ships to go in and others to come out, which would tend to deceive other persons, and would therefore vitiate the effect of the notification. And I confess, if I was satisfied of the fact that such instances did occur, I should be disposed to admit the conclusion that such a mode of keeping up, or rather of relaxing the blockade, would altogether destroy the effect of it. For what is a blockade but a uniform universal exclusion of all vessels not privileged by law? If some are permitted to pass, others will have a right to infer that the blockade is raised. If it was shown, therefore, that ships not privileged by law have been allowed to enter or come out, from motives of civility, or other considerations, I should be disposed to admit that other parties would be justified in presuming that the blockade had been taken off.

1807 *June* 3.

THE ROLLA.

Sir W. Scott.

A list is exhibited of the number of instances in which this is said to have occurred. The first two are of the date of the 20th of September, previous to the notification, and therefore may be put out of the question. The next is the *Minerva*, which appears to have been guilty of no breach of blockade whatever. That vessel had been detained and examined, but was driven in by the violence of the storm, and is therefore no instance of a liberty given by Sir Home Popham to go in. The rest that follow are slave ships, with respect to which it appears that Sir Home Popham had come to the humane resolution of permitting them to pass. . . . .

Then it is said that some were permitted to go out; but the fact is, as far as I understand it, that none were permitted to come out. . . . . I am of opinion, therefore, that the blockade existed under competent authority; that it was notified in a credible manner; and that it came to the knowledge of these parties in such a way as must bind them; that no circumstances occurred to invalidate the notice previous to the capture; and that nothing which happened since can have the effect of relieving this ship and cargo from the penalty of condemnation.

A similar question was decided in the *Hare* in reference to the blockade of Cadiz. The *Hare* was an American vessel which sailed from New York to Cadiz, and there took in a return cargo, which was loaded in June and July. On July 21st she sailed and was captured. [1 Acton, 260.]

SIR W. GRANT.—From the evidence adduced in this cause, originally or since invoked, there can be no doubt that the fact of the fleet having appeared off the harbour must have been known on the 10th of June, and was also considered to have arrived there for the purposes of blockade. From this period to the shipment of the cargo, which was not completed until late in July, enough must have transpired to display the intention of that squadron. Various vessels were warned off. Previous to that time, in May and the early part of June, many American vessels entered, as

1810 *March* 25.

1810 *March* 25. — THE HARE. — Sir W. Grant.

appears by the list introduced amongst the papers of this cause. From the 6th of June no more vessels enter the port. This must have been a matter of notoriety, and must have excited attention. With regard to the egress from those ports, some vessels sailed subsequent to that date; of these part were in ballast; others, perhaps, had a right to depart, as being included within the exceptions of the general order in favour of vessels laden before the knowledge of the blockade; upon this, however, we are not called upon now to decide; and some were actually captured, brought in for adjudication, and condemned, of whom there are now a few on our list. The general order did not issue until the 23rd of June, yet we can draw no inference that the blockade was not as rigorously kept up from the time of the squadron's first appearing off the port, namely, on the 8th of the same month, as it was subsequent to the general order. We are of opinion it was not so much a blockade recommenced as a blockade *de novo*. From the general notoriety of the circumstances attending it, the parties should have considered it as an actual blockade in full force and effect. We therefore affirm the sentence of the Court below, condemning the property of the ship and cargo as lawful prize to the captors (*a*).

[6 C. Rob. 376.]

THE CHRISTIANSBERG.

Blockade—Permission to Trade to Neutral Port—Breach of Permission—Capture on Subsequent Voyage—Condemnation.

The port of A. being blockaded, vessels were, by an Order in Council, permitted to leave the port in order to carry cargo to a neutral port. *Held*, that a vessel which infringed the permission by sailing to an enemy port, and was captured on her next voyage, was liable to condemnation for breach of the blockade.

1807 *June* 10.

THIS was a case of a ship which had sailed in February, 1807, with a cargo of cheese and butter from Rotterdam, ostensibly for Smyrna, but had put into Alicant, as asserted, in distress. The outward cargo was there sold and another cargo taken on board, with which the vessel sailed on a destination to Copenhagen, and was captured on that voyage. A claim was given for the ship and cargo on behalf of Mr. R. Rugge, of Altona.

For the captors, the *King's Advocate* and *Laurence*.—The plea of distress is falsified by the manner in which the entries appeared to be made in the log by interlineation. The original voyage is to be considered as in breach of the instructions of the 7th of January, and under false papers. In analogous cases of blockade a vessel that had violated the blockade inwards was still liable to capture

(*a*) See the *Hoffnung*, *ante*, p. 533.

on her returned voyage (*a*), though in a situation otherwise innocent, viz., even though she was coming out in ballast. 1807 *June* 10.

For the claimant, *Arnold* and *Adams*.

SIR W. SCOTT.—The first point to be considered in this case is the matter of fact on which the question of law is raised. It is a new question undoubtedly, but supported by such considerations that if the facts are established I shall feel no hesitation in pronouncing that they are sufficient to subject this ship and cargo to condemnation. It appears that the vessel had come out of Rotterdam under the benefit of that indulgence or limitation of the Order in Council of the 7th of January, 1807, which directs that the restriction should not be applied to vessels going to a neutral port. To avoid the effect of this Order an ostensible destination was assumed "to Smyrna"; but, as I collect from all the circumstances of the case, without the slightest intention of going to that port. The ship went to Alicant, as it is asserted, under distress, and there the former cargo was disposed of. The mate and the master have been examined, and the account which they give of the deviation is "that they met with bad weather, which obliged them to put into Alicant, where the master sold the former cargo and repaired the ship, and purchased another cargo." This is the result of the depositions, that it was merely an act of necessity; and if that is proved, a clear necessity will be a sufficient justification for everything that is done, fairly and with good faith, under it.

[The Court then examined the evidence, and concluded.]

Taking all these facts together, I have no hesitation in pronouncing that the evidence of the log is sufficient to convince me that the excuse set up for running into Alicant is false.

Then comes the question of law, whether the ship is not, under such circumstances, liable to condemnation? It is, as already

(*a*) So decided in the *Waeksamkeit*, 31st July, 1807; also *Instruction*, 5th August; also in more ancient cases—the *Jonge Fredericus*; the *Good Hope*, 15th October, 1799, agreeable to the dictum in the *Frederick Molke*, *ante*, p. 58.

1807 June 10.

THE CHRISTIANSBERG.

Sir W. Scott.

noticed, a new question of considerable importance; and more particularly if it is viewed in the extent of the consequences to which it may lead, as connected with the present restricted state of commerce. I am to consider, first, the situation in which the ship was shut up at Rotterdam. She was in fact blockaded in the port of Rotterdam, and could not come out with a cargo, unless going to a neutral port. The permission to go to a neutral port, if accepted, implies a contract that that destination should be *bonâ fide* pursued. The vessel avails herself of the indulgence, and comes out with a professed intention of acting conformably to the Order. But the fact turns out afterwards that she deposits her cargo in a port to which she would not have been permitted to go if the real intention of the voyage had been disclosed. This is unquestionably an act of perfidy; and I ask, by what means can the Order be maintained, or such a conduct be repressed, unless by the application of the penalty to the subsequent voyage? Until the vessel had actually entered the interdicted port, nothing appeared, whether she was *in delicto* or not. Cruisers see nothing; she goes in and then the offence is consummated, and the intention is for the first time declared. It is not till the vessel comes out again that any opportunity is afforded of vindicating the law, and of enforcing the restriction of this Order. It is objected that if the penalty is applied to the subsequent voyage, it may travel on with the vessel for ever. In principle, perhaps, it might not unjustly be pursued further than to the immediate voyage (*a*).

(*a*) So in an old case recorded in the Reports of the Court of Session in Scotland. "That the ship was taken in her return, having taken contraband to the enemy in that voyage, which is founded upon evident reason, because, that whilst ships are going towards the enemy, it is but an intention of delinquency against the King in assisting his enemies, but when they have actually gone in and sold the contraband, it is *delictum commissum;* and though it might infer a quarrel against the delinquent, whenever he could be found, yet the law of nations hath, for the freedom of trade, abridged it to the immediate return of the same voyage, because quarrels would be multiplied upon pretence of any former voyage": *Parkman* v. *Allen*, Stair's Decis. vol. 1, p. 529.

Agreeable to this distinction in the *Randers Bye* (23rd February), captured on her course from Cette to Randers, it appeared that the voyage immediately preceding had been from Marseilles to Cette in ballast, but that the voyage preceding that had been from Almeira to Marseilles,

But we all know that in practice it has not been carried further than to the voyage succeeding, which affords the first opportunity of enforcing the law. I shall, therefore, on these grounds pronounce the ship and cargo subject to condemnation.

1807 *June* 10. THE CHRISTIANSBERG. Sir W. Scott.

Prayer for the master's private adventure, which was considerable, refused.

THE HOFFNUNG (No. 3).

[6 C. Rob. 383.]

Capture—Ship and Cargo—Claim against Ship—Proceeds of Cargo Applied to Repair of Ship.

Where part of a cargo which was condemned as enemy's property had been sold, and the proceeds applied to the repair of the ship, which had been captured, and was subsequently restored. *Held*, that the captors could not, in a Prize Court, claim from the ship the value of the cargo spent upon her.

1807 *May* 1.

THIS was a case of a demand of average on the part of the Admiralty against a Swedish ship seized in the port of Ilfracombe, on account of the cargo, which was seized and condemned as Prussian property on the breaking out of Prussian hostilities. The demand was to recover against the ship the value of part of the cargo, which had been applied to the reparation of the vessel in the port of Ilfracombe before the seizure. The ship had been restored on bail given to answer the adjudication on this reserved question.

with ostensible papers to Trieste. It was argued, on the authority of the *Christiansberg*, that the effect of the former fraudulent destination would render the vessel liable on this subsequent voyage, more particularly as the voyage pretended to have been interposed was but of very short extent, and only a mere passage from one port of the same coast to another for the purpose of taking the cargo on board. On the other side it was contended, that the circumstance of an intermediate voyage, though in ballast, raised a ground of material distinction, inasmuch as it had afforded an opportunity of vindicating the law by capture on that voyage; that the Court had not extended the penalty further than to the next subsequent voyage, and would not be disposed to extend it. So decreed.

Restitution.

1807
May 1.

THE HOFFNUNG.

Sir W. Scott.

SIR W. SCOTT.—This is a claim of average against the ship, on the part of the captors of the cargo, which has been condemned as Prussian property. The vessel had been brought to Ilfracombe and was there detained, but before the seizure some part of the goods had been sold by the master to defray the expenses of the repairs of the ship, and that account was closed before the seizure. The monition was first taken out against the ship and the goods seized, and properly, because it could not be against the cargo generally. The law of war operates by force, and cannot be extended beyond that which is the object of practical seizure as a tangible object, which those parts of the cargo which had been sold clearly were not. If the term "cargo" was introduced afterwards in the subsequent stages of the proceedings, it is to be interpreted in the same sense of the cargo actually on board, and cannot be taken more generally as embracing the whole cargo, or as meaning to enlarge the object of the proceedings beyond what was on board at the time of seizure.

When the condemnation passed, it was not improperly suggested in argument that there might be a demand of average or contribution against the ship, and that question was reserved. The registrar and merchants have reported what would be the sum due if on the point of law anything should be held to be due, and that is the question which the Court has now to determine.

It is a case, as far as my experience goes, *primæ impressionis.* I do not recollect any instance of a demand of this nature, and in this I am confirmed by the recollection of the registrar. Cases of average on the part of the ship against the cargo are not unfrequent, but a demand of the cargo against the ship is perfectly novel in this Court. The distinction is obvious; the right of war is a right *in re*, and the Court of Prize accordingly attends only to the *res ipsa* and the *onera* attaching on the property in right of possession. The ship has the possession of the cargo, which the master is not bound to deliver till he has been satisfied for his demand of average, if he has such, in the same manner as for his demand of freight. He has the *res ipsa* in his possession and may legally detain it.

The captor succeeds to the rights of the owner of the ship when that is condemned, and may detain the cargo also in virtue of these rights when they exist. But with respect to the cargo it is very different. That has not, in any manner, a right of possession against the ship; it may have the *jus in rem*, possibly, but it has not the *jus in re*, and consequently no right of detention existing at the time of seizure. If there is any demand on that side, it must be enforced by a new process; there can be no detention, and consequently no right of detention. The demand must be of that description of interests only, which are collateral and extrinsic, and which are to be enforced on principles of law of another species and by a new process. They are not tangible objects to which the hand of war can be applied, and therefore the Prize Court will not take notice of them. Indeed, how could the claim of the cargo against the ship be enforced in this Court? If the ship goes into the country of the owners of the cargo, it may be reached by process of another kind; but only in virtue of an implied contract in law. That is the state of this demand, it is one that could be enforced only in the country to which the parties belong.

It has been said in argument that the captor succeeds to all the rights attending the property, and that he is subject to all the obligations belonging to the property seized. But this is not an accurate description. It is not, I conceive, a complete representation of all the interests and obligations of the proprietors that is devolved by act of seizure on the captor. The right of capture attaches according to the state in which the property is found; but if a former freight is due to the ship, the captor could not exact it, since he has not earned it. The owner of the ship has parted with his lien, and must look to his remedy of another species. Neither does the captor become subject to the obligations to which the owner is liable. Antecedent collateral contracts, as bottomry, may exist, that will not affect him; he becomes possessed of the *res ipsa* but without being made liable to the personal contracts in which the proprietor is engaged. Therefore, unless it can be shown that the hand of capture was employed on these goods in quality of cargo (*a*), the Court cannot go back to affect them in

(*a*) This principle was exemplified in the case of the *Charlotte* (March 25th, 1808), an American vessel which had sailed from America with a cargo of pitch and tar to the Cape of Good Hope, under a false destination to

1807 *May* 1.

THE HOFFNUNG.

Sir W. Scott.

any other character. This cannot be maintained. The ship had been totally restored, and part of the cargo had been converted before seizure. What has become of it the Court will not inquire, nor look back to rights of this extrinsic nature.

If the whole cargo had been applied to the repairs of a ship in a foreign port and incorporated with it, and the vessel had afterwards become prize, the captors might have had the benefit of that conversion, yet they would not have been subject to any demand on that account; still less could they in that case say, "You must find me a cargo," when in fact they had received it in the amelioration of the ship. So in this case they are not entitled to demand the proceeds of a cargo applied in the repairs of the ship. I am of opinion, therefore, that the debt, if it is to be so called, due from the vessel to the owner of the cargo, is amongst those *onera*, which the Prize Court does not notice, and that the claimant of the ship is entitled to his dismissal.

Madras and a market in India. The vessel had arrived at the Cape a short time prior to the capture of that settlement by the English forces. The chief part of the cargo had been sold to the Dutch Government. The proceeds had been deposited by the master in the hands of a merchant at the Cape as his agent there, and one hundred kegs of butter and eighty boxes of soap had been purchased and shipped by the master on the joint account of himself and the co-owner in America. On the surrender of the Cape, the vessel and the goods on board were seized, and a bond was taken of the agent to abide adjudication on the value of the proceeds of the cargo sold to the Dutch Government. There being no Vice-Admiralty Court at that time at the Cape, the case was brought before the High Court of Admiralty, when the Court condemned the ship, and the goods on board belonging to the owners, as implicated in the act of carrying contraband to a settlement of the enemy with false papers which would affect even the returned voyage: *Rosalie and Betty*, *ante*, p. 246. But the Court held the proceeds of that part of the cargo which had been delivered, and had not been subject to seizure, to be not amenable to the jurisdiction of the Court, and dismissed that part of the case.

THE LISETTE.

[6 C. Rob. 387.]

Blockade—Capture—Withdrawal of Blockade.

A ship or cargo is not liable to condemnation for breach of a blockade if captured after the cessation of such blockade.

1806 *December* 5. 1807 *July* 2.

THIS was a case of a vessel which had sailed from the Elbe to Tonningen under a charter-party, to take on board a cargo of goods for Malaga, which were to be sent from the Elbe in lighters. The goods were accordingly so shipped, and sailed on the 6th of September, and were captured on the 26th of September, after the blockade of the Elbe had been notified to be withdrawn on the 25th September, 1806.

[After argument, the Court on the 19th of December ordered the ship to be restored without giving judgment.]

On the 2nd July, 1807, the case was brought before the Court again in respect to the cargo.

SIR W. SCOTT.—This ship was taken on a voyage from Tonningen to Malaga, but a voyage accompanied with this fact that she had gone from Hamburg to Tonningen, under a charter-party formed at Hamburg for this ulterior voyage, and had there taken on board the cargo, which was brought from Hamburg in lighters. The Court has already restored the ship. But it is said that this passed on grounds which will not apply to the cargo; that the ship had gone from Hamburg in ballast, but that the goods are to be considered as taken in one uninterrupted voyage, commencing in an actual breach of the blockade and continuing as the same identical shipment, on the original destination from the blockaded port to Spain.

[The Court then examined the evidence and concluded.]

In the former case of the *Charlotte Sophia* (*a*), both the ship and the cargo were condemned; and this ship had been engaged in precisely the same course of trade. There is no doubt, then, that this vessel must have been condemned upon the authority of that

(*a*) *Ante*, p. 547, note.

1806 December 5. 1807 July 2.

THE LISETTE.

Sir W. Scott.

case, unless one other material distinction of fact had existed, leading to a rule of law to which the Court is strongly disposed to adhere. It is this, that this vessel was not captured till the blockade had ceased. It is said that the offence was consummated by the act of sailing; so it is, in a certain sense. But the ship was not taken *in delicto*, and I have not had any case pointed out to me in which the Court has pronounced an unfavourable judgment on a ship seized for the breach of a bygone blockade. I know of no such case, and certainly the same reason for rigour does not exist, because the blockade being gone, the necessity of applying the penalty to prevent future transgression cannot continue. That was the ground on which my opinion was formed in restoring the ship, though I did not then express my reasons for that judgment, in a case that came on at the conclusion of a very long and laborious sitting. It is true, as has been observed, that the offence incurred by a breach of blockade generally remains during the voyage. But that must be understood as subject to the condition that the blockade itself continues. When the blockade is raised a veil is thrown over everything that has been done, and the vessel is no longer taken *in delicto*. The *delictum* may have been completed at one period, but it is by subsequent events entirely done away. On these considerations I pronounce that this cargo is not subject to condemnation on the ground of the blockade.

[6 C. Rob. 391, note.]

THE TRENDE SOSTRE.

Contraband—Port of Destination—Change of Nationality.

A contraband cargo destined for an enemy's port was seized after such port became a British port. *Held*, that at the moment of seizure there was no *delictum*, and that the cargo could no longer be considered contraband.

1807 *August 5.*

THIS was a Danish vessel claimed for the Royal Danish College of Commerce, captured May 14, 1806, at the Cape of Good Hope, where the vessel had touched, on an ulterior destination to Tranquebar, with a cargo of cordage, and tar, gin, iron, and wine, and with despatches on board from Mr. Schimmelpenninck, the

Minister of State in Holland, for Governor Jansen, at the Cape of Good Hope. The vessel arrived at the Cape after that settlement had surrendered to the British forces, and was there seized as prize.

On the part of the captor, the *King's Advocate* and *Arnold* contended that a vessel was not at liberty to go to an enemy's port, having articles of contraband on board, under an asserted intention of proceeding on an ulterior destination; that though the settlement had become British the penalty would not be defeated, as the intention and the act continued the same; that there was no case in which such a distinction had been allowed on the question of contraband. The distinction, which had been admitted in blockade cases, stood altogether on particular grounds as arising out of a class of cases depending on the blockade of neutral ports, in which the Court had expressed a disposition to admit all favourable distinctions. This, on the contrary, was an offence of a noxious nature, and not entitled to any indulgence.

On the other side, *Laurence* and *Stoddart* adverted to the facts of the case as tending to exculpate the Danish College of Commerce from any intention of delivering the naval stores at the Cape, or from being privy to the conveyance of the Dutch despatches, and contended that on the interpretation to be put upon their acts it might be a question whether a great commercial company, trading under the authority of its own government and sending out stores for the Danish settlements in the east, could justly be restrained on the same terms as individuals from touching at an enemy's port for provisions, notwithstanding there might be on board articles that could not be carried to that port for sale. That the declarations of a public company as to its intentions were more entitled to credit and respect than the declarations of individuals; that, with respect to any forcible application of such articles to the use of the enemy that might be apprehended, there was also less danger that such a constraint would be put upon them when going in that manner under the special protection of the State; that this question was rendered unnecessary, however, by the date of the capture, which did not take place till the 14th May, 1806, when the Cape was in British possession; that

1807 *August 5.*

THE TRENDE SOSTRE.

the offence of carrying such articles to an enemy's port was no longer in existence. The *delictum* was done away, as the Court had held in analogous cases (*a*); that the judgment of the Court in the blockade cases was strictly in point, and did not stand on special grounds of lenity and forbearance, but on the just application of a general rule of law.

The *Court* observed:—If the port had continued Dutch, a person could not, I think, have been at liberty to carry thither articles of a contraband nature under an intention of selling other innocent commodities only, and of proceeding with the contraband articles to a port of ulterior destination; but before the ship arrives a circumstance takes place which completely discharges the whole guilt, because from the moment when the Cape became a British possession the goods lost their nature of contraband. They were going into the possession of a British settlement, and the consequence of any pre-emption that could be put upon them would be British pre-emption. It has been said that this is a principle which the Court has not applied to cases of contraband, and that the Court in applying it to cases of blockade did it only in consideration of the particular hardships consequent on that class of cases; but I am not aware of any material distinction, because the principle on which the Court proceeded was that there must be a *delictum* existing at the moment of seizure to sustain the penalty. It is said that the offence was consummated by the act of sailing, and so it might be with respect to the design of the party, and if the seizure had been made whilst the offence continued the property would have been subject to condemnation. But when the character of the goods is altered, and they are no longer to be considered as contraband going to the port of an enemy, it is not enough to say that they were going under an illegal intention. There may be the *mens rea*, not accompanied by the act of going to an enemy's port. I am of opinion, therefore, that the same rule does apply to cases of contraband, and upon the same principle on which it has been applied in those of blockade; I am not aware of any cases in which the penalty of contraband has been inflicted on goods not *in delicto*, except in the recent class of

(*a*) The *Lisette*, *ante*, p. 587; the *Conferenzrath*, *ante*, p. 571.

cases respecting the proceeds of contraband carried outward with false papers. But on what principle have those decisions been founded? On this, that the right of capture having been defrauded in the original voyage, the opportunity should be extended to the return voyage. Here the opportunity has been afforded till the character of the port of destination became British. Till that time the liability attached; after that, though the intention is consummated, there is a material defect in the body and substance of the offence, in the fact though not in the intent. I am of opinion that it is a discharge and a complete acquittal, that long before the time of seizure these goods had lost their noxious character of going as contraband to an enemy's port.

1807
August 5.

THE TRENDE SOSTRE.

Sir W. Scott.

THE MINERVA.

[6 C. Rob. 396.]

Capture—Neutral Ship—Ship of War Purchased by Neutral—Condemnation.

The sale of an enemy ship of war lying in a neutral port to a neutral is invalid, and if such vessel after such sale be captured, she will be condemned.

1807
August 12.

THIS was a case of a vessel under Kniphausen colours, and claimed for Count Bentinck, Lord of Kniphausen, as a ship lately purchased by him in April, 1807, in the port of Bergen, and coming, as it was asserted, according to his directions, to the river Jade, the port of Kniphausen. It appeared that at the time of the capture the vessel was sailing towards the Texel, and about ten or twelve miles from the coast of Holland; that she had been a Dutch ship of war belonging to the Dutch East India Company that had been chased into North Bergen, after an action with a British frigate at the beginning of the war, and had been lying in that port ever since.

For the captors, the *King's Advocate* and *Laurence*.

For the claim, *Arnold* and *Robinson*.

SIR W. SCOTT.—This question arises on the purchase of a vessel which is asserted to have been made by a highly distinguished

1807
August 12.

THE MINERVA.

Sir W. Scott.

person, described to be the Prince of Kniphausen. The circumstances of the transaction are these:—It is stated by all the witnesses that the ship had been a vessel of war, belonging to the Government of Holland, or to that great branch of the State, the East India Company; and it appears that the crew were all hired at Amsterdam to go to Bergen, and "to bring home an East India ship." The account which one of the witnesses gives is very natural on this subject; he says "that he was hired to bring home an East India ship, and to his great surprise found that it was a sloop of war, and expressed his apprehensions as to the consequences," as well he might. It is clear, also, from other parts of the evidence, that this vessel had been a Dutch ship of war that had maintained a conflict with a British frigate, and had been driven into Bergen, where she had remained sealed up ever since, for nearly three years.

The first question is, whether such a purchase can be legally made? I am not aware of any case in this Court, or in the Court of Appeal, in which the legality of such a purchase has been recognized. There have been cases of merchant vessels driven into ports out of which they could not escape, and there sold, in which, after much discussion and some hesitation of opinion, the validity of the purchase has been sustained. Such cases (*a*), I believe, did occur during the first war in which I attended this Court, or the Court of Appeal. But whether the purchase of a

(*a*) The *Nieuwe Vriendschap* (Lords, 7th March, 1786), and other Dutch ships that had been lying with their cargoes on board, at Curaçao, near two years in expectation of convoy, and were asserted to have been sold in that situation to imperial subjects, and other neutral claimants.

From a note of the *Nieuwe Vriendschap*, which seems to have been the first of that class of cases, it appears that the point of law was strongly argued. On the part of the claimant some precedents were cited, especially the *Felicity*, in 1756, a French ship which had sailed from Martinico, and had put into Cadiz, and was there sold, and was afterwards taken and condemned as not proved to be Spanish property. But that judgment was reversed in the Court of Appeal.

In the *Nieuwe Vriendschap*, the Court of Appeal seems to have inclined rather to the argument of the claimant, but did not give any decision upon the question of law affirming the sentence of condemnation of the Vice-Admiralty Court expressly on the ground of defect of proof of an actual *bonâ fide* transfer.

1807 *August* 12.

THE MINERVA.

Sir W. Scott.

vessel of this description, built for war, and employed as such, and now rendered incapable of acting as a ship of war by the arms of the other belligerent, and driven into a neutral port for shelter; whether the purchase of such a ship, I say, can be allowed, which shall enable the enemy so far to rescue himself from the disadvantage into which he has fallen, as to have the value at least restored to him by a neutral purchaser, is a question on which I shall wait for the authority of the Superior Court before I admit the validity of such a transfer. That a private merchant could lawfully do this I shall not hold till I am so instructed by the Superior Court. That a sovereign prince should embark in such a transaction, unless under such guards as would effectually remove all possibility of abuse, is what, but for the instance before us, could scarcely have been expected. Some communication, at least, we might suppose would be made to the belligerent government, accompanied with a disclosure of every circumstance of caution that should exclude the suspicion of what is always to be apprehended, the danger of such a vessel finding her way back again into the navy of her own country. It has not appeared to my recollection, in any case before the Court, that Count Bentinck was the owner of merchant vessels, or that he was engaged, as we know some Italian princes have been, in mercantile adventures. This perhaps is not a material circumstance, further than as it may add a little to the improbability of the present transaction, without much affecting the principle on which I shall determine this case, the illegality of such a purchase. It is the purchase of a ship of war lying in the port of Bergen, with eighteen guns and ammunition, of which fourteen guns and the ammunition are taken out for the mere convenience of conveyance. Can such things be allowed to be transferred as articles of commerce, and under the known pressure under which the enemy's marine has laboured? It can, at most, only be expected to be allowed under all circumstances of communicated preventive caution, that might secure the belligerent from the just apprehension of abuse, which I have before stated; some previous acquiescence signified on the part of the belligerent government—some consent obtained, upon an entire disclosure of the intention fully substantiated.

Now, what is the course of this transaction? Has any such

1807
August 12.

THE MINERVA.

Sir W. Scott.

communication been made, or any such acquiescence signified? Nothing appears to either effect. Is there any person sent from the neutral port whose character in the service of his sovereign might afford any guarantee or protection against abuse? No such thing. On the contrary, the whole contract has been carried on at Amsterdam, and the management of the vessel is at last entrusted to an old Dutchman, who, though he says he is burgher of Kniphausen, has never set his foot in that place. I can hardly persuade myself that there must not have been some imposition practised in this affair, since I cannot conceive that the august person for whom the claim is given, and who is no doubt desirous of preserving, with most perfect honour, his relations of amity with this country, should put a vessel of this description into the hands of such a master as this is, accompanied by a crew all picked up at Amsterdam. Admitting, as we must, that he was privy to the purchase, we can hardly doubt, at the same time, that those persons who have had the management of this business have conducted it in a manner very opposite to his inclinations and interests.

Where is the vessel found? The mate says, "within two or two and a half Dutch miles of the Vlie;" and the master, who takes the utmost latitude, admits, "within four." In the month of June, and in such weather as we have notoriously had during that month, that a man should not find his way into the Jade without getting immediately close to the land of Holland, that he should be found in this situation, without having attempted to alter his course or to retrace his steps, and that he should be continuing to steer on towards the coast of Holland, though it is not pretended that he did not know where he was, are such circumstances as convince me that some imposition has been practised. To say precisely what it is may be presumptuous, though all the circumstances tend to establish a belief that the parties entrusted with the execution of this project looked to a restitution of this ship into the possession of Holland. I cannot doubt that there has been some imposition practised on the august person whose name has been used. If there are any circumstances which can be brought forward on this part to elucidate this transaction, they will be addressed with better effect to the Superior Tribunal, which may be composed of persons better enabled to judge of the conduct of persons in that elevated station than I can consider myself to be. My judgment is, that the transaction of this purchase, taking it to have been made, has been conducted in a manner that cannot be considered as legal.

1807 *August* 12.

THE MINERVA.

Sir W. Scott.

Claim rejected.

THE NEPTUNUS (No. 5).

[6 C. Rob. 403.]

Cargo—Capture—Trade of Ally with Enemy.

Trade with the enemy by an ally in contraband articles, or articles in the nature of contraband, is illegal.

1807 *August* 12, 14.

THIS was one of an important class of cases of Swedish ships, captured on a voyage from the ports of Sweden to Amsterdam with cargoes of pitch and tar, in which the question turned on the effect of a modified permission of trade with the common enemy, in innocent articles, on the part of an ally in the war.

SIR W. SCOTT.—This is the case of a ship and cargo of pitch and tar going from Gottenburgh to Amsterdam, on which several questions arise, first as to the liberty of carrying such cargoes under the present situation of this country and Sweden; and, secondly, whether there is anything of a special nature to vary the general rule which would be otherwise applicable to the case. The right of carrying pitch and tar has long been a subject of much contention; this country contending that they were to be considered as contraband, Sweden, on the contrary, maintaining that they were not contraband when they were the produce of the exporting country. After long and passionate discussion on this subject, which has irritated the feelings of the two countries for two centuries, a sort of compromise was at length adopted, and the late treaty was formed as a kind of middle term, in which both parties abated something of their original pretensions. It was agreed that these articles should be considered not as absolutely contraband, nor yet as entirely free and innocent, but as liable to this exercise of the right of war, "that they should be subject to seizure for pre-emption." This was the substance of the treaty that was formed for the regulation of the trade of Sweden, when

1807 August 12, 14. THE NEPTUNUS. Sir W. Scott.

that country was at peace and in a state of neutrality towards each of the belligerent powers.

That, however, is not the present situation of the two countries, since Sweden has long been engaged with this country in hostility against a common enemy. The question, therefore, is to be taken up on different grounds, as depending on the general principles belonging to such a state of warlike confederacy, on what has passed between the two Courts immediately applicable to this subject, and on the public orders which have issued for the regulation of trade. It is well known that a declaration of hostility naturally carries with it an interdiction of all commercial intercourse; it leaves the belligerent countries in a state that is inconsistent with the relations of commerce. This is the natural result of a state of war, and it is by no means necessary that there should be a special interdiction of commerce to produce this effect. At the same time it has happened, since the world has grown more commercial, that a practice has crept in of admitting particular relaxations; and if one State only is at war, no injury is committed to any other State. It is of no importance to other nations how much a single belligerent chooses to weaken and dilute his own rights. But it is otherwise when allied nations are pursuing a common cause against a common enemy. Between them it must be taken as an implied, if not an express contract, that one State shall not do anything to defeat the general object. If one State admits its subjects to carry on an uninterrupted trade with the enemy the consequence may be that it will supply that aid and comfort to the enemy, especially if it is an enemy depending, like Holland, very materially on the resources of foreign commerce, which may be very injurious to the prosecution of the common cause and the interests of its ally. It should seem that it is not enough, therefore, to say that the one State has allowed this practice to its own subjects; it should appear to be at least desirable that it could be shown that either the practice is of such a nature as can in no manner interfere with the common operations or that it has the allowance of the confederate State.

If Sweden and Holland are at war there is no occasion for a special prohibition, as is intimated in Mr. Alderberg's letter. But if it is taken on the evidence of the correspondence, that the

Swedish Government has given an express liberty to its subjects to freight vessels for the ports of Holland, this must necessarily admit of some limitations; for can it be maintained, under the latitude of that expression, that they might carry gunpowder, or any other article in a state of preparation for the purposes of war? It is not enough to say that it is the natural produce of the country, because that principle must have its limits in acknowledged principles of self-defence on the part of the allied belligerent. Suppose the case of a country so unfortunately framed by nature as to produce nothing but sulphur, wood, and nitre, or that iron was the only production, can it be said that the inhabitants of that country should be at liberty to export their own manufacture of gunpowder or cannon to the ports of the enemy? There must be some limitation assigned to pretensions of this kind. Where are they to be found? In the order that has been issued by our own government (*a*), reciting "that information had been received that Sweden allows a trade in innocent articles only," and confirming the liberty of trade to that extent. It appears from Mr. Canning's letter that some discussion had taken place on this subject between the Secretary of State and the Swedish Minister, in which a confident persuasion is expressed on the part of this government that Sweden could not mean to suffer a supply of naval stores to be carried to the ports of the enemy. That being the construction which this government has put upon the permission, it must be binding on this Court. Permission is understood to be granted for innocent articles, but with an exclusion of naval stores. Then waiving the question of contraband, it is sufficient to ask whether the articles, of which this cargo is composed, fall under the description of naval stores, and that is a question which answers itself.

It is said that the terms of the letter seem to reserve the consideration of naval stores for further discussion, and the Court is requested to suspend its judgment till that discussion has taken place. But it is not to be inferred from the request made for additional security, on the part of this country, that we should suspend our own declaration on the subject, which is expressed in

(*a*) July 31st, 1807.

1807 *August* 12, 14.

THE NEPTUNUS.

Sir W. Scott.

definite terms. Nothing is reserved as to the question whether pitch and tar are to be considered as innocent articles or not. That is expressly determined by the restriction of naval and military stores, regarding which it cannot admit of a doubt that these articles are to be included under that description. I am of opinion that, where such articles occur, though the word contraband may be kept out of sight, the Court is bound to consider them as of the nature of contraband, in such a sense as renders it impossible that they could be included under the description of innocent articles.

This is the general principle that I feel myself bound to apply to the whole class. And in no instance can the penalty of confiscation be applied with more propriety than in this first case which occurs, in which the parties exporting these articles to the enemy are British subjects domiciled in Sweden. It has been decided, both in this Court and in the Court of Appeal, that though a British subject, resident abroad, may engage generally in trade with the enemy, he cannot carry on such a trade in articles of a contraband nature. The duties of allegiance travel with them, so as to restrain them from supplying articles of that kind to the enemy. This, however, I only mention as an aggravation of this particular case. On the general question I have no hesitation in pronouncing that the pitch and tar will be subject to condemnation.

But it is contended that the innocent parts of the cargo also and the ship itself will be subject to condemnation, on the known principle that the infection of contraband extends also to all interests included in the same claim on behalf of the same proprietor. I could assent to that argument if the case stood only on the general law; but when I look to the order of government I find "that all other goods are directed to be restored." So with regard to the ship. It has been uniformly held on general principles that the vessel belonging to the proprietor of contraband goods is liable to confiscation. But the order itself, in directing the restitution of all other goods, implies that this class of cases is not to be decided strictly on the general principle of contraband. Swedish vessels have been allowed to go to the ports of the enemy with permitted goods, and this country has acquiesced in that indulgence. I shall not, therefore, apply the principles of contraband to the ship under this modified state of the general rule. 1807 *August* 12, 14.

There is one parcel of goods, I perceive, in which the bill of lading has been endorsed over to the consignee in Holland, and the master in his deposition says, "that he believes they would have become the property of the consignee on arrival." This, I conceive, is such a transfer of the property as will render those particular goods liable to confiscation. The innocent goods, it appears, were going under a special licence granted by the King of Holland to Andersen & Co. at Amsterdam, to import a certain number of cargoes in Swedish ships. This has so much the appearance of a special *indulto* that it may not be without its consequence in determining on the national character of a trade so carried on, even on the part of Swedish subjects. If it is pressed I shall require some explanation to be given of the nature of these licences, and of the manner in which they are obtained and applied.

THE NEPTUNUS.

Sir W. Scott.

THE FRIENDSHIP. [6 C. Rob. 420.]

THE OROZEMBO. [6 C. Rob. 430.]

Neutral Vessel—Employment by Belligerent—Conveyance of Troops—Condemnation.

The carriage by a neutral ship of military persons irrespective of numbers in the service of a belligerent, even if the master is ignorant of the character of the service, renders such ship and her cargo liable to condemnation (*a*).

This was the case of an American ship bound from Baltimore to Bordeaux with thirty tons of fustic and 4,414 hogshead staves, and ninety passengers, French sailors shipped by direction of the French Minister in America. The ship was claimed by M. Gaultier, a Frenchman by birth, but a subject of the United States.

1807 *August* 19, 20. *September* 24.

For the captors, *Arnold*.

For the claimant, *Laurence* and *Swabey*.

(*a*) See the *Carolina*, *ante*, p. 385.

1807
August 19, 20.
September 24.

THE FRIENDSHIP.
THE OROZEMBO.

Sir W. Scott.

SIR W. SCOTT.—This is an American ship with a few goods of small bulk and little value, about thirty tons of fustic, and some staves, which are frequently taken as dunnage or ballast, but very seldom as a principal cargo. But there is a cargo on board of a different kind: ninety passengers, one American, five French merchants, and the rest French military officers and mariners. It has been objected that the seventh interrogatory must have been improperly addressed to the witnesses, since it has extracted an answer from the master which could not have been suggested by the interrogatory addressed in its usual and proper form. The master says "that the vessel was not a French transport; that there were about ninety passengers on board, but who paid for their passage he does not know; that the provisions were supplied by the owner of the ship." These are facts which do not naturally arise out of the interrogatory, and so far the question must have been irregular. But the answer is not of a nature that raises any imputation of improper deviation from duty on the part of the Commissioners; because, if the question had not been put to the witnesses by them, it is one which I should certainly have thought it necessary to address to them. How persons, appearing like those on board, in a military character, were taken on board as passengers, how their provisions were supplied, are questions of fact very proper to be answered. Notwithstanding there may have been some little irregularity in the form in which the interrogatories have been put, with reference to which the answer has been given, that the ship was not a French transport, it will not be necessary to delay the cause for the purpose of having them put again, under the authority of the Court. That is a point which the Court has to determine, on a view of all the evidence, and which cannot be taken either way merely on the master's representation. The master knows little, and with respect to what he has to disclose, the Court may very safely proceed on his deposition in the present form.

The instructions of the owner are produced, directing the master "to go to Annapolis, there to take as many passengers as you can"; as if they were to be picked up accidentally, and without previous contract. They then go on in these terms: "You must go to Bordeaux, and deliver the fustic; you will endeavour to preserve a good understanding between the passengers and the crew, and see that they have their due allowance, according to the instructions which will be communicated to you." "In case of British capture" (an event which seems very reasonably to have been apprehended), "or being carried into a British port, you will apply to," &c. It is evident from these papers, and from other circumstances, that there must have been a formal contract between the owner and the person who was to pay the passage-money for these mariners. No such instrument is produced, and on inquiring for it, I am told that it is not in this country. I am, therefore, left in the dark as to the terms of the contracting parties, and I am to determine from other parts of the case what the character of this vessel is—whether she is to be considered as a neutral vessel carrying on an innoxious commerce, or as a transport vessel engaged in the immediate military service of the enemy.

In order to determine how far the vessel was engaged in a commercial employment, I have little more to do than to look at the nature of this part, or parcel of the cargo, which she carries, for so it is called by the mate, and also by the master. So little, however, do the French officers know of the lading, that they depose "that there was no cargo on board," and repeat "that there was not any lading" over and over again. I observe this also more particularly with respect to the deposition of one person, M. Septans, who was more immediately concerned in the transaction, being a sort of superintendent over the rest. He says in three distinct places "that there was no cargo on board." I am rather led by this manner of deposing to conjecture that it would be found to be one of the conditions of the contract (if it could be inspected) that there should not be any cargo taken on board, but that the whole space should be reserved for the accommodation of the passengers; and that these witnesses speak correctly under the impression of their understanding of the contract, "that no cargo was on board."

On this evidence I may, I think, dispose of that part of the case which depends upon character, and may determine that the vessel has no commercial character belonging to her that can be said to arise out of the nature of her lading. As far as it is contended that the ship cannot be considered as a transport, because she had a cargo on board, I am of opinion that all such argument is

1807
August 19, 20.
September 21.

THE FRIENDSHIP.
THE OROZEMBO.

Sir W. Scott.

effectually answered, and that there was, in the understanding of the parties, no cargo on board, as indeed it is a common stipulation with transports that none shall be taken. It is said that there is nothing in the form of a charter-party to denote the vessel to have been a transport under contract with the enemy's Government. I know of no precise technical definition of transport vessels more than this, that they are vessels hired by the Government to do such acts as shall be imposed upon them in the military service of the country. In this country there is a particular department of office called the Transport Board, and the vessels which are hired by that board are distinguished in common language by the name of transport vessels. Other nations may have different modes of conducting this service, and it is by no means essential to the character of a transport that she should be chartered in any particular manner, or in any particular form of words, or by any particular department of the Government. In contracts made abroad, more especially where the same opportunities may not occur, it would be still less to be expected that they should be confined to particular forms. If French vessels are not to be found, others must be employed on their own terms. The form, therefore, is of no importance. The substance of the thing is this, whether they are vessels hired by the agents of the Government, for the purpose of conveying soldiers or stores in the service of the State. That is the substance; and it signifies nothing whether the men so conveyed are to be put into action on an immediate expedition or not. The mere shifting of drafts in detachments, and the conveyance of stores from one place to another, is an ordinary employment of transport vessels, and it is a distinction totally unimportant, whether this or that case may be connected with the immediate active service of the enemy. In removing forces from distant settlements, there may be no intention of immediate action; but still the general importance of having troops conveyed to places, where it is convenient that they should be collected, either for present or future use, is what constitutes the object and employment of transport vessels. I therefore discard that distinction, that these persons were not going on an immediate active expedition.

Then what are the circumstances that disclose themselves in this case? If the contract is not on board, but is industriously concealed from the master, who professes to know nothing about it, or if he wilfully suppresses the fact, though it is in his knowledge, that will not defeat the Courts of the belligerent of their right of putting the proper construction on the act done. This then appears that it was a transaction entered into with the privity and consent of the French Government. It was done under the authority of what the French call their public functionary, their Minister Plenipotentiary in America. There is an order from the representative of the French Government, dated May 31st, "directing an officer by the name of Aubrey, in virtue of the disposition of the Minister Plenipotentiary resident in the United States, to disembark from the *Eole* and to go on board the American ship the *Union*, destined immediately to France." There is also another paper, from the Commissary of Marine at St. Domingo, which grants "permission to Mr. Septans, late accountable agent to the French ship the *Felicite*, to return to France in a neutral vessel, on condition that he should present himself to the constituted authority of the port at which he should land." So in the public papers the other persons also are required "to render themselves at the port of their arrival in France to the Bureau Maritime, there to receive further orders." There cannot be stronger evidence than this that these persons are still retained in the public service. Then comes the certificate of the French consul at Maryland, which orders Mr. Septans to go on board as accountable agent in this ship, to "preserve the police," which is a strong term, and may be supposed to include something of military discipline, "and to act with the senior officers among the passengers," manifestly keeping up a military subordination, "according to instructions which he would receive." No such instructions are produced, but it is clear that some must have been delivered which are now withheld. Then comes the muster-roll, which describes these passengers in their several capacities as military and naval officers, and mariners of all classes, being the relics of the crews of two vessels going back to France, still preserving their professional character and situation as part of the marine of France, subject to the orders of the marine department on their arrival, and going at the expense of the French Government. Is it not ludicrous, then, to speak of the cargo of this vessel as being

1807
August 19, 20.
September 24.

THE FRIENDSHIP.
THE OROZEMBO.

Sir W. Scott.

any other than these passengers for whom the ship was freighted? I have no doubt that if the charter-party was produced, which is now skulking in obscurity, it would appear to be a fundamental condition of that contract that no cargo should be taken on board.

Under these circumstances I am of opinion that this vessel is to be considered as a French transport; it would be a very different case if a vessel appeared to be carrying only a few individual invalided soldiers or discharged sailors, taken on board by chance and at their own charge. Looking at the description given of the men on board, I am satisfied that they are still as effective members of the French marine as any can be. Shall it be said, then, that this is an innoxious trade, or that it is an innocent occupation of the vessel? What are arms and ammunition in comparison with men, who may be going to be conveyed perhaps to renew their activity on our own shores? They are persons in a military capacity, who could not have made their escape in a vessel of their own country. Can it be allowed that neutral vessels shall be at liberty to step in and make themselves a vehicle for the liberation of such persons, whom the chance of war has made in some measure prisoners in a distant port of their own colonies in the West Indies? It is asked, will you lay down a principle that may be carried to the length of preventing a military officer in the service of the enemy from finding his way home in a neutral vessel from America to Europe? If he was going merely as an ordinary passenger, as other passengers do, and at his own expense, the question would present itself in a very different form. Neither this Court nor any other British tribunal has ever laid down the principle to that extent. This is a case differently composed. It is the case of a vessel letting herself out in a distinct manner, under a contract with the enemy's Government, to convey a number of persons, described as being in the service of the enemy, with their military character travelling with them, and to restore them to their own country in that character. I do with perfect satisfaction of mind pronounce this to be a case of a ship engaged in a course of trade which cannot be considered to be permitted to neutral vessels, and without hesitation pronounce this vessel subject to condemnation.

The fustic and staves were condemned also.

THE OROZEMBO.

1807 *August* 19, 20. *September* 24.

THE OROZEMBO.

Sir W. Scott.

Sir W. Scott.—This is the case of an admitted American vessel; but the title to restitution is impugned, on the ground of its having been employed at the time of the capture in the service of the enemy in transporting military persons first to Macao, and ultimately to Batavia. That a vessel hired by the enemy for the conveyance of military persons is to be considered as a transport subject to condemnation has been in a recent case held by this Court, and on other occasions. What is the number of military persons that shall constitute such a case it may be difficult to define. In the former case there were many, in the present there are much fewer in number; but I accede to what has been observed in argument, that number alone is an insignificant circumstance in the considerations on which the principle of law on this subject is built, since fewer persons of high quality and character may be of more importance than a much greater number of persons of lower condition. To send out one veteran general of France to take the command of the forces at Batavia might be a much more noxious act than the conveyance of a whole regiment. The consequences of such assistance are greater; and therefore it is what the belligerent has a stronger right to prevent and punish. In this instance the military persons are three, and there are, besides, two other persons, who were going to be employed in civil capacities in the government of Batavia. Whether the principle would apply to them alone, I do not feel it necessary to determine. I am not aware of any case in which that question has been agitated; but it appears to me, on principle, to be but reasonable that, whenever it is of sufficient importance to the enemy that such persons should be sent out on the public service at the public expense, it should afford equal ground of forfeiture against the vessel that may be let out for a purpose so intimately connected with the hostile operations.

It has been argued that the master was ignorant of the character of the service on which he was engaged, and that, in order to support the penalty, it would be necessary that there should be some proof of delinquency in him or his owner. But I conceive that is not necessary; it will be sufficient if there is an injury arising to the belligerent from the employment in which the vessel is found. In the case of the Swedish vessel (*a*), there was no *mens rea* in the owner, or in any other person acting under his authority. The master was an involuntary agent, acting under compulsion put upon him by the officers of the French Government, and, so far as intention alone is considered, perfectly innocent. In the same manner, in cases of *bonâ fide* ignorance, there may be no actual delinquency; but if the service is injurious, that will be sufficient to give the belligerent a right to prevent the thing from being done, or at least repeated, by enforcing the penalty of confiscation. If imposition has been practised, it operates as force; and if redress in the way of indemnification is to be sought against any person, it must be against those who have, by means either of compulsion or deceit, exposed the property to danger. If, therefore, it was the most innocent case on the part of the master, if there was nothing whatever to affect him with privity, the whole amount of this argument would be that he must seek his redress against the freighter, otherwise such opportunities of conveyance would be constantly used, and it would be almost impossible, in the greater number of cases, to prove the knowledge and privity of the immediate offender.

It has been argued throughout as if the ignorance of the master alone would be sufficient to exempt the property of the owner from confiscation. But may there not be other persons, besides the master, whose knowledge and privity would carry with it the same consequences? Suppose the owner himself had knowledge of the engagement, would not that produce the *mens rea*, if such a thing is necessary? or if those who had been employed to act for the owner had thought fit to engage the ship in a service of this nature, keeping the master in profound ignorance, would it not be just as effectual, if the *mens rea* is necessary, that it should reside in those persons as in the owner? The observations which I shall have occasion to make on the remaining parts of this case will, perhaps, appear to justify such a supposition, either that the owner himself, or those who acted for him in Lisbon or in Holland, were connusant of the nature of the whole transaction. But I will first state

(*a*) *Carolina*, *ante*, p. 385.

distinctly that the principle on which I determine this case is, that the carrying military persons to the colony of an enemy, who are there to take on them the exercise of their military functions, will lead to condemnation, and that the Court is not to scan with minute arithmetic the number of persons that are so carried. If it has appeared to be of sufficient importance to the government of the enemy to send them, it must be enough to put the adverse government on the exercise of their right of prevention, and the ignorance of the master can afford no ground of exculpation in favour of the owner, who must seek his remedy in cases of deception as well as of force against those who have imposed upon him.

1807 *August* 19, 20. *September* 24.

THE FRIENDSHIP. THE OROZEMBO.

Sir W. Scott.

Having stated the principle on which my judgment must be understood to rest, I will advert a little to some incidental circumstances of the case.

[The Court then examined the evidence, and concluded:]

On every view which I take of the case, on the principle of law or on the evidence of the facts, I have no hesitation in pronouncing that this vessel is liable to be considered as a transport, let out in the service of the Government of Holland, and that it is, as such, subject to condemnation.

THE ATALANTA.

THE CAROLINE.

[6 C. Rob. 440.]
[6 C. Rob. 461.]

Capture—Neutral Ship—Despatches of Enemy—Fraudulent Concealment—Condemnation of Ship and Cargo.

The carrying of despatches of a belligerent on a neutral ship places such ship in the service of the belligerent, and the fraudulent concealment of such despatches subjects both ship and cargo to condemnation. But this rule does not apply to despatches from the ambassador of a belligerent in a neutral State to his Government. Definition of despatches.

THIS was a case of a Bremen ship (*a*) and cargo, captured on a voyage from Batavia to Bremen, on the 14th of July, 1807,

1808 *March* 4. *April* 1.

(*a*) The ship in this case had been recently purchased as an American vessel, in the Isle of France, in the place of the former vessel which had

1808 *March* 4. *April* 1.

THE ATALANTA. THE CAROLINE.

having come last from the Isle of France, where a packet containing despatches from the government of the Isle of France to the Minister of Marine at Paris was taken on board by the master and one of the supercargoes, and was afterwards found concealed, in the possession of the second supercargo, under circumstances detailed in the judgment.

[The first portion of the judgment dealt entirely with the facts of the case, and the Court in conclusion found that "the fact of a fraudulent concealment and suppression [of public despatches] is most satisfactorily demonstrated."]

The case was argued by the *King's Advocate*, *Laurence* and *Adams*, for the captors; and by *Robinson* and *Stoddart* for the claimants.

SIR W. SCOTT.—. . . . . The question then is, what are the legal consequences attaching on such a criminal act [fraudulent concealment of despatches], for that it is criminal and most noxious is scarcely denied. What might be the consequences of a simple transmission of despatches I am not called upon by the necessities of the present case to decide, because I have already pronounced this to be a fraudulent case. That the simple carrying of despatches between the colonies and the mother country of the enemy is a service highly injurious to the other belligerent is most obvious. In the present state of the world, in the hostilities of European powers, it is an object of great importance to preserve the connection between the mother country and her colonies; and to interrupt that connection, on the part of the other belligerent, is one of the most energetic operations of war. The importance of keeping up that connection, for the concentration of troops and for various military purposes, is manifest; and, I may add, for the supply of civil assistance also and support, because the infliction of civil distress, for the purpose of compelling a surrender, forms no

been driven into the Isle of France in great distress, and there sold under the authority of the Court of Admiralty of that island with so much of the cargo as was required to defray the expenses of transhipment, and the purchase of the present vessel.

inconsiderable part of the operations of war. It is not to be argued, therefore, that the importance of these despatches might relate only to the civil wants of the colony, and that it is necessary to show a military tendency; because the object of compelling a surrender being a measure of war, whatever is conducive to that event must also be considered, in the contemplation of law, as an object of hostility, although not produced by operations strictly military. How is this intercourse with the mother country kept up in time of peace: by ships of war, or by packets in the service of the State? If a war intervenes, and the other belligerent prevails to interrupt that communication, any person stepping in to lend himself to effect the same purpose under the privilege of an ostensible neutral character, does in fact place himself in the service of the enemy State, and is justly to be considered in that character. Nor let it be supposed that it is an act of light and casual importance. The consequence of such a service is indefinite, infinitely beyond the effect of any contraband that can be conveyed. The carrying of two or three cargoes of stores is necessarily an assistance of a limited nature; but in the transmission of despatches may be conveyed the entire plan of a campaign that may defeat all the projects of the other belligerent in that quarter of the world. It is true, as it has been said, that one ball might take off a Charles the XIIth, and might produce the most disastrous effects in a campaign; but that is a consequence so remote and accidental, that, in the contemplation of human events, it is a sort of evanescent quantity of which no account is taken; and the practice has been accordingly, that it is in considerable quantities only that the offence of contraband is contemplated. The case of despatches is very different; it is impossible to limit a letter to so small a size as not to be capable of producing the most important consequences in the operations of the enemy. It is a service therefore which, in whatever degree it exists, can only be considered in one character, as an act of the most noxious and hostile nature.

It has accordingly been so held in decided cases that fully recognize the principle, for on this principle the *Constitution* (*a*), was condemned; and how is that case to be distinguished? It is

(*a*) Lords, 14th July, 1802.

1808 March 4. April 1.

THE ATALANTA. THE CAROLINE.

Sir W. Scott.

said that that was not a case of despatches simply, but that it was dependent on the modified relaxation of the principle of exclusion from the colonial trade of the enemy in the West Indies; that it was also a case of carrying backwards and forwards, in two separate instances, from the Havannah to Truxillo, and back again. But can these circumstances make any difference? The exclusion being taken off, that trade stood upon the common footing; and if the carrying of the original despatches is no offence, will the circumstance of being made the vehicle of carrying the answer to those dispatches make it so?

The case of the *Sally* (*a*) has been mentioned as one in which this principle was not applied at the commencement of the late war; but there the despatches were not referable to the operations of war, or even to the existence of war. The vessel had sailed before the knowledge of hostilities; and the despatches were altogether of a commercial nature, from the French Minister in America, relating to a contract for flour, which had been made (wholly unconnected with the war, and prior to the expectation of such an event) for the purpose of supplying France and the French colonies in the West Indies in a year of great scarcity.

The *Hope* (*b*) is another case which has been mentioned as an instance in which the Superior Court passed over an imputation of this kind, without suffering it to obstruct the sentence of restitution, which was finally decreed. But in that case it was admitted that no such paper was on board. There was merely a receipt, appearing to have been given by the captain, for a packet taken by him from the Governor of Batavia, to be transmitted to the Dutch Minister in America, and to be forwarded ultimately to Amsterdam. In fact, the question was not raised; it was argued that the packet might not have been on board, and that it might, notwithstanding the receipt, have been sent by some other American ship, of which there were several lying at Batavia at the same time. The case came before the Court of Appeal from the Vice-Admiralty Court at the Cape of Good Hope, and the Superior Court acted on the presumption that the Court below had made the necessary inquiry and had been satisfied on that point. The

(*a*) *Ante*, p. 28. (*b*) Lords, 23rd April, 1803.

appeal proceeded on other grounds, and therefore the question did not fairly present itself, and the Court of Appeal, adopting the conclusion of the Court below upon the point, did not think it necessary to direct further inquiry to be instituted upon this fact when the cause came on to be heard and when the opportunity of investigating it was gone by. The effect of that decision, therefore, has no application to the present question.

In the *Trende Sostre* (*a*), in which the same fact came incidentally before this Court, the question of law was avoided, as was also that of contraband, by the circumstance that before the seizure the Cape of Good Hope, to which port the vessel was going, had ceased to be a colony of the enemy and had become an English settlement.

In the *Lisette* (*b*), which had carried a Dutch packet in the Danish mail bag, the vessel was captured on the return voyage, and then also a paper of this description was produced by a woman, who had so discredited herself by the manner in which she appeared to have acted, being the person who had taken the papers on board by fraud against the master (who had conducted himself *optima fide*, and had exerted his utmost influence and authority to prevent any papers from being put on board), that the Court repudiated her evidence altogether, and refused to act upon it in a case of that description.

In all these cases the principle was uniformly asserted, although the circumstances under which the fact appeared did not lead the Court to consider it with that particularity which the nature of the present case requires. Unless, therefore, it can be said that there must be a plurality of offences to constitute the delinquency, it has already been laid down by the Superior Court, in the *Constitution*, that the fraudulent carrying the despatches of the enemy is a criminal act which will lead to condemnation. Under the authority of that decision, then, I am warranted to hold that it is an act which will affect the vehicle, without any fear of incurring the imputation which is sometimes strangely cast upon this Court, that it is guilty of interpolations in the laws of nations. If the Court took upon itself to assume principles in themselves novel, it might

(*a*) *Ante*, p. 588. (*b*) 5th May, 1807.

1808 *March* 4. *April* 1.

THE ATALANTA. THE CAROLINE.

Sir W. Scott.

justly incur such an imputation, but to apply established principles to new cases cannot surely be so considered. All law is resolvable into general principles; the cases which may arise under new combinations of circumstances, leading to an extended application of principles, ancient and recognized by just corollaries, may be infinite, but so long as the continuity of the original and established principles is preserved pure and unbroken the practice is not new, nor is it justly chargeable with being an innovation on the ancient law, when, in fact, the Court does nothing more than apply old principles to new circumstances. If, therefore, the decision, which the Court has to pronounce in this case, stood on principle alone, I should feel no scruple in resting it on the just and fair application of the ancient law. But the fact is that I have the direct authority of the Superior Court for pronouncing that the carrying the despatches of the enemy brings on the confiscation of the vehicle so employed.

It is said that this is more than is done even in cases of contraband, and it is true with respect to the very lenient practice of this country, which in this matter recedes very much from the correct principle of the law of nations, which authorizes the penalty of confiscation. This is rightly stated by Bynkershoek to depend on this fact, whether the contraband is taken on board with the actual or presumed knowledge of the owner—I say presumed knowledge, because the knowledge of the master is, in law, the knowledge of the owner: "*Si sciverit, ipse est in dolo, et navis publicabitur*" (*a*). This country, which however much its practice may be misrepresented by foreign writers, and sometimes by our own, has always administered the law of nations with lenity, adopts a more indulgent rule, inflicting on the ship only a forfeiture of freight in ordinary cases of contraband. But the offence of carrying despatches is, it has been observed, greater. To talk of the confiscation of the noxious article, the despatches, which constitutes the penalty in contraband, would be ridiculous. There would be no freight dependent on it, and therefore the same precise penalty cannot, in the nature of things, be applied. It becomes absolutely necessary, as well as just, to resort to some other

(*a*) Bynker. I. P. c. 12, p. 95.

measure of confiscation, which can be no other than that of the vehicle.

Then comes the other question, whether the penalty is not also to be extended further, to the cargo, being the property of the same proprietors, not merely *ob continentiam delicti*, but likewise because the representatives of the owners of the cargo are directly involved in the knowledge and conduct of this guilty transaction? On the circumstances of the present case, I have to observe that the offence is as much the act of those who are the constituted agents of the cargo as of the master, who is the agent of the ship. The general rule of law is, that where a party has been guilty of an interposition in the war, and is taken *in delicto*, he is not entitled to the aid of the Court to obtain the restitution of any part of his property involved in the same transaction. It is said that the term "interposition in the war" is a very general term, and not to be loosely applied. I am of opinion that this is an aggravated case of active interposition in the service of the enemy, concerted and continued in fraud, and marked with every species of malignant conduct. In such a case I feel myself bound, not only by the general rule, *ob continentiam delicti*, but by the direct participation of guilt in the agents of the cargo. Their own immediate conduct not only excludes all favourable distinction, but makes them pre-eminently the object of just punishment. The conclusion therefore is, that I must pronounce the ship and cargo subject to condemnation (*a*).

(*a*) Other cases that have occurred on the question of despatches, are the *Constantia* (15th March, 1808), a Danish ship taken on a voyage from the Isle of France to Copenhagen, having on board a packet which was to be delivered to the French Ambassador at Copenhagen, to be by him forwarded to the departments of government in France. Hostilities with Denmark having intervened, the claims of the Danish proprietor could not be given. The case was argued only, with respect to the interest in the prize, between the Crown and the captors, and therefore no special explanations were offered on the part of the master. The Court observed, upon the evidence, that the master appeared to have taken charge of this packet knowingly; and though there did not appear to have been any fraudulent concealment, he had been in the custody of a British frigate fifteen days without making any disclosure of the fact; that he was part owner of the vessel and of the cargo, and had been entrusted with the management of the expedition, as agent, by his co-partner; that the case, therefore, must

1808
March 4.
April 1.

The Court observed afterwards:—I will mention, though it is a circumstance of no great consequence, that I have seen the des-

The Atalanta.
The Caroline.

follow the course of the *Atalanta*, independent of the breaking out of Danish hostilities, on which only the claim of the Crown was founded. That the captors were entitled to the condemnation of the ship and cargo.

Sir W. Scott.

The *Susan* (1st April, 1808), an American vessel, captured on a voyage from Bordeaux to New York, having on board a packet addressed to the Prefect of the Isle of France (of which it did not appear that it contained more than a letter providing for the payment of that officer's salary). The master had made an affidavit averring his ignorance of the contents, and stating that the packet was delivered to him by a private merchant as containing old newspapers and some shawls to be delivered to a merchant at New York. The insignificance of such a communication, and its want of connection with the political objects of the war, were insisted upon. But the Court overruled that distinction under observations similar to those above stated; and on the plea of ignorance observed, that without saying what might be the effect of an extreme case of imposition practised on a neutral master, notwithstanding the utmost exertions of caution and good faith on his part, it must be taken to be the general rule that a master is not at liberty to aver his ignorance, but that, if he is made the victim of imposition practised on him by his private agent, or by the government of the enemy, he must seek for his redress against them. That in this instance the master did not appear, even from his own account, to have used any caution to inform himself of the nature of the papers; that with respect to the disclosure, although the papers were not so kept as to implicate him in the charge of a fraudulent concealment, they were not produced to the captors as they ought to have been. That since it appeared that cases of this description were multiplying so fast as to have produced four instances of neutral vessels making themselves in this manner subservient to the purposes of the enemy within the present sitting, it was necessary to be known that it would be considered as a proof of fraud if papers of this description being on board were not produced voluntarily in the first instance. In this case the ship was condemned, but the cargo was restored, and even that part belonging to the owner of the ship, as it did not appear that the master had been appointed agent for the cargo. But (2nd June, 1808) on prayer that the master might be allowed his private adventure, the Court observed that this was a description of cases in which the usual indulgence of the Court, in that respect, would be misapplied. That it was an offence originating chiefly in the misconduct or culpable negligence of the master, and that whilst he was acting thus culpably and wantonly with respect to the property of his owner, it could not be expected that he himself should escape with impunity as far as his own adventure in that transaction was concerned.

Also the case of the *Hope* (9th April, 1808), an American vessel, captured on a voyage from Bordeaux to New York, having on board various despatches to the officers of government in the French West India

patches in this case, and that they are of a noxious nature, stating the strength of the different regiments, &c., and other particulars entirely military.

1808
March 4.
April 1.

THE ATALANTA.
THE CAROLINE.

Sir W. Scott.

THE CAROLINE.

[6 C. Rob. 461.]

Sir W. Scott.—This is the case of a ship which was captured, having on board despatches from the Minister and Consul of France in the United States to the Government of France. The Court has before had repeated occasion to express its opinion that the carrying the despatches of the enemy from the colonies to the mother country is a criminal interposition in the war that will lead to condemnation. In this case a distinction was taken, very briefly in the original argument, which, I confess, struck me very forcibly at the moment, that carrying the despatches of an ambassador, situated in a neutral country, did not fall within the reasoning on which the general principle is founded; and I cannot but say that

islands and the Isle of France. There was also on board a military officer of rank, *aide de camp* to General Villaret, who had lately come from Martinique, and was returning to that island, and who had been shipped in the character of a merchant's clerk, going to settle some outstanding accounts in New York. The master made an affidavit protesting his ignorance, and stating, "that in answer to a request made to him, he had refused publicly in the coffee-house at Bordeaux, to take any public papers; that the papers in question were brought on board in the officer's baggage, and had been stowed away in the hold for want of room in the cabin assigned to him." The veracity of this account was contradicted by a shipping paper on board, from the custom house at Bordeaux, which described this trunk "as sent on board originally with a direction that it should be stowed in the hold." The Court observed again, that the general rule must be held strong against the averment of ignorance; that the circumstances of the present case did not even approach to a case of that kind; that it was scarcely credible that the master could have been deceived with respect to the character of a military officer of high rank so as to be imposed upon by the disguise of a merchant's clerk which he had pretended to assume; that he was further discredited, by the representation which he had attempted to impose upon the Court, respecting the manner in which the trunk was concealed. The Court condemned the ship, but restored the cargo, though the property of the owner, as the master did not appear to have been appointed super-cargo or agent with regard to the cargo.

1808 *March* 4. *April* 1.

THE ATALANTA. THE CAROLINE.

Sir W. Scott.

the further argument which I have heard on that point, and my own consideration of the subject, have but confirmed the impression which I then received of the solidity of this distinction. That the carrying the despatches between the mother country and her colonies is criminal can hardly be doubted; and I have never heard of a claim of privilege of this kind being asserted on the part of any nation or by any individual. On the contrary, the artifices of clandestinity and concealment, with which such acts have always been accompanied, strongly betray the opinion which the individuals themselves entertain of the right.

It has been asked, what are despatches? to which, I think, this answer may safely be returned: that they are all official communications of official persons on the public affairs of the government. The comparative importance of the particular papers is immaterial, since the Court will not construct a scale of relative importance, which in fact it has not the means of doing, with any degree of accuracy or with satisfaction to itself; it is sufficient that they relate to the public business of the enemy, be it great or small. It is the right of the belligerent to intercept and cut off all communication between the enemy and his settlements, and to the utmost of his power to harass and disturb this connection, which it is one of the declared objects of the ambition of the enemy to preserve. It is not to be said, therefore, that this or that letter is of small moment; the true criterion will be, is it on the public business of the State, and passing between public persons for the public service? That is the question. If individuals take papers coming from official persons and addressed to persons in authority, and they turn out to be mere private letters, as may sometimes happen in the various relations of life, it will be well for them, and they will have the benefit of so fortunate an event. But if the papers so taken relate to public concerns, be they great or small, civil or military, the Court will not split hairs and consider their relative importance. For on what grounds can it proceed to make such an estimate with any accuracy? What appears small in words, or what may, perhaps, be artfully disguised, may relate to objects of infinite importance known only to the enemy, and of which the Court has no means of judging. The Court, therefore, will not take upon itself the burthen of forming such a scale, but will look only to the fact whether the case falls within the general description or not.

The circumstances of the present case, however, do not bring it within the range of these considerations, because it is not a case of despatches coming from any part of the enemy's territory whose commerce and communications of every kind the other belligerent has a right to interrupt. They are despatches from persons who are, in a peculiar manner, the favourite objects of the protection of the law of nations, ambassadors, resident in a neutral country, for the purpose of preserving the relations of amity between that State and his own government.

On these grounds a very material distinction arises with respect to the right of furnishing the conveyance. The former cases were cases of neutral ships, carrying the enemy's despatches from his colonies to the mother country. In all such cases you have a right to conclude that the effect of those despatches is hostile to yourself, because they must relate to the security of the enemy's possessions and to the maintenance of a communication between them; you have a right to destroy these possessions and that communication, and it is a legal act of hostility so to do. But the neutral country has a right to preserve its relations with the enemy, and you are not at liberty to conclude that any communication between them can partake in any degree of the nature of hostility against you. The enemy may have his hostile projects to be attempted with the neutral State; but your reliance is on the integrity of that neutral State, that it will not favour nor participate in such designs, but, as far as its own councils and actions are concerned, will oppose them. And if there should be private reason to suppose that this confidence in the good faith of the neutral State has a doubtful foundation, that is matter for the caution of the government, to be counteracted by just measures of preventive policy, but is no ground on which this Court can pronounce that the neutral carrier has violated his duty by bearing despatches, which, as far as he can know, may be presumed to be of an innocent nature, and in the maintenance of a pacific connection. One material ground, therefore, is wanting on which the judgment of the Court proceeded in the former cases. Another distinction arises from the character of the person who is

1808 *March 4. April 1.*

THE ATALANTA. THE CAROLINE.

Sir W. Scott.

employed in the correspondence: he is not an executive officer of the government, acting simply in the conduct of its own affairs within its own territories, but an ambassador resident in a neutral State for the purpose of supporting an amicable relation with it.

I have before said that persons discharging the functions of ambassadors are, in a peculiar manner, objects of the protection and favour of the law of nations. The limits that are assigned to the operations of war against them by Vattel and other writers upon those subjects are, that you may exercise your right of war against them wherever the character of hostility exists. You may stop the ambassador of your enemy on his passage; but when he has arrived, and has taken upon himself the functions of his office, and has been admitted in his representative character, he becomes a sort of middleman, entitled to peculiar privileges, as set apart for the protection of the relations of amity and peace, in maintaining which all nations are in some degree interested. It has been argued that he retains his national character unmixed, and that even his residence is considered as a residence in his own country. But that is a fiction of law invented for his further protection only, and as such a fiction it is not to be extended beyond the reasoning on which it depends. It was intended as a privilege, and I am not aware of any instance in which it has been urged to his disadvantage. Could it be said that he would, on that principle, be subject to any of the rights of war in a neutral territory? Certainly not. He is there for the purpose of carrying on the communications of peace and amity; for the interest of his own country primarily, but, at the same time, for the furtherance and protection of the interests which the neutral country also has in the continuance of those relations.

It is to be considered, also, with regard to this question, what may be due to the convenience of the neutral State: for its interests may require that the intercourse of correspondence with the enemy's country should not be altogether interdicted. It might be thought to amount almost to a declaration that an ambassador from the enemy shall not reside in the neutral State if he is declared to be debarred from the only means of communicating with his own. For to what useful purpose can he reside there, without the opportunities of such a communication? It is too much to say that all the business of the two States shall be transacted by the minister of the neutral State resident in the enemy's country. The practice of nations has allowed to neutral States the privilege of receiving ministers from the belligerent States, and the use and convenience of an immediate negotiation with them.

It is said, and truly said, that this exception may be liable to great abuses, and so, perhaps, will any rule that can be laid down on this subject:—

> ——— *Mille adde catenas;*
> *Effugiet tamen hæc*——

Opportunities of conveying intelligence may always exist in some form or other. It may happen that much mischief may arise by the communication of news in the private letters of intriguing private men, or, as the French Government has been much in the habit of employing such characters, of intriguing women; but if they are not stamped with the character of public communications, this Court cannot pursue the consequence to the penalty of those persons who may be made the vehicles of conveying such a correspondence. It has been argued truly that whatever the necessities of the negotiation may be, a private merchant is under no obligation to be the carrier of the enemy's despatches to his own government. Certainly he is not; and one inconvenience to which he may be held fairly subject, is that of having his vessel brought in for examination, and of the necessary detention and expense. He gives the captors an undeniable right to intercept and examine the nature and contents of the papers which he is carrying, for they may be papers of an injurious tendency, although not such on any *à priori* presumption as to subject the party who carries them to the penalty of confiscation, and by giving the captors the right of that inquiry he must submit to all the inconvenience that may attend it.

Ship and cargo restored on payment of captor's expense.

INDEX TO VOLUME I.

PRINTED BY C. F. ROWORTH, GREAT NEW STREET, FETTER LANE, E.C.

Made in the USA
Monee, IL
13 September 2026

62976474R00411